Principles of Business: Accounting

Principles of Business: Accounting

The Editors at Salem Press

SALEM PRESS

A Division of EBSCO Information Services, Inc.
Ipswich, Massachusetts

GREY HOUSE PUBLISHING

Publisher's Cataloging-In-Publication Data
(Prepared by The Donohue Group, Inc.)

Names: Salem Press, editor.
Title: Principles of business. Accounting / [the Editors at Salem Press].
Other Titles: Accounting
Description: [First edition]. | Ipswich, Massachusetts : Salem Press, a division of EBSCO Information Services, Inc. ; Amenia, NY : Grey House Publishing, [2018] | Includes bibliographical references and index.
Identifiers: ISBN 9781682176702 (hardcover)
Subjects: LCSH: Accounting.
Classification: LCC HF5636 .P75 2018 | DDC 657--dc23

PRINTED IN THE UNITED STATES OF AMERICA

Contents

Publisher's Note vii
Introduction ix
Contributors xi

Accounting for Complex Financial Structures 1
Accounting for Mergers and Acquisitions 8
Accounting for Stock-Based Compensation 18
Accounting Systems and Controls 23
Accounting Systems for Managerial Decisions . . . 33
Accounts Receivables and Inventories 37
Applied Global Money Management 43
Assurance Services 49
Audit Services 56
Auditing 63

B2B Business Models 74
Balance of Payments 80
Bankruptcy and Organization 87
Business Applications on Spreadsheets 94
Business Conditions Analysis 100
Business Cycle 106
Business Estate Planning 112
Business, Ethics and Society 118
Buyout of Acquisitions 124

Capital Budgeting 130
Cloud Computing Security 135
Communications, Networking and Security 139
Computer Applications in Business 144
Consulting to Growth Companies 149
Corporate Accountability 155
Corporate Financial Policy 162
Cost Accounting 167
Cost Management Systems 177
Cost-Benefit Analysis: Decision-Making in the
    Public Sector 182
Crowdfunding in Business 189

Entrepreneurship 194
Entrepreneurship and Business Planning 200
Entrepreneurship and Venture Initiation 206
Ethical Responsibilities of Business 212
Ethics in Accounting 218

Financial and Accounting Compliance 224
Fundamental vs. Technical Financial Analysis . . . 229
Funding New Ventures 234

Global Finance 240
Globalization and International Accounting 247
Gold Standard 254
Governmental Accounting 260
Growth of Nations in the Global Economy 267

History and Processes of the Stock Market 274

Income Distribution 281
Income Tax Accounting 288
Information Systems Auditing 293
International Corporate Finance 300
International Financial Accounting 306
Internet Security 311
Issues in International Banking 318
IT Management Applications 323

Law of Property 330
Liability Risk Management 341
Loss Distributions 347

Money, Banking, and the Economy 353

Nonprofit Accounting 359

Principles of Macroeconomics 368
Principles of Microeconomics 375
Principles of Taxation 384
Property and Liability Insurance 392

Role of International Financial Markets 402

Statistical Applications in Accounting 408
Stock Markets 413
21st Century IT Applications 420

Tax Administration 426
Tax Impact on Decisions 432
Tax Planning and Preparation 438
Taxes and Business Strategy 443
The Global Financial Crisis of 2007–2010 447
The U.S. Financial Crisis of 2007–2010 453
Theory of Interest 459
Time Value of Money 465

Wills, Trusts, Estates, and Taxation 471

Glossary 479
Index 493

PUBLISHER'S NOTE

Principles of Business: Accounting is the fifth volume of a new series on business information. The first four volumes cover *Finance, Marketing, Entrepreneurship,* and *Management.* The next volume will discuss *Economics.* This series is intended to offer the fundamentals of business topics in easy-to-understand language to students, researchers, and those interested in clear, current information on a wide variety of important and far-reaching business subjects.

Accounting is an integral part of business, government activity, and personal life. This volume provides the reader with a clear introduction to accounting principles and application. With topics like "Crowdfunding," "Cloud Computing Security," "Ethics in Accounting," "Funding New Ventures," and "Tax Impact on Decisions," *Accounting* offers detailed information on what is involved in starting and running your own business, how best to manage accounts on a day-to-day basis, and how to apply accounting principles to your work and personal life.

The entries in this volume are arranged in an A to Z order, from "Accounting for Complex Financial Structures" to "Wills, Trusts, Estates, and Taxation,"

making it easy to find a topic of interest. Each entry includes the following:

- *Abstract* giving a brief introduction to the topic;
- *Overview* that presents key terms and concepts;
- Clear, concise *presentation of the topic,* including a discussion of applications and issues;
- *Further reading* to help readers dig deeper with more specific material on the topic.

Added features include illustrations and helpful diagrams of relevant topics. The back matter in *Principles of Business: Accounting* contains a detailed glossary to support the meaning of the articles, as well as an index.

Salem Press thanks the contributors, whose names are listed with each essay. Their diverse backgrounds include graduate degrees in accounting, business expertise, and non-business experience that offers material that is often more accessible that that of accounting specialists. Without their expert contributions, a project of this nature would not be possible. A full list of contributor's names and affiliations follows this Publisher's Note.

Principles of Business: Accounting is, as are all titles in this series, available in print and as an e-book.

Introduction

Principles of Business: Accounting is the latest volume in the *Principles of Business* series by Salem Press. Other volumes cover *Management, Finance, Marketing* and *Entrepreneurship*. A volume on *Economics* will follow. *Principles of Business: Accounting* discuss topics vital to the understanding of this critical field, including accounting structures, business and entrepreneurship issues, ethical responsibilities, ramifications of a growing global economy, and taxation, as well as both the Global and U.S. Financial Crises of 2007-2010.

Understanding the principles of accounting is vital for all businesses and government entities, as well as for individuals. Anyone who is involved in an activity that requires the use of monetary transactions must keep accurate records of such transactions for a variety of reasons. Individuals maintain budgets of income and expenses to ensure that they do not succumb to a heavy debt load. Businesses keep accurate records to determine their profitability, answer to their boards of directors, and help meet the requests of their creditors. Both businesses and individuals must also report the status of their financial situations to the Internal Revenue Service on an annual basis. The preparation and maintenance of such records is the basis of all accounting methods.

Financial and Managerial Accounting

In business, the goal of financial accounting is to gather data and prepare financial statements that will provide the recipient of such materials, including boards of directors, shareholders, investors, banks and various government agencies, with the information necessary to make sound financial decisions regarding this business entity, as well as to meet all regulatory requirements.

Businesses are responsible for two tasks: acquiring financial and productive resources and combing the two resources in order to create new resources. Acquired resources are called assets, and the different types of assets are called equities.

Although organizations tend to focus significant time preparing financial reports for external stakeholders, the demands of an organization's management team are equally important. This group of individuals is responsible for providing direction to the organization. Therefore, it is crucial that they have access to the most up-to-date information regarding the organization's financial status. The organization tends to select an accounting system that would provide the management team with information that will assist and validate why they make certain decisions. The process of providing the management team with financial information that will assist in decision making is referred to as managerial accounting.

Managerial accounting is an internal function that focuses on using present financial information to anticipate and predict future events. All types of organizations can benefit from the use of managerial accounting information. The information obtained may assist organizations with their mission statement, vision, goals, and objectives.

The goals of these two types of accounting methods differ in their objectives. The goal of financial accounting is to provide information to external decision-makers while managerial accounting focuses on the needs of the businesses' internal decision-makers. Two types of techniques are utilized by decision-makers in the planning process: cost/value/profit (CVP) analysis and financial budgeting. An organization's income and profit is based on the structure of its revenues and costs as well as the volume of activity that it achieves. The financial budgeting process can be accomplished by utilizing an information system to perform a spreadsheet analysis. This process will eliminate the need for paperwork.

Accounting Systems and Controls

Accounting systems are comprised of hardware, software applications, and the people who design and administer the system as a whole. An accounting system has three distinct components: analysis, design, and implementation. These components generally incorporate databases, user applications, and the designers and end-users of the entire system. An organization's internal controls help determine its accounting systems.

Internal controls function as the administrative and procedural framework of an accounting system and can be thought of as a sub-system within the overall accounting system. The elements of an internal controls system are the control environment, risk assessment, control activities, information and communication, and monitoring of the controls.

Today, many companies are turning their attention to implementing an internal control framework that supports an overall risk management strategy within an organization. The benefits of implementing strong internal controls are not just a benefit or a requirement of public companies. Today, private companies are implementing accounting systems and internal controls as a means to improve operations, accountability, and efficiency.

NEED FOR ACCOUNTING UNDERSTANDING

In today's growing global economy, it has become increasingly important for individuals as well as businesses and government to have a firm understanding of accounting practices and responsibilities. Individuals who understand the basics of accounting will be able to handle their income and expenses better, thus being able to avoid financial pitfalls and be able to save for the future. Understanding accounting procedures will also help avoid being taken advantage of by those in powerful financial situations, such as banks and credit card institutions. Furthermore, understanding basic accounting methods allows the individual to understand the world around him or her better, including the recent tax cut enacted by Congress in 2017.

BIBLIOGRAPHY

Alino, N. U., & Schneider, G. P. (2012). Conflict reduction in organization design: budgeting and accounting control systems. *Academy of Strategic Management Journal, 11,* 1–8.

Applebaum, D., Kogan, A., Vasarhelyi, M., Yan, Z. (2017). Impact of business analytics and enterprise systems on managerial accounting. *International Journal of Accounting Information Systems, 25,* 29–44.

Diamond, E. (2007). What private companies need to know about internal controls. *New Jersey Tech News, 11.*

Drury, C. (1996). *Management and cost accounting* (4th ed.). London: International Thompson Business Press.

Florin, B., & Carmen, B. (2013). Management control systems: a review of their components and their underlying independence. *Annals of the University of Oradea, Economic Science Series, 22,* 1424–1433.

Fotache, G., Fotache, M., Bucsa, R., & Ocneanu, L. (2011). The changing role of managerial accounting in decision making process research on managing costs. *Economy Transdisciplinarity Cognition, 14,* 45–55.

Horngreen C. T., Stratton, W. O., & Sundem, G. L. (2002). *Introduction to management accounting* (12th ed.). New Jersey: Prentice Hall.

Page, J., & Hooper, P. (1985). *Microcomputer accounting and business applications* . Reston: Reston Publishing Company, Inc.

Rogoski, R. (2004). Investment pay off with financial information systems. *Health Management Technology, 25,* 14–17.

Thitiworada, S.,& Phapruke, U. (2013). Best managerial accounting information system and firm performance: an empirical investigation of information technology and communication bussiness in Thailand. *Review of Business Research, 13,* 47–66.

This introduction is based on essays Accounting Systems for Managerial Systems by Marie Gould and Accounting Systems and Controls by Carolyn Sprague

CONTRIBUTORS

MICHAEL P. AUERBACH

Michael P. Auerbach holds a BA from Wittenberg University and MA from Boston College. Mr. Auerbach has extensive private and public sector experience in a wide range of arenas: political science, business and economic development, tax policy, international development, defense, public administration, and tourism.

SETH M. AZRIA

Seth M. Azria earned his JD, magna cum laude, from New York Law School, where he was an editor of the *Law Review* and research assistant to a professor of labor and employment law. He has written appellate briefs and other memorandum of law on a variety of legal topics for submission to state and federal courts. He is a practicing attorney in Syracuse, New York.

SUE ANN CONNAUGHTON

Sue Ann Connaughton is a freelance writer and researcher. Formerly the manager of Intellectual Capital & Research at Silver Oak Solutions, a spend management solutions consulting firm, Ms. Connaughton holds a BA in English from Salem State College, a MEd from Boston University, and a MLS from Florida State University.

EDWIN D. DAVISON

Edwin D. Davison is an attorney from Dayton, Ohio and holds a MBA and a Ph.D in Law from the University of Wisconsin-Madison. He has completed professional management training at the University of Michigan Ross School of Business, UCLA Anderson School of Management, and the University of South Carolina Moore School of Business and has more than 20 years' experience as a management consultant, a business professor, an entrepreneur, and a U.S. Navy JAG attorney. He has published research on multinational human resource practices and is employed with the Educational Testing Service of Princeton, NJ.

NANCY DEVENGER

Nancy Devenger, FACMPE, holds a BS from the University of New Hampshire and a MS in health policy from Dartmouth College's Center for the Evaluative and Clinical Sciences. Ms. Devenger was a registered nurse before earning her undergraduate degree in business. She has worked in private medical practice, home health, consulting, and as director of ambulatory operations for a large academic medical center. Her operational experience as a business manager in private medical practice and in a tertiary medical center have allowed Ms. Devenger broad insight into both private and academic business endeavors.

MARLANDA ENGLISH

Dr. Marlanda English is president of ECS Consulting Associates, which provides executive coaching, management consulting, and online professional development content. Dr. English was previously employed in various engineering, marketing, and management positions with IBM, American Airlines, Borg-Warner Automotive, and Johnson & Johnson. Dr. English holds a doctorate in business with a major in organization and management and a specialization in e-business.

MICHAEL ERBSCHLOE

Michael Erbschloe is an information technology consultant, educator, and author. He has taught graduate level courses and developed technology-related curriculum for several universities and speaks at conferences and industry events around the world. Mr. Erbschloe holds a MS in Sociology from Kent State University. He has authored hundreds of articles and several books on technology.

SIMONE I. FLYNN

Dr. Simone I. Flynn earned her Ph.D in cultural anthropology from Yale University, where she wrote a dissertation on Internet communities. She is a writer, researcher, and teacher in Amherst, Massachusetts.

MARIE GOULD

Marie Gould is an associate professor and the faculty chair of the Business Administration Department at Peirce College in Philadelphia. She teaches management, entrepreneurship, and international business.

In a career that spans both academia and corporate, Ms. Gould has always enjoyed helping people learn through teaching, developing, or mentoring.

STEVEN R. HOAGLAND

Dr. Steven Hoagland holds BS and MS in economics, MS in urban studies, and a Ph.D in urban services management with a cognate in education, all from Old Dominion University. His experience includes senior-level university administration, adjunct professor of economics, consultant to grant development, and expertise in research design and program evaluation in the health care, information technology, and education sectors. In 2007, he founded a nonprofit organization to address failures in the education marketplace by guiding college-bound high school students toward objective information relevant to college selection and application processes.

HEATHER NEWTON

Heather Newton earned her JD, cum laude, from Georgetown University Law Center, where she served as articles editor for *The Georgetown Journal of Legal Ethics*. She worked as an attorney in Washington, D.C., before moving to Atlanta, where she is currently an editor for a legal publishing company. Prior to law school, she was a high school English teacher and freelance writer. Her work has appeared in numerous print and online publications.

ELIZABETH RHOLETTER PURDY

Elizabeth Rholetter Purdy earned a BA in political science graduating summa cum laude from Columbus College, an MA from Emory University as a Phi Kappa Phi fellow, and a Ph.D in political science from Georgia State University. She has published articles on subjects ranging from political science and women's studies to economics and popular culture.

CAROLYN SPRAGUE

Carolyn Sprague holds a BS from the University of New Hampshire and a MLS from Simmons College.

Ms. Sprague gained business experience by owning and operating a restaurant 10 years. Since earning her graduate degree, Ms. Sprague has worked in numerous library/information settings within the academic, corporate, and consulting worlds. Her operational experience as a manager at a global high tech firm and as a web content researcher have afforded Ms. Sprague insight into many aspects of today's challenging and fast-changing business climate.

VANESSA A. TETTEH

Dr. Tetteh earned her Ph.D from the University of Buckingham in England, United Kingdom, where she wrote a dissertation on tourism policy, education, and training. She is a teacher, writer, and management consultant based in Ghana, West Africa. Her work has appeared in journals such as *International Journal of Contemporary Hospitality Management*, *Consortium Journal*, and *Ghana Review International*.

RICHA S. TIWARY

Dr. Richa S. Tiwary holds a Ph.D in marketing management with a specialization in consumer behavior from Banaras Hindu University, India. She earned her second MLS with dual concentration in information science technology, and library information services from the Department of Information Studies, University at Albany-SUNY.

RUTH A. WIENCLAW

Dr. Ruth A. Wienclaw holds a Ph.D in industrial/organizational psychology with a specialization in organization development from the University of Memphis. She is the owner of a small business that works with organizations in both the public and private sectors, consulting on matters of strategic planning, training, and human/systems integration.

SCOTT ZIMMER

Scott Zimmer has earned a MLS, a MS in computer science, and a JD. He is an attorney and a librarian at Alliant International University.

A

ACCOUNTING FOR COMPLEX FINANCIAL STRUCTURES

According to a Bureau of National Affairs report, complexity in accounting principles and practices is one of the top challenges of accounting professionals and businesses. The knowledge economy and global marketplace have spawned larger, more diverse, and more complex organizations. Accounting standards and practices have increased in complexity in proportion to the organizations for which they are written. The Financial Accounting Standards Board (FASB) in the United States is the organization that is primarily responsible for writing accounting standards for both public and private companies in the United States. The FASB maintains Generally Accepted Accounting Principles (GAAP) for use by public and private businesses to prepare their financial statements. FASB has been criticized by various stakeholders for adding to the complexity of accounting standards in the United States. The FASB has been working on an internal codification project that will reorganize GAAP into a much more user-friendly and accessible format. The FASB is also working with other American boards and entities to reduce redundancy in the writing and interpretation of accounting principles. The FASB and the Securities and Exchange Commission (SEC) teamed up in 2007 to address the issue of complexity in accounting and financial reporting and are addressing major issues that have been raised by stakeholders in the public and private sectors. International Financial Reporting Standards (IFRS's) are being converged with U.S. GAAP standards to eliminate the need for two different sets of accounting standards in the United States. The topics covered in this article highlight some of the challenges that complex accounting practices are posing to public and private businesses in the United States. This article also highlights a number of steps that are being taken to reduce complexity in accounting for complex organizations.

OVERVIEW

The topic of complexity as related to accounting is like the chicken-or-the-egg scenario. Is complexity related to accounting as the result of the complexity of today's organizational structure, or have the rules just become more complicated in an effort to account for complex organizations? The answer to this question lies somewhere in the middle. Certainly the nature of American corporations has changed rapidly and radically over the years, and accounting rules have struggled to keep up. The following comments were made in 2006 by then SEC commissioner Cynthia Glassman.

> "The economy continues to evolve at a rapid pace, while reporting standards and mechanisms are in a "catch-up" mode. "Advances in technology, including the emergence of the Internet, faster and more ubiquitous communication and other technological developments, have changed the way companies do business, as well as changing the types of financial arrangements and instruments that businesses utilize. As the business world has become more complex, so have financial reports and accounting standards" (Glassman, 2006).

The comments by Commissioner Glassman indicate that accounting rules are being written in response to the changing nature of American and global business.

According to the Bureau of National Affairs' (BNA) *Accounting Policy & Practice Series(tm)*, "The advisory board members—high level corporate accountants from Corning, Microsoft, and Eli Lilly and Co., as well leading academics and advisors —named complexity as a key topic when asked to name top [accounting] issues for 2007" ("Surviving Complexity," 2007). This article focuses on the complexity of today's accounting standards and how organizations

US Security and Exchange Commission Office is located in Washington, D.C. (Courtesy of Don Ramey Logan via Wikimedia Commons)

are responding to the myriad of changes that affect their financial and accounting practices.

The following comments underscore just how big the issue of complexity is for those who must interpret accounting rules in today's economy. The comments were delivered to the FASB and the SEC by a committee from Financial Executives International (FEI).

- Every effort should be made to work with stakeholders "to end the proliferation of detailed rules"; the general consensus from FEI and its subcommittee, the Committee on Corporate Reporting (CCR), is that accountants are struggling to understand and keep up with the deluge of new accounting standards.
- "Over the past ten years, the Board (FASB) has issued a significant number of standards that are among the most complex we have ever encountered. These standards have caused significant difficulties in practice due to one or more of the following: Scopes that are broad and hard to comprehend; complex accounting principles that require extensive supplemental interpretive guidance; and measurement principles that pre-

sume a level of valuation capabilities that do not exist uniformly across the preparer community" (Difabio, 2007).

Globalization, the rise of multinational corporations, compliance, government oversight, and mergers and acquisitions have greatly impacted accounting practices at public companies. "Accountants, investment bankers, and clients are structuring financial instruments around the provisions of highly technical, complex accounting pronouncements. The game is based on whether the security falls either inside or outside of the established principle. The predictable recipe resulting from this cookbook is what one observes in Enron, WorldCom, Adelphia, and so on" (McCarthy, 2004).

Currently, regulatory and financial reporting is much more demanding for public companies than for private companies—as are the stakeholders who have the most invested in sound accounting practices and accurate reporting of company financials. Common stakeholders for public and private companies include employees, customers, partners, and boards of directors. Private companies' biggest stakeholders are company owners and banks and institutions that finance the company's growth. Public companies' stakeholders include executive managers, investors, and creditors.

Private Companies
Private companies, while not subject to the same government oversight as public companies, are faced with increasingly complex accounting rules as well. GAAP for public companies are increasingly diverging from the GAAP standards for private companies.

In reference to the proliferation of complex accounting principles, one critic points out that the FASB is rewriting accounting standards to support publicly traded companies, which constitute the minority of businesses in the United States.

"To whom is FASB pandering when it promulgates these principles? The answer is the international accounting firms, their multinational public clients, and the relative few financial analysts and investment bankers that say they need this kind of information.

Understand this phenomenon for what it is. The historical record of economic activity in the United States is being replaced with a system tailored to these specific constituencies" (McCarthy, 2004).

Privately held companies still comprise the vast majority of businesses in the United States, and many are convinced the FASB is rewriting accounting standards to support the minority of businesses (public companies).

To fully understand how and why accounting standards are changing so rapidly, one must also look at the changing nature of American business as it moves steadily to a knowledge-based economy. Many of the standard industrial-age accounting practices do not accurately address the changing nature of American and international business. In today's knowledge economy, businesses have fewer tangible, "hard" assets on their balance sheets. More typically, today's corporation derives much of its value from intangible assets such as customer relationships, intellectual property, brand recognition, and other knowledge-based activities.

The sheer number and breadth of current accounting standards contributes to the difficulty and complexity for public and private companies to stay on top of current accounting procedures. "The proliferation of codified accounting principles has, in large part, led to the distress that the profession currently is experiencing. Codified principles issued by the Accounting Principles Board (APB), then by FASB, have led to a 'cookbook' approach to financial reporting" (McCarthy, 2004).

Few investors and other stakeholders would disagree that corporations have become complex entities. Many corporations (U.S.-based and others) have operations in many different countries. Operations continue around the clock in different time zones, and many corporations rely on far-flung but highly integrated supply chains. Investment capital is readily available along with a more diverse set of creditors and investors. The vast changes that globalization and the "flattening" of the world have initiated are reflected in the financial and accounting standards that have attempted to keep pace with these changes.

This article investigates the current topic of reducing financial reporting complexity that is being studied by the SEC, FASB, and the U.S. Treasury Department. Topics include

- SEC efforts to study practices that will reduce complexity in the creation and application of accounting principles.
- increasing numbers of financial restatements.
- what information investors and owners really want on financial statements.

This article concludes with a look at the move toward the adoption of IFRS's, the future role of the FASB, and some of the implications affecting private companies.

APPLICATIONS

The FASB is the specified private-sector organization that determines financial reporting and accounting standards.

Financial statements should be

- credible
- concise
- transparent
- understandable
- responsive to a changing economic environment
- useful to public and others for decision making
- promote, whenever possible, convergence with existing standards

This article investigates different viewpoints regarding just how well stakeholders from public and private companies think the FASB is adhering to its stated core mission and directives.

Public Companies—GAAP

Private companies are largely exempt from many of the prescribed accounting and compliance standards that affect public companies. As accounting standards are revised, many would say with an emphasis on public companies, GAAP standards for public and private companies diverge to a greater extent.

Complexity has become part of the business landscape in the United States when it comes to accounting practices. Officials at the Public Companies Accounting Oversight Board (PCAOB) "acknowledged that, as a result of the enactment of the

Sarbanes-Oxley Act, auditing standards for public companies now differ substantially from those of nonpublic companies. The differences are factual and no longer arguable" (McCarthy, 2004).

Private companies greatly outnumber public companies in the United States. Critics of the FASB contend that the board has largely ignored private companies, as many of the recent standards are slanted toward publicly traded companies. "Private companies have a significant impact on our economy, and the attention given to this sector by our standard setters has been largely nonexistent compared to that given to public companies, which represent only a fraction of the 22 million businesses in the United States" (Kranacher, 2006). As FASB accounting standards and GAAP are written for different constituencies—public and private companies—the volume and complexity of standards increase. Private companies are not subject to the same regulatory reporting and financial transparency as public companies, and as such may be erroneously regarded as having a lower bar for financial reporting and for applying GAAP.

"The intention is not for private-company GAAP to be less significant or less prestigious than public-company GAAP. It would be different, that is all. Auditing standards for public companies are not considered superior to those required for nonpublic companies. Neither should private-company accounting principles be considered less significant than those promulgated for multinational companies" (McCarthy, 2004). The future of the FASB is in question— particularly in regard to its role as a standard setter for public companies. As IFRS standards take the place of GAAP standards for public companies, it has been suggested that the FASB may refocus its attention on setting standards for private companies. It remains to be seen if maintaining GAAP alongside IFRS standards will help to reduce accounting complexity for private companies.

Creation of the SEC & Treasury Board Oversight Committees

Early in 2007, it seemed that Congress was finally ready to address the topic of complexity in accounting. This time, the FEI sounded the warning that complexity in accounting standards is likely compromising American market competitiveness. While concerns about increasing complexity in accounting standards

had been a topic for some years, in 2005 the FEI filed comment letters with the FASB expressing concerns about FASB statement 141 (Business Combinations). The FEI stated that the "cumulative consequences of these statements leave accountants struggling to understand what to do." According to the FEI (a perennial watchdog of the FASB), the complexity of FASB statements was increasing company reliance on outside subject matter experts to apply requirements. Fast forward to 2007 and the FEI once again voiced concerns about reducing complexity, while concurrently the FASB was working to finalize standards on business combinations and release new or revised statements such as FIN 48 and statement 133 (DiFabio, 2007). In June of 2007, "Washington responded to the crisis by forming a commission to study the problem" (DiFabio, 2007). The SEC chair at the time, Chris Cox, with support from the FASB and the PCAOB, announced the establishment of SEC's Advisory Committee on Improvements to Financial Reporting (CIFR).

"Cox said the SEC-sponsored group will focus on reducing complexity in U.S. financial reporting, while an effort promoted by U.S. Treasury Secretary Henry Paulson will examine the business of U.S. accounting, now dominated by the Big Four accounting firms. Still, Cox didn't rule out potential overlap between the two studies and said the SEC will coordinate closely with Treasury Department officials on the committee's work" (SEC Unveils Effort To Attack U.S. Accounting Complexity, 2007).

The goals outlined by the SEC-sponsored group included the following goals and objectives addressed in 2007-2008 ("Surviving Complexity," Top 2007):

- creating less complex accounting rules and clear direction for companies applying them
- determining better ways to communicate financial results to sophisticated and ordinary investors
- reducing irrelevant financial reporting
- moving toward convergence with international standards
- pushing toward fair value reporting for financial instruments
- continuing the FASB codification project

While the FASB chair did not dispute that accounting standards are overly complex, he was quick to point out the mission of the FASB in creating current standards. Accounting standards are written to meet business needs through accurate application and creation of financial reports (Glassman, 2006).

- Standards allow companies to present their business and financial conditions based on current knowledge and expectations for the future.
- Standards provide accurate reports of companies' operating results and cash flows.
- Financial statements reflect economic and business reality and help investors formulate investment decisions.
- Statements decrease the probability of distorted business reality and cause capital to be deployed suboptimally.
- Standards allow companies to provide investors with accurate information about the value of investing in a given company.
- Standards provide customers and suppliers with accurate data to make important business decisions.
- Standards inform lenders about the true risk associated with loans.
- Standards provide employees with an accurate picture of employer's financials.

Financial complexity can be as devastating to corporate reputation and confidence as fraud (Glassman, 2006).

CODIFICATION

The FASB has its eyes on a convergence of American accounting standards with international standards, but first the United States needs to reign and codify its own disperse accounting regulations. According to Glassman, "Accounting standards and literature flow from a vast array of standard setters, regulators and other sources. The financial reporting landscape is littered with pronouncements from the FASB, the AICPA, the EITF, the APB, the SEC and the PCAOB. We have pronouncements, rules, regulations, guides, bulletins, audit standards, interpretations and practice aids in the form of SOPs, FAQs, SABs, Q&As and FSPs" (Glassman, 2006).

Estimates put the number of separate pronouncements that apply to U.S. GAAP at more than 2,000. According to Glassman, the SEC, like many government agencies, has a "bureaucratic tendency to create ever thicker rule books." The standard setters simply add another layer of complexity with each pronouncement until "the original regulatory goal becomes obscured amid thousands of words of detailed dictates. Some SEC rules, intended to guide market participants in daily decisions, have become a kind of Latin liturgy, comprehensible only to those of us who have devoted our professional lives to abstract regulatory nuances" (Glassman, 2006).

Before the United States can even hope to converge U.S. GAAP and other accounting principles with international standards, a huge amount of work needs to be done with the U.S. codification project. "Codification has been cited as a top issue in 2007 and will serve to move toward the development of a uniform set of accounting standards. The standards will be more objective-oriented and principles-based. The codification project will integrate accounting guidance from the FASB, AICPA, EITF, and SEC into a single, consistently written source" (Iannaconi & Schinas, 2007).

Robert Pozen also took a stab at the myriad of standards that are inundating companies and their financial preparers. The SEC group blames the complexity buildup on the wealth and length of accounting standards from the FASB in the past several years, and on the mounting interpretations of those rules coming from regulators and the accounting firms. "We have too much GAAP running around," Pozen said during the CIFR's first meeting. "We need to figure out what is and isn't GAAP and grab hold of it" (Johnson, 2007).

FINANCIAL RESTATEMENTS

One big concern around complexity in financial and accounting reporting is the increase in financial restatements by companies. A restatement refers to the revision of a company's earlier financial statements. Restatements can result from clerical error, fraud, or misinterpretation of accounting standards. The increasing number of restatements has been seen by the SEC committee as an indication that the financial reporting system is overly complex (SEC Unveils Effort To Attack U.S. Accounting Complexity, 2007).

Robert Pozen, then chair of the CIFR, stated "We need clearer accounting standards." He also suggested that firms are finding it difficult to comply with accounting rules and added that costly and confusing financial restatements could be improved if American accounting rules "were simpler to understand and apply" (SEC Unveils Effort to Attack U.S. Accounting Complexity, 2007).

Value of Financial Statements

Complexity in accounting standards has led to complexity in financial reporting as well. In general, financial statements are not only difficult to prepare, but are also difficult for many holders to understand. The use of press releases by corporate management is thought to be an indication that many users do not want or need the complex level of information that is provided on many financial statements (Iannaconi& Schinas, 2007). The Governmental Accounting Standards Board (GASB) has committed to using plain language in its communications with constituents (Governmental Accounting Standards Board, 2013).

Comments provided by constituents to the FASB are being taken seriously. The end result of all the complexity associated with creating accurate and usable financial statements is having the opposite effect for many end-users. According to Glassman, "Commentators have suggested that our current prescriptive accounting rules have contributed to a lack of transparency in financial reporting, where boilerplate conceals what is really going on" (Glassman, 2006).

Glassman added, "Reducing accounting complexity and migrating to a more principles-based accounting system would encourage more accurate and complete financial disclosure. Therefore, standard setters and regulators should consider how accounting standards and disclosure rules can be re-designed to elicit information that is complete, clear and concise, and thus, more useful to investors" (Glassman, 2006).

The SEC's CIFR group also examines what type of financial information investors and other stakeholders need and want going forward. The CIFR is aware that companies may be more interested in key performance indicators (KPI) and forward-looking information rather than complex financial statements. According to the CIFR, "Financial performance summaries, compressed into a few pages, might be helpful for individual investors, provided firms include links to supplemental details that are useful to analysts and sophisticated investors" (SEC Unveils Effort to Attack U.S. Accounting Complexity,

2007). This information may be more useful than much of the current information that is provided on financial statements (Iannaconi & Schinas, 2007). The CIFR helps make financial statements more useful and relevant to end-users.

CONCLUSION

In the third quarter of 2007, the SEC issued a statement that proposed eliminating the requirement of international companies to reconcile its IRFR-prepared financial statements with GAAP. Some question if U.S.-domiciled businesses (multinationals) should have a similar choice. Critics of this move state that the SEC is pushing too fast for the adoption of IFRS standards. These are related questions:

- What is the future of GAAP?
- How will this move affect the ongoing convergence of GAAP and IFRS standards?
- What will be the role of the FASB going forward if GAAP is eliminated?

There is certainly a suggestion that the FASB will still lose its standing as the official standard setter for the accounting rules that govern American-based public companies. There have been suggestions that the FASB could serve as the new standard setter for private companies and nonprofits in the United States. The FASB could also take on a role in educating companies about the new IFRS standards or serve in an advisory capacity to the board (Is FASB fading away? 2007).

This proposal is a clear signal that there is an international movement to adopt one strong global accounting standard. The major accounting firms have voiced favor for the SEC proposal and concede not only the inevitability of IFRS adoption, but also a speedier time line for adoption. There are numerous concerns about any course of action; some fear that allowing for a dual set of standards (GAAP and IFRS) will slow down the convergence to a global standard. Others feel that the SEC is being hasty in its proposal, as many feel that IFRS standards are not yet ready.

TERMS & CONCEPTS

Accounting complexity: Refers to the proliferation of American accounting principles, which have become increasingly bureaucratic, complex, and prolific. In 2007 the SEC established an independent committee to investigate how to address the debilitating issue of accounting complexity for American corporations.

Bureau of National Affairs (BNA): The largest independent information and analysis publisher for tax, law, business, and government professionals.

Business combination: A transaction or other event where one entity takes control of one or more businesses through acquisition. A business combination can occur in a number of situations but usually happens through the purchase of the net assets or equity interests of one or more businesses.

Codification Project: See FASB Codification Project.

Convergence with U.S. GAAP: In 2002 the IASB and the FASB agreed to coordinate their agendas to minimize differences between IFRS and U.S. GAAP (the Norwalk Agreement).

Financial Accounting Standards Board (FASB): The specified private sector organization responsible for determining financial reporting and accounting standards. The FASB is recognized by the SEC as the official setter of accounting standards.

FASB Codification Project: This project organized the thousands of articles in the U.S. GAAP based on accounting topic. All 90 or so topics are presented using a standardized structure (Federal Accounting Standards Board, 2012).

FEI (Financial Executives International): FEI has become the leading advocate for ensuring that corporate financial management voices get heard. Its 15,000 members hold numerous policymaking positions as chief financial officers, treasurers, and controllers. The FEI is a watchdog organization of the FASB.

Financial restatement: Refers to the revision of a company's earlier financial statements. The need for restating financial figures can result from fraudulent practices or the misrepresentation of financial or accounting standards through human error.

Generally Accepted Accounting Principles (GAAP): The standardized structure for financial accounting guidelines. Mainly used in the United States, it includes standards, conventions, and rules followed by accountants while recording and summarizing transactions and preparing financial statements.

Intangible assets: Nonmonetary assets that cannot be physically measured but that are created through time and effort. The two main types of intangibles are legal intangibles—such as trade secrets, copyrights, patents, trademarks, and goodwill—and competitive intangibles—such as knowledge activities, collaboration activities, leverage activities, and structural procedures.

International Financial Reporting Standards (IFRS): Standards and interpretations adopted by the International Accounting Standards Board (IASB).

BIBLIOGRAPHY

Bryan, S., & Lilien, S. (2013). How fair values and accounting structures allow triple-counting income: Implications for standard setters, market participants, and academics. *Journal of Accounting, Auditing & Finance, 28,* 79–98.

DiFabio, C. (2007). Washington poised to tackle complexity in reporting. *Financial Executive, 23,* 66.

Etheridge, H., & Kathy Hsiao Yu, H. (2013). Financial instrument credit impairment models—a rift in the convergence of IASB and FASB accounting standards. *Academy of Accounting & Financial Studies Journal, 17,* 119–126.

Facts about FASB. (2007).

Federal Accounting Standards Board. (2012). FASB Learning Guide: For the Codification Research System.

Glassman, C. (2006). Complexity in financial reporting and disclosure regulation. SEC.

Goodwill games: How to tackle FASB's new merger rules. (2001). CFO.com.

Governmental Accounting Standards Board. Plain Language Documents. (2013).

Iannaconi, T. & Schinas, W. (2007). SEC advisory committee to study ways to reduce complexity in financial reporting system. KPMG.

Is FASB fading away? (2007). CFO.com.

Johnson, S. (2007). Here's how to fix accounting's complexity. *CFO*.

Kranacher, M. (2006). The GAAP between public and private companies. *CPA Journal*.

Matthew Austin J., et al. (2017). From board to bedside: How the application of financial structures to safety and quality can drive accountability in a large health care system. *The Joint Commission Journal on Quality and Patient Safety, 43*(4), 166–175.

McCarthy, P. (2004). Unnecessary complexity in accounting principles. *CPA Journal*.

Scheig, G., & Perrone, D. (2004). Bringing intangible assets into focus: Customer relationships. *Natural Gas & Electricity, 20*, 18–23.

Schmidt, J., Wilkins, M. S. (2013). Bringing darkness to light: The influence of auditor quality and audit committee expertise on the timeliness of financial statement restatement disclosures. *Auditing, 32*, 221–244.

SEC unveils effort to attack U.S. accounting complexity. (2007). *Dow Jones Newswires*.

Shortridge, R., Schroeder, A. & Wagoner, E. (2006). Fair value accounting. *CPA Journal*.

Surviving complexity top accounting challenge for 2007, leading accountants say. (2007). BNA.

U.S. GAAP vs IFRS: The basics. Ernst & Young.

Womack, B. (2005). Mind the GAAP: Private companies want accounting fixes. *Orange County Business Journal, 28*, 31.

SUGGESTED READINGS

Business combinations II. (2007). IASB.

Johnson, K., & Richson, C. (2007). The global M&A boom continues: Are boards getting shareholders their money's worth? *Corporate Governance Advisor, 15*, 25–31.

Massoud, M. & Raiborn, C. (2003). Accounting for goodwill: Are we better off? *Review of Business, 24*, 26.

Summary of FASB tentative decisions on business combinations. (2004). FASB.

Tysiac, K.(2013). New mechanisms eyed by FASB, IASB in long march toward global comparability. *Journal of Accountancy* (Nov. 2013).

Essay by Carolyn Sprague, MLS

ACCOUNTING FOR MERGERS AND ACQUISITIONS

This article explains the basic principles relating to accounting for mergers and acquisitions. The article provides an overview of mergers and acquisitions, with explanations of the most common types of mergers, merger procedures, and the means by which companies finance a merger or an acquisition. The two most common types of accounting methods for mergers and acquisitions are also described, including the pooling method, which was traditionally used but was phased out in 2001, and the purchase method. In addition, this article also describes the valuation procedures for accounting for mergers and acquisitions, including valuation methodologies using the purchase method, calculating the purchase price, and the required disclosures using the purchase method. Finally, various applications of accounting in business combination activities are described, such as tax considerations in a merger or an acquisition, pension liabilities, and the accretion or dilution of earnings following a merger or an acquisition.

OVERVIEW

Mergers and acquisitions are types of business combinations in which separate entities or operations of entities are merged into one reporting entity. Mergers occur when two or more corporations become one. In a typical merger, the assets and liabilities of one company are transferred to another, and the two companies no longer operate independently. Shareholders of the merging company become shareholders of the resulting company or are entitled to compensation for their shares. Mergers occur for many reasons such as improved market share or ownership of supply or distribution channels. Mergers can be either friendly or unfriendly. Friendly mergers develop with the management of the merging firms approving and supporting the combination. Hostile mergers are known as take-overs, because they are met with resistance and opposition from the merging firm.

An acquisition occurs when one company acquires, or takes control, of another company. This can occur when the acquiring company assumes total control of the target, or the company that has been identified for acquisition, or when the acquiring company purchases the majority of another company's stock or all of its assets. Although acquisitions can be unfriendly, as in a hostile takeover, in a purchase of assets, the acquiring company must still negotiate the asset acquisition with the management of the target. The following sections provide a more in-depth explanation of mergers and acquisitions, and the accounting techniques used in these business combinations.

Understanding Mergers and Acquisitions

Mergers and acquisitions are methods by which corporations legally unify ownership of assets formerly subject to separate controls. Mergers and acquisitions are regulated by federal and state laws that are aimed at monitoring the effects of the elimination of competition in an industry, which increases the potential for the dominant company to raise prices or reduce output. However, mergers and acquisitions often result in a number of social benefits. Mergers can bring better management and technical skills to smaller companies and can streamline production processes resulting in reduced costs, quality improvement, and product diversification. The following sections explain the types of mergers and acquisitions and the procedures and methods companies use to complete and finance the business combination.

Types of Mergers and Acquisitions

Three common forms of mergers are the result of the relationship between the merging parties.

- In a horizontal merger, a company acquires a competitor firm that produces and sells an identical or a similar product in the same geographic area.
- In a vertical merger, a company acquires a customer or supplier.
- Conglomerate mergers include a number of other types of business combinations, regardless of common geographic location or industry affiliation. Conglomerate mergers may arise when a

company wants to expand for reasons not directly related to competition in the marketplace, such as when a furniture manufacturer buys an appliance manufacturer or when a sales agency in Ohio buys a sales agency in Florida.

Like mergers, acquisitions can take several forms. In a tender offer, the acquiring company makes a public offer to purchase a majority of shares from the target company's shareholders, thus bypassing the target company's management. In order to induce the shareholders to sell, or "tender," their shares, the acquiring company typically offers a purchase price higher than the market value of the shares, although the acquiring company may require that enough shares must be tendered in order for the acquiring company to gain control of the target company. If the tender offer is successful, the acquiring company may change the management and certain procedures of the target company or the acquiring company may use its newfound control to effect a merger of the two companies. For instance, in a cash-out merger, the target company is merged into the acquiring company, and the shareholders of the target company are given the right to receive cash for their shares.

Procedures for Mergers and Acquisitions

There is no single corporate law in the United States that governs business combinations. Instead, each individual state has its own domestic corporation law. However, companies involved in a merger or an acquisition must generally obtain the approval of the board of directors for certain significant corporate changes. In addition, the shareholders of a target company are typically required to give their approval for a merger or an acquisition.

The approval of the boards of directors of the companies has to include such information as the terms of the merger and the entities that will survive or be acquired in the transaction. Once the required approvals are obtained, a notice is filed by the surviving entity with the Secretary of State within the state where the entity has been formed. Statutes often provide that corporations formed in different states must follow the rules of the respective states for a merger to be effective.

In addition, companies involved in a merger or an acquisition may need to comply with federal securities laws, unless the transaction is exempt from registration under the Securities Act of 1933. For transactions that are not exempt, a registration with the Securities and Exchange Commission (SEC) is required if the transaction includes corporate modifications, reorganizations or transfers of control in a company.

Financing Mergers and Acquisitions

There are several different methods by which companies finance mergers and acquisitions.

- First, payment may be by cash from the acquiring company's reserves or from cash that has been borrowed from a bank or raised by an issue of bonds.
- Companies may also participate in a leveraged buyout, in which most of the debt is financed by selling off some of the target company's divisions or assets while the acquiring company pays only a small percentage of the total purchase price.
- Also, an acquisition can involve a combination of cash and debt, or a combination of cash and stock of the purchasing entity.
- Finally, there are Employee Stock Ownership Plans (ESOPs), which call for a firm to tender its own stock, paying for it by borrowing at a bank and then repaying the loan from the employee stock fund.

Ideally, mergers are implemented to facilitate synergism, whereby the value of the merged firm is greater than the sum of the two separate entities. However, mergers are not always this neat. The combined company after a merger can become too large, which can create management problems. Also, company founders or top performers who have aggressively pursued profits at an individual company may become disenchanted by heavy-handed managerial oversight from an acquiring company. Or, the combined operations of the merged companies may not operate as efficiently and effectively as a smaller, streamlined business.

Methods of Accounting for Mergers and Acquisitions

Mergers and acquisitions are reported and analyzed using unique accounting methods. Historically, there were two accepted methods of accounting for business combinations: the pooling method and the purchase method, sometimes referred to as the purchase

acquisition method. However, the pooling method is no longer permitted for new business combinations initiated after June 30, 2001. Although the pooling method has been phased out, it is still an important accounting method to understand, as many business combinations used this accounting method until it was eliminated. The following sections will provide greater details about these two accounting methods.

Pooling Method

Under the *pooling method*, all assets and liabilities were recorded at existing book values while goodwill was not recorded. As a result, the values for the assets and liabilities listed in the accounting records and financial statements of each company involved in a merger or an acquisition were carried forward to the surviving company that remained or was created after the business combination. Under the pooling method, no new assets or liabilities were created by the business combination. Further, the income statement of the surviving company included all of the revenues and expenses of the fiscal year for each company. Ultimately, the operating results for both companies were combined for all periods prior to the closing date, and previously issued financial statements were restated as though the companies had always been combined.

The pooling method was not designed to be used whenever it would produce favorable accounting records. Instead, it was intended to be used only for mergers of two entities of approximately equal value. This method came under increasing scrutiny and disfavor because over time it created disparate financial outcomes in transactions that were otherwise relatively similar, and thus became a tool that could be misused for financial gain. For instance, if an acquiring company paid cash for an acquisition, the accounting records created using the pooling method could appear to reflect that the acquiring company had lower earnings and financial returns compared to companies that paid using debt or a cash and stock combination because an acquiring company paying cash could amortize the additional goodwill on its income statement. In addition, the pooling method was unique to the United States, and this raised concern among the global accounting community that the use of different accounting methods may produce unequal or biased financial statements. As a result, the pooling method was eliminated as an approved accounting method in July of 2001.

Purchase Method

The *purchase method* is now the preferred accounting method used for business combinations. Under the purchase method, the purchase price and costs of the acquisition are allocated to the identified assets that are acquired, whether tangible or intangible, and to any liabilities that are assumed based on the current fair market value of the assets and liabilities. If the purchase price exceeds the fair value of the purchased company's net assets, the excess is recorded as goodwill. Goodwill, or the excess of the cost of an acquired entity over the net of the amounts assigned to assets acquired and liabilities assumed, is almost always present because the purchase price of a target or its assets is almost always higher than the sum of the fair values of all of the assets being purchased. This is because a company is more than just the sum of its assets. It also has intangible qualities such as its reputation in the business community that add to its value beyond the market value of its assets. However, the purchase method does not allow the allocated purchase price for any asset to exceed its fair value. Thus, the excess is recorded as goodwill as a type of catchall category.

In addition, under the purchase method, earnings or losses of the purchased company are included in the acquiring company's financial statements beginning on the closing date of the acquisition. The total liabilities of the combined firms equal the sum of the two firms' individual liabilities. The equity of the acquiring firm is increased by the amount of the purchase price. Short-term or current liabilities have a current fair value equal to their book value. Long-term liabilities may have fair values different from current book value should the face amount of the interest rate not fluctuate with current market conditions.

Attitudes toward the purchase method are not altogether positive. The method was blamed by Gerard Cassidy, a director of equity research, for merger and acquisition activity in the banking industry slowing down considerably following the thrift and banking crises of the late 1980s and early 1990s (Anason, 2012).

Accounting Procedures for Mergers and Acquisitions

Under the purchase method of accounting for mergers and acquisitions, all assets acquired and liabilities assumed are recorded at their current fair market value. This process follows certain valuation procedures.

- First, the process of allocating valuation among the various assets purchased starts with the determination of tangible assets purchased, such as inventory, equipment, or furniture.
- Next, any identifiable intangible assets are classified and valued, such as trademarks, patents, or covenants not to compete.
- Finally, if appropriate, goodwill is recorded and expensed down to its fair value.

In addition to the valuation of a target's assets and liabilities, an appropriate purchase price for the target must also be calculated. This calculation involves determining the minimum and maximum price that an acquiring company should pay for the target. Once this range has been established, the negotiations between the acquiring company and the target get underway. Finally, when the transaction has been completed, certain information must be disclosed in the financial statements of the companies. The following sections will provide further explanation of these valuation procedures.

Valuation Using the Purchase Method

Under the purchase method of accounting, there are specific methodologies for valuing each major balance sheet category, and each of these categories must be assessed and valued in order to properly calculate the assets of the target company. For cash and accounts receivable, these items are reduced for bad debt and returns and are then valued at their values on the books of the target company prior to the acquisition. Marketable securities are valued at their realizable value after any transaction costs. Inventories are broken into finished goods and raw materials. Finished goods are valued at their liquidation value; raw materials inventories at their current replacement cost. Last-in, first-out inventory reserves maintained by the target before the acquisition are eliminated. Property, plant and equipment are valued at fair market value.

In addition, accounts payable and accrued expenses are valued at the levels at which they were recorded in the accounting records of target prior to the acquisition. Pension fund obligations are valued in relation to any excess or deficiency in the value of the fund relative to its obligations, and by calculating the present value of the projected benefit obligations given the present value of pension fund assets. Intangible assets are valued at their appraised values. All other liabilities are recorded at their net present value of future cash payments.

After this process of valuing all of the target's assets and liabilities, the target's net identifiable assets are calculated. This is done after both eliminating the target company's goodwill and valuing all assets and liabilities according to their fair value. Then, any difference between the target's identifiable assets and liabilities is calculated. This difference represents the target company's net identifiable assets. Further, a target's net identifiable assets provide an accurate approximation of the fair value of the target. Any excess of the purchase price paid above that fair value is considered transaction goodwill and recorded as such.

On July 1, 2013, the Financial Accounting Standards Board (FASB) issued two proposed Accounting Standards Updates on the subject of goodwill in private-company accounting. PCC Issue 13-01A, Accounting for Identifiable Intangible Assets in a Business Combination, would allow private companies relief from the requirement to separately recognize certain intangible assets that are acquired in business combinations. In other words, a private company would have the option not to recognize an intangible asset separate from goodwill, unless that asset arises from a non-cancelable contract or other legal right. PCC Issue 13-01B, Accounting for Goodwill Subsequent to a Business Combination, would allow private companies to amortize goodwill and use a simplified goodwill impairment model. Specifically, a company would amortize goodwill using the useful life of the primary asset acquired in the business combination for a timeframe of up to 10 years (Evans, 2013).

Calculating the Purchase Price
In addition to valuing all assets and liabilities, accounting for mergers and acquisitions requires that companies determine an appropriate purchase price for a target firm. In order to make this calculation, acquiring companies generally seek to establish both the minimum price and the maximum price that they might be willing to pay for the target company, and these figures help shape the ensuing negotiations. The minimum price is the actual price of the target company's stock, as quoted in the market, times the number of its shares outstanding. Because a target company's shareholders are unlikely to sell all or most of their shares for no more than they could obtain in the open market, the acquiring company generally has to offer to purchase shares at a premium in order to induce stockholders to part with their shares. However, an acquiring company must be mindful of the market activity that inevitably follows news of a possible merger or an acquisition. As shareholders and investors catch wind of a potential merger or an acquisition, the price of the target share's stock often rises, sometimes significantly.

While this process is important, in many merger cases, the price paid for target companies is higher than is justifiable under objective financial principles because of goodwill or relative bargaining positions of the two companies. If the target company is strong financially and unwilling to settle except for a high premium over the minimum price, its final acceptance will be closer to the maximum price. Thus, the minimum price that an acquiring company can pay for a target will likely be greater than the price of the market value of the number of shares the acquiring company wishes to purchase. However, once the minimum price for a target is determined, it represents the lowest value for the purchase price of the target and furnishes a starting point for negotiations for a merger or an acquisition.

The maximum price of a target company must take into account the total synergistic benefits that may result from the merger while still accounting for any investments an acquiring company must make in order for the merger or an acquisition to yield a profitable outcome. As in the calculations to determine the minimum price for a target company, establishing the maximum price is also an approximation, as some of the factors that must be calculated cannot be determined to any exact figures before the business combination occurs. However difficult they may be to calculate, the minimum and maximum price levels for a target company create bookmarks that represent an appropriate negotiating range for the final acquisition price of the target.

Required Disclosure Under the Purchase Method
Once a merger or an acquisition has occurred, certain financial information must be publicly disclosed

in financial statements or their footnotes. For the period in which a purchase occurs, a schedule disclosing the fair values of assets purchased must be included in the financial statement footnotes. Additionally, other key information must also be included within the financial statement footnotes, including the name of the company acquired, the percentage of voting shares acquired and the reasons for the acquisition and the determination of goodwill. In addition, whether and to what extent any research and development costs were acquired and expensed during the period must be revealed. And finally, full disclosure must be given if any portion of the purchase price was not yet determined, along with the reason why such determination had not yet been finalized, and any subsequent allocations must also be disclosed.

During the acquisition period, there must also be footnote disclosure as to the results of operations as if the purchase was made as of the first day of the acquisition period, as well as the operating results for the immediately prior period if comparative financial statements are issued. Finally, footnote disclosure must include revenue, income before extraordinary items and cumulative effect of accounting changes, net income and earnings per share.

Factors Affecting the Purchase Price

Although an acquiring company may determine a minimum and maximum price for the book value of the target company, as described above, the purchase price of a target company can be affected by certain factors such as pre-acquisition contingencies or acquisition-related costs and fees. Pre-acquisition contingencies, in particular, can significantly alter not only a target's purchase price, but the level of interest an acquiring company maintains in pursuing the transaction through to closure. For instance, a contingent liability such as a possible or pending lawsuit could hinder the ability of the companies to complete a merger or an acquisition, and the expense and potential liability of the litigation or a final judgment could impact the financial position of the companies. These factors must be considered and factored into any purchase price calculations. In addition, professional fees associated with the merger or an acquisition process must be factored into the purchase price, including any legal, investment banking, accounting, appraisal and environmental

costs. The following sections describe these factors, which can have a significant impact on the purchase price of a target firm, in greater detail.

Pre-acquisition Contingencies

A contingency is an economic event, usually negative, that may occur or is in the process of occurring and, therefore, has not yet been resolved. A pre-acquisition contingency is a contingency of the target that is in existence before the merger or an acquisition is completed. For instance, a pre-acquisition contingency could include pending or threatened litigation, obligations relating to product warranties or product defects and actual or possible assessments to be levied against a company. These assessments could include income tax examinations, assessments by environmental agencies or guarantees of certain debts owed by other affiliated or unaffiliated entities.

The techniques used in accounting for mergers and acquisitions are designed to enable acquiring companies to determine whether a pre-acquisition contingency should be included in the calculation of the purchase price. For instance, according to these accounting principles, if the fair value of the pre-acquisition contingency can be determined during the allocation or valuation period, the pre-acquisition contingency is included in the allocation of purchase price based on the fair value of the contingency. If the fair value of the contingency cannot be determined during the valuation period, the pre-acquisition contingency is included in the calculation of the purchase price only if, before the end of the valuation period, the acquiring company can obtain information to show that a contingent asset or liability existed or an existing asset might be impaired at the close of the merger or acquisition. Thus, in order for a pre-acquisition contingency to be included in the calculation of the purchase price of the target, even if the fair value of the contingency cannot be readily determined during the valuation period, the acquiring company must at least be able to point to one or more future events that will occur to either confirm the contingency or aid in estimating the amount of the contingent asset or liability. Contingencies that arise from the acquisition and that did not exist prior to the acquisition are the buyer's contingencies rather than pre-acquisition contingencies of the target company.

Acquisition-Related Expenses

Expenses, costs, and fees related to the search for and process of merging with or acquiring a target company can be significant, and thus can impact the price that an acquiring company can or will pay for a target firm. For instance, companies that desire to merge with or acquire a competitor, supplier, or some other company must spend the money necessary to search for the proper candidate. Since a merger or an acquisition is very difficult to undo, companies seeking to grow through this process must be very sure that the target company will be the right fit. Once a good target company is identified, the acquiring company must pay the necessary legal fees to ensure that an antitrust violation would not arise from the business combination. Also, the shareholders of the target company may object to the merger and raise legal challenges, which can add to the legal costs associated with the merger or an acquisition. Aside from the legal fees, many companies hire professionals such as investment bankers to facilitate the process of searching for and negotiating with a target company in order to complete a merger or an acquisition. Finally, even if a business combination is consummated with relatively few problems, the acquiring company will face significant administrative costs associated with completing and filing the necessary paperwork and registrations, issuing new shares and registering stock in the name of new stockholders and handling other matters that arise as the transaction is finalized.

APPLICATIONS

Tax Considerations

The gains from an acquisition may result in significant changes to the tax liabilities of companies involved in a merger or acquisition. These changes may stem from gains from enhanced revenues, cost reductions or a lower cost of obtaining operating capital. Increased revenues may come from stronger market power or more effective advertising, supply and distribution channels and product quality. However, a merger or an acquisition may also create tax losses, especially on the part of the target companies. Tax losses are not always a negative factor, though, since any tax losses of target firms may be used to offset the acquiring company's future income, within certain restrictions. For instance, although tax losses can

be used to offset income for up to 15 years or until the tax loss is exhausted, only tax losses for the three years preceding the merger or an acquisition can be used to offset future income.

Tax advantages can also arise from an acquisition when a target firm carries an asset on its books with a basis, or the value of the asset that is subject to taxation, below its market value. If these assets could become more valuable if acquired by a corporation that could increase the tax basis of the assets following the acquisition, an acquiring company may depreciate the assets based on the higher market values of the assets after the acquisition, thereby enabling the company to gain additional depreciation tax benefits.

While companies engaged in a merger or an acquisition face the potential for tax gains or losses because of changes in asset ownership, they may also initiate a merger or an acquisition based solely on tax gain or loss considerations. For instance, loss carryforwards, which involve an accounting technique that applies the current year's net operating losses to future years' profits to reduce tax liability, can motivate a business combination in that a company that has earned significant profits may search for a target company facing tax losses, which can then be used to offset the earnings of the acquiring company. Also, firms that have accrued surplus funds may choose to acquire another firm based upon tax considerations. This is because distributing the money as a dividend or using it to repurchase shares will increase income taxes for shareholders, while shareholders pay no income tax when a company acquires another entity.

However, in factoring tax considerations into business combination transactions, companies must be careful to comply with tax laws and regulations. The tax regulations, which often require detailed recordkeeping and complex calculations, can affect the tax gains or losses that acquiring companies ultimately realize. Further, companies may not structure a merger solely for tax purposes. In addition, an acquiring company must continue to operate the pre-acquisition business of a target company in a net loss position for a period of time, and as a result the tax benefits obtained by the acquiring company may be reduced.

Regarding employment taxes in particular, while costs related to such taxes do not drive decisions relating to merger and acquisition transactions, pre-transaction planning, and post-transaction review of the available employment tax opportunities and reporting requirements can result in significant tax savings and help companies avoid penalty and interest assessments for late notifications and filings (Russo, 2011).

Finally, the tax implications of a merger or an acquisition may be felt long after the deal has been completed. If an acquiring company assumed significant levels of debt in the transaction, the interest payments on the debt are a tax-deductible expense while the dividend payments to stockholders for equity ownership are not. This is why some companies view the assumption of debt as a means of financing merger and acquisition transactions as more advantageous than any type of equity financing, such as through the sale of additional shares. However, although the use of financial leverage produces tax benefits, significant levels of debt also raise the possibility of future financial problems if the acquiring firm cannot make the required interest payments on the acquisition debt.

Pension Liability Considerations

When two companies merge, they will have to decide whether to terminate one of the firm's employee benefits plans or whether to incorporate one or both of the plans into another existing plan. In addition, accounting for mergers and acquisitions must take into account any assets or liabilities created by these plans. If the target company sponsors a single-employer defined-benefit pension plan or any other postretirement benefit plan, the acquiring company must recognize a liability or an asset for the unfunded or over-funded portion of the projected benefit obligation that exists on the acquisition date. Similarly, any accumulated postretirement benefit obligation ("APBO") for defined-benefit post-retirement benefit plans assets or liabilities must also be accounted for. If the plans are over-funded, then the acquiring company recognizes a long-term asset, thus reducing transaction goodwill, instead of a long-term liability, which would increase transaction goodwill.

Also, 401(k) plans are a common employee benefit and pose unique challenges to companies interested in a merger or an acquisition. For instance, employers and plan sponsors have certain fiduciary duties to beneficiaries in that they are responsible for overseeing the 401(k) plan. These duties may include

selecting the best investment options for the plan or monitoring the plan's performance. If a company is interested in acquiring another company that has not met these fiduciary responsibilities, the acquiring company runs the risk of facing future litigation from participants who have experienced investment losses or other problems with their 401(k) plans. To avoid this, the acquiring firm may choose to have the target firm terminate its plan prior to the merger or an acquisition and resolve any ensuing litigation before proceeding with the business combination. However, terminating employee benefits plans raises several additional issues relating to proper distributions, and thus companies must carefully consider any potential problems stemming from terminating or altering employee benefits plans that could slow or halt the merger or an acquisition process.

Accretion and Dilution of Earnings

After the acquisition date, the projected earnings of both the acquiring company and the target company are reported on a combined basis. Accretions reflect the growth of an asset through an addition or expansion such as a merger or an acquisition. A dilution refers to a reduction in the earnings per share of a company's common stock. Thus, if the projected earnings of the acquiring company and the target company increase on a per-share basis, the transaction has facilitated the accretion, or increase, of earnings. If the projected earnings decrease on a per-share basis, the results are dilutive to earnings in that they reflect a decrease.

Determining the accretion or dilution of earnings from a business combination is a four-step process.

- First, the expected operation structure of the combined company is analyzed and the best approach for projecting the target company's operating results is determined.
- Second, based on the outcome of the first step, either the target company's results are combined with the acquiring company's results for the transaction period and then the combined operating results are projected forward, or the target company's operating results and the acquiring company's operating results are projected separately and then these results are combined and projected into each forecast period.

- The third step is accounting for the effects of the transaction on the earnings of the combined firm. This includes accounting for matters such as synergies stemming from the merger or acquisition, changes in corporate interest and dividends of the acquisition and target companies and amortization of certain other items included in the transaction.

- The final step is that the difference between the acquiring company's own per-share earnings results and the earnings results of the combined entity are analyzed. The results, whether positive or negative, are generally presented as a percentage of accretion or dilution of earnings. Determining the accretion or dilution of earnings as a function of a business combination can help accountants and investors make informed decisions about a particular merger or acquisition or in regard to the merits of a potential business combination.

CONCLUSION

Accounting for mergers and acquisitions under generally accepted accounting principles in the United States relies upon the purchase method. The purchase method records the target company's identifiable assets and liabilities at fair value, and the excess of the purchase price over the net identifiable assets is recorded as an asset called goodwill. Transaction goodwill is positive whenever the purchase price exceeds the fair value of the net identifiable assets. When considering a business combination, companies must consider what form of merger or acquisition best suits their needs. Mergers can take several forms, such as horizontal mergers, vertical mergers and conglomerate mergers. Each type of merger has different attributes and offers different benefits. Acquisitions can also take different forms in that they can be friendly, as in a tender offer, or unfriendly, such as a hostile takeover. When initiating and implementing a merger or an acquisition, companies must follow state laws as well as any relevant federal securities regulations. To finance a merger or an acquisition, companies may pay by cash or a combination of cash and stocks, or they may finance the deal through debt, as in a leveraged buyout. In order to determine the value of the target firm, each major balance sheet category of the target company must be assessed and valued. Then, the purchase price of the target company is calculated, and any pre-acquisition contingencies or acquisition-related expenses factored in. Certain information related to the transaction must also be disclosed in corporate financial statements. Finally, in accounting for mergers and acquisitions, various factors are important considerations, such as the tax gains or losses resulting from the transaction, pension liabilities and the accretion or dilution of earnings following a merger or an acquisition.

TERMS & CONCEPTS

Adjusted grossed-up basis: The amount for which the new target is deemed to have purchased all of its assets in the deemed asset sale.

Carryback: Deductions or credits that cannot be utilized on the tax return during a year that may be carried back to reduce taxable income or taxes payable in a prior year.

Carryforward: Deductions or credits that cannot be utilized on the tax return during a year that may be carried forward to reduce taxable income or taxes payable in a future year.

Contra accounts: Offsetting accounts that are normally presented on the face of the financial statements or in footnote disclosures, as in accumulated depreciating offsetting the property, plant, and equipment account.

EBITDA: Earnings before interest, taxes, depreciation and amortization. EBITDA is often used as a proxy for cash flows from operations.

Earnings per share (EPS): The amount of earnings attributable to each share of common stock. EPS is also used to refer to either earnings or loss per share.

Financial accounting standards board (FASB): The designated standards board in the United States for establishing financial accounting and reporting standards.

Generally accepted accounting principles (GAAP): The rules, standards, laws, and common practices that firms must adhere to when preparing financial statements for presentation to auditors or to outside users.

Goodwill: An account that can be found in the assets portion of a company's balance sheet that typically reflects the value of intangible assets such as a strong brand name, good customer relations, good employee relations, and any patents or proprietary technology. Also, in an acquisition, the amount paid for the company over book value usually accounts for the target firm's intangible assets.

Income statement: A financial statement that measures a company's financial performance over a specific accounting period.

Net identifiable assets: A firm's total assets minus its total liabilities minus recorded goodwill.

Net operating loss: The excess of the deductions allowed for by the Internal Revenue Code (IRC) over gross income.

Old target: The target for periods ending on or before the close of the target's acquisition date, or the target while it is still in the hands of the seller as part of the seller's consolidated selling group.

Realize: In accounting terminology, realize is a concept relating to *when* revenues should be recorded in the income statement.

Recognize: In accounting terminology, events or items are recognized by recording them in the financial accounting books, the tax books, or both.

Salvage value: The amount for which an asset can be sold or disposed of at the end of its useful depreciable life.

Target: A firm that has been targeted by another firm for a takeover.

Valuation: The process of determining the current worth of an asset or a company.

Bibliography

Anason, D. (2012). RBC blames slowness in MA on accounting. *American Banker, 177,* 16– 13.

Cohen, J. (2007). Street sees sun setting on horizon deal. *Mergers and Acquisitions Report, 20,* 1-12.

Cvach, G.& Patterson, M. (1999). Taxation of compensation and benefits. *Corporate Business Taxation Monthly, 1,* 27.

Evans, L. (2013). FASB issues first new private company proposals for comment. *Financial Executive, 29,* 3– 5.

Jenkins Jr., E. (2007). "Uncertainty" with mergers and acquisitions. *Pennsylvania CPA Journal, 78,* 6–7.

Landsberg, R. (2007). Section 409A-payments and distributions. *Journal of Financial Service Professionals, 61,* 24–26.

Lee, J. & Bader, M. (1987). Contingent income items and cost basis corporate acquisitions: Correlative adjustments and clearer reflection of income. *Journal of Corporation Law, 12,* 137.

O'Connell Jr., & F., Powers, K. & Reinbold, M. (2007). Deductibility of nonqualified deferred compensation in mergers and acquisitions. *Tax Adviser, 38,* 496 – 98.

Russo, D. (2011). Mergers, acquisitions, and consolidations: managing employment tax liability. *Journal of State Taxation, 29,* 37–66.

Unger, J. (2004). Tax issues arising with IRC section 338(h) acquisitions. *CPA Journal, 74,* 48–51.

Venema, W. & Cheskiewicz, S. (2007). Purchase-price adjustment: A trap for the unwary. *Practical Accountant, 40,* 48.

Suggested Reading

Ayers, B., Lefanowicz, & C. Robinson, J. (2007). Capital gains taxes and acquisition activity: Evidence of the lock-in effect. *Contemporary Accounting Research, 24,* 315–344.

De Haven, T., Moran, F. & Fox, C. (2006). Buyer beware: Deferred compensation issues lurk where you may least suspect. *Journal of Pension Benefits: Issues in Administration, 13,* 44–50.

Harrell, M. & McCarthy, A. (2007). ERISA and the 25% exception. *Mergers Acquisitions: The Dealermaker's Journal, 42,* 66–67.

Essay by Heather Newton, J.D.

ACCOUNTING FOR STOCK-BASED COMPENSATION

While employee stock option incentives provide a significant benefit for employees, such incentives have been the focus of great controversy and debate, particularly in terms of accounting for such practices. This paper will take an in-depth look at the evolution of stock-based compensation over the last few decades and how accounting and reporting of such company expenses has changed during that period. As a result, the reader will glean a stronger understanding of this practice.

OVERVIEW

Dot.coms and Stock Options

By the 1990s, the Internet, which only a decade earlier was virtually unknown outside of academic and intergovernmental circles, had become a juggernaut of personal and commercial activity. Entrepreneurs saw the nearly limitless potential for conducting their business. Companies like Amazon.com, eBay and WebMD got their start at this time, along with countless smaller companies offering similar, web-based commerce. These commercial start-up enterprises conducted the latest fad in business known as "e-commerce." Investors shared these companies' faith in web-based business, infusing a great deal of capital into their development, monies which were used for online marketing campaigns, lavish office space and employee perks. In the latter case, many employees of these "dot.coms" were paid not with salaries but with perks such as stock options.

Stock options in those cases helped inflate the perceived value of dot.coms on the open market, where a great many of these companies went public via initial public offerings (IPOs). In 2000, however, such inflation of stock was eventually corrected to account for the true value of these companies, and because of the sheer volume of dot.coms on the market, the NASDAQ technology index quickly fell by about 50 percent in the first few months of that year, leading observers to state that the "dot.com bubble" had burst.

Although it is an extreme example, the leveling of the dot.com industry provides an interesting case of a growing form of employee incentive. In order to provide competitive salary and benefits packages to their employees, many companies will offer stock options

to their personnel. The rationale for this revenue-sharing concept is simple — in addition to pay and insurance, employees have an opportunity to reap the benefits of the company's success.

While employee stock option incentives provide a significant benefit for employees, such incentives have been the focus of great controversy and debate, particularly in terms of accounting for such practices. This paper will take an in-depth look at the evolution of stock-based compensation over the last few decades, and how accounting and reporting of such company expenses has changed during that period. As a result, the reader will glean a stronger understanding of this stock-based employee compensatory practice.

A Look at the Practice

The practice of offering stock-based compensation to employees centers on giving the employee the option to purchase shares in the company at discounted rates. Also known as "share-based payment," stock options are typically offered to senior-level executives of a company (although the dot.com example above is illustrative of the fact that it may be offered to other employees as well) as a performance incentive or as an employee retention benefit.

The practice of offering stock options to executives has generated controversy for two main reasons. The first is philosophical in nature, centering around the assertion that such practices give even more power and access to wealth for executives, while the profits from a company's market performance could be distributed among all employees on a more equitable level. This philosophical aversion to the practice came to light during the 2008 collapse of the financial markets. Like most personnel strata, senior executives like CEOs lost much of their compensatory benefits and incentives when the recession took root. Even their stock options fell significantly — about 90 percent of the $1.2 billion offered to company CEOs in 2008 fell "under water," which means that they were too low to yield a profit. In partial response, these companies have attempted to retain their high-level personnel by introducing even more stock options, giving them the ability to buy future shares in those companies at current prices ("Recession

Amazon founder Jeff Bezos. (Courtesy of Senior Master Sgt. Adrian Cadiz, U.S. Department of Defense via Wikimedia Commons)

Takes," 2009). During a period of economic frailty and stagnation, many consumer advocates and activists are railing against such incentives.

The second controversy about the practice of share-based payments is what one industry expert calls "a moral hazard." By design, stock-based compensation acts as an incentive for the executive to foster the success of the company. The underlying principle involved in this venture is shared risk — if the executive succeeds, then the company succeeds, and if he or she fails, then the company falters. The company's failure or success dictates the value of the stock that is part of the executive's benefits package.

The headquarters of eBay in San Jose, California. (Courtesy of Coolcaesar via Wikimedia Commons)

Hence, he or she has a vested interest in seeing that stock perform well. In this regard, the executive in effect becomes a shareholder of the company as well as an administrator. Some experts argue that shared risk forces the executive into a conflict of interest between the activities of the company's management and the agenda of the shareholders (Chhabra, 2008).

Adding to the above-mentioned issues surrounding stock-based compensation is the fact that a company must account for any expenses and benefits paid to employees. In many ways, accounting for share-based executive payments has become an even more controversial issue than concerns over the morality and equity of such practices. Cannon and Kessel (2013) go so far as to call the accounting rules for stock options "Byzantine" and, as such, provide possible modifications or alternatives to stock option programs.

Korn, Paschke, and Uhrig-Homburg (2011) assert that designing stock-option plans for robustness at the outset is essential for reliable accounting valuations. They explain how robustness can be achieved by combining certain design elements of stock-option plans. They add that robustness of these plans is in itself an element of good corporate governance, in that it could impede managers' ability to understate the values of their compensation packages.

FURTHER INSIGHTS

Accounting for Share-Based Benefits: Policy Guidelines

In the mid-1980s, considerable attention was paid by the Internal Revenue Service (IRS) to better quantify the income of U.S. businesses. Upon the direction of Congress in 1986, the IRS modified its code pertaining to the income and deductions of publicly shared corporations to account for "intangible" property transfers. In a one-sentence addition, the IRS code included the statement that, in "the case of any transfer or license of intangible property, the income with respect to the transfer or license shall be commensurate with the income attributable to the intangible(s)" (Internal Revenue Service, 2009a).

The 1986 phraseology in that code was invoked less than a decade later when interest developed in Washington to regulate the practice of stock-based compensation. In 1995, after three years of careful study, a series of regulations were issued that outlined the manner by which cost sharing would be defined.

Société Générale's central branch, in Paris, now a historic monument. (Courtesy of Benh Liue Song via Wikimedia Commons)

In doing so, the IRS was in effect dictating to companies and taxpayers that stock-based compensation was in fact a component of a company's operating expenses as they pertain to employee benefits.

Still, although the inclusion of stock-based compensation was implied in the 1995 IRS regulations, it was not officially confirmed as such. That lack of clarity led to court challenges that argued that such inclusions were inserted on an arbitrary basis and lacking any uniformity or definition. It was not until 2003 that the IRS offered a further regulation that clarified that stock-based compensation was in fact an "intangible development cost" that, where applicable, should be included in any expense reports.

The Sarbanes-Oxley Act of 2002 may have influenced stock-option accounting practices as well.

A 2011 study compared the accruals-based earnings-management patterns for a group of firms that were implicated by the Securities and Exchange Commission for backdating stock options with a matched control group of nonimplicated firms during the enactment of the Sarbanes-Oxley Act. The results suggest that the Sarbanes-Oxley Act had effects on management's reporting choices beyond those resulting from improvements in governance and internal control over financial reporting (Hossain, Mitra, Rezaee & Sarath, 2011).

Fair Value Method
In March of 2004, the Financial Accounting Standards Board (FASB), the organization charged with establishing standards of accounting, issued a set of proposals geared toward accounting for such expenses. In language that would immediately meet with controversy, the FASB recommended that stock-based compensation costs would be based on the fair value of the employee's right to purchase stock at a set price. Fair value in this case was determined by existing market prices or relevant option pricing models.

Within three months of the proposal's promulgation, the FASB received more than 4,000 comment letters from businesses and taxpayers. One of the most prominent arguments was that while market prices and stable models give some indication of a stock option's value, stock options contain an element of depth and fluidity that could not be quantified under this framework. One expert suggests that rather than reliance on market and modeling systems, the accounting measures should instead operate from a more simple basis — the ultimate cost to the company of the stock options is equal to the amount of cash proceeds forgone at the date the employee exercises those options (Dyson, 2004).

The proposal was handed other criticisms as well. Some simply disagreed with the idea that employee stock options were expenses — in their view, stock options were merely pieces of paper that stated that an individual could purchase such stock, and that as a result, cost nothing for the company while giving a benefit to the employee. Other critics complained that there was a wide range of variables, such as the time at which the employee purchases the stock, which added an air of complexity to stock options for which simply valuating at market value could not account.

One of the most common criticisms, however, came from those who felt the policy would adversely impact business. After all, this school of thought professed, expensing stock options meant reporting lower net earnings. In the case of small business, lower earnings could put a startup business at risk to lose venture capital dollars. Additionally, expensing stock-based compensation could, in critics' eyes, give larger companies a competitive advantage over smaller businesses in terms of attracting high-quality employees (Carruth, 2003).

Still years after the proposals were released, criticism continued. Howe and Lippitt (2013) put forth that disparities between accounting expenses and actual exercise-date economic effects reflect a substantial wealth transfer that is not recognized or disclosed. Even within the context of the equity approach, they wrote, one can argue that the expenses, as currently measured, significantly understate the value of the services rendered. They offered an alternative "expected value approach."

Intrinsic Value Method

Since the release of the 1995 FASB statements, that organization has also allowed for other methods for equity valuation. One such method is intrinsic value-based, which focuses not on the market value but on the actual value of the share in question. Under the intrinsic value-based method, the cost of employee compensation is the difference between the quoted market price at the time the stock is granted and the amount the employee must pay to acquire the shares. The FASB leans against intrinsic value methodologies, however, as the most common type of stock option plan, the fixed stock option, does not have an intrinsic value by the date at which the option is exercised. Absent this intrinsic value, accounting for compensation in this arena is extremely difficult (Financial Accounting Standards Board, 2009).

Restricted Stock

Another form of share-based compensation is restricted stock. In this form, the stock has any number of limitations in terms of how and when the stock is exercised. Accounting for such restricted stock (also known as "nonvested stock") is conducted using the fair market value method, taking into account any restrictions that are imposed.

Stock purchase plans entail a group of employees who are allowed to purchase stock at a discounted price from the market rate. However, such plans are generally not considered compensation in accounting terms, due to the fact that most of them are relatively small and limited in terms of their dividend-generating capabilities.

Stock-based compensation appears in a number of manifestations. The stock option, which is extremely common among executives, offers the employee the option to purchase shares at a specified price within a certain period of time. Valuating stock option expenses entails accounting for the stock price at the time it is granted, the exercise price, the life of the option, the stock's volatility and the expected dividends.

Accounting for these types of stock options has been enmeshed in controversy since the FASB and IRS statements and policies pertaining thereto. Assertions that the parameters surrounding the inclusion of stock-based compensation present an incomplete image of the value of such stocks have been paralleled by the overall philosophical opposition to such inclusion. In general, however, the recommendations of the FASB and IRS have largely been adhered to, although begrudgingly among some.

ISSUES

Public Perception of Stock-Based Compensation

The use of stock options as an employee benefit and/or incentive was highly popular during the latter twentieth century. The practice was particularly of use for high-level executives, although in the case of the dot.coms, was offered to all levels of staff (and in high quantities in this business arena). However, in the early twenty-first century, the practice had been so widespread among executives that it caught the attention of both lawmakers and the general public when these executives' respective companies began to falter.

In one case, French investment giant Societe Generale had offered its highest-level executives stock options, a benefit France's third-largest bank had also offered 5,000 of its employees. In 2009, the company received about $2.3 billion in government support after the collapse of the financial markets. After considerable public backlash against large corporations around the world who had received state "bailout" money yet continued the practice of offering executives stock options and bonuses, Societe Generale made a policy move. In March of 2009, the company's chairman announced that four of its upper-level executives would return their stock options to the company. The change in policy was a clear attempt to quell mounting criticism not only from the general public but also from the French Parliament, which was threatening to levy sanctions against companies that offer stock options and bonuses to employees after receiving government aid (Frost, 2009).

From an accounting perspective, the Societe Generale move had minimal fiscal impact on the company. Rather, it was seen as an effort to mitigate public dissent over high-level benefits. The company continued to receive state funds; its upper management simply opted to decline any stock options. The policy therefore cost Societe Generale very little financially, since such options have no value until they are exercised, an action from which these targets of controversy would refrain.

The Societe Generale example provides an illustration of two important points. First, public opinion presently holds that stock-based compensation offers executives great returns even if the company is failing. This view is not entirely accurate, as the practice of offering stock options is not limited to upper-level executives (the 5,000 employees of the bank held stock options that amounted to about 98 percent of the program's total value). Still, public opinion, especially during times of recession, remains high in the eyes of lawmakers who act upon it with restrictive regulations and laws.

Second, this case underscores the latent nebulousness about the value of stock-based compensation for accounting purposes. Placing a value on stock options depends on when the employee exercises them — if they do not take advantage of such benefits, such options are not worth the price of the paper on which they are printed.

CONCLUSIONS

The British lawyer and novelist John Mortimer once said, "The freedom to make a fortune on the stock exchange has been made to sound more alluring than freedom of speech." Words of the sort uttered by Mortimer are illustrative of the value people place in the potential for return on investments in the markets. It is for this reason that, among the items in many employees' benefits packages, stock options are highly prevalent. In cases like the dot.coms of the 1990s, they are often seen as potentially more valuable than cash, especially when the company shows signs that it will continue to grow in profits.

However, the government and the FASB have collectively deemed such policies as similar to other employee payroll expenses. This mandate was initially met with a number of different criticisms. Some of the objections were philosophical in nature, speaking against regulation of an important employment incentive. Others were with the fair value approach, offering alternatives to such a formula. The latter of these criticisms resulted in some flexibility in accounting guidelines among the IRS and FASB, and also spurred more diversity in the types of stock-based compensation created for employees.

The virtual collapse of several of the world's largest financial institutions in 2008 created a firestorm of public sentiment against the practice of offering stock options, particularly to high-level employees of financially distressed institutions that received government "bailout" monies. From an accounting standpoint, however, this issue has underscored the prevalence of this practice from upper management to rank-and-file employees, at minimal cost to employers. Indeed, share-based compensatory benefits remain an important tool in employee recruitment and retention, in strong and even weak economic times.

Terms & Concepts

Fair value-based method: Accounting measure preferred by FASB for determining share-based compensation benefit value using existing market prices or relevant option pricing models.

Financial accounting standards board (FASB): A quasi-public organization that oversees the management and policies of accounting practices.

Intrinsic value-based method: Accounting principle for determining value of shares that focuses not on the market value but on the actual value of the share in question.

Restricted stock: Stock-based compensation with limits on when and how the individual may exercise the option.

Stock option: Employee benefit offered in lieu of or in addition to cash benefits as an incentive for employee recruitment and retention.

Stock purchase plan: Share-based compensatory program in which a group of employees are able to exercise stock options at a reduced or discounted rate.

BIBLIOGRAPHY

Carruth, P. (2003). Accounting for stock options: a historical perspective. *Journal of Business and Economics Research, 1,* 9–14.

Chhabra, A. B. (2008). Executive stock options: Moral hazard or just compensation? *The Journal of Wealth Management, 11,* 20 – 35.

Dyson, R. (2004). Accounting for stock-based compensation: A simple proposal. *The CPA Journal, 74,* 6–10.

Financial Accounting Standards Board. (2009). Summary of Statement 123.

Frost, L. (2009, March 22). Societe Generale executives bow to pressure, drop stock options.

Hossain, M., Mitra, S., Rezaee, Z., & Sarath, B. (2011). Corporate governance and earnings management in the pre- and post-Sarbanes-Oxley Act regimes: evidence from implicated option backdating firms. *Journal of Accounting, Auditing & Finance, 26,* 279 – 315.

Howe, H., Lippitt, J.W. (2012). An evaluation of fair value accounting for employee stock options. *International Business Economics Research Journal, 11,* 821–826.

Internal Revenue Service. (2009a). Stock based compensation audit techniques guide (02-2005).

Internal Revenue Service. (2009b). Cost sharing stock based compensation.

Korn, O., Paschke, C., & Uhrig-Homburg, M. (2012). Robust stock option plans. *Review of Quantitative Finance & Accounting, 39,* 77– 03.

Nonstop English. (2009). Stock market quotations.

Recession takes toll on CEO pay in 2008. (2009, May 1). *The Economic Times.*

SUGGESTED READING

Balsam, S. (1994). Extending the method of accounting for stock appreciation rights to employee stock options. *Accounting Horizons, 8,* 52–60.

Barth, M., Bell, T., & Collins, D. et al. (1994). Response to the FASB exposure draft "Accounting for Stock-Based Compensation." *Accounting Horizons, 8,* 114–116.

Canada: Stock-based compensation. (2000). *Accountancy, 126* (1288), 107.

Dechow, P., Hutton, A. & Sloan, R. (1996). Economic consequences of accounting for stock-based compensation. *Journal of Accounting Research, 34,* 1–20.

Simon, R. (2003, September 4). Popular stock perk faces cutbacks. *Wall Street Journal — Eastern Edition, 242,* D1–D2.

Talmor, E. & Wallace, J. (1998). Computer industry executives: An analysis of the new barons' compensation. *Information Systems Research, 9,* 398–414.

Essay by Michael P. Auerbach, M.A.

ACCOUNTING SYSTEMS AND CONTROLS

Accounting systems are comprised of hardware, software applications, and the people who design and administer the system as a whole. An accounting system has three distinct components: analysis, design, and implementation. These components generally incorporate databases, user applications, and the designers and end-users of the entire system. This essay looks closely at the role that an organization's internal controls have in an accounting system. Internal controls function as the administrative and procedural framework of an accounting system and can be thought of as a sub-system within the overall accounting system. The elements of an internal controls system are the control environment, risk assessment, control activities, information and communication, and monitoring of the controls. Internal controls are very much in the spotlight at organizations as a result of implementation of the Sarbanes-Oxley Act of 2002. Much scrutiny has been placed on internal controls that monitor financial transactions. The Sarbanes-Oxley Act has been blamed for adding complexity and cost to overall corporate governance. The costs of implementation and compliance have steadily risen since 2002 and many companies continue to struggle with SEC guidelines for administering Sarbanes-Oxley directives. A chief accounting officer at General Motors Corp. was quoted as saying of the Act, "The real cost isn't the incremental dollars, it is having people that should be focused on the business [being instead] focused on complying with the details of the rules." This essay discusses trends in the cost of compliance as well as SEC efforts to clarify the guidelines for companies. Today, many companies are turning their attention to implementing an internal control framework that supports an overall risk management strategy within an organization. The benefits of implementing strong internal controls are not just a benefit or a requirement of public companies. Today, private companies are implementing accounting systems and internal controls as a means to improve operations, accountability, and efficiency. Lastly, this essay reviews a number of trends and best practices for internal controls for enterprise risk a means to illicit further discussion and research.

OVERVIEW

Internal Controls

Merriam-Webster's dictionary defines a "system" as a regularly interacting or interdependent group of items forming a unified whole. A "control" is defined as a device or mechanism used to regulate or guide the operation of a machine, apparatus, or system. It is important to define the individual terms within the topic of "accounting systems and controls" to clarify the scope of what is meant by it.

An accounting system consists of the following three components: analysis, design, and implementation. These three components define the accounting system framework and should provide businesses with a uniform way in which to use their data and financial information. Accounting systems are, in-part, comprised of the hardware, software and applications that allow for storage of important organizational information-both financial and non-financial. For purposes of clarification, this essay concentrates on discussing "internal controls" as they impact accounting systems and not the electronic storage of financial data.

Internal controls can be thought of as a sub-system within the accounting system ("Internal controls," 2007). Internal controls offer guidance, practices and procedures that the accounting system needs to operate within an organization. Internal controls are designed to protect against fraud and abuse, ensure accuracy and timeliness of information, and ensure that an organization is in compliance with regulatory guidelines ("Internal controls," 2007). Internal accounting controls are a series of procedures and practices designed to promote management practices — both financial and general. Internal controls can be further outlined as being designed to insure the following within an organization ("Developing an internal accounting control system," 2007)

- Financial information is reliable and that managers and boards have assurance that financial data is accurate.
- Company assets and records (information) are protected from fraud.
- Policies are followed by employees and stakeholders.
- All applicable regulations are met by the organization.

Five Key Elements of Internal Controls

The elements of an internal controls system are generally accepted as having the following five elements ("Internal controls," 2007).

Control Environment — This refers to the general attitude of management or others who administer the internal controls of an organization. A high level of commitment to ethical values and good business practices should be exhibited at the executive, management, and board level to instill employees with a similar attitude to implementing effective controls. The control environment may include background checks for key employees, technical competence of staff,and thorough written procedures to support the controls.

Risk Assessment — Identifies areas of potential risk in an organization and asks the following questions: What assets are at risk? What can go wrong? Who is in a position of risk? The role of the controls administrator is to identify methods to control risk and analyze associated costs.

Control Activities — Refers to activities that provide a "reasonable" level of assurance that the goals and objectives of the organization or a business unit will be met. Absolute assurance is not possible because of a number of factors including: prohibitive costs, human error, and management's ability to over-ride controls.

Information and Communication Systems — Communication lets employees know what is expected of them and how to accomplish given objectives. Clear communication also identifies who has responsibility for a given task and provides needed clarity for employees. Information systems include data repositories as well as the reports that monitor progress related to operational, financial, and compliance objectives. Information provides a means to monitor progress toward specific accomplishments and provides administration with the information to make decisions.

Monitoring — This step involves checking on the internal control system and making certain that it operates as expected. The focus of monitoring should always be on areas of highest risk. It is the role of the controls administrator to change internal controls to reflect any changes in operational circumstances as they may occur.

History of Internal Controls

Internal controls are probably most often thought of within the context of corporate compliance and specifically as a means to comply with section 404 of Sarbanes-Oxley (SOX) legislation that was passed in 2002. SOX Section 404 falls under the heading "Management Assessment of Internal Controls." Section 404 states, "Issuers are required to publish information in their annual reports concerning the scope and adequacy of the internal control structure and procedures for financial reporting. This statement shall also assess the effectiveness of such internal controls and procedures" (Sarbanes-Oxley Act Section 404," 2004).

Donald C. Langevoort (2006) states the following regarding SOX section 404:

"Today, the vocal criticism is largely reserved for just one piece of the legislation: The internal controls requirement found in section 404, which in some circles has become almost synonymous with SOX itself. Doubts about the balance of costs and benefits and whether the result will be increased de-listings and going to private transactions to avoid 404's burdens have made this the portion of the Act that has encountered the most political resistance" (p. 950).

Given the amount of ink that has been devoted to SOX legislation and in particular section 404 over the past five years, one might think that the subject of internal controls and corporate transparency issues didn't exist before this decade's now famous accounting scandals. However, corporate scandals have been around for a long time and will likely continue despite the best intentions and government intervention.

From a historical perspective, one should consider the following quote:

"Concern about the adequacy of internal controls-and corporate accountability generally-was one of the most important issues in securities regulation in the 1970s. Because a handful of large corporations had funded the break-in of the Democratic headquarters, the Watergate scandal led directly to questions about the legitimacy of corporate managers' opaque dominion over corporate assets, especially as it related to foreign and domestic bribery and illegal political campaign contributions" (Langevoort, 2006, p. 951).

In another citation, Langevoort points outs the following:

"Revisiting section 3.4.2 of Clark's *Corporate Law*" ("Duty of Care as Responsibility for Systems") reminds us, however, that the internal controls story actually goes back many decades, and that many of the strategic issues that are at the heart of section 404 have long been contentious"(2006, p. 950).

By now it should be clear that internal controls are not a new concept for corporations. Depending upon the size and complexity of an organization, the implementation of internal controls to mitigate financial and operational risk may vary, but few businesses operating today can afford not to implement a base-level of checks and balances—particularly for publicly traded companies. Public companies must not only satisfy regulatory requirements but also meet stakeholder expectations when setting up and monitoring internal controls. The most visible "testing" of internal controls remains the auditing of a company's financial statements. With increasing frequency, internal controls are put in place to mitigate risk throughout all functional areas of an organization and as such, financial audits are being replaced by enterprise risk audits.

"The primary stakeholders of internal audit — the board of directors, audit committees and senior executive management — have come to recognize the valuable role that internal audits should perform and have set their expectations accordingly" (Gregory, 2007, ¶4).

Similarly, executive managers have set their expectations higher; they look to internal audits for a reliable appraisal of the system of internal control — for which they are responsible — and, most importantly, they want advice as to how internal control should be improved (Gregory, 2007, ¶7).

Good corporate governance relies on risk management to identify the problems faced by the organization and on internal controls to achieve that organization's objectives. Internal auditors, apart from supporting the organization and enabling it to identify and monitor the upcoming risks, must also understand and monitor the functioning of the internal controls system, which is the key to implementing the corporate governance principles (Florin & Carmen, 2013).

APPLICATIONS

Clarification of Internal Controls
(Specific to Sarbanes-Oxley Section 404)
In 2005, the Securities and Exchange Commission (SEC) issued the *"Statement on Management's Report on Internal Control Over Financial Reporting."* This statement was written to address many of the questions that had surfaced by corporate management teams

and auditors in the first few years of SOX 404 compliance. Adrian P. Fitzsimons and Gerard A. Lange noted the following in their article about the SEC statement:

> "The SEC staff noted in the statement that the establishment and maintenance of internal accounting controls has been required of public companies since the enactment of the Foreign Corrupt Practices Act of 1977 (FCPA). The significance of Section 404 of the SOA is that it re-emphasizes the important relationship between the maintenance of effective internal control over financial reporting and the preparation of reliable financial statements" (2006, p. 42).

The SEC statement pointed out some of the high-level issues and concerns that had been brought to their attention regarding SOA 404 compliance. The SEC noted that in many cases, "significant costs" had been incurred by companies — the SEC noted that some of the expense could be attributed to 'start-up expenses' associated with implementing the increased internal controls. The SEC also admitted that it was aware of cases where "excessive, duplicative and mis-focused efforts" had resulted at some companies with SOA 404 compliance. The SEC countered that with time and experience, "management and external auditors should bring reasoned judgment and a top-down risk-based approach to section 404 compliance" (Fitzsimons Lange, 2006, p. 41).

The SEC's clarification statement encouraged corporate management to take more ownership and responsibility for implementation — specifically regarding the following:

- Management must determine the format and level of appropriate controls.
- Management must determine the scope of assessment of internal controls as well as the methods and timeframe for testing controls.

The clear message given in the SEC statement was that individual organizations and their management teams must take the responsibility, along with their auditors, to use their judgment in interpreting the application of internal controls (as applied specifically to accounting practices).

Benefits of the SEC

"We expect that the SEC proposed management guidance, along with the proposed auditing standard of the Public Company Accounting Oversight Board (PCAOB), will result in a reduction of total Section 404 efforts due to various specific positive changes such as:

- The ability of management to undertake or accelerate a controls rationalization process through the principles in the proposal to better focus its assessment on those controls that impact its financial statement reporting.
- The ability of an auditor to increase the use of the work of others, if certain conditions are met (Fitzsimons Lange, 2006).

The following are positive aspects of the SEC's proposal ("Center for audit quality," 2007):

- A principles-based approach to the internal control assessment that can be scaled based on the size and complexity of the issuer.
- A top-down risk-based approach to management's assessment of ICFR that requires testing of only those controls necessary to prevent or detect material misstatements in the financial statements.
- With respect to internal control, the SEC staff concluded that "one size does not fit all and that internal control effectiveness is affected by many factors" (Fitzsimons & Lange, 2006, p. 41).

SEC Clarification Statements

In the statement, "the SEC staff notes that compliance with Section 404 has produced benefits, including a heightened focus on internal controls at the top levels of public companies and that focus should produce better financial reporting" (Fitzsimons & Lange, 2006, p. 41).

The following are a few notable statements of clarification that were provided in the SEC statement and help to inform the reader of the nature and scope of questions that had arisen as a result of SOA 404 legislation, according to Hall and Gaetanos (2006):

- The SEC staff cautions that, due to their inherent limitations, internal controls cannot prevent or detect every instance of fraud.
- Internal controls are susceptible to manipulation, especially in instances of fraud caused by the collusion of two or more people including senior management.
- In performing these steps, management and auditors should keep the "reasonable assurance" standard in mind.
- The application of judgment by management and the auditor will typically affect the nature, timing and extent of control testing such that the level of testing performed for a low-risk account will likely be different than it will be for a high-risk account.
- Overly conservative interpretations of the applicable requirements and hesitancy by the independent auditor to use professional judgment in evaluating management's assessment resulted, in many cases, in too many controls being identified, documented and tested.
- The SEC staff stated it expects that, through the natural learning process, management will achieve efficiencies as it completes future assessments of internal control.

Costs of Internal Accounting Controls

While companies have an existing obligation to maintain an adequate system of internal accounting controls under the Foreign Corrupt Practices Act (FCPA), preparing an annual report on controls by management involves additional costs. Moreover, compliance is not a one-time effort or a one-year project; it is an ongoing process requiring extensive investment. For example:

- Senior management must be involved in the evaluation of controls.
- Internal audit departments may need to be enlarged, or in some cases formed.
- Consultants may be engaged to analyze and design control systems.
- The company may need to purchase additional computer software or hardware.
- Audit fees will undoubtedly increase.

Additional section 404 compliance costs are attributed to documentation, legal requirements, detailed policy development, self-assessment, attest requirements and certifications, and staff training. Information technology consultants believe that companies will also invest heavily in technologies such as workflow, document management, and identification management tools to automate section 404 compliance processes (Hall & Gaetanos, 2006, p. 58).

ISSUES

Cost of Compliance

The SEC *"Statement on Management's Report on Internal Control Over Financial Reporting"* addressed the "cost" of compliance with SOA 404. The 2005 statement noted that "significant costs" had been incurred by many companies as a direct result of SOA legislation-with section 404 adding the most overhead. The SEC optimistically stated that "integrating internal audit of general controls with financial controls will help reduce costs" (Fitzsimons & Lange, 2006). It was the view of the SEC and many others that companies would simply "get better" at meeting compliance objectives and that the costs of meeting 404 compliance would level off in time — this has not proven to be the case.

"According to the fifth edition of an annual study conducted by law firm Foley and Lardner LLP on the costs associated with corporate governance reform, companies of all sizes experienced double-digit percentage increases in compliance costs during fiscal year 2006 in comparison to fiscal year 2001, the year before the Sarbanes-Oxley Act was implemented"(Taylor, 2007, ¶2).

Some predictions were made that "external audit fees would decrease after the initial implementation of Section 404 audits as external auditors became more familiar with their client's accounting controls and therefore more efficient in conducting their audits," Tom Harman, a Foley partner, stated. "Our study results do not support this prediction. Indeed, external audit fees have been the only cost our study has shown to increase every year since the Sarbanes-Oxley Act was passed" (cited in Taylor, 2007).

There are a number of reasons that costs associated with accounting and internal controls have increased. One will recall from evidence cited earlier in this essay that there are a number of elements recommended for successful implementation of internal controls. They include: Communication, documentation, education, risk management, information systems and monitoring of internal controls. All of these elements contribute directly or indirectly to implementation and administration of internal controls for accounting.

Thanks to the SOX, the SEC and the Basel II Capital Accord, companies are spending a fortune on internal controls and other processes that add only a negligible value to governance, risk management and accurate reporting of financial results (Hampton, 2006, ¶2).

The following trends and statistics are taken from *The Cost of Being Public in the Era of Sarbanes-Oxley*, the annual report conducted by Foley Lardner LLP.

- The average cost of compliance for companies with under $1 billion in annual revenue has increased more than $1.7 million to approximately $2.8 million since the enactment of the SOX. This represents a 171 percent overall increase between fiscal years 2001 and 2006.
- Out-of-pocket costs associated with the SOX compliance were up 13 percent in fiscal year 2006 from fiscal year 2005 for public companies with annual revenue of under $1 billion, and were up 12 percent over the same period for public companies with annual revenues over $1 billion. The increased cost of audit fees, board compensation, and legal fees were the primary drivers of these out-of-pocket percentage increases.
- On average, external audit fees have increased 271 percent between fiscal years 2001 and 2006 for companies with under $1 billion in revenue. Between fiscal years 2005 and 2006, external audit fees for these companies increased by 4 percent.
- The increases seen in connection with the initial implementation of Section 404, which required all public companies to go through an internal audit enhancement program, have been sustained from its introduction in 2004 to fiscal years 2005 and 2006.
- External audit fees necessitated by the SOX have continued to increase and represent a "significant expense" for public companies (Hartman, 2007, p. 1).

As companies move toward enterprise implementation of internal controls, the hope remains that compliance costs associated with the SOX will fall as redundancies in controls are eliminated. Today, many are skeptical about the ability to contain compliance costs — as companies err on the side of "over-compliance."

"Companies are probably spending more time and resources on 404 compliance than a reasonable reading of the legislation and the rules necessarily requires, heavily influenced by those who gain from issuer over-compliance" (Langevoort, 2006).

However, a Financial Executives International annual survey of SOX compliance done in 2008, which polled 185 companies to find trends in the act's perceived impact and effectiveness during the prior four years, pointed to the overall value of section 404 as follows:

- 50.3 percent of respondents agreed that financial reports were more accurate, up from 46 percent in 2006.
- 56.0 percent agreed that financial reports were more reliable, up from 48 percent in 2006.
- 43.6 percent agreed that compliance with Section 404 had helped prevent or detect fraud, up from 34 percent in 2006.
- 69.1 percent agreed that compliance with Section 404 had resulted in more investor confidence in their financial reports, up from 60 percent in 2006.

The survey also showed an overall decline in cost of compliance during those previous four years.

Furthermore, three years later, in 2011, Chelikani and D'Souza used logistic regression analysis to show that the implementation of SOX resulted in "greater reliability of market information, lower levels of mispricing, and hence a more efficient market." They also argued that their results provided evidence that the SOX-imposed compliance costs were not as burdensome as critics claimed.

Mergers and Acquisitions — Internal Controls
There is evidence to suggest that the cost of maintaining internal controls for accounting practices and financial reporting is affecting corporations in profound ways. Corporate mergers and acquisitions have been popular since the mid-1990s. An abundance of global capital has enabled global players to snatch up competitors at an astonishing rate. Mergers and acquisitions have long been seen as an opportunity for an acquiring firm to capitalize on a target company's strengths, while reducing operational redundancies.

"Mergers can result in combined entities that can more easily absorb the significant compliance costs associated with SOX (Koehn & DelVecchio, 2006). With costs being so significant as has been cited within this essay, corporate mergers may be the one way to ultimately reduce compliance costs in the long run. When two companies become one, the compliance requirements could be expected to drop by 50 percent.

Even if a merger provides the resources needed to absorb compliance costs, the initial expenses associated with compliance and maintaining internal controls will be significant. "While the number of deals after SOX has not declined, SOX has still affected MA activity by impacting the due diligence required to support merger transactions. Acquiring companies must carefully review financial records, vendors, and key customers of target companies, and assume accountability after the merger for those records and relationships. Such increased time and scope for due diligence has increased the transaction costs associated with mergers and acquisitions" (Koehn & DelVecchio, 2006).

Staying Private — Internal Controls
The Cost of Being Public in the Era of Sarbanes-Oxley, the annual report conducted by Foley and Lardner LLP, contends that "companies looking to go public may be discouraged by financial hurdles presented by the SOX, the corporate governance reforms enacted by the U.S. government in 2002 — and the growing trend of private equity buyout in the tech industry may be directly related to those increased costs" (Taylor, 2007).

According to Don S. Peters, Director of Collins Industry Inc., the cost of complying with SOX was estimated at $1 million. Peters questioned whether being publicly listed justified the cost, stating: "It's a heck of a mess for companies our size" (Koehn & DelVecchio, 2006).

SOX has "made it more time-consuming and expensive to function as a public company. And the executives and directors of publicly held outfits face greater scrutiny — putting them personally at risk if things go wrong — from regulators such as the SEC and New York Attorney General Eliot Spitzer. The new responsibilities add to the growing sense that status as a public company means a lot more hassles than it used to" (Rosenbush, 2005, ¶5).

Benefits of Maintaining Internal Controls

While private companies may shy away from going public to avoid the costs and complexity associated with SOX compliance, every company can benefit from maintaining internal controls for accounting practices. "The world of internal controls is not only for public companies. Private companies as well should be analyzing and improving their internal controls" (Diamond, 2007). Accounting systems and internal controls have become synonymous with corporate compliance and SOX. While publicly traded companies must bear the "burden" and cost of federal legislation and compliance, it is important to remember that internal controls are put in place to benefit the company. Compliance issues aside, there are many benefits that can be gained by implementing effective internal controls at private companies. The following list offers the benefits to both public and private companies.

Internal controls can:

- create value by helping to maximize potential and enable growth
- reduce the risk of financial statement fraud
- promote a culture of integrity and high values
- give confidence to customers and shareholders
- improve processes and operational efficiency
- prepare for the process of becoming a public company (Diamond, 2007)

The AICPA recently issued (SAS no. 104–111) *Risk-Based Audit Standards*. Auditors will be assessing the need to conduct risk-based audits; their criteria will include industry, business size, and internal control structure. COSO has recently issued guidelines to assist small companies with internal controls frameworks. The benefits of maintaining strong and well-designed internal controls for accounting practices cannot be overstated. While it is easy to associate the need for accounting systems and controls with government mandates, this is a short-sighted view. Strong accounting systems and supporting internal controls are tools that can help any company maintain sound financial practices, high ethical standards, and many other best practices that can help with an overall enterprise risk management strategy.

CONCLUSION

According to a 2007 Ernst and Young survey of chief audit executives (CAEs), there's a renewed interest by boards in monitoring internal controls through the audit process. Greater scrutiny and knowledge about internal controls is providing greater assurance to stakeholders about the responsiveness of organizations to risk. The "adequacy and operational effectiveness of internal controls" is paramount — and analysis of the effectiveness of controls has become a major driver for decision-making (Gregory, 2007). Communication is now expected to be near real-time and very exhaustive in its scope. Comprehensive reporting should help identify the root cause of identified problems and subsequent feedback to improve the controls. The following list outlines some future trends that are seen as essential in leveraging internal controls and audits for improved operational efficiency. According to Gregory,

- An organization should be able to draw conclusions on the quality of risk management and internal control by each major business area within the company.
- The most significant control exposures the group face should be defined in detail; the impact and root cause of control weaknesses should be highlighted and the appropriateness of management's remediation plans documented.
- Management needs a clear understanding of the risks and must also have the capability to manage the most crucial risks.
- Identify new and emerging control themes that the business needs to address.
- Ensure consistency with the views of other risk and assurance related functions to create an overall risk strategy.
- Compare risk strategies and solutions against other firms as a chance to take advantage of new trends and best practices.
- Prioritize company portfolios of improvement opportunities arising from reviews of the control environment.
- Communicate views on management's proposed approach and capability to fix control weaknesses and their track record in fixing known issues.

- Assess the suitability of internal controls in the light of strategic plans/anticipated change; both market and internally initiated.
- Take advantage of opportunities to reduce the overall cost of c ontrols (Gregory, 2007).

TERMS & CONCEPTS

Accounting controls: Procedures to assure accuracy in record keeping functions; using a system of controls to insure that data and reports are accurate and correct.

Accounting system: Comprised of computer software that records transactional and financial data along with the documentation, procedures, and strategies that control implementation and administration of the system.

The American Institute of Certified Public Accountants (AICPA): The national, professional organization for all Certified Public Accountants (CPAs). Its mission is to provide members with the resources, information, and leadership that enable them to provide valuable services in the highest professional manner to benefit the public as well as employers and clients (AICPA).

Assurance: CPA examination of a given process or system which attests to the correctness or appropriateness which therefore allows a given level of confidence that the system or process under review is correct in its reporting.

Chief audit executive (CAE): Refers to an executive-level position responsible for helping to determine an enterprise's risk/reward picture and keep management informed of scenarios. The CAE must take a holistic approach to the management of risks across the enterprise.

Committee of Sponsoring Organizations of the Treadway Commission (COSO): A voluntary private sector organization dedicated to improving the quality of financial reporting through business ethics, effective internal controls, and corporate governance (COSO.org).

Control environment: The general attitude of management or others who administer the internal controls of an organization. It can be thought of as level of commitment or adherence to controls by management.

Corporate compliance: The rules and regulations imposed by federal law to insure that organizations comply with a given regulatory environment — typically refers to compliance in financial reporting under Sarbanes-Oxley Section 404.

External audit: An audit or assessment of controls that is conducted by someone who does not work for the company being audited (aka independent audit).

Internal controls: Broadly defined as a process, affected by an entity's board of directors, management, and other personnel, designed to provide reasonable assurance regarding the achievement of objectives in financial reporting and record keeping (COSO.org).

Private company: A company whose shares are not publicly traded on the open market.

Public company: A company whose shares are publicly traded or publicly held. A public company offers securities for trade in an open market (stock market).

Public Company Accounting Oversight Board (PCAOB): A private sector, non-profit corporation created by the Sarbanes-Oxley Act of 2002. The role of the PCAOB is to oversee auditors of public companies and protect the interests of investors and to insure that the creation of independent audit reports (PCAOB.org).

Risk-based audit: An audit of one of an organization's major activities; processes or activities are ranked according to strategic importance and where risk may have the greatest impact on the organization from a financial or reputational risk standpoint.

Sarbanes-Oxley (Sarbox or SOX or SOA): AKA Public Company Accounting Reform and Investor Protection Act of 2002. Wide-ranging legislation that establishes new or enhanced standards for all U.S. public company boards, management, and public accounting firms. The act was created and implemented after a number of high profile corporate accounting scandals in early 2000s.

Sarbanes-Oxley-section 404: Issuers are required to publish information in their annual reports concerning the scope and adequacy of the internal control structure and procedures for financial reporting. This statement shall also assess the effectiveness of such internal controls and procedures (Sarbanes-Oxley Act Section 404, 2004).

(SAS no. 104-111) Risk-based audit standards: New standards to enhance the application of the long-standing audit risk model and improve the quality of audits because they specifically require auditors to: Have a more comprehensive understanding of the client's business and its environment, including its internal control; perform a more exacting assessment of the risk of material misstatement resulting from such understanding, and; perform procedures that more clearly link the risk assessment to the decision of what audit procedures to perform, and when (Freelibrary.com).

Securities and Exchange Commission (SEC): The primary federal regulatory agency for the securities industry, whose responsibility is to promote full disclosure and to protect investors against fraudulent and manipulative practices in the securities markets (Investorwords.com).

BIBLIOGRAPHY

Center for audit quality submits comment letter to the SEC on internal control proposals. (2007). AICPA.

Chelikani, S., & D'Souza, F. (2011). The impact of Sarbanes-Oxley on market efficiency: evidence from mergers and acquisitions activity. *International Journal of Business & Finance Research (IJBFR), 5*, 75–88.

Choi, B., Kim, J. (2017). The effect of CEO stock-based compensation on the pricing of future earnings. *European Accounting Review, 26(4)*, 651–679.

Diamond, E. (2007). What private companies need to know about internal controls. *New Jersey Tech News, 11*.

Developing an internal accounting control system. (2007).

Fitzsimons, A., & Lange, G. (2006). SEC staff issues guidance on the implementation of internal control reporting requirements. *Bank Accounting & Finance (08943958), 19*, 41–52.

Florin, B., & Carmen, B. (2013). Management control systems: a review of their components and their underlying independence. *Annals of the University of Oradea, Economic Science Series, 22*, 1424–1433.

Gregory, S. (2007, October 4). Internal audit: Power surge. *Accountancy Age*.

Hall, L., & Gaetanos, C. (2006). Treatment of section 404 compliance costs. *CPA Journal, 76*, 58–62.

Hampton, J. (2006). 'Push' and 'pull' in enterprise risk management. *Business Insurance, 40*, 19-19.

Hartman, T. (2007). The cost of being public in the era of Sarbanes-Oxley. Foley Lardner, LLP, Annual Report.

Internal controls. (2007). Office of Audit and Compliance Review.

Koehn, J., DelVecchio, S. (2006). Revisiting the ripple effects of the Sarbanes-Oxley Act. *CPA Journal, 76*, 32–39.

Langevoort, D. (2006). Internal controls after Sarbanes-Oxley: Revisiting corporate law's duty of care as responsibility for systems. *Journal of Corporation Law, 31*, 949–973.

Lenn, L.E. (2013). Sarbanes-Oxley Act 2002 (SOX)-10 years later. *Journal of Legal Issues Cases In Business, 2*, 1–14.

Rosenbush, S. (2005, March 29). The allure of going private. *Business Week*.

Sarbanes-Oxley Act Section 404. (2004) SoxLaw.com.

Taylor, C. (2007). SOX costs could be cause of surge in private equity buyouts, study finds. *Electronic News (10616624), 52*, 2.

Turner, L., & Weirich, T. (2006). A closer look at financial statement restatements. (Cover story). *CPA Journal, 76*, 12–23.

SUGGESTED READING

Flexible finance systems. (2007). *Accounting Technology, 23*, 19.

Kranacher, M. (2006). Transparency and accountability (for some?). *CPA Journal, 76*, 80.

Wojcik, J. (2007). Risk managers bringing data in-house to gain greater control. *Business Insurance, 41*, 57.

Essay by Carolyn Sprague, MLS

Accounting Systems for Managerial Decisions

This article provides a foundation for the basic accounting equation and how different types of accounting processes assist managers in making decisions. Financial accounting and managerial accounting are defined and compared and contrasted. There are nine different types of accounting transactions that can take place as a result of the basic accounting equation. However, only five of the nine transactions have a common effect on the accounting equation. The objective of financial accounting is to provide information to external decision makers, whereas, the objective of managerial accounting is to provide information to internal decision-makers. There are two types of techniques utilized by decision makers in the planning process: cost/value/profit (CVP) analysis and financial budgeting.

OVERVIEW

Being familiar with financial transactions and their effects on financial reports can help accounting professionals with creating new reports that will assist decision makers, developing financial strategies in response to what may occur in the future, creating methods of filing and tracking financial information, automating financial records, and filing the required income taxes (Page & Hooper, 1985). If a business or an individual is involved in any type of activity that requires money, there will be a need to keep detailed and accurate records on the financial operations of all activities that transpire. Businesses are accountable to entities such as boards of directors, creditors, and various governmental agencies. Individuals tend to report information to banks and other creditors. Both businesses and individuals must report to the Internal Revenue Service (IRS) at least once a year. The reports prepared tend to give the reader an idea of the financial state of the businesses or individual's affairs. Basically, the reports tell a story of how the money is being managed. The process of collecting the financial information and preparing a report has been referred to as financial accounting.

Financial Accounting

Financial accounting focuses on preparing financial statements for external decision-makers such as banks and government agencies. The primary purpose of the field is to review and monitor an organization's financial performance and report the results of the evaluation to potential stakeholders. Financial accountants are expected to create financial statements based on generally accepted accounting principles (GAAP). Financial accounting exists in order to produce general purpose financial statements, provide information to decision-makers in the accounting field, and meet regulatory requirements.

Acquiring & Creating Resources

Businesses are responsible for two tasks: acquiring financial and productive resources and combing the two resources in order to create new resources. Acquired resources are called assets, and the different types of assets are called equities. Therefore, the foundation for the basic accounting equation is "Assets = Equities." However, since equities can be divided into two groups, the basic accounting equation can be revised to read as "Assets = Liabilities + Owners' Equity."

Assets. Although assets consist of financial and productive resources, not all resources are considered to be assets. In order to determine if a resource is to be considered an asset, it must satisfy all three of the following criteria:

- The resource must possess future value for the business. The future value must take the form of exchange ability (i.e. cash) or usability (i.e. equipment).
- The resource must be under the effective control of the business. However, legal ownership is not mandatory. As long as the resource can be freely used in business activities, the resource will meet the asset criteria. An example is a leased computer; although the organization may use the computer, legal rights still belong to the leasing company.
- The resource must have a dollar value resulting from an identifiable event or events in the life of

the organization. The value assigned to the asset must be tracked to an exchange between the organization and others (Page & Hooper, 1985).

If the resource does not meet all of the criteria, it cannot be reported as an asset.

Liabilities. When someone other than the owner provides an organization with an asset, the claims against the business take the form of a debt. Sources of assets from someone other than the owner are referred to as liabilities. Liabilities are the debts and legal obligations that a business incurs as the result of acquiring the assets from non-owners.

Owners' Equity. Some businesses may obtain assets via owner investment or sale of stock. When the owner supplies the organization with assets, the claim against those assets is called owners' equity (or stockholders' equity) in a financial report.

When a business accepts assets from a source other than the owner, it can be reported as a liability or owners' equity. However, there are some differences between these two sources.

Basic Accounting Equation Transactions
Nine different types of accounting transactions can take place as a result of the basic accounting equation. However, only five of the nine transactions have a common effect on the accounting equation. These transactions are:

- increase in assets and decrease in assets (i.e. when an organization collects money that is owed to it, there is an increase in cash and a decrease in accounts receivable)
- increase in assets and increase in liabilities (i.e. when an organization borrows money, there is an increase in cash and notes payable)
- increase in assets and increase in owners' equity (i.e. when an owner invests money in the business, there is an increase in cash and owners' equity)
- decrease in assets and decrease in liabilities (i.e. when a business pays off a loan, there is a decrease in cash and notes payable)
- decrease in assets and decrease in owners' equity (i.e. when an owner decides to withdraw some assets from the business, there is a decrease in assets, usually cash, and a decrease in owners'

equity since they tend to use the withdrawal for personal use)

Although organizations tend to focus significant time preparing financial reports for external stakeholders, the demands of an organization's management team are equally important. This group of individuals is responsible for providing direction to the organization. Therefore, it is crucial that they have access to the most up-to-date information regarding the organization's financial status. Therefore, the organization tends to select an accounting system that would provide the management team with information that will assist and validate why they make certain decisions. The process of providing the management team with financial information that will assist in decision making is referred to as managerial accounting.

Managerial Accounting
Managerial accounting is an internal function that focuses on using present financial information to anticipate and predict future events. All types of organizations can benefit from the use of managerial accounting information. The information obtained may assist organizations with their mission statement, vision, goals, and objectives. Some of the major objectives of managerial accounting are:

- provide information to decision makers so that they can plan for the future.
- direct and control the daily operational activities of an organization so that they can produce a quality product or service. Managers need information on the cost of providing products and services so that the organization can set the appropriate prices. Also, managers can use the accounting information to compare the actual costs to the projected costs of a product or service.
- guide managers to areas that may be problematic for the organization.

Financial Accounting versus Managerial Accounting
The objective of financial accounting is to provide information to external decision-makers, whereas, the objective of managerial accounting is to provide information to internal decision-makers. Although both areas need to use an organization's accounting records, there are differences between the two areas of accounting.

An organization's management team has the ability to create any type of internal accounting system. However, cost may be a key factor in deciding what type of system will be selected. The type and amount of information that needs to be stored is another factor in selecting the most appropriate information system.

Both financial and managerial accounting are bound by the Foreign Corrupt Practices Act. This act is a "U.S. law forbidding bribery and other corrupt practices, and requiring that accounting records be maintained in reasonable detail and accuracy, and that an appropriate system of internal accounting be maintained" (Horngreen, Stratton, & Sundem, 2002, p. 7). In summary, Drury (1996) stated that managerial accounting focuses on the provision of information to people within the organization so that they can make better decisions, whereas, financial accounting emphasizes the need of an organization to have the ability to provide financial information to stakeholders outside of the organization.

APPLICATION

Managerial Accounting
Techniques for the Planning Process
Two types of techniques are utilized by decision-makers in the planning process: cost/value/profit (CVP) analysis and financial budgeting. An organization's income and profit is based on the structure of its revenues and costs as well as the volume of activity that it achieves.

CVP Analysis
The CVP analysis is the decision-making model that most managerial accountants utilize when predicting future actions. Decisions, such as the pricing of products and services, selecting the appropriate advertising strategies, and deciding on which markets to enter, can be determined using this model. Page and Hooper (1985) determined that the steps in the cost/volume/profit analysis are as follows:

- Study cost behavior as volume changes and classify all costs as variable or fixed. Some costs may be classified if one understands the nature of the cost while other costs may need to the accountant to examine the organization's data on past activities in order to determine the amount of each cost at different volume levels and how each cost changed as volume changed.

- Determine total fixed costs (TFC) and variable cost per unit (VPU). Add the total amounts of all costs classified as fixed to get the TFC. Divide the amounts for each variable cost by the level of volume at which that cost was incurred to get the per unit amount for each variable cost. Then add the individual variable costs per unit to get the VCU for the business.

- Calculate contribution margin per unit (CMU). The selling price per unit of product or service should be available from the organization's records and CMU = SPU – VCU. CMU provides the amount left over from the sale of each unit after the direct costs of the unit are covered.

- Determine before-tax target profit (BTP). This figure is the after-tax desired profit of the business divided by the applicable income tax rate of the organization.

- Add TFC and BTP and divide the amount by CMU to get the number of units of product or service that must be sold to cover all costs and provide the desired profit for the business after taxes.

The CVP model is very versatile and can show the accountant the effect on the business given any change in one of the key variables in the equation.

The CVP model can be a powerful tool for managerial accountants because it allows one to evaluate different courses of action and see what their results would be before implementing a decision. Also, by looking at the relationship between the key variables, the accountant has the ability to analyze the total impact of a decision on the organization. However, it must be noted that the usefulness of the CVP model is dependent on the accountant's ability to properly classify the costs of the organization as variable or fixed. If one does not fully comprehend the organization's cost behavior patterns, errors can be made in the decision making process. On a positive note, an organization's information system can assist in documenting and storing the necessary information over a period of time.

Financial Budgeting
The second technique is financial budgeting. Financial budgeting is the function that connects a manager's ability to plan and control the process. The financial budget is a summary of the manager's decision making process for a particular project. It will show the overall impact of all of the possible

alternative decision making ideas. The projected financial statements are referred to as the master budget of the organization. The master budget becomes the standard benchmark with which all future performance will be measured and evaluated.

The master budget has three components that may influence an organization's future.

- profit plan—An income statement projected over a future period.
- cash budget—A statement of budgeted cash flows could be in many forms and may cover any period of timed deemed important by the managers. Most organizations will budget cash on a monthly basis to make sure that there is ample funds available to meet short term needs such as payroll and accounts payable.
- budgeted balance sheet—This statement summarizes everything by showing the final effects on the financial position of the organization based on the manager's decisions, assumptions and projections.

The financial budgeting process can be accomplished by utilizing an information system to perform a spreadsheet analysis. This process will eliminate the need for paperwork. One popular software package is VisiCalc. VisiCalc was one of the first spreadsheet programs designed for microcomputers, and was created by Dave Bricklin and Bob Frankston.

VIEWPOINT

Information Systems in Healthcare
According to Rogoski (2004), all expenditures and billings recorded will end up in the financial department. Unfortunately, most clinical applications and financial applications do not work together. They work independently, which causes duplication of efforts for the employees that have to process the information. As a result of this problem, some developers have created entirely integrated software; however, still others prefer to offer whatever is most effective at the time (best of the breed philosophy). Many chief financial officers are electing to do business with those organizations that create information systems that will satisfy their organization's needs. Top leaders such as Ron Bunnell, CFO of Banner Health, and Dan Deets, CFO of Hunterdone Healthcare, Inc., have found that as a result of integrated clinical and financial systems,

they have increased access to the information necessary to reduce costs and improve efficiencies within the delivery of healthcare services. The integrated systems allow for improved tracking of both clinical and business initiative revenue. Having the ability to have access to all types of financial data has provided the CFOs mentioned above the opportunity to have more negotiating power when dealing with managed care contracts. There is an ability to monitor the relationships that these healthcare systems have with payers over a period of time. In addition, the integrated systems allow the healthcare organizations to identify weak areas that need to be improved so that they can increase their revenue.

CONCLUSION

Being familiar with financial transactions and their effects on financial reports can help accounting professionals with (Page & Hooper, 1985):

- creating new reports that will assist decision makers
- developing financial strategies in response to what may occur in the future
- creating methods of filing and tracking financial information
- automating financial records
- filing the required income taxes

Financial accounting focuses on preparing financial statements for external decision-makers such as banks and government agencies. The primary purpose of the field is to review and monitor an organization's financial performance and report the results of the evaluation to potential stakeholders. Managerial accounting is an internal function that focuses on using present financial information to anticipate and predict future events. All types of organizations can benefit from the use of managerial accounting information.

Two types of techniques are utilized by decision-makers in the planning process: cost/value/profit (CVP) analysis and financial budgeting. An organization's income and profit are based on the structure of its revenues and costs as well as the volume of activity that it achieves. The financial budgeting process can be accomplished by utilizing an information system to perform a spreadsheet analysis. This process will eliminate the need for paperwork.

TERMS & CONCEPTS

Accounting systems: An organization's chronological list of debits and credits.

Assets: Those items owned by an individual or organization which hold economic value and have the potential to be converted to cash.

Financial accounting: Purposed with alerting external stakeholders of a business's performance through financial reports.

Generally accepted accounting principles (GAAP): Established by the Financial Accounting Standards Board (FASB), is the body of regulatory parameters recognized in the reporting of financial information.

Liabilities: Total assets minus total owners' equity.

Managerial accounting: Financial reporting that is aimed at helping managers to make decisions.

Owners' equity: Total assets minus total liabilities.

VisiCalc: One of the first spreadsheet programs designed for microcomputers; was created by Dave Bricklin and Bob Frankston.

BIBLIOGRAPHY

Alino, N. U., & Schneider, G. P. (2012). Conflict reduction in organization design: budgeting and accounting control systems. *Academy of Strategic Management Journal, 11*, 1–8.

Applebaum, D., Kogan, A., Vasarhelyi, M., Yan, Z. (2017). Impact of business analytics and enterprise systems on managerial accounting. *International Journal of Accounting Information Systems, 25*, 29–44.

Drury, C. (1996). *Management and cost accounting* (4th ed.). London: International Thompson Business Press.

Fotache, G., Fotache, M., Bucsa, R., & Ocneanu, L. (2011). The changing role of managerial accounting in decision making process research on managing costs. *Economy Transdisciplinarity Cognition, 14*, 45–55.

Horngreen C. T., Stratton, W. O., & Sundem, G. L. (2002). *Introduction to management accounting* (12th ed.). New Jersey: Prentice Hall.

Page, J., & Hooper, P. (1985). *Microcomputer accounting and business applications.* Reston: Reston Publishing Company, Inc.

Rogoski, R. (2004). Investment pay off with financial information systems. *Health Management Technology, 25*, 14–17.

Thitiworada, S., & Phapruke, U. (2013). Best managerial accounting information system and firm performance: an empirical investigation of information technology and communication bussiness in Thailand. *Review of Business Research, 13*, 47–66.

SUGGESTED READING

Brief, R., & Euske, K. (1988). Classifying and coding for accounting operations/decision support systems for management accountants. *Accounting Review, 63*, 721–723.

Driver, M., & Mock, T. (1975). Human information processing, decision style theory, and accounting information systems. *Accounting Review, 50*, 490–508.

Gordan, L., Larcker, D.; & Tuggle, F. (1978). Strategic decision processes and the design of accounting information systems: conceptual linkages. *Accounting, Organizations Society, 3* (3/4), 203–213.

Essay by Marie Gould

ACCOUNTS RECEIVABLES AND INVENTORIES

This article concerns the basic accounting principles for tracking accounts receivables and inventories, and how this relates to running an effective business. Whether the business entity is a small entrepreneurial enterprise or a large publicly traded corporation, maintaining sound accounting principles will help to ensure that the organization is well run and profitable. Both types of entities need to track business costs and maintain sufficient cash flows; and publicly traded corporations also need to ensure that their financial statements are accurate and in compliance with the Sarbanes-Oxley Act (SOX).

PayPal's corporate headquarters in San Jose, California. (Courtesy of Sagar Savla via Wikimedia Commons)

OVERVIEW

Effectively tracking accounts receivables and inventories is a necessary condition for running a successful business enterprise. In short, both small business owners and officers of publicly traded companies need to know how much money is owed to the business for work it has performed or the goods, services and merchandise it has provided on a credit basis. This is the definition of accounts receivables.

Not only must business owners and executives have a system for tracking accounts receivables, they must also be able to track the goods, services, and merchandise they can actually deliver or its inventories. A company that does not maintain sufficient inventories will not be able to deliver these assets to customers, and this will be detrimental to customer relationships. On the other hand, if a company has inventories that cannot be sold, the costs incurred in maintaining those assets, that is the actual dollar cost of as well as the risks associated with warehousing goods while not having a market for them, will increase the business expenses and adversely affect the company's profit margin.

APPLICATIONS

Accounts Receivables & Cash Flows
In order to keep track of accounts receivable, a company needs to establish a billing procedure. This will allow a customer to understand the terms of payment and give the company a method to keep accounts receivables current. The first step is for the company to provide the customer with an invoice and to have a system in place for tracking its invoices, such as a ledger.

Invoices
Invoices should be prepared on a company's stationery and indicate the items that were purchased (or the goods and services that were provided), the date of the purchase, purchase price (including applicable taxes and delivery fees), delivery date, invoice date and terms of payment — that is the due date, payment amount and the means of payment. The latter includes cash on delivery, check, money order, and credit card, as well as electronic methods such as PayPal, Square, and Safaricom's M-Pesa.

Of course, sending an invoice by whatever means (e.g., mail, email, telecopy) may not guarantee payment. So there must also be a procedure to handle payments and late payments. Usually, a customer who fails to pay by the due date after they have been provided with an initial statement is notified by mail or email, and then a follow-up call is made. In the event payments are not made, third-party collection agencies can be utilized to collect overdue payments, and if payments are still not made, further legal action may be required. One way to mitigate late payments is to have fewer payment terms; in particular, payments should be made in full by a certain date, and a penalty should be applied to late payments.

Working Capital & Cash Flow
For accounting purposes on income and financial statements, and in accordance with Generally Accepted Accounting Principles (GAAP), accounts receivables are listed as assets even though the cash is not on hand. Further, the cost of providing credit to customers is also a significant element in determining a company's working capital. A company's working capital is determined by cash flows, that is, an entity's cash receipts less its disbursements for a specific time period. Ultimately, a successful enterprise is one that has sufficient cash flows that will generate profits. Effective management of working capital will not only improve a company's profits but also reduce the risk of uncollected or delinquent receivables.

One way to enhance cash flow is to quickly collect accounts receivables by simplifying the invoicing process, minimizing payment terms, and having a collections procedure in place for delinquent accounts. Even if all these mechanisms are in place, a company still can experience problems collecting receivables and thus run into cash flow shortages. However, there is a means to mitigate the risk of late, uncollected or defaulted receivables, called factoring.

Factoring

Basically, factoring is the outright sale of a firm's account receivables to a third party. At one time, factoring was not viewed favorably; however, it is now a widely accepted and customary business practice. According to Feast (2013), research company BDRC reported that the use of such external financing as asset-based lending, invoice discounting, and factoring by UK small businesses increased to 21 percent in the second quarter of 2013, up from 15 percent in prior quarters.

But more importantly, it is good business management that enables a company to have sufficient working capital.

Factoring is usually made on a non-recourse basis. This means that the third party to whom the receivables are sold (the "factor"), is solely responsible for collection of the receivables. In so doing, the factor also assumes the risk of uncollected or defaulted receivables. To offset this risk, the sale of the receivables is usually made at a discount of the account's value. There are other forms of factoring, such as "recourse factoring" and "invoice discounting."

In short, factoring will enhance cash flows since payment of invoices becomes immediate. Ultimately, efficient cash flow will enhance a company's ability to re-invest in the company as well as to invest in interest-bearing investments. Effectively tracking accounts receivables is one tool for managing working capital that can enhance profits.

Inventory & Cash Flows

Another essential component of managing working capital is the effective management of inventory. This is a complex but necessary task since excess inventory (like uncollected or defaulted receivables) can adversely affect cash flows. At the same time, insufficient inventories can result in lost sales and delays for customers — and if such delays become a pattern, customers will seek out a company that can provide goods and services expediently. Not only will this affect a company's profits, but lost sales and lost customers can also have a significant adverse impact on a company's professional reputation — a bad name is bad for business.

JIT Manufacturing

One key to effectively managing inventory is to know how quickly stock is moving, and this can vary depending on the type and size of the business. Today, for example, many large manufacturing companies utilize a just-in-time (JIT) method for maintaining inventories. This means that all the components of the good being manufactured on a particular day are delivered early that morning — no earlier or later (Flanagan 2005).

JIT inventorying reduces manufacturing costs since JIT stocks take up little space and this reduces the need for warehousing. Supplies that remain warehoused for excessive periods of time have a greater propensity for being damaged, and in some cases such supplies can become obsolete, and there is no market for obsolete goods. The key for a company is to determine which supplies move quickly and which move slowly. Inventory that does not move quickly means that cash flow will be hindered.

Although the JIT method reduces manufacturing costs, it should be noted that profitability ratios (such as return on assets, return on equity, and basic earning power) that aggregate all of a firm's activities may not be suitable metrics to determine the effect of JIT and lean manufacturing methods on a firm's financial performance (Klingenberg, Timberlake, Geurts, & Brown, 2013).

As with accounts receivables, for accounting purposes, inventories are listed as assets on a company's balance sheet — but this does not mean that inventory is cash. In addition to employing JIT, there are other ways to achieve inventory reductions and therefore enhance cash flows. The goal here is to reduce the time it takes to deliver goods and services to a customer. There are three means to reaching this end: Increasing sales, decreasing production and disposing of obsolete inventories.

Increased Sales

If sales rates are increased to the point that sales exceed creation of inventory, the amount and value of the inventory will decrease. Increasing sales rates are directly tied to the company's business model — included in that model should be an effectively trained sales force that is aware of inventory levels and the related pricing options. Moreover, the administrative costs associated with maintaining and training a sales force must also be minimized.

Reduced Production Rates

Another way companies reduce inventory is by reducing production rates, and this is greatly determined by demand. If demand is declining, then production rates obviously need to be decreased. In addition, the business needs to consider another cost associated with maintaining inventory — labor costs. There are a number of ways to reduce labor costs: cut shifts, hold wages steady, or reduce the workforce when needed.

Obsolete Inventory Disposal

Finally, there is an accounting mechanism in place for reducing inventory. A company can resort to declaring its inventory obsolete and disposing of it. The expense associated with this a permissible write off in accordance with GAAP. This can be considered an expense that reduces profit and that likewise reduces taxable income.

In the end, reducing inventory frees up cash for other investments, and this will be reflected in the company's books and records or its financial statements.

The Accuracy of Financial Statements

In addition to the business basics associated with accounts receivables and inventories, and the need for effective management of these items to ensure cash flows that enable a company to have sufficient working capital to cover its business costs, reinvest in the company, or to invest in interest bearing investment vehicles, there is another crucial matter to consider — the accuracy of financial statements.

As we have seen, accounts receivables and inventories are considered assets on a company's income statements and balance sheets. For a small, non-publicly traded company, these items must be accurately reflected on its income statements as those will be included in its federal and state income tax filings. If these items are incorrectly booked and subsequently incorrectly reported to tax authorities, the consequences can be significant.

For publicly traded companies that are required to file financial statements with the Securities Exchange Commission (SEC) on a quarterly basis (such filings are made on "Form 10-Q" and must be filed within 45 days of the end of a particular quarter) or on an annual basis (on "Form 10-K," now required to be filed within 60 days of a company's fiscal year end), the need for accurate financial statements has far-reaching implications.

SOX & Accounting Procedures

While the need for effective internal controls of accounting procedures are not new to the industry, the Sarbanes-Oxley Act of 2002 (SOX) imposed many new rules and procedures on publicly traded entities. First and foremost, executive officers are required to attest to the accuracy of the financial statements, under penalty of perjury. Moreover, there are numerous internal controls required to ensure that financial statements are accurate. These controls not only relate to the actual quantitative accuracy of financial statements, but also require audits of all corporate functions. Each and every business group, from the controller's office right down to the document retention functions are required to undergo thorough and exhaustive internal examinations to ensure that all the company's policies and procedures are being followed.

As SOX has worked its way through the business community over the years, various accounting deficiencies have been discovered. With respect to determining revenue, numerous companies have been shown to have deficiencies in their revenue recognition policies. These deficiencies are usually related to the timing of revenue recognition as well as contracting practices (Weili 2005). The timing of revenue recognition and contracting practices are directly related to accounts receivable, accounts payable, and inventory accounts.

Channel Stuffing & Invoice Backdating

Essentially, certain companies were found to have practices that were deemed to be improper revenue recognition. One such practice has been termed channel stuffing. This is a scheme whereby a company attempts to boost sales results by shipping more products to subsidiaries or vendors prior to the end of a reporting quarter (Weili 2005). This gives the appearance of higher sales figures, and reduced inventory, and thus greater revenue for that quarter. Another deficient practice that has been revealed concerns the treatment of accounts receivables. Certain companies were found to have been back dating invoices in an attempt to lower their outstanding or uncollected receivables for a particular quarter which gave the appearance of greater cash flows at the close of a quarter.

In any case, manipulating financial statements is an egregious violation of the SOX. By employing such devices, not only have companies (and the responsible individuals) been convicted of fraud under SOX, investors have also suffered undue hardship as the value of the companies' stock price has fallen dramatically in these cases. And this has opened a Pandora's Box of class action lawsuits. Defending against these suits can be quite expensive and this can have a material adverse effect on a company's profits and its reputation as well as its viability as a business entity.

Not only have violations and deficiencies discovered by virtue of SOX proven to be costly, implementing policies and procedures to ensure compliance with the Act have also increased the cost to conduct business. In order to perform the required extensive internal audits and verify that responsible individuals connected to accounting procedures are well trained, many companies have had to add significant personnel to their staff or to outsource these functions to consultants, and the increase in labor costs has had an impact on working capital.

CONCLUSION

Accounts receivables and inventories might seem like a mundane matter, but this is not the case. The complexities involved in accurately tracking and managing receivables and inventory require an expertise in accounting. More importantly, it requires a business entity to have "best practices" in place aimed at maintaining business ethics. Accounting expertise and business ethics are intangible assets that will have a serious effect on a company's bottom line, positively or negatively. As a result, it is necessary to have effective systems in place.

Accounts receivables essentially represent the value of the goods and services a company provides. This value is directly related to the company's profitability. Having efficient systems for invoicing and collections enables a company to mitigate the time it takes to get paid for items it has basically sold on credit. Moreover, having a handle on outstanding accounts receivables enables a company to devise a strategy for enhancing cash flows. As we have seen, one such approach is factoring. The outright sales of an entity's receivables will enhance cash flow — albeit the receivables are sold at a discount of the original value of the good or service. However, effective accounting procedures will result in adequate pricing models that will ensure profitability.

Inventories are the actual goods or services that a business entity provides to customers. The amount of time it takes to deliver these goods and services to customers also affects available working capital. Items that remain in inventory for excessive periods become costly as they are more likely to be damaged, or can become obsolete. While there are ways a company can mitigate losses for obsolete merchandize by permitted write-offs, business enterprises are established to sell goods and services, not to have their products become obsolete. A company needs to have a responsible individual aware of what is in inventory, and this information must be effectively communicated to its sales force. An effectively trained sales force can use this information by knowing what pricing models to employ. At the same time, sales managers can use this information and develop unit based incentives for its sales staff in order to increase sales rates.

Not only is effectively managing accounts receivables and inventories a crucial function in establishing business plans and models, such management enables a company controller as well as the responsible compliance officer to establish policies and procedures throughout all the company's business lines to ensure compliance with SOX and guarantee that the financial statements accurately reflect the company's financial well-being at any given time.

In the final analysis, a company that fails to have "best practices" in place for maintaining accounts receivables and inventories will not be profitable and can, if public, subject itself and its employees to criminal prosecution. Moreover, not adhering to these practices can cause unnecessary losses for its investors and eventually trigger regulatory scrutiny and legal actions that will hinder business growth. Having qualified accounting and compliance personnel is one way to prevent these things from occurring and will prove quite beneficial to a company's profits, and that is the bottom line.

TERMS & CONCEPTS

Accounts receivables: Money owed to a business entity for goods, services and merchandise purchased on a credit basis.

Business model: The means by which a company generates revenue and profits, how it serves its customers and the strategy and implementation of procedures to achieve this end.

Cash flow: Cash receipts minus cash disbursements from a given operation for a specific period. Cash flow and cash inflow are used interchangeably in accounting terminology.

Channel stuffing: A manipulation of revenue on a company's books where sales results are boosted by shipping more products to subsidiaries or vendors prior to the end of a fiscal quarter.

Compliance officer: Responsible individual in a company who ensures that procedures adhere to applicable federal, state and regional laws, rules, and guidelines.

Controller: Responsible individual in a publicly traded company who maintains corporate financial books and records or financial statements.

Delinquent receivables: Receivables that have not been paid by a customer by the due date. (The due date is usually 45 days from the date of the invoice.)

Defaulted receivable: A receivable that has not been paid and is referred to a collection agency.

Factoring: Outright sale of a firm's account receivables to a third party (the "factor") without recourse; that is the factor is solely responsible for collection of the receivables. Accordingly, such sales are usually made at a discount of the accounts value.

Generally accepted accounting principles (GAAP): Universally practiced principles established by the Financial Accounting Standards Board (FASB).

Invoice: A bill used by a person or business that provides goods or services to a customer.

Inventory: The name given to an asset of a business relating to merchandise or supplies on hand or in transit at a particular point in time.

Just in time (JIT): A method for maintaining inventories where components of a good being manufactured on a particular day are delivered that morning — no earlier or later.

Securities Exchange Commission (SEC): Federal regulatory agency responsible for enforcing the federal laws regarding the purchase and sale of stocks, bonds and other investments. One such law is the Sarbanes-Oxley Act (SOX) of 2002.

Sarbanes-Oxley Act (SOX): Federal law enacted in 2002 that requires executives of publicly traded companies to attest to the accuracy of its financial statements and which also requires the establishment of extensive internal procedures and controls to ensure compliance with the law.

BIBLIOGRAPHY

Ameiss, A. P. Kargas, N. A. (2001). *Accountant's desk handbook.* New Jersey: Prentice Hall.

Feast, S. (2013). Factoring enjoys resurgence in demand. *Credit Management,* 6.

Flanagan, B. (2005). Managing working capital. *Business Credit, 107,* 26–29.

Klingenberg, B., Timberlake, R., Geurts, T.G., Brown, R.J. (2013). The relationship of operational innovation and financial performance–a critical perspective. *International Journal of Production Economics, 142,* 317–323.

Kutler, J. (2012). Leading the e-money revolution. *Institutional Investor, 46,* 269.

Mason, R. (2004). *Credit controller's desktop guide.* London, UK: Thorogood Publishing.

Prince, C. J. (2004). Catch your cash. *Entrepreneur, 32,* 57–58.

Rosenberg, J. M. (1983). *Dictionary of business and accounting*. New York: John Wiley and Sons.

Siegal, J. E. Shim, Jae, K. (2000). *Barron's dictionary of accounting terms*. New York: Barrons Educational Services Inc.

Singh, H., Kumar, S., Colombage, S. (2017). Working capital management and firm profitability: a meta-analysis. *Qualitative Research in Financial Markets, 9(1)*, 34-47.

Yu-Lee, R. T. (2004) Inventory is not cash. *Industrial Management, 46*, 8–15.

Weili, G. McVay, S. (2005). The disclosure of material weaknesses in internal control after the Sarbanes-Oxley Act. *Accounting Horizons, 19*, 137–158.

Wiersema, W. H. (2001). *Planning cash flow when cash is short*. Chicago: Barks Publications.

Corrigan, L. (1999, September 8) Why accounts receivable and inventories matter. Retrieved November 25, 2006 from The Motley Fool.

Encyclopedia Britannica Online

The New York public library business desk reference. (1998). New York: Stone Song Press and the New York Public Library.

Suggested Reading

Lavingia, N. (2006). How to create a world class project management organization. *Ace International Transactions, 1*.1–1.5.

Teague, P. E. (2006). How to speak like a CEO. *Chemicals Edition, 135*, 34–37.

Nagarkatte, A. (2006). The small business customer is ready to switch — For payment products. *Banking Strategies, 82*, S2–S8.

Edited by Richa S. Tiwary, Ph.D., MLS

Applied Global Money Management

This article focuses on various global money management systems and practices. Three of the featured topics include the international monetary system, the international financial system, and the international capital budgeting process. There is an explanation as to why the international monetary system is necessary as well as some of the problems that are encountered in the international capital budgeting process. Finally, there is a discussion about the international financial system, especially the new international financial architecture (NIFA).

OVERVIEW

What is money management? Money management is the method of controlling and governing money, which can involve investing, budgeting, banking, and the implementation of taxes. This article provides a preview of how it is applied in a global economy. Some of the highlighted areas include the international monetary system, the international financial system, and international capital budgeting.

INTERNATIONAL MONETARY SYSTEM

The Gold Standard

The international monetary system is needed in order to better describe an ordinary form of value for the world to use as its currency. During the late nineteenth and early twentieth centuries, the gold standard became the first international monetary system. "It has often been assumed in the international political economy literature that the classical gold standard of the late 19th century represented a turning point in monetary history because it marked the end wherein states manipulated their currency to increase their revenues" (Knafo, 2006, p. 78). One advantage of this type of system is that gold has a stabilizing influence. However, a disadvantage of the system is that it lacks liquidity. In addition, if there was an unexplainable increase in the supply of gold, prices could rise abruptly. Given the number of disadvantages, the international gold standard failed in 1914 and was replaced by the gold bullion standard during the 1920s. However, the gold bullion standard ceased to be used in the 1930s.

The Gold-Exchange Standard

The gold-exchange standard was used to conduct international trade during the period after World War II. This system encouraged countries to set the value of their currency to some foreign currency, which was set and redeemed in gold. Many countries set their currency to the dollar and maintained dollar reserves in America. The United States was seen as the leading country for currency. It was during the 1944 Bretton Woods International conference that a method of fixed exchange rates was conceived and implemented. In addition, the International Monetary Fund was established and charged with conserving stable exchange rates globally.

The Bretton Woods System

The Bretton Woods system was charged with developing and implementing the rules and regulations for global commercial and financial transactions. The International Bank for Reconstruction and Development was established as a result of this endeavor. It was the first effort at creating a system that would control monetary relationships between autonomous nation-states. The greatest accomplishments of the Bretton Woods system occurred when rach country agreed to implement a monetary policy that would maintain the exchange rate of its currency in a fixed amount through the value of gold. The countries also agreed that the International Monetary Fund had the right to connect fleeting inequalities of payments. Unfortunately, the method broke down in 1971 because of Americas' suspending of conversion from dollars to gold.

The Growth of the Global Economy

According to a new report conducted by Oliver, Wyman Company for Strategic Finance, global net revenue from money management is expected to triple to $900 billion by 2010, which is up from $277 billion in 1996 (Chernoff, 1998). The report predicts that revenue will grow at a 9 percent annual clip. As a result, money management will become one of the quickest spreading sectors in the global financial industry.

Chernoff (1998) alleges that growth is driven by a variety of factors such as "modest economic growth; faster wealth buildup among the affluent; continued growth in investments as a share of total financial assets: aging populations in Western countries; and an emerging middle class in developing companies" (p. 8).

APPLICATION

International Capital Budgeting

When the financial management team determines whether or not to invest in specific capital projects, the process is called capital budgeting. An organization usually has to deal with capital budgeting issues when it plans to acquire new assets or replace existing obsolete assets in order to maintain efficiency. The financial management team must determine which projects are good investment opportunities, which projects are the most desirable to acquire, and how much the organization should invest in each asset.

International capital budgeting refers to when projects are located in host countries other than the home country of the multinational corporation. Some of the techniques (i.e. calculation of net present value) are the same as traditional finance. However, "capital budgeting for a multinational is complicated because of the complexity of cash flows and financing options available to the multinational corporation" (Booth, 1982, p. 113).

Challenges Unique to Capital Budgeting for the Multinational Corporation

Capital budgeting for the multinational corporation presents many problems that are rarely found in domestic capital budgeting (Shapiro, 1978; Ang & Lai, 1989). Financial analysts may find that foreign projects are more complex to analyze than domestic projects due to the need to:

Distinguish between parent cash flow and projects cash flow. Multinationals will have the opportunity to evaluate the cash flow associated with projects from two approaches. They may look at the net impact of the project on their consolidated cash flow or they may treat the cash flow on a stand-alone or unconsolidated basis. The theoretical perspective asserts that the project should be evaluated from the parent company's viewpoint since dividends and repayment of debt is handled by the parent company. This action supports the notion that the evaluation is actually on the contributions that the project can make to the multinational's bottom line.

Some organizations may want to evaluate the project from the subsidiary's (local) point of view. However, the parent company's viewpoint should supersede the subsidiary's point of view. Multinational corporations tend to compare their projects with the subsidiary's projects in order to determine where their investments should go. The rule of thumb is to only invest in those projects that can earn a risk-adjusted return greater than the local competitors performing the same type of project. If the earnings are not greater than the local competitors', the multinational corporation can invest in the host country's bonds since they will pay the risk free rate adjusted for inflation.

Although the theoretical approach is a sound process, many multinationals tend to evaluate their projects from both the parent and project point of view because of the combined advantages. When looking from the parent company's viewpoint, one could obtain results that are closer to the traditional net present value technique. However, the project's point of view allows one to obtain a closer approximation of the effect on consolidated earnings per share. The way the project is analyzed is dependent on the type of technique utilized to report the consolidated net earnings per share.

Recognize money reimbursed to parent company when there are differences in the tax system. The way in which the cash flows are returned to the parent company has an effect on the project. Cash flow can be returned in the following ways:

Dividends — It can only be returned in this form if the project has a positive income. Some countries may impose limits on the amounts of funds that subsidiaries can pay to their foreign parent company in this form.

Intrafirm Debt — Interest on debt is tax deductible and helps to reduce foreign tax liability.

Intrafirm Sales — This form is the operating cost of the project and it helps lower the foreign tax liability.

Royalties and License Fees — This form covers the expenses of the project and lowers the tax liability.

Transfer Pricing — This form refers to the internally established prices where different units of a single enterprise buy goods and services from each other.

- Anticipate the differences in the inflation rate between countries given that it will affect the cash flow over time.

Analyze the use of subsidized loans from the host country since the practice may complicate the capital structure and discounted rate. The host country may target specific subsidiaries in order to attract specific types of investment (i.e. technology). Subsidized loans can be given in the form of tax relief and preferential financing, and the practice will increase the net present value of the project. Some of the advantages of this practice include adding the subsidiary to project cash inflows and discount; discounting the subsidiary at some other rate, risk free, and; lowering the risk adjusted discount rate for the project in order to show the lower cost of debt.

Determine if the political risk will reduce the value of the investment. Expropriation is the ultimate level of political risk, and the effects of it depends on when the expropriation takes place, the amount of money the host government will pay for the expropriation, how much debt is still outstanding, and the tax consequences of expropriation and the future cash flow.

Assess the different perspectives when assessing the terminal value of the project. Estimating the salvage value or terminal value depends on the value of the project if retained, the value of the project if purchased by outside investors, and the value of the project if it were liquidated. The corporation would use the assessment that yields the highest value.

Review whether or not the parent company had problems transferring cash flows due to the funds being blocked. An example would be when a host country limits the amounts of dividends that can be paid. If this were to occur, the multinational corporation would have to reexamine its reinvestment return and other methods in which the funds could be transferred out of the country. The blocked funds can be used to repay bank debt in the host country and allow the organization to have open lines of credit to other countries.

- Make sure that there is no confusion as to how the discount rate is going to be applied to the project.

Adjust the project cash flow to account for potential risks. One must assume that every project has some level of risk. The risk is usually seen as part of the cost of capital. International projects tend to have more risk than domestic projects. Therefore, it is advantageous to review the risk based on the parent's and project's perspective. Each perspective has a different way of adjusting risk. For example, the parent company may propose to treat all foreign risk as a single problem by increasing the discount rate applicable to the foreign projects or incorporate all foreign risk in adjustments to forecasted cash flows of the project. The first option is usually not recommended because it may penalize the cash flows that are not really affected by any sort of risk and ignore events that are favorable to the organization. The four components are initial investment outlay, net cash benefits (or savings) from the operations, terminal cash flow, and net present value (NPV) technique.

VIEWPOINT

International Financial Systems

There was much growth and change in national and international financial systems in the twentieth century. During the Post War period, many countries had the opportunity to experience economic increases, steady low unemployment and continuous deregulation in their respective economic markets. Positive steps have been taken to change the way business was done through acts such as the implementation of the European Union (EU), the North America Free Trade Agreement (NAFTA), and the Asia Pacific Economic Cooperation (APEC). In addition, international institutions like the World Bank, the International Monetary Fund and the Bank for International Settlements have assisted in the management of the changes that have occurred in the international financial arena. All the efforts mentioned above have been an attempt to produce a sound international financial system that will be able to sustain over the years. "The financial system in the 21st century should provide a financial environment that is conducive to contributing to further global financial integration as well as better macroeconomic coordination" (Moshirian, 2002, p. 274).

Importance of International Cooperation

Some key issues may have an effect on the international financial system. Therefore, it is imperative that all the organizations and initiatives listed above come together to create an international financial architecture versus working in isolation. "Globalization and increasing interdependence amongst all the nations of the world have allowed people to have a better understanding of key factors which affect the welfare and interest of all people and nations and their absence could harm both developed and developing countries. Some of these issues are sustainable development, world peace and security, sound global environmental policies, international trade, stable monetary systems, sound financial institutions, universal education and health, sound and all embracing technological changes and effective and universally accessible telecommunication" (Moshirian, 2002, p. 276).

The establishment of the International Monetary Fund and the World Bank is probably one of the most important success stories for international economic cooperation. Since the mid-twentieth century, there have been many changes in terms of the political and economic climate on a global level, which has caused the world's top international financial institutions to shift in terms of how they operate their businesses. Given the number of financial crises that have surfaced during in the twenty-first century, many scholars and practitioners in the field have called for a reform in how the international financial system is structured. These crises have exposed the weaknesses that are in the international financial system and highlighted the fact that globalization has pros (benefits) and cons (risks).

The New International Financial Architecture

"The new international financial architecture (NIFA) was created by the G-7 countries due to the growing volatility in developing countries. Some key components of the NIFA include: The G-20, the Financial Stability Forum and the Reports on Observance of Standards and Codes, the latter involving areas such as corporate governance" (Soederberg, 2002, p. 612). The purpose of the architecture is to offer governments, businesses, and individuals a mechanism (i.e. institutions, markets) to conduct economic and financial activities. The goal is to create an environment that strengthens and stabilizes the international financial system and minimizes the global exposure to financial dilemmas. Some advances have been made in order to reach these goals. The International Monetary Fund (IMF) has been instrumental in making some of these goals a reality. According to the IMF's fact sheet (2000), some of the major accomplishments include:

- increased availability of information from governments and other institutions to the general public
- increased usage of codes of healthy practices that are needed for an economy to function successfully
- the creation of the Contingent Credit Lines

International Monetary Fund (IMF) Improvements

IMF is working diligently to provide continuous improvements to practices that affect many sectors. For example, this body continues to:

- stimulate the release of public information reports that detail the IMF executive board's evaluation of a nation's financial state and economic policies
- encourage members to reveal the description of policies that the members might adhere to in order to maintain financial stability through the IMF-supported program
- help countries implement guidelines, such as the Reports on the Observance of Standards and Codes, that will evaluate a nation's development in practicing globally accepted standards and codes
- address gaps in regulatory standards through the Basel Committee on Banking Supervision
- encourage members to put procedures in place when they are not experiencing any problems so that they are not responding to a crisis. It's an opportunity to be proactive versus reactive
- aid countries in assessing their extrinsic liabilities and choosing the proper exchange rate programs

CONCLUSION

The international monetary system is needed in order to better describe the shared standards of value for global currencies. During the late nineteenth and early twentieth centuries, the gold standard became the first international monetary system. One of the advantages of this type of system is that gold has a stabilizing influence. However, a disadvantage of the system is that it lacks liquidity. In addition, if there was unexplainable increase in the supply of gold, prices could rise abruptly. Given the number of disadvantages, the international gold standard failed in 1914 and was replaced by the gold bullion standard during the 1920s. However, the gold bullion standard ceased to be used in the 1930s.

The Bretton Woods system was charged with developing and implementing the rules and regulations for global commercial and financial transactions. The International Bank for Reconstruction and Development was established as a result. It was the first effort at creating a system that would govern monetary relations among independent nation-states. The greatest accomplishments of the Bretton Woods system occurred when each country agreed to implement a monetary policy that would maintain the exchange rate of its currency in a fixed amount through the value of gold. They also agreed that the International Monetary Fund (IMF) had the right to connect fleeting inequalities of payments. Unfortunately, the method broke down in 1971 when the United States suspended conversion from dollars to gold.

International capital budgeting refers to when projects are located in host countries other than the home country of the multinational corporation. Some of the techniques (i.e. calculation of net present value) are the same as traditional finance. However, "capital budgeting for a multinational is complicated because of the complexity of cash flows and financing options available to the multinational corporation" (Booth, 1982, p. 113). Capital budgeting for the multinational corporation presents many problems that are rarely found in domestic capital budgeting (Shapiro, 1978; Ang & Lai, 1989).

There was much growth and change in national and international financial systems in the twentieth century. During the Post War period, many countries had the opportunity to experience economic growth, low unemployment and gradual deregulation in their respective financial markets. Positive steps have been taken to change the way business was done through acts such as the emergence of the European Union (EU), the North America Free Trade Agreement (NAFTA), and the Asia Pacific Economic Cooperation (APEC). In addition, international institutions such as the World Bank, the IMF and the Bank for International Settlements have assisted in the management of the changes that have occurred in the international financial arena. All the efforts mentioned above have been an attempt to produce a sound international financial system that will be able to sustain over the years. "The financial system in the 21st century should provide a financial environment that is conducive to contributing to further global financial integration as well as better macroeconomic coordination" (Moshirian, 2002, p. 274).

According to a report conducted by Oliver Wyman Company for Strategic Finance in the 1990s, global net revenue from money management was expected to triple to $900 billion by 2010, up from $277 billion in 1996 (Chernoff, 1998). In fact, by 2013, money management was a $53-trillion-dollar industry (Bradford, 2013).

TERMS & CONCEPTS

Asia Pacific Economic Cooperation (APEC): A financial forum for an alliance of Pacific Rim nations to altercate over issues regarding the global and regional economy, the level of cooperation needed to function successfully, and the ins and outs of trading and investing.

Bank of International Settlements: An institution that extends its service to central banks around the world in addition to other global and national financial institutions. Individuals and businesses, however, are not allowed to deposit or otherwise receive services from this bank.

Basel Committee on Banking Supervision: A company first establishing by the central bank Governors of the Group of Ten nations. It was instilled in 1974 and joins together quarterly.

Capital budgeting: The process by which the financial manager decides whether to invest in specific capital projects or assets.

European Union (EU): A financial and governmental alliance created in 1993 following the ratification of the Maastricht Treaty by members of the European Community. The union - which includes Austria, Finland, Sweden, Syprus, the Czech Republic, Estonia, Hungary, Latvia, Lithuania, Malta, Poland, Slovakia, and Slovenia – increased the political scope of the European Economic Community, particularly in foreign policies and security initiatives. The union also initiated the establishment of a common European bank and central currency known as the euro.

International Monetary Fund (IMF): An institution of more than 180 nations motivated to promote worldwide monetary cooperation and the wellbeing and security of the international monetary system. Every member fulfills its position by contributing to quota payments that relates directly to the nation's size and position in the global economy. The size of the nation also determines its voting control within the IMF. The United States, for example, has a 17 percent voting stake. The IMF contributes to global financial gains through loan grants and technical aid directed at underdeveloped or needy countries. The institution was developed in 1944 with the help of 45 nations as a means to counter the issues raised by the catastrophic events following the stock market crash of 1929.

International monetary system: Guidelines and policies by which differing currencies are traded for each other during global exchanges. The system is needed in order to create and impose a universal standard of value for finances across the globe.

Money management: The process of controlling and governing finances through investing, budgeting, banking, and taxing.

North America Free Trade Agreement (NAFTA): An agreement that supports the implementation of free trade between Mexico, America, and Canada.

World bank: An organization whose focus is on foreign exchange reserves and the balance of trade.

BIBLIOGRAPHY

Ang, J., & Lai, T. (1989). A simple rule for multinational capital budgeting. *Global Finance Journal, 1,* 71–76.

Booth, L. (1982). Capital budgeting frameworks for the multinational corporation. *Journal of International Business Studies, 13,* 113–123.

Bradford, H. (2013). Report gives money managers pause. *Pensions & Investments, 41,* 2–43.

Chernoff, J. (1998). Global money management boom predicted. *Pensions $amp; Investments, 26,* 8.

Dent, C. M. (2013). Paths ahead for East Asia and Asia-Pacific regionalism. *International Affairs, 89,* 963–985.

Knafo, S. (2006). The gold standard and the origins of the modern international monetary system. *Review of International Political Economy, 13,* 78–102.

Moshirian, F. (2002). New international financial architecture. *Journal of Multinational Financial Management, 12,* 273–284.

Shapiro, A. (1978). Capital budgeting for the multinational corporation. *Financial Management (1972), 7,* 7–16.

Soederberg, S. (2002). On the contradictions of the new international financial architecture: Another procrustean bed for emerging markets? *Third World Quarterly, 23,* 607–620.

SUGGESTED READING

Appell, D. (2007). So that's where the money goes. *Pensions & Investments, 35,* 8.

Garrone, F., Solnik, B. (1976). A global approach to money management. *Journal of Portfolio Management, 2,* 5–14.

Top 40 money managers. (2007). *Benefits Canada, 31,* 36–37.

Essay by Marie Gould

ASSURANCE SERVICES

Assurance services refer to independent professional services offered by CPAs and others to improve information quality or its context for decision-makers ("Assurance services, 2006). Traditional auditing services have focused on financial and governance issues and not on broader functional business units within organizations. Assurance services encompass a broad approach to assessing risk associated with and, potentially, touching all functional areas within an organization. Assurance service offerings have grown proportionally with advances in information technology. Assurance services focus on issues related to information security management, privacy and data governance issues, and nearly every other aspect of digital data management. Core competencies required of CPAs will need to change in order for these professionals to meet the growing demand and expertise in assurance services. CPA professionals need to be well versed in how information technology is affecting core business as well as the accounting profession. CPAs will also need to increase their overall customer service skills and business knowledge in order to fully meet their client's needs for assurance. Accounting firms will need to invest in training for their professional services personnel as CPAs will be required to have more in-depth knowledge of specific industries. Assurance services afford ample opportunity for accounting firms to expand into non-financial auditing markets. The competition to provide future assurance services will be fierce and will require a much broader set of competencies than have been traditionally relied upon by CPAs.

OVERVIEW

Assurance services are defined by the American Institute of Certified Public Accountants (AICPA) as independent professional services that enhance the quality or context of information for decision makers. The aim of assurance services is to reduce the risks that information provided is incorrect. Assurance services are founded on the CPA tradition of valuing the independent certification of data veracity by an outside party. Assurance is not just an assessment of financial data, but addresses the risks associated with a company's non-financial information and processes as well. Auditing services and attestation services provided by CPAs could be confused with assurance services, but there are some important distinctions.

Auditing services are well known and have been provided by CPAs for many years. In the context of CPA services, an audit can be defined as "an independent assessment of the fairness by which a company's financial statements are presented by its management. It is performed by competent, independent and objective persons, known as auditors or accountants, who then issue a report on the results of the audit. When a CPA provides attestation, he or she expresses a conclusion about the reliability of a written statement that is the responsibility of someone else" (Wordweb, 2007). Attestation and auditing have typically been defined around financial services, while assurance services may cover all functional business areas in an organization. Given the definitions of audit and attestation, it is easy to see how assurance services are a natural extension of the traditional CPA auditing services.

The following list describes some of the types of assurance services available to companies. These represent services that are non-financial in nature ("Assurance services," 2006).

- customer satisfaction
- information technology assurance services (ITAS)
- information systems security
- business risk assessment
- internal audit outsourcing
- accounts receivable review

Timeline: Auditing to Assurance Services

CPAs have been auditing financial statements since the early part of the twentieth century. The examination of a company's financial records insures that financial information is presented in conformance with federal rules and regulations such as generally accepted accounting principals (GAAP). In the 1970s, companies were looking for lower level/lower cost options to typical CPA financial statement audits. CPAs began to provide "reviews" of financial statements which were based on inquiry and analysis of data rather than the physical inspection of financial data. The resulting reports provided "limited assurance" of a company's financial statements. Another service provided by a CPA was called a "compilation" in which the CPA simply helped a company put its financial data into a statement form ("Assurance services," 2006). This report provided no assurance about the integrity of a company's financial data because no testing of the data had been done.

In the 1980s, the role of the CPA expanded to include what we now know as assurance services. CPAs began to report on non-financial subjects, and included internal controls, contracts, and compliance. The resulting reports were termed "attestation engagements."

"In an attestation engagement, the CPA applies the tools used in audits and reviews to provide assurance on whether the subject matter of the engagement (such as internal control or management's discussion and analysis of operations) complies with applicable criteria for measurement and disclosure. The result is a report much like an audit (reasonable assurance) or review (limited assurance) of financial statements" ("Assurance services," 2006).

Throughout the 1990s, revenues generated from traditional auditing and accounting services became flat. Accounting firms realized that financial statement auditing was a mature product and that the market expansion lay in offering expended services. Auditing of financial statements provided objectivity and integrity to users, clients and capital markets and the value that CPAs provided could be transferred to other services. In 1995, the American Institute of CPAs (IACPA) special committee on assurance services began a study of the audit-assurance function. The report of the AICPA was focused on looking forward beyond traditional CPA services to identify new opportunities for the accounting professional (Pallais, 1997). It was really the explosion of digital information and the knowledge economy that afforded new opportunities for assurance services. The risks associated with the easy sharing and movement of digital data is well documented in security and data privacy breaches. While risks to companies rose, so too did opportunities for companies to implement strategic solutions with increased access to metrics and data. The need for assurance services associated with information technology advances exploded as the digital economy developed. Issues specific to technology and the accounting field will be explored in greater detail later in this essay.

Avenues of Assurance Services

Assurance services were viewed as being aligned with audit-attestation but focused on a more comprehensive approach to reviewing specific subject matter within a given organizational context. The focus of assurance services was on improving information rather than advice or installing systems (Pallais, 1997). Assurance services encompass the following parameters:

- financial or non-financial subjects
- direct or indirect information
- internal or external processes/information
- improved reliability and context

The AICPA committee's study released in 1997 identified the following "six broad areas of potential "hot" assurance services for the accounting profession ("Special committee...," 1997):

- electronic commerce assurance
- health care performance measurement
- entity performance measurement
- information systems quality
- comprehensive risk assessments
- elder care assurance

A seventh area may be added (Schneider, 2013; Perego & Kolk, 2012).

- sustainability and greenhouse gas emissions

Stakeholders and users of assurance services represent a wider audience than users of typical CPA auditing reports. Financial statements provide valuable information for senior managers and chief financial officers, but stakeholders for assurance services may come from any area of an organization. Because assurance services are subject-specific, and placed in a specific business context, stakeholders may include: (subject expert) Decision-makers, boards of directors, creditors, or customers. Managers, accustomed to making decisions with incomplete data, benefit from assurance services which can lead to better decisions and decreased risk. Assurance services aim to evaluate the veracity of past business cycle data and benefit stakeholders across an organization ("Assurance services," 2006).

Assurance services can be provided by a number of individuals, depending upon expertise within an industry. Generally, assurance services may be delivered by accountants, attorneys, or management or technical consultants (Elifisen, Wallage, Knechel, & Van Praag, 2004). This article focuses on the role of the CPA in providing assurance services, along with the new competencies that will be needed by CPAs in the future.

APPLICATIONS

Role of the CPA in Providing Assurance Services

This essay has already reviewed some of the changes that occurred in the 1990s in the accounting industry. The market for financial accounting has become increasingly saturated and auditing is viewed as a compliance requirement rather than a service. Advances in information technology have impacted the field of accounting in a number of ways that will be examined later in this article. Other factors that are driving the need for new accounting services are: Globalization, risk assessment, internal controls governance, and corporate governance failure (Elifisen, Wallage, Knechel, & Van Praag, 2004).

Business cycles are being compressed and firms need to raise the bar in terms of providing services to their clients. Within the accounting industry, competition is fierce and merger mania continues (Nisberg, 2007). Assurance services provided by CPAs require enhanced communication skills and an emphasis on customer service. CPAs now need to understand the decision making process of end-users and customers in non-financial business units. Accounting curriculum must equip CPAs to be leaders in providing assurance services. In addition to enhanced communication skills, CPA training should focus on a number of areas. The following competencies are required for CPAs who wish to be adept at delivering strategic assurance services (Pallais, 1997):

- understanding of the strategic implications of information technology and accounting
- comprehensive understanding of business strategy
- enhanced research skills- knowledge of customer (decision maker) information needs
- measurement criteria — non-financial
- enhanced reporting of non-financial information
- criteria for identifying business risk
- knowledge of E-commerce solutions and security
- systems design

The new basics for future CPAs are intrapersonal skills and technological competence, but those skills are just the beginning. CPA firms that provide specialized assurance services may need to organize into "intrapreneurial units" where innovative design and narrow market specialization will be required to meet customer demands. Globalization and increased international trade will also require new expertise in the accounting profession (Nisberg, 2007).

All indications are that the accounting industry will continue to change rapidly as the profession aligns its services and personnel by specialization. The perception is that there is a huge market opportunity for

CPAs to provide assurance services as value-added billings for their firms. However, there are questions about what companies are willing to pay for in terms of assurance services (Elifisen, Wallage, Knechel, & Van Praag, 2004).

- Will the market want assurance services and are customers willing to pay?
- Will CPAs be able to maintain their independence?
- Will CPAs be able to develop the necessary expertise and specificity required to advise organizations in non-financial matters?
- Will assurance services provided meet compliance requirements?

Development of Assurance Services
In 1999, the International Standards for Professional Practice of International Auditing encouraged the use of the "strategic audit plan" as a means of expanding auditing services to non-financial areas. Historically, organizations had functional areas that maintained internal auditing procedures such as Legal and Quality Assurance that were responsible for internal oversight of some key controls. By implementing a strategic audit plan, auditable units were to be identified with the hope that over time, all business units would be audited. However, the changing dynamics of organizations didn't allow for enough continuity to successfully implement strategic audits. Functional business units changed so quickly that the risk environment was often very different by the time the audit was conducted and thus no longer applicable to the audit plan.

The challenges in implementing strategic audit plans led to the adoption of risk-based audit plans as an alternate solution. Risk-based audit plans tended to focus on perceived risk and avoided "unnecessary" review activities. As a consequence, some functional activities or areas were never reviewed. Neither the strategic audit nor risk-based audit strategies were ideal in assessing and monitoring total organizational risk, so a hybrid solution was developed.

The IAAS
An Internal Audit and Assurance Strategy (IAAS) was the proposed solution. An IAAS enables an organization to bridge the gap between a strategic audit plan and a risk-based audit. "An IAAS defines the customers and purpose of the internal assurance process, outlines the approach to obtaining that assurance, and details internal auditing's role in providing it" (Parkinson, 2004, p.64).

The IAAS can be thought of as a mechanism for filling the gaps between the strategic and risk-based audit so that no part of an organization is ignored in terms of the review process. An IAAS plan documents and identifies those requirements of an organization, and lays out a strategy for delivering on the strategy. Additional benefits to a well thought out IAAS insure that auditors and audit reviews clearly support organizational goals.

An IAAS takes into consideration an organization's mission, business context, assets, governance and risk models and tailors an approach to overall assurance programs. Only by examining an organization's purpose or the business it is in, can the relative importance or risk be assigned. Risk to an organization can be internal or external and may include:

- legal, political or economic risks- such as adherence to laws regulations or a response to social conditions
- major business relationships with customers or suppliers can pose risk to an organization, as can the loss of a key asset such as business reputation, intellectual property, or a business advantage

In 2004, the Chartered Institute of Management Accountants (CIMA) published a report called *Enterprise Governance, Getting the Balance Right*. The report proposed an interesting model that included two distinct aspects of a corporate governance model:

- corporate governance = conformance
- business governance = performance

In essence, the report states that there's more to success in business than following rules; systems must operate efficiently and the delivery of core services must be reliable. Risk can affect an organization from either of the above mentioned areas. Internal controls need to be put in place on both the corporate and business sides of governance to insure that risk is being addressed. "Because assurance concerns itself with controls, a comprehensive IAAS addresses both arms of the governance model. An assurance program cannot take credit for good organizational performance any more than it can for the organization obeying the law but, it can help improve performance and mitigate illegal activity" (Parkinson, 2004, p.65).

Risk

Risk is defined as the chance of something happening that will impact an organization's objectives. Risk doesn't have to result in a negative impact to an organization and having internal controls in place can identify risk opportunities that a company may want to act upon for competitive advantage. In either case, an organization must determine an acceptable level of risk, implement control systems and continuously assess processes to identify those that may not be properly controlled.

"Assurance is information that confirms the correct or incorrect operation of a function. If boards could know from personal examination that the organization was functioning as intended, they would not need an assurance function. It is because of the size and complexity of organizations that the need for internal assurance arises" (Parkinson, 2004, p.66).

Assurance services are concerned with identifying operational risks and places the risks within the context of the business being reviewed. A comprehensive IAAS document will identify the scope and depth of assurance services, but the International Standards for Professional Practice of International Auditing also recommends the development of a comprehensive risk assessment document that will serve as an overview for an organization's executive managers. The comprehensive risk assessment document should consider major processes and high-level inherent risks and how often key control systems should be reviewed. The executive management team of an organization needs to sign off on any comprehensive risk assessment document. All organizations need to be mindful that the assurance process needs to be tailored to their specific business context. Large organizations will need more audit resources than small organizations. The size and complexity of an organization will also require additional resources to implement assurance plans.

ISSUES

Top Tech Issues-Assurance Services

The AICPA conducts a yearly survey to monitor how professional accountants see their profession changing and being affected by advances in information technology. In 2007, CPAs identified Information Security as the top technological initiative, as it had been the top initiative for the previous five years. In 2006, Identity Access Management was sixth on the survey list; in 2007, it had jumped to number two. Other top initiatives included: Privacy Management, Securing and Controlling Information Distribution and Mobile and Remote Computing.

If one considers the following list of top Assurance Services that the AICPA identified in 2006, it is easy to see that accounting technology will play a huge role in the delivery of assurance services ("Assurance services," 2006).

- comprehensive risk assessments
- business performance
- electronic commerce
- systems reliability
- elder care
- policy compliance
- trading partners
- mergers and acquisitions

"'This top technology survey provides the CPA's unique perspective regarding the impact of technology on financial management and the fulfillment of other fiduciary responsibilities, such as the safeguarding of business assets, oversight of business performance and compliance with regulatory requirements,' said Barry Melancon, CPA, President and CEO of the AICPA. 'We sponsor this survey each year because we believe that it is critical for CPAs to stay abreast of the latest technology initiatives and provide guidance regarding its impact to their clients and employers'" (AICPA, 2007).

The top ten technology initiatives as defined by the AICPA for 2007 were:

- Information security management—rrefers to the overall approach to security that takes into account, people, processes and technology systems that safeguard critical systems and information from internal and external threats.
- Identity access management— includes hardware, software, and processes used to authenticate user identity and control access to appropriate systems and data- based on pre-established rights and privileges.
- Conforming to assurance and compliance standards— refers to the strategies and systems that

address organizational goals and statutory requirements that include collaboration and compliance tools to report on specific controls.

- Privacy management- governance over the disclosure and retention of personal information; convergence of security and privacy and adherence to applicable laws.
- Disaster recovery planning (DRP) business continuity management (BCM) —encompass an overall approach to addressing risk or threats (natural or man-made) to provide stability and improve chances of business survival in the event of a disaster.
- IT Governance— refers to the relationships and processes that help an organization balance risk vs return over IT and processes.
- Security and controlling information distribution—protecting and controlling the distribution of digital data (secure distribution, access to protected resources, and prevention of illegal distribution).
- Mobile and remote computing— Technology that enables secure connection to information at any time regardless of physical location.
- Electronic archiving and data retention —Technology and processes that enable archiving and retrieval of information over a given period of time. Policies to insure destruction and archiving of information to meet compliance objectives.
- Document, content and knowledge management refers to the process of controlling electronic information through the capture, indexing, storage, retrieval, search, and management of data (AICPA, 2007).

The integration of technology and business practices will help organizations achieve organizational goals, support employees and improve services to customers. Thoughtful and deliberate planning, execution and oversight of information technology initiatives will be an integral part of managing risk within organizations. Management, auditors and IT collaboration are key components of successful security and governance programs.

Competition for Assurance Services

Assurance service, like auditing, tax and compliance are the bread and butter of many accounting firms. With traditional financial accounting services on the wane, accounting firms are anxious to capitalize on the lucrative assurance services market.

Improving the audit choices for organizations (large and small) is challenging because most large companies go with the Big Four accounting firms and it is difficult for mid-tier firms to break into the market. It is true that the Big Four accounting firms have a global reach that many mid-tier accounting firms can only dream of, but there's a concern about the lack of competition within the industry as well.

Investors and boards of directors are known for being conservative and adverse to change which explains much of the allegiance of large multinationals to the Big Four Accountants. There's certainly an economy of scale that factors into the "reach" of the Big Four firms — the largest accounting firms have the depth and breadth of knowledge and expertise to service large international companies. Big Four audit fees are perceived as high and implementation of the IFRS accounting standards are only driving up fees (Perrin, 2007).

Room for Mid-Tier Accounting Firms

According to some critics, incumbent accounting firms (Big Four) don't have any incentive to improve services, quality, or be innovative. Since the largest accounting firms have a virtual monopoly on providing services to large/multinationals, many companies feel that they are a captive audience. With the growth in assurance services, there's an opportunity for smaller accounting firms to steal some of the market away from the big guys. Mid-tier providers will likely fill in specialized gaps; particularly in assurance services where subject matter expertise is paramount. It will be difficult for mid-tier accounting firms to invest in the training, expertise and personnel to compete with global giants. However, the idea of the "intrapreneurial units" (Nisberg, 2007) with subject matter expertise in a particular business or industry could help to level the playing field. With billions at stake in the assurance services marketplace, mid-tier accounting firms will be anxious to find their niche by offering more customized service and industry specific assurance services in the future.

Terms & Concepts

Audit: A situation where an independent CPA gives an opinion regarding the fairness of a given financial statement. The CPA bases their opinion on generally accepted accounting guidelines and principles such as cash basis or income tax basis.

Attestation services: A situation where a CPA expresses their conclusion in writing regarding the reliability of a statement made by another party.

Assurance services: Take into account the specific needs of individuals or groups; information put into a specific context for decision making.

AICPA: "National, professional association of CPAs, with approximately 330,000 members, including CPAs in business and industry, public practice, government, and education. It sets ethical standards for the profession and U.S. auditing standards for audits of private companies; federal, state and local governments; and non-profit organizations" (AICPA, 2007).

Big four accounting firms: Refers to a group of professional services firms that handle auditing and accounting services for most publicly-traded companies; the Big Four include: PricewaterhouseCoopers, Deloitte Touche Thomatsu, Ernst Young and KPMG.

Internal audit and assurance strategy (IAAS): A wholistic approach to assessing organizational risk; includes the implementation of key controls within two distinct areas: Corporate governance (conformance) and business governance (performance). The IAAS strategy has been proposed as the best solution for identifying and managing organization-wide risk within an organization's business context.

Risk-base audit: Focuses on areas within an organization that pose a perceived "high risk" of impacting an organization's business. Depending upon the criteria used, not all business units are audited-leaving companies vulnerable to unforeseen risks.

Strategic audit: Refers to a plan to audit an organization's unique business units over time; emphasis on aligning risk assessment to business strategy.

Trust services: "Trust Services (including WebTrust® and SysTrust®) are defined as a set of professional assurance and advisory services based on a common framework (that is, a core set of principles and criteria) to address the risks and opportunities of IT. Trust Services principles and criteria are issued by the Assurance Services Executive Committee of the AICPA" (AICPA, 2007).

BIBLIOGRAPHY

AICPA. (2007). 2007 top technology initiatives survey. *Information Technology Center.*

AICPA. (1997, March). Special committee on assurance services releases recommendations to improve, expand CPAs' offerings. *The CPA Letter.*

Assurance services. (2006). *Encyclopedia of Business and Finance.*

Elifisen, A, Wallage, P, Knechel, W, & Van Praag, B (2004) The demand attributes of assurance services and the role of independent accountants. Norwegian School of Economics and Business Adminstration.

Farooq, M., Villiers, C. (2017). The market for sustainability assurance services: A comprehensive literature review and future avenues for research. *Pacific Accounting Review, 29(1),* 79-106.

Hasan, M., Maijoor, S., Mock, T., Roebuck, P., Simnett, R., & Vanstraelen, A. (2005). The different types of assurance services and levels of assurance provided. *International Journal of Auditing, 9,* 91–102.

Li, Z., Pawlicki, A. R., McQuilken, D., & Titera, W. R. (2012). The AICPA Assurance Services Executive Committee Emerging Assurance Technologies task force: The Audit Data Standards (ADS) initiative. *Journal of Information Systems, 26,* 199–205.

Nisberg, J. (2007). Future trends and accelerated change. *Practical Accountant, 40,* 16–17.

Pallais, D. (1997, June 1). Are you ready for new assurance services? *Journal of Accountancy.*

Parkinson, M. (2004). A strategy for providing assurance. *Internal Auditor, 61,* 63–68.

Perego, P., Kolk, A. (2012). Multinationals' accountability on sustainability: the evolution of third-party assurance of sustainability reports. *Journal of Business Ethics, 110,* 173–190.

Perrin, S. (2007, June). Four get choice. *Financial Director,* 34-35.

Schneider, B. A. (2013). Assurance opportunities broaden. *Journal of Accountancy, 215,* 32–36.

SUGGESTED READINGS

Greenlees, E. M. (2006). Auditing & assurance services: A systematic approach. *Accounting Education, 21*, 330.

Janvrin, D.J. & Kurtenbach, J.M. (2006). The influence of disclosure regulation on selective disclosure: Impact on difficult-to-measure reporting activities and the importance of assurance services. *Accounting & the Public Interest, 6*, 70–94.

Nouri, H. & Machinga, R.J. (2003, September). Reports for assurance services. *National Public Accountant*, 16–19.

Top tech 2006 predictions. (2006). *Practical Accountant, 38*, 21–22.

Essay by Carolyn Sprague, MLS

AUDIT SERVICES

This article discusses audit services as they are related to an organization's financial reporting, finance operations, and enterprise risk. In large organizations, there are often three types of auditors and audit functions: internal, external (independent), and third party or consulting auditors. Auditing committees play an important role as liaisons between organizations and independent and external auditors. The current role of audit committees as overseeing compliance and governance issues is investigated—as is the changing role of the committee—as it moves toward the oversight of enterprise risk management. Enterprise risk assessment includes oversight of financial reporting compliance, but also encompasses a holistic approach to integrated risk within organizations. Risk assessment from the standpoint of finance is discussed in terms of an organization's entities, processes, and systems.

OVERVIEW

Auditing is often thought of in terms of complex oversight of a company's financial statements. However, auditing services vary widely depending upon the size and nature of the business contracting the service. For small businesses and firms, auditing services are most likely a relationship between the business and a CPA (certified public accountant). The CPA likely conducts a yearly audit (assistance with tax filing) and serves as an independent set of eyes and ears to check the work of the internal accounting department.

At large organizations, auditing of company financials and the associated risk can be extremely complex and costly and can involve relationships with multiple auditing-services firms. Financial disclosures and reports may be required on a quarterly basis and may be made available to employees, investors, and financial institutions to apprise customers of the financial health of an organization.

History of Auditing Services

Auditing services have a long history of interaction in American business. The expansion of global markets and the growth of multinational companies have increased the complexity of financial management, reporting, and auditing in larger enterprises. As the accounting function grew in importance, organizations began to rely on outside auditors to help interpret fast-changing accounting rules, regulatory missives, and the overall pace at which finance functions were growing.

The notorious accounting scandals of the early 2000s (such as those involving Enron, Tyco, and Worldcom) were the impetus for passage of Sarbane-Oxley (SOX) in 2002. However, as early as 1993, auditing failures were being documented. The estimated cost to investors was $88 billion from 1993 to 2000 (McNamee, Dwyer, Schmitt, & Lavelle, 2000).

In 2000, Arthur Levitt, chairman of the Securities and Exchange Commission (SEC), launched a personal crusade to expose what he considered "a massive conflict of interest between accountants' duties as auditors and the profits they earn as consultants to the same corporate clients" (McNamee, Dwyer, Schmitt, & Lavelle, 2000). By the year 2000, estimates put consulting revenues at 51 percent of the total revenues of many accounting firms. The big five accounting firms were well established as providers of

Arthur Levitt (Former Chairman, Securities and Exchange Commission) at *Financial Times* and Goldmans Sachs Business Book of the Year Award 2012. (Courtesy of *Financial Times* via Wikimedia Commons)

accounting services for many of the largest corporations in the United States. The big five were Arthur Andersen, Deloitte & Touche, Ernst & Young, KPMG, and PricewaterhouseCoopers; all five were opposed to SEC intervention. The big five saw Levitt's action as potentially cutting the accounting firms "off" from new growth markets (consulting). That the big five accounting firms provided both accounting services and consulting services was not in itself problematic. However, it had become clear that these firms were signing up the same clients for accounting and consulting services, which created a conflict of interest. "The trend [offering accounting and consulting] has convinced Levitt that auditors are relaxing their vigilance and growing cozier with management. And the SEC is developing evidence in at least two cases (Waste Management Inc.'s [WMI] $3.54 billion write-down of 1992-97 profits and the $55.8

million earnings restatement at high-flying software developer MicroStrategy Inc. [MSTR]) that accountants' consulting work and financial ties to clients compromised their audits. Levitt's solution was to split auditing and consulting. On June 27 [2000], the SEC voted unanimously to issue a proposed rule that would bar accountants from providing a range of consulting services to companies that they audit. Levitt also wants to beef up public oversight of accountants, all with an eye to send the profession back to its roots as vigorous guardians of investor interests. `When the public loses confidence in our markets, or when the reliability of the numbers is diminished, the whole system is jeopardized,' said Levitt. `The sanctity of the numbers and of their reliability must be there'" (McNamee, Dwyer, Schmitt, & Lavelle, 2000).

Just two years after Levitt's call to action, the major accounting scandal involving Enron and its accounting firm Arthur Anderson became a watershed event in the way that auditing services were provided. Congressional intervention had stalled developments on Levitt's request for action in 2000. The big five accounting firms and their trade association (American Institute of CPAs) contributed millions of dollars in funds to election campaigns; they had hoped to retain the ability to provide both accounting and consulting services to the same clients. However, by 2002, Congress would become involved in crafting the landmark SOX law that was meant to restore investor confidence in corporate America.

An article from 2002 described the shift in political thinking in the following statement:
"Now, with both Congress and the FBI investigating Enron's close relationship with Arthur Andersen, the SEC is tackling the [Levitt] issue again. Enron's critics say because Arthur Andersen also provided $27 million worth of consulting services to Enron, the auditor failed to properly review the company's financial statements, allowing Enron to overstate its earnings by nearly $600 million. The SEC, now headed by Harvey Pitt, has proposed creating a watchdog panel that would oversee the accounting industry" (Center for Responsive Politics, 2002).

The issues of financial disclosure, compliance, and reporting in corporations have been profoundly affected by the passage of SOX. Auditing services also made course corrections in response to compliance and regulatory mandates. The distribution of auditing services and duties between internal, external, and consulting auditors are discussed in detail in this article. The role of audit committees related to the oversight of compliance and enterprise risk is also detailed within the context of SOX and beyond.

APPLICATIONS

Trends in Auditing Services

Years after the passage of SarbOx legislation, companies are still struggling to meet the requirements of the most costly (in terms of people and dollars) mandate: Section 404. Section 404 requires the auditing and testing of internal controls related to financial reporting and the generation of an internal audit report. Compliance with SarbOx 404 is proving to be costly when deficiencies in internal controls are found. These annual tests, "stipulated by Section 404 of the SOX, require external auditors to thoroughly test the adequacy of clients' key controls over financial reporting" (Banham, 2006). When deficiencies are found to exist in processes or controls, the cost can be enormous in terms of company share price or reputation. One such example is the case of Genlyte Group Inc., a Louisville, Kentucky lighting manufacturer.

"The auditors uncovered several deficiencies in the financial controls at Genlyte, including material weaknesses in three of the company's financial-statement accounts. The failing grade meant [that because of] the $1.2 billion (in revenues) Genlyte had to disclose the problems to the Securities and Exchange Commission. In the aftermath, the company's share price fell 9 percent. Recalls [CFO] Bill Ferko: `The Sarbox standards of evidence were more rigorous than we'd expected'" (Banham, 2006).

In the case of Genlyte, the company finance team had worked diligently with their external auditors at PricewaterhouseCoopers (PwC) for more than one year to ensure that the company was going to pass its audit. Still, when PwC sent its representative to review Genlyte's controls, the deficiencies described above were found. CFO Ferko decided not to take any chances, and instead contracted with yet another third party to conduct a pre-audit. Ferko actually hired Genlyte's former independent auditor, Ernst & Young, to conduct the pre-audit. The reliance on third-party consultants has become familiar in many companies that do not want to take chances with SarbOx 404 compliance.

Third-Party Consultants

"Typically, the third-party consultants come from the Big Four accountancies, second-tier firms like BDO Seidman and Grant Thornton, or business-process specialists such as Protiviti Inc. or Paisley Consulting. And there appears to be no shortage of work, either. In a survey of public-company executives conducted by CFO magazine earlier this year nearly 60 percent of managers said they had hired third-party consultants to help with Section 404 certification" (Banham, 2006).

There are a number of reasons cited by CFOs and managers as to why third-party consultants are worth the extra dollars they cost in meeting compliance mandates.

- Many companies need help documenting and testing internal controls because the task is daunting and there are not enough internal resources to complete the task.
- Finance chiefs say that they are not getting the answers they need from external auditors—external auditors are "spooked" by the auditor-independence provision of SarbOx.
- Consultants help document workflow and provide advice on processes and documentation.
- Legally, independent auditors are not allowed to provide internal-controls consulting to audit clients.
- External auditors do not want companies testing their own internal controls; they want third-party auditors to do it.

Auditing Practices

Before the passage of SarbOx legislation, many auditors saw themselves as business advisors to companies. Auditors would offer advice on accounting transactions and new ventures; auditors really knew the core business of their clients because they were involved in operational processes. The nearly "real-time" advice that auditors gave to clients enabled organizations to consult with them regarding complex accounting transactions.

"Some auditors have taken the position that continuous dialogue with registrants on accounting issues runs counter to the Securities and Exchange Commission's position that an accounting firm cannot be deemed independent with regard to auditing financial statements of a client if it has participated closely in maintenance of basic accounting records and preparation of financial statements, or if the firm performs other accounting services through which it participates with management in operational decisions" (Spinella, 2006).

Contracting of third-party auditors is a trend that is likely to continue. Organizations and their respective external auditors feel better having an objective third party to test controls, advise on processes and documentation, and alleviate fears about auditor-client independence. There is no question that organizations regard objective third-party advice to be valuable, and many are turning toward audit committees to provide oversight as well.

Audit Committees

"In no small part, audit committees help to create the right environment for confident investing around the world. They do this by playing a substantial and growing role in matters of financial responsibility and accountability to shareholders, regulators and the business and government communities at large" (Lloyd, 2007).

Reasons for Increased Auditor Dependence

Meeting financial reporting, testing, and compliance in the post SarbOx era has been tough on CFOs. The following points illustrate why companies are so anxious to disperse compliance risk by seeking advice of third-party auditors and audit committees (Banham, 2006).

- A material weakness (defined as a deficiency in an internal control) can result in a 4 percent drop in share price for a company.
- Sixty percent of finance chiefs at companies who reported materials weakness were replaced within six months.
- Even with the dire consequences of bungled compliance and reporting, many companies feel like they have SarbOx 404 compliance under control.

"With Sarbanes-Oxley Act Section 404 compliance processes widely in place, many audit committees are refocusing on the issues they view as critical to the integrity of the company's financial reporting process. Oversight of internal controls remains a top issue, as does risk management. But many audit committees have identified accounting judgments and estimates as their top priority, and they're looking to the CFO to help them better understand this increasingly complex area of oversight" (Daly, 2007). Because of the failures and extreme costs of Section 404, a 2011 article called for Congress to amend the section to require the opinions of CEOs, CFOs, and external auditors on "the effectiveness of risk management processes" (Leech Leech, 2011). The authors argue that "this legislative change will result in significantly more reliable financial statements, [will] reduce long-term Section 404 compliance costs, [will] better align with the new global regulatory focus on risk management and risk oversight and, most importantly, [will] restore global confidence in US corporate governance and capital markets" (Leech & Leech, 2011).

Auditor Responsibility

Audit committee members are increasingly under pressure from responsibilities that are cited under section 204 of SarbOx. Some of the responsibilities include the following (Daly, 2007):

- The audit committee must review all critical accounting policies and practices with external auditor.
- The audit committee must review major issues and changes regarding accounting principles and financial presentations—per NY Stock Exchange listing standards (Sec. 303A, 07(c)).
- The audit committee must review analyses of management or external auditor regarding significant issues and judgments related to financial statements, including alternative GAAP methods.
- The audit committee has an obligation to exercise "duty of care," which requires staying informed of company matters, asking probing questions, and being actively engaged.

Management Accountability

Because of their increased responsibilities, audit committees are demanding more accountability from management, especially the CFO and external auditors. Generally, audit committees are only somewhat satisfied that they are getting the information they need from management and auditors to fulfill their responsibilities. The rise in the number of financial restatements is driving audit committees to demand more and better information from management and external auditors.

As Daly reports, "Whatever the actual cause of restatements, the growing intolerance—by investors, regulators, and others—for management miscues has put a premium on `getting the numbers right'" (Daly, 2007).

Committee members acknowledge that their responsibility is to take a "deep dive" into vital issues regarding accounting. Audit committees are relying most heavily on CFOs to provide a greater level of understanding of critical accounting issues. While there are many points that CFOs can help audit committee members understand, the biggest opportunity is to increase the depth and frequency of communication between the CFO and the committee. It is critical that the CFO and the audit committee speak the same language, understand critical issues, and devote appropriate time to discussion of key points.

Auditing Risk

Mazur reports that "Audit committee chairs are becoming more aware of risk as recent events have rocked the corporate world. When asked how they felt about the personal settlements by company directors in certain high-profile cases, more than half polled said they were concerned. In addition, a vast majority (83 percent) stated that their risk as an audit committee chair has increased since the SOX was passed. Still, even with this growing concern, a majority of respondents did not believe it was either easier or harder to recruit audit committee members" (Mazur, 2007)

One cannot overstate the impact that the passage of SOX legislation has had on auditing services and corporate auditing committees. However, there is a growing call for audit committees to focus on broader risk management issues and their potential impact of the financial health of organizations. Audit committees will also benefit greatly from recruiting a younger and more diverse membership.

The Changing Focus of Audit Committees
A 2006 Ernst & Young survey indicated some interesting facts about corporate audit committees. The top four reported risk issues were

- regulation and compliance
- merger and acquisitions/divestitures
- information technology
- market dynamics

Ironically, the same survey indicated that only 18 percent of respondents had established a risk committee. The majority of respondents indicated that their audit committees had the following standing committees—as required by their corporate boards (Koppes, 2007):

- compensation committee
- corporate governance committee
- nomination committee

Audit committees have long provided oversight and guidance to corporations, but with the passage of SOX legislation, the scope of responsibilities and the visibility of the audit committee have increased greatly. Global investor confidence relies on the work that audit committees do in an expanding landscape. Multinational corporations have an obligation to diversify their audit committees to look more like their customers and markets (younger and more diverse). An Ernst Young survey in 2006 reported that more than 91 percent of audit committee members were age 50 years or older, more than one-half were between the ages of 61 and 70, and only 42 percent were employed full-time. "In response to the hot-house growth of global business, now—more than ever—it is time to think beyond the traditional resume when looking to strengthen the audit committee composition" (Lloyd, 2007).

Recommendations for changing the composition of the audit committee include the recruiting of younger members, global candidates, entrepreneurs, members with legal experience, women, and other diverse populations. Recruiting the correct committee mix is just one aspect of assembling a world-class auditing committee. Supporting audit committee members with in-house and continuing education is critical, according to a poll by the Audit Committee Institute. SEC reporting requirements make up just one example of the complex regulations that audit committee members are required to understand. Continuing education initiatives should include the following participants: management, internal and external auditors, corporate counsel, and outside experts—all of whom can help to educate committee members. On-boarding (new member orientation) is crucial for member success and retention (Daley, 2006).

Refocusing the Auditing Committee Agenda

As organizations work toward the creation of more diverse auditing committees, there should also be a focus on more enterprise risk management. An Ernst & Young survey from 2006 reported that respondents thought that compliance issue distracted audit committee members from "other" critical risk issues. The majority of respondents to the Ernst & Young survey reported that only 20 percent of the typical audit committee agenda was devoted to risk. Risk management is uncharted territory for most audit committees, and committee chairs are aware that the topic of enterprise risk management must play a much larger role on audit committee agendas.

Enterprise Risk Management

Lloyd states that "Whether scrutinizing financial statements or exploring the possible risk from a cross-border transaction, the work of audit committees is vital to the future success of the companies they serve, particularly as the competition for global market share intensifies" (Lloyd, 2007).

The experience that many companies have in managing financial risk through SarbOx regulations can be transferred to other risk management areas.

SarbOx disclosure has raised the expectations of stakeholders who want transparency in all areas of business reporting. Stakeholders are paying attention to how companies conduct their businesses, and their perception of an organization is critical (Nabel, 2007).

Enterprise risk management (ERM) can be defined as an organization's planned efforts to identify the myriad risks that exist as an organization conducts its business operations. Some common business risks include credit risks, market risks, product risks, and risks to reputation or brand. Managing enterprise risk is not about eliminating all risks—an impossible task. Instead, "Risk Intelligent Enterprises" (Deloitte, 2007) modify their overall strategic plans to include risks assessment and management.

Steps for Dealing with Risk

The most effective steps for dealing with the inevitable risks of doing business are the following (Sammer, 2006):

- understand key risks in an organization; this should be a comprehensive list
- measure the tolerance for the identified risk
- develop a process to manage the risk
- continuously update the risk profile

It is critical to remember that some risk is inevitable and will occur. The ERM approach is designed to make risk more predictable and less volatile when it does occur. Organizations that understand key risks and have shared information with other functional areas will be better prepared to deal with risk. The more decentralized that business units are, and the more easily information flows through a company, will determine how quickly risk can be managed.

The faster pace of business has increased risk for many companies. Identifying stakeholders, their interests, and the "what ifs" of risk is an absolute necessity in managing enterprise-wide risk. Mapping out risks and the interdependencies and potential effects is really the key to ERM, but the assessment of risk impact is also a mission- critical part of the process.

"Many companies base their risk management program on the probability of certain negative events occurring. This approach is especially well-established in the internal audit profession and in the financial services and energy industries. Unfortunately, probability-based risk assessments do not always suffice. As a recent Deloitte Research study noted, major-value losses are often high-impact, low-likelihood events.

If senior management is biased toward mitigating high-impact, high-likelihood events, [an] internal audit should draw attention to and advocate for resources to address other events relevant to the business that could have a high negative impact if they do occur. Simply stated, if a risk is relevant to the business and is extremely high impact, it should be addressed, regardless of probability. This is particularly true of risks associated with value creation as they have higher uncertainty (such as the development and launch of new products)" (Deloitte, 2007).

CONCLUSION

Companies have been relying on external auditors to help meet Sarbanes-Oxley compliance mandates. Client-external auditor relationships are under scrutiny because of a renewed focus on objectivity and transparency in financial disclosure. Relationships with consulting (third-party) auditors provide companies with an additional set of objective (nonbiased) eyes for assessing business processes and internal controls. Financial restatements (reissuance of past financial statements) have become commonplace. Restatements can be costly for a company in terms of reputation and negative effects on stock prices. Company executives, anxious to avoid having to file a financial restatement, are relying on third-party auditors to serve as an additional line of defense in the process.

Auditing committees play an important role in managing relationships between independent auditors and management. They also provide objective oversight and guidance to an organization on a number of issues. The responsibilities of the audit committee continue to increase as accounting rules and regulations become more complex. Companies are reshaping the look of their audit committees by recruiting a younger and more diverse demographic mix. Audit committee members are spending more time per year in their oversight duties and will benefit from company-sponsored training and education. Audit committees will shift their focus from financial compliance to overall risk management in organizations. Enterprise risk management will include financial oversight, but that is only one aspect of a company's overall risk. Enterprise risk management is most effective when integrated into an organization's strategic plan—the overall goal being to help the organization achieve business objectives and improve business performance while planning and managing company-wide risk.

Terms & Concepts

Audit committee: The committee established to monitor oversight of an institution's financial reporting process and enterprise risk.

Certified public accountant (CPA): Refers to individuals (accountants) in the United States who have successfully passed the Uniform Certified Public Accountant Examination and other requirements for CPA status. In most U.S. states, only licensed CPAs are allowed to contribute to the public attestation, including auditing opinions on financial statements.

Enterprise risk: A management strategy focused on risk that includes static planning, operations management, and internal controls. This approach is adapting to satisfy the various needs of stakeholders who wish to comprehend the wide array of risks faced by complicated organizations to make sure that they are managed appropriately.

External auditor: In the United States, CPAs are the only nongovernmental external-auditing entity allowed to conduct audits and attestations regarding an organization's financial statements and submit public audit reports for review. This person is independent of the company that they are auditing.

Financial restatement: The reissuance of a past financial statement because of some error or omission in reporting.

Inherent risk: Inherent risk identifies the risk that already exists before one acts on it. In other words, this is the risk your company faces without any action you might take to change the probability or the effects of the risk.

Materials weakness: Materials weakness refers to a situation where a company's internal controls—established to avoid major financial statement irregularities—prove ineffective. If a failure of an internal control is considered a material weakness, it could result in a major material mistake in the company financial statements.

Restatements: correction of a previously issued financial statement, usually because of an accounting irregularity or misrepresentation.

Registrant: A client or company that has established a relationship with an auditor for oversight of financial statements and reporting.

Residual risk: The risk that remains after a company has tried to address the inherent risk. Residual risk is also referred to as "vulnerability" or "exposure."

404 compliance: Section 404 of the Sarbanes-Oxley Act of 2002 necessitates that publicly traded companies implement and uphold internal controls for the financial reporting process. ..ST.

BIBLIOGRAPHY

Banham, R. (2006). Party of three. *CFO, 22,* 56–64.

Barlas, S., Shillam, P., & Williams, K. (2006). Companies still struggle with enterprise risk. *Strategic Finance, 88,* 25.

Accounting industry. (2002). *OpenSecrets.org* Retrieved August 22, 2007.

Daly, K. (2006). Refocusing the audit committee's agenda. *Directorship, 32,* 35.

Daly, K. (2007). On critical accounting issues, CFOs can add value. *Financial Executive, 22,* 33–35.

Deloitte (2007) The risk intelligent chief audit officer.

Du, L., Masli, A., Meschke, F. (2017). Credit default swaps on corporate debt and the pricing of adult services. *AUDITING: A Journal of Practice & Theory.*

Koppes, R. (2007). The growing role of the nominating/corporate governance committee. *Corporate Governance Advisor, 15,* 7–8.

Leech, T., & Leech, L. (2011). Preventing the next wave of unreliable financial reporting: Why US Congress should amend Section 404 of the Sarbanes-Oxley Act. *International Journal Of Disclosure Governance, 8,* 295–322.

Lloyd, K. (2007). The evolving audit committee. *Investment Dealers' Digest, 73,* 13–14.

Mazur, M. (2007). A closer look at bank audit committees. *Community Banker, 16,* 67.

McNamee, M. Dwyer, P. Schmitt, C. & Lavelle, L. (2000, September 25) Accounting wars. *Business Week.*

Mitra, S., Jaggi, B., & Hossain, M. (2013). Internal control weaknesses and accounting conservatism: Evidence from the post–Sarbanes–Oxley period. *Journal of Accounting, Auditing & Finance, 28,* 152–191.

Nabel, D. (2007). Getting serious about reputational risk. *Business Finance, 13,* 9.

Sammer, J. (2006). Customizing enterprise risk management. *Business Finance, 12,* 33-36.

Spinella Jr., J. (2006). Basic communications: For auditors and registrants, it's that simple. *Accounting Today, 20,* 6–9. Retrieved August 21, 2007, from EBSCO Online Database Business Source Premier.

Verschoor, C. C. (2012). Olympus scandal shows need for U.S. standards. *Strategic Finance, 93,* 12–1.

SUGGESTED READING

Jackson, B., Goodridge, E. (2005). New auditor? You're not the only one. *American Banker,* 170, 1–5.

Koppes, R. (2007). The growing role of the nominating/corporate governance committee. *Corporate Governance Advisor, 15,* 7–8.

Landsberg, R. (2007). Understanding the role of a corporate compensation committee. *Journal of Financial Service Professionals, 61,* 22–3.

Essay by Carolyn Sprague, MLS

AUDITING

This article explains the process of auditing. The overview provides an introduction to the basic objectives and procedures involved in the auditing process. In addition, this article explains the process that auditors undertake as they plan and perform their audit and then prepare the audit report. This process includes such steps as designing the audit approach, performing tests of controls and transactions, performing analytical procedures and tests of details of balances, completing the audit and issuing an opinion. Explanations of factors affecting the audit process are also provided, such as materiality and risk, professional ethics and legal liability. Finally, examples of the various forms of auditing, including internal financial auditing, government financial auditing and operational auditing, are included to

The General Accounting Office Building is the headquarters of the U.S. Government Accountability Office. It is located at 441 G Street NW in Washington, D.C. (Courtesy of AgnoticPreachersKid via Wikimedia Commons)

information providers are at odds with the objectives of those who use the information. Thus, there is a need for objective third parties who will verify reported information and summarize their findings to the information users. In some industries, these third parties are known as independent auditors and the process they undertake to collect, track and verify information is called an audit. Independent auditors are highly trained professionals who are guided by ethical and legal standards that are designed to safeguard the social need for accurate information and the high regard given the reports they produce.

This article explains the basic concepts and techniques of the auditing profession. It explains the attestation function and the other objectives and procedures of the auditing process. It also provides a description of the internal control evaluations that take place to ensure the accuracy of the information being audited and the reports that are drafted to summarize the audit findings. Also, factors that affect the auditing process are discussed, which include materiality and risk, professional ethics and legal liability. Finally, the various types of auditing are explained, including internal financial auditing, government financial auditing and operational auditing. The following sections describe these concepts in more detail.

help illustrate the roles that auditing plays in various industries and in differing aspects of the business model.

Heather Newton earned her J.D., Cum Laude, from Georgetown University Law Center, where she served as Articles Editor for *The Georgetown Journal of Legal Ethics.* She worked as an attorney at a large, international law firm in Washington, DC, before moving to Atlanta, where she is currently an editor for a legal publishing company. Prior to law school, she was a high school English teacher and freelance writer, and her works have appeared in numerous print and online publications.

OVERVIEW

Our society depends on timely and accurate financial information. Businesses and investors alike need current, reliable information in order to make the decisions that must be made every day. Much of the information that investors, companies and even the government receive and incorporate in their business decisions is provided by third parties. Investors depend on corporate financial statements, lenders depend on consumer applications and the government relies upon tax returns filed by individuals and businesses. However, investors, business leaders and government agents do not have the time or ability to verify all of the information on which they rely. Further, in many cases, the objectives of the

Basic Concepts & Techniques of Auditing

Professional auditors serve as objective intermediaries who lend credibility to financial information by reporting whether the information conforms to generally recognized accounting and auditing standards. Auditing consists only of the review of reported information, and thus does not include the actual production of financial reports. That function is performed by a company's accountants and financial analysts, who generally work under the direction of its controller or management team. Auditors collect evidence, which consists of financial statements and the supporting documentation, which they cross-check and verify in order to determine whether the information in the financial statements is reliable. After completing this process, auditors compile a report that summarizes whether the information reported in the company's financial statements is reliable. This report is essentially a professional opinion expressed by the auditing firm as to whether the company's reported financial position, operational capabilities, and any changes in its financial position, have been documented in accordance with generally accepted accounting principles.

This process is critical because reliable and timely information enables capital markets to operate efficiently and allows individuals who depend on reported financial information to make informed decisions on a wide variety of economic issues. The following sections will explain in more detail the objectives and procedures that guide auditors during the auditing process (Whittington & Pany, 2006).

Audit Objectives

Independent auditors are hired and paid by clients. A client is the person, company, board of directors, agency or group that retains the auditor to complete the auditing process, often called an "engagement," and pays the fee for the auditor's services. Audits may be financial, in which the client's financial statements and other economic data are examined, or operational, whereby an auditor examines the efficiency and effectiveness of a client's business operations. In financial audits, the client and the auditee are usually the same. The auditee is the company or entity whose financial statements are being audited. Occasionally, the client and the auditee are different, such as when Corporation A hires and pays the auditors to audit Corporation B in conjunction with a proposed merger or acquisition. In such cases, Corporation A is the client and Corporation B is the auditee (Whittington & Pany, 2006).

Once independent auditors have reviewed the financial information provided by a client, the auditors prepare a report that expresses an opinion as to whether the financial information provided by the client has been compiled and presented in accordance with generally accepted accounting principles. This third-party scrutiny lends a certain amount of credibility to the financial information and is often referred to as an attestation. Thus, to attest to information means to provide assurance as to its reliability. A financial statement audit is, by far, the most common type of attest function that auditors perform. However, professionally licensed auditors, known as certified public accountants (CPAs),

also attest to the reliability of a wide range of other types of information including financial forecasts, internal control policies and procedures, compliance with laws and regulations and advertising claims. No matter what type of information is being examined, the objectives and techniques of the auditing process remain essentially the same.

The basic objectives for an audit are to:

- understand the responsibilities for the audit
- divide the financial statements into cycles
- know management's assertions about the accounts
- know the general audit objectives for classes of transactions and accounts
- know specific audit objectives for classes of transactions and accounts

In order to meet these objectives, auditors gather evidence that enables them to determine the accuracy of management's assertion as to the reliability of the information. A company's financial statements are generally submitted with an assertion by its management that the financial records have been prepared in accordance with generally accepted accounting principles (GAAP). After reviewing the financial records, the auditors issue a report summarizing their findings. In order to issue a report, auditors must ensure that the objectives for the audit have been met. Although not an insurer or a guarantor of the fairness or reliability of the information in the financial statements, the auditor has considerable responsibility for notifying users whether the statements are properly stated. If the auditor believes that the statements are not fairly presented or is unable to reach a conclusion because of insufficient evidence, the auditor has the responsibility to convey this by altering the opinion expressed their report.

Audit Procedures

The amount of evidence collected and reviewed by the auditors and the content of the audit report depends on the nature of the engagement. The two most common forms of attestation engagements are examinations, which are referred to as audits when they involve the review of financial statements, and reviews.

An examination or audit provides the highest level of managerial assurance that its financial statements have been prepared following generally accepted accounting principles is reliable. In an audit, the auditor must obtain independent evidence to substantiate the assertions made by the association's employees and management.

In a review, unless deemed necessary, the auditor is not required to obtain any independent corroboration to substantiate the financial statements. A review is designed to lend only a limited, or moderate, amount of assurance about the management's assertions.

Auditors must follow careful procedures in order to preserve the objectivity and dependability of their reports. In a financial statement audit, the auditors begin by creating and drafting an audit plan that will guide every step of the audit process. The audit plan dictates not only the scope of the audit, but also the responsibilities of the auditors and accountants involved in the review of the financial records. Once the audit plan has been finalized, the audit begins. An audit involves searching and verifying the accounting records and examining other evidence supporting those financial statements. Auditors must also gain an understanding of the company's internal controls over errors or other misstatements in its financial records. In addition, auditors inspect documents and account for listed assets and make appropriate inquiries within and outside the company in order to satisfactorily perform the audit procedures. Through this process, the auditors gather the evidence necessary to issue an audit report. The evidence gathered by the auditors focuses on whether the financial statements are presented in accordance with GAAP.

In essence, an audit seeks to verity and lend credence to management's assertions that the assets listed in the balance sheet actually exist and remain at the values expressed, that the company has title to the assets and that the valuations assigned to the assets have been established in conformity with GAAP. Likewise, auditors also gather evidence to show that all the liabilities of a company are included on the balance sheet. Alterations or omissions of a company's liabilities could skew the information contained on a balance sheet and in other financial statements, thus misleading users who make investment and other financial decisions based on a company's financial well-being as expressed in its financial statements. Finally, the auditors gather evidence about the company's income statement. The auditors collect and verify evidence demonstrating that reported sales actually occurred, that the goods were indeed shipped to customers, that the recorded costs and expenses are applicable to the current period and that all expenses have been recognized.

Only if sufficient evidence is gathered in support of all these significant assertions can the auditors issue an audit report. The audit report states that it is the auditors' opinion that the financial statements follow generally accepted accounting principles. If the auditors find information that leads them to conclude that the financial statements do not follow generally accepted accounting principles or are missing essential information, the auditor may issue a qualified or an adverse opinion. A qualified opinion is a statement written upon the front page of an audit that suggests that the information provided by management was limited in scope or the company's financial statements were not maintained in accordance with generally accepted accounting principles. An adverse opinion is the most severe opinion an auditor can issue and it indicates that a company's financial statements were misrepresented, misstated and/or did not accurately reflect its financial performance and health.

The Auditing Process
The auditing process requires careful planning and close attention to detail. The preparations begin even before the actual audit commences. In preparing for a potential audit engagement, auditors first investigate a prospective client in order to obtain an understanding of the client's business operations and to decide whether to accept the engagement. If the engagement is accepted, auditors then work on developing an overall strategy to organize, coordinate and schedule the activities of the audit staff. Even after the audit is underway, the planning process continues throughout the engagement. Whenever a problem is encountered during the course of the audit, the auditors must develop a response to the situation and determine how the problem affects their ability to continue the audit and issue an opinion. The following sections describe the dynamic process of planning and performing an auditing engagement, beginning with the acceptance of a client and proceeding through the design and completion of the audit and issuance of the audit report.

Planning & Designing an Audit Approach
Before accepting any engagement, auditors must first consider the financial strength and credit rating of a

prospective client in order to assess the overall risk of association with that business entity. When a potential client is facing financial difficulties, is in need of an inflow of additional capital or is facing government investigation, there is a risk that management will overstate or misstate financial information or operating results in an attempt to deflect the gravity of the company's standing. Auditors must be aware of this incentive and consider carefully whether to proceed with an audit engagement with such a client. If an audit client goes bankrupt or faces further financial turmoil, the auditors can be sued directly or named as defendants in lengthy and costly lawsuits. Thus, some auditors simply avoid accepting engagements that would expose them to the potential for an inflated risk of overstated or misstated financial or operational records or for future litigation. Other auditors may accept riskier engagements but implement greater controls over the scope and level of scrutiny in the document review process.

After the auditors have completed their review of a potential client, they then assess the levels of risks involved with completing the audit and make a final determination whether to accept or refuse the engagement. Even if an auditing or accounting firm decides to perform an audit for a potential client, the auditors may face a competitive bid process whereby the firm will be required to submit a competitive proposal that will include information on the nature of the services it provides, a fee structure, the qualifications of the firm's personnel and other relevant information.

Once the client has hired an auditing firm and the engagement has been accepted, the preparations for the audit escalate as the auditors work to gain a detailed understanding of the client's business and industry and compile and finalize an overall audit strategy. The auditors must obtain a detailed understanding of such factors as the client's organizational structure, accounting policies and procedures, capital structure, product lines and methods of production and distribution. In addition, the auditors generally need to become knowledgeable about current issues that may affect the client's business or industry, such as reigning economic conditions and financial trends, current and proposed governmental regulations that may impact the client and changes in technology or operational processes. Without obtaining this information, the auditor would not be in a position to properly apply the relevant accounting principles or evaluate the soundness of the estimates and assumptions contained in the client's financial statements.

After obtaining knowledge of the client's business, the auditors design the overall audit strategy for the upcoming engagement. The best audit strategies are formulated to accomplish the most efficient audit, in which the firm completes an adequate audit at the least possible cost. The audit strategy, along with other aspects of the planning process, is documented in the audit working papers, which also include audit plans, time budgets and audit programs. The audit plan is an overview of the engagement, outlining the nature and characteristics of the client's business operations and the overall audit strategy. A time budget consists of time estimates for the work that is required at each step in the audit program. Finally, an audit program is a detailed list of the audit procedures to be performed in the course of the examination. The audit program usually is divided into two major sections. The first section deals with the procedures to assess the effectiveness of the client's internal control structure and the second section deals with the substantive testing of financial statement amounts as well as the adequacy of financial statement disclosures. Together, these planning documents provide evidence of the auditing firm's planning and preparation procedures in the event of subsequent litigation or other investigations and also provide the lead auditor with a means of coordinating, scheduling and supervising the activities of the audit staff members involved in the engagement.

Performing Tests of Controls & Transactions

The soundness of a client's internal controls and the ability of these controls to ensure reliable financial information while safeguarding assets and relevant records is a critical component of the auditing process. Internal controls refer to methods that are put into place by a company to ensure the integrity of financial and accounting information, meet operational and profitability targets and transmit management policies throughout the organization. If a client has solid internal controls, auditors are generally able to collect significantly less evidence for their review than would be required for a client with inadequate internal controls. Thus, before beginning an audit and collecting financial statements and other audit evidence, the auditors must first gain an understanding of the client's internal control procedures. This is done by gathering and reviewing organization charts and procedure manuals, through interviews with client personnel, by completing internal control questionnaires and flowcharts and by observing client activities.

Once the auditors have gained a satisfactory understanding of a client's internal controls, the auditor is able to determine the measures that must be taken to accumulate sufficient audit evidence and to prevent and detect errors and fraud. In order to make this determination, the auditors are required to identify specific control procedures that must be implemented during the audit in order to reduce the likelihood that errors and fraud will occur and not be detected and corrected on a timely basis. This process is called assessing control risk.

When the auditor has reduced assessed control risk based on the identification of controls, the auditor may then reduce the extent to which the accuracy of the financial statement information directly related to those controls must be supported through the accumulation of evidence. However, to justify reducing planned assessed control risk, the auditor must test the effectiveness of the controls. The procedures involved in this type of testing are commonly referred to as tests of controls. For example, if a client's internal controls require that an employee verify and initial all unit selling prices on sales before the invoices are mailed to customers, the auditors might examine a sample of the clerk's initials that he or she was required to put on each duplicate sales invoice after verifying the unit selling price as well as various invoices to ensure that this internal control procedure was routinely followed. Auditors also evaluate the client's recording of transactions by verifying the monetary amounts of transactions. This is called substantive tests of transactions. An example is for the auditor to compare the unit selling price on a duplicate sales invoice with the approved price list as a test of the accuracy objective for sales transactions. Often, auditors perform tests of controls and substantive tests of transactions at the same time.

Performing Analytical Procedures & Tests of Details of Balances

Once the tests of controls and transactions have occurred, auditors then perform analytical procedures and tests of details and balances to further check for the accuracy and reliability of the client's financial and operational records. Analytical procedures use comparisons and relationships to assess whether account balances or other data appear reasonable. These procedures vary depending on the kind of client involved and the amount of financial information under review. These procedures can range from simple basic comparisons of items to complex analytical models of relationships. Key areas that are examined during a financial statement review are previous financial information, expected results, industry information and the interrelation of financial and non-financial data.

Tests of details of balances are specific procedures intended to test for monetary misstatements in the balances in the financial statements. An example related to the accuracy objective for accounts receivable is direct written communication with the client's customers. Tests of details of ending balances are essential to the conduct of the audit because most of the evidence is obtained from a source independent of the client and therefore considered to be of high quality.

There is a close relationship among the general review of the client's circumstances, results of understanding internal control and assessing control risk, analytical procedures and the tests of details of the financial statement account balances. If the auditor has obtained a reasonable level of assurance for any given audit objective through performing tests of controls, substantive tests of transactions and analytical procedures, the tests of details for that objective can be significantly reduced. In most instances, however, some tests of details of significant financial statement account balances are necessary.

Completing the Audit & Issuing an Audit Report

After the auditor has completed all procedures for each audit objective and for each financial statement account, it is necessary to combine the information obtained to reach an overall conclusion as to whether the financial statements are fairly presented. This is a highly subjective process that relies heavily on the auditor's professional judgment. In practice, the auditor continuously combines the information obtained as he or she proceeds through the audit. The final combination is a summation at the completion of the engagement. When the audit is completed, the CPA must issue an audit report to accompany the client's published financial statements. The report must meet well-defined technical requirements that are affected by the scope of the audit and the nature of the findings.

Factors Affecting the Auditing Process

Expressing an independent and expert opinion on the fairness of financial statements is the most frequently performed attestation service rendered by the public accounting profession. The auditor's standard report meets this service by stating that the auditors' examination was performed in conformity with generally accepted auditing standards and by expressing an opinion that the client's financial statements are presented fairly in conformity with generally accepted accounting principles. However, if there are material deficiencies in the client's financial statements or limitations in the auditors' examination, or if there are other unusual conditions about which the readers of the financial statements should be informed, auditors *cannot* issue the standard report. Instead, they must carefully modify their report to make these problems or conditions known to users of the audited financial statements. Auditors are guided by professional ethics that provide further governance as to the appropriate reporting requirements and auditors face legal liability for the accuracy and veracity of their reports. The following sections explain these factors in more detail.

Materiality & Risk

In planning an audit, the auditors must carefully consider the appropriate levels of materiality and audit risk. Materiality, for planning purposes, is the auditor's preliminary estimate of the smallest amount of misstatement that would probably influence the judgment of a reasonable person relying upon the financial statement. The auditor's responsibility is to determine whether financial statements are materially misstated. If the auditor determines that there is a material misstatement, he or she will bring it to the client's attention so that a correction can be made. If the client refuses to correct the statements, a qualified or adverse opinion must be issued, depending on how material the misstatement is. Auditors must modify their opinions whenever there are material deficiencies in the client's financial statements. However, they may issue an unqualified report if the deficiencies are immaterial.

Another factor that auditors must consider is risk. There is a close relationship between materiality and risk. Auditors must accept some level of risk, or uncertainty, in performing the audit function. The auditor recognizes, for example, that there is uncertainty about the competence of evidence, uncertainty about the effectiveness of a client's internal controls and uncertainty about whether the financial statements are fairly stated when the audit is completed.

An effective auditor recognizes that risks exist and deals with those risks in an appropriate manner. Most risks auditors encounter are difficult to measure and require careful thought to respond to appropriately. There are four primary types of risks that auditors face.

- First, planned detection risk is a measure of the risk that audit evidence for a segment will fail to detect misstatements exceeding a tolerable amount, should such misstatements exist. Planned detection risk determines the amount of substantive evidence that the auditor plans to accumulate, inversely with the size of planned detection risk. If planned detection risk is reduced, the auditor needs to accumulate more evidence to achieve the reduced planned risk.

- Another type of risk is inherent risk, or a measure of the auditor's assessment of the likelihood that there are material misstatements in a segment before considering the effectiveness of internal control. Inherent risk is the susceptibility of the financial statements to material misstatement, assuming no internal controls.

- In addition, control risk is a measure of the perceived level of risk that a material misstatement in the client's unaudited financial statements, or underlying levels of aggregation, will not be detected and corrected by the management's internal control procedures. Control risk also represents the auditor's intention to make the assessment of whether a client's internal controls are effective for preventing or detecting misstatements within the audit plan.

- Finally, acceptable audit risk is a measure of the potential risk that the financial statements that may be materially misstated after the audit is completed and an unqualified opinion has been issued. When the auditor decides on a lower acceptable audit risk, it means the auditor wants to be more certain that the financial statements are not materially misstated. Complete assurance, or zero risk, of the accuracy of the financial statements is not economically practical and the auditor cannot guarantee the complete absence of material misstatements.

Professional Ethics

A professional is often understood to mean a person whose conduct while engaging in their source of livelihood is exemplary and extends beyond satisfying the person's responsibility to himself or herself and beyond the basic requirements required by society's laws and norms. Auditors, who are often CPAs, have a unique role in their responsibility to the public, to the client and to fellow practitioners in upholding the highest standards of professionalism. The underlying reason for a high level of professional conduct is the need for public confidence in the quality of service by the professional. For the CPA, it is essential that the client and external financial statement users have confidence in the quality of audits and the professional opinions expressed by auditors.

The CPA profession is guided by high standards of professionalism in several ways. For instance, in order to become a CPA, one must sit for the CPA examination, which is a rigorous exam designed to protect the public interest by helping to ensure that only qualified individuals become licensed as CPAs. In addition, peer review and continuing education requirements serve to keep CPAs abreast of changes and developments within their field. Also, the American Institute of Certified Public Accountants (AICPA) is the national, professional organization for all CPAs. Its mission is to provide members with the resources, information, and leadership that enable them to provide valuable services in the highest professional manner to benefit the public as well as employers and clients. The AICPA maintains a *Code of Professional Conduct* that provides both general standards of ideal conduct and specific enforceable rules of conduct for CPAs.

There are four parts to the *Code of Professional Conduct*: principles, rules of conduct, interpretations of the rules of conduct, and ethical rulings.

- The principles include ideal standards of ethical conduct that are stated as preferred conduct but are not enforceable.
- The rules of conduct include minimum standards of ethical conduct that are stated as specific rules, and they are enforceable.

- The interpretations of the rules of conduct are not enforceable, but a practitioner must justify a departure from the interpretations.
- The ethical rulings are published explanations and answers to questions about the rules of conduct that have been submitted to the AICPA by practitioners and others interested in ethical requirements. They also are not enforceable, but a practitioner must justify a departure from them.

Legal Liability

CPAs and other audit professionals have a responsibility to meet the ethical and legal guidelines that govern their profession. In addition to the AICPA's *Code of Professional Conduct*, auditors also face legal liability stemming from other sources for their conduct in carrying out their professional responsibilities. Under common law, auditors are liable to their clients for failure to exercise due professional care. Accordingly, ordinary negligence, or a violation of a legal duty to exercise a degree of care that an ordinarily prudent person would exercise under similar circumstances, is a sufficient degree of misconduct to hold CPAs liable for damages caused to their clients.

Auditors' liability to third parties under common law varies from state to state. In some states, CPAs are held liable for ordinary negligence only to third-party beneficiaries, or those known users who use the information for a particular purpose. Other third parties must prove gross negligence, or reckless disregard for professional responsibilities, on the part of the auditors. In other states, liability for ordinary negligence to third parties is extended to include any limited class of parties that could be foreseen to rely upon the financial statements, even if the auditor does not know the particular user of the information. In still other states, auditors' liabilities for ordinary negligence is extended even further to include any third party the auditors could reasonably foresee as users of the financial statements.

In addition to common law liability, auditors may also be held liable to third parties under the federal securities laws, which allow class action lawsuits by purchasers or sellers of a company's securities. The Securities Act of 1933, which applies to registrations and prospectuses, is unique in that it imposes civil liability on accountants and others for making misstatements or omissions of material facts in a registration statement or failing to find such misstatements or omissions. The Securities Exchange Act of 1934 also places liability on accountants and others, although third parties must prove the intent to manipulate, deceive, or defraud before damages can be recovered. CPAs are also subject to criminal prosecution for violation of various statutes. To protect themselves from liability, auditors must strive to adhere to a high level of professional performance, and may take necessary proactive steps, such as attempting to avoid engagements that have a very high risk of litigation.

APPLICATIONS

Types of Audits

There are several different types of services provided by auditors. For instance, external auditors, such as CPAs and auditing firms, focus on providing attestation services and audit reports on behalf of their clients. CPA firms also do considerable financial auditing of governmental units. However, internal and government auditors also perform similar financial auditing services on behalf of their respective employers. Finally, operational auditors work to determine the internal controls of an organization and even test those controls for effectiveness. The following sections will describe these responsibilities in more detail.

Internal Financial Auditing

There are many similarities between the responsibilities of internal and external auditors of business entities. For instance, both types of auditors must remain objective in performing their work and reporting their results, and both use materiality and audit risk in deciding the extent of their tests and evaluating results. The primary difference between external and internal auditors is whom each party is responsible to. The external auditor is responsible to financial statement users who rely on the auditor to add credibility to the statements. The internal auditor is responsible to management.

Internal auditors are employed by companies to do both financial and operational auditing. Their role in auditing has increased dramatically in the past two decades, primarily because of the increased size and complexity of many corporations. Because internal auditors spend all of their time with one company, their knowledge about the company's operations and internal controls is much greater than the external auditors' knowledge.

Internal auditing encompasses the examination and evaluation of the adequacy and effectiveness of the organization's system of internal control and the quality of performance in carrying out assigned responsibilities. For instance, internal auditors review the reliability and integrity of financial and operating information and the means used to identify, measure, classify and report such information. They also review the systems established to ensure compliance with those policies, plans, procedures, laws, regulations and contracts, which could have a significant impact on operations and reports and should determine whether the organization is in compliance. Internal auditors also review an organization's means of safeguarding its assets and, as appropriate, verify the existence of such assets. Finally, internal auditors review operations or programs to review the efficiency with which resources are employed and to ascertain whether results are consistent with the company's established objectives and goals.

Government Financial Auditing

The federal and state governments employ their own auditing staff to perform audits in much the same way as internal auditors. At the federal level, the U.S General Accounting Office ("GAO") is the agency that functions as the investigative arm of Congress and is charged with examining matters relating to the receipt and payment of public funds. At the state level, all states have their own audit agencies. In addition, CPA firms do considerable financial auditing of governmental units. For example, some states require the audit of the financial statements of city agencies and departments by CPA firms. In addition to audits of financial statements of government units, government financial auditing includes audits of government contracts and grants, internal control, fraud and other noncompliance with laws and regulations. Thus, government financial auditing is complex in that the auditor must be familiar with both generally accepted auditing standards as well as government audit laws and regulations.

Operational Auditing

Operational auditing differs from financial accounting in that it is focused on the review of organizations for efficiency and effectiveness. Effectiveness is a function of how well an organization's objectives are accomplished, while efficiency examines the resources that are used to achieve those objectives. Another way in which operational auditing differs from financial auditing is that financial audits are oriented to the past, whereas an operational audit concerns operating performance for the future. In addition, for financial auditing, the report typically goes to many users of financial statements, such as stockholders and bankers; whereas operational audit reports are intended primarily for management. Finally, financial auditing reports are carefully worded because of the widespread distribution of the reports and users' reliance on the information they contain. Operational reports have a limited distribution and their content may vary considerably from audit to audit.

CONCLUSION

Audits are carried out to ensure the validity and reliability of reported information and to provide an assessment of an organizational system's internal control. A financial accounting audit is an independent assessment of the objectivity with which a company's financial statements are reported by its management. An audit is performed by competent, independent and objective people, auditors or accountants, who issue an independent report on their findings and results. The auditing process involves such actions as planning for all stages of the audit, performing tests of controls and transactions, performing analytical procedures and tests of details of balances and summarizing the results and releasing an audit report. In planning for and performing an audit, auditors must consider such factors as the materiality of any erroneous or omitted information in the audit evidence and the risk that such information will not be identified during the audit or that the financial statements will be altered after the audit. The conduct and work product of auditors is governed by a system of professional ethics and various forms of legal liability. Although traditional audits were primarily thought of as a way to gain information about the finances and financial records of a company or business, auditing now includes other information about the systems, such as information about the operational performance of business entities. Thus, there are now various forms of auditing that CPAs and auditors perform, including internal financial auditing,

government financial auditing and operational auditing. Financial accounting provides assurance for management, third parties or external users that a company's financial statements fairly present its financial and operational results, while operational accounting focuses on the effectiveness and efficiency of an organization.

TERMS & CONCEPTS

Adverse opinion: An opinion presented by an auditor that financial statements do not conform with generally accepted accounting principles in terms of fairly representing the operations and finances of the company.

Attest function: Refers to independent audits of financial statements, and also to review services, associations with forecasts and projections and compilation services where lack of independence is not acknowledged.

Attestation: When auditors serve as objective intermediaries, they lend credibility to financial or other information.

Audit program: An outline of audit procedures deemed necessary to obtain sufficient, competent evidence from the audit that will serve as the basis for the audit report.

Audit risk: The likelihood that an audit will fail to sufficient evidence equal to or greater than the tolerable misstatement assigned to the account.

Client: The entity (person, company, board of directors, agency or other group) who hires the auditor and pays for the service.

Common law: Previous cases and precedents that guide judges' decisions in suits or litigation for damages; monetary or other.

Disclaimer of opinion: The lowest level of assurance, in which auditors explicitly state that they give no opinion and no assurance, thus taking no responsibility for a report on the fair presentation of financial statements in conformity with generally accepted accounting principles.

Error: A departure from a prescribed internal control activity in a particular case. Also known as a deviation.

External auditor: Independent CPA who audits financial statements for the purpose of rendering an opinion.

Internal auditor: A person employed within an organization for the purpose of making recommendations about the economic and efficient use of resources, effective achievement of business objectives and compliance with company policies.

Internal control structure: Consists of a management's control environment, risk assessment, control activities, monitoring and communication. Satisfactory control reduces errors and irregularities in the company's accounts.

Operational auditing: Observing and reporting on business operations in order to make recommendations regarding adequate economic and efficient use of resources, satisfactory achievement of business objectives and compliance with company policies.

Sampling risk: The probability that an audit report based on a sample will be different from the report conclusions based on an audit of the entire population.

Vouching: A process in which an auditor reviews sample items from an account by looking backward through the accounting and control system until the source documentation that supports the item is found.

BIBLIOGRAPHY

Abbott, L., Parker, S., Peters, G. & Rama, D. (2007). Corporate governance, audit quality, and the Sarbanes-Oxley Act: Evidence from internal audit outsourcing. *Accounting Review, 82,* 803–835.

Auditing. (2013). *Journal of Accountancy, 216,* 11–13.

Burns, J. (2007). Audit firms, partners face SEC charges for not registering. *Wall Street Journal — Eastern Edition, 250,* C3.

Chenhall, R. & Euske, K. (2007). The role of management control systems in planned organizational change: An analysis of two organizations. *Accounting, Organizations & Society, 32* (7/8), 601–637.

Denyer, C. (2007). Ask the auditor: Maintaining acronym awareness with SOX, SAS and HIPAA. *Employee Benefit News, 21,* 14.

Hoitash, R., Markelevich, A., & Barragato, C. (2007). Auditor fees and audit quality. *Managerial Auditing Journal, 22,* 761–786.

Lillis, B. & Lane, R. (2007). Auditing the strategic role of operations. *International Journal of Management Reviews, 9,* 191–210.

Marshall, J. & Heffes, E. (2007). Internal audit becoming standardized globally. *Financial Executive, 23,* 15.

O'Leary, C. & Stewart, J. (2007). Governance factors affecting internal auditors' ethical decision-making: An exploratory study. *Managerial Auditing Journal, 22,* 787–08.

Prawitt, D.F., Sharp, N.Y., & Wood, D.A. (2012). Internal audit outsourcing and the risk of misleading or fraudulent financial reporting: Did Sarbanes-Oxley get it wrong? *Contemporary Accounting Research, 29,* 1109–1136.

Shin, I., Lee, M., & Park, W. (2013). Implementation of the continuous auditing system in the ERP-based environment. *Managerial Auditing Journal, 28,* 592–627.

Simunic, D., Ye, M., Zhang, P. (2017). The joint effects of multiple legal system characteristics on auditing standards and auditor behavior. *Contemporary Accounting Research, 34(1),* 7–38.

Whittington, O. R. & Pany, K. (2006). Principles of Auditing and Other Assurance Services, 15th ed. New York: McGraw-Hill.

Ye, M., & Simunic, D.A. (2013). The economics of setting auditing standards. *Contemporary Accounting Research, 30,* 1191–1215.

SUGGESTED READING

Beldona, S. & Francis, V. (2007). Regression analysis for equipment auditing. *Managerial Auditing Journal, 22,* 809–822.

Burr, B. (2007). Auditors see 64% boost in corporate fees over 5 years. *Pensions Investments, 35,* 29.

Snow, A. & Warren Jr., R. (2007). Audit uncertainty, Bayesian updating, and tax evasion. *Public Finance Review, 35,* 555–571.

Essay by Heather Newton, J.D.

B

B2B Business Models

ABSTRACT

Information technology is revolutionizing not only the way that enterprises do business with consumers but also the way that they do business with each other. In addition, many experts predict that business-to-business (B2B) transactions will eventually exceed those of business-to-consumer e-commerce. Just as there are different business models for non-electronic businesses, there is also more than one model for business-to-business e-commerce. Two revolutionary new business models that have come out of this movement are the business-to-business e-commerce models of Dell and Cisco. However, these models are not appropriate for every organization. In addition to these new paradigms for individual firms, other changes in business-to-business e-commerce are occurring that are revolutionizing the traditional paradigms.

OVERVIEW

Traditionally, when one thinks of business paradigms, one of the first things that comes to mind is the concept of companies selling to consumers. The department store or the big-box store down the street are prime examples of this business model. Historically, this meant that the business had a brick-and-mortar location where it employed its own personnel. Even with the advent of the Information Age, this model changed only slightly, with information technology being used to support the way that business is done by making standard operations more efficient. For example, manual cash registers have been replaced in most modern businesses by high-tech models that keep track of various aspects of transactions including tender type (i.e., whether the transaction is cash, check, charge, etc.) and amount paid, as well as inventory control information or other administrative data. Such automated information collection makes closing the store at night and balancing the books a much easier task and can also help store and chain managers make decisions about the type of inventory to carry, new services that could be offered to customers, and demographics that can be used in marketing efforts.

However, information technology not only allows organizations to perform various business processes more efficiently, in many cases it also allows them to reengineer organizational processes by improving the effectiveness and efficiency of the various processes within an organization. With advances in information systems, however, this model can be taken a step farther. Electronic business-to-consumer paradigms allow a business to market and sell directly to consumers. Examples of this business model include Amazon.com (online purveyor of books and a wide variety of other items) and Travelocity (online travel agency), businesses that sell electronically directly to consumers.

However, not all businesses sell directly to consumers, nor should they. Automobile parts manufacturers frequently sell to the automotive industry rather than to the car owner. Precious stones' miners sell to the gem industry where the stones are cut and sold, in turn, to jewelers and suppliers who, in turn, sell to suppliers. Pharmaceutical companies sell directly or indirectly to pharmacies and hospitals that sell the products to customers. As with business-to-consumer (B2C) paradigms, the model of business-to-business (B2B) commerce has been revolutionized by advances in information technology and systems.

Despite the increasing popularity of business-to-consumer e-commerce, with its ease of ordering and comparing items online, many experts have predicted that business-to-business transactions will exceed those of business-to-consumer e-commerce. This makes sense. For example, although a consumer

Electronic components shops in Guangzhou. There is a whole area - several blocks not far from the Guangta Mosque - mostly taken over by these shops. They apparently supply local companies that assemble various electronic and electric products. (Courtesy of Vmenkov via Wikimedia Commons)

may order a book over the Internet, the business from which the book is purchased not only has to interact with the purchaser but also with the publisher that printed the book. The publisher, in turn, needs to interact with the paper and ink suppliers, the maintenance firm that keeps the printing presses running, the authors who submit their manuscripts online, and so forth.

Business Models for Conducting B2B E-Commerce. Just as there are different business models for non-electronic businesses, there is also more than one model for business-to-business e-commerce. In general, a business model is an organization's approach to doing business. Although many different business models are available, most business models have several core concepts in common.

- At the level of the most basic business model, an organization must have something of value to offer to the marketplace, whether it is goods, products, or services. A bookstore, for example, may offer books and magazines as well as various services such as special ordering. To be successful, whatever the organization offers its customers needs to be of value—something that the customer either wants or needs (or both).
- Another part of the business model is the customer—the target market to whom the organization is trying to sell its offering. The business

model needs to articulate how the business will gain, maintain, and foster relationships with customers.

- In order to get the product into the hands of the customer, the organization also needs an infrastructure in place. The infrastructure may include having the right mix of people and skills necessary to produce the product as well as run the business. This may include the people working directly for the organization and also partners who provide skills or services that the business does not provide for itself but are necessary to get the product into the hands of the customer. This may include companies that provide complementary skills necessary to make the product (e.g., suppliers) as well as supply-chain partners that provide raw materials, supplies, or components or distribute, warehouse, or sell finished products.
- The business model also needs to include consideration of the company's income and cash flow as well as its cost structure.

Electronic Data Interchange & E-Commerce Models. One of the outgrowths of information technology that has enabled the development of business-to-business e-commerce models is electronic data interchange, a standard format used in exchanging business data such as price or product identification number. Electronic data interchange technology is particularly important for international commerce, in which paperwork required for international trade creates costs that can be up to 7 percent of the value of the items being traded. With electronic data interchange technology, on the other hand, shippers, carriers, customs agents, and customers all can send and receive documents electronically, thereby saving both time and money for international transactions.

Advantages of E-Commerce for B2B Businesses. As shown in Figure 1, the traditional business model for business-to-business operations involves a procurement staff that negotiates with various suppliers. For example, a bookstore may procure books from several distributors and office supplies from one or more other suppliers. In the e-commerce business model, a procurement staff (typically smaller than the staff necessary in the traditional business-to-business model) shops online for supplies and other items necessary to the business. Just as it does for the consumer in the business-to-consumer business model, the Internet allows businesses to comparison shop online in order to find the most appropriate product at the best price. This reduces many of the front-end costs for finding goods and products that are incurred in the traditional model.

Figure 1: Business-to-Business Business Models (From Lucas, H. C. Jr. (2005). Information technology: Strategic decision making for managers. New York: John Wiley and Sons, p. 52)

Electronic Exchanges. Another way that this can be done is through the use of electronic exchanges (also known as electronic markets or B2B hubs). These hubs are sites on the Internet where buyers and sellers can come together to exchange information and buy and sell products and services. As shown in Figure 2, electronic interchanges typically have one of three structures.

Public Exchange. In a public exchange (also known as an independent exchange), a third-party market operates the electronic market, displays information, and provides the tools necessary to conduct e-business. Independent exchanges may be vertical (i.e., serving members of a specific industry) or horizontal (i.e., simultaneously serving businesses in different industries). Public exchanges are independently owned by the third party that displays the content and provides electronic tools for conducting business.

Consortia-backed Exchange. The second general type of electronic exchange is the consortia-backed exchange. These are e-markets created by consortia of traditional firms within an industry who band together to create a common forum for business-to-business transactions of goods and services. One of the primary purposes of consortia-backed exchanges is to drive down costs for all participants.

Private Exchange. Another type of electronic exchange structure is the private exchange. These exchanges are structured around the needs of a specific sponsoring business and its trading partners and can be joined by invitation only. There are several advantages to private exchanges over other types of electronic exchanges. First, the owners of these exchanges can regulate access to both buyers and sellers. This means that the owners have the ability

to exclude competitors and their suppliers from the exchange so that the exchange only benefits its members. The owners of a private exchange can also offer pricing incentives or alternatives so that they can streamline business processes and benefit participants. In addition, as opposed to public exchanges, most private exchanges can be tailored to serve specific products.

APPLICATIONS

For many years, the traditional mass manufacturing (or Fordist) model followed the principles of assembly-line manufacture that revolutionized production when first implemented by Henry Ford. Certainly, the assembly line allowed products to be made more quickly and cheaply than ever before, but it did so at a price. Assembly lines are set up to produce masses of products that are all the same; custom options were—at least in the beginning—difficult to acquire. Even though the assembly-line process improved over the years, it was not until the flexibility and power brought about by information technology that a true revolution of the manufacturing process occurred. The use of the Internet to facilitate business-to-business transactions promises reduced costs, better access to buyers and sellers, improved marketplace liquidity, and more efficient and flexible transaction methods.

The Dell Business Model. One of the business models for business-to-business operations that was enabled by information technology was Dell's former business model. As shown in Figure 3, in this model, orders for computers were placed with Dell by telephone or through the Internet. Through a process called just-in-time (or lean) manufacturing, waste was reduced and productivity improved by only having the required inventory on hand when it is actually needed for manufacturing. This reduced both lead times and set-up times for building a computer. Under the just-in-time philosophy, Dell only ordered the parts for a computer when it had a firm (and in the case of non-corporate orders, prepaid) order. As a result, Dell operated with little in-process and no finished goods inventory: products were shipped as soon as they were manufactured.

This approach also enabled Dell to forego having brick-and-mortar storefronts with inventory that must be kept on the books or might become obsolete, thereby significantly reducing overhead. In addition, items that were not built by Dell were shipped directly to the customer by the manufacturer. These features helped Dell reduce the costs of production and sales. Far from being inflexible, however, this process also allowed Dell to custom design systems for its customer within certain parameters as well as to offer a range of items rather than a single system. However, in 2012, Dell began to shift its business model to keep pace with changes in the tech industry. As of 2016, it employed a service-based model, concentrating its business less on individual consumers and more on government and corporate entities. For example, in 2015, Dell bought EMC, which specializes in cloud computing and data storage for large corporation. However, despite Dell's switch in business model, lean principles are still generally considered to be relevant for other types of corporations.

The Cisco Model. Another lean business-to-business model enabled by information technology was that used by Cisco beginning in the 2000s (Figure 4). This successful network communications manufacturer received approximately 90 percent of its orders over the Internet. The orders were routed to contract electronics manufacturers that built the products to Cisco's specifications. Not only were the majority of Cisco's orders received over the Web, but 70 to 80 percent of its customer service requests were also dealt with online.

Other Business Model Innovations. Although the business models used by Dell and Cisco helped revolutionize the way that these and similar organizations do business over the Internet, these models are not appropriate for every organization. Companies must analyze their needs and pursue a model that best fits their goals in selling to or buying from other businesses. As technology and systems evolve and improve, new models arise to take advantage of such changes and provide better, more efficient transactions.

E-Hubs. In addition to these paradigms for individual firms, other changes in business-to-business e-commerce have occurred that have changed traditional paradigms. Electronic hubs (also known as vertical portals) are business-to-business websites that bring together buyers and sellers in a particular industry such as information technology or retail. These hubs facilitate business transactions within an industry and may charge a transaction fee for purchases. The value of hubs is that they reduce transaction costs by aggregating buyers and sellers in an electronic marketplace. As opposed to business-to-consumer hubs that are one-way networks that primarily create value for sellers, business-to-business hubs are two-way networks that mediate between buyers and sellers and create value for all parties. Business-to-business hubs create value in a number of ways including reducing search costs, standardizing systems, and improving matches for both buyers and sellers. Business-to-business hubs offer more choices to buyers and give sellers more access to buyers. For example, if five buyers and five sellers were potentially interested in doing business with each other, they would first have to locate each other. The sellers would have to determine who the potential buyers are through advertising or a direct sales force. The sellers would then have to make contact with each potential buyer. This would involve 25 separate searches and 25 separate contacts each time a seller wants to sell. With the hub system, however, this number is drastically reduced. The hub finds the potential sellers and buyers, reducing the total number of postings to ten: five postings on the hub by the sellers and five views by the buyers. Hub systems also allow information such as credit checks, product descriptions, and evaluations to be transferred more easily.

Vertical Hubs. Vertical hubs are set up to specialize within an industry or other vertical market. They provide domain-specific content and relationships that are of value to their participants. Vertical hubs are particularly advantageous when there is much fragmentation among the buyers and sellers, and inefficiency in the existing supply chain. Vertical hubs that are successful tend to have a high degree of domain knowledge and industry relationships, create master catalogs, and allow advanced search options. Examples of vertical hubs have included Band-X for the telecommunications industry and PlasticsNet.com for the plastics industry.

Functional Hubs. Functional hubs, on the other hand, are horizontal hubs that provide the same functions across different industries rather than more functions within a single industry. Functional hubs are successful in situations where there is a greater degree of process standardization and sufficient knowledge about the processes and the ability to customize the business process to respond to differences in various industries. Examples of functional hubs include iMark, a buyer and seller of used capital equipment across industries, and Employease for employee benefits administration.

Systems for Improving B2B E-Commerce. Business-to-business e-commerce has been in a state of flux as enterprises learn how to leverage information technology in general and the Internet in particular into systems that help them more efficiently and effectively do business. Observers have noted several particularly relevant criteria.

- First, to make business-to-business e-commerce worthwhile, systems need to evolve to handle not only simple transactions but complex ones as well. To facilitate this need, standards need to be developed and put into place.
- In addition, as markets become more competitive, transaction fees will most likely decrease or even disappear. Among other implications, this means that providers will need to shift from dealing in transactions to offering more comprehensive solutions to business needs. For example, products can be bundled with related information and services in an effort to forge customer loyalty and long-lasting relationships.

New business-to-business models will continue to appear as technology continues to evolve and enterprises seek creative solutions. Among business-to-business e-commerce models that have emerged in the early twenty-first century are the mega exchange that maximizes liquidity and sets common transaction standards, the specialist originator that deals with complex and relatively expensive products, the e-speculator model that has a high degree of product standardization and moderate to high price volatility, the solution provider in which product costs are only a small portion of the overall costs, and the sell-side asset exchange with high fixed costs and a relatively fragmented supplier and customer base. In addition, the rapid twenty-first century rise of improved mobile devices, such as smartphones and tablet computers,

as well as wireless technology, has created new platforms for B2B commerce that require the development of new features.

CONCLUSION

E-commerce and the information technology that enables it allow organizations to conduct business together in new ways. Two revolutionary business models that came out of this movement were the business-to-business e-commerce models of Dell and Cisco, which supported lean manufacturing and improved transaction efficiency. In addition, new models for business-to-business e-commerce continue to evolve as enterprises find new and creative ways to do business with each other.

Terms & Concepts

Business model: The paradigm under which an organization operates and does business in order to accomplish its goals. Business models include consideration of what the business offers of value to the marketplace, building and maintaining customer relationships, an infrastructure that allows the organization to produce its offering, and the income, cash flow, and cost structure of the organization.

Business process: Any of a number of linked activities that transforms an input into the organization into an output that is delivered to the customer. Business processes include management processes, operational processes (e.g., purchasing, manufacturing, marketing), and supporting processes, (accounting, human resources).

Business-to-business (B2B) e-business: E-business in which a business markets and sells to other businesses.

Business-to-consumer (B2C) e-business: E-business in which a business markets and sells directly to consumers.

E-commerce: E-commerce (i.e., electronic commerce) is the process of buying and selling goods or services—including information products and information retrieval services—electronically rather than through conventional means. E-commerce is typically conducted over the Internet.

Electronic exchanges: Sites on the Internet where buyers and sellers can come together to exchange information and buy and sell products and services.

Enterprise: An organization that uses computers. Although this term is often applied to large organizations, it can be applied to both small and large organizations.

Hub: A business-to-business website that brings together buyers and sellers in a particular industry. Web hubs may charge a transaction fee for purchases. Also known as a vertical portal.

Information system: A system that facilitates the flow of information and data between people or departments.

Information technology: The use of computers, communications networks, and knowledge in the creation, storage, and dispersal of data and information. Information technology comprises a wide range of items and abilities for use in the creation, storage, and distribution of information.

Just-in-time manufacturing (JIT): A manufacturing philosophy that strives to eliminate waste and continually improve productivity. The primary characteristics of JIT include having the required inventory only when it is needed for manufacturing and reducing lead times and set-up times. Also called "lean manufacturing."

Portal: A website that acts as a point of access to the World Wide Web. Portal sites typically offer a search engine or catalog of websites as well as other features.

Target market: The people or businesses to whom the entrepreneur wishes to sell goods or services.

BIBLIOGRAPHY

Getner, D., Stelzer, B., Brecht, L. (2017). Analyzing customers' readiness for digital B2B business models. *The International Society for Professional Innovation Management.*

Jackson, R. W., & Wood, C. M. (2013). The marketing environment: A new paradigm. *Academy of Marketing Studies Journal, 17* (1), 35–50.

Lackman, C. (2011). Game theory framework for B2B channel policy. *Proceedings for the Northeast Region Decision Sciences Institute (NEDSI),* 1383–1411.

Lucas, H. C. Jr. (2005). *Information technology: Strategic decision making for managers.* New York: John Wiley and Sons.

Reisinger, D. (2015). How an EMC buyout will make Dell a more capable enterprise IT player. *Eweek,* 1.

Rogers, B., & Clark, L. (2016). CABS: A conceptual model for context-aware B2B sales applications. *Journal of Research in Interactive Marketing, 10*(1), 50–60.

Sawhney, M. & Kaplan, S. (1998). Let's get vertical. *Imagine Media Inc.*

Senn, J. A. (2004). *Information technology: Principles, practices, opportunities* (3rd ed.). Upper Saddle River, NJ: Pearson/Prentice Hall.

Wise, R. & Morrison, D. (2000). Beyond the exchange: The future of B2B. *Harvard Business Review, 78*(6), 86–96.

Zakaria, M., & Janom, N. (2011). Developing and validating readiness measures of inter-organizational e-commerce on SMEs. *Journal of Internet Banking & Commerce, 16* (3), 1–15.

SUGGESTED READING

Huang, E. (2007). Entry to the e-commerce markets of China and Taiwan: An application of content analysis. *International Journal of Management, 24*(1), 82–91.

Juntunen, M., Juntunen, J., & Juga, J. (2011). Corporate brand equity and loyalty in B2B markets: A study among logistics service purchasers. *Journal of Brand Management, 18* (4/5), 300–311.

Laudon, K. C., & Traver, C. G. (2015). *E-Commerce 2015: Business. Technology. Society.* Harlow, England: Pearson Education Limited.

McAfee, Andrew. (2000). The Napsterization of B2B. *Harvard Business Review, 78*(6), 18–19.

Sarin, S. (2016). *Strategic brand management for B2B markets: A road map for organizational transformation.* 2nd ed. Thousand Oaks, CA: SAGE.

Teschler, L. (2000). New role for b-to-b exchanges: Helping developers collaborate. *Machine Design, 72*(19), 52–57.

Williams, D. (2007). Going from push to pull. *Brand Strategy, 209,* 36–37.

York, J. (2011). Social media websites advance businesses. *Home Accents Today, 26* (6), 67.

Essay by Ruth A. Wienclaw, Ph.D.

BALANCE OF PAYMENTS

This article focuses on balance of payments. It provides an overview of the main categories of balance of payments accounts including current accounts, capital accounts, and financial accounts. The double-entry bookkeeping method used for balance of payments accounting is described. The article provides a close look at the United States' balance of payments accounts and practices. The connections between trade liberalization, economic globalization, and balance of payments are addressed.

OVERVIEW

Balance of payments (BOP) is a method used by countries to monitor and record international financial activities and transactions. The Federal Reserve Bank of New York defines balance of payments as "an accounting of a country's international transactions for a particular time period." The balance of payments records all private and public sector trade activity and records the total of all money moving into and out of a country during a particular time period. The balance of payments may be recorded on a quarterly or annual basis. The balance of payments includes credits and debits.

- Credit refers to the money or payments a country has received during the balance of payments time period. Balance of payments credits include any transaction that causes money to flow into a country.
- Debit refers to the payments a country has made during a balance of payments time period. Balance of payments debits include any transaction that causes money to flow out.

A nation's balance of payments includes three separate accounts: The current account, the capital account, and the financial account, related to different types of international financial activity or transactions. The balance of payments should ideally or theoretically stand at zero. In practice, the balance of payments of most countries usually includes a trade surplus or deficit (Fieleke, 1996).

The following sections provide an overview of the three main categories in the balance of payments accounts and balance of payments record keeping practices. These sections serve as the foundation for later discussion of the United States' balance of payments accounts and practices. The issues associated with international governance of balance of payments practices are addressed.

Balance of Payment Accounts

Balance of payments includes three categories of accounts. These three accounts: current accounts, capital accounts, and financial accounts, are described and analyzed below.

The Current Account

The current account reflects a country's inflow and outflow of goods, services, income, and current transfers. The current account includes a summary of a country's balance of trade. Revenue produced from investments and income-generating assets are included in the current account. The current account is considered to be a measure of a country's economic health and strength. Countries tend to have either a balance of trade surplus or deficit depending on the health and scale of their import and export programs. The current account includes four sub-categories: Merchandise trade, services, income receipts, and unilateral transfers.

- Merchandise trade refers to all raw materials and manufactured goods bought, sold, or given away.
- Services refer to activities such as tourism, transportation, engineering, and business services, such as law, management consulting, accounting, and fees from patents and copyrights.
- Income receipts refer to income derived from ownership of assets including dividends on holdings of stock and interest on securities.
- Unilateral transfers refer to one-way transfers of assets including worker remittances from abroad and direct foreign aid (Federal Reserve Bank of New York, 2004).

The Federal Reserve Bank of New York Building at 33 Liberty Street as seen from the west. (Courtesy of Beyond My Ken via Wikimedia Commons)

The Capital Account

The capital account reflects all of a country's international transfers. Examples of international capital transfers include the acquisition or disposal of non-financial assets. Capital transfers include debt forgiveness, migrants' transfers, the transfer of title to fixed assets, the transfer of funds connected to the sale or purchase of fixed assets, gift and inheritance taxes, death duties, and uninsured damage to fixed assets. In addition, capital accounts include transfers of non-produced, non-financial assets. Non-produced, non-financial assets refer to the sales and purchases of the rights to natural resources, leases, patents, copyrights, and trademarks (Federal Reserve Bank of New York, 2004).

The Financial Account

The financial account reflects all international monetary flows related to investment, business, real estate, bonds, stocks, foreign reserves, and direct foreign

investments and assets. Foreign-owned assets include official reserve assets, government assets, and private assets. Examples of these assets include gold, foreign currencies, foreign securities, foreign credits, direct foreign investment, corporate securities, and direct investments (Federal Reserve Bank of New York, 2004).

Countries work to balance their capital and financial accounts. In practice, the goal of balanced accounts is not possible due to factors such as record keeping practices and exchange rate fluctuations, described in the next section.

Balance of Payments Record Keeping

Balance of payments record keeping follows double-entry bookkeeping accounting practices. For example, the amounts and figures involved are recorded on each of the two sides of the balance-of-payments accounts. While the two sides of the account would ideally be equal, this is rarely the case. The imbalances reflect surpluses or deficits in the national economy.

Balance of payments accounting practices and records include three main categories:

- accounts dealing with goods, services, and income
- accounts recording gifts or unilateral transfers
- accounts on financial claims including bank deposits and stocks and bonds (Fieleke, 1996)

Common transactions recorded in the balance of payments record include the following:

- commercial exports
- payment for commercial exports
- receipt of income from investment abroad
- commercial imports
- expenditures on travel abroad
- gifts to foreign residents
- loans to borrowers abroad

Challenges to Balance of Payments Data Collection

Challenges, errors, and omissions are common in balance of payments data collection. For example, some international financial transactions go unreported. Purchases and sales of short-term financial claims are often underreported. Some transactions are consistently estimated rather than measured. There is often a difference in the value stated in accounting records and the value actually paid for a good or service. This difference in valuation can lead to disparity between debits and credits. In response to this problem, a residual account for statistical discrepancies has become standard practice in balance of payment accounting practices. This residual account gives strategy for satisfying the rule of double entry bookkeeping so that total debits must equal total credits (Fieleke, 1996).

In addition to statistical discrepancies, fluctuating exchange rates and the change in the value of money, can add to balance of payments discrepancies by changing the recorded value of transactions. An exchange rate is a comparison between a national currency and a foreign currency. Exchange rates and the global or macroeconomy are closely related. A country's exchange rate influences exports, imports, job rates, working conditions, external purchasing power of residents abroad, and trade balances. For example, a rising exchange rate depresses exports, boosts imports, and depresses the trade balance (Piana, 2001). International capital markets respond to exchange rate fluctuations and exchange rate volatility. Exchange rate variability and volatility depress trade and the economy in general. In an effort to limit exchange rate variability, international governance organizations, such as Group of Seven (G-7) industrialized countries and the European Union (EU) have explored the possibility of establishing informal target ranges for exchange rates. Currently, there is no international consensus on how currency relations among major regions should be approached or governed (Obstfeld, 1995). Ultimately, statistical discrepancies, accounting conventions, and exchange rate movements may combine to create significant discrepancies in balance of payments accounts. International governance organizations promote shared or standardized balance of payments record keeping in an effort to facilitate comparable accounting records and balanced trade relations.

APPLICATIONS

The United States' Balance of Payments
The U.S. government and economic analysts track and monitor three measures of the balance of payment: The balance on goods and services, the balance on current account, and transactions in U.S. official reserve assets and in foreign official assets in the United States.

A picture from the gold vault of the Federal Reserve Bank of New York. (Courtesy of Federal Reserve Bank of New York via Wikimedia Commons)

- The balance of payments on goods and services is measured by figuring the net excess of debits or credits in those accounts.
- The balance of payments on the current account is the net excess of debits or credits in the accounts for goods, services, income, and unilateral transfers.
- Transactions in U.S. official reserve assets and in foreign official assets in the United States measure the difference between the change in U.S. official reserves and the change in foreign official claims on the United States (Fieleke, 1996).

Federal Reserve Bank of New York
The Federal Reserve Bank of New York publishes information about United States' balance of payments terms and issues. General information about the process and purpose of balance of payments is included in the government document entitled "International Affairs Fedpoints." "Fedpoints" is a

reference series explaining the structure and functions of the Federal Reserve System and the economic concepts relevant to its work. The Federal Reserve Bank of New York, as part of the Federal Reserve System, sets monetary policy to help promote national economic goals; promotes financial stability and banking stability in the United States and abroad; operates and oversees the United States' electronic wire transfer system commonly known as Fedwire; and provides banking and financial services to international institutions (Federal Reserve Bank of New York, 2004).

Bureau of Economic Analysis

The Bureau of Economic Analysis (BEA) is a sub-agency of the Department of Commerce. The Bureau of Economic Analysis produces economic accounts statistics that enable government and business decision-makers, researchers, and the American public to follow and understand the performance of the Nation's economy. The Bureau of Economic Analysis prepares national, regional, industry, and international account information on such key issues as economic growth, regional economic development, inter-industry relationships, and the nation's position in the world economy (Bureau of Economic Analysis, 2007).

The Bureau of Economic Analysis includes balance of payments information as part of the data it prepares on international economic accounts. The Bureau of Economic Analysis refers to balance of payments as international transactions. It prepares quarterly and annual estimates of transactions with foreigners, including trade in goods and services, receipts and payments of income, transfers, and transactions in financial assets (Bureau of Economic Analysis, 2007). The Bureau of Economic Analysis publishes current and historical data about U.S. International transactions with the following geographical areas: Europe (1960–present), Canada (1960–present), Latin America and other western hemisphere (196 0–present), Asia and the Pacific (1999–present), Middle East (1999–present), Africa (1999–present), and International organizations and unallocated areas (1960–present).

The United States includes the following categories within their current accounts, capital accounts, and financial accounts.

Current Account

The current account is comprised of:

- exports of goods and services such as transfers under U.S. military agency sales contracts, passenger fares, and U.S. government miscellaneous services
- income receipts
- compensation of employees
- imports of goods and services such as direct defense expenditures, royalties, and license fees
- income payments on foreign-owned assets in the United States
- U.S. government grants
- U.S. government pensions
- private remittances

Capital Account:

The capital account is comprised of net capital account transactions.

Financial Account:

The financial account is comprised of U.S.-owned assets abroad such as:
- U.S. official reserve assets of gold, special drawing rights, and foreign currencies.
- toreign-owned assets in the United States such as U.S. government securities, U.S. treasury securities, and U.S. liabilities reported by U.S. banks.
- net financial derivatives
- statistical discrepancy amounts

In the second quarter of 2007, the U.S. International Transactions News Release reported the following balance-of-payments data:

- Current account: The U.S. current-account deficit decreased to $190.8 billion in the second quarter of 2007 from $197.1 billion in the first quarter. A decrease in net unilateral current transfers to foreigners and increases in the surpluses on services and on income more than accounted for the decrease.
- Capital account: Net capital account payments were virtually unchanged at $0.6 billion in the second quarter.
- Financial account: Net financial inflows were $150.9 billion in the second quarter, down from

$181.9 billion in the first. Net U.S. acquisitions of assets abroad picked up more than net foreign acquisitions of assets in the United States (Bureau of Economic Analysis, 2007).

The example of the United States' balance of payments data demonstrates the tendency of current accounts, capital accounts, and financial accounts to be out of balance (Weinberg, 2007).

ISSUES

Balance of Payments & International Governance Organizations

Trade liberalization and balance of payments policies are closely connected in the new global economy. With the increase in capital flows during the 1980s and 1990s, countries lifted trade restrictions to promote and facilitate economic liberalization. The global economy is characterized by growth (in populations and in output and consumption per capita), interdependence of nations, and international management efforts. Indicators of global growth and interdependence include the huge increases in communication links, world output, international trade, and international investment since the 1970s. The global economy is built on global interdependence of economic flows linking the economies of the world. The global economy is characterized by economic sensitivity. National economic events in one region often have profound results for other regions and national economies (Thurow, 1995). Business opportunities, including international investments and joint ventures, in the global economy are increasingly tied to trade pacts such as the North American Free Trade Agreement (NAFTA) between the United States, Canada, and Mexico, the Mercosur trade pact among South American countries, and the Asia Pacific Economic Cooperation (APEC) trade zone.

Global Financial Governance

Global financial governance, including the development and management of international financial architecture, is an increasingly important practice in the global arena. National economies exist not in isolation but in relationship and tension with other economies worldwide. The global economy includes numerous economic phenomena and financial tools shared between all countries. Examples include the price of gold, the price of oil, and the related worldwide movement of interest rates. The new global economy is characterized and controlled through global management or governance efforts. International organizations, both public and private, work to establish norms, standards, and requirements for international financial governance. These international organizations, including the International Monetary Fund (IMF), the World Trade Organization (WTO), the Financial Stability Forum, the International Organization of Securities Commissions Organization for Economic Cooperation and Development (OECD), and the Basle Committee on Banking Supervision, develop and encourage implementation of standards, principles, best practices, and economic architecture (Preston, 1996).

The relationship between capital markets and international standards for financial governance is evolving as established and emerging markets and nations grow into one another. International economic organizations began forming in the twentieth century to manage and promote strong national economies. Economic development has been in existence, in some form, since the end of World War II. The modern era of aid to developing countries began in the 1940s as World War II ended. Developing countries, found primarily in Africa, Asia, and Latin America, are characterized by low per capita income, widespread poverty, and low capital formation. After World War II, world leaders and governing bodies put structures into place, such as the World Bank, United Nations, World Trade Organization, and International Monetary Fund (IMF), to prevent the economic depressions and instability that characterized the years following World War I. The efforts of the International Monetary Fund and the World Trade Organization to promote trade, in part through efforts to publish balance of payments data and promote standardized balance of payments practices, are described below.

The International Monetary Fund (IMF)

The International Monetary Fund (IMF), founded in 1945, is an international organization of 185 member countries established to promote international monetary cooperation, exchange stability, and orderly exchange arrangements; to foster economic growth and high levels of employment; and to provide temporary financial assistance to countries to help ease balance of payments adjustment. The IMF develops standards and codes of good practice and economic responsibility.

The IMF's Statistics Department publishes information about balance of payments of countries worldwide. Examples of IMF materials include data, statistical publications, metadata, research, methodology, and coding systems (International Monetary Fund, 2007).

IMF data about balance of payments includes the following types:

- data on the international reserves and foreign currency liquidity of selected countries
- data on external debt
- data on portfolio investment from the Coordinated Portfolio Investment Survey (CPIS)

IMF metadata about balance of payments include the following types: Metadata describing the practices of 56 countries for compiling their data on foreign direct investment (FDI) and metadata describing the practices of 63 economies for compiling their data on the coordinated portfolio investment survey (CPIS). IMF research on balance of payment issues includes the following:

- revision of the fifth edition of the *Balance of Payments Manual*
- manuals on balance of payments, external debt, financial derivatives, and statistics on international trade in services
- guidelines for the dissemination of data on international reserves and foreign currency liquidity, and for foreign exchange reserve management; information on the Coordinated Portfolio Investment Surveys (CPIS) and the Surveys on the Implementation of Methodological Standards for Direct Investment (SIMSDI)
- information on remittances statistics; the annual reports of the International Monetary Fund Committee on Balance of Payments Statistics, and the statistical papers presented to that Committee
- country experiences in estimating data on travel services (International Monetary Fund, 2013)

In addition, the IMF publicizes the coding system it uses for the balance of payments statistics.

The World Trade Organization
The World Trade Organization (WTO), established in 1995, is one of the main international governance organizations promoting rules of trade between nations. In 2013, the WTO had 159 member nations. The WTO actively works to help member nations understand the provisions of Articles XII and XVIII of the General Agreement on Tariffs and Trade (GATT) passed in 1994 and of the Declaration on Trade Measures Taken for Balance-of-Payments Purposes adopted in 1979. These international agreements govern and direct international trade activity, reporting, and accounting. The WTO asks member nations to confirm and agree to four main principles about balance of payments:

- Members confirm their commitment to announce publicly time-schedules for the removal of restrictive import measures taken for balance-of-payments purposes.
- Members confirm their commitment to give preference to those measures which have the least disruptive effect on trade such as import surcharges and import deposit requirements.
- Members should avoid the imposition of new quantitative restrictions for balance-of-payments purposes unless price-based measures cannot stop a decline in the external payments position.
- Members confirm that restrictive import measures taken for balance-of-payments purposes will only be applied to control the general level of imports and will not exceed what is necessary to address the balance-of-payments situation.

Current international economic organizations, such as the IMF and WTO, are not responding to a particular war or political crisis, as they did post World War II, so much as responding to the economic and political forces of globalization. International economic organizations have far-reaching influence on the economies of nations worldwide. International lending institutions, both corporate and non-profit, use the policy recommendations and standards created and promoted by international economic institutions as a guide for investment decisions.

CONCLUSION

In the final analysis, balance of payments, which is a method used by countries to monitor and record international financial activities and transactions, is a crucial measure of a country's economic health. The balance of payments, informed by current accounts, capital accounts, and financial accounts, provides information about nations' trade deficits and surpluses. Nations make trade and economic policy based on quarterly and annual balance of payments reports.

TERMS & CONCEPTS

Balance of payments: An accounting of a country's international transactions for a particular time period (Federal Reserve Bank of New York, 2004).

Capital account: A balance of payments account which reflects all a country's international transfers.

Current account: A balance of payments account which reflects a country's inflow and outflow of goods, services, income, and current transfers.

Deficit: The amount of money which a government, company, or individual spends which exceeds its income.

Developing countries: Countries characterized by an underdeveloped industrial base, low per capita income, and widespread poverty.

Double-entry bookkeeping: An accounting practices in which the amounts and figures involved are recorded on two separate sides or columns of a ledger.

Exchange rate: A comparison between a national currency and a foreign currency.

Financial account: A balance of payment account in which all international monetary flows related to investment, business, real estate, bonds, stocks, foreign reserves, and direct foreign investments and assets are included.

Globalization: A process of economic and cultural integration around the world caused by changes in technology, commerce, and politics.

Markets: Social or economic arrangements that allow buyers and sellers to discover information and carry out voluntary exchanges of goods and services.

Nations: Large aggregations of people sharing rules of law and an identity based on common racial, linguistic, historical, or cultural heritage; rarely act unilaterally.

World Bank: An international economic development assistance organization that was founded in 1944.

BIBLIOGRAPHY

Akpansung, A. O. (2013). A review of empirical literature on balance of payments as a monetary phenomenon. *Journal of Emerging Trends In Economics Management Sciences, 4,* 124–132.

Currie, D. (1976). Some criticisms of the monetary analysis of balance of payments correction. *Economic Journal, 86,* 508–522.

Feldmann, L. (2011). The International Monetary Fund's international financial statistics database. *Journal of Business Finance Librarianship, 16,* 243–246.

Federal Reserve Bank of New York. (2004). Balance of payments. Retrieved October 11, 2007,

Fieleke, N. (1996). What is the balance of payments? Federal Reserve Bank of Boston.

Finn, T. (1977). The monetary approach to balance of payments theory and policy: Explanation and policy implications. *Economica, 44,* 217–229.

Hipple, F. (1979). The optimal frequency of adjustment to balance of payments disturbances. *Southern Economic Journal, 46,* 549.

Komiya, R. (1969). Economic growth and the balance of payments: A monetary approach. *Journal of Political Economy, 77,* 35.

Paun, C., Mustetescu, & R., Munteanu, C. (2013). The monetary approach of the balance of payments: empirical evidences from emerging markets. *Economic Computation Economic Cybernetics Studies Research, 47,* 133–150.

Piana, V. (2001). Exchange rate. The Economics Web Institute.

Preston, L. (1996). Global economy/global environment: Relationships and regimes. EarthWorks.

Sites, J. (1995). Going forward with global investments. *Risk Management, 42,* 12–17.

The Bureau of Economic Analysis. (2007). U.S. international transactions accounts data.

The International Monetary Fund. (2007). Balance of payments and international investment position statistics.

Thurow, L. (1995). Surviving in a turbulent environment. *Planning Review, 23,* 24.

Vines, D. (2017). Absorption approach to the balance of payments. *The New Palgrave Dictionary of Economics,* 1-4.

Weinberg, D. (2007). News release: U.S. international transactions. Bureau of Economic Analysis.

SUGGESTED READING
Graeser, P. (1968). Money, growth, and the balance of payments. *Journal of Finance, 23,* 542.

Hopkin, B. (1970). Aid and the balance of payments. *Economic Journal, 80,* 1–23.
Scammell, W. (1976). The monetary approach to the balance of payments. *Journal of Economic Studies, 3,* 186.

Essay by Simone I. Flynn, Ph.D.

BANKRUPTCY AND ORGANIZATION

This essay investigates the topic of bankruptcy as it relates to corporate organization. Bankruptcy is a proceeding that is governed by federal law and offers protection to debtors from creditors under certain guidelines and for a certain period of time. The most common options that corporations have for gaining protection from creditors are to file Chapter

Notice of closure attached to the door of a Computer Shop outlet the day after its parent company declared "bankruptcy" (strictly, put into administration) in the United Kingdom. (Courtesy of Andrew Dunn via Wikimedia Commons)

7 (liquidation) or Chapter 11 (reorganization). This article focuses on issues and topics related to Chapter 11.

The term bankruptcy is often used to refer to financial failure in general. However, in the United States, bankruptcy has a specific legal meaning; in fact, bankruptcy is federal law. Congress has the power to enact "uniform laws on the subject of bankruptcy" and "restricts the ability of states to provide a discharge or collect assets that are not in the state. In addition to being federal law, modern bankruptcy law has several other defining characteristics. Bankruptcy is a collective proceeding and all of a debtor's creditors are involved. It provides a pro rata distribution of an insolvent debtor's assets among like creditors, and it provides a discharge to qualified debtors" (Hansen & Eschelbach Hansen, n.d.).

History of Bankruptcy Law
In the twentieth century, bankruptcy laws generally favored the creditor rather than the debtor; debtors were often considered criminals and might be punished with imprisonment or death as a result of the inability to re-pay their debt. U.S. bankruptcy laws were originally modeled after English law but were enacted as Article 1, Section 8, Clause 4 of the U.S. Constitution. Article 1, section 8 became known as uniform laws on the subject of bankruptcies throughout the United States. Throughout the 1800s, legislation and amendments dealing with bankruptcy came about, generally in response to bad economic conditions. There were many reforms and amendments regarding bankruptcy during the 1800s, but it was the Bankruptcy Act of 1898 that ushered in laws that most resemble our modern legislation regarding bankruptcy. The emergence of a "credit economy" and the Industrial Age changed the focus to the discharge of debt or liquidation of assets

rather than punishment of the debtor ("A brief history of bankruptcy in the US," 2007).

1898 Bankruptcy Act

Today's modern bankruptcy law has its roots in the 1898 Bankruptcy Act. This revised law focused on liquidation of a debtor's property or assets but also contained several chapters that dealt with the reorganization of distressed businesses. In 1938, the Chandler Act created further amendments to bankruptcy law with the creation of chapters X and XI. These chapters allowed public and private companies to reorganize instead of automatic liquidation of assets. The Chandler Act also introduced the role of the "bankruptcy referee" who had "quasi-judicial powers" ("A brief history of bankruptcy law," 2002) and served as an appointed representative to act as an intermediary in the proceedings.

Bankruptcy Reform Act of 1978

Bankruptcy law had been part of federal legislation from the beginning of the nineteenth century but it was not until the Bankruptcy Reform Act of 1978 and the introduction of Chapter 11 that the practice of bankruptcy was "legitimized" as a viable option for businesses in distress to re-organize. Prior to the revision of Chapter 11, bankruptcy had been avoided by businesses as a "ghetto" and not a viable business tool for re-organization and restructuring. The 1978 Bankruptcy Reform Act introduced a reorganization tool for corporate debtors ("A brief history of bankruptcy in US," 2007).

The Bankruptcy Code has been amended several times since 1978, most recently in extensive amendments in 2005 through the Bankruptcy Abuse Prevention and Consumer Protection Act of 2005, or BAPCPA.

The U.S. Bankruptcy Court handles all bankruptcy cases through the U.S. district court system. Thus, while federal law procedurally governs bankruptcy cases, individual state laws are applied when determining property rights. State law therefore plays a major role in most bankruptcy cases.

Filing for Bankruptcy

When a public company is unable to maintain operation because of "crippling debt," the organization may seek protection under federal bankruptcy laws.

In 2013, Detroit filed one of the largest municipal bankruptcy cases in U.S. history. (Courtesy of Haljackey via Wikimedia Commons)

Bankruptcy laws provide guidance about the course of action that a business may take—whether it is to go out of business or to re-organize. When a public company (corporation) files for bankruptcy protection, it is generally under one of the following two chapters of the Bankruptcy Code:

Chapter 11, which will "reorganize its business and try to become profitable again. Management continues to run the day-to-day business operations but all significant business decisions must be approved by a bankruptcy court."

Chapter 7, in which the company "stops all operations and goes completely out of business. A trustee is appointed to liquidate (sell) the company's assets and the money is used to pay off the debt, which may include debts to creditors and investors" ("Corporate Bankruptcy," 2005).

When a business fails, a number of stakeholders likely have a vested interest in what happens to the organization. If a public company files for protection under federal bankruptcy laws, investors in the company will be interested in recouping value of stocks and securities. Of course, a corporation's creditors or debtholders will also seek reparations if a company needs to liquidate or re-organize. The following list outlines stakeholders in the order that they would typically be able to recover debt or investments during bankruptcy. Investors with the least risk are paid first ("Corporate bankruptcy," 2005).

- Secured creditors: Typically a bank is paid first. Debt is secured by assets or collateral.
- Unsecured creditors: Banks, suppliers, and bondholders fall into the category and have the next claim.
- Stockholder: Owners of the company (stocks) may not receive anything. Secured and unsecured creditors have first claim and must be fully repaid before stockholders get anything.

Securities Trading for Companies under Bankruptcy Protection

Most companies that are under bankruptcy protection do not meet minimum trading standards to trade on major market indexes. No federal law exists prohibiting the trading of securities of companies in bankruptcy ("Corporate bankruptcy," 2005). There are several alternatives for the trading of securities, and even an index that trades shares from companies in financial trouble.

According to the Securities & Exchange Commission

"The reorganization plan will spell out your rights as an investor, and what you can expect to receive, if anything, from the company. The bankruptcy court may determine that stockholders don't get anything because the debtor is insolvent. (A debtor's solvency is determined by the difference between the value of its assets and its liabilities.) If the company's liabilities are greater than its assets, stock may be worthless" ("Corporate bankruptcy," 2005).

APPLICATIONS

The Bankruptcy Abuse Prevention and Consumer Protection Act

The implementation of the Bankruptcy Abuse Prevention and Consumer Protection Act (BAPCPA"") in October of 2005, signaled the largest change in bankruptcy code in 20 years (Cecil, 2005). BAPCPA"" shifted the focus of the code to the rights of the creditor and away from debtors. The act's "creditor-friendly" provisions, in contrast to the old law's "debtor-friendly" provisions, make it much more important for prospective Chapter 11 filers to think and plan ahead and significantly easier for creditors to collect on certain types of debt ("Chapter 11 then and now," 2006).

BAPCPA came about as a result of much lobbying by creditor banks, credit card companies, and others who wanted to curb alleged abuse of the bankruptcy system. There was little doubt that changes to the code would make it more difficult for companies to restructure, and many predicted that there would be more filings for Chapter 7 (liquidation) as a result of the code changes. In one article alone, the author makes the following statements regarding the burden of BAPCPA's new provisions on debtors (Cecil, 2006):

- "There are some businesses that will find it almost impossible to re-organize after October 17th" (date of the BAPCPA's implementation).
- "New laws make re-organization more difficult."
- "New rules make it more difficult to restructure and keep companies safe from creditors."

Chapter 7 business filings did increase, as many predicted, hitting a peak of 40,977 filings for the year ending in September 2010, up from 18,258 in 2006 (Administrative Office of the US Courts, 2014). Prior to October of 2005, the U.S. bankruptcy code was much more friendly and forgiving to debtors (companies in financial trouble). Financially strapped companies took advantage of the leniency in the code and its more flexible timelines and schedules to investigate re-organization options. According the Securities and Exchange Commission, the following statement applies in many cases ("Corporate bankruptcy," 2005):

"Most publicly-held companies will file under Chapter 11 rather than Chapter 7 because they can still run their business and control the bankruptcy process. Chapter 11 provides a process for rehabilitating the company's faltering business. Sometimes the company successfully works out a plan to return to profitability; sometimes, in the end, it liquidates."

BAPCPA's' Potential Burdens

Before the adoption of the 2005 act, much had been written about the abuses of consumers and businesses in not taking enough responsibility for their personal or corporate debt. Even in the twenty-first century, debt is still seen by many as a personal or professional failure and accountability is still seen by many as a necessary step for restitution. A Deloitte white paper, "Chapter 11, Then and Now," adds a word of caution (2006): "Some of the changes [to BAPCPA] could be an added burden to legitimately troubled companies." In general, the changes that could hurt ailing companies are

- added cost and time
- stricter deadlines
- curtailment of court discretionary power
- greater creditor involvement

According to Thomas M. Mayer, a bankruptcy specialist and partner in a New York law office, "Cases will be quicker and more brutal," since the law gives creditors more leverage; however, "suppliers, landlords, and investment banks will fare especially well" (Borrus, 2005, par. 3).

There was a marked increase in the number of corporate bankruptcy filings prior to October 2005. Companies that filed for protection prior to the October 17th deadline could count on operating under the prior bankruptcy rules. Many took advantage of the opportunity rather than taking their chances under the new code.

"From the way many companies raced to file chapter 11 before the Bankruptcy Abuse Prevention and Consumer Protection Act of 2005 """" took effect on October 17, 2005, you probably caught on that the Act meant potentially bad news for corporate bankruptcy filers" ("Chapter 11 then and now," 2006).

Major Changes to the Bankruptcy Act of 2005

According to Deloitte's Reorganization Services division, seven significant areas of change affect corporate bankruptcy filings as a result of the adoption of the 2005 act:

- Changes to rules involving leadership compensation and KERPs programs.
- Filing Timeline: 18-month cap for filing a plan of reorganization.
- Avoidance powers: Give more power to creditors to protest transfers of debt or KERPs-type payments that may have occurred prior to filing Chapter 11.
- Reclaiming inventory: Increased power for creditors to get back inventory.
- Handling of leases: Shortened window for debtors to decide on status of leases.
- Utilities payments: Debtors have stricter guidelines; must pay cash or prove good payment history.

- Creditor committees: More room for creditors at the negotiating table and more transparency in information sharing.

The following four changes resulting from the 2005 act are the most commonly cited and will have the most universal impact of the parties involved in bankruptcy proceedings (from Borrus, 2005).

ISSUES

Trading of Securities

According to the Securities and Exchange Commission's (SEC) information on corporate bankruptcy, there is no federal law prohibiting the trading of securities of companies in bankruptcy. The SEC warns that it is a risky investment strategy to buy common stock of a company in Chapter 11 bankruptcy and it "is likely to lead to financial loss" ("Corporate bankruptcy," 2005).

A common stockholder in a company that has filed for Chapter 11 protection will not be paid until secured and unsecured creditors are paid from a company's assets or ongoing operations. Creditors and bondholders become the new owners of the company as they have claim to company assets before stockholders. A more likely scenario is that a company's plan of reorganization (POR) will actually cancel all existing shares. Under Chapter 11 reorganization, a company usually keeps doing business, and its stock and bonds may continue to trade in securities markets. Even if a company has shares that remain in active trading upon filing Chapter 11, the shares are likely to have lost a great deal of value (aka: substantial dilution).

Securities Tied to Bankruptcy

Old Common Stock: On the market when the company went into bankruptcy. Stock may not meet criteria for trading on open stock indexes. Stock may be traded on OTCCB or Pink Sheets. In this case, the ticker symbol is five letters and ends with a "Q," which indicates that the stock was involved in a bankruptcy.

New Common Stock: Issued as part of a reorganization plan and has a different ticker symbol than the old stock. If a company plans to issue a stock and the stock has been authorized to trade, the ticker symbol will end with a "V." This designation simply indicates that the company plans to issue a stock for trading. Once the stock is issued, the "V" will no longer appear as part of the ticker symbol.

The SEC warns "would be" investors to stay informed about such investments. "Be sure you know which shares you are purchasing, because the old shares that were issued before the company filed for bankruptcy may be worthless if the company has emerged from bankruptcy and has issued new common stock" ("Corporate bankruptcy," 2005).

Jeffries Index

The Wall Street firm of Jeffries and Company launched a number of specialty indexes that track specific asset classes and segments. The smallest index that Jeffries maintains is unique in its tracking of post-bankruptcy stocks. The Jeffries universe is centered on small and mid-cap companies and their stocks. The index has been created to serve as a benchmarking tool for investors. According to Ross Stevens, head of equity investing at Jeffries, these stocks represent "value investing in the truest sense of the word" (Hahn, 2007).

The purpose of the Jefferies Re-Org IndexSM is to "track returns for newly emerged post-reorganization (i.e., post-Chapter 11) equities that have effected a re-characterization of equity ownership through the bankruptcy process, within the two-year period after bankruptcy emergence. This benchmark index is intended to be used by Jefferies' post-reorganization clients and other participants for this unique investment category" (Jefferies Re-Org Index, 2007).

Criteria for inclusion include
- stocks are small or mid-cap
- trading volume of 1 million per day
- stocks must reflect a change in equity ownership (post reorganization)

One initial challenge in maintaining the index is that the supply of eligible stocks is relatively small because there were not many bankruptcies from 2003–2006 (the years that the index has been tracking performance). Still, cumulative returns for 2003–2006 were stated at 234 percent as compared to returns for Standard & Poor's Index at 172 percent and Russell Index at 134 percent (Hahn, 2007).

RESTRUCTURING BOUTIQUES & WALL STREET Investment Firms

Passage of the Bankruptcy Abuse Prevention and Consumer Protection Act (BAPCPA) afforded Wall Street firms a waiver of a rule that guarded against conflict of interest on the part of advisors to companies under bankruptcy protection. "No longer will investment banks that underwrote securities for companies that ended up in bankruptcy be barred from offering advice to the same companies" (Borrus, 2005).

With "the bankruptcy reform bill signed into law, Wall Street investment banks can finally advise bankruptcy bound clients whose securities they have underwritten & a business previously prohibited due to conflicts of interest" (Hahn, 2005, p. 14). The act, previously described in this paper as being "creditor friendly," is also described as being "Wall Street friendly." The act is Wall Street friendly because banks stand to benefit in several ways from new rules governing corporate bankruptcy. The new 18-month window for companies to file restructuring plans (PORs) is certain to speed up bankruptcy proceedings that once could be delayed for years on end. The shortened period for drafting reorganization plans has the potential to lead to more sales of ailing companies, which makes bankers very happy. Ailing companies may also continue to fuel corporate mergers that have been a mainstay of Wall Street business for several years.

Wall Street is opportunistic in terms of seeking out future business and all eyes are on the shrinking credit markets and the potential increase in corporate failures. One analyst noted that there has been an increase in the number of B-ratings loans in the past few years. Credit has been cheap and plentiful and lower grade (B-rated) and higher risk loans have been made. "Default rates have a tendency to increase considerably two or three years after a peak in B and below issuance. If 2004 was indeed a peak in this type of issuance, default rates could be headed significantly higher in the 2006-2007 time frame" (Hahn, 2005, p. 14).

An increase in defaults on loans is a likely indicator of increasing bankruptcies. Because of the new rules that will allow some Wall Street banks to advise bankruptcy-bound clients, Wall Street firms see lots of potential business. It is important to note that under the new law, prohibitions for advising clients will exist for universal banks like JP Morgan and Citibank. These large banks are big lenders. Creditors cannot advise debtors under the new bankruptcy law or the old law. The new law does allow banks to advise clients whose securities they have underwritten.

"Banks that have been big underwriters of junk bonds, including players like Lehman Brothers, Bear Stearns, Goldman Sachs and Merrill Lynch & Co., are all expected to go after restructuring talent, either by acquiring or by poaching, as the financing bubble begins to deflate." In addition, "bankruptcy work is time consuming and requires specific expertise, which makes it difficult to build a restructuring group by transferring bankers from other groups" (Hahn, 2005, p. 14).

Turnaround management services is the term used to describe the niche that has developed around advising struggling companies regarding reorganization options. Wall Street firms had been prohibited from advising debtors under the old bankruptcy laws, but there was a limited amount of work because of the relatively low number of bankruptcies. With the potential number of bankruptcies projected to increase and the "go ahead" from the act's new rules, Wall Street is ready to jump into a sector that has been mainly the domain of specialized restructuring firms. Said one financial restructurer, "There is a view out there that when the next restructuring wave comes, it will come fast and heavy, and banks will recruit heavily" (cited in Hahn, 2005, p. 14).

Money to be Made in Restructuring
The attraction is obvious for companies that provide turnaround management services. Large [corporate] bankruptcies "can generate millions of dollars in fees each month for restructuring experts, lawyers, accountants, and other professionals. The extra help is needed to guide a company through a maze of litigation, negotiations, and bureaucracy" (Snavely & Nussel, 2006).

The following figures are representative of the costs that can be incurred by companies that are undergoing turnarounds or corporate restructuring. The following examples apply to the troubled automotive industry that, like the airline industry, has not been exempt from industry failure in the past couple decades (Snavely & Nussel, 2006):

- FTI Consulting is the financial adviser for Tower Automotive and the restructuring and financial adviser for Delphi. FTI was paid $6.7 million in fees and expenses for its work with Tower from May through July 2006.
- Kroll Zolfo Cooper was paid $1.9 million in fees and expenses for its work with Collins & Aikman in June 2005.

CONCLUSION

Bankruptcy laws have been in existence in the United States since the early 1800s. The first bankruptcy laws heavily favored creditors and dealt harshly with debtors. Over the years, options were afforded to debtors that allowed for liquidation of assets to pay off debt service. In the case of businesses, Chapter 11 provided a chance to reorganize while allowing a business to continue operations. There have been many amendments made to the bankruptcy code throughout the years with the most recent revisions occurring in October of 2005. The Act of 2005 tipped the bankruptcy scales in favor of creditors and away from debtors as had been written into the previous code revisions. The act of 2005 was heavily supported by creditor organizations (banks, credit card companies) as a way to shorten the process of bankruptcy. The act sets out stricter time limits for debtors to submit reorganization plans, gives more leverage to creditors in reclaiming inventory, and also gives creditors more input into the process as a whole. Bankruptcy law is constantly changing in response to credit markets and economic trends; and as such, the 2005 act will also be subject to amendments and changes as business needs and conditions change.

TERMS & CONCEPTS

Antecedent debt: An obligation to reimburse another that has previously been in existence and is legally enforceable.

Avoidance powers: Rights given to the bankruptcy trustee (for Chapter 11, the debtor in possession) to recover some kinds of transfers of property such as those deemed fraudulent or to void liens instituted before the start of a bankruptcy case.

Bankruptcy: Financial failure. A collective proceeding involving all of a debtor's creditors. It provides a pro rata distribution of an insolvent debtor's assets among like creditors and a discharge to qualified debtors" (Hansen & Eschelbach Hansen, n.d.).

Bankruptcy Abuse Prevention and Consumer Protection Act (BAPCPA): Signed into law by President George Bush in April of 2005, the act"" took effect in October of 2007. The revised law gives more leverage to creditors in the bankruptcy process.

Chapter 7: When a company ceases all operations, goes completely out of business, and may liquidate assets to pay off creditors.

Chapter 11: A reorganization of a business in an attempt to once again become profitable. "Management continues to run the day-to-day business operations but all significant business decisions must be approved by a bankruptcy court" (SEC.gov).

Key Employee Retention Programs (KERPs): Retention programs for senior management (or managers), often referred to as key employee retention plans (KERPS). These bonuses are meant to retain key talent that is needed to see a company through a restructuring effort.

Over-the-Counter (OTC) Security: A security not traded over a formal exchange such as the NYSE, TSX, or AMEX. The reason a stock is traded over-the-counter is usually because the company is small, making it unable to meet exchange listing requirements. Stock of companies in Chapter 11 typically trade in this manner.

Pink sheet: The leading provider of pricing and financial information for the over-the-counter (OTC) securities markets. Stocks of companies in Chapter 11 typically trade as OTC securities.

Plan of Reorganization (POR): "The U.S. Trustee, the bankruptcy arm of the Justice Department, will appoint one or more committees to represent the interests of creditors and stockholders in working with the company to develop a plan of reorganization to get out of debt" ("Corporate Bankruptcy," 2005).

Restructuring boutiques: Alternative investment firms to large financial entities that provide a highly personalized environment for investing. In the context of bankruptcy law, many boutiques specialize in reorganization services.

Risk-return tradeoff: The idea that as risk increases, so does potential return. The risk-return tradeoff holds that invested money can return higher profits only if it is subject to a higher possibility of being lost.

Solvency: The ability of an organization to meet its long-term fixed expenses and to accomplish long-term expansion and growth. Insolvency indicates a company is under bankruptcy protection.

Turnaround management services: Professionals or boutique firms offering turnaround, crisis management, liquidation, bankruptcy, and related services. These firms develop specialized expertise and operation in a niche industry that helps struggling companies reorganize under Chapter 11.

Universal banks: Also known as financial services companies, engage in several activities such as commercial and retail lending and have subsidiaries in tax-havens to offer offshore banking services to customers in other countries.

BIBLIOGRAPHY

A brief history of bankruptcy law. (2002). *The Vault.*

A brief history of bankruptcy in the US. (2007). *Bankruptcy Yearbook and Almanac.*

Administrative Office of the US Courts. (2014). *Bankruptcy Statistics: 12-Month Period Ending September.*

An overview of corporate bankruptcy. (2005) *Investopedia.*

Baird, D. G., & Casey, A. J. (2013). No exit? withdrawal rights and the law of corporate reorganizations. *Columbia Law Review, 113*(1), 1–52.

Borrus, A. (2005). Creditors will crack the whip. *Business Week,* (3941), 82–83.

Cecil, M. (2005). Bankruptcy code changes in the Fall loom. *Mergers & Acquisitions Report, 18*(25), 1–12.

Chapter 11 then and now. (2006). *Deloitte.*

Corporate bankruptcy. (2005). U.S. Securities and Exchange Commission.

Hahn, A. (2007). Finding beauty in bankruptcy. *Investment Dealers' Digest, 73*(1), 7–8.

Hahn, A. (2005). Winners and losers in bankruptcy bill. *Investment Dealers' Digest, 71*(17), 14–15.

Hansen, B. & Eschelbach Hanson, M. (n.d.) The transformation of bankruptcy in the United States. Princeton.edu.

Jefferies Re-Org Index. (2007). Jeffries & Company.

Landers, J. M. (2013). Recent developments in business bankruptcy cases. *Pratt's Journal of Bankruptcy Law, 9*(2), 158–184.

Meyerowitz, S. A. (2013). Financings and bankruptcy. *Pratt's Journal of Bankruptcy Law, 9*(6), 485–486.

Oellermann, C. M., & Douglas, M. G. (2013). Safe harbor redux: The second circuit revisits the bankruptcy code's protection against avoidance of securities contract payments. *Pratt's Journal of Bankruptcy Law, 9*(7), 651–661.

Snavely, B., & Nussel, P. (2006). Busy restructuring firms attract investors. *Automotive News, 81*(6232), 32.

SUGGESTED READING

Freed, D. (2007). Are bankruptcies set to speed up? *Investment Dealers' Digest, 73*(30), 3–34.

Miller, H. & Waisman, S. (2004). Does Chapter 11 reorganisation remain a viable option for distressed businesses for the twenty-first century? *American Bankruptcy Law Journal, 78*(2), 153–200.

Oellermann, C. M., & Douglas, M. G. (2013). The Year in Bankruptcy: Part I. *Pratt's Journal Of Bankruptcy Law, 9*(2), 127–57.

Robertson, A., & Khatibi, A. (2013). The influence of employer branding on productivity-related outcomes of an organization. *IUP Journal of Brand Management, 13.*

Sherefkin, R. (2006). Even in bankruptcy, cash can flow to CEOs. *Automotive News, 80*(6203), 38.

Essay by Carolyn Sprague, MLS

BUSINESS APPLICATIONS ON SPREADSHEETS

This article examines how spreadsheet applications software is used as a business data processing tool. Problems with the accuracy of spreadsheets are examined along with the implications for compliance with various regulatory requirements such as Sarbanes-Oxley (SOX). The growth of the spreadsheet template industry is explained and the types of templates available for purchase are reviewed. The efforts of the European Spreadsheet Risks Interest Group (EuSpRIG) and the Spreadsheet Standards Review Board (SSRB) to improve the quality of spreadsheets are also reviewed.

OVERVIEW

Spreadsheet software packages are widely used applications for analyzing and displaying data. Spreadsheets can help users develop graphs, charts, reports of financial data, or statistical analyses. Typical spreadsheet software has a wide variety of features including file creation and retrieval, report generation and printing, graphics, sorting, mathematical and statistical computing. The most widely used spreadsheet software packages are Microsoft Excel, Lotus 1-2-3, and Quattro Pro. Spreadsheet software packages can be used on almost any type of computer including personal computers, workstations, and mainframes and can run on virtually all the major operating systems (Chou & Gensler, 1993).

The functionality available in spreadsheets continues to be enhanced with some products now having capacities of one million rows by 16,000 columns. In addition, 3-D, soft shadowing and transparency effects help to spiff up charts and graphs. Conditional formatting features allow users to highlight cells with colors and icons to spot trends in data (Baig, 2007).

A critical part of an MBA's education is learning how to build business models that are adaptable to real-life situations. It's particularly useful for students to learn spreadsheet modeling techniques, which allow them to make mathematical models of relatively unstructured business problems and organize them via a spreadsheet. Such models help them think through a problem and even determine what data will be most useful to solve problems (Powell & Shumsky, 2007).

Spreadsheets can aid in analytical tasks that range from the simple to the very complex. Analysis of tabular data is a rather straightforward and simple use of spreadsheets. Decision support processes, on the other hand, involve the analysis of business intelligence using problem-specific methodologies. The purpose of an SDSS is to solve an unstructured problem in a business environment. Therefore, knowledge of procedures for problem solving is critical in the process of building an SDSS. Knowledge of the decision-making process is also critical in performing decision selection (Chou & Gensler, 1993).

Problems with Spreadsheets

Spreadsheets may be a liability in the Sarbanes-Oxley era because they could hold important corporate financial data. The Sarbanes-Oxley Act of 2002, also known as the Public Company Accounting Reform and Investor Protection Act of 2002 and commonly called SOX, is a U.S. federal law. The law requires, in part, that corporations certify the internal control of financial information and data and retain data relating to the financial management of the company. In simple terms, this law requires that the spreadsheets used in financial management or decision-making need to be audited for adequacy of controls and accuracy of information. The law also requires that copies of the relative spreadsheets be retained.

Various studies report that 47 percent to 64 percent of companies use stand-alone spreadsheets for planning and budgeting. Although spreadsheets were originally invented as a personal productivity tool, they may not be well suited to collaboration, data quality, or regulatory compliance. Spreadsheets often contain substantial errors. As corporations seek consolidated planning and financial reporting, spreadsheets pose challenges not dreamed of when they were first used on personal computers.

Many company spreadsheets have errors, and surveys have shown that up to 91 percent of the spreadsheets used by large organizations had errors. The mistakes range from mechanical errors (such as pointing to the wrong cell when entering a formula) to logic errors (such as entering the wrong formula) when setting up the spreadsheet. Washington-based Fannie Mae, for example, made a $1.2 billion accounting error because of what it called honest mistakes made in a spreadsheet used in the implementation of a new accounting standard (Horowitz & Betts, 2004). In 2012, a formula error resulted in traders at J. P. MorganChase undervalueing risk by 50 percent and contributed to a loss of $6.2 billion (Herbert, Lowth & Buckner, 2013).

To some extent, the criticism, or demonization of spreadsheets, may come from software producers pushing their own, more expensive financial software such as business performance applications packages.

Although spreadsheets have significant shortcomings, they provide the benefits of usability, analysis, and presentation graphics. Most observers say that spreadsheets will be around for the foreseeable future.

Many IT departments are embracing new business intelligence tools that aim to forge a balance between strident user demands for spreadsheets and corporate requirements that financial data be consistent and accurate. This includes spreadsheet development environments for building enterprise-class systems with customized user interfaces and strong management controls. To maintain an audit trail, automated write-back systems are deployed that update central data stores so transactional systems reflect user changes. In instances where data should not be changed, system lockdown methods are being implemented (Havenstein, 2005). In addition, many companies are gradually moving away from using spreadsheets and are adopting data warehouse systems that combine several database sources together and have sophisticated business analysis tools to support users (Horowitz & Betts, 2004).

Regardless of how the control of spreadsheets and spreadsheet data is handled, the SOX legislation requires that the IT Department conduct risk assessments to determine the type of controls necessary and to implement an appropriate level of control for spreadsheets. This includes establishing policies and procedures that assure necessary actions are taken to address risks. Information systems auditing processes, in turn, must test to determine if controls for spreadsheets are adequate and properly implemented.

Spreadsheet Templates

Although many people benefit from using spreadsheets, they do not have sufficient skills or enough time to actually create a reliable spreadsheet. A spreadsheet template industry has emerged that provides off-the-shelf ready-to-use spreadsheets for a wide variety of management or analytical activities. Most sellers of spreadsheet templates tout reliability and accuracy of their products. The templates vary in price and typically cost between $100 and $200. Applications that templates can support include:

- bond yield calculation
- customer invoicing
- event planning
- inventory management

- investment and business valuation
- multiple regression analysis and forecasting
- personal finance
- portfolio optimization, monitoring, and valuation
- project planning and management
- real-option valuation.

Business valuation templates can be designed to accept information from publicly-available 10-K reports in order to calculate the total and per-share value of a business. Valuation models can include a basic income statement and balance sheet, a cost of equity calculator, and a detailed ratio analysis. This type of template often allows the user to vary their analysis based on forecast of items such as the expected return on the overall investment or expected new investments. Changes made to one part of the model can automatically flow through to the other parts modifying the projected per-share valuation of the company.

Spreadsheet templates are also available for inventory management that allow small business owners to track inventory and view automatic alerts when reordering is necessary. This often involves the ability to pre-define reorder levels and customize reorder levels. When the number of units of an item currently in stock, falls below a certain number or pre-defined percentage, alerts can be generated.

There are also a wide variety of spreadsheet templates available in the realm of freeware. These templates were created by individuals, small companies, or organizations and are made available to users on a no charge basis. Some of the free or low-cost software available online suffers from design deficiencies that make it difficult to install or uninstall and may cause problems with operating systems. Other software downloads may come packed with adware that bombards you with marketing pitches (Mainelli, 2002). Freeware does take caveat emptor to a whole new level, though. You're not a buyer, so whatever problems you encounter are often yours, not the developer's. If free software comes with tech support, it's usually through online forums, and many freeware apps are plagued with bugs (Steinhart, 2005).

APPLICATIONS

Spreadsheets to Manage Construction Work
Spreadsheets can been used to develop computer-based modeling tools to help manage a wide variety of companies. One way spreadsheets can be used to help manage construction companies is by employing a simplified spreadsheet-based subcontractor information system (SIS). The SIS design involves the setup of several data lists, establishing relationships among them, and designing related reports.

In this model, resource data lists are stored in different worksheets for labor, equipment, crews, material, and subcontractors. These resource lists are referred to in the methods sheet, which defines alternative construction methods for various tasks. Once the general spreadsheets of the resources and construction methods are filled with data (ideally using the company's past records), they are ready for use in any project. The worksheets are as follows:

Labor. The labor list contains five fields: code, description, total hourly rate, basic hourly rate, and availability constraints.

Equipment. The equipment basic rate includes rental cost and operating costs such as fuel, oil, and routine maintenance. An average of 10 percent is often added to the basic rate for overhead to calculate the rate per hour.

Crews. Crews are defined by assigning up to five labor and equipment resources, using their codes as reference.

Materials. The material basic unit cost includes delivery to the site, including the sales tax or allowance for wasted material. An average of 10 percent is often added to the basic unit cost for overhead to calculate the cost per unit.

Subcontractors. This sheet defines various subcontractors, providing their unit cost for the required tasks. An average of 10 percent is often added to the subcontractor's rate to calculate the cost per unit for subcontractor's work.

Various methods of construction are defined in a separate worksheet that defines the resources used in each construction method (crews and material, or subcontractor), the overtime strategy they use, daily production rate, and assumed seasonal productivity factors for winter, spring, and fall. Several business rules can be established to calculate productivity and costs:

- Normal workday is eight hours.
- The hourly rate of the first four overtime hours is 1.2 of normal rate.
- The hourly rate of the overtime hours over the first four hours is 1.5 of normal rate.
- An overtime hour has 90 percent productivity of a regular hour.
- Different methods can have different overtime and/or resources.

Cost estimating is one of the most important functions to any contractor, as it is the basis for bid proposals, procurement plans, and job cost control. Construction estimating is a complex process due to the many interactions involved and the absence of standardization of conditions. Special care has to be given to cost estimation in order to be able to win a job and maintain a fair profit. One of the main functions of the SIS is to establish a realistic and automated estimating and cost control system utilizing the resource and method lists described previously.

Different levels of reports that summarize the data stored in the system become essential for supporting a project and for identifying important trends that can be used as the basis for corrective actions. Helpful reports can include a bid proposal, summary of methods of construction, and unit price deviations in contracts (Hegazy & Ersahin, 2001).

ISSUE

Developing Standards for Spreadsheet Design

Research has repeatedly shown that an alarming proportion of corporate spreadsheets are not tested to the extent necessary to support directors' fiduciary, reporting and compliance obligations. Uncontrolled and untested spreadsheet models therefore pose significant business risks. These risks include lost revenue, poor decision-making due to prevalent but undetected errors, and difficulties in demonstrating fiduciary and regulatory compliance. To counter these risks and address the pertinent management issues, the European Spreadsheet Risks Interest Group (EuSpRIG) holds annual conferences to discuss problems with spreadsheets and their solutions (EuSpRIG, 2007).

Studies from Coopers & Lybrand, KPMG, NYNEX, University of Hawaii and University of Michigan have revealed staggering error rates in spreadsheets. Although these studies assert that nine out of every ten spreadsheets contain errors, spreadsheets are still the choice of four out of ten engineers for doing calculations (Randles, 2006). Problems have been found in many well-known companies. At Rolls-Royce, for example, engineers faced problems when using spreadsheet programs not explicitly designed for engineering calculations and did not readily identify the errors. Several instances were documented in which a popular spreadsheet program returned wrong answers and problems worsened as size of a data set increased (Thilmany, 2005).

The use of spreadsheets is certainly increasing, and many organizations develop their own spreadsheets or use a commercially supplied template. As the use of spreadsheets for important financial or forecasting activity increases, users need assurance of reliability and accuracy. The Spreadsheet Standards Review Board (SSRB) develops and maintains the Best Practice Spreadsheet Modeling Standards. The standards are publicly available at no charge.

The SSRB meets periodically to evaluate and consider proposals to add, delete or modify the Standards that are submitted to the SSRB by any party. The SSRB also invests significant resources into comprehensively analyzing every aspect of spreadsheet development, maintenance and usage in order to establish universally applicable standards and conventions for spreadsheet modeling activities. The primary objectives of the standards are to:

- improve quality and transparency
- ensure user-friendliness
- decrease spreadsheet model development time and cost
- minimize risk of errors
- allow efficient sharing of model development methodologies
- prevent model redundancy
- align model developers and model users

The standards are rapidly gaining acceptance from banks, advisors, governments, and large companies. By adopting the standards, organizations initiate a process of ongoing improvement in the efficiency and quality of financial analytics used for decision-making. The standards are comprehensive and cover every area of the spreadsheet development, maintenance, and usage process. The standards are split into 16 spreadsheet modeling areas:

- general concepts
- workbook structure
- sheet structure
- formats and styles
- assumption entry interfaces
- sensitivity analysis
- outputs and presentations
- calculation formulae
- naming principles
- time series analysis
- error checks
- printing and viewing
- multiple workbooks
- security and protection
- visual basic programming
- miscellaneous

Any party may participate in the further development of the standards by submitting a proposal form to the SSRB. In order for a standard or convention proposal to qualify for inclusion in the standards, it must contain universally applicable methodologies or approaches to spreadsheet development, maintenance and use. The proposed standard must also reduce the likelihood of errors or mistakes in spreadsheets (SSRB, 2007).

CONCLUSION

Spreadsheet software packages have become widely used tools for analyzing and displaying data. Spreadsheets can help users develop graphs, charts, reports of financial data, or statistical analysis. Typical spreadsheet software has a wide variety of features, including file creation and retrieval, report generation and printing, graphics, sorting, mathematical and statistical computing. A critical part of an MBA's education is learning how to build business models that are adaptable to real-life situations.

Spreadsheets can aide in analytical tasks that range from the simple to the very complex. Analysis of tabular data is a rather straightforward and simple use of spreadsheets. Decision support processes, on the other hand, involve the analysis of business

intelligence using problem-specific methodologies. However, various studies report that 47 percent to 64 percent of companies use stand-alone spreadsheets for planning and budgeting. As a result of these problems, spreadsheets may be a liability in the Sarbanes-Oxley era because they could hold important corporate financial data.

To eliminate the problems with spreadsheets, many IT departments are embracing new business intelligence tools that aim to forge a balance between strident user demands for spreadsheets and corporate requirements that financial data be consistent and accurate. This includes spreadsheet development environments for building enterprise-class systems with customized user interfaces and strong management controls. To maintain an audit trail, automated write-back systems are deployed that update central data stores so transactional systems reflect user changes. In instances where data should not be changed, system lockdown methods is being implemented. Other companies are gradually moving away from using spreadsheets and are adopting data warehouse systems that combine several database sources together and have sophisticated business analysis tools to support users.

Spreadsheets are likely to remain popular and a spreadsheet template industry has emerged that provides off-the-shelf ready-to-use spreadsheets for a wide variety of management or analytical activities. Most sellers of spreadsheet templates tout reliability and accuracy of their products. The templates vary in price and typically cost between $100 and $200.

There are also efforts to establish standards for spreadsheets. The European Spreadsheet Risks Interest Group (EuSpRIG) holds annual conferences to discuss problems with spreadsheets and their solutions. The standards set by the Spreadsheet Standards Review Board (SSRB) are rapidly gaining acceptance from banks, advisors, governments, and large companies. By adopting the standards, organizations initiate a process of ongoing improvement in the efficiency and quality of financial analytics used for decision-making.

TERMS & CONCEPTS

Business valuation spreadsheet templates: A spreadsheet template designed to calculate various aspects of business value including benchmarks such as the total and per-share value of a business or the cost of equity.

European Spreadsheet Risks Interest Group (EuSpRIG): An interest group of academia and industry promoting research regarding the extent and nature of spreadsheet risks, methods of prevention and detection of errors and methods of limiting damage.

Sarbanes-Oxley: The Sarbanes-Oxley Act of 2002, also known as the Public Company Accounting Reform and Investor Protection Act of 2002 and commonly called SOX, is a U.S. federal law designed to improve integrity in corporate management.

Spreadsheet errors: Factors that have the ability to alter/compromise the information being placed in and gleaned from spreadsheets. Mistakes range from mechanical errors (such as pointing to the wrong cell when entering a formula) to logic errors (such as entering the wrong formula) when setting up the spreadsheet.

Spreadsheet modeling techniques: In relation to business, spreadsheet modeling techniques allow them to make mathematical models of relatively unstructured business problems and organize them via a spreadsheet. Such models help them think through a problem and even determine what data will be most useful to solve problems.

Spreadsheet template: A spreadsheet template is an off-the-shelf ready-to-use spreadsheet designed to support specific management or analytical activities.

Spreadsheet software: Widely used applications for analyzing and displaying data.

Spreadsheet Standards Review Board (SSRB): Body that develops and maintains the Best Spreadsheet Modeling Standards; the highest professional spreadsheet modeling standards that are publicly available in the world.

BIBLIOGRAPHY

Baig, E. (2006, November 30). Microsoft Office makes encouraging strides. *USA Today*, 6B.

Chou, D., & Gensler, P. (1993). Using spreadsheets to teach decision support systems in business schools. *Journal of Education for Business, 69*, 116–120.

European Spreadsheet Risks Interest Group (EuSpRIG) Website.

Havenstein, H. (2005). Tools clamp down on spreadsheet abuse. *Computerworld, 39*, 72.

Hegazy, T., & Ersahin, T. (2001). Simplified spreadsheets solutions. I: Subcontractor information system. *Journal of Construction Engineering Management, 127*, 461.

Herbert, I., Lowth, G., & Buckner, E. (2013). Spreadsheets under the spotlight. *Management Services, 57*, 36–38.

Horowitz, A., & Betts, M. (2004). Spreadsheet overload? *Computerworld, 38*, 46–47.

Leon, L., Kalbers, L., Coster, N., & Abraham, D. (2012). A spreadsheet life cycle analysis and the impact of Sarbanes–Oxley. *Decision Support Systems, 54*, 452–460.

Mainelli, T. (2002). Disasterware? *PC World, 20*, 22–24.

Powell, S., & Shumsky, R. (2007). Covering the spread. *BizEd, 6*, 46–50.

Randles, C. (2006). The hidden cost of mismanaging calculations. *Manufacturing Engineer, 85*, 28–29.

Steinhart, M. (2005). Free software: Good, for nothing. *PC Magazine, 24*, 76–77.

Spreadsheet data manipulation using examples. (2012). *Communications of the ACM, 55*, 97–105.

The Spreadsheet Standards Review Board (SSRB) Website.

Thilmany, J. (2005). Don't trust that tool. *Mechanical Engineering, 127*, 16–167.

SUGGESTED READING

Cahill, M., & Kosicki, G. (2001). A framework for developing spreadsheet applications in economics. *Social Science Computer Review, 19*.

Enns, S. (1999). A simple spreadsheet approach to understanding work flow in production facilities. *Total Quality Management, 10*, 107–119.

Greulich, F. (2003). Airtanker initial attack: A spreadsheet-based modeling procedure. *Canadian Journal of Forest Research, 33*, 232.

Kowar, T. (2001). A spreadsheet for the estimation of chemical exposure. *Professional Safety, 46*, 26.

Kräger, B. (2004). Why you should use a relational database instead of a spreadsheet. *Cybernetics Systems, 35* (7/8), 683–696.

La Trobe-Bateman, J., & Wild, D. (2003). Design for manufacturing: use of a spreadsheet model of manufacturability to optimize product design and development. *Research in Engineering Design, 14*, 107.

Luttrell, G. (2004). Reconciliation of excess circuit data using spreadsheet tools. *Coal Preparation, 24* (1/2), 35–52.

Pickard, S. (1997). Integrated spreadsheets. *Civil Engineering (08857024), 67,* 44.

Savel, T. (1999). Organize your data with Microsoft Excel. *Family & Practice Management, 6,* 51.

Tohamy, S., & Mixon, J. (2002). Comparing trade instruments using spreadsheets. *Social Science Computer Review, 20,* 187.

Essay by Michael Erbschloe

BUSINESS CONDITIONS ANALYSIS

This article identifies five discernible areas conducive to the development and maintenance of a successful business environment. Using examples from the United States and abroad, the essay defines and illustrates the following concepts as integral elements for business and economic development: market demand, workforce development, political considerations, the cost of doing business, and access to technology. Each of these components are manifest or lacking in many high-profile industries, including Honda's U.S. expansion in central Ohio, Google's 2007 operation in western North Carolina, and the U.S. lodging industry in sub-Saharan Africa.

OVERVIEW

In the early 1980s, residents of Midwestern America thought they were under siege. The prevalence of foreign-made automobiles, many of which were imported from a surging Japanese motor industry, intimidated U.S. automakers and those loyal to them. United Auto Workers were rumored to be behind a rash of vandalism to Japanese vehicles, using keys to scrape the paint of privately owned Hondas as retribution for purchasing a foreign car instead of an "American" automobile. In the eyes of these miscreants, the Honda plant that had opened in 1979 in Marysville, Ohio, took away jobs from American workers in greater Detroit, which is only a few hours north (Brat, 2006).

It did not take very long for attitudes to shift, however. "Rust Belt" communities like Marysville have since enjoyed a thriving local economy due to Honda's operations there. More than 16,000 Ohio residents are currently employed by Honda, and since the plant's opening, layoffs have been virtually nonexistent. $1.1 billion is pumped annually into Ohio's economy. Two decades after Honda arrived in the United States, the very same communities whose residents used keys to express their displeasure at Japanese vehicles were offering the keys to the city to the same company as it considers expanding Midwestern operations (Honda, 2004).

Determining a fertile business climate can be based on a simple word: needs. This refers to the needs of the market, the needs of the workforce, and the needs of company itself. This essay illustrates the areas in which these multiple "needs" manifest themselves as five quantifiable factors that contribute to a successful business model. These elements are market demand, workforce development and base, political considerations, operating costs, and access to technology.

APPLICATIONS

Market Demand

Arguably, one of the industries in which the concept of demand is most well-defined is automobile manufacturing. The significant rise in crude oil prices that began in the early 2000s in the United States and abroad, coupled with increased public attention to the issue of global warming, spawned a trend toward fuel-efficient vehicles. After a sustained preference for large, low-mpg trucks and SUVs during a period of cheap fuel, car buyers began seeking smaller vehicles that use much less regular gasoline or diesel. Hybrid vehicles (which alternate between gasoline and electricity as fuel sources) became popular, and cars that operate on alternative fuel sources, such as biodiesel, hydrogen and 100 percent electricity, entered the market as well.

Periodic plateaus and declines in gas prices somewhat placated consumers' initial frenzy for jettisoning

Aerial view of the Googleplex core buildings in California. (Courtesy of Austin McKinley via Wikimedia Commons)

their gas guzzlers. One study at the time revealed that 50 percent of new car buyers were considering a hybrid, down from 57 percent in the previous year ("Hybrid," 2007). This slight decline in market demand was largely attributed to consumers' increased understanding that the fuel-cost savings offered by certain hybrids was not necessarily enough to justify the premium vehicle price when compared with some other conventional cars in the same class. In other words, consumers, who only two years earlier had decried the skyrocketing cost of fuel (and were more inclined to accept the hype surrounding hybrid vehicles) adjusted to those increases and became more critical when shopping for new vehicles. Car buyers remained concerned about fuel efficiency, however, and hybrids continued to be one response among many to the overarching issues of oil prices and environmental responsibility. As one industry analyst put it (North, 2007):

Any doubt that a focus on environmentally friendly vehicles is of growing importance to consumers should be gone by now. Regardless of which side you come down on in the global warming debate, fuel efficiency, low emissions, and recyclability are all becoming more important in vehicle design and production.

Indeed, Lienert (2006) reported that among the 10 top-selling vehicles in the United States, seven were small and mid-sized cars, each of which boasts better-than-average mileage. According to *Forbes*, "Gas prices used to be a consideration in car purchasing. Then they became a decisive factor. Now they are the decisive factor." *Forbes*'s 2013 list of 20 bestselling vehicles in the United States once again saw a boost in (considerably more fuel-efficient) trucks and SUVs, and small and mid-sized cars still dominated the list.

The example of environmentally friendly automobiles demonstrates the significance of market demand on a business's viability. Successful business development relies on the needs and concerns of the customer. In terms of the automobile industry, hybrid gasoline/electric vehicle sales soared immediately upon placement on the market because those cars directly responded to the rising cost of gasoline as well as the issue of global warming. Interestingly, in this case, the concerns over oil prices and the environment created a market and even a product concept rather than a single product that would address that demand. The "green" car market continues to evolve, with customer demand still strong.

Workforce Base & Development

Joseph Joubert once proffered, "Genius begins great works; labor alone finishes them."

Indeed, without a strong workforce on which to hang a business's hat, a corporation cannot thrive very long. An interesting example of this premise can be found in the lodging industry. To the casual observer, a hotel's employees are few and identifiable: the front desk employee, the housekeeper, room service, and a small handful of miscellaneous staff. In fact, the lodging industry employs an enormous number of employees whose talents require specific training and whose pay scale spans from minimum wage through the highest echelons of management. The lodging industry employs millions of these personnel in locations around the globe.

To illustrate this point, one may look at one of the larger international hotel chains, the Hilton Hotel Company. In addition to its well-known eponymous properties, Hilton owns such brands as Doubletree, Embassy Suites, and the luxurious Waldorf Astoria. Hilton has more than 2,500 managed and franchised hotels and employs an impressive 105,000 people worldwide.

Unfortunately, recruiting well-trained staff for a hotel is no easy undertaking. Most U.S. colleges and universities that offer hospitality degrees are located near major lodging and tourist centers, such as New York, California, and Florida. Despite the plethora of hotels, motels, inns and B&Bs that operate in greater Washington DC, only six programs offer hospitality certifications within an hour's drive'. (There are eight law schools and 10 MBA programs in that same radius.)

In the case of the lodging industry, it is clear that jobs are available in great numbers. The problem is two-fold. First, while there are enough people to fill posts, they may not choose to do so because of the low pay and/or poor benefits. Economist David Rosenberg echoes this concept. Those who claim there is a shortage of employees, he argues, may be overlooking the fact that the manpower is

The Honda East Liberty Auto Plant as seen from Ohio State Route 347. (Courtesy of Nheyob via Wikimedia Commons)

there — employers are simply not willing to pay for what they seek (Herbst, 2007).

Training is another issue. Training is absolutely pivotal to ensuring the success of any business. The hospitality industry requires individuals trained in sales, culinary arts, engineering, management, marketing, administrative, and customer service..

It is always a challenge to draw a pool of eligible workers from any region. Adequate training of staff is therefore essential. As is the case in a variety of large-scale industries, the lodging industry sometimes calls upon foreign-born workers to perform some of the more low-level jobs. Despite the relatively basic parameters of these minimum-wage positions, some training is required (including, for many, coursework on English as a second language). On any level, a well-trained workforce can make the difference. This point remains sage and yet challenging for any major industry.

A biodiesel hybrid bus in Montreal, Canada. (Courtesy of Happyfamily via Wikimedia Commons)

Political Considerations

"I would have voted for a 100% tax incentive if that's what it would have taken to land them," said Herbert H. Greene, a County Commissioner of Caldwell County, of which the small city of Lenoir, North Carolina, is the county seat (Burns, 2007). Commissioner Greene was understandably excited for Lenoir. Earlier in the year, that community of about 17,000 residents was skyrocketed into the public arena, thanks to its newest local business: Internet giant Google.

Greene was not alone in his excitement about luring Google to the Blue Ridge Mountain environs of Lenoir. The community was still reeling from the loss of seven furniture factories and, with those closures, 2,100 jobs over a three-year period. Communities like Lenoir do not recover so quickly from such a hit; the arrival of Google, which remains a stable leader of the volatile world of Internet commerce, represented a cure for such ills.

Drawing this corporate icon to Lenoir was easy and certainly not without expense. Google negotiated $212 million in tax incentives and infrastructure modifications from North Carolina. Using one of the large factory spaces left vacant by the departing furniture industry, Google adapted the space as one of its "server farms," filling it with row after row of computer systems and recruiting a mere 212-person staff to run the facility.

Nevertheless, the notion of reversing a downward trend, creating sustainable jobs and, of course, enhancing the town's profile as a "business friendly" environment made the investment in accommodating Google worthwhile for Lenoir's leaders. Lenoir is hardly the first community to adopt such an attitude when it comes to luring big-name corporations (and industries) to its city limits (and away from other competing communities). Marysville, Ohio, discussed earlier in this paper, is one such example. Freeport, Maine (home of outdoor apparel giant LL Bean) is another. Virtually any community that seeks to generate local corporate tax revenues and spur job growth will do what it can to entice a potentially lucrative business to locate there.

As the example of Google demonstrates, however, a small community cannot always afford to entice a major corporation on its own. In addition to local tax exemptions, the state is quite often called into action to assist. This aid often comes in the form of tax exemptions, infrastructural improvements (such as roadway repairs, building refurbishment, and related projects) and even development grants.

How does the average taxpayer feel about "spending money to make money"? States often employ so-called economic stimulus packages to enable otherwise underperforming regions and communities to generate business and, therefore, local revenues. The Massachusetts Legislature passed two comprehensive stimulus packages between 2004 and 2006 ("Mass economy," 2006). Among the areas addressed in those initiatives are $3 million in grants "to promote defense industry-related development in Southeastern Massachusetts," an area that lost a major military reservation at the suggestion of the Base Realignment and Closure panel only one year earlier. Pennsylvania offers assistance for companies expanding in so-called "Keystone Opportunity Zones," which offer complete exemptions from state and local taxes. These economic development initiatives provide local residents with tangible resources for their local businesses, and as a result, taxpayers seem more than happy to see such assistance.

Clearly, the government can play a significant role in an industry's health as well as the long-term viability of an expanding corporation. There are risks and rules, of course, as seen in the examples I have just illustrated. First and foremost among them is a simple, inherent precept of a capitalist economy: There will be competition. Google was able to secure millions of dollars in tax exemptions and rehabilitation of its targeted expansion site, a deal that even some local residents complained was excessive, simply by reminding the people of Lenoir that there were other interested communities who *were* willing to give Google just what it asked of Lenoir, if the latter was reluctant to acquiesce. Put simply, government assistance is often available when a company is seen as a vehicle for breathing new life into a stagnant regional economy. Such packages can, however, be developed to the detriment of that same local economy. Nevertheless, such government involvement works to the benefit of the business itself and can spur new economic growth in that very same region.

Cost of Business

Of course, a truly representative assessment of a business climate cannot be conducted without taking into consideration the cost of business itself. This area of economics is arguably one of the more difficult concepts to truly grasp, as a wide range of mitigating factors play a role in "costs," and for some, certain areas are more cumbersome than others.

Thanks to Google, one may simply use "cost of doing business number one concern" as his or her search parameters to illustrate this point. Among business owners, these cost concerns include legal expenses (for regulatory compliance), health care and, of course, energy and fuel. Corporate and commercial taxes on the federal, state, and local levels are also cited, as are wages.

The varying costs businesses see as serious impediments to their successful operation make it difficult to assess what climates are more fertile for business growth. Indeed, one study presents a very diverse picture of the most business-conducive states: Hawaii, New York, and Alaska are cited as the most difficult states, in terms of costs, in which to do business. South Dakota is considered the least cost-cumbersome state. Two neighboring states, New Hampshire and Vermont, are cited as on opposite ends of the taxation spectrum, with Vermont's corporate rates far more business-unfriendly than they are across the Connecticut River in New Hampshire.

The aforementioned study, conducted by the Milken Institute, identifies several significant costs: Taxes, wages, electricity, industrial space, and office space. Absent are health care and oil prices, which are consistently cited among most American business leaders as the most impactful costs in 2007 (Marketwire, 2007).

Is there a single concern that weighs on business owners' minds, or is there a group thereof? In all likelihood, the cost of doing business, while a very real concern, is about as multifaceted and diverse as the range of businesses themselves.

Technologies & Infrastructure

If the cost of doing business in a region is so paramount a factor for entrepreneurs, why are the locales that most effectively mitigate those costs, such as New Hampshire and South Dakota, not attracting major corporations on the same scale as areas like New York, California, and Massachusetts? One factor might be the technologies available to run the business itself.

Along with a region's workforce base, the cost of doing business and the fiscal support of the local and state governments, the infrastructure and technology needed to effectively perform that business is a major factor affecting the business climate.

In the case of Lenoir, Google simply needed space, inexpensive utilities, and cooling systems. Google headquarters, however, is located in the greater San Francisco area, with nearly every resource available to it. Marysville, Ohio, located in central Ohio, has exactly what that facility needs: adequate factory space, nearby airports, and rail and highway transportation.

An outstanding example of the need for technology and similar resources comes from one of the world's larger economies. Since the end of the apartheid era, South Africa has emerged as the largest economy in sub-Saharan Africa. Foreign investment and business partnerships have surged into this once-isolated country. In 2007, communications giant Cisco announced that it was expanding operations in South Africa, enabling many black citizens to become part of junior, mid-level and even senior management (Cisco Systems, 2007). Unfortunately, with the exception of the safari and ecotourism industries, the economic success of South Africa is largely centered around cities like Johannesburg and Cape Town.

In rural areas, poverty and fiscal malaise remain commonplace. Some economists postulate that this disparity exists because of a lack of access to the technologies the modern world takes for granted: telecommunications (Skuse, 2007). A simple lack of access to cellular technology has prevented the establishment of interpersonal as well as business networks. Since the late 1990s, telecommunications companies, government, and international development groups have endeavored to correct this "digital divide," but progress has been slow. Nevertheless, the promises presented to rural South Africans in terms of enhancing their potential to find financial equity are significant enough to remain an ongoing endeavor.

While worlds apart culturally, geographically and socio-economically, the examples of underdeveloped rural America and undeveloped South Africa have a common thread relative to the central message of this essay: without the technological tools (and at times even the access to such resources) necessary for a business to thrive for the long term, stagnant business environments will likely remain so.

CONCLUSION

Only a few years ago, immense sport utility vehicles (SUVs) enjoyed great sales. The Ford Explorer and the Hummer, as well as a number of large pickup trucks, were among the most popular vehicles on the road. Of course, when the recession of the early twenty-first century took hold, gas prices began their upward climb. It was simply becoming more difficult for everyday citizens to afford to fill up their tanks, and SUV and truck sales slumped among everyday Americans. Adding to the mixture was the increased public awareness of global warming, caused largely by auto emissions. These two serious problems could have hurt the automobile industry but did not — they merely fostered the demand for a new breed of car.

Nearly 25 years after Honda opened its doors in Marysville (much to the consternation of a handful of xenophobes), the plant is a roaring success. For many residents of that once-sleepy community, it is hard to imagine life before Honda moved to Ohio. That plant has proven a shining example for others to follow, and others have: Marysville is now home to such thriving companies as Scotts Miracle-Gro, a Nestle research company, a Goodyear plant, and even Lamborghini Ohio.

Lenoir, North Carolina, was also a town hurting for business before 2007. With a painful unemployment rate, people and investors were leaving town before Google moved into the community this summer. Now, dozens of companies are seeing new life and potential with Google's arrival. Employees of that "server farm" are seeing salaries nearly double what Caldwell County is used to seeing.

The successes enjoyed by these business environments are exceptional, to be sure, and yet reflective of five major tenets of business analysis. The first is market demand, whose sources are so numerous that they might be the subject of a separate paper altogether. Interest in the product, whether real or as-yet unrealized, is essential to the health of a business climate.

The second factor is prevalent in every example provided in this essay. Without a well-trained workforce, a business cannot survive. Marysville, Lenoir, the hotel industry, and even the presently undefined business landscape of rural South Africa, all serve as illustrations of the potential benefits of a local workforce suited to the needs of a successful business.

Third among the strongest determinants of the health of a business environment is the government's input. This factor is pervasive throughout the other four elements of this paper, as government intervention has protected against high tax rates (and therefore business costs), provided grants for workforce development and technology and even, in the case of global warming, spurred market demand. While conservative rhetoric may involve calls for government to keep its hands out of business, clearly, many economies owe their success to government assistance.

There are many forms of the fourth arena: whether commercial taxes, energy and fuel prices, facilities expenses, health care, salaries, or regulatory compliance, there are countless costs associated with business. Some can be effectively mitigated; others remain a perennial thorn in the side of entrepreneurs. All are factors to be considered in the analysis of a business climate.

technology and resources that are easily obtained in more established commercial and urban centers majorly contribute to an entrepreneur's decision to operate in a certain environment. Even the simplest of resources, placed in an otherwise cost-effective area with an abundance of workers and even the assistance of the local, regional and national governments, can mean the difference between a business mistake and a commercial success.

Terms & Concepts

Business climate: An environment in which conditions are conducive for the development of independent commerce as well as industrial development.

Corporation: A business entity established for the purposes of providing goods and/or services to customers for profit.

Economic development: The practice of creating a sustainable business climate within a certain geographic area, industry, or group of industries.

Economic stimulus package: Legislation or regulations designed to spur economic growth within a particular geographic, socio-economic, or industry area.

Market demand: Consumer interest in or need for a product or service offered by an entrepreneur, a corporation, or an industry.

Public policy: Legislation, laws, or regulations generated at federal, state, county, or local levels.

Tax incentives: Special arrangements between government entities and private entities wherein the latter are exempted from certain taxation requirements at local, state, and/or federal levels in exchange for conducting business under certain agreed-upon conditions.

Technologies: Hardware, software, products, and networks designed to foster interconnectivity, efficiency, and convenience.

Workforce: Current and potential employees of a certain industry or economic region.

BIBLIOGRAPHY

Advantage West Economic Development Group. (2007, July 11). New jobs, new opportunities click in Caldwell County.

Atherton, A. & Fairbanks, A. (2006). Stimulating private sector development in China: The emergence of enterprise development centres in Liaoning and Sichuan Provinces. *Asia Pacific Business Review, 12,* 333–354.

Brat, I. (2006, June 22). Indiana town woos Honda. *CNNMoney.com.*

Burns, N. & Cowan, C. (2007, July 23). The high cost of wooing Google. *Business Week,* (4043), 50–56.

Cisco deepens commitment to economic transformation in South Africa with Black economic empowerment initiative. (2007, September 4). Cisco Systems, Inc.,

Company history. (2004). Honda of America Manufacturing, Inc.

Economic stimulus programs. (2006). University of Massachusetts/MassEconomy.org.

Herbst, M. (2007, August 22). Labor shortages: Myth and reality. *Business Week Online,* 1.

Honda's Marysville auto plant at 25 Years: Historic yet 'new.' (2007, August 26). *Topix.*

Hospitality schools and universities. (2007). American Hotel and Lodging Association Education Institute.

Hybrid lovers: The honeymoon may be over. (2007, July 20). *CNNMoney.com.*

Keystone opportunity zones. (2007). Commonwealth of Pennsylvania Department of Community and Economic Development.

Lienert, D.(2006, September 15). *Best-Selling Cars of 2006.*

Luger, M. & Bae, S. (2006). Speaking falsehoods to power: States' misguided use of 'cost-of-doing-business' studies in economic development policy. *Review of Regional Studies, 36,* 15–43.

Milken Institute. (2007, August 16). Hawaii, New York and Alaska most costly states for business, according to Milken Institute. *Marketwire.*

Muller, J. (2013). The best-selling cars of 2013 aren't really cars at all. *Forbes.com, 12.*

Skuse, A. & Cousins, T. (2007). Managing distance. *Journal of Asian & African Studies, 42,* 4.

SUGGESTED READING

Forsyth, J. S. (2007). Soaring rents pinch businesses across U.S. *Wall Street Journal — Eastern Edition, 250,* A1–A10.

Kramer, L. (2007). Training local workers instead of outsourcing. *New York Times, 156*(54027), 19.

Owen, B. & French, N. (2007, July 21). Getting it together. *Estates Gazette,* 138–139.

Vemuri, Ashok. (2007). Technology as an Agent of Change. *American Banker, 172,* 7.

Essay by Michael P. Auerbach

BUSINESS CYCLE

This article focuses on the business cycle in the U.S. economy. The business cycle, with its peaks, recessions, troughs, and expansions, will be described and analyzed. The concepts of economic contraction and expansion will be introduced. The process of determining and dating the business cycle will be described. The tactics for managing the business cycle, particularly risk management, will be summarized. Case studies of business-cycle sensitive industries will be investigated.

OVERVIEW

The business cycle, which includes a peak, a recession, a trough, and an expansion, is a cycle of economic contraction and expansion. A recession, as defined by the National Bureau of Economic Research (NBER), is a significant decline in economic activity spread across the economy, lasting more than a few months, normally visible in real gross domestic product (GDP), real income, employment, industrial production, and wholesale-retail sales. Expansion is considered the normal state of the economy. According to the NBER's Business Cycle Dating Committee, the most recent peak in the business cycle occurred in March 2001. This economic peak followed a 10-year expansion that began in 1991. The most recent trough in the business cycle, followed by an expansion, occurred in November 2001.

Business cycles refer to type of fluctuation found in the aggregate economic activity of nations that organize their work mainly in business enterprises. A complete business cycle consists of expansions occurring at about the same time in many economic activities, followed by similarly general recessions, contractions, and expansions or revivals. There are two types of business cycles: classical cycles and growth cycles. Classical cycles refer to hills and valleys in a series representing the general level of economic activity. Growth cycles refer to recurring fluctuations in the rate of growth of aggregate activity relative to the long-run trend rate of growth. The measurement and analysis of business cycles is crucial for the economic health of the public and private sectors. Economic indicator analysis is one of the main tools used in measuring and analyzing business cycles. Economic indicator analysis involves using leading and coincident indexes of economic activity as strong forecasting factors or tools (Boehm, 1999).

The business cycle is a prevalent concept, in part, due to the shared nature of the experience across the economy. The majority of economic sectors expand and contract together in the business cycle. Comovement refers to the synchronized movement of sectors of the economy during periods of economic recession and expansion (Christiano, 1998). Business cycles are created by severe economic and geopolitical shocks and crises. Examples of events that create turbulence sufficient to move the business cycle include recessions, inflation, war, terrorism, nuclear threats, housing bubbles, drought, disease, pandemics, earthquakes, tsunamis, rising oil-price shocks, Federal Reserve rate hikes, soaring budgets, trade deficits, and falling dollar values. The shocks and crises that cause economic contraction and recession include both exogenous and endogenous events (Navarro, 2006). Exogenous refers to change from outside the system and endogenous refers to change from inside the system.

Business-cycle sensitivity varies by industry and product. For example, durable goods manufacturers are sensitive to business cycles while nondurable and "necessary" services are not. In addition, industries that represent the early stages of the production chains are particularly sensitive to business cycles due to the need for businesses to adjust their inventory levels during business cycles (Schwartz, 1992). Despite the variations in business-cycle sensitivity by industry and product, business cycles are known to depress the strength of the aggregate economy. Knowing that business cycles reduce long-run growth, governments work to avoid and resolve economic recessions (Rafferty, 2004).

The history of the modern business cycle goes back to the late eighteenth century. The mid-medieval period of feudalism in Europe was a pre-capitalist period. This period was characterized by manor production with little market exchange and barter with little money and credit. Three specific differences between the pre-capitalist and capitalist economies created the modern business cycle. Business cycles require market exchange, production for profit, and money to be present in the economy. Thus, the first business cycle did not appear until Europe transitioned from feudalism to capitalism. The first business cycles appeared in England in the 1790s along with industrial capitalism and the Industrial Revolution (Sherman, 2001). Business cycles, since the late 1800s, have tended to last between two and eight years.

The following section describes the processes of determining and dating the business cycle. This section serves as a foundation for later discussions of managing the business cycle and case studies of business-cycle sensitive industries.

Determining & Dating the Business Cycle

The National Bureau of Economic Research (NBER), the United States' leading nonprofit economic research organization, determines and records dates for

The Marriner S. Eccles Federal Reserve Board Building (commonly known as the Eccles Building or the Federal Reserve Building) is located at 20th Street & Constitution Avenue, NW in the Foggy Bottom neighborhood of Washington, D.C. It was designed by architect Paul Philippe Cret in 1935. Construction of the Art Deco building was completed in 1937. (Courtesy of AgnosticPreachersKid via Wikimedia Commons)

business cycles in the United States. The NBER published its first business cycle dates in 1929. The NBER, established in 1920, is a private, nonprofit, nonpartisan research organization dedicated to promoting a greater understanding of how the economy works. NBER associates, including 600 professors of economics and business, develop new statistical measurements, estimate quantitative models of economic behavior, assess the effects of public policies on the U.S. economy, and project the effects of alternative policy proposals. The NBER established itself as the predominant research organization on the topic of business cycles through the bureau's early research on the aggregate economy, business cycles, and long-term economic growth.

The NBER has developed a recession-dating procedure, which is standardized to ensure continuity. The recession-dating procedure takes a broad view of the economy to determine recessions, as recessions are never limited to one business sector. The committee prioritizes the GDP, a strong measure of aggregate economy estimated by the U.S. Department of Commerce when determining whether or not a recession has occurred and in identifying the approximate dates of the peak and the trough. The NBER's Business Cycle Dating Committee uses monthly economic indicators to determine the months of peaks and troughs of a business cycle. The monthly economic indicators used by the Business Cycle Dating Committee to develop its business cycle chronology include monthly estimates of real GDP; personal income less transfer payments; employment; industrial production; and the volume of sales of the manufacturing and whole-sale-retail sectors adjusted for price changes.

The NBER's Business Cycle Dating Committee keeps a historical chronology of the U.S. business cycle. The U.S. business cycle chronology identifies the dates of peaks and troughs that frame economic recession or expansion in the United States. The NBER's Business Cycle Dating Committee has recorded the following historical averages for U.S. business cycle expansions and contractions:

- 1854–2001: 32 cycles
- 1854–1919: 16 cycles
- 1919–1945: 6 cycles
- 1945–2001: 10 cycles

According to the NBER's Business Cycle Dating Committee and its historical chronology of the business cycle, the most recent peak occurred in March 2001 and the most recent trough occurred in November 2001.

APPLICATIONS

Managing the Business Cycle

Business cycles have a profound effect on business stakeholders, owners, employees, investors, and society at large. The expansions and contractions of the economic business cycles create an environment of economic risks and uncertainties in the business sector. Firms use management strategies, tactics, and forecasting tools to survive through the economically challenging times during a business cycle.

Business cycles must be managed by businesses to avoid economic collapse during periods of economic contraction. Executives with high levels of business-cycle literacy may be referred to as master cyclist executives. There are three broad and general objectives that businesses use to manage the business cycle:

- Evaluate the capabilities and resources that a firm may deploy to hedge or leverage business cycle risk.
- Articulate strategies and tactics that companies may use to better manage business cycle volatility.
- Develop prescriptive measures in areas ranging from marketing, pricing, and human resources management to M&A activity in order to improve business cycle management.

Business cycle orientation, which refers to a firm's level of business cycle preparedness, is influenced by a firm's organizational culture and structure, how it deploys its forecasting resources, and how business cycle literate its executive team is. A high level of business cycle orientation usually translates to superior performance during times of recession and expansion. Business cycle literacy requires understanding basic macroeconomic concepts like fiscal and monetary policy, interpreting key leading economic indicators like the yield curve and stock prices, and complex adjustment processes such as the effect of Federal Reserve interest rate hikes on exchange rates, global capital flows, and world trade.

's business cycle management will influence all sectors of business operations including human resource management, production and inventory control, marketing and pricing, risk management, capital expenditures, and acquisitions and divestitures.

- Human resource management: Human resource management for business cycles includes protecting a firm's high-skilled workforce during recessions and using cross-training, wage and work hour flexibility, and supportive organizational culture to make a "no layoffs" policy feasible.
- Production and inventory control: Production and inventory control management for business cycles includes macro-managing a firm's production and inventory turnover in anticipation of recession and recovery and creating production-to-order systems in order to reduce inventory needs.
- Marketing and pricing: Marketing and pricing management for business cycles include building brand and market share through countercyclical advertising, retargeting the customer and market as economic conditions dictate, and cutting prices in bad times to protect market share.
- Risk management: Risk management for business cycles includes diversifying, outsourcing, and offshoring to hedge business cycle risk; using options, futures, and swaps to hedge commodity price, interest rate, and exchange rate risk; and developing new products and markets in response to macroeconomic shocks.
- Capital expenditures: Capital expenditure management for business cycles includes cutting capital expenditures countercyclically in anticipation of a recession in order to protect cash flow; in-

creasing capital expenditures during the recession to develop innovative products and new capacity in time for the recover; and modernizing existing facilities during economic slowdowns.
- Acquisitions and divestitures: Acquisitions and divestitures management for business cycles includes timing key strategic acquisitions and divestitures to the stock market cycle and using the patterns of sector rotation to fine tune this tactical timing.

A successful business cycle manager will oversee business cycle preparedness in all the areas of business operations described above. Ultimately, successful business cycle management requires a supportive and cooperative organizational culture (Navarro, 2006).

Risk management, the identification and assessment of the collective risks that affect firm value, and the implementation of a firm-wide strategy to manage those risks, is particularly suited to the job of business cycle management. Risk managers develop and implement the firm's risk management strategy by modifying the firm's operations, adjusting its capital structure, and employing targeted financial instruments. A risk management strategy allows a firm to alter its risk profile. A risk management strategy or system, appropriate for managing a business cycle, involves the following steps (Meulbroek, 2002):

- Inventory all risks faced by the corporation.
- Estimate the probability of each risk occurring.
- Assess the cost of losses should they occur.
- Identify ways to reduce risk and estimate the cost of risk reduction.
- Build a model of firm value using all the information gathered as inputs.
- Use this model to identify the risk management policy that maximizes the firm's value.

Risk managers perform two main tasks in business cycle management. First, they hedge general business cycle risk by using tools such as business units and geographical diversification. Second, risk managers hedge the more specific risks associated with movements in commodity and oil prices, interest rates, and exchange rates by using financial derivatives such as call options and futures (Navarro, 2006). Savvy risk managers, who are literate about business cycles, can often predict an economic recession and prepare and protect their business accordingly.

Case Study: How Cyclical Industries Respond to Business Cycles

The following case studies describe how cyclical industries, such as the airline industry and the home improvement supply industry, respond to and prepare for business cycles.

The Airline Industry

The airline industry is highly sensitive to business cycles as are the paper industry, real estate markets, commodity markets, and the shipping industry. The airline industry has, in general, poor profitability and low shareholder return. The airline market has experienced two complete business cycles since 1970. Its' cyclical behavior began after the deregulation of the airlines in the United States through the U.S. Airline Deregulation Act of 1978. Major economic and geopolitical incidents, between 1970 and 1998, that have affected the business cycles of the airline industry include the introduction of the Boeing 747, the oil crisis, frequent flier programs, European Union's decision to liberalize the airline market, and the Gulf War.

The majority of airline managers believe that the business cycles in the airline market are related to fluctuations of the gross domestic product and are, as a result, out of their control. This bias leaves airlines poorly prepared to handle the issues that arise during the recessions and contracts of business cycles. Economic fluctuations challenge the majority of airlines, and those that succeed tend to have established strategies for cycle-oriented behavior. Lufthansa German Airlines, for example, has implemented numerous business cycle management strategies. The goal of Lufthansa German Airlines is to keep profits up and outperform the industry. Lufthansa German Airlines developed and implemented stabilizing policies for aircraft ordering, network planning, flexibility in leasing and retirement policies, and seat pricing to prepare for the economic destabilization of business cycles (Liehr, 2001).

Southwest Airlines Company, with 30 years of profitability, is also an example of an airline that works to protect and stabilize its business during business cycles. Southwest Airlines prepared its business cycle strategy by hedging to neutralize risk. Its' business approach is characterized by low-budget, no-reserved-seats, ticketless travel system, charismatic CEOs, and a unique organizational culture known for humor and high employee morale. Southwest Airlines' internal business cycle forecasting model incorporates energy price forecasting, global supply and demand, monetary aggregates, exchange rates, and geopolitical risk. Southwest Airlines' forecasting model has allowed the company to forecast changes in the business cycle and lock in fuel prices before the prices soared in response to economic recessions (Navarro, 2006).

The Home Improvement Supply Industry

The Lowe's Companies Inc. is a home improvement supply business. During the expansion phase of the 2000 business cycle, Lowe's CEO Robert Tillman sought out business opportunity. Tillman was highly literate about business cycles and worked to connect changes in the economy to changes in Lowe's business practices. Tillman believed that when the economic climate changes during a business cycle, successful retailers look for opportunity. He foresaw an industry adjustment process during the upcoming recession that could potentially benefit Lowe's. Tillman believed home remodeling and repairs would increase as new home sales decreased; lowered interest rates would drive home remodeling as consumers refinanced their homes for expensive remodeling; and lower interest rates would drive a new-house building-boom.

In addition, in 1999, Tillman,' authorized the opening of 300 new stores by the end of 2001. Opening new stores in the years before an expected recession is a highly unusual business strategy but for cyclical industries, aggressive capital expansion tends to be successful. Tillman understood how Lowe's business sector would be affected by the business cycle

A typical Lowe's storefront in Santa Clara, California. (Courtesy of Coolcaesar via Wikipedia)

and by the highly related interest rate cycle. Tillman's business cycle strategy for Lowe's was highly effective. Profits during 2001 were $149 million. Net income in 2002 increased to almost $500 million. Lowe's remained profitable in 2003 and began to control an increasingly large section of the home improvement market (Navarro, 2006).

CONCLUSION

In the final analysis, business cycles, characterized as wavelike fluctuations of peaks and troughs in economic activity, have gotten less severe and economically destructive since World War II. Factors that have moderated the severity of the business cycle since World War II include the increased role of government in economic activity, changes in the private sector such as the growth of international trade, changes in producer and consumer behavior, a more stable financial system, greater wage and price flexibility, greater exchange rate flexibility, and better inventory management (Garner, 1990). Examples of the business cycle management strategies and tactics, as described in this article, include the majority of the major decision-making areas of the modern corporation such as marketing and pricing, production and inventory control, human resource management, capital expenditures, risk management, and acquisitions and divestitures (Navarro, 2006). Business cycles cannot disappear as long as economic and geopolitical shocks such as recessions, inflation, war, terrorism, nuclear threats, housing bubbles, drought, disease, pandemics, earthquakes, tsunamis, rising oil-price shocks, Federal Reserve rate hikes, soaring budgets, trade deficits, and falling dollar exist but business cycles may become increasingly more manageable through public and private sector efforts.

TERMS & CONCEPTS

Aggregate economy: The total workings of a national economy, such as income, output, and the interrelationship among diverse economic sectors.

Business cycle: A type of fluctuation found in the aggregate economic activity of nations that organize their work mainly in business enterprises.

Business cycle orientation: A firm's level of business cycle preparedness.

Classical cycles: Hills and valleys in a plot representing the general level of economic activity.

Co-movement: The synchronized movement of sectors of the economy during periods of economic recession and expansion.

Endogenous: Change from inside the system.

Exogenous: Change from outside the system.

Growth cycles: Recurring fluctuations in the rate of growth of aggregate activity relative to the long-run trend rate of growth.

Recession: A significant decline in economic activity spread across the economy, lasting more than a few months, normally visible in real GDP, real income, employment, industrial production, and wholesale-retail sales.

Risk management: The identification and assessment of the collective risks that affect firm value and the implementation of a firm-wide strategy to manage those risks.

Risk management strategy: A risk management system that includes modifying the firm's operations, adjusting its capital structure, and employing targeted financial instruments.

BIBLIOGRAPHY

Christiano, L., & Fitzgerald, T. (1998). The business cycle: It's still a puzzle. *Economic Perspectives, 22,* 56.

Fusari1, A. (2013). Radical uncertainty, dynamic competition and a model of the business cycle: The implications of a measure and an explanation of what is supposed non-measurable and non-explainable. *International Journal of Business & Management, 8,* 8– 8.

Garner, C. (1990). Is the business cycle disappearing? *Economic Review, 75,* 25–40.

Hackenburg, P. (2003). Cycles. *Risk Management, 50,* 56–57.

Hall, R & Feldstein, M. (2003). *The NBER's recession dating procedure.* Business Cycle Dating Committee, National Bureau of Economic Research.

Kin-Yip, H., Tsui, A.K., & Zhaoyong, Z. (2013). Conditional volatility asymmetry of business cycles: evidence from four OECD countries. *Journal of Economic Development, 38,* 33–56.

Liehr, M., Grö ler, A., Klein, M., & Milling, P. (2001). Cycles in the sky: understanding and managing business cycles in the airline market. *System Dynamics Review (Wiley), 17,* 311–332.

Meulbroek, L. (2002). The promise and challenge of integrated risk management. *Risk Management and Insurance Review, 5,* 55–67.

National Bureau of Economic Research. (2003). *Business cycle expansions and contractions.* Cambridge, MA: National Bureau of Economic Research, Inc.

Navarro, P. (2006). Help your clients manage the business cycle. *Consulting to Management — C2M, 17,* 32–49.

Navarro, P. (2006). Sustainable strategies for a world of economic shocks. *Financial Executive, 22,* 40–45.

Pagan, A. (1997). Towards an understanding of some business cycle characteristics. *Australian Economic Review, 30,* 1–15.

Rafferty, M. (2004). Growth-business cycle interaction: a look at the OECD. *International Advances in Economic Research, 10,* 191–202.

Rizzi, J. (2006). Managing the credit cycle: a behavioral risk interpretation. *Commercial Lending Review, 21,* 3–9.

Schwartz, R. & Righini, G. (1992). Hedging the business cycle. *Institutional Investor, 26.* 21–24.

Sherman, H. (2001). The business cycle theory of Wesley Mitchell. *Journal of Economic Issues, 35,* 85–97.

Van Heerde, H.J., Gijsenberg, M.J., Dekimpe, M.G., & Steenkamp, J.M. (2013). Price and advertising effectiveness over the business cycle. *Journal of Marketing Research (JMR), 50,* 177–193.

SUGGESTED READING

Backus, D., Kehoe, P., & Kydland, F. (1992). International real business cycles. *Journal of Political Economy, 100,* 745.

Bodman, P., & Crosby, M. (2005). Are business cycles independent in the G7? *International Economic Journal, 19,* 483–499.

Schmitt-Grohe, S. (2000). Endogenous business cycles and the dynamics of output, hours, and consumption. *American Economic Review, 90,* 1136–1159.

Essay by Simone I. Flynn, Ph.D

BUSINESS ESTATE PLANNING

ABSTRACT

This article focuses on business estate planning. It will provide a general overview of the business estate planning process for both closely held businesses (CHB) family owned businesses (FOB). Topics of discussion include business estate planners and advisers, business estate planning goals and objectives, the connection between Internal Revenue Code (IRC) and business estate planning, and succession planning. The issues associated with post-mortem business estate planning will be addressed.

OVERVIEW

In the United States, small businesses, which characterize the majority of closely held businesses (CHB) and family owned businesses (FOB), drive the economy.

According to a 2014 report by the Small Business Administration (SBA), 99.7 percent of U.S. employer firms were classified as small businesses with fewer than 500 employees in the first decade of the twenty-first century, and of the 27 million small businesses in 2011, about 75 percent were nonemployer firms (sole proprietorships, partnerships, and incorporated businesses). Despite the strength and power of small CHBs and FOBs, numerous small businesses do not survive the transition from first- to second-generation ownership and management. When a business owner dies or retires, the business may be liquidated, continued, or sold to family, employees, or an outside party. Small businesses, both COBs and FOBs require successful business estate planning to survive the transition from first- to second-generation ownership (Grassi, 2007).

'Business estate planning refers to the minimization of estate or transfer tax as well as active

The Trump Organization is a family owned business. Its headquarters is located in Trump Tower in New York City. (Courtesy of Martin Dürrschnabel, de:Benutzer:Martin-D1, via Wikimedia Commons)

succession planning undertaken when transferring a CHB or FOB to the next generation. Small businesses are all at risk for failure when the business owner dies or retires. For example, the lack of a clear business successor and estate taxes as high as 40 percent can ruin businesses. Business estate plans are intended to minimize business disruption during the transition phase between business owners or managers (Hess & Havlik, 2005).

Effective business estate planning involves the following steps and stages: educating business owners and heirs about the estate planning processes and issues; coordinating and sharing plans with all significant shareholders; addressing the next generation's estate plans; soliciting multiple opinions from estate planners; sharing the business owner's intentions and plans fully with the board of directors; and reviewing the estate plans regularly with business estate advisers. Business estate planning requires that business owners and heirs address potentially uncomfortable issues such as mortality, aging, privacy, power, business operations and goals, resources, family dynamics, and leadership. Common problems associated with the choice to delay or forgo business estate planning include making irrevocable decisions, fearing disclosure, and clinging to privacy. Business owners fear and delay business estate planning due to the potential complications, loss of privacy, and the risk of heirs losing their companies to estate taxes, family fighting, and lack of clear leadership (Ward & Aronoff, 1993).

The following section provides a general overview of business estate planning processes for both FOBs and CHBs. Topics of discussion include business estate planners and advisers, business estate planning goals and objectives, the connection between the Internal Revenue Code (IRC) and business estate planning, and succession planning. This section serves as a foundation for later discussion of the issues associated with post-mortem business estate planning.

APPLICATIONS

Preparing a Business Estate Plan

Ideally, business estate planning should begin at the very start of a business venture. To maximize the advantages available from effective business estate planning, business owners should choose their business entity or type with their estate plans in mind. The business type will limit or expand the options and financial tools available to the business upon the business owner's retirement or death (Grassi, 2007). The following sections describe the key elements of the business estate planning process.

Business Estate Planners & Advisers

Business estate planning, which generally includes business succession decisions, requires the input of multiple parties including business owners, family business counselors, estate planning advisers, accountants, lawyers, managers, and human resources personnel. The lawyer involved in the business estate planning process will review the following documents: articles of incorporation, articles of organization, by-laws, operating agreements, partnership agreements, other governance documents, loan agreements, and any other relevant documents and contracts. In some business estate planning processes, multiple lawyers will be required to review and prepare documents. For example, a business lawyer prepares the buy-sell agreement, a labor lawyer prepares the employment agreement, a tax lawyer prepares the retirement and deferred compensation plan, and an estate planning attorney prepares the wills and trusts (Grassi, 2007).

Business Estate Planning Objectives & Goals

Business owners develop estate plans for multiple financial and personal reasons. Business owners generally make their estate planning goals and objectives explicit as part of the estate planning process. Common estate planning objectives and goals include the following: treat all heirs fairly; provide heirs who are active in the business with an opportunity to progress in the business; minimize transfer estate and gift taxes; avoid a forced liquidation of the business in the event of the business owner's death; retire and receive a monthly pension from the business; receive an income from business for perpetuity; provide for the surviving spouse and any minor or dependent children; design a succession plan for the business that provides stability for the business and its owners as well as certainty as to the transfer of ownership and control of the business; engineer a smooth transition of the business without the loss of revenue or consumer confidence; and design a business estate plan that coordinates with and facilitates the business succession plan (Grassi, 2007).

Internal Revenue Code & Business Estate Planning

The Internal Revenue Code (IRC), particularly IRS Revenue Ruling 59–60, and numerous other laws, such as the Economic Growth and Tax Relief Reconciliation Act (EGTRRA) of 2001 and the Pension Protection Act (PPA) of 2006, control and regulate business estate planning. Federal estate taxes, as described in the IRC, rely on accurate business valuations. IRS Revenue Ruling 59–60, passed in 1959, accomplished the following: provides a framework for the best way to value shares of capital stock of CHCs for estate and gift tax purposes and defines fair market value as the general standard of value for

Walmart is a publicly traded, family-owned business controlled by the Walton family. Its headquarters is located in Bentonville, Arkansas. (Courtesy of Brandonrush via Wikimedia Commons)

federal estate and gift tax purposes (Maccarrone & Warshavsky, 2003).

The IRC permits the following techniques and strategies to be used for business estate management and execution: installment sale, private annuity, gift or sale leaseback, intentionally defective irrevocable trusts (IDIT), special-use valuation, and buy-sell agreements (Rattiner, 2004).

Installment sale: The sale of a business to a family member through a manageable payment schedule. This strategy spreads the business estate tax burden over the life of the transaction.

Private annuity: Arrangements in which the buyer of a business receives an asset, such as real estate, from the seller in return for a promise to pay an annuity for life to the seller. IRC section 72 governs the taxation of private annuities. In most cases, the exchange in a private annuity transaction is viewed as even and goes untaxed.

Gift or sale leaseback: Arrangements in which the parent company disposes of an asset to reduce the size of the estate but leases the asset back for company use. To prevent fraud, the IRS reviews and oversees all gift or sale leaseback agreements to ensure that the company does not retain total control of the leased asset and appropriate rent is paid for the use of the asset.

Buy-sell agreements: Agreements between business owners to sell the interests of a deceased owner to the other remaining partners at a price determined beforehand. Buy-sell agreements often use business insurance to fund the purchase of the deceased owner's interest in the company. There are two main forms of buy-sell agreements: cross-purchase and stock redemption.

Stock redemptions: IRC allows businesses to control and minimize business estate taxes through stock redemptions. Section 303 of the IRC gives each business estate the opportunity to remove cash from the business without a tax penalty through a partial redemption of company stock.

Succession Planning

Business estate planning must include decisions about how, when, and to whom to transfer control of the business. Business owners tend to focus attention on choosing the best successor, while estate planners tend to focus on strategies and techniques for minimizing estate taxes. Succession planning must explicitly describe the channels of ownership succession and management succession. The following tools are useful for succession planning: "shareholder agreements, stock recapitalizations, voting trusts, voting agreements or irrevocable proxies, and trust arrangements" (Hess, 2005, p.56).

Shareholder agreements: ""Explicit agreements between a company's shareholders that outline the way the company should be managed as well as shareholders' rights and responsibilities. Shareholder agreements, which include information on the regulation of shareholder relationships and the management of the company, expedite the transfer of control from one business owner to his or her heir through limits on share transfers by shareholders who are not active in the family business as well as purchase obligations for the company or the heir. In addition, a shareholder agreement may explicitly state that when the owner dies or retires, control of the business passes to a designated successor. Lastly, shareholder agreements clarify succession issues by identifying officers, selecting the size of a company's board of directors and the procedure for selection of board members, and explicitly providing guidelines on the restrictions for issuing additional shares.

Stock recapitalizations: A technique used by business owners who choose not to specify a business successor in the shareholder agreement. "Stock recapitalization" refers to the process of trading in a single class of company stock in favor of two separate classes: voting and non-voting. The U.S. Supreme Court defined "recapitalization" as a capital structure reorganization within the existing framework of an established corporation. A business must satisfy three requirements to prove that its stock recapitalization is valid: First, the stock recapitalization must be part of an overall plan of reorganization. Second, the stock recapitalization must include exchanges of stock or securities of the corporation for other similar stock or securities. Third, the stock recapitalization must have a valid business purpose. Stock recapitalization, which may legally be structured as a tax-free transaction, provides large potential tax benefits to the business and shareholders.

Voting trusts: Voting trusts are a common tool for transferring control from one party or generation to another. A "voting trust" refers to an agreement in which shareholders transfer stock and voting rights, but not economic rights, to a small group of individuals for a specified time period. The voting trust transfers voting power but not wealth; therefore, the voting trust does not change the economic ownership of the business. In fact, despite the transfer of voting rights, no financial change is reported for income tax purposes after the transfer of stock to a voting trust. Voting trusts occur when company shareholders establish a voting trust agreement and switch their company stock shares over to the voting trustees. The process involves the issuance of voting trust certificates to the shareholders that match the number of shares transferred. The voting trustees become the legal owners of the stock and exercise all rights to vote.

Voting agreements and irrevocable proxies: Informal arrangements that control voting of the company shares without officially altering company ownership. Voting agreements differ from voting trusts due to the absence of legal transfer of share title. In addition to the voting agreement, a business owner generally augments the arrangement by granting an irrevocable voting proxy to his or her specified successor to vote the shares of stock of the company.

Trust arrangements: Business owners who plan to transfer business control to a chosen successor without including shareholders often create trust arrangements. Trust arrangements grant business control to the chosen successor without altering ownership or getting shareholder approval.

Ultimately, successful business estate planning will include tax planning, estate planning, and succession planning. Despite the importance of succession planning, and business estate planning in general, to the passage of wealth, resources, and power between generations, approximately 80 percent of all family businesses operate without a succession plan, according to a 2007 white paper by the Family Business Institute. It reports that as a result, only 30 percent of family businesses are successfully transferred from one generation to the next.

ISSUES

Post-Mortem Business Estate Tax Planning
Advanced or lifetime business estate planning has the potential to eliminate some or all business estate taxes and create a clear successor to the business owner and business manager. While business estate planning is most effectively undertaken prior to a business owner's death, post-mortem business estate planning strategies and techniques are available to heirs to reduce or eliminate federal estate taxes.

their life or who engaged in inadequate or inaccurate business estate planning (Oliver & Granstaf, 1998).

Alternate valuation: In the event of the death of an owner of a FOB or CHB, business heirs or estate executors may petition for alternate valuation to lessen the burden of estate tax. Business estates that decline in value after the death of the business owner are eligible for alternate valuation. Alternate valuation, which values and taxes business property on the date of distribution, sale, exchange, or other disposition within six months of the death, is governed and controlled by IRC section 2032.

Special-use valuation: In the event of the death of an owner of a FOB or CHB, business heirs or estate executors may petition for special-use valuation to lessen the burden of estate taxes by up to $500,000. The special-use valuation, which determines a

business's value by looking at its usefulness in the activity for which it is mainly employed instead of looking at its ideal use, is governed and controlled by section 2032a of the IRC. Eligibility requirements for the special-use valuation include the following: The deceased business owner or member of the deceased family must have both owned and used the property in the business for a minimum of five of the last eight years; and the deceased business owner must have actively and physically participated in the business.

Disclaimer and qualified terminable interest property (QTIP) election: In the event of the death of an owner of a CHC, business heirs or estate executors may use a disclaimer or qualified terminable interest property (QTIP) election to make it easier to use the deceased's unified tax credit or marital deduction. A disclaimer or qualified terminable interest property election legally allows the use of a deceased business owner's unified tax credit applicable to certain amount of property tax-free. Disclaimers are governed and controlled by IRC section 2518, qualified terminable interest property elections under IRC section 2056.

Delaying payment of business estate taxes: In the event of the death of an owner of a CHC, business heirs or estate executors may be able to delay the payment of business estate taxes. Delayed business estate taxes are subject to interest charges.

Post-mortem stock redemption: In the event of the death of an owner of a CHC, post-mortem stock redemption can be used to cover expenses related to death taxes, funeral costs, and administration expenses. Post-mortem stock redemption is governed and controlled by the IRC section 303. The IRC section 303 states that stock redemption may be used if the stock of a closely held corporation exceeds 35 percent of an individual's adjusted gross estate. Post-mortem stock redemption is not usually subject to income tax.

Ultimately, a business owner's death poses a real threat to the health of his or her business, creates the very real possibility of significant business interruption, and often results in a cash shortage. Federal business estate tax rates may reach 40 percent of the value of the business. Post-mortem business estate planning, while inferior to lifetime business estate planning, may help keep the business operational and profitable.

CONCLUSION

In the final analysis, business estate planning is a vital activity for all FOBs and CHB. Business estate planning is a collaborative effort and process involving valuing the company, determining succession, establishing transfer or sale of business control, assets, and property, and planning for and minimizing estate and gift taxes. Factors and variables that influence the business estate planning process and the business estate value include the following: "Lifetime gifting and gift tax computation; the transfer tax basis; business stability and continuity; generation-skipping taxes; estate taxes; business interest valuation; special use valuation; alternate valuation date; the family owned business deduction; and estate liquidity" (Maccarrone & Warshavsky, 2003). Ultimately, business estate planning is most effective when undertaken prior to a business owner's death or retirement.

TERMS & CONCEPTS

Business estate planning: The minimization of estate or transfer tax as well as active succession planning undertaken when transferring a family owned business (FOB) or closely held business (CHB) to the next generation.

Buy-sell agreements: Buy-sell agreements refer to agreements between business owners to sell the interests of a deceased owner to the other remaining partners at a price determined beforehand.

Closely held business (CHB): A business in which most of the stock is held by a few shareholders who have no plans to sell.

Fair market value: The price that a buyer would be willing to pay and a seller would be willing to accept when neither party has any obligation to buy or sell.

Family owned business (FOB): A business mainly controlled by members of a single family. Two or more family members must be actively involved in the business for it to be designated a family owned business.

Installment sale: The sale of a business to a family member through a manageable payment schedule.

Private annuity: Arrangements in which the buyer of a business receives an asset, such as real estate, from the seller in return for a promise to pay an annuity for life to the seller.

Shareholder agreements: An explicit agreement between a company's shareholders that outlines the way the company should be managed as well as shareholders' rights and responsibilities.

Stock recapitalization: The process of trading in one class of company stock in favor of two different classes: voting and non-voting.

Succession: The process of handing over the control of an organization from a current leader to a new leader.

Voting trust: An agreement in which shareholders transfer stock and voting rights but not financial rights to a small group of individuals for a specified time.

BIBLIOGRAPHY

Blackman, I.L. (2013). Estate plan secrets they don't reveal in law school. *Modern Machine Shop, 86,* 40–42.

Blesy, D. (1993). Estate planning for business owners: A case study. *Journal of Financial Planning, 6,* 179–187.

Grassi, S. (2007). Estate planning for the closely held business after the pension protection act of 2006. *Gifts and Trusts Journal, 32,* 87–131.

Hess, D & Havlik, K. (2005). Attitude adjustment. *Trusts & Estates, 144,* 56–62.

Kess, S., & Mendlowitz, E. (2015). Helping business owners with succession planning. *CPA Journal, 85*(8), 76– .

Maccarrone, E., & Warshavsky, M. (2003). Estate planning for business owners. *CPA Journal, 73,* 34–38.

McAlister, J.R. (2010). Test your planning with a 'fire drill.' *Family Business, 21,* 18–20.

Nelton, S. (1994). What I've learned — part two. *Nation's Business, 82,* 74.

Oliver, J. (1998). Postmortem estate planning for small business owners. *Journal of Accountancy, 186,* 31–35.

Prince, R. & Schutz, A. (1989). Marketing estate planning to small business owners. *Trusts & Estates, 128,* 47–55.

Rattiner, J. (2004). Small estates. *Financial Planning, 34*, 133–137.

Rivers, W. (2012). Classic family business estate planning mistakes: A case study. *Family Business Advisor,* 1–2.

Scroggin, J. (2000). Two realities for a business owner. *Advisor Today, 95*, 50.

Solomon, M. (2000). Estate planning for the business owner. *Ohio CPA Journal, 59*, 51.

Ward, J. The fears of estate planning. (1992). *Nation's Business, 80*, 57–59.

SUGGESTED READING

Garman, A., & Glawe, J. (2004). Succession planning. *Consulting Psychology Journal: Practice & Research, 56*, 119–128.

Hisrchfeld, C. (2002). ESOPs as an estate planning vehicle for business owners. *Journal of Financial Planning, 15*, 92–97.

Lansberg, I., & Gersick, K. (2015). Educating family business owners: The fundamental intervention. *Academy of Management Learning & Education, 14*(3), 400–413.

Lurz, B. (2003). End games. *Professional Builder, 68*, 54–54.

Essay by Simone I. Flynn, Ph.D.

BUSINESS, ETHICS AND SOCIETY

This article focuses on how corporations and the government have responded to unethical behavior by employees. There will be a discussion of the role of whistleblowers as well as how regulations such as the False Claims Act, Sarbanes-Oxley Act (SOX), and the Lloyd-La Follette Act have been implemented in order to encourage employees to report acts of misconduct. In addition, there will be a review of how employees use organizational justice as a factor in the whistle blowing process.

OVERVIEW

Given the competitiveness in the world today, many people are tempted to go outside of the rules and regulations of society in order to get ahead. Although many would argue that traits such as honesty and credibility are valued, temptations have lured some to act irresponsibly. Actions such as cheating, stealing, lying, and bribing have become common in the workplace. Good moral values and actions are becoming the exception rather than the rule. How can the trend turn? Organizations must put policies in place that will encourage employees to do the right thing and inform the proper authorities when illegal actions and dishonesty take place.

Unfortunately, when employees step forward and alert the organization of wrongdoings, they are labeled whistleblowers and negative labels are applied to them. Instead of being considered heroes for doing the right thing, they tend to be chastised and some never fully recover from the experience. For many of these individuals, there is a loss of trust in fellow employees and the organizations in which they work.

> For some, the earth moves when they discover that people in authority routinely lie and that those who work for them routinely cover up. Once one knows this, or rather once one feels this knowledge in one's bones one lives in a new world. Some people remain aliens in the new world forever. Maybe they like it that way. Maybe they don't have a choice (Alford, 2001, p. 52).

This can be a devastating moment for many. Everything that they have believed and trusted is turned upside down. In some cases, these employees may have been friends with the culprits outside of the workplace, which may place an additional burden on the potential whistleblower. It is unfortunate that society has come to a point where individuals with moral values and a sense of right and wrong are treated as outsiders of societal norms. Whistleblowers have been ostracized, reprimanded, forced to transfer, referred to receive psychiatric care, assigned to menial duties, dismissed and blacklisted. There are reports of where they have been unable to seek employment at other companies because there is a fear that the same situation will occur. Organizations respond to whistle blowers with hostility and fear.

The federal government and some states have passed legislation to protect employees who decide to become whistleblowers. According to Sheeder (2006), the federal False Claims Act provides protection for:

> Any employee who is discharged, demoted, suspended, threatened, harassed, or in any other manner discriminated in the terms and conditions of employment by his or her employment because of lawful acts done by the employee on behalf of the employee or others in furtherance of an action under this section (i.e. a whistleblower action) shall be entitled to all relief necessary to make the employee whole (p. 39).

Many courts will provide protection when:

- an employee becomes a participant in a "protected activity" (i.e. when an employee decides to confront an employer about illegal activities such as fraud)
- the employer becomes aware of the "protected activity"

The employee is penalized as a result of coming forth about the "protected activity" (i.e. termination, harassment). When it has been determined that an employee is a victim of retaliation, he or she may petition for:

- reinstatement with the same seniority that he/she would have had if the adverse action did not occur
- two times back pay
- interest on the back pay
- special damages (i.e. compensation for emotional distress, recovery of litigation costs, and reasonable attorney's fees)

Any type of relief that will assist the employee in becoming a whole person again (Sheeder, 2006, p. 39-40). An employee is entitled to all of the relief listed above as well as any recovery obtained by the government based on the regulations of the False Claims Act (FCA).

Given the financial penalties for acts of wrongdoing, employers are encouraged to monitor the activities of their organization so that these fines are not imposed.

- In order to avoid the costly expenses of these types of situations, many organizations are encouraged to draft policies that will assist employees in feeling comfortable about coming forward to advise the senior management team and the outside world of fraudulent behavior occurring in companies today. Tennebaum provided four elements of a good whistleblower policy. The four elements are:
- A policy that has a clear purpose and a statement of intent to protect whistleblowers to the fullest extent possible. The purpose may include creating an environment where the whistleblower can feel safe.
- Guidelines that provide a detailed explanation of how the organization will attempt to protect the whistleblower.
- Procedures on who, when and how to contact the organization in order to report unethical and/or illegal behavior.
- A statement declaring what the organization will do as a result of the whistleblowing activity (Associations Now, 2007, p. 12).
- In addition, employers should be proactive and see if they can determine the types of behaviors or situations that encourage employees to participate in unethical behavior and the types of actions that encourage employees to step up and become whistleblowers. Sheeder (2006) identified six common factors that have encouraged employees to become whistleblowers. In most cases, the lack of organizational support was enough for the employee to seek external assistance in correcting improper behavior. Each of the mentioned scenarios is based on a real life case study.

Expect employees to participate in fraudulent conduct. In many situations, senior managers are the culprits. To try to improve the organization's image and financial records, some executives have encouraged and mandated employees to participate in unethical behavior. Excuses such as "it's really not hurting anyone," "we are getting what we deserve," "be a team player," and "this action offsets the system" have been used to justify the organization's behavior. When an employee refuses to play the game, he or she may be terminated, which forces the former employee to file a retaliation lawsuit.

Dismiss employee concerns or complaints. Some employees have attempted to alert the appropriate officials only to find out their concerns have been ignored. Once they have worked through the appropriate channels within the organization, they may feel as though their only recourse is to go externally and hire an attorney to champion their cause.

Forget about a professional's ethical duty to report. Some employees may feel that they are obligated to report unethical practices to maintain the image of their profession. For example, a police officer may become aware that his partner is working with criminals. After attempting to reason with the partner, the police officer may feel a need to alert Internal Affairs to maintain a positive image of police officers in the eyes of the community and protect the public from criminal activities.

Don't give "Public Duty" enough respect. There have been cases where an organization may be overbilling another entity and the employee may not be able to support the deception. For example, some hospitals have been accused of overcharging Medicare programs. There may be an employee who believes that the process is unethical and innocent people may suffer as a result of the deceptive actions. Therefore, the employee feels obligated to turn the hospital in to the proper authorities. The employee may believe that it is his or her civic and public duty to do so.

Fail to take prompt and proper action correction. Many employees have followed the company's policy on reporting fraudulent activity only to find out that their good deed has been ignored. They believe their only alternative is to expose the situation externally since the system has failed internally.

Underestimate the perseverance of an employee. Some organizations wrongly assume that if they ignore the employee, the problem will go away. However, employees with a conscience will pursue their cause until the problem has been resolved.

Organizations need to realize there are people who value their conscience over their job. The government recognized that big business may not always do the right thing. Therefore, it has introduced and implemented some regulations to level the playing field and allow employees to come forth. Examples of such legislation are:

False Claims Act (FCA) A qui tam provision that was enacted during Abraham Lincoln's tenure as president. This legislation was aimed at preventing the sale of faulty war equipment by fraudulent suppliers to the government (during the Civil War). Revisions were made to the Act in 1943 and 1986. In 1986, there was a significant expansion of the rights of whistleblowers and their attorneys. The law allows individuals to file actions against federal contractors claiming fraud against the government. People filing under the Act may receive 15–25 percent of any recovered damages.

Sarbanes-Oxley Act (SOX) Legislation passed in 2002 with the purpose of encouraging employees to become effective corporate monitors and report misconduct and unethical behavior in corporations. The act has two approaches that encourage employees to become corporate whistleblowers (Moberly, 2006). The first step is a clause that provides protection to whistleblowers from employer retaliation once they have disclosed improper behavior. The second step requires employers to provide employees with guidelines, policies, and procedures to report organizational misconduct within the organization.

Lloyd-La Follette Act. This Act was enacted in 1912 and was designed to protect American civil servants from retaliation. The purpose was to ensure the right of employees when they wanted to provide the House of Congress, a committee or individual congressman with information about fraud. The intent was to provide conferring job protection rights to federal employees.

No-FEAR Act The Notification and Federal Employee Antidiscrimination and Retaliation (No-FEAR) Act of 2002 went into effect on October 1, 2003. The law applies to federal agencies and is aimed at keeping employees informed of their rights under anti-discrimination and whistleblower protection laws. The No-FEAR Act also protects against retaliatory actions on the part of employers and provides for the reimbursement of current and former federal employees and federal applicants for costs incurred in the course of asserting their rights under said anti-discrimination and whistleblower protection laws.

APPLICATION

Life of a Whistleblower

Two of the most discussed fraud cases in history have been Enron and Worldcom. Coincidentally, both of the whistleblowers in these two cases were women who had risen to the ranks of vice president in their respective organizations. A study conducted by two professors at St. Mary's College in Indiana found that female business students value honesty and independence more than their male counterparts (Allen, 2002). Women may be more prone to expose wrongdoing due to their value system.

Cynthia Cooper was a vice president at Worldcom, and Sherron Watkins was a vice president at Enron. The circumstances surrounding both cases were so shocking that it made the public acknowledge how corrupt some organizations had become. Worldcom would become known as the company that created the largest accounting fraud in history (Ripley, 2002). "Enron and Worldcom have become America's twin symbols of business malfeasance, but share a different kind of similarity: In each case the public learned the extent of the scandal in large part through the actions of a brave woman who did the right thing by going over her boss' head" (Colvin, 2002, p. 56).

Worldcom

Worldcom's headquarters was located in Clinton, Mississippi. The founder, Bernie Ebbers, went to college there and wanted to move his company to the area. Cynthia Cooper had grown up in the area as well and was proud of the organization. She became the vice president of internal auditing. Unfortunately, in June of 2002, she had to tell the audit committee of Worldcom's board that the organization was unethical in its accounting practices (Ripley, 2002).

Worldcom had started out as a small company in 1983, but became a major powerhouse in the 1990s. Most of the executives were in their late thirties and making millions of dollars. However, there was a glut of companies like Worldcom by early 2001. Many believe that this was the time that the organization

started to use creative accounting practices. Cooper was not part of the illegal activities, but many of the people whom she had respected were a part of the scandal. Even the organization's external auditor, Arthur Andersen, was alleged to be part of the cover-up. Many of the activities were geared toward providing fraudulent information to the Securities Exchange Commission (SEC).

Cooper stayed at Worldcom once she became a whistleblower. Although she became physically and emotionally exhausted, she persevered because she did not want the innocent employees of the company to suffer. Even though Cooper can be credited as a major influence for the country starting to take corporate governance to heart, no one from the senior management team at Worldcom acknowledged the sacrifice that she had made. When speaking at different conferences, she has offered the following advice to corporations:

- Protect whistleblowers so that they can continue to provide information to support their allegations.
- Set an ethical tone at the top. In the Worldcom situation, the deceitful few were members of the senior management team.
- Hold more committee meetings and consider going into executive sessions.
- Remain flexible in the course of auditing and maintain an element of surprise (Peterson, 2005).

VIEWPOINT

Organizational Justice

Alford (2001) has been quoted as saying that "the whistleblower is a political actor in a nonpolitical world" (p. 97). This statement should be interpreted as meaning that the whistleblower responds to his/her value system in an organization where the value system has no role. Employees may view situations in terms of right or wrong, whereas, the employer may view situations in terms of the bottom line and financial profit. In essence, the purpose of the employee is to make sure that the business makes money. The end justifies the means. What can an organization do to support employees who want to do the right thing and view the organization as a fair and ethical place to work?

Organizational justice is a concept that explores an employee's perception about whether or not an organization is fair in making decisions and/or the decision making processes within organizations and the influences of those perceptions on behavior. Research has shown that organizational performance is improved as a result of improved ethical decision making (Hatcher, 2002; Swanson, 1999). Many have researched this area in hope of understanding why and how ethical decisions are made in order. By understanding the thought process behind an employee's decision making, human resource professionals may be able to create an environment that encourages ethical actions in the organization. "According to a national business ethics survey, 40% of professionals in human resource management and development roles must respond to their organization's ethical situations and in 70% of organizations, these same professionals are viewed as their organization's experts on ethics" (Joseph & Esen, 2003).

As the business community embraces a global economy, there has been a push to speed up processes in order to make more profit. As a result, some employees see taking shortcuts as the only way to stay on top in a competitive environment. In order to accomplish ambitious goals, some may be tempted to participate in unethical behavior. Thus, organizational acceptance may be a factor as to why some people make unethical decisions. Research supporting the understanding of the ethical decision-making process may assist human resource professionals in creating an environment where employees are encouraged to make ethical decisions.

"The result of justice research suggests that the effects of injustice within organizations may be much broader than previously thought" (Cropanzano, Golman & Folger, 2003). "Not only do victims directly affected by organizational injustice consider and sometimes take retributive actions, but so do neutral observers" (Kray & Lind, 2002). As a result of the recent scandals, institutions of higher education have been challenged to teach students the virtues of ethical behavior and organizations have been challenged to create an ethical environment. Those who have devoted their time to researching the importance of organizational justice may be of assistance to this cause.

CONCLUSION

Given the competitiveness in the world today, many people are tempted to go outside of the rules and regulations of society in order to get ahead. Although many would argue that traits such as honesty and credibility are valued, temptations have lured some to act irresponsibly. Unfortunately, when employees step forward and alert the organization of wrongdoings, they are labeled whistleblowers and negative labels are applied to them. Instead of being considered heroes for doing the right thing, they tend to be chastised and some never fully recover from the experience. Once Cynthia Cooper realized her work had been done at Worldcom, she left and formed her own consulting firm. Cynthia decided to branch out and speak at corporations, associations, and universities about ethics and leadership and how it related to her situation at Worldcom (Amer, 2007).

The government recognized that big business may not always do the right thing. Therefore, it has introduced and implemented some regulations to level the playing field and allow employees to come forth. The federal government and some states have passed legislation to protect employees who decide to become whistle blowers. In order to avoid the costly expenses of litigation, many organizations are encouraged to draft policies that will help employees feel comfortable about coming forward to advise the senior management team and the outside world of fraudulent behavior occurring in companies today.

Organizational justice is a concept that explores an employee's perception about whether or not an organization is fair in making decisions and/or the decision making processes within organizations and the influences of those perceptions on behavior. By understanding the thought process behind an employee's decision making, human resource professionals may be able to create an environment that encourages ethical actions in the organization.

TERMS & CONCEPTS

Cynthia Cooper: The whistleblower who exposed the corporate scandal at Worldcom.

Ethics: The philosophical study which concentrates on tenants of right and wrong, good and evil, and responsibility within groups or cultures; has a strong correlation with the values and customs of individuals and groups alike.

Enron: Formerly applauded and successful electricity, natural gas, pulp and paper, and communications supplier based out of Houston, Texas. In 2001, it was discovered that Enron's financial status was maintained through carefully executed accounting fraud; the company now serves as an infamous example of corruption.

False Claims Act (FCA): A qui tam provision that was enacted during Abraham Lincoln's tenure as president. This legislation was aimed at preventing the sale of faulty war equipment by fraudulent suppliers to the government (during the Civil War). Revisions were made to the Act in 1943 and 1986. In 1986, there was a significant expansion of the rights of whistleblowers and their attorneys.

Lloyd-La Follette Act: This Act was enacted in 1912 and was designed to protect American civil servants from retaliation.

Organizational justice: An umbrella term used to refer to individuals' perceptions about the fairness of decisions and decision-making processes within organizations and the influences of those perceptions on behavior

Sarbanes-Oxley (SOX) Act: Legislation passed in 2002 with the purpose of encouraging employees to become effective corporate monitors and report misconduct and unethical behavior in corporations.

No-FEAR Act Legislation passed in 2002 that ensures federal agencies keep employees informed of their rights under anti-discrimination and whistleblower protection laws, and seeks to create a workplace free from discrimination or retaliation.

Securities Exchange Commission (SEC): Government body which is tasked with enforcing federal securities laws as well as industry and stock market regulation.

Sherron Watkins: Former vice president of corporate development at the Enron Corporation; rumored to have been the whistleblower of the 2001 Enron scandal.

Whistleblowers: An employee, a former employee, or a member of an organization, especially a business or government agency, who reports misconduct to people or entities that have the power and presumed willingness to take corrective action. Generally, the

misconduct is a violation of law, rule, regulation and/or a direct threat to public interest — fraud, health, safety violations, and corruption are just a few examples.

BIBLIOGRAPHY

Alford, C. (2001). *Whistleblowers: Broken lives and organizational power.* Ithaca and London: Cornell University Press.

Allen, J. (2002). Women who blow whistles... *U.S. News World Report, 133,* 48.

Amer, S. (2005). Do the right thing. *Successful Meetings, 54,* 72.

Baden, D. (2014). Look on the bright side: a comparison of positive and negative role models in business ethics education. Academy Of Management Learning Education, 13, 154–170.

Colvin, G. (2002). Wonder women of whistle blowing. *Fortune, 146,* 56.

Cropanzo, R., Golman, B., & Folger, R. (2003). Deontic justice: The role of moral principles in workplace fairness. *Journal of Organizational Behavior, 24,* 1019–1024.

Elements of whistleblower policy. (2007). *Associations Now, 3,* 12.

Floyd, L. A., Xu, F., Atkins, R., & Caldwell, C. (2013). Ethical outcomes and business ethics: toward improving business ethics education. *Journal Of Business Ethics,* 117, 753–776.

Hatcher, T. (2002). *Ethics and HRD: A new approach to leading responsible organizations.* Cambridge, MA: Perseus Publishers.

Joseph, J., & Esen, E. (2003). *SHRM/Ethics resource center 2003 business ethics survey.* Alexandria, VA: SHRM.

Joshi, J. (2012). Ethics, business and society: managing responsibility. *South Asian Journal of Management, 19,* 148–150.

Kelly, J. (2002, December 30). The year of the whistleblowers. *Time South Pacific (Australia/New Zealand edition),* (51/52), 10.

Kray, L., & Lind, A. (2002). The injustices of others: Social reports and the integration of others' experiences in organizational justice judgments. *Organizational Behavior and Human Decision Processes, 89,* 906–924.

Lin-Hi, N., & Blumberg, I. (2012). Managing the social acceptance of business: Three core competencies in business ethics. *Business Professional Ethics Journal, 31,* 247–263.

Moberly, R. (2006). Sarbanes-Oxley's structural model to encourage corporate whistleblowers. *Brigham Young University Law Review, 2006*, 1107–1175.

Peterson, A. (2005). Inside the WorldCom fraud. *Credit Union Magazine, 71*, 15–20.

Rakas, S. (2011). Global business ethics - utopia or reality. *Megatrend Review, 8*, 385–406.

Ripley, A. (2002). The night detective. *Time Canada, 160/161 (27/1)*, 36.

Ruud, J., & Ruud, W.N. (2011). Law and ethics: society and corporate social responsibility: is the focus shifting?. *Journal of Academic & Business Ethics*, 41–31.

Sheeder, F. (2006). Whistleblowers are not born that way — We create them through multiple system failures. *Journal of Health Care Compliance, 8*, 39–73.

Swan, R. (1999). Foundations of performance improvement and implications for practice. In R. Torraco (Ed.), *Performance Improvement Theory and Practice*, (pp. 1–25). San Francisco: Berrett-Koehler.

SUGGESTED READING

Abend, G. (2013). The origins of business ethics in American universities, 1902-1936. Business Ethics Quarterly, 23, 171–205.

Aguilera, R., Rupp, D., Williams, C., & Ganapathi, J. (2007). Putting the S back in corporate social responsibility: A multilevel theory of social change in organizations. *Academy of Management Review, 32*, 836–863.

Barrier, M., & Cooper, C. (2003). One right path. *Internal Auditor, 60*, 52–57.

Gleeson, W., & Minier, J. (2003). Why companies need to adopt whistleblower policies now. *Banking Financial Services Policy Report, 22*, 1–6.

McNamee, M., & Fleming, S. (2007). Ethics audits and corporate governance: The case of public sector sports organizations. *Journal of Business Ethics, 73*, 425–437.

Essay by Marie Gould

BUYOUT OF ACQUISITIONS

This article focuses on acquisitions, especially leveraged and management buyouts. These types of transactions are very unique and have been around since the 1970s. There is a discussion of Frankel's strategic transaction process. There are several types of investors. Two types of private capital equity are venture capitalists and angel investors.

OVERVIEW

"Merger and acquisitions, buyouts, leveraged buyouts (LBOs), management buyouts (MBOs), private equity, venture capital, corporate development, and a myriad of other terms are used to describe large transactions that fundamentally change the nature or course, and control, of a company" (Frankel, 2005, p. ix). However, this article focuses on LBOs and MBOs. These types of transactions are very unique and have been around since the 1970s. Once a rarity, it is very common for a business to be bought out in order to strengthen its worth. Unlike other commercial contracts and agreements, these types of transactions tend to be dramatic and sudden with many businesses losing their independence once the deal has been sealed.

The Players

According to Frankel (2005), all the transactions have some things in common even though the focus and process may be different. Who are the key players in what Frankel calls the "Strategic Transactions" process? These players are the buyer, seller, investors/owners, corporate staff, advisors, regulators, and others. However, this article will focus on the buyers, sellers, and investors/owners.

Buyers

The buyer usually refers to a group of individuals that forms an entity in order to maximize the interest of the corporation and the shareholders. There are many types of buyers, including strategic buyers, repeat players, newbies or one-timers, financial buyers, private equity firms, and management buyers.

- Strategic buyers are usually corporations that are interested in making an acquisition in order to strengthen and upgrade their poor business performance.
- Repeat players tend to go through the acquisition process more than once. As a result, they can rec-

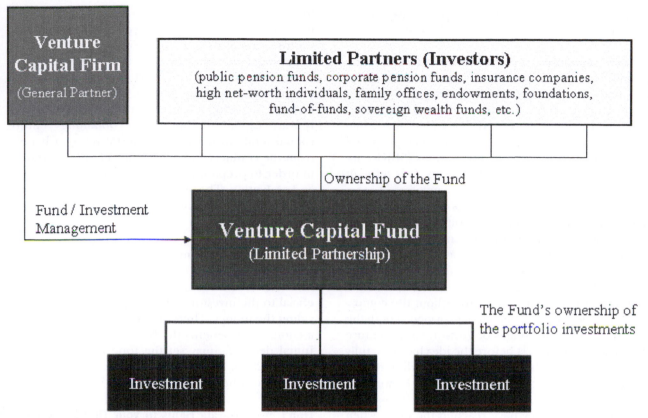

Diagram of the structure of a generic venture capital fund. (Courtesy of Urbanrenewal via Wikimedia Commons)

ognize what they have done well and strive to improve what they do not do well.

- Most first-time buyers are nervous in the beginning, but strive to get the experience of making strategic transactions so that they can become repeat buyers.
- Financial buyers tend to use some form of investor capital in order to acquire control over a target company with the goal of selling the company for a profit.
- Private equity firms are those that collect a pool of capital from others and then make investments in a portfolio of companies.
- Management buyers tend to partner with a private equity firm in order to acquire a company.

Sellers

There are three types of sellers: partial sellers, full sellers, and unwilling sellers. Many acquisitions involve the sale of part of the company versus the whole thing.

- In most cases, partial sales are usually the first step in a series of transactions of selling the entire company.
- Full sellers have a desire to get rid of the company as soon as possible.
- Unwilling sellers may be the target of another company and the process can be hostile.

Investors/Owners

There are several types of investors. However, this article will focus on entrepreneurs, private equity firms, angels investors, venture capitalists, and leveraged buyout (LBO) and management buyout (MBO) firms. Entrepreneurs are very creative. Many seek to see their vision become a reality. Once the business is successful, they may decide to "step aside" and let the management team run the company. Many businesses are started with the founders' capital. However, once the business gets started, they may find that they need additional funding and seek the assistance of private equity firms. Two types of private capital equity are venture capitalists and angel investors.

Venture capitalists: Venture capital is usually available for start-up companies with a product or an idea that may risky but has a high potential of yielding above-average profits. Funds are invested in ventures that have not been discovered. The money may come from wealthy individuals, government sponsored Small Business Investment Corporations (SBICs), insurance companies, and corporations. It is difficult to obtain financing from venture capitalists. A company must provide a formal proposal such as a business plan so that the venture capitalist may conduct a thorough evaluation of the company's records. Venture capitalists only approve a small percentage of the proposals they receive and tend to favor innovative technical ventures.

Funding may be invested throughout the company's life cycle with funding being provided at both the beginning and later stages of growth. Some venture capital firms may invest before the idea has been fully developed while others may provide funding during the early stages of the company's life. However, a group of venture capitalists specializes in assisting companies when they have reached the point when the company needs financing in order to expand the business. Finally, the venture capitalists may provide funding in order to buy (acquire) a business.

Angel investors: Many firms receive some type of funding prior to seeking capital from venture capitalists. Angel Investors have been identified as one source that organizations, especially entrepreneurs, may reach out to for assistance (Gompers, 1995). "In a nationwide survey of more than 3,000 individual angel investors conducted by the Angel Capital Association (ACA), more than 96 percent predict they'll invest in at least one new company in 2007. Also, 77 percent expect to invest in three to nine startups, and 5 percent think they'll fund 10 or more new companies" (Edelhauser, 2007, "Angel"). This is beneficial for future entrepreneurs who have a dream they would like to pursue.

Including angel investors in the early stages of financing could improve the chances of receiving venture capital financing. Madill, Haines, and Rlding (2005) conducted a study with small businesses and found that "57% of the firms that had received angel investor financing had also received financing from venture capitalists" (p. 107). Firms that did not receive angel investing in the early stages (approximately 10 percent of the firms in the study) did not obtain venture capital funding. It appears that angel investor financing is a significant factor in obtaining venture capital funding. Since obtaining venture capital tends to be difficult, businesses can benefit from the contacts and experience of angel investors in order to prepare for a venture capital application and evaluation. The intervention of an angel investor may make the company appear more attractive to the venture capitalists.

Forming an Agreement

Regardless of how a company decides to finance the venture, it will have to make an agreement that is beneficial to the investor since he or she is the one providing the money. Therefore, it is important to select a choice that benefits the business in the long run. Initial decisions may set the tone for future deals. Advani (2006) has provided some recommendations to consider when determining what will work best:

Don't give pro-rata rights to your first investors. If your first investor is given pro-rata rights, chances are your future investors will want the same agreement. It would be wise to balance the needs of your early investors to protect their stake in the company with how attractive the company will be to future investors.

Avoid giving too many people the right to be overly involved. If too many people are involved, it could create a bureaucracy and make it difficult for decisions to be made in a timely manner. In addition, the daily tasks of a business may be prolonged due to the need for multiple authorization signatures.

Beware of any limits placed on management compensation. Some investors may place a cap on the earning potential of senior management personnel. This type of action could create a problem with human resource needs such as attracting and hiring quality talent to run and grow the business.

Request a cure period. Many investors will request representation for every legal agreement to protect themselves if the management of a company is not in compliance with laws, licenses, and regulations that govern the operation of the business. Although all parties may have good intentions, errors do occur. If a "cure period" is added to the financing agreement, the entrepreneur will have the opportunity to find a solution to the problem within a given period of time (e.g., two to four weeks).

Restrict your share restrictions. Having unrestricted shares is often a good negotiating factor with future investors. Therefore, it would be wise to evaluate any requests to restrict the sale of shares owned by the founders and/or management team.

APPLICATION

Leveraged & Management Buyouts

A leveraged buyout (LBO) is the process of acquiring a company where the purchase price is financed by borrowing money. The major advantage of a LBO is that a buyer can purchase a large company with a small amount of money. Another form of a private equity acquisition is the MBO. In an MBO, the management team acquires the company with funding that comes from their personal finances combined with funding from a private equity firm.

As mentioned in the previous section, buyouts tend to occur when an entity borrows money in order to acquire a company. It may be a private equity firm or it may be a combination of the private equity firm with the management team of the organization.

The Appeal of Leveraged Buyouts (LBO)

According to Dartmouth College's Center for Private Equity and Entrepreneurship (2003), LOBs have a number of appealing characteristics for managers. Some of these characteristics include:

- tax advantages associated with debt financing;
- freedom from the scrutiny of being a public company or a captive division of a larger parent;
- the ability for founders to take advantage of a liquidity event without ceding operational influence or sacrificing continued day-to-day involvement; and
- e opportunity for managers to become owners of a significant percentage of a firm's equity (p. 3).

Many considering whether or not to pursue a LBO/MBO acquisition may be swayed by the following advantages:

- Internal process and transfer of responsibilities remain confidential and are often handled quickly.
- Continuity with the company's business will reduce the risk.
- Experienced management team understands the needs of the business.
- The company's existing clients and business partners are reassured.
- Opportunity to obtain interesting return on investment (BDC, nod., p. 1).

Steps to LBO & MBO Transfers

Some of the common steps that need to be taken in order to transfer power include:

- Buyer and seller agree on a sale price that may result in a win-win transaction.
- A valuation of the business confirms the agreed upon price.
- Managers assess the portion of the shares that can be purchased immediately and draft the shareholder agreement.
- Financial institutions are approached.
- A transition plan is developed that incorporates tax and succession planning.
- Managers buy out the owner's interest with financial support.
- Decision-making and ownership powers are transferred to the successors. This process can take place gradually over a period of a few months or a few years.
- Managers pay back the financial institution (BDC, n.d. p. 2).

In order to be successful, there are steps that a LBO and MBO must take. For example, a LBO should:

- Research the company to be purchased and make sure that the company's assets are sufficient to secure the necessary loans.
- Make sure that the management team is strong and will continue with the company once the buyout has taken place.
- Hire a professional to act as a middleman in the negotiations with the management team, shareholders, potential investors and board members.

- Assemble a team of LBO specialists, investment bankers, accountants and attorneys (eHow, n.d., "Step 1 – 5").

When there is an opportunity for a MBO acquisition, the team of managers will need to make sure that (ThisIsMoney, n.d):

- They possess a diverse spread of skills and talents.
- The business is viable.
- The existing owner of the business is willing to sell.
- A realistic price for the business has been established.

CONCLUSION

"Merger and acquisitions, buyouts, leveraged buyouts (LBOs), management buyouts (MBOs), private equity, venture capital, corporate development, and a myriad of other terms are used to describe large transactions that fundamentally change the nature or course, and control, of a company" (Frankel, 2005, p. ix). However, this article focuses on LBOs, MBOs, and employee buyouts. These types of transactions are very unique, and have been around since the 1970s. Once a rarity, it is very common for a business to be bought out in order to strengthen its worth. Unlike other commercial contracts and agreements, these types of transactions tend to be dramatic and sudden with many businesses losing their independence once the deal has been sealed.

All entrepreneurs believe in the success of their dream and expect their ventures to take off and expand. One of the greatest challenges for new ventures is the ability to secure capital for investments that will allow the company to grow. All projects will reach a crossroad where sufficient cash flow is necessary in order to go to the next level. It could be after a period of time or it could be because the venture was so popular that the company is growing at a rapid rate due to demand. Regardless of the situation, the company's management team will need to determine when and how they will invest in items such as purchasing new equipment, hiring new staff, and putting more money into marketing initiatives. Raising money can be a difficult task if the company has not established a reputation or is still new.

When determining the amount of capital needed, the decision makers must analyze the situation and decide how much and what type of capital is required.

Since the situation is not the same for all businesses, there is no magic formula. Some businesses may only need short-term financing for items such as salaries and inventory; whereas, other businesses may need long-term financing for major items such as office space and equipment. Each business must develop a customized plan that will meet its unique needs.

Securing capital is a choice made after weighing the pros and cons of various options. There are three popular sources for obtaining funding for new ventures: borrowing from financial institutions, partnering with venture capitalists, and selling equity/ownership in exchange for a share of the revenue (Goel & Hasan, 2004). All financing options can be classified into two categories: debt financing and equity capital.

Many considering whether or not to pursue a LBO/MBO acquisition may be swayed by the following advantages:

- Internal process and transfer of responsibilities remain confidential and are often handled quickly.
- Continuity with the company's business will reduce the risk.
- Experienced management team understands the needs of the business.
- The company's existing clients and business partners are reassured.
- Opportunity to obtain interesting return on investment (BDC, n.d., p. 1).

Some of the common steps that need to be taken to transfer power include (BDC, nod. p. 2):

- Buyer and seller agree on a sale price that may result in a win-win transaction.
- A valuation of the business confirms the agreed upon price.
- Managers assess the portion of the shares they could purchase immediately and draft the shareholder agreement.
- Financial institutions are approached.
- A transition plan is developed that incorporates tax and succession planning.
- Managers' buy out the owner's interest with financial support.
- Decision-making and ownership powers are transferred to the successors. (This process can take

place gradually over a period of a few months or a few years.)

- Managers pay back the financial institution.

Terms & Concepts

Acquisition: The obtainment of control of a business or target by purchasing or exchanging stock through friendly or hostile means.

Angel investors: Someone who provides capital to one or more startup institutions or corporations. The provided capital is constituted from beneficial and powerful contacts and a superior expertise in the field.

Investments: The attainment of a portion of a financial product or item of value that is made in the hopes of receiving larger returns in the future. Generally, investment is using and risking money in order for it to grow and replicate over time.

Leveraged buyout (LBO): The takeover of a corporation or control over the interests of a business by utilizing a sum of borrowed money. The business's assets usually stand as collateral for the money that is loaned.

Management buyout (MBO): The acquisition of all or part of a business made by the company's own managers or executives.

Merger: The combination of two or more corporations into one, usually as a result of a purchase or joining of interests. Mergers differ from consolidations because mergers are simply joined together, and a new entity is not created.

Venture capitalists: A term that defines a type of investor who offers capital to startup ventures or smaller businesses with potential for expansion, but does so without the aid of public funding.

Bibliography

Advani, A. (2006, November 10). Start-up financing trends for 2007. *Entrepreneur.com.*

Advani, A. (2006, October 12). Raising money from informal investors. *Entrepreneur.com.*

The Business Development Bank of Canada. (n.d.). Management buyout demystified.

Center For Private Equity and Entrepreneurship. (2003, September 30). Note on leveraged buyouts.

Edelhauser, K. (2007, April 11). Angel investing to grow in '07. *Entrepreneur.com.*

Frankel, M. (2005). *Mergers and acquisitions basics: The key steps of acquisitions, divestitures, and investments.* Hoboken, NJ: John Wiley & Sons, Inc.

Goel, R. K., & Hasan, I. (2004). Funding new ventures: Some strategies for raising early finance. *Applied Financial Economics, 14*, 773–778.

Gompers, P. A. (1995). Optimal investment, monitoring, and the staging of venture capital. *Journal of Finance, 50*, 1461–1490.

Guo, S., Hotchkiss, E. S., & Song, W. (2011). Do buyouts (still) create value? *Journal of Finance, 66*, 479–517.

How to perform a leveraged buyout. (n.d.). *eHow.*

Madill, J., Haines Jr., G., & Rlding, A. (2005). The role of angels in technology SMEs: A link to venture capital. *Venture Capital, 7*, 107–129

Management buyouts. (n.d.). *Thisismoney.co.uk.*

Wirz, M. (2012, December 17). Debt loads climb in buyout deals. *Wall Street Journal - Eastern Edition.* pp. C1–C2.

Suggested Reading

Brody, H. (2007). The buyout cash-out. *Smart Money, 16*, 71.

Platt, G. (2007). M&A activity to stay hot in some sectors. *Global Finance, 21*, 64.

Ryan, F. (2007). HIMA acquires NOVA Infusion in leveraged buyout. *Caribbean Business, 35*, 2.

Essay by Marie Gould

C

CAPITAL BUDGETING

ABSTRACT

Capital budgeting is the procedure for establishing whether or not a company should invest in projects such as new facilities or products. This article presents the most common methods of capital budgeting; discusses economic issues in capital budgeting unique to three types of companies: steel producers, small companies, and U.S. multinational subsidiaries; and provides a glossary of relevant terms.

OVERVIEW

When a company plans to invest in new facilities, equipment, or products, it may engage in capital budgeting. Capital budgeting is a strategy that a company can utilize to plan future investment projects.

A company utilizes capital budgeting to establish whether a project's benefits will outweigh the costs of investing in the project. The process generally involves constructing a formula that considers total funds needed for the project, including working capital; the financial benefits expected from the project; the length of time needed to reap the financial benefits of the project; and whether it is better to forego the project completely. For example, a company that manufactures furniture is considering whether or not to also start manufacturing its own fabric for the furniture. The furniture manufacturer can use capital budgeting to determine the most financially profitable option for manufacturing fabric among the following four investment projects:

- Remodel a current facility to accommodate a fabric manufacturing operation
- Build a new fabric manufacturing facility
- Purchase an existing fabric manufacturing company.

- Continue to purchase the fabric rather than manufacture it. (If this option is chosen, the project is then removed from consideration as a capital budgeting project.)

FURTHER INSIGHTS

As part of the capital budgeting process, companies consider their access to funds; their need for cash flow to operate the company throughout the time line for any capital budgeting project; and in some instances, their responsibility to shareholders.

Capital Budgeting Valuation Methods
A variety of approaches and mathematical formulas may be used in capital budgeting. Four of the most common approaches used in capital budgeting are based on the following four valuation methods:

- Net Present Value (NPV)
- Internal Rate of Return (IRR)
- Discounted Cash Flow (DCF)
- Payback Period

Net Present Value (NPV)
The first capital budgeting valuation method is net present value (NPV). NPV reflects the variance between the current amount of cash inflows and the current amount of cash outflows. "Present value" refers to the current worth of money that will be received in the future, based on a particular rate of return.

Internal Rate of Return (IRR)
The second capital budgeting valuation method is internal rate of return (IRR). IRR, which is sometimes called "economic rate of return," refers to

The U.S. Steel Tower in New York City, now One Liberty Plaza. (Courtesy of Team Tiara as part of the Commons: Wikis Take Manhattan project, via Wikimedia Commons)

the discount rate that renders the NPV of all cash flows for a specific project equal to zero. Usually, the higher the IRR for a specific project, the more financially attractive the project will be.

Discounted Cash Flow (DCF)

The third capital budgeting valuation method is discounted cash flow (DCF). In DCF, future free cash flows are discounted to arrive at a present value. For a project to be considered worthwhile according to this valuation method, the DCF must be greater than the present investment cost.

Payback Period

The last capital budgeting valuation method is the payback period, which refers to the amount of time needed to recapture the cost of an investment. In general, the sooner a company can recover the cost of its investment, the more financially attractive the project will be.

The payback method of valuation does not measure the time value of money or reflect any financial benefits that would occur after the payback period. Therefore, this method of capital budgeting is considered less effective than the NPV, IRR, or DCF methods.

ISSUES

Economic Issues in Capital Budgeting Decisions

In addition to considering their corporate financial goals, companies need to also consider how national and international economic issues will affect their capital budgeting decisions.

This section explores three topics that consider the economic issues that affect capital budgeting:

- a capital budgeting issue for U.S. steel producers
- the capital budgeting decisions of small companies
- the results of an analysis of capital budgeting strategies of U.S. multinational subsidiaries

A Capital Budgeting Issue for U.S. Steel Producers

The first economic issue in capital budgeting covers a capital budgeting issue for U.S. steel producers.

Should U.S. steel producers expand their capacity to avoid being the lowest-cost suppliers to the U.S. market? At least one industry analyst says "No." Michelle Applebaum, an independent steel industry analyst, discusses why she disagrees with those who think that U.S. steel producers need to expand their capacity (production) to prosper in the marketplace.

Applebaum offers three reasons why expanding capacity is not desirable:

- Limited resources, such as scrap metal, are available.
- The delivery of steelmaking equipment requires an exceptionally long lead time.
- The potential for a surge in exports from China remains an economic threat.

She reasons that any capital budgeting that includes a new capacity project would have to assume a period of negative returns to yield a net positive return (Applebaum, 2007, p. 91).

Instead of investing in capital budgeting projects to increase production capacity, Applebaum suggests that it would be more mutually beneficial for steel producers and their customers to engage in the following practices:

Steel producers: Allow for flexible arrangements with customers. Reduce volume when business conditions warrant this practice, rather than forcing customers to buy according to previous contract arrangements.

Customers: Honor your price commitments with the producers.

Steel producers and customers: Share surcharge responsibility. Surcharges allow visibility into pricing for raw materials and as such are necessary, but producers can show flexibility; when the prices of raw materials decrease, they can decrease the surcharges.

The Capital Budgeting Decisions of Small Companies

The second economic issue in capital budgeting covers the capital budgeting decisions of small companies.

Based on data compiled by the National Federation of Independent Business (NFIB), Danielson and Scott (2006) analyzed the capital budgeting decisions of small businesses. Although the U.S. Small Business Administration (SBA) defines small businesses as those with fewer than 500 employees, Danielson and Scott based their study on companies with fewer than 250 employees.

Danielson and Scott based their study on 792 observations and segmented the industries into four groups: service; construction and manufacturing; retail/wholesale; and other. Their analysis of the data addressed three aspects of capital budgeting in small companies:

- investment activity
- planning activity
- project evaluation technique

Investment Activity

The first aspect of capital budgeting in small companies that is addressed is investment activity. For companies in the construction and manufacturing industries, their most significant investments during the previous year were almost evenly distributed among replacement of equipment, expansion of existing products, and introduction of a new product line.

Planning Activity

The second aspect of capital budgeting in small companies that is addressed is planning activity. For companies in the construction and manufacturing industries, 68 percent made cash flow projections before making a major investment; 32 percent wrote a business plan; and 71 percent considered their tax situation.

Project Evaluation Technique

The last aspect of capital budgeting in small companies that is addressed is project evaluation technique. The majority of construction and manufacturing companies (22 percent) used an informal "gut feel" method to determine whether a project was financially attractive. At 19 percent, the payback period method was the second most popular evaluation technique in capital budgeting among this group of companies.

Analysis Conclusions

In summary, Danielson and Scott (2006) concluded that the capital budgeting strategies of small companies are often characterized by the following factors:

- They frequently balanced wealth maximization against objectives such as maintaining the independence of the business.
- They often lacked the personnel and resources to complete in-depth capital budgeting analyses.
- They frequently relied upon either the payback period method of capital budgeting or the owner's "gut feeling." This practice contrasts with that of large companies, who were more likely to use the discounted cash flow analysis method.

The Results of an Analysis of Budgeting Strategies of U.S. Multinational Subsidiaries

The last economic issue in capital budgeting covers the budgeting strategies of U.S. multinational subsidiaries.

According to a study by Hasan, Shao, & Shao (1997) of 159 foreign subsidiaries of U.S.-based multinational manufacturing enterprises operating in 43 companies, additional influences complicate the capital budgeting decisions of multinational subsidiaries.

They identified the following five complicating factors (Hasan, Shao, & Shao, 1997, p. 68):

- complex cash flow estimates;
- foreign exchange rate fluctuations;
- varying accounting systems;
- financial risks;
- political uncertainties.

The authors determined that the capital budgeting process for multinational enterprises is affected by factors that do not affect domestic companies.

Based on their analysis of the respondents' responses to the survey, they reached the following conclusions (Hasan et al., 1997, p. 75):

- The refinement of the capital budgeting strategies of foreign subsidiaries correlated to levels of ownership status and financial leverage. In general, in those situations where the parent companies owned most of the subsidiaries' shares, more sophisticated capital budgeting strategies were likely to be employed.
- The sources used to determine discount rates were positively related to the age of the firm, the total asset size, and whether the subsidiaries were publicly traded.
- Publicly traded subsidiaries, firms with credit regulations implemented by outside creditors, and asset size were closely associated with refined risk-adjustment capital budgeting strategies.

CONCLUSION

When a company engages in capital budgeting, it carefully assesses which projects are most important to the company's strategy and financial future because capital budgeting projects will consume a large financial investment and greatly affect operating cash flow. Capital budgeting projects therefore must take into account whether the future benefits of the projects will outweigh the financial investment and whether the company can afford to financially support the project and also continue operating the company for the duration of the capital projects.

Various methods and mathematical formulas are available for capital budgeting. Most large companies will choose one of the three most popular capital budgeting methods: net present value (NPV), internal rate of return (IRR), or discounted cash flow (DCF). Small

companies with fewer than 250 employees, choose the "gut feeling" approach to capital budgeting most frequently, followed by the payback period method. The payback period method is more attractive to smaller companies because it relies upon the shortest possible time to recapture the cost of the investment in the project. However, the payback period method does not measure profitability because it does not take into account any benefits that accrue after the payback period and also does not account for the time value of money. For these reasons, the payback method of capital budgeting is not used as frequently by larger companies, who are usually in a better position to wait longer to recoup their investments. The capital budgeting strategies for the foreign subsidiaries of U.S multinational companies are complicated by five unique factors: complex cash flow estimates; foreign exchange rate fluctuations; varying accounting systems; financial risks; and political uncertainties.

TERMS & CONCEPTS

Capital budgeting: The strategy used by businesses to plan out the viability of future investments.

Cash flow: The cash flow statement demonstrates the amount of cash produced and spent by a company during a certain time period, measured by adding non-cash charges (including depreciation) to net income post-taxes. Cash flow can be associated with a certain project or to a whole company. Cash flow can be used to represent a company's financial viability.

Cash inflows: Mainly generated from one of three activities: financing, operations, or investing. Cash inflows can also occur through donations or gifts.

Cash outflows: Result from expenses or investments.

Discounted cash flow (DCF): A valuation strategy utilized to determine the benefits of an investment opportunity. DCF analysis looks at future free cash flow predictions and discounts them (usually using the weighted average capital cost) to reach a present value, which is then used to assess the investment possibility. If the value derived from DCF is greater than the present investment cost, the opportunity might be an attractive one.

Free cash flow: A measurement of financial strength measured by subtracting capital expenditures from operating cash flow. Free cash flow demonstrates the cash that a company can produce without including the funds necessary to upkeep or add to its base assets.

Internal rate of return (IRR), also known as economic rate of return (ERR): The discount rate employed during capital budgeting analysis that equates the net current value of all cash flows from a given project to zero. Usually a higher internal rate of return means that a project is a more attractive proposition. Companies can use this rating to evaluate a number of potential projects. With all other factors staying consistent between projects, the project with the highest IRR would most likely be chosen.

Manufacture: To make a product from raw materials by hand or by machine.

Net present value (NPV): The variation between the current amount of cash inflow and the current amount of cash outflow. NPV is used during capital budgeting to assess the profitability of a potential investment or future project.

Payback period: The amount of time necessary to recapture an investment cost. If all other factors are consistent, the best investment is the one with the shortest payback period.

Present value (PV), or discounted value: The present value of a future sum of money or cash flows given a certain return rate. Future cash flows are discounted at the discount rate. The higher the discount rate is, the lower the current value of the future cash flows will be. Identifying the accurate discount rate is critical to effectively determining the value of future cash flows, regardless of whether they are earnings or obligations. The basic premise is that receiving $1,000 now is more valuable than receiving the same $1,000 in five years because during the intervening five years, you could have invested it and received additional returns.

Small businesses: Danielson & Scott (2006) cite the U.S. Small Business Administration (SBA) definition of small businesses as "firms with fewer than 500 employees." However, the SBA actually limits the size based on industry according to the North American Industry Classification System (NAICS).

BIBLIOGRAPHY

Applebaum, M. (2007). Three reasons why upping U.S. capacity doesn't add up. *American Metal Market, 116,* 91.

Bower, J. L, & Gilbert, C. G. (2007). How managers' everyday decisions create or destroy your company's strategy. *Harvard Business Review, 85,* 72–79.

Danielson, M. G., & Scott, J. A. (2006). Capital budgeting decisions of small businesses. *Journal of Applied Finance, 16,* 45–56.

Gervais, S., Heaton, J. B., & Odean, T. (2011). Overconfidence, compensation contracts, and capital budgeting. *Journal of Finance, 66,* 1735–1777.

Ghahremani, M., Aghaie, A., & Abedzadeh, M. (2012). Capital budgeting technique selection through four decades: With a great focus on real option. *International Journal of Business & Management, 7,* 98–119.

Goodman, T. H., Neamtiu, M., Shroff, N., & White, H. D. (2014). Management forecast quality and capital investment decisions. *Accounting Review, 89*(1), 331–365.

Hasan, I., Shao, L. P., & Shao, A. T. (1997). Determinants of capital budgeting strategies: An econometric analysis of U.S. multinational subsidiaries. *Multinational Business Review, 5,* 68–76.

Investopedia. (2007). *Dictionary.*

Merriam-Webster's collegiate dictionary (10th ed.). (2000). Springfield, MA: Merriam- Webster.

U.S. Small Business Administration.

Wolffsen, P. (2012). Modification of capital budgeting under uncertainty. *Applied Economics: Systematic Research, 6,* 143–159.

SUGGESTED READING

Bimal, N., et al. (2007). A quality-based business model for determining non-product investment: A case study from a Ford automotive engine plant. *Engineering Management Journal, 19,* 41–56.

Dedi, L., & Orsag, S. (2007). Capital budgeting practices: A survey of Croatian firms. *South East European Journal of Economics & Business, 2,* 59-67.

Hyde, J., Dunn, J. W., Steward, A., & Hollabaugh, E. R. (2007). Robots don't get sick or get paid overtime, but are they a profitable option for milking cows? *Review of Agricultural Economics, 29,* 366–380.

Soloman, M. J. (2015). *Investment decisions in small business.* Lexington: University Press of Kentucky.

Essay by Sue Ann Connaughton, MLS

Cloud Computing Security

ABSTRACT

Cloud computing security is a concept that has arisen in recent years in response to the broader move of personal and enterprise computer operations into "the cloud." As the infrastructure and popular usage of the Internet has matured and become more robust, more and more entities have chosen to move their data, their data processing, or both, to third-party computing facilities. On diagrams of network architecture, such third-party facilities were traditionally represented by a drawing of a cloud—hence the term "cloud computing." Cloud computing security concerns the measures that can be taken to protect user data that is being stored or processed in third-party systems.

OVERVIEW

Cloud computing generally involves an architecture in which users of the cloud computing service access their cloud remotely. For example, a university library might run its day-to-day operations using library management software that is running on a cloud server located hundreds or thousands of miles away. This means that there are multiple physical sites where there is the potential for a security issue to occur. In large organizations, it is likely that this situation will be made still more complex because there are many different departments in the organization, each of which may use multiple cloud services (Halpert, 2011).

The university library in the example above might be located in Maine, store its data in Oklahoma, and host its management software in California. An organization like a university could easily have its operations using dozens of cloud services, each creating a new set of security issues at the user's location and at the cloud computing facility.

Cloud computing security issues that can arise at the location of the user tend to be associated with users who either do not follow established security procedures or who deliberately misuse the access they have legitimately been given. Users who do not follow security procedures can leave the entire cloud computing system vulnerable to attack.

Some such users choose passwords that can easily be guessed by hackers because they are simple words like "password" or can easily be guessed by anyone who knows basic personal information about the user. This is why security professionals strongly advise against users using their birth date as their password, their children's names, or similar information.

Another type of security issue that can arise at the user location is a failure to secure the physical workstation that is used to access the cloud services. This could happen if a user were to log into his or her computer and then step away for a few moments, giving another person the opportunity to access the systems on the user's computer. A similar issue can arise when users carry identification badges that permit them to enter sensitive areas; if a badge is stolen, then an unauthorized person may be able to enter a restricted area and gain access to cloud computing resources (Chee & Franklin, 2010).

The types of security issues that arise at cloud computing facilities tend to be more complex. Not only are the same types of security problems associated with the user side of the equation capable of occurring at the cloud computing facility, but the facility is also vulnerable to a variety of remote attacks that could be executed by individuals at a distance, using the Internet to compromise the cloud facility's resources (Winkler, 2011). There is also a significant risk of unintentional security issues at cloud computing facilities because cloud computing facilities, by their very nature, host data and software from many different entities, some of whom may be in direct competition with one another. For example, two drug manufacturers might both store their research with the same cloud storage provider. Even a minor error in system configuration or user permissions could conceivably allow a researcher at one company to view the data developed by the other company. To prevent incidents like this from occurring, cloud facilities must create strict policies governing how their systems are designed to protect user data, and they must monitor their operations continuously to determine whether these policies are being followed. This can become extremely complicated because the cloud facility must protect not only the live systems that it operates, but also the data that it backs up (Erl, Puttini & Mahmood, 2013). Modern business operations and research programs routinely produce many terabytes of data per year, so keeping this information secure, safe, and still accessible in the event of an emergency is decidedly challenging (Manuel, 2015). The problem of cloud computing security, particularly at the enterprise level, has been likened to a family that owns large homes all over the world, because each home—like each cloud facility—must be kept in good condition, protected from accidents and intrusion, and yet remain available for use at a moment's notice.

APPLICATIONS

To prevent intrusions and mishaps, cloud computing services implement a cloud security architecture, which is a set of policies and procedures designed to prevent systems from being compromised and, if they are compromised, to contain the breach by keeping it as compartmentalized as possible. A cloud computing architecture utilizes several different types of controls to prevent unauthorized access (Tauwhare, 2015).

Preventive Controls
One type of security control concentrates on preventing security issues from occurring. For example, a critical preventive control is to require users with access to the cloud computing system to use strong passwords composed of random assortments of many different symbols and letters, rather than common words that can be easy to guess.

Another preventive control may be to ensure that all software applications associated with the cloud environment are the latest versions available and all security updates have been installed. All too often, the cause of breaches has been traced back to a small number of computers on a network running out-of-date software that is known to be vulnerable to hackers. All the hackers have to do is connect to such an old system, use "malware" (malicious programs developed to compromise the security of other systems) to break into it, and then use the compromised computer's network connections to "leapfrog" to other computers on the network (Hugos & Hulitzky, 2011).

Computer scientist Murugiah Souppaya investigates security techniques for protecting virtuallized computing environments and cloud computing systems. His virtualization lab serves as a testbed to develop and implement controls that reduce security vulnerabilities and minimize exposure to cyber attacks, and also provides virtualized computing services for other ITL research projects. (Courtesy of National Institute of Standards and Technology (Cloud Computing) via Wikimedia Commons)

Detection Controls
A second category of cloud security control concentrates on detection. Regardless of how effective the preventive measures an organization has in place may be, there will inevitably be a breach or mishap at some point, simply because there is no such thing as a completely invulnerable computer system. Detection controls exist in order to alert system administrators as soon as a breach has occurred, or even while it is still occurring. Detection control measures usually have two purposes: notification of parties and implementation of countermeasures. Intrusion countermeasures can take a variety of forms—such as terminating all active network connections, disabling all user accounts, and so on—and are intended to make it difficult or impossible for an intruder to benefit from the act of having broken into the system (Krutz & Vines, 2010). This buys time for the system administrators to be notified of the breach and to take further action.

Corrective Controls
To a certain extent, cloud security countermeasures overlap with a third category of security controls, those that are corrective in nature. Corrective security controls are intended to restore the cloud computing system's functionality after a breach has occurred. The main difference between countermeasures and

corrective controls is one of timing. Countermeasures are usually automated steps that are followed during or immediately following a breach, while corrective controls are initiated quite a while after a breach. One type of corrective control might be restoring a cloud system from a secure backup that was made prior to a breach, ensuring that it contains data that could not have been tampered with by the intruders. Another corrective control might be requiring users of the cloud computing system to reset their passwords after a breach that might have exposed those passwords to prying eyes; this would prevent the intruders from using stolen passwords and other account information to enrich themselves (Buyya, Broberg & Gos cin ski, 2011).

Deterrent Controls

Finally, some security controls are intended to act as a deterrent to intruders. Some regard deterrent controls as only one specific type of preventive control, but there is a meaningful difference between the two. Preventive controls are put in place to guard against all types of breaches, both deliberate and inadvertent, while deterrent controls target those who would intentionally seek to compromise the cloud computing environment for their own purposes. Deterrent controls seek to make such activity less appealing to would-be hackers by making clear what the consequences of such illicit behavior may be and by describing some of the measures in place that make it likely that intrusion attempts will both fail and reveal the hacker's identity to authorities.

VIEWPOINTS

Cloud computing security is an important part of the technology sector of the economy for several reasons. The most obvious of these pertains to public perceptions. Customers seeking to use cloud services for business or personal reasons have many different cloud providers to choose from, and one of the factors upon which they base their decision is reputation. Customers want to be sure that the cloud computing provider they choose has a superior reputation for protecting the integrity of user data (Ali, Kahn & Vasilakos, 2015), so there is a powerful incentive for companies to make sure that the general public has a high opinion of their security practices (Rittinghouse & Ransome, 2010).

When a security breach occurs, there are profound implications on several levels. First, losses may be inflicted directly on the user of the cloud computing service in the form of lost data, lost productivity, or both. For example, a company whose cloud-based customer database is compromised just before their busiest sales season experiences a direct loss. Second, losses may be incurred after a cloud computing breach that affects not only the user of the cloud services, but also those who rely on some service that the user performs with the cloud computing facility. For example, in the case of the company whose customer database was compromised, the customers would also experience a loss, because they would be unable to use their accounts to make purchases until the cloud computing system is restored.

Third, generalized losses may result from cloud security incidents that affect the reputation of the cloud facility and the customers who use it. If the breach is significant enough, the reputational damage may be catastrophic. This has occurred, for example, when major retailers have experienced data breaches so distressing to their customers that for weeks or even months afterward, the retailer's sales have drastically declined.

Each of these categories of loss carries with it the potential for liability on the part of the cloud computing facility, should one or more parties who suffered a loss due to a security breach choose to pursue a legal claim. Because of the large potential for legal repercussions following security incidents, a system of laws and regulations governing the conduct of the cloud computing industry is gradually developing (Jamsa, 2013). This process is hampered somewhat by the rapidly changing nature of the technologies being used and because the process of law making moves much too slowly to keep pace with the rate of innovation. Oftentimes, laws governing risk allocation in the technology sector are obsolete as soon as they are enacted because the technologies the laws were written to regulate have been replaced by newer generations of hardware and software.

Companies have strong incentives to avoid taking on excessive risk in the cloud computing security market because the price of failure (in the form of a security breach) can be incredibly high: If a firm's reputation as a responsible steward of customers' cloud data is compromised severely enough, sales can take a nosedive, and companies can see their leadership change or go out of business entirely. Cloud computing is a rapidly growing field and if its growth is to continue, then security must remain a top priority (Weinman, 2012).

TERMS & CONCEPTS

Data isolation: This concept describes the need, from a computer security perspective, to store sensitive data separately so that if one piece of it is breached, its utility remains limited. For example, a customer's credit card number should not be stored in the same file as his or her Social Security number because keeping these pieces of data in the same place makes it easier for unauthorized parties to use the data for illicit purposes. Data isolation can also be used to describe the need to keep data from different users separate when it is stored on the same virtual or physical machine.

Encryption: Encryption is the process of converting data into another set of symbols, using a cipher, so that unauthorized parties cannot extract meaning from it even if they gain access to it. Only parties with the proper encryption key can decode the data to access its meaning.

Infrastructure as a service (IaaS): One of the three main forms of cloud computing. IaaS provides hardware, software, and network infrastructure to users so they do not have to maintain these systems at their own site.

Platform as a service (PaaS): A type of cloud computing designed for software developers. It provides the infrastructure needed for application development so that users can concentrate on their development efforts without having to maintain their own development platforms at their local sites.

Software as a service (SaaS): A type of cloud computing in which users pay a license fee to use software that is based in the cloud; for example, a SaaS image editing program might allow users to upload a photo and then use the SaaS software to edit the image in the cloud. SaaS is different from the traditional model in which users purchase software, install it on their local hardware, and then use it.

Virtualization: One of the core technologies underlying cloud computing. Whereas traditional computing involves the installation of software and operating systems on physical media such as hard disks, virtualization makes it possible for an entire server to exist without having it installed on physical media. This means that whole servers and the software they run can be rapidly deployed and even run in parallel on the same physical infrastructure.

BIBLIOGRAPHY

Ali, M., Khan, S. U., & Vasilakos, A. V. (2015). Security in cloud computing: Opportunities and challenges. *Information Sciences, 305,* 357–383.

Buyya, R., Broberg, J., & Gos cin ski, A. (2011). *Cloud computing: Principles and paradigms.* Hoboken, NJ: Wiley.

Chee, B. J. S., & Franklin, C. (2010). *Cloud computing: Technologies and strategies of the ubiquitous data center.* New York, NY: CRC.

Erl, T., Puttini, R., & Mahmood, Z. (2013). *Cloud computing: Concepts, technology, & architecture.* Upper Saddle River, NJ: Prentice Hall.

Halpert, B. (2011). *Auditing cloud computing: A security and privacy guide.* Hoboken, NJ: John Wiley & Sons.

Hugos, M. H., & Hulitzky, D. (2011). *Business in the cloud: What every business needs to know about cloud computing.* New York, NY: Wiley.

Jamsa, K. (2013). *Cloud computing: SaaS, PaaS, IaaS, virtualization, business models, mobile, security and more.* Burlington, MA: Jones & Bartlett Learning.

Krutz, R. L., & Vines, R. D. (2010). *Cloud security: A comprehensive guide to secure cloud computing.* Indianapolis, IN: Wiley.

Manuel, P. (2015). *A trust model of cloud computing based on quality of service.* Annals of Operations Research, 233(1), 281–292.

Rittinghouse, J. W., & Ransome, J. F. (2010). *Cloud computing: Implementation, management, and security.* Boca Raton, FL: CRC Press.

Tauwhare, R. (2015). Cloud computing, export controls, and sanctions. *Journal of Internet Law, 19*(2), 1–14.

Weinman, J. (2012). *Cloudonomics: The business value of cloud computing.* Hoboken, NJ: Wiley.

Winkler, J. R. (2011). *Securing the cloud: Cloud computer security techniques and tactics.* Waltham, MA: Syngress.

Yong Y., Atsuko M., Man H. Susilo W. (2017). Cloud computing security and privacy: Standards and regulations. *Computer Standards & Interfaces, 54*(1), 1–2.

Suggested Reading

Ardagna, C. A., Asal, R., Damiani, E., & Quang Hieu, V. (2015). From security to assurance in the cloud: A survey. *ACM Computing Surveys, 48*(1), 2–50.

Liu, Y., Sheng, X., & Marston, S. R. (2015). The impact of client-side security restrictions on the competition of cloud computing services. *International Journal of Electronic Commerce, 19*(3), 90–117.

Sarrab, M., & Bourdoucen, H. (2015). Mobile cloud computing: security issues and considerations.

Journal of Advances in Information Technology, 6(4), 248–251.

Srinivasan, S. (2013). Is security realistic in cloud computing? *Journal of International Technology & Information Management, 22*(4), 47–66.

Wheeler, A., & Winburn, M. (2015). *Cloud storage security: A practical guide.* Amsterdam, Netherlands: Elsevier.

Essay by Scott Zimmer, JD

Communications, Networking and Security

ABSTRACT

One of the keys to success in most twenty-first-century businesses is the ability to exchange data and information quickly and accurately. Networks of computers enable organizations to better perform their tasks and meet the needs of their customers. Networks are particularly useful for enabling the fast transmission of messages, information, and documents and for allowing virtual meetings over long distances. Such technologies are not without their drawbacks, however. Networks are at risk from numerous threats both internally and externally. Although network threats continue to evolve, a number of general precautions and specific technologies can be used to reduce network security risks.

OVERVIEW

Most organizations need to be able to access data and communicate within the organization and with outside agencies. For example, a dry cleaner needs to be able to quickly locate the customer's contact information as well as the customer's clothes. The mom-and-pop grocery store needs to know what items it has in stock and what items it needs to order, It also needs to communicate with suppliers to continue to serve its customers. Banks need access to multiple types of sensitive personal and financial information about their customers and must be able to account for every cent in a customer's account. Engineering firms need to be able to share and coordinate information between employees and work teams, order supplies and equipment, and communicate with customers and government agencies. No matter the type of organization, information management and communication are vital to success in the twenty-first century. Modern technology offers organizations better ways to communicate, manage, and exchange information than ever before. The ability to network, or electronically link computers together, further enhances an organization's ability to optimize these technologies to enhance performance and improve viability in the marketplace. In the Information Age, communications networks have become a necessity for most businesses to facilitate information flow, reduce data transmission time, and enable employees across the company or across the globe to work together more effectively.

There are a number of impetuses to the use of communications networks in organizations, such as the trend toward globalization in which businesses no longer operate only locally but have customers and operations around the world. This trend creates an interconnected, global marketplace operating outside the constraints of time zones or national boundaries. To be successful in the global marketplace, businesses also need to be able to communicate and exchange information outside of these constraints.

In addition, the increasing use of high-speed communication technologies for information exchange has changed the expectations of many industries. Businesses are no longer willing to wait for information to be delivered via the mail but need and expect immediate access to keep their processes going. This better and faster communication has also helped businesses become more aware of what is going on in other departments and form strategic alliances with other businesses for their mutual benefit. This trend extends to suppliers and agencies that have an impact on the business's operation'.

Communications networks can be used for a number of purposes. They are commonly used to transmit messages and documents. These include email, voice mail, electronic document exchange, electronic funds transfer, and Internet access. In addition, communications networks can be used for purposes of e-commerce to buy and sell goods or services, including products and information retrieval services, electronically rather than through conventional means. Networks also support group activities such as the ability to hold meetings with participants at geographically dispersed sites. Audio and videoconferencing capabilities combined with electronic document exchange capabilities can obviate the need for extensive travel to meetings.

Although data communications and networking bring capabilities to businesses that enhance performance and allow them to perform tasks that were previously more laborious and time-consuming, the use of this technology is not without its risks and complications. Without adequate safeguards in place, networked computers are open to both external and internal attacks. Such attacks can affect the validity of data and the reliability of network processes. They can harm not only the organization's reputation and ability to do business but the customer's security and safety as well. The impact of security breaches on the customer can range from false charges to the theft of sensitive information or even identity theft of the individuals whose data are contained in compromised databases. Therefore, it is essential that a business protect its information technology assets. The destruction or sabotage of information technology hardware, software, or data can be expensive for the organization.

Threats to the enterprise's network security can come from both external hackers who gain access to the system illegally and from the business's own employees. The enterprise must protect its data and processes from both sources of threat. Computer systems and networks are also vulnerable to computer viruses and worms. These are malicious programs or pieces of code, which are loaded onto a computer without the user's knowledge and against the user's wishes. They alter the way the computer operates or modify the data or programs that are stored on

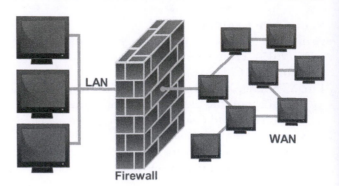

An illustration of where a firewall would be located in a network. (Courtesy of Bruno Pedrozo via Wikimedia Commons)

the computer. Simple viruses can be self-replicating and use up a computer's memory or otherwise slow down or disable a computer; more complex viruses can transmit themselves across networks and bypass security systems to infect other computers or systems, corrupting or erasing programs or data. Computer viruses can be loaded onto the computer intentionally by internal or external hackers, but also through the receipt of infected email attachments.

There are a number of categories of computer crimes to which an enterprise may become susceptible if sufficient security measures are not in place. One such category involves the unauthorized entry of criminal hackers into the enterprise's computer system. Piggybacking falls into this category. When piggybacking, the criminal uses the codes or passwords of an authorized user to gain illegal access to the system. Piggybacking also refers to the unauthorized use of a terminal in the system. Another type of computer crime involving illegal access is entry through a trapdoor, an unknown entry point in a program or network that allows criminals to gain access to and control the system.

A second category of computer crime involves intentionally damaging to the system's data. Data diddling involves the changing of data and information before they enter the system. As opposed to honest mistakes or keyboarding errors, data diddling is intentionally done to damage the enterprise's ability to conduct business. Similarly, data leakage is the intentional erasure or removal of files or even entire databases from a system without leaving any trace that they have been removed or even that they existed. Data leakage can result in cost to the enterprise in the recovery or replacement of the lost data as well as from loss of customers' confidence due to errors resulting from the data loss. Customers can also be harmed from data leakage if the leakage results in receipts or credits not being posted correctly or at all. Another way in which the enterprise's communications networks can be harmed is through zapping, the process of damaging or erasing data and information. Scavenging is another type of crime in this category. It involves searching through the physical trash can in the computer center or the electronic trash can in the computer to find discarded data or other information about the system's programs or processes. Zapping typically occurs as a result of the criminal bypassing the enterprise's security systems.

Another category of computer crime revolves around the attempt to steal or capture data in the enterprise's systems. Eavesdropping is the use of electronic surveillance devices to either listen to or capture the content of electronic transmissions. Similarly, wiretapping is the use of any device to electronically capture data during transmission or to listen to conversations that take place over the network. Both wireless transmissions and those that occur over copper wire are susceptible to wiretapping. In addition, small amounts of the enterprise's data can be captured or rerouted through salami or data slicing. This crime involves the development or modification of software to capture small amounts of financial transactions and redirect them to a hidden account. Because the amounts ("slices") are so small, they typically go unnoticed. However, over time, a large volume of small losses can yield significant amount of stolen money.

Sometimes, however, computer criminals are not out to steal data or money from a business but aim to sabotage its computer systems. Logic bombs are programs that are designed to sabotage data, programs, or processes. Logic bombs are set to execute when certain conditions exist in the system. Similarly, time bombs are programs that monitor the computer's internal calendar and execute on a specific date. Trojan horses are programs that look as if they perform one function but actually do something else. Although Trojan horses appear to be harmless applications, once they are loaded into the computer, they wreak damage.

Because of the potential for external and internal attacks, information technology systems need to address several levels of security issues. In general, a business needs to protect its information technology resources from both intrusions by forced, unauthorized entry into the system as well as interception and capture of data by unauthorized personnel. The security of the computer centers and other rooms where information technology processing activities take place and data and other resources are stored must be ensured. This includes the security of equipment and facilities. Unauthorized users need to be denied access through the use of security protocols and procedures. Similarly, the security of both the data and application software needs to be taken into account. The enterprise needs to put into place security procedures to limit access to data and processes by those who do not need to access them. In addition, the communications networks, access to the Internet, and any intranets or extranets must be carefully controlled to limit the potential for viruses and other opportunities for hackers.

APPLICATIONS

There are A number of general measures can be taken to help protect the enterprise and its communications networks from security breaches. An obvious first step is to hire trustworthy, reliable employees who will not sabotage the system or steal data and who will safeguard the system from possible intruders. To assist employees in this task, a number of other general policies and procedures can be put into place to help reduce the risk of computer crime. The enterprise's computer networks should only be accessible using a code word and password. Employees should keep these confidential and not allow any unauthorized access to their terminal. Employees should be encouraged to report any suspected security breaches immediately. In addition, it is often helpful to set up the system so that it requires users to change their access passwords frequently. For situations where sensitive, classified, or otherwise restricted data are stored, used, and processed, in some cases it is cost effective to use biometric devices such as retinal, fingerprint, or palm scanners. Such devices are extremely difficult to access without authorization. Similarly, many organizations set up security procedures to control who is allowed to gain access to the system and the data. Employees should be educated on the importance of data and system security, the ways that computer criminals gain access to systems, and guidelines on how to respond when unauthorized access is suspected.

Other ways to keep data secure include not allowing users unlimited access to the system. Users should only be able to access those data and functions they need to use for their jobs. For those functions that are critical in terms of value or risk, procedures can be set in place so that more than one authorized employee is necessary to gain access to those functions or data. In addition, data can be scrambled, coded, or otherwise encrypted to make it more difficult for potential hackers to use them. Similarly, network and database administrators should be given separate responsibilities for controlling system access. In some situations, it can also be helpful to keep a record of all transactions and user activities and the person responsible for each. From time to time, the system should also be audited by an independent party. In an audit, the transactions and processing should be analyzed to determine if there were any unauthorized activities and what impact they had on the system.

In addition, an enterprise can take some specific measures to reduce the possibility of experiencing a security breach. Virus protection software comprises special application programs that scan the computer to detect or intercept viruses before they gain access to the computer. There are two types of virus protection software. Scanning programs search the computer's memory for viruses, typically notifying the user if any are found. The user can then use the software to destroy the virus and repair any damage if possible. Detection or interception programs monitor the computer's processing and stop viruses from accessing and infecting the computer. Another way to prevent damage from viruses is through the use of digital signature encryption. This technology transmits a mathematically encoded signature that can be used to authenticate the identity of the individual sending a message.

Another application of encryption technology is to code data transmissions so that they cannot be easily intercepted by hackers or other computer criminals. One way to encrypt data is through the use of a public key infrastructure. This technology uses an algorithm to create a public and a private key. The private key is given only to the requesting enterprise, whereas the public key is a searchable directory. To transmit a message, the sender searches a digital certificate directory to find the recipient's public key and uses it to encrypt the message. The message is decoded by the recipient using the private key. Security credentials and public keys are issued and managed by an independent certificate authority. Messages can also be encrypted through the use of a "pretty good privacy" (PGP) program. This program is available as freeware or shareware and works with most popular email programs. The public key is part of the program and is registered with a pretty good privacy server. A third option for data encryption is through the use of a virtual private network. This technology uses a public telecommunications infrastructure to provide secure communications between individual users or the enterprise and remote locations.

Firewalls are another security measure employed by many enterprises. A firewall is a special-purpose software program or piece of computer hardware that is designed to prevent authorized access to or from a private network. Firewalls are often used to prevent unauthorized access to a private network from the Internet. The firewall is located at the network gateway server and examines incoming messages to determine their origin, destination, purpose, contents, and attachments before making the decision whether to forward the message to the intended recipient. Although firewalls are useful for protecting against intruders, they often filter out executable programs or attachments of excessive length on the assumption that they may contain harmful contents. Historically, firewalls have been separate application programs that were loaded onto a system. Increasingly, however, they are being built into operative systems and communication devices.

Another information technology security device is the proxy server. These devices are used as an intermediary between a personal computer and the Internet. They separate the enterprise network from the Internet or other outside networks. Proxy servers are often used in tandem with firewalls. When they receive a request to access the Internet, they determine whether the user is allowed to make the request and then look to see if a copy of the requested web page is stored in cache. If the web page is stored in cache, it is sent to the user; otherwise, the server requests the page from the Internet.

TERMS & CONCEPTS

Cache memory: Special high-speed random access memory that temporarily holds frequently used data or information.

Firewall: A special-purpose software program or piece of computer hardware that is designed to prevent unauthorized access to or from a private network. Firewalls are often used to prevent unauthorized access to a private network from the Internet.

Hacker: Although the term is used by some to refer to any clever programmer, it is used specifically to refer to an individual who attempts to break into a computer system without authorization.

Information technology: The use of computers, communications networks, and knowledge in the creation, storage, and dispersal of data and information. Information technology comprises a wide range of items and abilities for use in the creation, storage, and distribution of information.

Local area network (LAN): Multiple computers that are located near each other and linked into a network that allows the users to share files and peripheral devices such as printers, fax machines, and storage devices.

Metropolitan area network (MAN): Computer networks that transmit data and information citywide and at greater speeds than a local area network.

Network: A set of computers that are electronically linked together.

Security: The process of safeguarding and protecting the data, hardware, software, and processes of a business's information technology assets.

Virus: In computer science, a virus is a program or piece of code that is loaded onto the computer without the user's knowledge and against the user's wishes that alters the way that the computer operates or modifies the data or programs that are stored on the computer. Simple viruses can be self-replicating and use up a computer's memory or otherwise disable a computer; more complex viruses can transmit themselves across networks and bypass security systems to infect other computers or systems.

Wide area network (WAN): Multiple computers that are widely dispersed and linked into a network. Wide area networks typically use high-speed, long-distance communications networks or satellites to connect the computers within the network.

BIBLIOGRAPHY

Dey, D., Lahiri, A., & Zhang, G. (2012). Hacker behavior, network effects, and the security software market. *Journal of Management Information Systems, 29,* 77–108.

Gupta, A., & Zhdanov, D. (2012). Growth and sustainability of managed security services networks: An economic perspective. *MIS Quarterly, 36,* 1109–A7.

Juels, A., & Oprea, A. (2013). New approaches to security and availability for cloud data. *Communications of the ACM, 56,* 64–73.

Lucas, H. C., Jr. (2005). *Information technology: Strategic decision making for managers.* New York: John Wiley and Sons.

Mangili, M., Martignon, F., & Paraboschi, S. (2015). A cache-aware mechanism to enforce confidentiality, trackability and access policy evolution in Content-Centric Networks. *Computer Networks,* 76126–145. doi:10.1016/j.comnet.2014.11.010.

Prince, B. (2014). Cybersecurity. *Forbes, 194,* 136–142.

Security of the Internet and the Known Unknowns. (2012). *Communications of the ACM, 55,* 35–37.

Senn, J. A. (2004). *Information technology: Principles, practices, opportunities* (3rd ed.). Upper Saddle River, NJ: Pearson/Prentice Hall.

Strauss, K. (2015). How small businesses can improve their cyber security. *Forbes.com, 8.*

SUGGESTED READING

Engebretson, D. (2004). The beginnings: Beyond the PC. *Distributing & Marketing, 34,* 74–76.

Hui, K.-L., Hui, W., & Yue, W. T. (2012). Information security outsourcing with system interdependency and mandatory security requirement. *Journal of Management Information Systems, 29,* 117–156.

Kamens, M. (2007). Making user access policies work for you. *Network World, 24,* 33.

McPherson, D. (2007). IP network security: Progress, not perfection. *Business Communications Review, 37,* 54–58.

The practice of network security monitoring. (2014). *Network Security*, 2014, 4.

Sax, D. (2016). State-of-the-art safeguards. *Bloomberg Businessweek, (4467),* 51–52.

Stallings, W. (2013). *Business data communications: Infrastructure, networking and security.* (7th ed.). Boston, MA: Pearson.

Essay by Ruth A. Wienclaw, PhD

COMPUTER APPLICATIONS IN BUSINESS

Although computing devices are not as recent an invention as one might think, it was not until the latter part of the twentieth century that they reached a level of sophistication that enabled them to become common in the workplace. Computers enhance productivity at work, quickly and accurately performing many of the repetitive and tedious chores associated with document creation and editing, accounting, publishing, and record keeping. In addition, computers are invaluable for enhancing the way that people work together by providing the capabilities to share data, coordinate tasks, and quickly communicate. Computers also are invaluable for managing data and allow organizations to maintain and manipulate databases in ways that would be impossible without technology. The use of computers for business is not without risks and concerns, however, including both issues of security and concerns for the individual's right to privacy.

OVERVIEW

As human beings, we are infinitely inventive and constantly searching for ways to improve our lives. Many important accomplishments and innovations resulting from this quest have changed the course of history along the way. Within the current lifetime, however, arguably none is more important than the progress that has been made in countless disciplines as well as in everyday activities as a result of computer technology. The application of computers both at home and at work helps us to better organize our lives, more easily perform repetitive or logical tasks, and access our creativity. Like the Renaissance and the Industrial Revolution before it, the Information Age continues to transform our lives and the ways in which we perform many of our tasks. The trend does not appear to be coming to a quick end, however, so it is reasonable to assume that the proliferation of technological invention and innovation will continue to change the way we do things well into the future.

The use of computers to assist in performing tedious tasks, however, is not a recent concept. For centuries, human beings have looked for ways to improve the accuracy of their computations and better control the world around them. For example, the Antikythera Mechanism — the world's oldest known computing device — dates to the first century B.C.E. This complex, multi-geared device is believed to be an early analog computer that was designed to calculate astronomical positions. Despite this intriguing example, however, computers did not come into their own until the mid-twentieth century. The cumbersome mainframe devices of the time were revolutionized in the 1970s with the invention of the

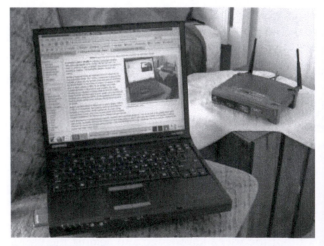

The notebook computer is connected via radio waves to the wireless access point (seen in the background), which in turn is connected to the internet or a LAN (Local Area Network). Computers connected via the LAN/WLAN can interact with each other. The wireless devices need to have a WiFi adapter, such as the card protruding from the notebook computer (though more commonly the adapter is built-in these days). (Courtesy of Wikimedia Commons)

microprocessor. This innovative technology led to the development of the personal computer that soon became commonplace both at home and at work.

Computers have become so much a part of many people's lives that it is difficult to imagine life without them. In the workplace, computers allow workers to write letters, record financial transactions, and send both quick messages and lengthy documents to colleagues across the room or across the world. Computers automatically spell check correspondence and make suggestions on how to improve grammar. Computers allow workers to circumvent the art department and use presentation software to design business presentations in full color, illustrated with high-quality photographs and graphics, with just a few clicks of a mouse. Computers automatically synchronize the calendars in personal digital assistants or smartphones and chime merrily to remind us of appointments, tasks, and deadlines.

In the mid-twentieth century, computers were cumbersome machines that belonged to the realm of big business problems and scientific research. For most people, correspondence and technical writing was literally penned by hand and sent to a secretary or a typing pool to be formalized on that modern wonder, the electric typewriter. The phrase "cut and paste" was literal: workers received the crisp white sheets of paper back from the unseen typing pool and proceeded to edit by hand, frequently using scissors and tape to rearrange paragraphs. Then suddenly lives were revolutionized with the advent of

the word processor. Although these devices still were not on every desktop, the secretaries and typists were thrilled because they no longer had to type each draft from scratch; they could rearrange paragraphs, edit, and correct on electronically stored documents and print out a freshly edited copy in a fraction of the time that the work would have taken on a typewriter.

The first word processors were crude, however, when compared to the capabilities that are housed today within personal computers and laptops. They were uni-taskers, useful only for typing, editing, and printing documents. Since the introduction of the personal computer to the workplace, the way that we do work has been transformed. Depending on the software applications that are installed on the computers, one can not only type and edit documents but also create layouts and designs for print. Electronic spreadsheets that automatically total columns of figures and quickly paste cells to other pages make the task of double-entry bookkeeping almost fun. Whether they work on independent personal computers or are part of a network, the ability to carry out work using computers has impacted workers in a wide range of industries. The application of computers to business is virtually as unlimited as the tasks performed in the workplace.

APPLICATIONS

The examples above illustrate just a few of the ways that computers can enhance individual productivity in the workplace. However, computers in the workplace are useful for much more than enhancing individual productivity. Numerous applications of computer technology can enhance the way that workers interact with each other and collaborate to enhance the productivity and effectiveness of the organization as a whole. Computers also are invaluable for storing and manipulating large collections of data in support of numerous tasks across the organization. In addition, the Internet has given businesses an entirely new medium for advertising products and services, gathering data about prospective customers and competitors, and selling products online.

Enterprise-Wide Computer Applications
By definition, an organization is a group of people that is organized to perform work or some other task. The fact that organizations are made up of more than

Replica of Zuse's Z3, the first fully automatic, digital (electromechanical) computer. (Courtesy of Venusianer via Wikimedia Commons)

one person gives them the opportunity to achieve synergy and accomplish more together than they could as isolated individuals. Modern computer technology can help in this task. In many businesses, computers are linked together over a local area network that allows multiple computers located near each other (e.g., in the same room or building) to share files and peripheral devices such as printers. This capability is particularly useful if a number of people need to work on the same document (e.g., inputting data, commenting on a document, creating reports from a database). Similarly, computers that are widely dispersed can be linked into a wide area network. Wide area networks typically use high-speed, long-distance communications networks or satellites to connect the computers within the network. Through them, employees can communicate and cooperate with colleagues in the next office and across the globe.

The linking of computers through networks can enhance the productivity and effectiveness of the entire enterprise. For example, computerized cash registers in a retail store or other points of sale can be linked together so that sales clerks can search across the network to see whether other stores have a particular item in stock. Similarly, the computers at the point of sale can be linked directly to the corporate headquarters so that the store's closing data each evening can be directly and immediately shared with corporate management. Computerized inventories can help individual stores keep track of what they have in stock, what products are most in demand, and when it is time to reorder and can even assist in automatically ordering stock. Enterprise-wide computer systems can also automatically invoice customers and perform other billing tasks.

Computers are also used to organize and manage tasks. On a personal productivity level, application software is readily available that can help people keep track of their calendars, including scheduling of appointments, meetings, and tasks to be done. However, on a higher level, application software is available for project management. This type of application allows a project manager to track and control schedules for complex projects and communicate status, risks, and other information about the project status to customers and team members.

Another important computer application frequently used in the business world is the database management system. A database is a computer program that allows the user to create, change, and organize data items that are related to each other. What differentiates a database from other collections of data is that the data in a database are used for multiple purposes. The data in a database are placed into a series of tables that are keyed to each other and can be manipulated into a variety of reports that display only that portion of the database in which the user is currently interested. The process of database management comprises inputting data into the database, updating the data, and representing all or part of the data in various reports that meet the user's specific needs. Computer technology enables the creation and manipulation of large databases that could not be managed through another medium.

Database management systems are used in a wide array of businesses. The inventory control system of a retail store or chain discussed above is one example of a database management system. Another example is a medical records management system in a hospital. These systems may help a hospital or physician's office control, organize, and manage a wide range of demographic information about their patients and their medical histories, information about their medical insurance coverage, and other data that are important to the healthcare system. Medical records management systems can allow users to pull together the information in a variety of ways for various forms and records.

Another application of a database management system is in marketing. Database systems in this area can help marketers better understand their target market, collect and analyze data on prospective customers, and keep track of current customers' buying history, needs, and other characteristics. A database management system can be used to develop targeted mailing lists for new products based on customer demographics or buying history or to track customer purchases so that better solutions can be offered or new products developed to better meet their needs.

Internet Applications for Business

No discussion of computer applications in business would be complete without mention of the Internet. The advent of this "network of networks" has revolutionized the way that many tasks are carried out. The Internet links together numerous smaller networks, including many from government, business, and academia, and allows users to communicate through various communication media, including email, online chat, instant messaging, forums, social-networking sites, and blogs.

From a marketing perspective, the rise of the Internet and the ease of designing and maintaining a professional website has brought with it the potential to reach far greater numbers of potential customers than was previously possible. The Internet can provide a wealth of information that an organization can use in marketing efforts. Whether the organization is offering goods or services, the Internet offers an array of opportunities for gathering information, testing marketing approaches, and advertising. For organizations offering products for sale, the Internet also offers effective ways to put one's catalog online and even to take orders and receive payment without the expense of a physical storefront or extensive staff. E-commerce also allows businesses to sell directly to customers and reach a larger potential market.

Another marketing application of Internet technology is the ability to research the competition. Data about what competitors are selling, how and to whom they are advertising, and what the latest buzz words are for attracting potential customers is readily available to those who are willing to gather it. The Internet can also provide a wealth of information about prospective customers. Demographic data are frequently available from government sources online, and lists of businesses or organizations that might be part of the target market can be readily generated.

Security & Ethical Considerations for Computers in the Workplace

Business applications for computer technology are not an unmixed blessing. The same technology that offers new opportunities to honest businesspersons also offers new opportunities to criminals. Cybercrime can affect both those buying and selling products. Organizations using the Internet for financial transactions or the collection of other sensitive or personal information must be diligent in ensuring that their websites are secure to protect both themselves and their customers. For those organizations storing or transmitting sensitive information over the Internet, security becomes an even greater concern as criminals increasingly find innovative ways to outwit the security measures instituted by Internet users.

It is essential that a business protect its information technology assets. The impact of security breaches can be far reaching. The physical destruction or sabotage of information technology hardware can be expensive for the organization, as can the destruction of data or software. Software can be not only erased but also altered or corrupted so that it produces invalid results and the system becomes unreliable and unusable. In addition to the threat to the organization, security breaches can also result in identity theft for the individuals whose data are contained in the databases. Threats to enterprise security can come not only from external hackers — individuals who gain access to the system illegally — but from the business's own employees as well.

A good security program for information technology needs to address several levels. First, the security of the computer centers and other rooms where information technology processing activities take place and data and other resources are stored must be ensured. Second, the security of equipment, facilities, and application software needs to be taken into account. Third, the communication networks (both local area and wide area), access to the Internet, and any intranets or extranets must be considered. Care must be taken to protect the enterprise's information technology resources from both intrusions by forced, unauthorized entry into the system and interception and capture of data by unauthorized personnel.

However, security issues are not the only ethical issues faced by enterprises using computer technology, particularly database management systems containing sensitive information about people. Although in Europe it is illegal to use information about a customer in ways that a customer did not intend for it to be used — including selling the customer's information to another company for marketing purposes — this is both a legal and an accepted practice in the United States. However, ethical concerns about an individual's right to privacy should not be taken lightly.

Computers offer another opportunity to businesses: the opportunity to closely monitor their employees. For example, computers can gather data concerning the time it takes for an individual to fill out an insurance claim form or process a travel reservation or how many phone calls an individual takes during a shift. On production lines, computers can enable businesses to keep track of errors and trace them to the employee who made them.

Some organizations monitor the employees' emails. Although there may be legitimate reasons for doing such things, employees often take exception to such close monitoring. Employee dissatisfaction, sabotage, or other negative consequences can result from such computer applications in business.

Terms & Concepts

Application software: A program that performs functions not related to the running of the computer itself. Application software includes word processing, electronic spreadsheet, computer graphics, and presentation software.

Database: A collection of data items used for multiple purposes that is stored on a computer.

Desktop publishing: The use of a personal computer to create high-quality printed documents such as brochures, newsletters, and books. Desktop publishing uses various types of computer software (e.g., word processing, page layout, graphics) to create professional-quality documents.

Double entry bookkeeping: An accounting technique in which each transaction is recorded as both a credit (the source of financing) and a debit (the use of the financing). Each credit typically has more than one debit posted against it. This system aids in balancing credit and debit ledgers.

E-commerce: E-commerce (electronic commerce) is the process of buying and selling goods or services — including information products and information retrieval services — electronically rather than through conventional means. E-commerce is typically conducted over the Internet.

Enterprise: An organization that uses computers. Although this term is often applied to large organizations, the term can be applied to both small and large organizations.

Information technology: The use of computers, communications networks, and knowledge in the creation, storage, and dispersal of data and information. Information technology comprises a wide range of items and abilities for use in the creation, storage, and distribution of information.

Local area network (LAN): Multiple computers that are located near each other and linked into a network that allows the users to share files and peripheral devices such as printers.

Network: Computers that are electronically linked together.

Presentation software: A type of graphics software that allows the user to create a series of visual aids (slides) that can be used to support a speaker in giving a speech or public presentation. Typically, the slides are displayed via a projector connected to a computer on which the software resides. Presentation software often also allows the user to print out paper versions (hard copy) of the slides for various uses, including handouts for the audience or memory aids for the presentation.

Security: The process of safeguarding and protecting the data, hardware, software, and processes of a business's information technology assets.

Spreadsheet: A table of values arranged in rows and columns in which the values have predefined relationships. Spreadsheet application software allows users to create and manipulate spreadsheets electronically.

Synergy: The process by which the combined product resulting from the work of a team of individuals is greater than the results of their individual efforts.

Wide area network (WAN): Multiple computers that are widely dispersed and linked into a network. Wide area networks typically use high-speed, long-distance communications networks or satellites to connect the computers within the network.

Word processing: The use of a computer to create, edit, and store documents electronically.

Bibliography

Elmasri, R. & Navathe, S. B. (1989). *Fundamentals of database systems.* Redwood City, CA: The Benjamin/Cummings Publishing Company.
Grover, V., & Kohli, R. (2013). Revealing your hand: Caveats in implementing digital business strategy. *MIS Quarterly, 37,* 655–662.

Junglas, I., & Harris, J. (2013). The promise of consumer technologies in emerging markets. *Communications of the ACM, 56*, 84–90.

Leonardi, P. M. (2013). When does technology use enable network change in organizations? A comparative study of feature use and shared affordances. *MIS Quarterly, 37*, 749–775.

Lucas, H. C. Jr. (2005). *Information technology: Strategic decision making for managers.* New York: John Wiley and Sons.

Senn, J. A. (2004). *Information technology: Principles, practices, opportunities* (3rd ed.). Upper Saddle River, NJ: Pearson/Prentice Hall.

SUGGESTED READING

Aponte, M. J. (2007). DevNet educates customers to maximize productivity. *Caribbean Business, 35*, S25.

Berman, S. (2007). The changing landscape of it security (part 1). *Business Communications Review, 37*, 26–31.

Case study V: BT exact: Intelligent business analytics — turning data into business benefit. (2004). *Journal of Database Marketing & Customer Strategy Management, 12*, 73–79.

Clark, L. (2007, February 27).Get the IT productivity message across, CIOs told. *Computer Weekly*, 5.

Gupta, P., Seetharaman, A. A., & Raj, J. (2013). The usage and adoption of cloud computing by small and medium businesses. *International Journal of Information Management, 33*, 861–874.

Mohamed, A. (2007, February 6). How to get it right when shopping for a database management system. *Computer Weekly*, 30–32.

Oppliger, R. (2007). IT security: In search of the holy grail. *Communications of the ACM, 50*, 96–98.

Peterson, K. (2007). Organizing business staff for greater productivity. *Kitchen & Bath Design News, 25*, 40.

Ryan, S., & Tucker, C. (2012). Heterogeneity and the dynamics of technology adoption. *Quantitative Marketing & Economics, 10*, 63–109.

Essay by Ruth A. Wienclaw, Ph.D.

CONSULTING TO GROWTH COMPANIES

This article will focus on consulting to growth companies. It will provide an overview of the role that consultants play in growth companies, a description of global growth companies, and approaches to identifying and ranking growth companies. In addition, the strategies that companies use to promote growth, performance, and innovation and the issues associated with human capital in growth companies will be addressed and analyzed. This article will be of particular use and interest to consultants to growth companies. As this article will explain, consultants, with domain expertise and suggestions for optimization of a company's strategic assets, are vital to the success of growth companies.

OVERVIEW

Growth companies are those companies whose rate of growth significantly exceeds that of the average in its field or the overall rate of economic growth. Growth companies, which increase at significantly faster rates than the overall economy, differ from mature companies that have stable earnings and little or no growth. Growth companies are classified into high-, moderate-, and low-growth companies. High-growth companies refer to companies that grow at an average rate greater than 20 percent per year for at least four or five years in a row. Growth companies tend to reinvest their earnings back into the company to expand the business and promote increased growth and performance.

The stakeholders of growth companies, including mangers, investors, consultants, and the public, are influenced by the performance of growth companies. Managers seek out these companies for the profit and challenge. Investors seek out these companies for the higher-than-normal return on investment dollars. Consultants seek out growth companies for the abundant work and opportunity they provide. The public seeks out growth companies as an expanding source of employment. Growth companies are characterized by the leadership position that they claim in an expanding product or market area. Growth companies, common in the technology industries, tend to develop, promote, and capitalize

World Economic Forum headquarters in Geneva, Switzerland. (Courtesy of Alexey M. via Wikimedia Commons)

may or may not be licensed, depending on their field. Consultants in the legal and accounting fields must be licensed while the fields of computer programming, business strategy, and marketing have no licensing requirements for consultants. Consultants can help traditional companies achieve growth. Consultants to growth companies may assist in the preparation of a business plan, raising capital, conducting market research, or advising in the development of a company's product, manufacturing process, or marketing strategy. Consultants help companies develop the following strategies that promote substantial, long-term growth (Zielasko, 2006):

Sense of purpose: Companies must have a purpose and a mission outside of profits. The purpose can be product, service, or market related. The sense of purpose will unite employees and create increased loyalty and efficiency.

Market intelligence: Companies must move beyond internal focus and analyze market trends and how their company can capitalize on the market.

Customer-driven processes: Companies must concentrate their efforts in developing and implementing customer-driven processes that put the customers' needs first.

Smart technology: Companies must develop smart and interconnected tools.

Seeing the future: Companies must develop forecasting tools.

Finding and keeping the best and the brightest people: Companies must seek out and work to keep industry talent.

Consultants to growth companies generally work on a contract basis and do not earn fringe benefits. They generally sign consulting agreements that refer to contracts between companies and advisors who are

in new and technologically focused goods or services (Kotter & Sathe, 1978).

Growth companies, characterized as learning organizations, make use of consultants to guide choices, build structures, develop goals, and allocate resources that promote growth. The following sections provide an overview of the role that consultants play in growth companies, a description of global growth companies, and approaches to identifying and ranking growth companies. These sections serve as a foundation for later discussion of the strategies that companies use to promote growth and the issues associated with human capital in growth companies. This article will be of particular use and interest to consultants to growth companies. As this article will explain, consultants, with domain expertise and suggestions for improvement and optimization, are vital to the success of growth companies.

Consulting to Growth Companies

Consultants refer to professionals who perform specific services for a fee. Consultants work in numerous fields including human resources, investment, financing, production, research and design, marketing, shipping and distribution, forecasting, safety, risk management, and regulatory oversight. Consultants not their employees. The contracts cover the scope of the consultant's obligations, understandings as to who owns his or her work product, the limitations on his or her authority, and the company's fee payment obligations. The following issues are described or addressed to varying degrees in every consulting agreement (Hanson, 2004):

- Scope of work: The consulting agreement must specifically state what services the consultant will provide. The time given for the consultant to perform the services must also be explicitly stated.
- Compensation: The consulting agreement must specifically state the compensation that will be for paid to the consultant for the provided services. Examples include flat fees, salary, expenses, bonuses, and company shares.
- Independent contractor status: The consulting agreement must indicate that the contractor' is an independent contractor rather than a full-time employee. This distinction is a requirement of tax-reporting law.
- Term and termination: The consulting agreement must specifically state the term of the contract in months or years. The client and the consultant may also choose to add specific details and requirements for the termination of the contract by either party. Common criteria for termination of consulting agreements include breach of contract and illegal activities.
- Rights and data: The consulting agreement must specifically address the allowable and legal uses of the consultant's work produced while under contract. The consulting agreement should, if relevant, specify copyrights and ownership rights of work or products.
- Conflict of interest: The consulting agreement often includes a non-competition clause for at least the length of the contract. This clause prohibits the consultant, while under contract, from doing similar work that would compete with the client for business or market share.
- Non-solicitation: The consulting agreement usually includes a non-solicitation clause that forbids the consultant, while under contract, from soliciting the client's employees.

Consultants, as described above, participate in similar ways in growth companies across businesses and industries. Consultants to growth companies help companies learn to be flexible, handle change, work as a team, and work at a high level of efficiency and performance despite risk and uncertainty.

Global Growth Companies
The potential for growth across businesses, industries, and markets is increased by the emergence of new economic markets and transnational companies. New business opportunities abound in the new global marketplace for emerging and established corporations. The World Economic Forum (WEF), an independent international organization committed to improving the state of the world by engaging leaders in partnerships to shape global, regional, and industry agendas, tracks global growth companies. Economic globalization and related practices are changing business practices worldwide. WEF developed the Community of Global Growth Companies as a resource to support emerging businesses as they navigate the challenges of new geographies, markets, cultures, and regulatory systems. WEF hopes to support and align with companies that will become future industry leaders.

Global growth companies, as defined by WEF, are businesses that have demonstrated a clear potential to become leaders in the global economy based on such factors as a company's business model, growth record, leadership, and the markets it serves. Global growth companies meet or exceed the following criteria:

- Global growth companies expand outside their traditional boundaries.
- Global growth companies experience annual growth rates exceeding 15 percent.
- Global growth companies have revenues between $100 million and $2 billion.
- Global growth companies demonstrate leadership in a particular industry.

Economic indexes, such as the Standards & Poor's 500, suggest that global growth companies, which span multiple markets, will continue to outperform companies that remain tied to a single market.

Identifying & Ranking Growth Companies
The financial sector tracks company growth and performance data to evaluate the health of companies and the relative risk in investing in companies. Company

growth and company performance are not the same thing. Growth refers to economic expansion as measured by any number of indicators. Performance refers to the results an organization's activities or investments over a given time. Performance is a criterion for evaluating growth. Company growth and performance is measured and tracked by financial news organizations such as *Business Week* and financial investment organizations such as Standard & Poor's.

Growth companies tend to be measured and ranked within specific industries and markets. For example, in 2006, *Business Week* released the figures for the top 50 hot growth technology companies. *Business Week* determines and measures company growth by sales growth, total return to shareholders, return on equity, and overall sales. Examples of hot growth technology companies in 2006 include Amkor Technology, Apple Computer, AT & T, Google, Gilead Sciences, Cognizant Tech Solutions, Amphenol, Oracle, NII Holdings, and Lam Research. *Business Week* also produces a list of the 50 best performing companies. The top 2007 performers, measured by the two core financial measures of average return on capital and sales growth over the previous 36 months, include Google, Coach, Gilead Sciences, Nucor, Questar, Sunoco, Verion Communications, Colgate-Palmolive, Goldman Sachs group, and Paccar. The comparison between the top growth companies in technology and the top performers across industries illustrates the difference between growth and performance. They are related categories but not one in the same.

Business Week bases its list on the 10 economic sectors, including financials, technology, health care, basic materials, energy, consumer staples, industrials, telecom, utilities, and consumer discretionary, that make up the Standard & Poor's 500 (S & P 500) company index. The Standard & Poor's 500 ranks the leading companies in the U.S. economy's 10 largest industries. The S & P 500 market index began in 1923 and expanded to include 500 companies in 1957. Rankings and indexes, such as those described in this section, influence the public and financial sectors' investment choices.

APPLICATIONS

Growth Companies

There is A strong correlation exists between growth and managerial and operational strengths, ideas and vision, and investment and funding. Growth is related to how effectively companies understand and maximize their distinctive capabilities and strategic assets. Distinctive capabilities refer to skills that enable companies to operate at an exceptional level of effectiveness. Examples of distinctive advantage include an innovative corporate culture, talented management and development groups, and business networks that enhance supply and purchasing. Strategic assets refer to the resources companies have that they can exploit. Examples of strategic assets include intellectual property, reputation for quality and fast delivery, a desirable location, and exclusive licenses and copyrights.

Companies gain competitive advantage by understanding, promoting, and capitalizing on their distinctive capabilities and strategic assets. Distinctive capabilities and strategic assets only create competitive advantage and growth when they are managed correctly through the life cycle of a company or product. For example, startup or early-stage companies will go through distinct development phases, including pre-seed, seed, start up, early stage, and expansion, that require different management tools, tactics, and approaches. Management, during each of these phases, will be working on developing management structures and systems that build and exploit the company's distinctive capabilities.

Issues that affect growth include human capital, intellectual property, change management, and investment funding. Growth companies tend to have an operating business plan that guides the company toward growth choices and activities. An operating business plan refers to a dynamic document that highlights the company's strengths and weakness and guides the company toward learning and increased efficiency.

Companies depend on outside consultants to strategize and establish a company position on human capital, intellectual property, change management, and investment funding issues. Professional business consultants are often brought into the company to help develop the operating business plan. Legal consultants, often highly specialized intellectual property lawyers, are usually necessary to navigate and resolve the company's intellectual property issues. Change management consultants may help a company develop change management processes for initiating and implementing organizational change. Financial consultants may be used to brainstorm and attain funding. These consultants tend to have expertise in funding areas such as government grants, loan programs, private investment, and corporate ventures. Financial consultants help companies connect funding priorities to capital to create growth (Turner, 2006).

Management consultants help managers learn to manage in a way that creates and promotes growth. Consultants lead companies in maximizing the strengths associated with company financial resources, brand recognition, global reach, economies of scale, and human talent. Consultants also help companies develop a pro-growth business environment by improving business strategy, work strategy, and organizational arrangements and fostering a people-management approach (Nadler, 1997):

- Business strategy: The company business strategy refers to the context for specific business decisions and operating strategies. Examples include strategies for growth, business focus, product cannibalization, partnerships, and global focus.
- Work strategy: Company work strategy refers to the set of business decisions required to bring the vision to life and drive growth. Examples include competitive innovation, organizational speed, and cost-efficiency.
- Organizational arrangements: Growth companies tend to choose organizational arrangements such as structural simplicity, small and autonomous business units, pervasive growth mindsets, and shared organizational values and culture.
- Human capital: Growth companies are dependent on the talent and vision of their people. Top talent is often drawn to growth companies or ventures by the opportunity to work on cutting-edge projects in semi-autonomous work environments.

The following section describes the human resource issues common in growth companies.

ISSUES

Human Resources & Growth Companies

The greatest strategic asset of most growth companies is their human capital. A growth company's management team, research and design team, human resources team, financial team, production team, marketing team, distribution team, and consulting team, together, comprise the human capital that create growth. Growth companies, across businesses and industries, tend to experience similar human capital or human resource problems. The organizational approach to solving human resource problems (and eventual outcome and resolution) influences a company's ability to initiate and maintain growth.

Meanwhile, rapidly expanding job demands, large recruiting and training demands and constant change place a constant strain on resource. Consultants from outside the company often assist growth companies in resolving human resource problems. Growth companies tend to employ similar solutions to these human resource problems. Common solutions to human resource problems, as described above, include the following (Kotter & Sathe, 1978):

Recruiting, selection, and training: Growth companies tend to be extremely selective when hiring and devote extensive resources, both money and thought, to their training process. Characteristics of people hired into growth companies include the ability to perform the job without retraining; the potential for development and growth; the ability to handle and initiate change; and flexibility. Companies experiencing profitable growth tend to show a greater commitment to employee training than non-growth companies. Growth companies emphasize different training topics and approaches; these are often tailored, job-specific topics such as product and customer knowledge. They stress on-the-job training and develop their senior and middle managers through leadership training and regular management conferences. They promote informal communication within the organization.

Team structures and team building: Growth companies tend to have team or matrix structures and prioritize and promote team building within the organization. Team structures, in contrast to traditional hierarchical organizations, allow for success within changing and rapid decision-making work environments. Outside consultants are often utilized to lead team-building exercises intended to strengthen connections, learning, trust, and decision-making abilities.

Managing the culture: Growth companies tend to have an actively articulated and managed but informal company culture. Characteristics of the culture of growth companies include a shared belief in openness; a shared vision for the company; an explicit commitment to employee welfare and quality of life; and norms that support and value learning, flexibility, and change. This company culture is facilitated and promoted through shared, rather than hierarchical, decision-making, a work environment that may be aesthetically pleasing and offers food and exercise facilities, the practice of internal job postings, and flexible schedules.

Planning: Growth companies tend to engage in active organizational and human resource planning. The leaders and managers of growth companies tend to excel at understanding, assessing, and forecasting potential problems. This long-range vision allows managers to address problems and plan solutions before situations become destructive to the organization and inhibit growth.

Human resource staffing: Growth companies tend to employ full-time human resource managers to oversee employee hiring, training, and evaluation. Human resource managers in growth companies tend to go beyond traditional personnel management to work as problem solvers, life coaches, advisors, confidants, and mediators. The human resource manager of a growth company will play an integral role in company activities and regularly meet with managers, the company president, and team-members to assess both their performance and satisfaction in their rules.

Human resource or human capital in growth companies is considered one of the most important and malleable factors or variables effecting growth. Human resource consultants have the potential to help companies optimize their human capital and talent and, ultimately, promote increased growth.

CONCLUSION

Growth companies engage in constant evaluation and forecasting activities to assess how well the company is meeting its goals as well as to search out new opportunities. Consultants to growth companies can improve human resources, investment, financing, production, research and design, marketing, shipping and distribution, forecasting, safety, risk management, and regulatory oversight. Most importantly, consultants can help companies assess

their distinctive capabilities and strategic assets and develop their operating business strategies. Growth companies eschew industry assumptions, develop strategic focus, and value innovation as a means to growing their customer base. They tend to dare to innovate in products, services, and delivery. They optimize their unique strengths and focus on innovation to make their competitors irrelevant in the marketplace (Kim & Maugborgne, 1997). In the final analysis, consultants to growth companies have the opportunity to work in dynamic work environments and influence the direction and operation of the world's most innovative companies.

TERMS & CONCEPTS

Business environment: The combined factors, such as tax structure, public services, government regulations, labor force, and infrastructure, that affect the profitability and experience of conducting business in a particular business organization.

Business strategy: The context for specific business decisions and operating strategies.

Corporation: A firm that is owned by stockholders and operated by professional managers.

Consultants: Professionals who perform specific services for a fee.

Consulting agreements: Contracts between companies and advisors who are not their employees.

Distinctive capabilities: Skills that enable companies to operate at an exceptional level of effectiveness.

Growth: Economic expansion as measured by any of a number of indicators.

Growth companies: Those companies whose rate of growth significantly exceeds that of the average in its field or the overall rate of economic growth.

High-growth companies: Companies that grow at an average rate greater than 20 percent per year for at least four or five years in a row.

Operating business plan: Dynamic document that highlights the strengths and weakness of the company and guides the company toward learning and increased efficiency.

Performance: The results of activities of an organization or investment over a given period of time.

Strategic assets: The resources companies have to exploit.

BIBLIOGRAPHY

Baghai, M., Coley, S., White, D., Conn, C., & McLean, R. (1996). Staircases to growth. *McKinsey Quarterly,*, 38–61.

Gandossy, R., & Greenslade, S. (2005). Leading the way to double-digit growth. *Leader to Leader, 2005,* 15–20.

Global growth companies. (2007). World Economic Forum.

Growth companies share greater commitment to employee training. (1996). *Corporate Board, 17,* 29.

Hanson, M, Thompson, J, & Dahlgren, J. (2004). Overview of consulting agreements. Agriculture Marketing Resource Center.

Heneman, R., Tansky, J., Wang, S., & Wang, Z. (2002). Compensation practices in small entrepreneurial and high-growth companies in the United States and China. *Compensation & Benefits Review, 34,* 13.

Hot Growth. (2006). *Business Week.*

Kim, W., & Mauborgne, R. (1997). Value innovation: the strategic logic of high growth. *Harvard Business Review, 75,* 103–112.

Kotter, J., & Sathe, V. (1978). Problems of human resource management in rapidly growing companies. *California Management Review, 21,* 29.

Little, D. (2001, June 11). Hot growth companies. *Business Week,* pp. 107–110.

Nadler, D. (1997). How the big get bigger: Managing for growth. *Human Resource Planning, 20,* 11–14.

S & P 500. (2007). Standard and Poor's.

Tumer, R. (2006). Developing fast growth companies. *Engineering Management, 16,* 24–28.

Zielasko, D. (2006). Making the grade as a growth company. *Rubber & Plastics News, 35,* 6.

SUGGESTED READING

Beneda, N. (2003). Estimating free cash flows and valuing a growth company. *Journal of Asset Management, 4,* 247–257.

Bragg, S. (2000). How explosive growth companies can conserve cash. *Journal of Corporate Accounting & Finance (Wiley), 12,* 9– 4.

Sherman, A. (2003). Human capital — a critical growth driver. *Fast-Track Business Growth,* 73–82.

Treynor, J. (1994). Growth companies. *Financial Analysts Journal, 50,* 12–16.

Essay by Simone I. Flynn, Ph.D.

CORPORATE ACCOUNTABILITY

This article focuses on the different ways an organization can be held responsible for its activities. With scandals such as Enron, one would think that corporations would adhere to ethical standards. Recent scandals units, such as internal auditing, have been created, and the organization's initiatives with ethics and compliance directly report to the senior management team and the board of directors. Enterprise risk management addresses the risks and opportunities facing an organization by classifying objectives into four categories. Every business realizes that it will need to take some level of risk. Therefore, any approach to risk management should include competitive advantages. There will be a discussion of the role of whistleblowers as well as how regulations such as the False Claims Act (FCA), Sarbanes Oxley Act (SOX), and the Lloyd-La Follette Act have been implemented to encourage employees to report acts of misconduct.

Corporate accountability is a high priority in many businesses today due to the scandals that have occurred during the last decade. Ward (n.d.) believes that some of the dysfunctional behavior that has been witnessed can be traced back to two sources:

- The erroneous belief that a leader, or anyone for that matter, can "predict" and commit to delivering outcomes that he or she has little control over. This pressures leaders to take shortcuts and even "rig the results."

- Tying salary and bonuses to performance, and using them to motivate performance, when performance is difficult if not impossible to accurately measure and assign to cause-and-effect relationships. This encourages people to "fudge the results," using whatever mechanisms are at their disposal to protect their personal interests (par. 3).

Board members are requiring senior management teams to provide more operational information. External and internal stakeholders are requiring more information. In order to have an effective accountability system in place, organizations must commit to improving and encouraging the use of communication processes and education programs.

"Changing to the new accountability requires a change in culture. It is possible to change an organizational culture, but it requires champions who have a lot of courage, patience and persistence" (Ward, n.d., p. 2). Whistleblowers are an example of such champions. In addition, corporations must be committed to implementing systems that will act as a check-and-balance to ensure that the operations are being run properly. An attempt at addressing this scenario is the implementation of an enterprise risk management system.

Whistleblowers

Given the competitiveness in the world today, many people are tempted to go outside of the rules and regulations of society in order to get ahead. Although many argue that traits such as honesty and credibility are valued, temptations have lured some to act irresponsibly. Actions such as cheating, stealing, lying, and bribing have become common in the workplace. Good moral values and actions are becoming the exception rather than the rule. How can the trend turn? Organizations must put policies in place that will encourage employees to do the right thing and inform the proper authorities when illegal actions and dishonesty take place.

Unfortunately, when employees step forward and alert the organization of wrongdoings, they are labeled whistleblowers and negative labels are applied to them. Instead of being considered heroes for doing the right thing, they tend to be chastised and some never fully recover from the experience. Many of these individuals no longer trust their coworkers and their organization.

In 2013 Snowden, an American whistleblower, was charged with violating the Espionage Act for releasing confidential documents belonging to the National Security Agency (NSA). (Courtesy of Laura Poitras/Praxis Films via Wikimedia Commons)

For some, the earth moves when they discover that people in authority routinely lie and those who work for them routinely cover up. Once they realize this, they ' live in a different world. Some remain aliens in this new world forever. Maybe they like it that way. Maybe they don't have a choice (Alford, 2001, p. 52).

Realizing that they can no longer trust their coworkers can be devastating. Often times, whistleblowers may have been friends with their coworkers outside the office, so the loss of these friendships is especially painful. It is unfortunate that society has come to a point where individuals with moral values and a sense of right and wrong are treated as outsiders of societal norms. Whistleblowers have been ostracized, reprimanded, forced to transfer, referred to receive psychiatric care, assigned to menial duties, dismissed, and blacklisted. They may be unable to work at a different company because organizations respond to whistleblowers with hostility and fear.

Sen. Paul Sarbanes (D – MD) and Rep. Michael G. Oxley (R – OH-4) were the co-sponsors of the Sarbanes–Oxley Act. (Courtesy of U.S. House of Representatives (Oxley) and U.S. Senate (Sarbanes) via Wikimedia Commons)

Enterprise Risk Management

With scandals such as Enron, one would think that corporations would adhere to ethical standards. Unfortunately, many view companies such as Enron as the "ones that got caught," and changes have not occurred in the operations of some businesses because the issue has not been taken seriously. However, the trend is changing. According to a survey conducted in January, 2007, by the Risk Management Association (RMA), many organizations "are moving toward a fully integrated enterprise risk management approach where a myriad of risk types are measured and many of the processes automated and standardized" (p. 14).

Many situations—both positive and negative—can affect the future of a business. Situations with a negative impact may be viewed as risks; whereas situations with a positive impact can be viewed as opportunities. The overall objective of most businesses is to minimize risk and seize opportunities. Enterprise risk management addresses the risks and opportunities facing an organization by classifying objectives into four categories:

Strategic: "Big picture" goals focused on supporting an organization's mission.

Operations: Effective and efficient use of the organization's resources.

Reporting: Reliability of reporting.

Compliance: Compliance with laws and regulations.

Federal Protection

The federal government and some states have passed legislation to protect employees who decide to become whistle blowers. According to Sheeder (2006), the federal False Claims Act (FCA) provides protection for:

Any employee who is discharged, demoted, suspended, threatened, harassed, or in any other manner discriminated in the terms and conditions of employment by his or her employer because of lawful acts done by the employee on behalf of the employee or others in furtherance of an action under this section (i.e. a whistleblower action) shall be entitled to all relief necessary to make the employee whole (p. 39).

Many courts will provide protection when:

- an employee becomes a participant in a "protected activity" (i.e. when an employee decides to confront an employer about illegal activities such as fraud)
- the employer becomes aware of the "protected activity"
- the employee is penalized as a result of coming forth about the "protected activity" (i.e. termination, harassment)

When it has been determined that an employee is a victim of retaliation, he or she may petition for:

- reinstatement with the same seniority that he or she would have had if the adverse action did not occur.
- two times back pay
- interest on the back pay
- special damages (i.e. compensation for emotional distress, recovery of litigation costs, and reasonable attorney's fees)
- any type of relief that will assist the employee in becoming a whole person again (Sheeder, 2006, p. 39–40)

An employee is entitled to all the relief listed above as well as any recovery obtained by the government based on the regulations of the FCA. Given the financial penalties for acts of wrongdoing, employers are encouraged to monitor the activities of their organization so that these fines are not imposed.

Company-Drafted Whistleblower Policy

In order To avoid the costly expenses of these types of situations, many organizations are encouraged to draft policies that will assist employees in feeling comfortable about coming forward to advise the senior management team and the outside world of fraudulent behavior occurring in a company. Tennebaum provided these four elements of a good whistleblower policy:

- A policy that has a clear purpose and a statement of intent to protect whistleblowers to the fullest extent possible. The purpose may include creating an environment where the whistleblower feels safe.
- Guidelines that provide a detailed explanation of how the organization will attempt to protect the whistleblower.
- Procedures on who, when, and how to contact the organization in order to report unethical and/or illegal behavior.
- A statement declaring what the organization will do as a result of the whistleblowing activity (Associations Now, 2007, p. 12).

In addition, employers should be proactive and see if they can determine the types of behaviors or situations that encourage employees to participate in unethical behavior and the types of actions that encourage employees to step up and become whistleblowers. Sheeder (2006) identified six common ways employees are encourage to become whistleblowers. In most cases, the lack of organizational support was enough for the employee to seek external assistance in correcting improper behavior. Each of the mentioned scenarios is based on a real-life case study.

Expect employees to participate in fraudulent conduct.

There have been many situations where senior managers are the culprits. In an effort to improve the organization's image and financial records, some executives have encouraged and mandated employees to participate in unethical behavior. Excuses such as "it's really not hurting anyone," "we are getting what we deserve," "be a team player," and "this action offsets the system" have been used to justify the organization's behavior. When an employee refuses to play the game, he or she may be terminated, which forces the former employee to file a retaliation lawsuit.

Dismiss employee concerns or complaints.

Hire an attorney to champion their cause.

Forget about a professional's ethical duty to report.

Some employees may feel that they are obligated to report unethical practices to maintain the image of their profession. For example, a police officer may become aware that his partner is working with criminals. After attempting to reason with the partner, the police officer may feel a need to alert internal affairs to maintain a positive image of police officers of the community and protect the public from criminal activities.

Don't give "Public Duty" enough respect.

There have been cases where an organization may be overbilling another entity and the employee may not be able to support the deception. For example, some hospitals have been accused of overcharging Medicare programs. There may be an employee who believes that the process is unethical, and innocent people may suffer as a result of the deceptive actions. Therefore, the employee feels obligated to turn the hospital in to the proper authorities. The employee may believe that it is his or her civic and public duty to do so.

Fail to take prompt and proper corrective action.

Many employees have followed the company's policy on reporting fraudulent activity only to find out that their good deed has been ignored. They believe their only alternative is to expose the situation externally since the system has failed internally.

Underestimate the perseverance of an employee.

Some organizations wrongly assume that if they ignore the employee, the problem will go away. However, employees with a conscience will pursue their cause until the problem has been resolved.

Government Legislation

Organizations need to realize that there are people who value their conscience over their job. The government recognized that big business may not always do the right thing. Therefore, it has introduced and implemented some regulations to level the playing field and allow employees to come forth. These are examples of such legislation:

(FCA):This act is a qui tam provision that was enacted during Abraham Lincoln's tenure as president. The purpose of the legislation is to protect the government from the fraudulent suppliers of faulty war equipment during the Civil War. Revisions were made to the act in 1943 and 1986. In 1986, there was a significant expansion of the rights of whistleblowers and their attorneys. The law allows individuals to file actions against federal contractors claiming fraud against the government. People filing under the act may receive 15–25 percent of any recovered damages.

(SOX):Legislation passed in 2002 with the purpose of encouraging employees to become effective corporate monitors and report misconduct and unethical behavior in corporations. The sct has two approaches that encourage employees to become corporate whistleblowers (Moberly, 2006). The first step is a clause that provides protection to whistleblowers from employer retaliation once they have disclosed improper behavior. The second step requires employers to provide employees with guidelines, policies, and procedures to report organizational misconduct within the organization.

This act was enacted in 1912 and designed to protect American civil servants from retaliation. The purpose was to ensure the right of employees when they wanted to provide the House of Congress, a committee or individual congressman with information about fraud. The intent was to provide job protection rights to federal employees.

VIEWPOINT

Enterprise Risk Management (ERM)

By placing an organization's objectives into categories, one can focus on different aspects of enterprise risk management. Although the categories are different, they can overlap in terms of objectives. ERM is made up of eight interrelated components that define the manner in which a management team runs an organization and how the practices are processed (COSO, 2004). The components are:

Internal environment: The internal environment is an organization's tone and culture. It sets the bar for how risk is viewed by the organization and its employees. Organizations develop their philosophy, integrity standards, and ethical values on risk management.

Objective setting: Although an organization may have objectives in place prior to the implementation of a risk management plan, the ERM process ensures that the established objectives are in alignment with the organization's mission and position on risk.

Event identification: An organization must identify the internal and external events that may affect its ability to achieve goals, and the events have to be classified as risks or opportunities. Opportunities are shared with the management team to determine if they should be incorporated into the organization's goals and objectives.

Risk assessment: Risks are assessed and evaluated on a regular basis so that the organization can analyze what type of impact each has on the entity.

Risk response: The management team is responsible for selecting the appropriate action to risk events. Responses are based on an organization's risk tolerance and risk appetite.

Control activities. Policies and procedures are put in place to ensure that risk responses are effectively implemented.

Information and communication: Relevant information is identified and communicated in a timeframe that will allow employees to perform their responsibilities. The communication process should flow up, down, and across the organizational structure.

Monitoring: The ERM system is monitored and modified when appropriate. Monitoring is achieved through management interventions, separate evaluations, or a combination of both.

Ensuring ERM Success

If one wanted to determine the effectiveness of an organization's ERM, he or she would have to assess whether or not the eight components are working effectively. In order for the components to work, material weaknesses must be eliminated and the risk level has to be within the organization's risk appetite. In addition, the management team and board of directors must have an understanding of how the four categories of objectives are being achieved and know that the reporting process is reliable and addresses compliance with laws and regulations.

The senior management team could also implement a corporate risk policy to ensure that the ERM process is successful. Brown (n.d.) suggested a four-step process for this type of policy. The first step is to identify the major risks faced by the organization. Once they have been identified, the next step is to create an organizational approach to measure, monitor, and control the risks.

During the measuring phase, a value is assigned to each risk level, and it can be either quantitative or qualitative. The next phase, monitoring, requires the organization to track changes in risk over a period of time. The final step, controlling, requires the risk level to be modified in order to be in compliance with the risk-taking appetite and policies set by the shareholders and board of directors. This framework is applied to each risk category. Brown (n.d.) provided a summary of eight types of risk that fall into four different categories (i.e. financial risk, operational risk, strategic risk, and hazard risk).

CONCLUSION

Given the competitiveness in the world today, many people are tempted to go outside of the rules and regulations of society in order to get ahead. Although many argue that traits such as honesty and credibility are valued, temptations have lured some to act irresponsibly. Actions such as cheating, stealing, lying, and bribing have become common in the workplace. Good moral values and actions are becoming the exception rather than the rule. How can the trend turn? Organizations must put policies in place that will encourage employees to do the right thing and inform the proper authorities when illegal actions and dishonesty take place.

Unfortunately, when employees step forward and alert the organization of wrongdoings, they are called whistleblowers and negative labels are applied to them. Instead of being considered heroes for doing the right thing, they tend to be chastised and some never fully recover from the experience. Many of these lose trust in fellow employees and their organization.

With scandals such as Enron, one would think that corporations would adhere to ethical standards.

Unfortunately, many view companies such as Enron as the "ones that got caught," and changes have not occurred in the operations of some businesses because the issue has not been taken seriously. However, the trend is changing. According to a survey conducted in January, 2007, by the Risk Management Association (RMA), many organizations "are moving toward a fully integrated enterprise risk management approach where a myriad of risk types are measured and many of the processes automated and standardized" (p. 14).

The senior management team should also implement a corporate risk policy in order to ensure that the ERM process is successful. Brown (n.d.) suggested a four-step process for this type of policy. The first step is to identify the major risks faced by the organization. Once they have been identified, the next step is to create an organizational approach to measure, monitor, and control the risks.

During the measuring phase, a value is assigned to each risk level, and this value may be either quantitative or qualitative. The next phase, monitoring, requires the organization to track changes in risk over a period of time. The final step, controlling, requires the risk level to be modified in order to be in compliance with the risk-taking appetite and policies set by the shareholders and board of directors. This framework is applied to each risk category.

TERMS & CONCEPTS

Credit risk: The risk of loss due to a debtor's non-payment of a loan or other line of credit.

Enron: An American energy company based in Houston, Texas. Before its bankruptcy in late 2001, Enron employed about 21,000 people and was one of the world's leading electricity, natural gas, pulp and paper, and communications companies, with claimed revenues of $111 billion in 2000. Enron was hailed by many, including its workforce, as an overall great company, praised for its large long-term pensions, benefits for its workers, and extremely effective management until its exposure in corporate fraud.

Enterprise risk management (ERM): Methods and processes used to manage those risks, possible events, or circumstances that can have an influence on business enterprises. By identifying and proactively treating such potential effects, one protects the existence, resources (human and capital), products and services, or customers of the enterprise as well as external effects on society, markets, and environments.

False Claims Act (FCA): A qui tam provision that was enacted during Abraham Lincoln's tenure as president. The purpose of the legislation is to protect the government from the fraudulent suppliers of faulty war equipment during the Civil War. Revisions were made to the act in 1943 and 1986. In 1986, there was a significant expansion of the rights of whistleblowers and their attorneys.

Financial risk: Any risk associated with money.

Legal risk: Sometimes the government changes the law in a way that adversely affects an organization's position.

Liquidity risk: Situations in which a party interested in trading an asset cannot because no one in the market wants to trade that asset.

Lloyd-La Follette Act: This act was enacted in 1912 and was designed to protect American civil servants from retaliation.

Market risk: The risk that the value of an investment will decrease due to moves in the market factors.

Operational risk: The risk of loss resulting from inadequate or failed internal processes, people, and systems, or from external events.

Sarbanes Oxley Act (SOX): Legislation passed in 2002 with the purpose of encouraging employees to become effective corporate monitors and report misconduct and unethical behavior in corporations.

Whistleblowers: An employee, former employee, or member of an organization, especially a business or government agency, who reports misconduct to people or entities with the power and presumed willingness to take corrective action. Generally, the misconduct is a violation of law, rule, regulation and/or a direct threat to public interest – fraud, health, safety violations, and corruption are just a few examples.

BIBLIOGRAPHY

Alford, C. (2001). *Whistleblowers: Broken lives and organizational power.* Ithaca and London: Cornell University Press.

Brown, B. (n.d.) Step-by-step enterprise risk management. Risk Management Magazine.

Enterprise risk management – Integrated framework: Executive summary. (2004, September). Committee of Sponsoring Organizations.

Lenn, L. E. (2013). Sarbanes-Oxley Act 2002 (SOX) -10 years later. *Journal of Legal Issues & Cases in Business,* 21–14.

Mitra, S., Jaggi, B., & Hossain, M. (2013). Internal control weaknesses and accounting conservatism: Evidence from the post – Sarbanes – Oxley period. *Journal of Accounting, Auditing & Finance,* 28(2), 152–191.

Moberly, R. (2006). Sarbanes-Oxley's structural model to encourage corporate whistleblowers. *Brigham Young University Law Review, 2006*(5), 1107–1175.

Prawitt, D. F., Sharp, N. Y., & Wood, D. A. (2012). Internal audit outsourcing and the risk of misleading or fraudulent financial reporting: Did Sarbanes-Oxley get it wrong? *Contemporary Accounting Research, 29*(4), 1109–1136.

RMA announces results of enterprise risk management survey. (2007). *Secured Lender, 63*(1), 14.

Sheeder, F. (2006). Whistleblowers are not born that way – We create them through multiple system failures. *Journal of Health Care Compliance, 8*(4), 39–73.

Ward, B. (n.d.). The new accountability: Part 1.

SUGGESTED READING

Burrowes, A. & Sipple, S. (2007). Corporate accountability and continuing fraud. *Chartered Accountants Journal, 86*(10), 70–71.

Kinnear, J. (2002). Corporate governance: A system for accountability. *Directorship, 28*(6), 9–15.

Kosta, Karen da. (2017). Corporate accountability in the Samarco chemical sludge disaster, *Disaster Prevention Management, 26*(5), 540–552.

Walker, D. (2003, January 24). GAO forum on governance and accountability: Challenges to restore public confidence in U.S. corporate governance and accountability systems: GAO-03-419SP. *GAO Reports,* 1–38.

Essay by Marie Gould

CORPORATE FINANCIAL POLICY

A corporation's financial policy defines the company's overall approach to managing its financial decisions. A company's financial strategy is comprised of the following: capital budgeting, financing, and dividend policy. While every corporation typically deals with these three areas when setting its financial policies, each organization must examine many factors that are unique to its business and situation before setting up its overall policies. Trends in setting corporate financial policies have been changing over the past decade. While investors and shareholders want to ensure that there is capital available to grow the business, shareholders are increasingly comfortable in accumulating debt to do so. In today's fast changing marketplace, corporate managers and investors are looking for short-term gains as opposed to more traditional long-term financial strategies. The financial fitness of an organization is typically assessed from looking at its balance sheet; the ways that companies are willing to manipulate or dirty their balance sheets is discussed. Investors are keen to see a return on their equity investment in the form of dividends (also known as shareholder or investor value). Investors and shareholders have become increasingly active in determining corporate fiscal policy with an eye toward short-term financial rewards for themselves. U.S. corporations and their investors are much more comfortable operating at much higher risk levels than ever before; U.S. corporations have on average the lowest credit rating in history, which is another indication of how comfortable today's corporations are at operating in high-risk situations.

There are many aspects associated with planning and implementing a corporate financial policy. Historically, corporations have focused on both short-term and long-term planning when determining financial policies. Conventional wisdom indicates that investors favor companies with good fundamentals or a strong balance sheet. Corporations are faced with many decisions related to how to grow and finance their operations. The following are some factors that companies typically take into account when mapping out their financial strategy:

- Since the interest on debt is deductible, does it make sense to borrow more?
- What is the best thing to do with excess cash?
- Should cash be used to finance the business or returned to shareholders?

While these questions are rhetorical in nature, the answers are dependent upon linking financial strategy and business strategy. In terms of solid planning, companies should be looking into the longer term (typically 3 to 5 years) for direction. In essence, companies should have solid projections about what their cash flow or debt service will be for the next few years. If cash flow is strong, then companies are in a good position to acquire target companies in their industry, fund capital projects, or even improve existing operations. Cash allows companies much flexibility and security. Some mature companies may not have any acquisition targets and may well decide to distribute cash back to investors or shareholders. A couple of options are buying back stocks that are undervalued or paying dividends with them if they are overvalued (Godehart, Koller, & Rehm, 2006). Companies that are less mature or in highly competitive markets may have no choice but to take on debt to stay competitive—investments in infrastructure or target acquisitions are necessary to capture market share. A company's credit rating has historically been an important factor in securing competitive rates for borrowing. This essay discusses the changing trends in credit ratings in the United States and explains how these changes are affecting corporations. Debt is certainly not all bad, and many companies benefit from interest deductions on debt. Debt also keeps many companies honest by requiring discipline in making interest and principal payments.

Public corporations have long answered to shareholders by developing and executing solid financial policies. Much has been written about federal legislation that has been enacted to safeguard investor equity in corporations. Increasing numbers of public companies are "going private" as a way to escape the demanding regulatory environments imposed by federal legislation. This essay looks at the impact that private equity funds have had in the "going-private" movement and the effects that this trend has on corporate financial policy. Investors in public companies have become more involved in setting social and financial policies at their organizations. These so-called activist investors are shaping capital structures by influencing the debt-to-equity ratios of their companies. Finally, this essay looks at the high tolerance for risk that became prevalent in corporate America in the early 2000s. Access to cheap and abundant capital, emboldened shareholders and investors, and a high tolerance for risk have truly had a profound effect on corporate financial strategies.

APPLICATIONS

Investors typically look at a company's balance sheet as an indication of financial fitness. The company balance sheet illustrates the capital structure of an organization. Capital structure is a term that deals specifically with a company's debt-to-equity ratio. The ratio of debt to equity has always been an important consideration for investors and offers one of the best pictures of a company's leverage.

Managing capital structure is a balancing act that requires financial flexibility and fiscal discipline. Achieving a balance of debt and equity has been one of the biggest challenges to organizations, and it remains a major concern. The long-term impact of capital structure means managing operating cash flows and cost of capital. The interest exposure on debt is tax deductible, and a company can reduce its after-tax cost of capital by increasing debt relative to equity (Godehart, Koller, & Rehm, 2006).

Calculating Debt-to-Equity

Total Liabilities / Total Shareholders' Equity, where shareholder equity = common stock plus firm profits or losses (Adapted from McClure, n.d.)

The following is an illustration of the impact that the debt-to-equity ratio can have on an organization. In general, a debt ratio of 0.5 to 1.5 is considered a good ratio (McClure, n.d.).

If Company A has long-term debt (in a bond) of $10 million and has $10 million in equity, the debt-to-equity ratio is 1 (10 / 10 = 1). This ratio falls well within acceptable debt-to-equity ratios.

If Company B has long-term debt (in a bond) of $10 million and has $1 million in equity, the debt-to-equity ratio is 10 (10 / 1 = 10). This ratio is too high for most investors to feel comfortable. This company is debt laden.

It Company C has long-term debt (in a bond) of $10 million and has $20 million in equity, the debt-to-equity ratio is 0.5 (10 / 20 = 0.5). Investors will look upon this ratio favorably because the company has little debt compared to its equity.

Balancing Debt & Equity

"Indeed, the potential harm to a company's operations and business strategy from a bad capital structure is greater than the potential benefits from tax and financial leverage. Instead of relying on capital structure to create value on its own, companies should try to make it work hand in hand with their business strategy, by striking a balance between the discipline and tax savings that debt can deliver and the greater flexibility of equity" (Godehart, Koller, & Rehm, 2006).

Strong corporate fundamentals are a requisite for investors. Investors have long used criteria such as solid balance sheets and favorable credit ratings to decide where to invest their dollars. But just how much faith investors can put into balance sheets is being questioned. Baldwin describes tactics that create "dirty balance sheets." He describes tactics that reward companies to pile on debt by perpetuating the practice of allowing corporate deductions on interest from debt. "Financial engineers replace equity with debt and therefore cut tax bills" (Baldwin, 2006).

According to Baldwin, there are a couple of popular ways to turn equity into debt and spin the whole process as a being a sound financial strategy. The first way is to have a debt-financed takeover. This popular strategy allowed private equity firms to finance takeovers and buyouts with little money down and receive a reward in the form of an interest deduction on the huge debt. The second option for turning equity into debt involves the practice of companies buying back their own stock (shares), which shrinks their equity and their tax bills. The trend toward dirtying up balance sheets happened on a grand scale in the early-to-mid 2000s (Baldwin, 2006). There was a significant trend toward dirtying or repackaging existing corporate debt-to-equity figures (as well as buying and reselling of existing corporate stocks).

"This dirtying-up of corporate balance sheets [was] taking place on a grand scale. The graph below shows how much the retirement of equity (via buybacks, LBOs and merger activity) exceed[ed] the issuance of equity (through offerings of new shares)" (Baldwin, 2006, p. 18).

ISSUES

Corporate Credit Ratings

According to a January 2006 Deutsche Bank survey, respondents stated that the single most important factor in a firm's decision regarding overall capital structure was the credit rating of their company. In 2001, another survey had credit ratings as the second most important factor in determining capital structure. Some of the reasons why companies watch credit ratings closely include the following:

■ Rate changes on debt—a downgrade makes debt a lot more expensive to finance
■ Lower credit ratings result in diminished access to capital markets
■ Companies with lower ratings do not have access to debt capital as quickly (readily) as companies with higher credit ratings
■ A lower credit rating reflects the likelihood of financial distress—a downgraded credit rating indicates a question about a company's ability to make its principal and interest payments

Credit rating agencies look at short-term and long-term debt on a company's balance sheet in determining debt, even though there may be other debt on the books. Overall, the survey indicates that companies and managers consider credit rating to be a key determinant in how much debt they should have (Servaes & Tufano, 2006).

In another paper that provides research on the effect of credit rating on capital structure, the author says credit rating directly affects capital structure decision-making. Managers are concerned by the discrete costs (benefits) associated with rating levels. Ratings have a direct or an indirect effect on the following:

■ cost of capital
■ changes in bond coupon rates
■ potential loss of contracts
■ potential repurchase of bonds
■ loss of access to commercial paper markets

The author points out that credit ratings are significant in every financial marketplace and thus are critical when firms consider the impact of rating changes to their organizations (Kisgen, 2006). A number of factors can contribute to a downward trend in the credit rating profile and include investor's willingness to accept higher risk and the adoption of aggressive corporate financial policies that are aimed at appeasing stockholders (Riccio, 2007).

Rating Trends

More factors contributing to the rating slump included an increase in the number of new middle market-type companies tapping the bond and loan markets and the popularity of leveraged buyouts also contributing to the amount of debt used to finance many mergers and acquisitions. Despite market analysts' predictions of a nearly inevitable, sharp increase in companies defaulting on loans, the credit markets appeared a lot more comfortable with higher credit risks in the market, and many new issuers (companies entering the public markets) seemed unfazed by the B-ratings. New entries to the market added significantly to the higher number of B-rated companies, but there was also an exodus of companies from investment grade (A) down to B-ratings. Such companies are referred to as "fallen angels" as they have slipped from investment grade to speculative grade. Further, S&P stated in 2007 that it had issued more than 1,100 B-ratings in just the preceding four years, and even within the B-rating categories, the ratings were slipping. B+ ratings fell to a lower percentage than flat B-ratings, with B+ comprising 38 percent and the flat B comprising 46 percent (Riccio, 2007).

There is no question that companies benefited from cheap and abundant capital in the early-to-mid 2000s. Credit ratings can have a big impact on the cost of financing debt, but the rate spread between investment grade and speculative grade financing narrowed sharply. This simply means that companies with lower ratings grades have had access to equity that was quite inexpensive. A good credit rating cannot be discounted, however, as it affects decisions by investors when deciding to invest in companies. If capital becomes less readily available, it becomes more expensive for B-rated companies to finance debt and the market becomes more risk wary, then the credit rating may take back its prominent role related to debt financing.

Shareholder Value & Short-Term Earning Investment

Corporate financial policies are subject to many changes that result from economic conditions, market influences, and the influence of stakeholders. Investors in public and private companies have been playing a larger role in setting corporate financial policies.

Shareholders at public companies have only become actively involved in setting company policy since about the turn of the twenty-first century. The rise of shareholder activism apparently coincided with many of the major corporate scandals (Enron, Tyco, Worldcom) of the early 2000s. Most corporate investors did not play an active role in trying to influence management decisions and policies even though they are the true "owners" of the corporation; some estimates put the historical average percentage of dead (or un-cast) proxy votes by shareholders at 60 percent (Goff, 2004). The overwhelming lack of interest that these percentages show on the part of company shareholders has been blamed for corporate mismanagement on a grand scale. Shareholder activism started as a grassroots effort to influence social policies at corporations but later spread into the financial arena.

The easy availability of capital—including low interest rates and low-risk loans—emboldened many company shareholders to pursue "shareholder value," some might say at the expense of sound corporate financial policy. According to a PricewaterhouseCoopers (PwC) report, private equity funding has had a big impact on corporate financial decision-making. Private equity (PE) funding made a big splash in corporate financial markets in the mid-2000s. PE money has been around for a while, but after 2005 its influence in the marketplace soared. Between 2005 and 2007, according to PwC, there was an increase in the collaboration between corporate managers and PE firms, which resulted in a number of high-profile public companies defecting out of public markets by going private.

Many pundits blamed Sarbanes-Oxley's burdensome regulations with driving public companies to private status, when it may be PE that fueled the exodus. Consider the following statistics that show the percentage of going-private deals that were funded by PE between 1998 and 2007 (Private equity fuels larger, collaborate going-private transactions, 2007):

- 1998—$21 billion;
- 2005—$63 billion;
- 2006—$117 billion (86% increase in 1 year);
- 2007 (1st quarter)—$62 billion.

Additionally, beginning in 2005, there was an upsurge in larger companies going private (Private equity fuels larger, collaborate going-private transactions, 2007). The global economic crisis of 2008 and 2009 put a damper on the overall number of going-private deals made, with the size and frequency of such deals rising again in 2010 and 2011 but cooling off again slightly in 2012 (Weil, 2013). The significance of the going-private trend on corporate financial decisions points to an emphasis on creating shareholder value. The high returns of PE-financed deals translated into high value for both shareholders and companies. PE-financed going-private transactions typically encourage some or all of an existing company's management team to stay onboard. Executives that do transition to private status usually take an equity share in the company while maintaining their managerial duties. The goal is not just to reward shareholders but to grow the company's value and reap economic rewards for knowledgeable executives as well as the PE team. There is no question that the focus of many of these deals is on short-term growth and results, which is contradictory to many financial policies at more traditional public companies. Going private allows CEOs to escape investor scrutiny and many of the regulatory burdens that public companies must face (Private equity fuels larger, collaborate going-private transactions, 2007).

According to the Securities and Exchange Commission (SEC), "A company 'goes private' when it reduces the number of its shareholders to fewer than 300 and is no longer required to file reports with the SEC." For shareholders of public companies, the lure of high shareholder returns seen in PE going-private transactions did not go unnoticed. "The latest trend for shareholders is taking on hefty debt," Kim (2007) notes. The debt accumulation will serve two purposes. It allows shareholders to reward themselves monetarily using other people's money, and it serves as an alternative to the acceptance of going-private proposals.

"Activists have begun to clamor for companies to incur more debt, and the public increasingly embraces leveraged recapitalizations as alternatives to going-private transactions. Confident that leveraging tomorrow's cash flows to finance today's cash payments does not come at the expense of long-term prospects, companies have begun to float leveraged dividend recapitalizations in the market in order to return value to shareholders or preemptively ward off potential takeovers" (Kim, 2007, p. 6).

There is no question that many shareholders were captivated by a number of highly publicized PE deals that paid off big for investors. Investors at public companies still see high returns in PE deals as a product of financial engineering. That is to say, investors are under the impression that the promise of high returns is not necessarily dependent on investing in business operations and efficiencies. By emulating PE methods, activist shareholders are convinced that they too can reap high returns. The mantra for many public company shareholders has been as follows (Kim, 2007):

- Load up on debt.
- Sell company assets.
- Cut costs.
- Increase cash flow.
- Risk is no longer relevant.
- Debt is good, cash is bad.
- A strong balance sheet signals weak management.

Cash flow is still critical to fund ongoing investments, research and development, and opportunities to enter new markets. Putting a stranglehold on cash and taking on massive debt still holds the great potential to choke growth. There is plenty of speculation that practices of loading up on debt lead to credit deterioration and more fallen angels.

Investor activists are certainly driving corporate financial policy to a greater extent than ever before. Highly leveraged companies do not reflect well on the company balance sheet, but investors seem oblivious. Investors have been focused on short-term gains; according to Reuters, by 2010 the average holding period for a stock on the New York Stock Exchange (NYSE) was just six months (Saft, 2012), and there has been a precipitous move away from long-term value creation.

Corporate financial policies, once careful to balance debt and equity, manage risk for shareholders and plan for the long-term growth and stability of U.S. corporations appear subject to attention deficit.

TERMS & CONCEPTS

Activist shareholder: An individual who tries to utilize his or her rights as a shareholder of a publicly traded corporation to foment social change. Shareholder activism is a way in which shareholders can control a corporation's behavior by exercising their privileges as owners.

Capital structure: "A mix of a company's long-term debt, specific short-term debt, common equity, and preferred equity. The capital structure is how a firm finances its overall operations and growth by using different sources of funds" (Investopedia, 2007).

Debt: Debt comes in the form of bond issues or long-term notes payable.

Debt-to-equity ratio (D/E): "A measure of a company's financial leverage calculated by dividing its total liabilities by stockholders' equity. It indicates what portion of equity and debt the company is using to finance its assets" (Investopedia, 2007).

Equity: Classified as common stock, preferred stock, or retained earnings.

Fallen angels: Public companies that fell from investment grade ratings to speculative grade ratings in the eyes of credit rating agencies.

Financial engineering: "The creation of a new and improved financial products through innovative design or repackaging of existing financial instruments" (The Free Dictionary, 2007).

Going-private transactions: A company "goes private" when it reduces the number of its shareholders to fewer than 300 and is no longer required to file reports with the SEC (SEC.gov).

Leveraged buyouts (LBO): A highly leveraged transaction (HLT), or "bootstrap" transaction, occurs when a financial sponsor gains a majority of control a target company's equity through the use of borrowed money or debt.

Leveraged recapitalizations: A technique typically used to circumvent a hostile acquisition. Using this strategy, a company acquires additional debt to repurchase stocks through a buyback program or appropriates a large dividend among the shareholders.

Shareholder value: The idea that the prioritized goal for a company is to augment the wealth of its shareholders (owners) through activities such as paying dividends and causing the stock price to rise.

BIBLIOGRAPHY

Aslan, H., & Kumar, P. (2011). Lemons or cherries? Growth opportunities and market temptations in going public and private. *Journal of Financial & Quantitative Analysis, 16*(2), 489–526.

Baldwin, W. (2006). The equity vanishes. *Forbes, 777*(11), 18.

Ben Dor, A., & Zhe, X. (2011). Fallen angels: Characteristics, performance, and implications for investors. *Journal of Fixed Income, 20*(4), 33–58.

Godehart, M. Koller, T., & Rehm, W. (2006) Making capital structure support strategy. CFO.com.

Goff, J. (2004). Who's the boss? CFO.com.

Guo, S., Hotchkiss, E. S., & Song, W. (2011). Do buyouts (still) create value? *Journal of Finance,* 66(2), 479–517.

Kim, J. (2007). Shareholder activists get by with a little help from a lot of leverage. *Bank Loan Report,* 22(15), 4–12.

Kisgen, D. (2006). Credit ratings and capital structure. *Journal of Finance.*

Loth, R. (n.d.). Evaluating a company's capital structure. Investopedia.

McClure, B. (n.d.). Debt reckoning. Investopedia.

Private equity fuels larger, collaborate going-private transactions. (2007). PricewaterhouseCoopers.

Riccio, N. (2007, September 28). Corporate credit ratings hit a low point. Business Week Online, 25.

Saft, J. (2012, March 2). The wisdom of exercising patience in investing. Reuters.com.

Servaes, H., & Tufano, P. (2006). Corporate capital structure. Deutsche Bank.

Weil. (2013, May). A look back at sponsor-backed going private transactions.

SUGGESTED READING

Barclay, M., & Smith, C. (2005). The capital structure puzzle: The evidence revisited. *Journal of Applied Corporate Finance, 17*(1), 8–17.

Gordon, R., & Lee, Y. (2007). Interest rates, taxes and corporate financial policies. *National Tax Journal, 60*(1), 65–84.

Markides, C., & Oyon, D. (1994). Stealing from thy neighbour: Leveraged recapitalizations and wealth redistribution. *British Journal of Management, 5*(2), 139.

Myint, S., & Famery, F. (2012). *The handbook of corporate financial risk management.* [N.p.]: Risk Books.

Troughton, G. H., Fridson, M. S., & Clayman, M. R. (2012). *Corporate finance: A practical approach.* Hoboken, NJ: Wiley.

Essay by Carolyn Sprague, MLS

COST ACCOUNTING

ABSTRACT

This article explains the essential concepts of cost accounting. The overview provides an introduction to the basic cost accounting objectives and techniques, the roles of the controller and cost accountant within the corporate management structure, and the ethical considerations that guide cost accountants. This article also explains the basic cost accumulation methods that are used in cost accounting systems. These methods include job order costing, process costing, backflush costing, hybrid costing, and joint and by-product costing. Further, explanations of the most common costs that companies must plan for and control are included, such as direct labor, direct material and factory overhead costs. Finally, this overview describes how cost accounting techniques affect business considerations in areas such as budgeting, pricing and inventory costing methods, which include throughput, direct, absorption, and activity-based costing systems.

OVERVIEW

Cost accounting is the application of accounting and costing principles to the tracking, recording, and analysis of the costs associated with the products or services a business produces and the activities involved in the production process. Broadly speaking, cost accounting objectives include the preparation of statistical data, application of cost accumulation, and cost control methods to production processes and analysis of an organization's profitability as compared with previous periods of time and projected budgets. Cost accountants use basic accounting techniques to compile and analyze data to meet these objectives. In performing these tasks, cost accountants work within the controller's office or the accounting department of most companies. And in addition to any internal company policies that govern their duties, cost accountants must consider the ethical principles that guide the accounting and financial reporting industries. The following sections provide a more in-depth explanation of these concepts.

Introduction to Cost Accounting

Cost accounting identifies, defines, measures, reports, and analyzes the various elements of direct and indirect costs associated with producing and marketing goods and services. Cost accounting also measures performance, product quality, and productivity. Direct costs can be directly traced to producing specific goods or services, such as the cost of raw materials used in the production of a final consumer good. Indirect costs are expenditures on labor, materials, or services that cannot be economically identified with a specific saleable cost unit. Indirect costs include salaries for employees and rental or lease payments for office or factory space.

Cost Accounting Objectives & Techniques

The main objective of cost accounting is to compile, analyze, and transmit both financial and non-financial information to management for planning, controlling, and operational evaluation purposes. At its most basic, cost accounting measures the economic sacrifice an organization makes to achieve its goals. Costs are generally categorized by expenditure type. For instance, product costs represent the monetary measurement of resources an organization uses, such as material, labor, and overhead. Service costs are the

monetary sacrifices it makes to provide the goods or services. Cost accounting tracks these costs and provides this information to management so that the management team can make more informed business and administrative decisions. For this reason, modern cost accounting often is called "management accounting" because managers use accounting data to guide their decisions. In addition, managers oversee and distribute resources to most efficiently meet an organization's goals. Managers use the information produced by cost accounting techniques to direct day-to-day operations and supply feedback to evaluate and control performance.

Data Compilation & Analysis

To compile data for management, cost accountants obtain cost information on product and service costs from a variety of sources. For instance, they may use vendor invoices, engineering studies of production processes, employee timesheets, and planning schedules from production supervisors. Once they have compiled sufficient records, cost accountants use various means of analyzing the data, depending on the results they are seeking to obtain. Cost analysis techniques include break-even analysis, comparative cost analysis, capital expenditure analysis, and budgeting techniques.

- The break-even point for a product is the point at which the total revenue generated equals the total costs associated with the production and sale of a given product.
- Break-even analysis is the study of when it is profitable for a business to introduce a new product as opposed to modifying an existing product so that it becomes more lucrative.
- Comparative cost analysis involves identifying the costs associated with the baseline materials and processes and any available alternatives, and calculating the comparative costs between them.
- Capital expenditure analysis involves reviewing the funds spent for the acquisition of long-term assets.

Interpretation

After performing their analyses, cost accountants then use their professional judgment to interpret the results of each costing technique as they apply to different aspects of a company's financial analysis. For example, although break-even analysis indicates the capacity at which operations become profitable, it assumes a static condition in which sales prices and expenses are constant. However, such factors do not remain constant in the real world. Inflation and supply and demand cause sales prices and expenses to vary. Cost accountants, therefore, work with many people in other departments of a company (such as marketing, engineering, manufacturing, financial accounting, and human resources personnel) to obtain current information that may account for some of these fluctuations.

Finally, cost accountants collect all costs involved in the process of making goods or providing services and use such cost data for income measurement and inventory valuation. This information also helps management plan and make operational decisions. Because of these responsibilities, cost accountants must exercise initiative and good judgment and meet high ethical standards. Further, cost accountants must provide management with information that may indicate adverse economic conditions when these situations arise, such as reports about poor product quality, cost overruns, or abuses of company policies.

Roles of Controllers & Cost Accountants

A controller is the title that is often given to a company's chief accounting officer or manager of the accounting department. A controller plays a significant role in planning and guiding a company's financial decisions and is often charged with the tasks of designing systems to prepare internal reports for management and external reports for public and government users. A cost accountant is a member of the controller's department and is responsible for collecting product costs and preparing accurate and timely reports to evaluate and control company operations. As such, cost accountants assemble, classify, and summarize financial and economic data on the production and pricing of goods or services.

In addition, cost accountants play an important role in coordinating external and internal data so managers can formulate better planning and control activities. In the planning phases, cost accountants help management by preparing budgets that provide cost estimates of material, labor, and technology. A company uses this data to review alternative courses of action and select the best methods of achieving its goals and profit objectives. Cost accounting data are used for both planning and control activities. These activities differ in that planning activities are focused on future goals while control activities involve monitoring present production processes and tracking any variations from estimated budgets and plans. Cost accountants monitor these activities and issue progress reports that summarizing their costs and the efficiency of the processes associated with them. By comparing actual results with the forecasted budget amounts, cost accountants are able to identify areas of deviation where problems may be developing. Cost accountants also compile and relay this information to management so that appropriate decisions can be made to shore up inefficient or failing processes within an organization.

Ethical Considerations Facing Cost Accountants

Cost accountants face several types of ethical problems. A major one is confidentiality. This issue is particularly important because cost accountants typically have detailed access to sensitive information, such as payroll records, product costs, and individual product or departmental profits. Cost accountants must carefully safeguard such information because if improperly disclosed, it could be improperly used by other entities or even by hostile personnel within an organization.

Another issue that cost accountants face is integrity, particularly when faced with difficult tasks that may surpass their training or level of experience. This is critical because the reports and analyses that cost accountants generate become the foundation upon which management teams stake critical decisions, and thus it is imperative that the information contained in these materials be complete and accurate. Finally, cost accountants must maintain the ability to view information and strategies objectively. Objectivity allows a cost accountant to present cost analyses in a fair, well-balanced format that discloses all relevant information pertaining to a decision. Cost accountants may face considerable pressure from managers whose operations are being reviewed to skew reported information in such a way as to make the departments or products they oversee appear to be in better financial standing than they actually are. Thus, ethical considerations such as confidentiality, integrity, and objectivity are an important part of the responsibilities that cost accountants face and their observance, or lack thereof, can have a significant impact on a company's future.

Cost Accumulation

One of the most important tasks that cost accountants must accomplish is to gather or accumulate cost information and then assign that information to appropriate products or orders or other processes using a cost management system. The most commonly used costing methods are job order costing and process costing. However, many companies also use joint product or by-product costing or a hybrid costing system. The nature of the activities being analyzed determines which cost management system is most appropriate. The following sections describe these systems in more detail.

Job Order Costing

Job order costing is the typical method for compiling cost accounting information into a usable format. In job order costing systems, costs are assigned to each job, which may be an order, a contract, a unit of production, or a batch that is processed according to customer specifications. Thus, job order costing is appropriate for manufacturing and service industries such as design or publishing companies, manufacturing companies that produce special order products, accounting firms that perform audits or any organization producing a tailor-made good or service according to customers' specific requirements. For example, a graphic design company would likely use job order costing because graphic designers usually produce each design order to a specific customer request. Thus, job costing links all material and direct labor costs directly to a job or batch and all direct and overhead costs associated with that job or batch are accumulated for closer analysis (Bragg, 2005).

One of the major benefits of job costing is that a company's management team can easily determine all of the various costs being generated for each job being completed. This information allows management to examine each cost to determine why it was necessary and how it can be managed better in the future, thereby contributing to greater levels of profitability in the future. Another reason that companies use job costing is that they can more closely track the costs for each job as it is being fulfilled. Accounting software allows companies to use a job costing system to track costs as they arise rather than waiting until the job is complete to compile and assess overall costs. This is advantageous in that a company can oversee the costs incurred for more complex jobs during the production process so that there is sufficient time to make changes to the production process or sales price before the jobs close, based on the costing information provided by the job costing system (Bragg, 2005).

However, there are also considerable problems associated with job costing. An initial problem is that it concentrates attention on the costs incurred by specific products rather than on costs associated with different departments or activities. Another difficulty is that job costing is not always relevant. For example, some software manufacturers have high development costs but little direct costs associated with the marketing or advertising of their products. Finally, job costing requires a significant amount of data entry and data accuracy for the analysis to tender significant results. Minute data related to materials, labor, overhead, indirect labor, scrap, spoilage, and supplies must be entered into a system that can accurately assign these costs to their corresponding jobs. This process is open to errors stemming from keying errors or the misidentification of jobs or customers (Bragg, 2005).

Process Costing

Process costing is used in many industries where there are such large quantities of similar products that it makes no sense to track the cost of individual or small batches of products. Instead, costs are averaged over large quantities of production, which yields the same unit costs for all items in a production run. This type of costing requires accounting calculations that are considerably different from those used for job costing. Using a process costing system, accountants accumulate costs for each department for a time period and allocate these costs among all the products manufactured during that period. Companies that mass produce similar goods such as chemicals, bakery goods, or canned food in a continuous production process use process accounting. Direct material, direct labor, and factory overhead costs are accumulated for each department for a set period of time; usually a month. At the end of the period, departmental cost is divided by the number of units produced to obtain a cost per unit.

For instance, one type of process costing is known as first-in first-out ("FIFO") costing. This involves a complex calculation that creates layers of costs, one for units of production started in the previous production period but not completed, and another layer for production started for the current period. This type of costing is used when there are ongoing, significant changes in product costs from period to period—t o such an extent that management needs to know the new costing levels so that it can re-price products appropriately, determine if there are internal costing problems requiring resolution, or even replace managers or restructure their compensation or bonus packages.

Backflush Costing

Backflush costing is a simplified cost accumulation method that is sometimes used by companies that adopt just-in-time ("JIT") production systems. The JIT system is an approach that aims to reduce costs through the elimination of inventory. All materials and components are designed to arrive at a work station exactly when they are needed. Similarly, products are aimed to be completed and available to customers just when the customers want them.

In a backflush cost system, costing is deferred until products are completed. Standard costs are then run backwards through the system to determine which costs are associated with which products. The result is that time consuming meticulous tracking of costs is eliminated. The system is beneficial for companies that keep small inventories because costs are directly linked to the cost of products sold and manufacturing costs accrue in fewer inventory accounts than when using other methods. In extreme backflush systems, most accounting records are no longer needed because a higher percentage of the manufacturing costs become direct product costs and thus fewer cost allotments are necessary. However, the drawback to the JIT principle is that although the eradication of inventory stockpile eliminates storage and carrying costs, it also eliminates the cushion against production errors and imbalances that inventories provide.

Joint Product & By-Product Costing

Many industrial companies are faced with the difficult problem of assigning costs to their by-products and joint products. Chemical companies, petroleum refineries, flour mills, coal mines, meat packers and other similar producers' process, and sometimes create products to which some costs must be assigned, particularly for use in the preparation of financial statements.

Joint products are two or more products that are produced simultaneously by a common process or series of processes, with each product possessing a more than nominal value in the form in which it is produced. Pricing for joint products is somewhat more complex than pricing for a single product as fluctuations in demand may create a higher demand, and thus a higher price, for one product over another. A joint cost can be defined as the cost that arises from the simultaneous processing or manufacturing of products produced from the same process. Joint costs may be allocated to the joint products based on a physical measurement such as volume or weight, or they may be allocated to the joint products according to their relative sales value once they emerge as individually identifiable products.

By-products are products with a comparatively low total value that are produced concurrently with a product with a greater total value. The product with the greater value, commonly called the main product, is usually produced in greater quantities than the by-products. Thus, a by-product is an additional product that arises from a production process but with a potential sales value that is much smaller than that of the main product or joint products that were produced from the same process.

The split-off point is defined as the point at which joint products emerge as individual units. Before the split-off point, the cost of the products is almost inseparable and is often attributed to the process itself rather than the individual products. However, generally accepted accounting principles require that costs be assigned to products for inventory valuation purposes. Though costs incurred by a production process up to the split-off point cannot be clearly assigned to a single product, it is still necessary to find some reasonable allocation method for doing so in order to comply with standard accounting rules. By-product and joint product costing methods enable cost accountants to assign costs as accurately as possible while also furnishing management with data that can be useful in planning and managing various types of costs and in evaluating the actual profit performance of individual products and manufacturing processes.

Hybrid Costing

Hybrid or mixed costing systems are used when multiple cost accumulation methods are required. For example, some companies may use process costing to track direct materials and job order costing for such costs as direct labor and factory overhead. Other companies may use job order costing for direct materials and process costing for direct labor and overhead costs. Further, different departments or areas of focus within a company might need to use different cost accumulation methods. This is why hybrid or mixed cost accumulation methods are sometimes used so that the most effective cost accumulation system for each activity is used to record, track, and analyze costs.

Cost Management

Effective cost management is essential for businesses in order for them to provide the best price and service to customers, streamline production processes, and control their investment in inventories. In addition, businesses need systems to track and control costs involving direct materials, direct labor, and factory overhead expenses. These costs are fundamental to almost every business and comprise a significant portion of the costs associated with the production of goods and services. The following sections explain these basic costs in more detail.

Direct Material

Direct material is any raw material that becomes an identifiable part of the finished product. For example, in manufacturing women's clothing, the fabric is direct material. Accountants separately record and trace all direct material required in manufacturing to specific products. Companies buy direct materials in various forms. They buy some direct material in a finished state and assemble the component parts into their final product. Manufacturers of consumer electronic goods often purchase electronic components that workers assemble into finished appliances. Other companies purchase direct material in a raw state and apply labor, machinery, and equipment to change it into another form. Bakeries, for instance, obtain basic ingredients that are combined and baked in order to create a finished product.

The acquisition, control. and storage of direct materials requires different costing processes. To purchase direct materials, companies use purchase requisitions and purchase orders. When the materials are received, the receiving department inspects the items for quantity and quality and to ensure that all

items have arrived. Materials must then be stored in a safe, secure, and environmentally stable area until they are used. Finally, inventories must be continually monitored to ensure the steady flow of sufficient materials.

Labor

Direct labor costs are the wages earned by workers who transform direct materials from their raw state to a finished product. For example, the wages paid to factory workers who assemble parts and monitor the machinery are direct labor costs. However, only the wages earned by those workers involved in the physical manufacture of products are direct labor costs. Thus, labor costs consist of basic pay and fringe benefits. The basic pay for work performed is called the base rate. An equitable base rate or salary structure requires an analysis, description, and evaluation of each job within a plant or an office. Fringe benefits also form a substantial element of labor costs. Fringe benefits include the employer's share of FICA tax, unemployment taxes, holiday pay, vacation pay, overtime premium pay, insurance benefits, and pension costs. Fringe benefits must be added to the base rate to arrive at the full labor cost.

Factory Overhead

Factory overhead consists of all the costs that are incurred in production (not marketing and administration) and not traced directly to jobs. For example, the commissions earned by sales or product representatives are generally marketing expenses while salaries earned by top management are often classified as administrative expenses. However, the wages earned by a line manager in charge of overseeing production clerks are generally factory overhead costs. In addition, factory overhead includes indirect materials, which are the operating, repair and janitorial supplies used in the factory. Also, factory overhead includes such costs as rent, taxes, insurance, and depreciation on manufacturing facilities, as well as occupancy costs such as the light, heat, and power used to run the manufacturing facility.

APPLICATIONS

Cost Accounting in Business Considerations

Cost accounting plays an important role in the growth and development of a business organization. As businesses grow, their management teams set goals and objectives for future development benchmarks and then create and implement plans for achieving these aspirations. These plans developed by management are evaluated and tracked through the budgeting and accounting processes. In particular, cost accounting provides management with detailed statements of the actual cost of materials, labor, factory overhead, marketing expenses, and administrative expenses incurred in the development of the business. By analyzing and comparing a company's actual costs with those budgeted for specific time periods or processes, management is able to identify areas of both strength and weakness in a company. This knowledge enables management to make clearer and more informed decisions about a company's operations. In particular, by identifying significant deviations from a company's budget, a management team can develop and implement appropriate corrective action that is tailor-made for any situation. Some steps that a management team may take are to redesign a more suitable budget, restructure product pricings, and monitor inventory flow and valuation. The following sections describe these processes in more detail.

Budgeting

A budget is an estimation of the revenue and expenses an organization will incur over a specified future period of time. Beyond its financial component, budgeting provides a way for an organization to develop an informed plan of action to attain future objectives based on relevant indicators of past performance and expenses. This plan of action can then be communicated to key personnel and decision makers within an organization so that the entire management team is clear on the growth objectives of the organization. Without the discipline and framework a budget provides, individual managers may take actions that are in their best interest, but not ideal for the company as a whole.

During the budget-making process, cost accounting plays a critical role in helping to shape some or all of the key figures. Cost accountants may develop the entire budget, or may be assigned a partial role in developing a master budget. For instance, cost accountants may calculate overhead rates for the valuation of projected inventory levels, calculate unit or individual product costs during a production process, or evaluate the overall cost of producing each item in the company's sales budget. Cost accounting

also helps a company's management establish target costs for new products that are in the development stage and construct budgets for future time periods or significant investments. For instance, cost accountants may assist in developing a budget for capital expenditures. Capital expenditures are funds used by a company to acquire or upgrade physical assets such as property, industrial buildings, or equipment. Thus, because capital expenditures tie up significant resources of a company for an extended period of time, these acquisitions are considered more risky than short-term investments and much thought and planning goes into the evaluation of their acquisition.

Thus, the budget process is a critical component of the overall plan by which a company allocates its resources. Budgeting enables a company to channel funds to the most profitable activities while tracking and controlling expenditures in other, perhaps less profitable departments. This process enables a company to capture the information it needs to achieve its operational and financial objectives. Cost accounting plays an important role in assisting a company's management by providing key data on unit and production costs, capital expenditures, target costs, and departmental expenses that are central components of the budgeting process.

Pricing Issues

Some products — for instance such commodities as oil, wheat, corn, or gold — are priced based upon forces in the market. However, most of the time companies set and alter the prices they charge for their products. In establishing price points for a product, a company's management works closely with its cost accountants to determine a fair price for each product that is low enough so that the product is competitive in the market, but high enough so that the company is able to make a profit from its sales. Cost accounting also plays an important role in helping companies set pricing levels for both short-range and long-range pricing objectives. Short-range pricing scenarios occur when a company receives a special request from a customer to order products at a low or below-market price. When this occurs, the customer may be pitting one of its suppliers against another in an attempt to purchase goods at the lowest price, or it may desire to place a large order and is seeking to buy items in bulk at a lower price. When this occurs, the company must determine whether it will honor the request.

In order to determine whether a short-range pricing scenario is feasible for a company, the cost accountant will likely be asked to perform several types of analyses so that management has the information necessary to make a final decision. The basic rule for short-range pricing is that the lowest price that a company can charge for a product is one that at least covers all variable costs of production, plus a small profit. Anything lower would cost the company money to produce the product and therefore would not be an economically sound price point for a company. To complete these calculations, cost accountants must weigh the variable costs that are included in their analysis, which could include direct labor costs, direct machine costs, inventory carrying costs, raw materials, quality costs, and scrap costs. Once these costs have been calculated, the cost accountant can provide management with the minimum price that must be charged in order for a company to cover its expenditures and recoup at least some profit.

Another form of pricing that company must consider is long-range pricing, which is a common method for pricing sales of products sold in bulk. Long-range pricing factors several forms of overhead costs into the final price of products, including product-specific overhead costs, batch-specific overhead costs, product line-specific overhead costs, and facility-specific overhead costs.

Product-specific overhead costs include the expenses incurred in the production process of a single unit of a product.

Batch-specific overhead costs include the cost of labor required to set up or break down a machine for a production process. This might include the utility cost of running the machines throughout the production process, the cost of transporting component parts to the production area and finished products from the production area to a shipping area, and the depreciation on all machinery used in the production process.

Product line-specific overhead costs include the cost of maintaining a production manager, a design team, quality control personnel, customer service representatives, and distribution and advertising staff to monitor the production of a product line and promote its sales.

Finally, facility-specific overhead costs include the costs of building depreciation on the production facility, and the taxes, insurance, and maintenance costs involved in running the site.

All of these costs must be factored into the calculations of a final sales price for each product. Long-range pricing is difficult in that it can be challenging for cost accountants to accurately predict all the overhead costs that will be incurred in the production and promotion of an individual product. Thus, pricing is an extremely complex area of budget development, and cost accountants must often work closely with the marketing and business development departments to develop appropriate short-range and long-range pricing strategies. In addition, cost accountants must be mindful of federal laws that prevent collusive or predatory pricing and ensure that all pricing policies stay within the guidelines set by these laws.

Inventory Costing Methods

Cost accountants use different methods to track and analyze the costs associated with obtaining, storing, and restocking inventories. Traditionally, the most common inventory costing methods used by cost accountants were throughput or direct costing systems. However, many cost accountants have begun to use activity-based costing methods because of the holistic perspective this method affords of the entire production process. The following sections explain these inventory costing methods in greater detail.

Throughput Costing

The throughput method involves tracking the least amount of cost to the inventory. Using this method, only direct material costs are charged to the inventory. All other costs are expensed during the period. The throughput method does not provide proper matching, whereby expenses are recognized in the same reporting period as the related revenues for purposes of generally accepted accounting principles, except when direct materials are expensed at the time they are incurred rather than being capitalized in inventory costs. Therefore, the throughput method is not sufficient for external reporting in audits for public use, although it provides many advantages for internal reporting for management purposes (Martin, n.d.).

Direct Costing

In direct costing, more of the cost is traced than in the throughput method, but less than with the absorption method. In direct costing only the changeable manufacturing costs are charged to the inventory. Fixed manufacturing costs flow into expenses in the period during which they are acquired. This method has both advantages and disadvantages in regards to internal reporting. It does not allow proper matching for purposes of generally accepted accounting principles because the current fixed costs that accompany producing the inventory are charged to expense costs regardless of whether or not the output is sold during the designated time period. For this reason, direct costing is not useful for external reporting (Martin, n.d.).

Absorption Costing

Absorption costing is a traditional method where all manufacturing costs are capitalized or charged to the inventory, thereby becoming assets. Therefore these costs do not become expenses until the inventory is sold. In this way, matching is more closely estimated, although sales and administrative costs are charged to expense costs. Absorption costing is necessary for external reporting, and is also frequently used for internal reporting.

Activity-Based Costing

Activity-based costing (ABC) defines production processes, identifies costs associated with those processes, determines the unit costs of products and services, and create reports that assign the costs of resources to specific activities as a way of measuring the expenditures and profitability involved in specific processes. ABC is considered a more accurate cost management system than traditional costing systems because it enables managers to improve business process effectiveness and efficiency by determining the "true" costs involved in the production of a product or service.

ABC differs from traditional costing measures in several significant ways. First, traditional systems allocate costs to products using such allocation bases as units, direct labor input, machine hours, and revenue dollars. ABC systems allocate costs to products and services using allocation bases that correspond to cost drivers, or the factors that have the greatest effect upon activity costs, such as the number of machine setups, run times, or special inspection requirements. Also, because of the inability of traditional costing methods to align allocation bases with cost drivers, these methods can lead to overcosting and undercosting problems. ABC methods enable cost accountants to associate allocation bases with cost drivers, which provide managers with the most accurate information to support their decisions. Finally, ABC methods summarize the costs of organizational, or multi-department, activities while traditional costing techniques generally focus on the costs incurred in single departments.

CONCLUSION

Cost accounting is an important means by which businesses may compile, track, record, and analyze all aspects of the costs associated with producing, marketing, and selling goods and services. Cost accounting includes cost accumulation methods that enable cost accountants to compile the most accurate information about production processes, such as job order costing, process costing, backflush costing, hybrid costing, and joint and by-product costing systems. Cost accounting also involves helping an organization's management monitor and contain ongoing expenditures, which include direct labor, direct material, and factory overhead costs. To properly manage business operations, managers rely on the records and analyses prepared by cost accountants to create budgets, set prices, and control inventories. Thus, cost accountants play a critical role in the life cycle and development of individual products, product lines, and even businesses themselves.

TERMS & CONCEPTS

Activity-based costing (ABC): A system in which multiple overhead cost pools are allocated using bases that include one or more non-volume-related factors.

Activity-based management (ABM): Detailed analysis of activities and the expenses created by those activities (used as a basis for controlling and improving efficiency) or the use of information obtained from activity-based costing to make improvements in a firm.

Actual cost system: A method of collecting cost information as cost is incurred.

Backflush costing: A method of cost accumulation that works backward through the available accounting information after production is complete. This is useful in settings in which processing speeds are extremely fast.

Balance sheet: A financial statement showing financial position (assets, liabilities, and owner's equity at the end of a period. The balance sheet complements the income statement.

By-product: By-products are products with a comparatively low total value that are produced concurrently with a product with a greater total value.

Cost accounting: Calculation of costs for the purpose of planning and controlling activities, improving quality and efficiency and making decisions. Also referred to as management accounting.

Direct labor: Labor that converts direct materials into the finished product and can be assigned feasibly to a specific product.

Direct materials: Materials that form an integral part of the finished product and are included explicitly in calculating the cost of the product.

Factory cost: Usually, the sum of three cost elements: direct materials, direct labor, and factory overhead.

Factory overhead: Indirect materials, indirect labor and all other factory costs that cannot be conveniently identified with specific jobs, products, or final cost objectives.

Job order costing: A costing method in which costs are accumulated for each job, batch, lot, or customer order.

Joint cost: The cost that arises from the simultaneous processing or manufacturing of products produced from the same process.

Labor productivity: The measurement of production performance using the expenditure of human effort as a yardstick; the amount of goods or services a worker produces.

Process costing: A method in which materials, labor, and factory overhead are charged to cost centers. The cost assigned to each unit of product manufactured is determined by dividing the total cost charged to the cost center by the number of units produced.

Sunk cost: An expenditure that has already been made and cannot be recovered.

Variable cost: A cost that increases in total proportionately with an increase in activity and decreases proportionately with a decrease in activity.

BIBLIOGRAPHY

Baldenius, T., Dutta, S., & Reichelstein, S. (1991). Cost allocation for capital budgeting decisions. *Accounting Review, 82*, 837–867.

Bragg, S. (2005). *Controller's guide to costing.* Hoboken, NJ: John Wiley & Sons.

Dror, M. & Hartman, B. (2007). Shipment consolidation: Who pays for it and how much? *Management Science, 53*, 78–87.

Engle, P. (2015). How much does it cost? *Industrial Engineer: IE, 47*(5), 18.

Heitger, D. (2007). Estimating activity costs: How the provision of accurate historical activity data from a biased cost system can improve individuals' cost estimation accuracy. *Behavioral Research in Accounting, 19*, 133–159.

Kalicanin, D., & Kneževic, V. (2013). Activity-based costing as an information basis for an efficient strategic management process. *Ekonomski Anali / Economic Annals, 58*, 95–119.

Krug, K., & Weinberg, C. B. (2011). 6.3 Cost, management & activity-based accounting. *Foundations & Trends In Marketing, 6*(3/4), 228–230

Labro, E. & Vanhoucke, M. (2007). A simulation analysis of interactions among errors in costing systems. *Accounting Review, 82*, 939–962.

Martin, J. Costs accounting systems and manufacturing statements. *Management and Accounting Web.*

McWhorter, T. & Van Leuven, M. (2006). IRS clarifies direct labor costs cannot be MSC. *Tax Adviser, 37*, 318–321.

Norfleet, D. (2007). The theory of indirect costs. *AACE International Transactions,* 12.1–12.6

Ocneanu, L., & Bucsa, R. (2012). Advantages of using standard cost method in managerial accounting. *Economy Transdisciplinarity Cognition, 15*, 96–102.

Tsai, W. & Lai, C. (2007). Outsourcing or capacity expansions: Application of activity- based costing model on joint products decisions. *Computers & Operations Research, 34*, 3666–3681.

Williams, C. (2007). Are your cost allocations up-to-date? *Nonprofit World, 25*, 28.

Suggested Reading
Dowless, R. (2007). Your guide to costing methods and terminology. *Nursing Management, 38*, 52–57.

Liston, P. & Byrne, P. (2007). An evaluation of simulation to support contract costing. *Computers & Operations Research, 34*, 3652–3665.

Shields, M. D. (2015). Established management accounting knowledge. *Journal of Management Accounting Research, 27*(1), 123–132.

Wu, S. & Li, H. (2007). Warranty cost analysis for products with a dormant state. *European Journal of Operational Research, 182*, 1285–1293.

Essay by Heather Newton

Cost Management Systems

This article focuses on the tools that a cost accountant may need to use to supply managers with the information they require to make decisions for the organization. There is an exploration of the activity-based costing (ABC) cost management system as well as a comparison between the ERP and BoB applications.

Cost accounting is a type of accounting that measures, analyzes, and reports financial and nonfinancial data relating to the cost of acquiring or using resources in an organization. Cost accounting assesses product cost information that can be used by internal and external decision makers. These decision makers need reliable information to assist the organization in developing its mission, vision, and objectives. This information is also helpful when an organization is in the process of implementing a new strategy, devising and controlling the value chain, and evaluating organizational performance. By providing managers with such pertinent information, they will be equipped to complete their established goals.

Financial Accounting vs. Strategic Cost Management
Financial professionals such as cost accountants are primarily responsible for providing managers with information about cost and benefit measurements. However, cost accounting tends to be of limited value to some managers because they are focused on financial accounting issues. There are differences between financial accounting and strategic cost management.

- Financial Accounting: Cost information may be highly aggregated and historical, and it must be consistent with GAAP.
- Strategic Cost Management: Cost information may be segregated, current, and relevant to a particular purpose.

For cost accountants to be effective in completing their jobs, they will need assistance, such as the assistance provided by a cost management system, which collects data and information. Such systems help to provide managers with the cost and benefit information they need to make decisions for the organization.

Characteristics of Successful Cost Management Systems
A cost management system (CMS) consists of methods that are developed to assist in the planning and controlling of an organization's cost managing activities in the short and long term. As managers develop their strategies, they must address two main challenges—profitability in the short term and securing a competitive position in the long term.

Key Roles of a Cost Management System
In addition, a CMS should address two key roles:

- It should be able to manage the organization's core competencies in order to take advantage of opportunities and minimize potential threats.
- It should be able to link plans and strategies to the organization's performance.

Primary Goals of a Cost Management System

The primary goals of a cost management system include the following:

- Develop accurate product costs.
- Assess product/service life-cycle performance.
- Improve understanding of processes and activities.
- Control costs.
- Measure performance.
- Allow the organization to pursue different strategies.

A good CMS should be able to do the following:

- Provide a way to develop accurate product and service costs. Product and service costs are a factor when managers are planning, preparing financial statements, and assessing employee performance and productivity.
- Provide information about the life-cycle performance of a product or service. The financial statements do not list this type of information; therefore, it is imperative that financial professionals are able to collect the information from another source. This type of information will allow managers to assess costs incurred in one stage to the costs and profitability of other stages.
- Control costs.
- Generate information that will assist managers with measuring and evaluating performance.
- Generate information that allows the managers to define and implement organizational strategies.

Designing a Cost Management System

There are many factors to consider when designing a cost management system. However, one of the key factors is the need to integrate the organization's current information system. When evaluating this possibility, one should ask the following questions:

- What input data are being gathered in what form?
- What outputs are being generated and in what form?
- How do the current systems interact with one another, and how effectively?
- Is the current chart of accounts appropriate?
- What significant issues are not being addressed by the current system, and could these be integrated into the current "feeder" systems?

Motivation, information and reporting are three primary components of a cost system. An example of the motivational component is the use of performance rewards for the top management team members when they reach goals. Performance rewards could be short term (i.e., cash) or long term (i.e., stock options). The informational component focuses on whether there is a strong foundation for the financial budgeting process. An example of the reporting component is the continual collection of basic financial information such as statements.

Activity-Based Costing

In the past, many cost accountants would randomly add a broad percentage of expenses to the direct costs in order to account for the indirect costs. This practice became a problem when indirect and overhead costs started to rise. The cost accountants realized that the technique they had been using was not accurate. As a result of this situation, the accounting field sought to find a solution and the concept of activity-based costing was developed. Activity-based costing (ABC) can be defined as a method of allocating costs to products and services. It is a management tool that provides better allocation of resources; is applicable to both appropriations and revolving funds; and relates total costs (resources consumed) to work accomplished (outputs produced) (OSD Comptroller iCenter, n.d.). In most cases, outputs are

- produced to satisfy customer requirements;
- quantifiable, measurable, and auditable;
- consistent from fiscal period to fiscal period to allow cost comparisons;
- incorporated into existing or modified financial management systems;
- identifiable so that costs can be more easily allocated

Development of Activity-Based Costing

Activity-based costing was first introduced in U.S. manufacturing companies during the 1970s and 1980s. In 1988, Robin Cooper and Robert Kaplan began to promote the concept as a solution to problems created by traditional cost management systems. Activity-based costing was seen as a way to provide managers with accurate information so they could make the best decisions. Many experts believe that this method is the best way to measure an organization's performance (Accounting

Software Research, n.d.). The method can estimate costs for specific activities that occur in the organization.

Uses of Activity-Based Costing

Many will use the system to do the following:

- Focus on the total cost to produce a product or service.
- Have a system to serve as a basis for full cost recovery.

Benefits of Activity-Based Costing

According to Value Based Management.net (n.d.), some of the benefits of activity-based costing include the following:

- It can identify the most and least profitable customers, products, and channels.
- It can determine the true contributions to and detractors from financial performance.
- It can accurately predict costs, profits, and resource requirements associated with changes in production volumes, organizational structure, and resource costs.
- It can identify the root causes of poor financial performance.
- It can track costs of activities and work processes.
- It can equip managers with cost intelligence to drive improvements.
- It can facilitate better marketing mix.
- It can enhance the bargaining power with the customer.
- It can achieve better positioning of products (par. 2).

ABC has the potential to identify, describe, assign costs, and report on a company's operations. It can assist in improving business process effectiveness and efficiency by determining the true cost of a product or service. In most organizations, the true cost is critical because it identifies products and services that make and lose money; finds an economic break-even point; allows different options to be compared; and creates opportunities for cost improvement and strategic decision-making. The OSD Comptroller iCenter (n.d.) has reported that some of the advantages of using the system include the following:

- It avoids or minimizes distortions in product costing that could be a result of arbitrary allocations of indirect costs.

- It can generate useful information on how money is being spent, whether departments are being cost-effective, and how to benchmark for quality improvements.
- It provides a clear metric for improvement by encouraging managers to evaluate the efficiency and cost effectiveness of program activities

Implementing an Activity-Based Costing System

In addition, the center has listed a four-part process in implementing an activity-based cost management system.

Identify activities. The cost accountants will conduct an in-depth analysis of the operating process of each responsibility unit. Each process may consist of one or more activities required by the outputs.

Assign resource costs to activities. This step is sometimes referred to as tracing, which refers to the ability to trace cost-to-cost objects in order to determine why costs were incurred. There are certain organizations (i.e., the Department of Defense) that will divide the costs into categories such as

- Direct—Costs that can be traced directly to one output.
- Indirect—Costs that cannot be allocated to an individual output.
- General and Administrative—Costs that cannot reasonably be associated with any particular product or service produced (i.e., overhead).

Identify outputs. The decision makers will identify all of the outputs for which an activity segment performs activities and consumes resources.

Assign activity costs to outputs. The final step involves the assignment of activity costs to outputs using activity drivers. Activity drivers assign activity costs to outputs based on individual outputs' consumption or demand for activities.

APPLICATION

Software for Business

Many organizations began using computers in their business practices in the early 1960s. The main purpose of this was to provide a simple way of automating

179

many of the routine business tasks that had previously been performed manually. Sometime during the 1970s, some organizations elected to customize software packages to meet the needs of their individual businesses (Moriarty, 1999; Davenport, 2000; Shields, 2001&). As a result, these organizations felt a need to have someone make sure that the systems were meeting their needs, especially in relation to financial transactions. Given the nature of the system, some organizations have the information systems department reporting to the controller or vice president of finance (Shields, 2001). Vendors started to offer fully integrated suites of applications during the late 1980s, and the enterprise resource planning (ERP) packages became popular in the 1990s. There was a high demand for these packages because organizations realized that they had to accomplish the following: (Scapens, 1998; Moriarty, 1999; Davenport, 2000; Shields, 2001&):

- Maintain high-cost legacy systems.
- Continually look for new functionalities.
- Address Y2K issues.
- Keep pace in making sure that their systems were prepared to operate in a global economy.

At some point, the chief financial officer may request a gap analysis to be conducted of the system in place. A gap analysis is the study of the differences between two information systems. One of the reasons why it is conducted is to make sure that the organization is utilizing the best system. The goal of a gap analysis is to look for ways to reduce gaps that may be hindering the benefit and cost effectiveness of the system to the organization.

Enterprise Resource Planning Software

"Single vendor-based enterprise resource planning (ERP) software became the dominant strategic platform for supporting company-wide business processes" (Hyvonen, 2003, p. 156). Many organizations used an enterprise resource planning (ERP) system to link their feeder systems into an integrated cost management system, which will allowed them to

- standardize information systems and replace different "legacy" systems.
- integrate information systems and automate the transfer of data among systems.

- improve the quality of information, including purchase preferences of customers.
- and improve the timeliness of information by providing real-time, online reporting.

ERP System vs. BoB System

Although this was the favored method (Cooper & Kaplan, 1999), many expressed concern about the system's ability to have the proper degree of flexibility in order to meet organizational and industry requirements (Booth, 2000; Davenport, 2000; & Light, 2001). Given these concerns, there were some companies that continued to "use conventional best of breed (BoB) or standalone system components of standard package and/or custom software" (Hyvonen, 2003, p. 156).

Hyvönen (2003) conducted a study to evaluate how organizations determine if they should use an ERP or BoB system, especially as it related to management accounting functions. His data was gathered by mailing questionnaires to large and medium-sized industrial business units in Finland. The questionnaire highlighted questions that dealt with the background regarding the organization's implementation of its information system, perceived problems with the management accounting function, and the adoption of modern cost accounting and management accounting techniques. The following results were noted:

- When the IS project was introduced by the financial department, the solution tended to be BoB. However, when the idea originated from another department, the solution tended to be ERP.
- The two most articulated motives behind IS projects were the Y2K problems and the need to develop business processes. Therefore, information systems may be installed for technical reasons or to enhance strategy and competitiveness. It was found that a technologically focused implementation was intended only to provide core information systems functionality to an organization, with little business change as possible.

VIEWPOINT

According to Rogoski (2004), all expenditures and billings recorded will end up in the financial department. Unfortunately, most clinical applications and financial applications do not work together. They work independently, which causes duplication of efforts for the employees that have to process the information. Because of this problem, some vendors have chosen to create fully integrated clinical and financial software while others continue to sell whatever is best at the time (best of the breed philosophy). Many chief financial officers are electing to do business with those organizations that create information systems that will satisfy their organization's needs.

Top leaders such as Ron Bunnell, CFO of Banner Health, and Dan Deets, CFO of Hunterdon Healthcare Inc., have found that they have access to information that they need to cap costs and improve efficiencies in delivering health care services as a result of integrating the clinical and financial systems. The integrated systems provide a better way to track the inflow and outflow of revenue for both clinical and business initiatives. Having the ability to have access to all types of financial data has provided the CFOs mentioned above the opportunity to have more negotiating power when dealing with managed care contracts. There is an ability to monitor the relationships that these health care systems have with payers over a period. In addition, the integrated systems allow the health care organizations to identify weak areas that need to be improved so that they can increase their revenue.

CONCLUSION

Financial professionals such as cost accountants are primarily responsible for providing managers with information about measurements of costs and benefits. In order for cost accountants to be effective in completing their jobs, they will need assistance, such as the assistance provided by a cost management system. The cost management system helps to collect the cost and benefit information managers need to make decisions for the organization.

In the past, many cost accountants would randomly add a broad percentage of expenses to the direct costs in order to account for the indirect costs. This practice became a problem when indirect and overhead costs started to rise. The cost accountants realized that the technique they had been using was not accurate. As a result of this situation, the accounting field sought to find a solution and the concept of activity-based costing was developed.

However, there have been reports that suggest that ABC loses power in large-scale operations and can be difficult to implement and maintain (Kaplan & Anderson, 2005). As a result, Kaplan and Anderson (2005) made a recommendation that would simplify the process through an approach called "time-driven ABC."

Terms & Concepts

Activity-based costing (ABC): A method of allocating costs to products and services.

Activitybased management: Similar concept to activity-based costing. However, activity-based management analyzes activities for their degree of customer value added. After identifying activities that add little or no customer value, an activity-based management cost system looks for ways to reduce or eliminate them by redesigning activities and processes.

Balanced scorecard: An analysis technique designed to translate an organization's mission statement and overall business strategy into specific, quantifiable goals and to monitor the organization's performance in terms of achieving these goals.

Cost accounting: The process of identifying and evaluating production costs.

Cost management system (CMS): The process whereby companies use cost accounting to report or control the various costs of doing business.

Enterprise resource planning (ERP) system: A business management system that integrates all facets of the business, including planning, manufacturing, sales, and marketing. As the ERP methodology has become more popular, software applications have emerged to help business managers implement ERP in business activities such as inventory control, order tracking, customer service, finance, and human resources.

Financial accounting: Reporting of the financial position and performance of a firm through financial statements issued to external users on a periodic basis.

Life-cycle costing: A process to determine the sum of all the costs associated with an asset or part, including acquisition, installation, operation, maintenance, refurbishment, and disposal costs.

Target costing: A disciplined process for determining and realizing a total cost at which a proposed product with specified functionality must be produced to generate the desired profitability at its anticipated selling price in the future.

BIBLIOGRAPHY

Activity based costing. (2007). Accounting Software Research; Associated Research, Inc.

Booth, P., Matolcsy, Z., & Wieder, B. (2000). Integrated information systems (ERP-systems) an accounting practice—The Australian experience. *Australian Accounting Review, 10*(3), 4–18.

Brad, S. (2010). A general approach of quality cost management suitable for effective implementation in software systems. *Informatica Economica, 14*(4), 97–113.

Davenport, T. (2000). *Mission critical, realizing the promise of enterprise systems.* Boston, MA: Harvard Business School Press.

Hyvönen, T. (2003). Management accounting and information systems: ERP versus BoB. *European Accounting Review, 12*(1), 155–173.

Kaneko, P., Ussahawanitchakit, P., & Muenthaisong, K. (2013). Strategic target costing effectiveness and goal achievement: empirical evidence from exporting gem and jewelry businesses in Thailand. *International Journal of Business Strategy, 13*(3), 127–158.

Kaplan, R., & Anderson, S. (2005). *Rethinking activity-based costing.* Boston, MA: Harvard Business School Press.

Kaplan, R., & Bruns, W. (1987). *Accounting and management: A field study perspective.* Boston, MA: Harvard Business School Press.

Kaplan, R., & Norton, D. (2001). *The strategy-focused organization: How balanced scorecard companies thrive in the new business environment.* Boston, MA: Harvard Business School Press.&

Light, B., Holland, C., & Willis, K. (2001). ERP and best of breed: A comparative analysis. *Business Process Management Journal, 7*(3), 216–224.

Moisello, A. (2012). Cost measurement and cost management in target costing. *Annals of the University of Oradea, Economic Science Series, 21*(1), 533–547.

Moriarty, S. (1999). Breeding the best. *Management Accounting* (UK), *77,* 52.

OSD Comptroller iCenter (n.d.). Accounting for operational readiness.

OSD Comptroller iCenter (n.d.). Activity-based costing.

Rogoski, R. (2004). Investment pay off with financial information systems. *Health Management Technology, 25*(8), 14–17.

Scapens, R., & Jazayeri, M. (1998). SAP: Integrated information systems and the implications for management accountants. *Management Accounting: Magazine for Chartered Management Accountants, 76*(8), 46–48.

Shields, M. (2001). *E-business and ERP: Rapid implementation and project planning.* New York: John Wiley.

Value Based Management.net (n.d.). Activity based costing.

SUGGESTED READING

Beheshti, H. (2004). Gaining and sustaining competitive advantage with activity based cost management system. *Industrial Management & Data Systems, 104*(5), 377–383.

Irani, Z., Ghoneim, A., & Love, P. (2006). Evaluating cost taxonomies for information systems management. *European Journal of Operational Research, 173*(3), 1103–1122.

Nicolaou, A. (2003). Manufacturing strategy implementation and cost management systems effectiveness. *European Accounting Review, 12*(1), 175–199.

Essay by Marie Gould

COST-BENEFIT ANALYSIS: DECISION-MAKING IN THE PUBLIC SECTOR

This article will focus on cost-benefit analysis as a tool for decision-making in the public sector. Cost-benefit analysis, a tool for investment appraisal, is the federal government's main economic assessment tool to evaluate federal programs. The main types of cost analysis, the history of cost-benefit analysis, and the methodology of cost-benefit analysis will be described and analyzed. The federal government's official guidelines for cost-benefit analysis of federal programs will be explained. The article will summarize

Mick Mulvaney is the director of Office of Management and Budget under President Donald Trump. (Courtesy of U.S. Congress via Wikimedia Commons)

the main uses for cost-benefit analysis, including physical investment projects, loan guarantees, clean air initiatives, and big science. The main criticisms made against cost-benefit analysis will be addressed.

OVERVIEW

The public sector—including the economic and administrative enterprises of a local, regional, or national government—uses multiple analytical tools for fiscal, administrative, and policy decision-making. Examples of public sector decision-making tools include manpower planning, the social demand approach, and cost-benefit analysis. Cost-benefit analysis (CBA), a type of investment appraisal also referred to as benefit-cost analysis, is one

of the most prominent and widely used analytical and quantitative tools for decision-making in the public sector. The federal government recommends cost-benefit analysis to its agencies as the main technique to use in a formal economic analysis of government programs or projects. Cost-benefit analysis, as an analytical tool or methodological technique, is a practical tool for assessing the desirability of projects, particularly in situations when it is important to take a long-term view. In this process, costs and benefits will be enumerated and evaluated (Hough, 1994).

Cost-benefit analysis provides a systematic and formalized set of procedures for assessing whether to fund and implement a public policy or program. In instances where a choice must be made between public programs or policies, cost-benefit analysis can be used to compare the programs and select the most promising one (Mustafa, 1994). Cost-benefit analysis is the government's primary economic tool to assess and evaluate proposed resource allocation. The public sector is responsible for allocating public resources. Resource allocation influences economic development, quality of life, and opportunity for the public at large. The public sector works to make decisions about the allocation of resources in ways that promote and sustain economic productivity (Julnes, 2000). Cost-benefit analysis is implemented in instances when a cost analysis will provide information that will help decision makers determine how resources will be allocated (Beyea & Nicoll, 1999). Cost-benefit analysis is based on the idea that government should only undertake programs that promise favorable (usually monetary) return. It focuses on the economic efficiency aspects of governmental decision-making (Mustafa, 1994).

Cost-benefit analysis is used in all areas of public sector investment, including in nationalized industries, health expenditures, housing schemes, traffic networks, land-use and town planning problems, and regional development. Cost-benefit analysis, though developed in the early twentieth century in United States to assess public sector environmental projects, is practiced throughout the industrialized and developing world. The United States has most notably used cost-benefit analysis to assess reservoir projects and disease control. The United Kingdom has most notably used cost-benefit analysis to assess the

M1 motorway, the third London airport, London's Victoria Line underground, the Morecambe Bay barrage project and the re-siting of London's Covent Garden Market (Hough, 1994).

The following sections describe the main types of cost analysis, the history of cost-benefit analysis, and the methodology of cost-benefit analysis. These sections serve as the foundation for a later discussion on the main uses for cost-benefit analysis. Issues related to the main criticisms made against cost-benefit analysis will be introduced.

Types of Cost Analysis

The public sector uses multiple cost analysis tools to aid decision-making. There are four main "types of cost analysis including cost-benefit analysis, cost-effectiveness analysis, cost-minimization analysis, and cost-utility analysis" (Beyea & Nicoll, 1999, p. 129).

- cost-benefit analysis
- cost-effectiveness analysis
- cost-minimization analysis
- cost-utility analysis

All four types of cost analysis used by the public sector for decision-making, according to Beyea and Nicoll, share the same the same framework or guiding principles:

- Specify the analytic perspective that provided the framework for determining who pays the costs for and who benefits from a particular service or intervention.
- Define and specify the anticipated benefits and outcomes of a service or intervention.
- Identify all of the actual and potential costs using the specified analytic perspective to determine the costs.
- Account for how time may affect projected costs.
- Evaluate the results and consider alternative explanations for the conclusions.
- Calculate a cost-benefit or cost-effectiveness ratio as a summary measure (Beyea & Nicoll, 1999, p. 130).

While there are four related types of cost analysis, described above, cost-benefit analysis is the most popular and widely used analytical tool for economic decision-making in the public sector.

President Ronald Reagan at his desk in the Oval Office, Washington, D.C. (Courtesy of Library of Congress)

History of Cost-benefit Analysis

Cost-benefit analysis has been used by the United States' public sector, particularly in association with environmental projects, since the early 1900s. Cost-benefit analysis was a formal part of the River and Harbor Act of 1902 (Hough, 1994). The development of cost-benefit analysis, at the beginning of the twentieth century, was a way to gather objective measurements and information to use in public decision-making (Julnes, 2000). In the 1950s, cost-benefit analysis was used by the public sector to analyze large-scale environmental projects such as the development of large U.S. river valleys. The applications of the technique were extended to all areas of government operations and became a ubiquitous part of public sector decision-making practice in the second half of the twentieth century. Cost-benefit analysis, which began in the United States, has been adopted by the United Kingdom and most other industrialized and developing countries (Hough, 1994).

In the late twentieth century, the U.S. government formalized its approach to cost-benefit analysis for use by all of its agencies. In 1981, President Reagan enacted Executive Order No. 12291, which created the Office of Information and Regulatory Affairs

(OIRA) and "required regulatory agencies to prepare impact analyses for any regulations that are likely to result in annual effects on the economy of $100 million or more." Executive Order No. 12291 specifies that the "analyses must identify social costs and benefits and attempt to determine if the proposed regulation maximizes net benefits to society" (Mustafa, 1994). Section 3 of the Executive Order No. 12291, Regulatory Impact Analysis and Review, requires that all proposed rules be analyzed through cost-benefit analysis and that "all final regulatory impact analysis shall contain the following information:

- A description of the potential benefits of the rule, including any beneficial effects that cannot be quantified in monetary terms, and the identification of those likely to receive the benefits.
- A description of the potential costs of the rule, including any adverse effects that cannot be quantified in monetary terms, and the identification of those likely to bear the costs.
- A determination of the potential net benefits of the rule, including an evaluation of effects that cannot be quantified in monetary terms.
- A description of alternative approaches that could substantially achieve the same regulatory goal at lower cost, together with an analysis of this potential benefit and costs and a brief explanation of the legal reasons why such alternatives, if proposed, could not be adopted" (Section 3(d)1–5).

The federal government's institutionalized and formalized the practice of cost-benefit analysis, as the primary tool for economic decision-making, continues today in the majority of federal agencies.

Methodology of Cost-benefit Analysis

Cost-benefit analysis produces data about the cost and benefit of a program, practice, or investment. This data can be presented in three main ways to aid the evaluation stage of analysis:

First, data can be presented in a cost-benefit ratio. Second, data can be presented through a calculation of the present net value of the project. Third, data can be presented by calculating the internal rate of return of the investment. The third method, the internal rate of return or rate-of-return analysis, is the most common cost-benefit analysis tool used to evaluate investments and make decisions.

Cost-benefit analysis generally begins with a tabulation of all the costs and all the benefits of the proposed investment. Costs may include "direct and indirect costs for labor, programming, hiring, training, equipment and supplies, overhead, start-up costs, adverse effects, loss of productivity, and morbidity" (Beyea & Nicoll, 1999). The tabulation or computation of costs and benefits is often a process characterized by debate and disagreement. Benefits, in particular, can be extremely difficult to tabulate due to the differing subjectivity, philosophy, and values of the people involved in the assessment process. In theory, cost-benefit analysis leads the public sector to select all projects where the present value of benefits exceeds the present value of costs (Hough, 1994).

The federal Office of Management and Budget (OMB) issues guidelines (Circular No. A-94 Revised, 1992) to the heads of executive departments for conducting cost-benefit analysis of federal programs. These guidelines, released in 1992, are intended by the federal government to promote efficient resource allocation through well-informed decision-making by the federal government. The guidelines provide general guidance for conducting benefit-cost and cost-effectiveness analyses. The guidelines are designed to serve as a checklist of whether a government agency has considered all the elements for sound benefit-cost and cost-effectiveness analyses.

The Office of Management and Budget's *Guidelines for Benefit-Cost Analysis of Federal Programs* includes four main elements of cost-benefit analysis, including policy rationale, explicit assumptions, evaluation of alternatives, and verification (Circular No. A-94 Revised, 1992):

Policy rationale refers to the rationale for the government program being examined. Programs may be justified on efficiency grounds, and they may be justified where they improve the efficiency of the government's internal operations through cost-saving investments.

Explicit assumptions about the underlying assumptions used to arrive at estimates of future benefits and costs should be clear. The required analysis should include a statement of the assumptions, the rationale behind them, and a review of their strengths and weaknesses.

Evaluation of alternatives is a required step of federal cost-benefit analysis and decision-making. Analyses should consider alternative means of achieving pro-gram objectives by examining different program scales, methods of provision, and degrees of govern-ment involvement.

Verification of investment outcome is a required part of cost-benefit analysis. Federal agencies should have a plan for periodic, results-oriented evaluation of program effectiveness.

The federal guidelines for identifying and mea-suring benefits and costs include both intangible and tangible benefits and costs, such as incremental benefits and costs, interactive effects, international effects, and transfer payments.

Incremental benefits and costs: Calculation of net present value should be based on incremental ben-efits and costs.

Interactive effects: Possible interactions between the benefits and costs being analyzed and other govern-ment activities should be considered.

International effects: Analyses should focus on ben-efits and costs accruing to the citizens of the United States in determining net present value.

Transfer payments: Transfer payments should be ex-cluded from the calculation of net present value as there are no real economic gains from a pure transfer payment. The benefits to those who receive a transfer are matched by the costs borne by those who pay for it (Circular No. A-94 Revised, 1992).

While the federal government has generalized and formalized guidelines for the federal use of cost-benefit analysis, described above, multiple variables influence the applicability and effectiveness of cost-benefit analysis. The following section describes the varying uses for cost-benefit analysis for public sector decision-making and the varying outcomes.

APPLICATION

Uses of Cost-benefit Analysis

While cost-benefit analysis is used to varying degrees in nearly every area of public sector investment and decision-making—including nationalized industries, health expenditures, housing schemes, traffic net-works, land-use and town planning problems, and

regional development—there are areas of public sector decision-making where cost-benefit analysis proves to be the most applicable and useful and areas where cost-benefit analysis cannot be used effectively. The following examples—including physical invest-ment projects, loan guarantees, clean air initiatives and big science—illustrate the strengths and limita-tions of cost-benefit analysis when applied to real-world scenarios (Gramlich, 2002).

Environmental projects: Cost-benefit analysis is used routinely for assessing public sector physical invest-ment projects such as rivers, dams, and harbors. Cost-benefit analysis for physical investment projects involves the weighing of initial capital costs against project benefits, which often involve increased busi-ness activity. Complications of computing the cost-benefit analysis of physical investment projects in-clude the difficulties associated with tabulating the potential long-term environmental costs of projects.

Loan guarantees: Public sector loan guarantee pro-grams routinely use cost-benefit analysis to assess loan risk. Public sector loan guarantee programs, autho-rized by Congress, provide guaranteed loans to indus-tries—such as steel, oil and gas, and airlines—that may be facing economic challenges. The loan guarantee boards use cost-benefit analysis to find appropriate loans and to estimate the effects of the guarantee. The loan guarantee boards make loan decisions based on benefit-cost outcomes. Cost-benefit analysis by loan guarantee boards includes creating year-by-year models of repayment probabilities and calculations of the value of fees, collateral, and stock warrants.

Clean air programs: Cost-benefit analysis is used rou-tinely by the Environmental Protection Agency (EPA) to assess the benefits and costs of their clean air pro-grams. In particular, the Environmental Protection Agency uses cost-benefit analysis to evaluate ben-efits and costs of the Clean Air Act. For example, the Environmental Protection Agency estimates that the direct costs of its own agency's measures to reduce air pollution from 1970 to 1990 cost $689 billion and provided $29.3 trillion in benefits.

Big science: Cost-benefit analysis is used routinely by the public sector to assess and analyze big science proj-ects, such as the superconducting super collider. In the assessment of big science projects, costs can be calculated but benefits tend to remain difficult to tabulate or calculate. Valuing benefits for big science projects is nearly impossible as outcomes and applications are generally unknowable at early stages of research.

These four cases illustrate how cost-benefit analysis can be used in different ways to aid governmental decision-making.

ISSUES

Challenges to Cost-benefit Analysis

There are numerous conceptual, computational, and analytical criticisms of cost-benefit analysis including its apolitical nature, its level of effectiveness, its economic bias, and its methodological limitations:

Apolitical: Cost-benefit analysis, a formal approach to public policy decision-making, is used as a means of avoiding politics in public sector decision-making. The benefits and costs of a particular public policy program can be assessed, tabulated, and compared without weighing politics or requiring political evaluation (Gramlich, 2002). Cost-benefit analysis, as it is generally practiced in the public sector, is designed to be politically neutral. This methodological goal creates problems and limitations. Namely, cost-benefit analysis separates politics and policy making. Cost-benefit analysis obscures the conflict of multiple interests and competing agendas. Cost-benefit analysis is apolitical. Cost-benefit analysis does not provide all the information needed for policymakers to make informed decisions (Mustafa, 1994).

Level of effectiveness: Critics ask whether cost-benefit analysis has resulted in regulations with greater net benefits. There is little proof (no conclusive study) that compares the net benefit of federal regulations before Executive Order No. 12291 (i.e. President Ronald Reagan's executive order requiring cost-benefit analysis on some regulations) and the net benefit of federal regulations after Executive Order No. 12291. Since 1981, there have been near constant attempts to improve and strengthen cost-benefit analysis, including requirements in the private sector like the Unfunded Mandates Reform Act and the Congressional Review Act. This constant revision and updating signals to critics that cost-benefit analysis does not work (Shapiro,

2006). Shapiro and Morrall (2012) did find that, though there seemed to be no significant correlation "between the information provided by the analysis and the net benefits," the least politically salient regulations yield the highest net benefits.

Economic bias: Critics of the expanding scope of the American government argue for the need to make regulations more cost effective. These critics lobbied for greater regulatory oversight and assessment accountability. Executive Order No. 12291 created the Office of Information and Regulatory Affairs (OIRA) and the requirement that federal agencies use cost-benefit analysis to evaluate investment in programs (Shapiro, 2006). This federal institutionalization of cost-benefit analysis created an economic bias in policy evaluation and decision-making in the public sector. Further questions arise when counted costs extend beyond national concerns, as in the case of carbon emissions originating at a source that derives a clear benefit to the possible detriment of the wider world's climate (Heyes, Morgan, & Rivers, 2013).

Methodological limitations: Cost-benefit analysis has methodological limitations, particularly when applied to scientific fields. Gaps in scientific knowledge, in areas such as climate change or other types of extreme scientific uncertainty, make using benefit-cost analysis in real-world decision-making difficult (Gramlich, 2002). Some agencies combine cost-benefit analysis with simultaneous approaches to arrive at a more three-dimensional model (Popovic, Vasic, Lazovic, & Grbovic, 2012).

CONCLUSION

In the final analysis, cost-benefit analysis is one of several cost assessment techniques that tabulate and evaluate total costs and consequences of an investment or program in a systematic manner. Cost-benefit analysis is a useful economic tool that reveals a monetary and quantitative view of an investment or policy decision. Cost-benefit analysis tabulates costs and benefits in comparable units such as the monetary unit. As a result, cost-benefit analysis is a useful strategy for comparing distinct variables by giving each a price in dollars.

The public sector is increasingly called upon to find policy solutions to public problems such as poverty, child abuse, smoking, crime, aging, and terrorism.

Public problem-solving requires multiple types of analytical tools. Cost-benefit analysis is a fine tool for economic decision-making in the public sector but it does not account for social values and social need. As a result of the complexity of public problems, the future of decision-making in the public sector will likely evolve to include both cost-benefit analysis and political and social feasibility approaches (Mustafa, 1994).

TERMS & CONCEPTS

Cost-benefit Analysis: A systematic and formalized set of procedures for assessing whether to fund and implement a policy or program.

Cost-effectiveness: A comparison between the costs of two or more alternative means of achieving the same string of benefits or a specific objective.

Economic analysis: The study of trends, phenomena, and information that are related to the economics of a venture.

Federal government: A form of government in which a group of states recognizes the sovereignty and leadership of a central authority while retaining certain powers of government.

Net present value: The difference between the discounted present value of benefits and the discounted present value of costs.

Policy rationale: The rationale for the government program being examined.

Public problems: Undesirable conditions that impinge on a society.

Public problem-solving: The approaches and strategies that citizens and their elected representatives undertake to solve or alleviate public problems.

Public sector: The economic and administrative enterprises of a local, regional, or national government.

Transfer payment: A payment of money or goods.

Values: Personally and culturally specific moral judgments.

BIBLIOGRAPHY

Andranovich, G. (1995). Achieving consensus in public decision making: Applying interest-based problem solving to the challenges of intergovernmental collaboration. *The Journal of Applied Behavioral Science, 31*, 429–446.

Beyea, S. & Nicoll, H. (1999). Finding answers to questions using cost analysis. Association of Operating Room Nurses. *AORN Journal, 70*, 128–131.

Circular No. A-94 Revised. (1992). The Office of Management and Budget.

Executive Order 12291. (2007). *The Federal Register.*

Gramlich, E. (2002). The methodology of benefit-cost analysis. *Vital Speeches of the Day, 69*, 68.

Heyes, A., Morgan, D., & Rivers, N. (2013). The use of a social cost of carbon in Canadian cost-benefit analysis. *Canadian Public Policy, 39*, S67–S79.

Hough, J. (1994). Educational cost-benefit analysis. *Education Economics, 2*, 93.

Hy, R., & Mathews, W. (1978). Decision making practices of public service administrators. *Public Personnel Management, 7*, 148.

Irvin, R., & Stansbury, J. (2004). Citizen participation in decision making: Is it worth the effort? *Public Administration Review, 64*, 55–65.

Julnes, P. (2000). Decision-making tools for public productivity improvement: A comparison of DEA to cost-benefit and regression analyses. *Journal of Public Budgeting, Accounting & Financial Management, 12*, 625–647.

Mustafa, H. (1994). Conflict of multiple interests in cost-benefit analysis. *International Journal of Public Sector Management, 7*(3/4), 16.

Persky, J. (2001). Cost-benefit analysis and the classical creed. *Journal of Economic Perspectives, 15*, 199–208.

Popovic, V. M., Vasic, B. M., Lazovic, T. M., & Grbovic, A. M. (2012). Application of new decision making model based on modified cost-benefit analysis&— A case study: Belgrade tramway transit. *Asia-Pacific Journal of Operational Research, 29*, 1.

Razzouk, D. (2017). Cost-benefit analysis. *Mental Health Economics, 55*–70.

Shapiro, S. (2006). Politics and regulatory policy analysis. *Regulation, 29*, 40–45.

Shapiro, S., & Morrall III, J. F. (2012). The triumph of regulatory politics: Benefit-cost analysis and political salience. *Regulation & Governance, 6*, 189–206.

SUGGESTED READING

Ackerman, F., & Heinzerling, L. (2002). Pricing the priceless: Cost-benefit analysis of environmental protection. *University of Pennsylvania Law Review, 150*, 1553.

Johnston, J. (2002). A game theoretic analysis of alternative institutions for regulatory cost-benefit analysis. *University of Pennsylvania Law Review, 150*, 1343.

McIntosh, E., Donaldson, C., & Ryan, M. (1999). Recent advances in the methods of cost-benefit analysis in healthcare: Matching the art to the science. *PharmacoEconomics, 15*, 357–367.

Essay by Simone I. Flynn, Ph.D.

CROWDFUNDING IN BUSINESS

ABSTRACT

Crowdfunding is a method of acquiring the capital necessary to finance a new business, product, or project. Some innovators encounter difficulty in obtaining financing through traditional means, such as banks and venture capital firms. The Internet provides people in this situation with an alternative: They can raise the money needed by accepting small amounts of money from a large number of people (i.e., a crowd). Usually, members of the public who are interested in having the proposed product or service become commercially available will agree to donate a relatively small sum in exchange for some sort of incentive.

OVERVIEW

The usage of the term *crowdfunding* dates back only to about 2006. In its typical form, crowdfunding involves three different groups. The first group is the inventor, entrepreneur, or promoter of the new product or service. This person has what he or she thinks is a good idea for a commodity that many people would be interested in. Often, the commodity involves a "chicken-and-egg" dilemma: Many people would be willing to put their money behind the commodity if only it were commercially available (Chakradhar, 2015). However, the commodity is not commercially available precisely because no one is willing to take a chance on funding it. In traditional economics, this type of situation would be seen as a failure of the marketplace, because there is a need that actors in the market are aware of, but the dynamics of the marketplace make it impossible for this need to be met.

The investors make up the second of the three groups involved in crowdfunding. Prior to the advent of crowdfunding, investors tended to be established financial institutions such as banks. This is because banks, in the immortal words of bank robber Willie Sutton, "are where the money is"; that is, only banks had enough money to be able to finance ventures on the scale required to launch a new product or company. This began to change toward the end of the twentieth century, as venture capital firms arrived on the scene (Ennico, 2015). Venture capitalists operate in a manner similar to banks but on behalf of one or more wealthy investors who pool their investments into a fund that is used to support new ideas that the fund managers believe have a reasonable chance of turning a profit. Venture capital availability did help to encourage the Internet boom of the late 1990s by providing greater access to investment funding, but this still occurred on a very large scale, with huge amounts of money involved. This meant that smaller projects continued to have difficulty surmounting the chicken-and-egg dilemma. Creators of these smaller projects knew their product or idea could be successful because they knew many people who were interested in it, but they were unable to convince financial institutions or venture capitalists to give them a chance.

The third group involved in crowdfunding is the one that was able to fill this gap: the developers and managers of crowdfunding infrastructure services. By observing the unmet demand for financial backing of smaller projects, the crowdfunding developers were able to devise a solution to the problem. This solution is a combination escrow service and social media promotion platform, exemplified by the company Kickstarter (Lawton & Marom, 2013).

The purpose of the crowdfunding platform is to give people with ideas for products or services a place to describe their ideas—using text, pictures, or video—and a way to communicate that description to the rest of the world. It also includes a built-in mechanism by which members of the public can pledge their financial support for various projects.

For example, an inventor who came up with a way to make a standard lawn mower operate in complete silence, might nevertheless have difficulty obtaining the money needed to produce a prototype, file for patent protection, and begin production. To obtain those funds, the inventor could create a crowdfunding project and offer anyone who invested $100 a free lawn mower silencer from the first production run. The inventor could also create different contribution tiers, so that a person contributing $200 would receive three silencers, $300 would entitle one to five, and so on. As users contribute more money, it goes into a combined fund that has a predefined fundraising goal. The inventor of the lawn mower silencer would set this goal based on his or her calculations of the start-up costs. So, if the inventor had determined that creating an initial batch of silencers would cost $500,000, then the crowdfunding project would run until that goal had been reached.

Crowdfunding clearly serves an important role in the new Internet economy. It is especially apt for projects of such small scale that banks and venture capitalists would not be interested but whose start-up costs are out of reach for an individual or small group of investors. It is also attractive to some innovators because of its ability to act as its own advertising; this is because it exists almost entirely online and is designed from the ground up to take advantage of social media and word-of-mouth promotion. In addition, because the very concept of crowdfunding is still relatively new, it carries with it a certain cachet that sometimes spreads to the image of the product it is being used to fund and promote.

APPLICATIONS

Although crowdfunding as an online activity is quite new, its conceptual origins can be traced back at least a few hundred years. As early as the seventeenth century, there was something called the "subscription business model." Under this model, as with crowdfunding, projects were undertaken after first

Amanda Palmer singing at a barbeque in St. Kilda, Australia in March 2011. Palmer raised funds for her album using Kickstarter. (Courtesy of Many Hall via Wikimedia Commons)

obtaining financing commitments from members of the public. For example, if a small group wished to begin publishing a newspaper to disseminate its political views, it would begin by soliciting subscriptions for the as-yet unpublished paper. If enough people could be persuaded to commit to subscribing to the paper, then the publication could actually launch and begin producing issues, which would be distributed to the paying subscribers. This model was used to finance part of the construction of the Statue of Liberty.

Crowdfunding, despite its application to the Internet, has been adapted for a wide range of uses (Steinberg, 2012). In addition to the customary product development use, there are also crowdfunding platforms geared toward raising money for charitable purposes, such as defraying the cost of medical care for vulnerable individuals. A typical example of this type of crowdfunding might involve a person who has been in a serious car accident and has medical bills that are not covered by insurance. The injured person or those acting on his or her behalf might start the crowdfunding campaign. Artistic endeavors have also experimented with the crowdfunding model, particularly in the music industry, where several performers have used crowdfunding to finance the production of recordings and the logistics of performance tours.

VIEWPOINTS

Crowdfunding has been the source of controversy on several occasions. Typically, these incidents occur when the crowdfunding model is used by a person or organization that already possesses access to what most people would consider adequate resources to accomplish its goal. In these situations, prospective donors may resent that they are being asked to financially support activities that the person or organization could be paying for. This can result in backlash against the project, particularly on social media. In other cases, the mechanics of crowdfunding can prove to be the downfall of some projects (Sagall & Vega, 2014). This tends to happen when a project's financing phase takes longer than expected or encounters unforeseen challenges. The financing phase is the period in which contributions are solicited and stored. This phase generally lasts from the time the crowdfunding project is launched until the funding goal is reached and actual production begins. It is not uncommon for the financing phase to take several months or even a year or more, depending on the size of the project and the amount of starting capital needed to get it off the ground.

In some cases, funding may start out strong, with contributions from many interested parties, but then begin to taper off, slowing down gradually and even coming to a stop before the funding goal has been met. When this happens, it can cause those who have already contributed to become dissatisfied with the process. This is not because they have lost money, since the funds they have pledged are only committed if the funding goal is met—otherwise the investors keep their money. The dissatisfaction is usually a mixture of disappointment at the product continuing to be unavailable (this disappointment is perhaps more intense because the crowdfunding

project makes it more tantalizingly real) and frustration with the managers of the crowdfunded project, who may be perceived as not working hard enough to promote the idea and obtain buy-in from a large enough number of investors (Short, 2014).

Wisdom of the Crowd. One basic assumption that crowdfunding is built upon is the notion of the "wisdom of the crowd." This idea comes from the social sciences and information theory, and it attempts to explain the way that the behavior of crowds (i.e., groups of people affiliated in some way, either temporarily or on a long-term basis) can exhibit insights that transcend those possible for any individual member of the group. This is a phenomenon that has been observed in many contexts; one of the better-known examples comes from Victorian intellectual Sir Francis Galton and involves a crowd at a rural fair competition in which the goal is to correctly guess the weight of an ox. While no one in the crowd is able to accurately guess the weight, when all of the guesses from members of the crowd are viewed in the aggregate, the average guess comes remarkably close to the true figure. The lesson drawn from this vignette is that somehow a large number of people influence one another in subtle ways that cause the group to arrive at the correct answer to a problem, even if no single person in the group would be able to reach the same resolution on his or her own. Crowdfunding takes this lesson and applies it to the arena of business financing (Dresner, 2014). This means that some projects, products, or services have a potential market that justifies their creation, but that this justification is somehow imperceptible to banks, venture capitalists, and other traditional sources of capital. Only by presenting the idea for the new commodity to the crowd can the wisdom of the crowd have an opportunity to see the possibilities it represents.

Crowdfunding has inspired some interesting work in the fields of psychology and the social sciences, as its model appears to contradict the typical form of commercial transactions that people are accustomed to engaging in. Ordinarily, consumers search the marketplace for a product that will meet their needs. Once the product is located, consumers initiate a transaction in which they trade something of value—money, in most cases—for possession and ownership of the product. The merchant agrees to give up possession and ownership of the product in exchange for the money or other form of value. Scholars observe that this type of exchange is rooted firmly in the present and past, because the product has already been created and the money has already been earned and made available, and the trade between consumer and merchant occurs in the present (Bennett, 2015). Crowdfunding alters the entire landscape of such a transaction by placing its focus on the future. In this forward-looking model, the investors and the designer of the product or service make an agreement about what will happen in the future. The investors will give their money to the designer if the funding goal is met, and the designer will give the investors a reward for their financial support. Often, this reward takes the form of the product that the designer has designed.

Some psychologists liken this paradigm to one based on faith or trust, because both parties to the transaction must believe in each other on a fairly deep level—otherwise, there is no reason for them to engage in the transaction. Viewed in this light, the phenomenon of crowdfunding is seen as a positive development for society because it encourages so-called prosocial behaviors by creating opportunities for people with common interests to cooperate in order to produce a result not otherwise attainable.

Others make the observation that crowdfunding may produce positive effects, but it is usurping a role that might be better served by public spending. This view suggests that crowdfunding platforms are attempts at privatizing altruistic impulses and cooperative efforts and that a better approach would be to use tax revenue to provide greater access to startup capital and microloans to help people bring their ideas to fruition. Advocates of this tax-based approach point to the government programs enacted during the Great Depression, such as the Work Progress Administration's funding of the arts, as evidence that such programs could be successful and that they would do so without charging fees. There are difficulties with this argument—a portion of taxation is used to pay for government overhead, after all, and publicly funded projects might be able to assist small businesses but would be unlikely to help with social causes such as severe medical bills—yet it has proven problematic to discount entirely. Suggestions to increase funding to the Small Business Administration to test the theory have tended to fall afoul of the perennial political debate over the appropriate size of government and the impropriety of government entering the marketplace to the detriment of private enterprise (in this case, the crowdfunding platform developers).

Perhaps inevitably, the organizations that operate crowdfunding platforms online have begun to come under scrutiny. In some cases, this is related to the fee that the platforms charge, which is usually a percentage of the funds being raised. Critics argue that the fee is too large or that it is unfair because it takes advantage of projects that are already having difficulty obtaining funding. Defenders of crowdfunding argue that the fees are needed to make it financially viable to operate the crowdfunding platform. The fees cover the platform's online hosting, website development and maintenance, Internet bandwidth costs, as well as the salaries of the platform staff. Crowdfunding proponents also point out that crowdfunding services provide society and the economy with a valuable service and that without their efforts, huge numbers of worthwhile projects would be unable to launch due to lack of funding and lack of interest on the part of traditional investors.

TERMS & CONCEPTS

Barker: A person hired to assist in the promotion of a crowdfunded project by distributing information and links throughout various online communities and forums. The term comes from the carnival barkers who call out invitations to participate in different types of entertainment at fairs and festivals.

Equity investor: Some crowdfunded projects reward sponsors with the product being created, while others reward investors with a share in the ownership of the newly launched company; the latter type of investor is an equity investor because he or she gains an equity interest (ownership interest) in the company.

Progress bar: Most crowdfunding sites include a visual depiction of how close the project is to being fully funded. This usually looks like a computer's progress bar or an old-fashioned thermometer—as the project gains sponsors, the thermometer's "temperature" rises until the bar is completely full.

Social media: Online services that make it possible for users to create accounts and share information about themselves and their activities with friends, co-workers, and the public.

Sponsor: A term sometimes used to refer to someone who pledges money in support of a crowdfunded project.

Venture capital: Financial support given to a new product or service that is expected to be successful and highly profitable, thus earning a substantial return on the initial investment.

Bibliography

Assenova, V. (2016). The present and future of crowdfunding. *California Management Review, 58*(2), 125–135.

Banker R. et al. (2017). Cost management research. *Journal of Management Accounting Research In-Press.*

Bennett, L. K. (2015). *Crowdfunding the future: Media industries, ethics and digital society.* New York, NY: Lang.

Chakradhar, S. (2015). In new crowdfunding trend, donors decide fate of clinical trials. *Nature Medicine, 21,* 101–102.

Dresner, S. (2014). *Crowdfunding: A guide to raising capital on the Internet.* Hoboken, NJ: John Wiley & Sons.

Ennico, C. R. (2015). *Crowdfunding handbook: Using equity funding portals to raise money for your small business.* Place of publication not identified: Amacom.

Lawton, K., & Marom, D. (2013). *The crowdfunding revolution: How to raise venture capital using social media.* New York, NY: McGraw-Hill.

Sagall, R., & Vega, S. B. (2014). *Crowdfunding: A non-traditional financial assistance opportunity. Revenue-Cycle Strategist, 11,* 4–5.

Short, J. (2014). *Social entrepreneurship and research methods.* Branford, UK: Emerald Publishing.

Steinberg, D. (2012). T*he Kickstarter handbook: Real-life crowdfunding success stories.* Philadelphia, PA: Quirk Books.

Suggested Reading

Bruton, G., Khavul, S., Siegel, D., & Wright, M. (2015, January). New financial alternatives in seeding entrepreneurship: Microfinance, crowdfunding, and peer-to-peer innovations. *Entrepreneurship: Theory & Practice,* 9–26.

Macht, S. A., & Weatherston, J. (2014). The benefits of online crowdfunding for fund-seeking business ventures. *Strategic Change, 23,* 1–14.

Manchanda, K., & Muralidharan, P. (2014). Crowdfunding: A new paradigm in startup financing. *Global Conference on Business & Finance Proceedings, 9,* 369–374.

Perry, S. (2014). Caution! The downsides of crowdfunding. *Chronicle of Philanthropy, 26,* 1–10.

Rechtman, Y., & O'Callaghan, S. (2014). Understanding the basics of crowdfunding. *CPA Journal, 84,* 30–33.

Younkin, P., & Kashkooli, K. (2016). What problems does crowdfunding solve? *California Management Review, 58*(2), 20–43.

Essay by Scott Zimmer, MLS, MS, JD

E

ENTREPRENEURSHIP

This article focuses on the concept of entrepreneurship from its nascent beginnings to the present day. First, we shall review the various definitions applied to entrepreneurship, concluding with a fundamental definition of the term. Next, we'll consider entrepreneurial trait characteristics associated with successful entrepreneurship, highlighting a real-life entrepreneur as a prime example. Also, we'll explore entrepreneurship in its global context, examining the findings of a global survey that focused on entrepreneurship traits, motivations, demographics, and types of ventures undertaken.

OVERVIEW

As a global economic driver, entrepreneurship adds real value through the creation of new jobs and the production of innovative products and services. In short, entrepreneurship promotes the generation of wealth. Yet, a review of the literature indicates many definitions of entrepreneurship have been conceived over the years by researchers in the field. A single, commonly accepted definition of the term is simply nonexistent, though common elements tend to meet across the spectrum. Given this conundrum, a functional definition of entrepreneurship upon which to base our discussion is necessary.

Entrepreneurship Defined
The origin of the word entrepreneurship is derived from the French word "entreprende," which means "to undertake," as in undertaking a particular activity. Likewise, some researchers give credit for the word entrepreneur (in a business context) to eighteenth-century French businessman Richard Cantillon, who, in his published work *Essai Sur la Nature du Commerce en General,* "described entrepreneurs as 'undertakers' engaged in market exchanges at their own risk for the purpose of making a profit" (Roberts & Woods, 2005, p.46).

Definitions of entrepreneurship are generally situated within three broad categories: the *occupational notion* of entrepreneurship, the *behavioral notion,* and entrepreneurship on the basis of *new venture creation.* The *occupational notion* of entrepreneurship refers to owning and managing one's own business enterprise. "Its 'practitioners' are called entrepreneurs, self-employed or business owners" (Sternberg & Wennekers, 2005 p.193). An early nineteenth-century pioneer of the occupational notion (and behavioral notion) was French economist Jean Baptiste Say. According to Say, the entrepreneur is a business owner who creates value by transforming economic resources from areas of low productivity into areas of higher productivity, which in turn provide greater yields (Say, 1855). In essence, the entrepreneur is a creator of value.

The behavioral notion on the other hand, emphasizes the act of entrepreneurs recognizing and seizing economic *opportunity,* engaging in *innovative* practices, or assuming entrepreneurial *risk* —that is, pursuing new untapped markets, developing product innovations, etc. In fact, according to this behavioral notion, entrepreneurs need not be business owners — they may be what are referred to as intrapreneurs (Sterner & Wennekers, 2005). Contextually situated in ongoing businesses, intrapreneurship (also known as corporate entrepreneurship) encourages organizations' employees to engage in innovative entrepreneurial behavior. According to Pinchot (1985) — originator of the intrapreneurship concept — the intrapreneurial employee is an opportunistic innovator, engaging in creative business practices within his or her organization and introducing new products and services, production processes, and methods of distribution, all of which are pursued in the hope of achieving greater organizational growth and profits. However, in our present context, entrepreneurship should not to be substituted for or confused with the term intrapreneurship.

Ambassador-at-Large for Global Women's Issues Melanne Verveer greets participants in the African Women's Entrepreneurship Program at the Department of State in Washington, D.C. on June 14, 2012. (Courtesy of the U.S. Department of State via Wikimedia Commons)

Cantillon's work provided the intellectual foundation for three prominent twentieth-century economic theorists. Joseph Schumpeter emphasized the role of the entrepreneur as an *innovator*, Frank Knight stressed entrepreneurs' willingness to assume *risk*, and Israel Kirzner highlighted the pursuit of entrepreneurial *opportunity* (Roberts & Woods, 2005).

Schumpeter, a noted University of Chicago economist, identifies entrepreneurial *innovation* as a key driver in economic development. His definition of entrepreneurship focuses on *new combinations* of innovative behaviors felt to embody entrepreneurial behavior:

- developing new and innovative products
- proposing new forms of organization
- exploring new markets
- introducing new production methods
- searching for new sources of supplies and materials (Schumpeter, 1975)

Frank H. Knight, another notable University of Chicago economist, offers that it is the willingness to assume risks in the face of uncertainty that distinguishes entrepreneurship. Such risks may include a possible loss of business capital or the personal financial security risk associated with the uncertain

outcome of an entrepreneurial undertaking (Knight, 1921). On the other hand, leading economist Israel Kirzner's theory of entrepreneurship focuses on the detection of entrepreneurial opportunities for profit, which requires an *alertness of opportunity*. It is this alertness which allows the entrepreneur to exploit market arbitrage opportunities that have been overlooked or gone undiscovered by others—arbitrage being the identification of undervalued factors of production and the sale of them for an amount higher than the purchase price (Kirzner, 1973).

Similarly, acclaimed management theorist Peter Drucker states: "*Entrepreneurs* see change as the norm and as healthy. Usually, they do not bring about the change themselves. But, and this defines the *entrepreneu* and entrepreneurship — the *entrepreneur* always searches for change, responds to it and exploits it as an opportunity" (Drucker, 1985, p.28). In defining entrepreneurship, the general public most often associates entrepreneurship with small business ownership. According to Drucker, the act of starting or owning a small business does not in itself make one an entrepreneur, so much as the ability to innovate and exploit opportunity.

Carland (1984) follows a similar track, pointing out that one may be a small business owner but not necessarily engaged in entrepreneurship. He posits that while an entrepreneur and small business owner may establish and manage a business for profit, what sets the entrepreneur apart is the ability and willingness to employ innovative techniques and ways of thinking, as well as strategic management practices in the enterprise.

Another conception of entrepreneurship focuses on a more direct approach, defining entrepreneurship as new venture creation. Gartner (1988) believes entrepreneurship to be the act of creating Organizations: "What differentiates entrepreneurs from non-entrepreneurs is that entrepreneurs create organizations, while non-entrepreneurs do not" (Gartner, 1988, p.11). In simple terms, this concept of entrepreneurship focuses on the establishment of *new* business enterprises which create value.

Clearly, definitions for entrepreneurship are far from uniform, and each has its own merits. However, for the present dialogue, the most appropriate definition is that devised by the Global Entrepreneurship Monitor (GEM). Similar to Gartner (1988), GEM defines entrepreneurship as "any attempt at new business or new venture creation, such as self-employment, a new business organisation, or the expansion of an existing business by an individual, teams of individuals, or established business" (Harding, 2004, p.9). Later in this article, the purpose of GEM will be discussed, including a review of research findings concerning global entrepreneurship.

APPLICATION

Personality Traits of Entrepreneurs

A great deal of empirical research on the traits of successful entrepreneurs was conducted in the 1980s and 1990s. An early forerunner of entrepreneurial trait research was Harvard psychologist David McClelland (1961), who found that entrepreneurs are inclined to have the following characteristics:

- High need for achievement — Entrepreneurs display a higher need for achievement than the general population, and hence are motivated by this high achievement need.
- Moderate risk-taking propensity — Entrepreneurs tend to be moderate risk-takers. Unlike the common misconception, entrepreneurs are not high-rolling speculative gamblers. In short, entrepreneurs have a decided willingness to take calculated risks with a reasonable probability of success.
- In addition to the characteristics shown above, J.A. Timmons's study of entrepreneurial traits (as cited in Zimmerer and Scarborough, 1996) lists a number of trait characteristics associated with successful entrepreneurs:
- commitment and determination
- desire to accept responsibility for their venture's outcome
- opportunity Obsession — constantly seeking out opportunities
- high self-confidence in themselves
- creativity and flexibility in problem solving
- desire immediate performance feedback
- high levels of energy
- future oriented — i.e. possess a long-term perspective

Education campaigner Malala Yousafzai joined International Development Secretary Justine Greening in London to discuss the importance of getting girls through school around the world. Yousafzai is a Pakistani activist, social entrepreneur, and the youngest-ever Nobel Peace Prize winner, and named in the Forbes 30 list. (Courtesy of DFID – UK Dept. for International Development via Wikimedia Commons)

- willingness to learn from failure — they are unafraid of failure
- visionary leadership ability

It is important to note that successful entrepreneurs may or may not possess the majority of these characteristics, and in some cases, they may possess more of one trait and less of another. History dictates that entrepreneurs come in all shapes and sizes, yet these personal qualities serve as a general guide on what is known about the personality traits most associated with entrepreneurs.

Entrepreneurial Exemplar

An excellent example of a highly successful entrepreneurial venture is Federal Express and its founder and CEO, Frederick K. Smith. The following narrative provides ample evidence of the entrepreneurial prowess of Fred Smith, displaying risk-taking, opportunity-seeking, and innovative behaviors (American Enterprise Online, 2004).

Apple co-founder and longtime leader Steve Jobs (pictured in 2010) led the introduction of many innovations in the computer, smartphone and digital music industry. (Courtesy of Matthew Yohe via Wikimedia Commons)

- Risk-taker — While a student at Yale University in the mid-1960s, Fred Smith wrote an economics paper on the shortcomings of the delivery system for the air freight industry. He received a grade of "C" for his efforts, yet he persisted with his idea. In 1971, after serving four years of active duty as a pilot in the U.S. Marine Corps, (including tours in Vietnam) he started a company called Federal Express. In the early stages, Federal Express nearly went bankrupt, and it did not turn a profit until 1975; by the early twenty-first century, however, the company delivered billions of packages annually in over 200 countries. So, in spite of receiving an average grade from his college professor and almost going bankrupt in the early years of FedEx's operation, Smith persisted and made his company a success.

- Opportunity-seeker — The impetus for Federal Express rested on Smith's identification of an unrecognized opportunity — an air freight transportation system that could deliver packages faster, cheaper, conveniently, and more reliably than had ever been done previously. In addition, Smith recognized that FedEx was selling more than a delivery service — it was also in the business of selling knowledge. This knowledge asset is predicated on

the ability to show customers the exact location and expected delivery of their packages — in real-time.

- Innovator — A number of Federal Express innovations include the pioneering use of hand-held computers and satellite transponders on delivery trucks to keep track of packages and accurately estimate expected delivery times. Also, in order to eliminate the uncertainty of late package deliveries — FedEx guarantees a full refund for failure to provide on-time delivery. FedEx's just-in-time delivery system is especially important to businesses in that it reduces costly in-house inventory holding costs.

- Obviously, Smith embodies the spirit of entrepreneurship to the highest degree. With forward thinking and the ability to think outside the box, Smith and Federal Express created a new paradigm in the air freight industry, spurring economic growth and opportunity via just-in-time delivery of overnight packages.

Global Entrepreneurship

With the increasing globalization of the world's economies, the entrepreneurial mode of thinking must embrace a global mind-set. In line with this thinking, we'll proceed with an examination of what is known about global entrepreneurship based on the Global Entrepreneur Monitor (GEM) Results 2012, from a survey of respondents in 69 countries. Initially the GEM research project began in 1999 with 10 member countries; the scope of the survey has expanded significantly over the years. The project is the largest global study of entrepreneurship in the world, with a purpose of providing annual assessments of the national levels of entrepreneurial activity. Specifically, we'll examine the types of entrepreneurial activity, entrepreneurial traits and motivations, and demographic profiles.

In order to make proper use of the GEM data, a number of clarifications are necessary. GEM establishes several categories of entrepreneurs:

- Potential entrepreneurs are interested in potentially creating a business and have identified opportunities to do so.
- Early-stage entrepreneurs are engaged in the beginning steps of creating a business. If a business has not been operating for more than 42 months

it is considered nascent, and those managing it are early-stage entrepreneurs.

- Established entrepreneurs are those still managing a successful business after the first 42 months—the time in which a business is most likely to fail.

GEM considers early-stage entrepreneurship to be a good measure of the predisposition for entrepreneurial activity in a given country. Likewise, established entrepreneurs are used as a key indicator of the sustainability of entrepreneurial ventures. In analyzing these global entrepreneurial proclivities, GEM data makes a distinction between middle and high income countries, based on per capita GDP. Overall, countries with similar per capita GDP often display parallel levels of entrepreneurial endeavors. Early-stage entrepreneurship tends to be higher in countries with a lower per capita GDP. Conversely, early-stage entrepreneurial activity is relatively lower in higher income countries. Countries that have more early-stage entrepreneurial activity often have higher rates of successful business ownership.

Venture Types — In order of preference, most early-stage entrepreneurs and established business owners have businesses in consumer service activities (retail, restaurants, lodging, health and social services, education, recreation). Next are transformation businesses (construction, manufacturing, transportation, and wholesale distribution), followed by business to business services, and businesses extracting products from the natural environment (timber, mining, agriculture, etc.).

Traits — In comparing entrepreneurs' and non-entrepreneurs' traits, entrepreneurs tend to be more self-confident in their own skill-set, *and* they tend to be much like the opportunity-seekers described earlier by Knight (1927), in that they are more alert to the existence of unexploited market opportunities. Also, in line with other empirical research, entrepreneurs tend to be less apprehensive of failure than non-entrepreneurs.

Motivations — In this global environment, what motivates individuals to engage in entrepreneurial behavior? GEM data reveal that individuals are motivated to start new business ventures for two main reasons:

- They want to take advantage of a potential business opportunity (opportunity entrepreneurs). GEM data reveals that most early-stage entrepreneurs tend to be opportunity entrepreneurs.
- They pursue entrepreneurship because they have no other satisfactory options for employment (necessity entrepreneurs).

Findings indicate the rate of opportunity entrepreneurship is much higher than necessity entrepreneurship in high GDP countries than in middle GDP countries. Also, necessity entrepreneurship is relatively more common in middle GDP countries than in high GDP countries. This may be due to the fact that higher income countries tend to also have lower rates of unemployment, indicating more choices for generating a living wage and thus creating less of a need for entrepreneurship as a survival mechanism.

Demographics

Gender — Men are more likely to start businesses than women. In both high- and middle-income countries, the rate of male opportunity entrepreneurship is higher than that of women. The greatest gap exists in high income (GDP) countries, where men are significantly more likely to be early stage or established business owners than women.

Education — Entrepreneurial activity is higher among individuals with higher levels of education. Yet, in higher GDP countries, people lacking formal qualifications are also likely to become entrepreneurs.

Age — Overall, younger people (25–34 years old) are more likely to be early stage entrepreneurs. Yet, older people (45–54 years old) are more likely to be established business entrepreneurs. These results are consistent from country to country. Also, the age distribution of men and women are comparable as well, regardless of the stage of entrepreneurship or country context.

Looking across cultures, one might expect to find vast differences in the venture types, motivations, traits, attitudes, and demographics of entrepreneurs. With a few exceptions, the GEM 2012 data indicate otherwise. An interesting point is that most early-stage entrepreneurs tend to be of the type described by Kirzner and Drucker — i.e. opportunity-seekers. Likewise, as described by Knight, they perceive themselves as risk takers willing to bear the uncertainty of an entrepreneurial venture. Also, they view themselves as innovators, akin to the Schumpeterian notion of entrepreneurship. Indeed, entrepreneurial similarities span across cultures.

CONCLUSION

In theory, entrepreneurship may occur in a corporate environment or under the circumstance of starting and owning one's own business. In either case, entrepreneurship involves risk taking, innovative thinking, and an opportunity-seeking mindset. Likewise, successful entrepreneurship requires perseverance, determination, a long-term perspective, self-confidence, leadership ability, creativity, and imperviousness to failure. Also, as the Global Entrepreneurship Monitor results show, entrepreneurship is not a culturally bound phenomenon but a global phenomenon.

Also, to reiterate, there is no single typology of a successful entrepreneur. The Frederick Smiths of the world are but one example of successful entrepreneurship. History is replete with examples of individuals who possess more or less of the identified traits of successful entrepreneurs — some fail and some succeed in spite of perceived shortcomings. Regardless of the definition of choice for entrepreneurship, one thing is certain: entrepreneurship creates jobs and likewise produces innovative products and services, which subsequently add value to society.

Terms & Concepts

Arbitrage: The process of identifying undervalued factors of production and then selling them for an amount higher than the purchase price.

Corporate entrepreneurship: Another name for intrapreneurship.

Early-stage entrepreneurs: Individuals engaged in the beginning steps of creating a business. If a business has not been operating for over 42 months it is considered nascent, and those managing it are early-stage entrepreneurs.

Entrepreneurship: The act of new business creation, or the expansion of an existing business.

Established entrepreneurs: Individuals still managing a successful business after the first 42 months—the time in which a business is most likely to fail.

Global Entrepreneurship Monitor (GEM): A global research project with the purpose of providing annual assessments of the national levels of entrepreneurial activity.

Intrapreneurship: Also known as corporate entrepreneurship, intrapreneurship encourages organization's employees to engage in innovative entrepreneurial behavior within their respective organization.

Necessity entrepreneurs: Entrepreneurs who pursue entrepreneurship because all other options for employment are lacking or unavailable.

Opportunity entrepreneurs: Entrepreneurs exploiting a perceived business opportunity.

Bibliography

Alvarez, S. A., et al. (2014). Realism in the study of entrepreneurship. *Academy of Management Review, 39*, 227–33.

American Enterprise Online (2004, June) Frederick Smith. *Are we being run over by global capitalism?* Retrieved April 10, 2007.

Block, J., Thurik, R., & Zhou, H. (2013). What turns knowledge into innovative products? The role of entrepreneurship and knowledge spillovers. *Journal of Evolutionary Economics, 23*, 693–718.

Bosma, N. & Harding, R. (2006). *Global Entrepreneurship Monitor 2006 results*.

Carland, J. W., Hoy, F., Boulton, W. R., & Carland, J. C. (1984 April). Differentiating entrepreneurs from small business owners: A conceptualization. *The Academy of Management Review, 9*, 354–359.

Chaston, I. (2017). Entrepreneurship. *Technological Entrepreneurship*, 1–24.

Drucker, P. F. (1985). *Innovation Entrepreneurship*. New York: Harper and Row.

Gartner, W. B. (1988, Spring). "Who is an entrepreneur?" is the wrong question. *American Journal of Small Business, 12*, 11–32.

Global Entrepreneurship Monitor. (2013). GEM 2012 global report. Retrieved November 18, 2013.

Harding, R. (2004). *Global Entrepreneurship Monitor Report UK 2004.*

Kenworthy, T., & McMullan, W. (2013). Finding practical knowledge in entrepreneurship. Entrepreneurship: Theory & Practice, 37, 983–997.

Kirzner, I. M. (1973). *Competition and Entrepreneurship.* Chicago, IL: University of Chicago Press.

Knight, F. H. (1921). *Risk, Uncertainty, and Profit.* Library of Economics and Liberty. Retrieved April 9, 2007.

McClelland, D. A. (1961). *The Achieving Society.* Princeton, NJ: Van Nostrand.

Pinchot, G. (1985). *Intrapreneuring: Why You Don't Have to Leave the Corporation to Become an Entrepreneur.* New York: Harper and Row.

Raffiee, J., & Feng, J. (2014). Should I quit my day job? A hybrid path to entrepreneurship. *Academy of Management Journal, 57,* 936–63.

Roberts, D., & Woods, C. (2005, Autumn). Changing the world on a shoestring: The concept of social entrepreneurship. *University of Auckland Business Review, 7,* 45–51.

Say, J. B. (1855). *A Treatise on Political Economy.* Library of Economics and Liberty. Retrieved April 10, 2007.

Schumpeter, J. A. (1975). *Capitalism, Socialism, and Democracy.* New York: Harper.

Sternberg, R. & Wennekers, S. (2005, April). Determinants and effects of new business creation using global entrepreneurship monitor data. *Small Business Economics, 24,* 193–203.

Timmons, J. A. (1999). *New Venture Creation — Entrepreneurship for the 21st Century,* (5th ed.), Boston, MA: Irwin McGraw-Hill.

Warnecke, T. (2013). Entrepreneurship and gender: An institutional perspective. *Journal of Economic Issues, 47,* 455–464.

Zimmerer, T. W. Scarborough, N. M. (1996). *Entrepreneurship and New Venture Formation.* Upper Saddle River, NJ: Prentice Hall.

SUGGESTED READING

Estrin, S., Mickiewicz, T., & Stephan, U. (2013). Entrepreneurship, social capital, and institutions: Social and commercial entrepreneurship across nations. *Entrepreneurship: Theory & Practice, 37,* 479–504.

McGrath, R. G. MacMillan, I. (2000). *The Entrepreneurial Mindset.* Boston, MA: HBS Press.

Sautet, F. (2013). Local and systemic entrepreneurship: Solving the puzzle of entrepreneurship and economic development. *Entrepreneurship: Theory & Practice, 37,* 387–402.

Spinelli, S., & Timmons, J. (2004). *New Venture Creation for the 21st Century.* (6th ed.) New York: McGraw-Hill.

Vesper, K. H. (1980). *New venture strategies.* Englewood Cliffs: Prentice Hall.

Wei-Loon K., & Abdul Majid, I. (2014). A model for predicting intention towards sustainable entrepreneurship. *International Journal of Information, Business and Management, 6,* 256–69.

Essay by Edwin D. Davison, M.B.A., J.D.

Entrepreneurship and Business Planning

This article looks at the multifaceted relationships between entrepreneurship and business planning, and it considers the causes and effects of entrepreneurship in new and preexisting businesses. As a strategic management tool, business planning is seen as one of the activities undertaken in the entrepreneurial process. Types of plans and aspects of business planning are also discussed, along with several contradictory schools of thought on the factors that determine entrepreneurship, the outcomes of planning, and information analysis.

OVERVIEW

Business ventures fuel the economic growth and prosperity of nations and regions (Yusuf, 2002), and entrepreneurship has long been considered significant in encouraging such socioeconomic growth and development. Entrepreneurial ventures provide job opportunities, offer consumer goods and services, and increase general prosperity and competitiveness.

There is no universally accepted definition of the term *entrepreneurship. Entrepreneurship* is a derivative of the term *entrepreneur*, which historically referred to a businessperson, business owner, or owner-manager. In a narrow sense, entrepreneurship can be referred to as the creation of new enterprises, but over the years, the scope of this concept has expanded beyond basic new-venture creation (also known as corporate venturing or the setting-up of intra-firm "venture capital" processes).

The expanded scope of entrepreneurship is two-pronged: on the one hand, it refers to the growth-oriented and employment-generating creation of new ventures; on the other hand, it includes small businesses and microenterprises that provide self-employment, even if they do not foster employment growth. Naturally, entrepreneurship is fostered by entrepreneurial behavior, or behavior that fosters growth through innovative ideas, products, services, markets, and technologies (Stevenson & Jarillo, 1990).

Entrepreneurship can be stimulated by certain favorable environmental conditions that may promote or prevent success by the nature of the climate they engender. Such favorable environmental conditions include family and support systems, financial resources, local community, and government agencies. Additionally, "larger societal factors such as cultural, economic, political and social forces can combine to create threats or opportunities in the environments where entrepreneurs operate" (Lee & Peterson, 2000).

Entrepreneurship can also be viewed at three levels: the macro level, individual level, and firm level. In macro terms, the word *entrepreneurship* is synonymous with the advancement of an economy (Schumpeter, 1934) and the disruption of market equilibrium. Entrepreneurial activity in itself leads to the promotion of competition and innovation, and by doing so, it contributes to economic growth and development. It is not surprising, therefore, that entrepreneurship has rapidly become a dynamic field of study and research.

Entrepreneurs are creative, innovative, and opportunistic. At the individual level, entrepreneurship has been attributed to individuals with certain internal psychological traits, sociological background characteristics, and behaviors. Psychologically, it is believed that entrepreneurs have a propensity toward risk-taking, high achievement, and an internal concentration of control. Sociological characteristics

associated with entrepreneurs include being a first child, being an immigrant, and having early role models. Some writers, on the other hand, prefer to define entrepreneurship by what an entrepreneur does, not by who he or she is. For instance, a successful entrepreneur may be seen as one who most likely experiments with promising new technologies, seizes opportunities, or demonstrates initiative or decision-making competence in other ways (Lee & Peterson, 2000).

Entrepreneurship is widely recognized as a process that involves businesses of all sizes, be they new or preexisting, owner-managed, family-run, or corporations. At the firm level, three variables have been identified as underlying a firm's ability to behave in an entrepreneurial manner. These are opportunity recognition, organizational flexibility, and the firm's ability to measure, encourage and reward innovative and risk-taking behavior (Barringer & Bluedorn, 1999). The success of a firm in its entrepreneurial ventures depends on the commitment of top management in taking the firm through the entrepreneurial process, which consists of opportunity identification, definition of business concept, assessment of resources requirements, acquisition of resources, and management and harvesting of the venture. Thereafter, whether the firm can increase its entrepreneurial commitment is mainly up to the compatibility of its management practices with its entrepreneurial ambitions (Lee & Peterson, 2000).

Corporate entrepreneurship is motivated by the need to transform, create or grow a business, create wealth, or change the status quo in response to factors such as intensified competition, corporate downsizing, corporate delayering, and technological progress. Through its two subprocesses, discovery and exploitation, corporate entrepreneurship refers to the process by which an organization pioneers, innovates, and takes risks for growth and development. Corporate entrepreneurship is made manifest in the form of corporate venturing, strategic renewal, and spin-offs for ideas generated within organizations (Hayton, George, & Zahra, 2002).

There are three types of corporate entrepreneurship. The first is the creation of new businesses within a preexisting organization, also known as "corporate venturing" or "intrapreneurship," and the second is the activity associated with the transformation or renewal of preexisting organizations, which involves the creation of new wealth through a combination of resources. The third is where the enterprise changes the "rules of competition" for its industry.

Entrepreneurial firms are growth-oriented, proactive, innovative, creative, and flexible. They are pioneers and risk-takers, and they encourage their employees to be imaginative. Successful entrepreneurship will lead to the creation of value, through several means, including the following:

- the renewal of the organization itself
- the renewal of markets
- changes in the pattern of resource deployment
- the creation of new capabilities to add new possibilities for positioning in markets
- the breaking of new ground
- the remixing of old ideas to make seemingly new applications

Entrepreneurship levels differ from one geographic location to another due to variations in environmental conditions and, in particular, economic, political/legal, and social conditions. The main factors affecting entrepreneurship in a particular locality include the following:

- entrepreneurship policy
- social systems and institutions
- economic growth
- industry conditions
- industrial infrastructure
- population dynamics
- the cultural landscape

Entrepreneurial research has discovered, for instance, that countries whose populations are excessively skewed toward old or young individuals are likely to experience low levels of entrepreneurial activity. Furthermore, a culture's entrepreneurial orientation—the way that culture is inclined toward entrepreneurship in the areas of autonomy, innovativeness, risk-taking, proactiveness, and competitive aggressiveness—combined with key economic, political/legal, and social forces, will impact the degree of entrepreneurship experienced, and ultimately will impact the global competitiveness of a nation or nations (Lee & Peterson, 2000).

Within nations also, institutional patterns—such as access to research and educational institutions,

access to sources of financing, and the availability of educated labor—help to determine the manner in which an innovation—and hence entrepreneurship—emerges within a country. It is believed that differences in national institutions may bring about different levels of entrepreneurial activity across countries. Entrepreneurial activity is more likely to thrive when appropriate infrastructure is in place to enhance competition and problem-solving activities between a country's entrepreneurs (Busenitz, Gómez, & Spencer, 2000).

Cultural values will determine how much a society believes entrepreneurial behaviors such as risk-taking, proactiveness, and independent thinking are desirable. "Cultures that value and reward such behavior promote a propensity to develop and introduce radical innovation, whereas cultures that reinforce conformity, group interests, and control over the future are not likely to manifest risk-taking and entrepreneurial behavior" (Hayton, George, & Zahra, 2002).

Entrepreneurs are expected to allocate sufficient resources and implement a workable strategy capable of overcoming competitive and hostile adversaries. Planning, as a critical component of strategic management practice, is a major aspect of the entrepreneurial process, since planning has the potential to influence the degree of entrepreneurship taking place within an organization.

APPLICATIONS

The amount of business planning carried out within organizations ranges from no planning at all to the development of comprehensive and detailed long-term plans. There are four types of plans, ranging from the simplest to the most complex. These are unstructured plans, intuitive plans, structured operational plans, and structured strategic plans. Both the planning process (the creation, analysis, and implementation of strategy) and the planning content (the strategic choices, plans, and actions) are beneficial to entrepreneurs and entrepreneurial organizations.

Strategic plans focus on a firm's method of obtaining sustained competitive advantage, and a firm's strategic management practices must be tailored to support its organizational objectives and context. Therefore, the planning processes and practices will differ among industries. For instance, when planning, manufacturing organizations tend to identify their performance objectives and organizational expertise based on cost variables, quality, complexity, and available resources. Marketing organizations, on the other hand, frequently use SWOT analyses to identify competitive advantage through either market segmentation or identification of an effective marketing mix (Honig, 2004). Likewise, planning processes and their effects differ between small and large businesses.

Key aspects of the business planning process include environmental scanning, locus of planning (employee involvement), planning flexibility, planning horizon (planning time frame), and control attributes. Environmental scanning refers to the managerial activity of learning about events and trends in an organization's environment (Hambrick, 1981). By its very nature, the entrepreneurial process requires a high level of environmental scanning. Scanning may reveal new opportunities, but it may also unearth environmental uncertainty. Fortunately, scanning may help managers cope with the uncertainty, but only if they realize that uncertainty can only be reduced, not eliminated (Barringer & Bluedorn, 1999).

There are three types of uncertainty: state, effect, and response uncertainty. State uncertainty refers to the inability to understand or predict the state of the environment due to a lack of information or a lack of understanding of the interrelationships among environmental elements. Effect uncertainty refers to uncertainty over the consequences of environmental changes for the organization, and response uncertainty implies that decision makers do not know the response options, or they do not know the likely consequences of pursuing a particular option.

According to Barringer & and Bluedorn (1999), locus of planning "refers to the depth of employee involvement in a firm's strategic planning activities. Organizations can be described as having either a shallow or a deep locus of planning. A deep locus of planning refers to a high level of employee involvement in the planning process, where employees from virtually all hierarchical levels within the firm" are included. On the other hand, a shallow locus of planning denotes a fairly exclusive planning process, usually involving only the top managers of a firm.

It is believed that a deep locus of planning facilitates a high level of corporate entrepreneurship intensity, since a high level of employee involvement

in planning brings the frontline staff, those who are "closest to the customer," into the planning process. The involvement of nonmanagerial staff may allow a firm to see—and seize—opportunities that it otherwise could have missed. Hence, a deep locus of planning may facilitate opportunity recognition, which is vital in the entrepreneurial process (Schumpeter, 1936). A deep locus of planning also facilitates the entrepreneurial process by maximizing the diversity of viewpoints that a firm might consider in formulating its strategic plan.

A strong relationship has been discovered between planning flexibility and corporate entrepreneurship activity (Barringer & Bluedorn, 1999). Plans must be flexible: they should be easily changed as and when environmental opportunities or threats emerge. Unfortunately, some organizational decision makers hesitate to deviate from their plans, fearing that their deviations will be interpreted as flaws in the initial planning process. A flexible planning system will allow a firm to adjust its strategic plans quickly to pursue opportunities and keep up with environmental change.

A firm's planning time frame is known as its planning horizon, which is the length of the future time period that decision makers consider in planning. The planning horizon of individual firms varies from less than one year to more than 15 years. To facilitate successful entrepreneurship, planning horizons should be long enough to permit planning for expected changes in strategy and yet be short enough for a firm to have reasonably detailed plans.

An entrepreneurial firm "faces the dual challenge of remaining responsive to current environmental trends, which suggests the adoption of a short-term planning horizon, while at the same time remaining visionary, which suggests the adoption of a longer-term perspective" (Barringer & Bluedorn, 1999).

"A relatively 'short' average planning horizon of less than five years may be most advantageous, as entrepreneurial firms typically compete in turbulent environments that are characterized by short product and service life cycles. The main concern of an entrepreneurial firm is product and service innovation, which typically must be accomplished in the short term rather than the long term to maintain a sustainable competitive advantage. A short planning horizon, coupled with intensive environmental scanning and a high degree of organizational and planning flexibility, should provide an entrepreneurial firm with the capacity to quickly recognize environmental change and develop appropriate product and service innovations" (Barringer & Bluedorn, 1999).

Entrepreneurial firms must have systems in place to ensure that their business strategies meet predetermined goals and objectives. Such systems are known as control systems. Strategic controls base performance on strategically relevant criteria like customer satisfaction, new patent registrations, meeting deadlines, and the achievement of quality control standards. Conversely, financial controls base performance on objective financial criteria such as net income, return on equity, and return on sales. The control systems of entrepreneurial firms—particularly their strategic and financial controls—must stimulate innovation, proactiveness, and risk-taking (Barringer & Bluedorn, 1999).

VIEWPOINTS

As is the case in many fields of study, there are several contradictions in entrepreneurship theory and practice. For instance, scholars disagree on the very factors that determine entrepreneurship. While some believe that entrepreneurship is determined by the level of importance strategy making commands in a firm, others cite the personality traits of the leader, believing that entrepreneurship involves individuals with unique personality characteristics and abilities. Still others refer to the role played by the structure of the organization.

In response to this theoretical ambiguity, some researchers have conjectured that in small firms whose power is concentrated at the top, entrepreneurship would be determined by the characteristics of the leader. In larger firms, whose goal is smooth and efficient operation through the use of formal controls and plans, it appears that entrepreneurship would be facilitated by explicit and well-integrated product-market strategies. In firms that strive to be adaptive to their environments and emphasize expertise-based power and open communications, entrepreneurship may be a function of environment and structure (Miller, 1983).

Although many educational programs in entrepreneurship place much emphasis on business planning, there appears to be little evidence that planning—even pre-startup planning—leads to success. In fact, one often hears of notable cases where new businesses proved very successful despite the fact that pre-startup planning was limited. Business planning is often believed to interfere with the efforts of firm founders to undertake more valuable actions to develop their fledgling enterprises.

Empirical studies testing theoretical relationships between strategic planning and outcomes for preexisting businesses tend to be inconclusive, with some research pointing to the usefulness of long-term planning in organizations and other research failing to identify positive outcomes. Some of such studies have been faulted for methodological weaknesses. Some researchers found that outcomes differed across industry sectors, and others have shown that the effect of strategic planning on outcomes is conditional on the relative stability of the industrial environment under study.

It is therefore suggested that in entrepreneurship, entrepreneurs should avoid focusing their efforts on the production and evaluation of systematic detailed plans, developing instead the necessary skills to reevaluate, adapt, and revise their activities in a resourceful manner to suit new environmental contingencies. Outcomes are often impossible to predict and represent decisions that are impossible to anticipate (Honig, 2004).

While information gathering and analysis is crucial for the development and maintenance of successful innovation strategies in entrepreneurial firms, too much information—known as information overload—is detrimental to planning. In the form of a vicious cycle, it is often the case that the more information one collects, the more likely one is to receive conflicting pieces of information. In a quest to make sense of conflicting information, one then searches for more information, and eventually the law of diminishing returns sets in. Also detrimental is the overanalysis of a small amount of well-researched, comparable options.

To support a de-emphasis on planning, it has been observed that much of what entrepreneurs actually do is the product of tacit knowledge, also referred to as knowledge-by-doing, which is most often acquired through learning by experience. In general, entrepreneurial firms may thrive best if they have an experimental focus that makes use of environmental feedback.

TERMS & CONCEPTS

Control systems: Systems that ensure that an organization's strategies meet predetermined goals and objectives. Control systems include those that are both financial and strategic in nature.

Corporate venturing: The creation of new businesses within preexisting organizations. Corporate venturing is also known as intrapreneurship.

Entrepreneur: A creative, innovative, and opportunistic business owner or owner-manager who carries out new business permutations in a quest for growth through innovation.

Entrepreneurial behavior: The quest for growth through innovation, be this technological or purely managerial.

Entrepreneurship: In macro terms, this term is synonymous with the advancement of an economy, and in a micro sense, it refers to the process by which an individual or organization pioneers, innovates, and takes risks for growth and development.

Environmental scanning: The managerial activity of monitoring events and trends in an organization's environment.

Financial controls: Systems that base a firm's performance on objective financial criteria such as net income, return on equity, and return on sales (Barringer & Bluedorn, 1999).

Locus of planning: The depth of employee involvement in a firm's strategic planning activities (Barringer & Bluedorn, 1999).

Planning flexibility: The ease with which a firm can change its strategic plan in response to environmental change (Barringer & Bluedorn, 1999).

Planning horizon: The length of the future time period that a firm's decision makers consider in planning (Barringer & Bluedorn, 1999).

Strategic controls: Systems that base a firm's performance on strategically relevant criteria such as customer satisfaction, new patent registrations, meeting deadlines, and the achievement of quality control standards (Barringer & Bluedorn, 1999).

Strategic plans: Organizational plans that focus on a firm's method of obtaining sustained competitive advantage.

SWOT analysis: A method for determining the strengths, weaknesses, opportunities, and threats of an organization in order to define the ways in which a firm can accomplish its goals and which obstacles it must overcome or minimize.

Tacit knowledge: Knowledge gained through experience.

BIBLIOGRAPHY

Barringer, B., & Bluedorn, A. (1999). The relationship between corporate entrepreneurship and strategic management. *Strategic Management Journal, 20,* 421.

Bhide, A. (2000). *The origin and evolution of new business.* New York: Oxford University Press.

Birley, S., Moss, C., & Saunders, P. (1987). Do women entrepreneurs require different training? *American Journal of Small Business, 12,* 27–35.

Busenitz, L., Gómez, C., & Spencer, J. (2000). Country institutional profiles: Unlocking entrepreneurial phenomena. *Academy of Management Journal, 43,* 994–1003.

Castrogiovanni, G. J. (1996). Pre-startup planning and the survival of new small businesses: Theoretical linkages. *Journal of Management, 22,* 801–822.

Delmar, F., & Shane, S. (2003). Does business planning facilitate the development of new ventures? *Strategic Management Journal, 12,* 1165–1185.

Dess, G., Lumpkin, G., & McGee, J. (1999). Linking corporate entrepreneurship to strategy, structure, and process: Suggested research directions. *Entrepreneurship: Theory & Practice, 23,* 85–102.

Estay, C., Durrieu, F., & Akhter, M. (2013). Entrepreneurship: From motivation to start-up. *Journal of International Entrepreneurship, 11,* 243–267.

Fernández-Guerrero, R., Revuelto-Taboada, L., & Simón-Moya, V. (2012). The business plan as a project: An evaluation of its predictive capability for business success. *Service Industries Journal, 32,* 2399–2420.

Gumpert, D. (2007). What entrepreneurs need to know. *Business Week Online.*

Hambrick, D. C. (1981). Specialization of environmental scanning activities among upper level executives. *Journal of Management Studies, 18,* 299–320.

Hayton, J., George, G., & Zahra, S. (2002). National culture and entrepreneurship: A review of behavioral research. *Entrepreneurship: Theory & Practice, 26,* 33.

Honig, B. (2004). Entrepreneurship education: Toward a model of contingency-based business planning. *Academy of Management Learning & Education, 3,* 258–273.

Honig, B., & Samuelsson, M. (2012). Planning and the entrepreneur: A longitudinal examination of nascent entrepreneurs in Sweden. *Journal of Small Business Management, 50,* 365–388.

Lee, S., & Peterson, S. (2000). Culture, entrepreneurial orientation, and global competitiveness. *Journal of World Business, 35,* 401.

Levesque, M., & Minniti, M. (2005). Demographic structure and entrepreneurial activity. Entrepreneurship Conference Paper Abstract. *Academy of Management Proceedings.*

Matthews, C., & Scott, S. (1995). Uncertainty and planning in small and entrepreneurial firms: An empirical assessment. *Journal of Small Business Management, 33,* 34–52.

Miller, D. (1983). The correlates of entrepreneurship in three types of firms. *Management Science, 29,* 770–791.

Pentilla, C. (2007). I know too much! *Entrepreneur, 35,* 82–83.

Schumpeter, J. A. (1934). *The theory of economic development.* Cambridge: Harvard University Press.

Schumpeter, J. A. (1936). *The theory of economic development.* Cambridge: Cambridge University Press.

Stevenson, H., & Gumpert, D. (1985). The heart of entrepreneurship. *Harvard Business Review, 63,* 85–94.

Stevenson, H., & Jarillo, J. (1990). A paradigm of entrepreneurship: entrepreneurial management. *Strategic Management Journal, 11,* 17–27.

Stopford, J., & Baden-Fuller, C. (1994). Creating corporate entrepreneurship. *Strategic Management Journal, 15,* 521–536.

SUGGESTED READING

Baker, W. H., Addams, H. L., & Davis, B. Business planning in successful small firms. *Long Range Planning, 26,* 82–88.

Chwolka, A., & Raith, M. G. (2012). The value of business planning before start-up—A decision-theoretical perspective. *Journal of Business Venturing, 27,* 385–399.

Hechavarria, D., Renko, M., & Matthews, C. (2012). The nascent entrepreneurship hub: Goals, entrepreneurial self-efficacy and start-up outcomes. *Small Business Economics, 39,* 685–701

Porter, M. E. (1985). *Competitive advantage: Creating and sustaining superior performance.* New York: Free Press.

Schumpeter, J. A. (1934). *The theory of economic development.* Cambridge: Harvard University Press.

Essay by Vanessa A. Tetteh, Ph.D.

ENTREPRENEURSHIP AND VENTURE INITIATION

This article will focus on the process of venture initiation as it relates to the entrepreneurial process. To understand the process of initiating a new venture, one has to understand the field of entrepreneurship and the role of the entrepreneur. Entrepreneurship has become an important trend in the U.S. economy, and many individuals have elected this field as a career of choice. The increase in technology and globalization has changed the way that business is conducted as well as how entrepreneurs are categorized. It is important to understand the environment in which the new concept will operate, and most scholars would suggest providing a conceptual and process framework. Therefore, potential entrepreneurs will need to study the industry to develop a strategy.

"Entrepreneurship is a phenomenon that continues to excite the imagination of students interested in entering careers in which they must adapt to rapidly changing environments, inventors looking for ways to commercialize their discoveries, government leaders attempting to undertake economic development, and CEOs of large firms seeking to remain competitive in a global marketplace" (Allen, 2006, p. 4). All entrepreneurs believe in the success of their dreams, and expect their ventures to take off and expand.

ENTREPRENEURS

Webster (1977) classifies the title "entrepreneur" into five categories. He states that the distinctions among the different categories allow one to understand the different terminology in the field and practice.

Webster's Five Categories of Entrepreneur

The five categories of entrepreneur include the following:

The Cantillon Entrepreneur—Richard Cantillon introduced the term *entrepreneur* in the early eighteenth century to denote a person who is treated as one of the four factors of production (i.e., land, labor, capital, and the entrepreneur). The entrepreneur is considered the catalyst in the role of innovator and is responsible for fueling growth in a capitalist economy. Entrepreneurs can be successful and make a profit when they have the ability to create an opportunity in which they have a temporary monopoly to change market products and processes before the competition has an opportunity to dilute industry profits. Many economists do not view the entrepreneur as a real person. Rather, the entrepreneur is seen as a "silent theoretical entity that makes a rational decision, strives for profit maximization as defined by the economists, and assumes managerial and other uninsurable risks in exchange for profits" (Kilby, 1971, p. 2).

The Industry-Maker—Traditional management research views the entrepreneur as an industry-maker. Someone who builds the nation's economic system, is hardworking and willing to take risks, and invests personal assets. According to this school of thought, the entrepreneur establishes the foundation for an organization and then builds it into an industry leader.

The Administrative Entrepreneur—The entrepreneur role is viewed as an executive who establishes a new company, or a reorganization of an existing corporation, and becomes a permanent leader of the management team. Although there are similarities, there is a distinct difference between an industry-maker and an administrative entrepreneur. Administrative entrepreneurs are usually associated with an individual organization (e.g., Henry Ford), whereas industry-makers are usually considered manipulators (e.g., Jack Welch) of an entire industry or a large segment of an industry.

The Small Business Owner/Operator—During Webster's time, small business owners were perceived to be the local merchants and were tied predominantly to the retail and wholesale industry. Many scholars believe that these vendors were limited in scope in regards to sales, geographical outreach, and profit potential. However, technology, particularly the Internet, has allowed service businesses as well as retail businesses to reach an international market.

The Independent Entrepreneur—An individual who creates ventures from scratch and who does not generally commit long-term managerial responsibilities to one venture. These individuals tend to be very creative and get a thrill from developing the business.

Allen's Modern Categories of Entrepreneur

Webster's work was written in the 1970s and times have changed. As noted with the small business owner category, the increase in technology and globalization have changed the way that business is conducted as well as how entrepreneurs are categorized. Allen's categories (2006) are reflective of how business has been conducted in the twenty-first century. These categories include the following:

The Home-Based Entrepreneur—Millions of people operate home-based businesses. Although many of these businesses start out as sole proprietors, some have grown to the point that they can compete against large, well-known companies. Technology has made it possible for businesses to operate from any location, and home-based businesses are able to tap into resources via the Internet. Home-based businesses are usually the starting point for many businesses.

The Cyber Entrepreneur—This type of entrepreneur enjoys the fact that he or she is able to run a full-fledged business without a brick-and-mortar location.

Cyber entrepreneurs are able to process all of their business transactions with customers, suppliers, and strategic partners over the Internet. In addition, their businesses tend to be digital products and services that do not require a physical infrastructure (e.g., warehouse). Allen's 2012 edition of *Launching New Ventures* does not list the cyber entrepreneur as its own separate "path to entrepreneurship," as having an online component to one's business has become an essential part of entrepreneurship overall.

The Serial Entrepreneur—These entrepreneurs, also called portfolio entrepreneurs, enjoy creating businesses, but they tend to have a desire to move on when the business is up and running. They are motivated by the hype of the pre-launch and start-up phases of the business but do not have a desire to handle management responsibilities.

The Traditional Entrepreneur—Traditional entrepreneurs are classic entrepreneurs. They start brick-and-mortar businesses and stick with them as they begin to prosper. Traditional entrepreneurs will be around as long as there is a need to build sustainable businesses, especially in industries such as food services, manufacturing, and retail.

The Nonprofit Entrepreneur—Nonprofit entrepreneurs have a passion for work that involves socially responsible focuses such as educational, religious, and charitable initiatives. Many seek their 501(c) status so that they can solicit funding and donations from organizations and individuals who believe in their mission. Their businesses are allowed to make a profit as long as the profits are used for business purposes and not distributed to the owners of the company.

The Corporate Venturer—Corporate venturers are individuals who seek out new ventures while working within established large organizations. Organizations create skunk works so that they have a unit to explore potential opportunities. Skunk works are autonomous groups that are given the mandate to find and develop new products for a company that may be outside of the organization's core competencies. However, many have found this a difficult task due to the bureaucratic structure of many large organizations. To be a successful corporate venturer, it is important that the following factors are present:

1. Senior management commitment—Commitment from the leaders is important to be successful.
2. Corporate interoperability—The work environment must support collaboration and provide the venturer access to the organization's resources.
3. Clearly defined stages and metrics—There need to be established timelines and due dates for each stage so that the organization can decide whether to continue to pursue the initiatives.
4. A high-performance work team—Since these projects tend to be riskier, it is imperative that only the best employees are assigned to venture projects.
5. Spirit of entrepreneurship—Although success is the goal, failures may occur. Organizations must support the team as they explore the opportunities, even when efforts are failures.

Regardless of the type of entrepreneur, one objective is constant. Entrepreneurs enjoy seeing the fruition of their work. They enjoy creating and developing potential, whether it is from scratch or a restructure. Given the focus on technology, many entrepreneurs may be able to seek the assistance of venture capital organizations. The first venture capitalist firm was established in the 1940s with the purpose of providing financial and business support to entrepreneurs in exchange for repayment in capital gains. Venture capitalists tend to gravitate toward technology initiatives because of the potential for high returns. In addition, these organizations are interested in promoting their services nationally and internationally. Since the 1990s, venture capitalism has expanded to the global marketplace.

APPLICATION

New Venture Formation
"Since there is no consensus regarding the sequence of the identification of the idea/opportunity and the decision to initiate a new venture, there is no comprehensive process model of new venture formation" (Hunger, Korsching, & Van Auken, 2002). There are

different schools of thought concerning the process. Martin (1984) and Gartner (1989) state that the process commences when the entrepreneur decides to start a new business. This view is defined as decision driven because once a person decides to begin a venture, a venture opportunity is identified and the venture start-up is created. Another view (Wheelan & Hunger, 1992) suggests that recognition of a venture opportunity comes before deciding to start a new venture. This view supports the notion that an idea for a new venture leads to environmental evaluation to determine if a new venture opportunity is possible (Hunger, Korsching, & Van Auken, 2002). The remainder of this section will highlight the process of the second view.

In this model, starting a new venture takes place prior to the business opening its doors. Much time, energy, and research goes into determining whether to pursue an idea. The tests are conducted through a series of analytical tools, which are considered a feasibility analysis.

Entrepreneurial Environment

One of the factors that affects the direction in which the new venture initiation process begins is the environment in which the new concept will exist. According to Allen (2003), the environment includes the following:

- the industry in which a business operates
- the market the business serves
- the state of the national and international economy
- the people and businesses with which the business will interact (p. 75)

It is important to understand the environment in which the new concept will operate, and most scholars suggest providing a conceptual and process framework. Industries constantly change. Therefore, potential entrepreneurs will need to study the industry to develop a strategy. It has been suggested that Porter's "Five Forces" framework can be used to outline the process for exploring a new venture.

Five Areas for Competitive Environmental Analysis

This model lists five key areas that potential entrepreneurs should evaluate when analyzing the competitive environment. The five forces are threat of entry,

the power of buyers, the power of suppliers, the threat of substitutes, and competitive rivalry.

1. Threat of entry—Some barriers to entry may be so high that their presence will discourage entrepreneurs from attempting to enter. Some of these barriers include the following:

- **Economies of scale**—A new venture usually cannot achieve the same economies of scale as established businesses in the industry. One option would be to form alliances with other small firms to share resources in order to compete.
- **Brand loyalty**—New ventures may have to face customer loyalty to current products and services in the industry. As a result, entrepreneurs will need to spend a significant amount of money on marketing campaigns to get a foot in the door.
- **Capital requirements**—Upfront costs can be staggering. Therefore, entrepreneurs may need to outsource some services to keep costs down.
- **Switching costs for the buyer**—New ventures will have to spend time and money convincing customers that the new product is worth switching to.
- **Access to distribution channels**—Entrepreneurs must convince distribution channels that their product or service is worth distributing.
- **Proprietary factors**—New ventures may need patents in order to get started, and the holders of the patents may purposely withhold access to keep the new venture out of the market.
- **Government regulations**—The government can impose licensing requirements, high taxes, and/or zoning restrictions on new ventures.
- **Industry hostility**—Some industries have well-established firms that are hostile to new entrants.

2. Power of buyers—If buyers have bargaining power, it may be difficult for a new venture to gain access and grow.

3. Power of suppliers—Suppliers can raise prices or change the quality of a product that they supply in order to maintain control in the industry. Depending on the number of suppliers, it may not be advantageous for entrepreneurs to pursue certain ventures.

4. Threat of substitutes—A new venture must be able to compete against products and services in its own industry as well as potential substitutes in other industries.

5. Competitive rivalry—A highly competitive industry may reduce profits and the rate of return on investments. As a result, many organizations may resort to price wars and competitive advertising campaigns. Entrepreneurs will need to identify these potential rivalries in the proposed markets to determine the feasibility of entering the market.

Once a competitive analysis has been conducted and the position is still favorable, the entrepreneur can move to the next step in the process—developing and testing the business concept.

ISSUES

Joint Ventures

New venture firms tend to pick out joint ventures to expand internationally. International joint ventures (IJVs) represent a form of alliance that has increased in popularity over the years (Inkpen & Crossan, 1995). From a new venture perspective, IJVs allow small organizations an opportunity to pool their resources together to launch new ventures with an international scope. Small ventures have grown at a phenomenal rate. Unfortunately, research on multinational enterprises has often focused on the large established organizations. However, small ventures have earned their right to be key players in the global economy.

If an entrepreneur decides to enter the foreign market, the first attempt is often as a joint venture. Many entrepreneurs spend a large amount of time building networks so that they can provide necessary supplies for the new venture. These resources tend to be located across the border. In addition, they need to promote themselves as players in the international market. Entrepreneurs realize that it is important that the right partnerships and alliances be formed if they desire their product or service to obtain the necessary backing in order to survive.

New venture success is determined by the types of alliances an entrepreneur is able to establish and maintain with other organizations. Joint ventures are one way an organization can become a key player in the international arena. Trust is a key factor in making these types of relationships work. However, creating a new partnership can be risky. A joint venture involves creating a new entity, which has to

handle increased liabilities while making a name for itself. These relationships may become unstable over time. Therefore, the rate of failure tends to be high for these types of alliances.

Given the negative consequences and attributes of international joint ventures, the prospects are still encouraging, especially for small venture initiatives. Small businesses still have a place in the global economy. As more organizations attempt to build partnerships in the international market, there will be opportunity for IJVs to grow and expand. Scholars are challenged to continue their research on how joint ventures are formed and the process they use to launch new ventures. These types of ventures usually emerge rather than develop as the product of a strategic planning process. As a result, IJVs are entities that provide an opportunity for further research and study of international entrepreneurship.

CONCLUSION

"Entrepreneurship is a phenomenon that continues to excite the imagination of students interested in entering careers in which they must adapt to rapidly changing environments, inventors looking for ways to commercialize their discoveries, government leaders attempting to undertake economic development, and CEOs of large firms seeking to remain competitive in a global marketplace" (Allen, 2006, p. 4). All entrepreneurs believe in the success of their dreams and expect their ventures to take off and expand. Although many scholars have not attempted to distinguish the different types of entrepreneurs, Webster (1977), classifies the title into five categories. He states that the distinctions among these categories allow one to understand the different terminology in the field and practice. Webster's work was written in the 1970s and times have changed. The increase in technology and globalization have changed the way that business is conducted as well as how entrepreneurs are categorized. Allen's categories (2006) are reflective of how business has been conducted in the twenty-first century.

The field of entrepreneurship continues to boom as more individuals consider developing their ideas and passions—despite the estimate that 75 percent of all start-ups fail (Ghosh, as cited in Blank, 2013, p. 66). Scholars have not reached a consensus regarding the best way to initiate a new venture creation. Depending on the personality and characteristics of an individual, he or she may elect to enter this field in a number of ways. For example, the lean start-up business model, developed in the 2010s, lessens risk for new ventures by favoring experimentation and customer feedback over the more traditional big-plan approach (Blank 2013, p. 66). Carland, Carland, and Stewart (1996) believe it is the entrepreneur's vision that keeps the initiation process alive. A vision can initiate an opportunity that has not yet been created, and it can grow as a result of entrepreneurial drive. As long as an entrepreneur thinks about the vision, there is still an opportunity to initiate the venture.

Terms & Concepts

Administrative entrepreneur: An executive who creates an organization, or reorganizes an existing company, and becomes a permanent leader of the organization's management team.

Business enterprise: Organization that provides goods and services; involves finance, commerce, and industry.

Cantillon entrepreneur: A silent theoretical entity that makes rational decisions, strives for profit maximization as defined by economists, and assumes managerial and other uninsurable risks in exchange for profits.

Decision driven: Situation that is based upon a decision to do something as opposed to an idea or opportunity.

Entrepreneurship: A mindset or way of thinking that is opportunity-focused, innovative, and growth-oriented.

Entrepreneur: A person who assumes risk and management responsibility of the business enterprise.

Joint venture: A partnership or conglomerate, formed often to share risk or expertise.

New venture: An entrepreneurial effort, as in a new venture start-up.

Opportunity driven: Situation that is based upon an idea or opportunity as opposed to a decision.

Small business owner: An individual who starts an operating entity within the business environment and has a limited number of employees. Generally, an enterprise with less than 500 employees is considered a small business, especially if its owner(s) is involved in hands-on management.

Venture initiation: A start-up enterprise that is innovative in nature; often involves a certain amount of risk.

Bibliography

Allen, K. (2003). *Launching new ventures.* 3rd ed. Boston, MA: Houghton Mifflin Company.

Allen, K. (2006). *Launching new ventures.* 4th ed. Boston, MA: Houghton Mifflin Company.

Allen, K. (2012). *Launching new ventures.* 6th ed. Mason, OH: South-Western.

Arend, R. (2014). Entrepreneurship and dynamic capabilities: How firm age and size affect the 'capability enhancement-SME performance' relationship. *Small Business Economics, 42*(1), 33–57.

Blank, S. (2013). Why the lean start-up changes everything. *Harvard Business Review, 91*(5), 63–72.

Carland, J. A., Carland, J. W., & Stewart, W. H. (1996). Seeing what's not there: The enigma of entrepreneurship. *Journal of Small Business Strategy, 7*(1), 1–20.

Decker, R., Haltiwanger, J., Jarmin, R., & Miranda, J. The Role of Entrepreneurship in US Job Creation and Economic Dynamism. (2014). *Journal of Economic Perspectives, 28*(3), 3–24.

Feld, B. (2013). Creating start-up communities. *International Trade Forum,* (1), 13–14.

Gartner, W. (1989). Some suggestions for research on entrepreneurial traits and characteristics. *Entrepreneurship Theory & Practice, 14*(1), 27–37.

Hunger, J., Korsching, P., & Van Auken, H. (2002). *The interaction of founder motivation and environmental context in new venture formation: Preliminary findings.*

Inkpen, A. C., & Crossan, M. M. (1995). Believing is seeing: Joint ventures and organization learning. *Journal of Management Studies, 32*(5), 595–618.

Kilby, P. (1971). *Entrepreneurship and economic development.* New York: The Free Press.

Krzyzanowska, M., & Tkaczyk, J. (2013). Identifying competitors: Challenges for start-up firms. *International Journal of Management Cases, 15*(4), 234–246.

Martin, M. (1984). *Managing technological innovation and entrepreneurship.* Reston, VA: Reston Publishing.

Porter, M. E. (1980). *Competitive strategy.* The Free Press.

Timmons, J. (1999). *New venture creation: Entrepreneurship for the 21st century.* 5th ed. Boston, MA: Irwin/McGraw Hill.

Webster, F. (1977). Entrepreneurs and ventures: An attempt at classification and clarification. *The Academy of Management Review, 2*(1), 54–61.

Wheelan, T. & Hunger, J. (1992). The usefulness of strategic management concepts to small businesses and entrepreneurial ventures. *International Journal of Management, 9*(4), 399–405.

Yu, J., Gilbert, B., & Oviatt, B. M. (2011). Effects of alliances, time, and network cohesion on the initiation of foreign sales by new ventures. *Strategic Management Journal, 32*(4), 424–446.

SUGGESTED READING

Allen, K. R. (2012). *Launching new ventures: An entrepreneurial approach.* 6th ed. Mason, OH: South-Western, Cengage Learning.

Barringer, B. R., & Ireland, R.D. (2012). *Entrepreneurship: Successfully launching new ventures.* 4th ed. Boston, MA: Pearson/Prentice Hall.

Harnish, V. (2014). Finding the Route to Growth. *Fortune, 169*(7), 45.

Herron, L., & Sapienza, H. (1992). The entrepreneur and the initiation of new venture launch activities. *Entrepreneurship: Theory & Practice, 17*(1), 49–55.

Osgood, W., & Wetzel Jr., W. (1977). A systems approach to venture initiation. *Business Horizons, 20*(5), 42–54.

Greenberger, D., & Sexton, D. (1988). An interactive model of new venture initiation. *Journal of Small Business Management, 26*(3), 1–7.

Essay by Marie Gould

ETHICAL RESPONSIBILITIES OF BUSINESS

ABSTRACT

This article explores the ethical responsibilities of business. Business ethics became a hot-button issue in the wake of the corporate scandals that were exposed in the late 1990s through the early 2000s. Businesses do not exist in a vacuum, but rather they play a vital role in sustaining economic growth, providing jobs, giving employees access to health care, and more—businesses can and do exist for the betterment of our society. However, people run businesses, and human nature sometimes manifests itself in unethical conduct. The way toward maintaining ethical business standards is by examining the moral character of business people, employees, and consumers and adhering to the basic moral codes of trustworthiness, respect, responsibility, fairness, caring, and citizenship. In short, the ethical responsibility of business is to be a good corporate citizen, and adhering to moral codes is a responsibility that we all share.

OVERVIEW

Whether it was fraudulent accounting practices of publicly traded companies, front running of stocks and investments by mutual funds, the raiding of pension funds by businesses heading for bankruptcy, manipulative sales and lending practices by multinational banks, or the predatory lending practices of consumer finance companies, recent decades have seen an increase in the exposure of corporate malfeasance. These episodes are not limited to a particular industry, and a similar strain runs through all of these events: a lack of business ethics. However, there is a growing business ethics movement that has been ushered in through increased regulatory scrutiny by state and federal government agencies, class action lawsuits, and the initiatives of consumer advocates and not-for-profit organizations dedicated to the social responsibility of business.

Business ethics may seem like an ambiguous or even counterintuitive term. After all, the primary objective and responsibility of any business is to make and maximize profits. There are times, however, when the means employed to make profits conflict with a society's moral and legal codes. Essentially, business ethics are rules geared toward establishing and maintaining trustworthiness in a business or commercial setting. While it may be hard to identify, there is a growing business ethics movement in the wake of the aforementioned business scandals. Moreover, state and federal regulatory agencies have stepped up their monitoring activities across multiple lines of business.

Increasing Regulations and Legal Action. For example, the accounting scandals that ultimately led to the much-publicized demise of Enron (and the loss of thousands of jobs as well as the retirement funds of many former employees) and the prosecution of Tyco's former chief executive eventually prompted the U.S. Congress to enact the 2002 Sarbanes-Oxley Act. In 2004, the Financial Services Agency of Japan ordered a multinational bank to close one of its foreign private banking divisions after an investigation revealed manipulative sales and lending practices. Later, a major New York–based commercial banking institution was fined for laundering billions of dollars for criminal enterprises emanating from Russia, and this led to the bank's eventual acquisition by a larger banking entity. At the state level, following the subprime mortgage crisis of 2007 and 2008, a number of regulatory agencies responsible for overseeing consumer loans and mortgage lending were empowered by state legislatures to crack down on predatory lending practices. Quite a few consumer finance companies and multistate mortgage banks were held accountable for charging excessive points and fees for unsecured consumer loans as well as loans collateralized by residential dwellings.

Not only have the actions by regulatory agencies affected business practices, regulatory scrutiny has opened the door to class action lawsuits. Whether these were brought by firms representing shareholders who claim they were defrauded by accounting practices that did not truly represent the value of a company, or other actions on behalf of consumers who were harmed by so-called predatory lending practices of consumer finance companies, such lawsuits have resulted in multimillion dollar settlements and these, in turn, have had a significant impact on profits. However, in a controversial practice, several businesses adopted arbitration clauses in the 2010s that forced customers to settle disputes with the company though arbitration, preventing customers from joining others in a class action lawsuit. In some cases, regulatory oversight and legal actions were prompted by the initiatives of consumer advocates and not-for-profit organizations. In short, concerned citizens at the grassroots level are paying close attention to how companies operate and holding them accountable for their actions.

Corporate Ethics and Social Responsibility. While the Enron and Tyco scandals were front-page news, these prosecutions are not the norm. At times, the potential financial benefit from behavior that is short of ethical may seem to be worth the risk for some decision makers. However, in the long run, good ethics is good for business, as a company's professional reputation can have a positive impact on its relationships with customers and vendors and enable it to develop strategic alliances with other similar businesses. Professional reputation is a matter of perception, and society's perceptions closely link business performance to a company's social, environmental, and ethical conduct. Consumers have become increasingly concerned that businesses should be responsible not only for ensuring that they provide quality products but also for treating employees fairly. In light of the increased regulatory scrutiny, legal actions, and consumer advocacy, corporate social responsibility has become a growing concern for many business entities.

Compliance Procedures. To enhance corporate social responsibility, companies are increasingly concerned that they have efficient compliance procedures in place to ensure that their business practices adhere to the regulatory guidelines of their particular industry. Having a clearly defined compliance program enables a company to integrate compliance into its business model. By doing so, they have awareness of the potential regulatory issues that can arise in the event of an audit by a regulatory agency. This knowledge can empower an organization to take proactive corrective steps prior to the commencement of an adverse regulatory action. Moreover, having effective compliance systems in place will create positive working relationships with regulatory agencies.

The goal of regulatory agencies is not to be an impediment to business. After all, if their goal were merely to put companies out of business, there would be no business to regulate and no need for regulatory agencies. Thus, companies and governmental agencies must have a symbiotic relationship. By realizing this, business people will understand that there is no need for an adversarial posture with the agency that regulates their industry and that establishing harmonious relationships with regulators will be good for business in the long run.

Enforcing an Ethical Culture and Compliance. The challenge for many business enterprises goes beyond legal and compliance initiatives. Business owners and executives need to raise the bar and to consider whether their business decisions are ethical. This requires decision makers to develop and encourage a culture of ethics and compliance, and this can be a daunting task. There are numerous pressures confronting business in addition to increasing sales, maintaining competitive advantage and market shares, and being profitable. Mergers and acquisitions, downsizing, and outsourcing have dramatically changed the shape of corporations. In many cases they do not have the luxury of time to develop a "corporate culture" as their personnel goes through greater turnover today than in previous eras.

Despite these pressures and considerations, there is still a need for companies to develop a code of ethics that is communicated to all their employees. While ethical behavior should start at the top—with owners, executives, and managers adhering to moral standards—developing an ethical culture also requires having ethical employees. As we have seen, in order to adhere to regulatory guidelines and maintain its professional reputation, a company needs to have effective compliance procedures and internal controls in place. The goal is to create a code of ethics. In many instances, a corporate code of conduct is a written policy and is sometimes incorporated into a company's mission statement.

The Mission Statement. A mission statement defines the purpose of an organization, its reason for existing, and the goals of employees who work for the organization. If the goal of the organization is to provide quality products and adhere to a code of ethics, there are standard moral principles that should be incorporated into its code of ethics. These may be lofty notions to some, but ethics are essential virtues that many people learn from their families. Some of these virtues include integrity, justice, competence, and utility.

- Integrity means to be open, honest, and sincere.
- Justice relates to being impartial, having sound reasoning, and being conscientious.
- Competence is being capable, qualified, and reliable.
- Utility means being practical and useful.

Not only should a code of conduct be based on the foregoing virtues, the code should incorporate the following basic values of moral conduct:

trustworthiness, respect, responsibility, fairness, caring, and citizenship.

These are not merely theoretical notions, but rather virtues and ethical standards that will be reflected in the way a company conducts its business, how a business treats its employees, and the organization's relationship with its customers and vendors. Simply put, an ethical business enterprise is one that pays its bills expediently, treats its employees fairly, and provides quality products and service to its customers. Unethical behavior such as not paying vendors for their services, subjecting employees to hostile work environments, or not having reliable customer service will undo an organization in the end.

Financial Reporting and the Sarbanes-Oxley Act. Further, because of the Sarbanes-Oxley Act (SOX), publicly traded entities must have higher standards of ethical conduct as it relates to their financial reporting requirements. Essentially, a company's income statements and balance sheets must accurately reflect the company's financial standing. This means that their revenues, liabilities, and net worth must be bona fide, and executive officers are now required to attest to the accuracy of those statements.

In this regard, there have been numerous violations discovered where financial reports contained deficiencies. These deficiencies are usually related to the timing of revenue recognition as well as contracting practices. The timing of revenue recognition and contracting practices are directly related to relatively straightforward if not mundane matters such as accurately tracking accounts receivable and inventory accounts.

Essentially, certain companies were found to have practices that were deemed to be improper revenue recognition. One of these practices concerns the treatment of accounts receivable. Certain companies were found to have been backdating invoices in an attempt to lower their outstanding or uncollected receivables for a particular quarter that gave the appearance of greater cash flows at the close of a quarter. Another deficient practice has been termed "channel stuffing." Here, a company attempts to boost sales results by shipping more products to subsidiaries or vendors prior to the end of a reporting quarter. This gives the appearance of higher sales figures and reduced inventory, and thus greater revenue for that quarter.

Manipulating financial statements in such a manner is a violation of the SOX. Not only have companies and the responsible individuals been convicted of fraud under this law, investors have also suffered undue hardship as the value of the companies' stock price fell dramatically in these cases. This opened the door to class action lawsuits. Defending against these suits can be quite expensive, and this can have a material adverse effect on a company's profits, its reputation, and its viability as a business entity. In short, not having ethical standards can have serious implications as it relates to financial reporting requirements. Causing financial losses to its investors is not a theoretical matter, it is an endeavor that can stain a business's reputation and eventually cause its demise.

Hostile Work Environments. An ethical organization is one that also treats its employees well. Many companies meet this standard simply by providing jobs, giving employees access to health care, and creating professional work environments. However, there have been many instances where unethical conduct as it relates to work environments has been revealed. For example, sexual harassment lawsuits have been brought when employees were subjected to a hostile work environment. A hostile work environment can be one where a superior makes outright and unwanted sexual advances on a subordinate, or even where inappropriate comments by people running the mailroom take on a sexual tone. Most organizations have clearly defined policies regarding these matters and policies and procedures to ensure that hostile environments are not sustained.

Allegations of sexual harassment are not the only situations that indicate a hostile work environment. Such an environment also includes the use of obscene language, verbal abuse and intimidation, and derogatory comments about a person's ethnic or racial background, religious affiliation, gender, or and sexual orientation.

How does this relate to the virtues and moral values mentioned above? If a company adheres to the basic moral values of caring and citizenship, hostile work environments would not arise. A business that aspires to fairness and trustworthiness is one that expediently pays it vendors for services provided. By not treating its vendors fairly, a company can jeopardize its professional reputation by undermining its

professional relationships. An organization that believes in responsibility will ensure that its people are held accountable for their performance. That can be the performance of the controller, who is responsible for maintaining books and records and financial reporting; the human resource manager, who is responsible for implementing the company's policies and procedures as they relate to the treatment of employees; or the compliance officer, who is responsible for developing and implementing policies and procedures that adhere to regulatory guidelines.

The overriding moral value is respect. In fact, respect is the foundation of any relationship. Respect is not an abstract notion. To be respectful is to recognize the value of other people. At the end of the day, business organizations are not "brick-and-mortar" entities. Companies are not automated enterprises that run on their own. Business enterprises are made up of people. How people relate to one another within an organization is directly related to the ethical values of the business. Therefore, it is the shared responsibility of all the people in an organization to treat one another (the internal customer), as well as its customers, with respect. Customers who perceive a business is not treating them with respect will find another business to provide them with the goods or services they desire. Employees who feel that their coworkers or superiors are disrespectful will find another job. In the final analysis, though, the first relationship any individual has is with oneself. If people have self-respect, they will treat others respectfully, and they will respect the organizations that they work for, shop at, or invest in.

VIEWPOINTS

Business enterprises do not exist in a vacuum; they are integral to society. A company that seeks to maintain ethical standards will better serve society. Being a good corporate citizen is not much different from an individual being a good citizen. The moral values required for each are the same. Further, under the law, businesses are considered persons in many cases, and there are legal ramifications that go with that distinction. Beyond the legal ramifications that we are well familiar with by now, there is a difference between the letter of the law and the spirit of law, and the latter really speaks to ethics.

While we have seen many instances of unethical corporate behavior and the harm that arose from that behavior, it is a reasonable proposition that an unethical business will not survive in the long run. At the same time, if this is true, one might wonder why such instances of unethical conduct occurred in the first place. If unethical business practices can trigger regulatory scrutiny that might cause a business's demise, then it seems prudent for businesses to implement and maintain ethical practices.

Although government agencies and attorneys general have far-reaching abilities and ample resources, their regulatory enforcement actions are limited in scope and usually aimed at large organizations with so-called deep pockets; that is, businesses with financial resources that make it worthwhile to commence a regulatory action or a legal proceeding. While it may be of little value for an organization to spend needless amounts of time, resources, and money defending itself against regulatory enforcement actions or litigation, businesses that have ample financial resources are often successful in mitigating the damage of such proceedings. It is possible, therefore, that certain business decisions that might not appear ethical are made with the inherent regulatory or legal risks carefully considered. At times, the potential for financial gain may exceed the risk of financial losses that might occur in the event of an enforcement action or lawsuit. Moreover, in light of the fact that enforcement actions and class action lawsuits are more likely to be aimed at companies that have ample financial resources, smaller companies can engage in unethical practices and are less likely to be detected.

However, the energies and effort of a business enterprise are of better use when they are generating profits. To paraphrase the late economist Milton Friedman, the business of business is business. Friedman believed that the social responsibility of business is to generate profits. The purpose of this paper is not to debate the merits of Friedman's economic theories, but to some extent, perhaps he was right. A business that believes its social responsibility is to generate profits will conduct itself in a manner that will prove to be successful. In so doing, a business's success will contribute to the economic growth of a society. This will provide people with jobs and opportunities for growth.

Considering the importance of business ethics, then it is self-evident that to sustain itself, a business enterprise needs to attract and retain qualified and competent people. This reinforces one of the four virtues mentioned earlier. In addition to competence,

the other virtues include integrity, justice, and utility. With respect to the last of these, the simple question here is whether the goods or services a company is providing are useful. Of course, that is a matter of debate; after all, in a consumer-driven society, there are many goods sold to and purchased by the public that are of dubious utility. An organization that is delivering valuable and useful goods, services, or commodities is acting for the betterment of society. One can look to the technological innovations of recent years and see that our economies have become more efficient.

In the final analysis, the social responsibility of a business is to be profitable, as this will contribute to sustaining economic growth. A business that incorporates a code of ethics into its business practices will protect itself from regulatory and legal actions and will enhance its relationships with its employees, customers, and vendors. In so doing, a business can ensure its viability, and that is an ethical responsibility as well.

TERMS & CONCEPTS

Accounts receivable: Money owed to a business entity for goods, services, and merchandise purchased on a credit basis.

Business ethics: Rules geared toward establishing and maintaining trustworthiness in a business or commercial setting.

Business model: The means by which a company generates revenue and profits, how it serves its customers, and the strategy and implementation of procedures to achieve this end.

Compliance procedures: Business practices and procedures that adhere to federal, state, and regional laws, rules, and guidelines.

Corporate culture: The beliefs, attitudes, and behaviors of an organization and its employees that determine a corporation's character.

Financial services agency: The government organization in Japan responsible for overseeing the banking, securities and exchange, and insurance sectors.

Inventory accounts: The name given to an asset of a business relating to merchandise or supplies on hand or in transit at a particular point in time.

Mission statement: A statement that explains the core purpose of an organization, including why it exists, how it intends to conduct its business, and what the expectations of the employees in achieving these aims are.

Moral conduct: A rule or habit of behavior that is right or wrong according to socially accepted norms.

Predatory lending practices: Lending practices aimed at minority groups or senior citizens who have weaker credit ratings and financial resources than other demographic groups. Government investigations that began in the late 1990s have revealed that senior citizens and minority groups are ultimately charged more fees or offered higher interest rates for consumer loans.

Regulatory agencies: Federal, state, and regional government agencies that are responsible for enforcing laws, rules, and guidelines.

Sarbanes-Oxley Act (SOX): Federal law in the United States enacted in 2002 that requires executives of publicly traded companies to attest to the accuracy of their financial statements and requires the organization to establish extensive internal procedures and controls to ensure compliance with the act.

Social responsibility: The obligation of a business to conduct its business in a manner that is socially, environmentally, and ethically responsible.

BIBLIOGRAPHY

Ahmad, N., & Ramayah, T. T. (2012). Does the notion of 'doing well by doing good' prevail among entrepreneurial ventures in a developing nation? *Journal of Business Ethics, 106*, 479–490

Alzola, M. (2015). Virtuous persons and virtuous actions in business ethics and organizational research. *Business Ethics Quarterly, 25*(3), 287–318.

Atkinson, J., & Leandri, S. (2005). Best practices: Organizational structure that supports compliance. *Financial Executive, 21*, 36–40.

Banyard, P. (2006, June). Banking ethics: Some surprises along the way. *Credit Management,* 22–23

Cant, M. C., & van Niekerk, C. (2013). Survival or ethically correct? Small business owners' attitude towards ethical concerns. *Annual International Conference on Business Strategy & Organizational Behaviour (BizStrategy),* 1–7.

Millman, G. J. (2006). Black and white fever: The state of business ethics. *Financial Executive, 22,* 26–28.

Okoro, E. (2012). Ethical and social responsibility in global marketing: An evaluation of corporate commitment to stakeholders. *International Business & Economics Research Journal, 11,* 863–870.

Preuss, L., Barkemeyer, R., & Glavas, A. (2016). Corporate social responsibility in developing country multinationals: Identifying company and country-level influences. *Business Ethics Quarterly, 26*(3), 347–378.

Schrempf-Stirling, J., Palazzo, G., & Phillips, R. A. (2016). Historic corporate social responsibility. *Academy of Management Review, 41*(4), 700–719.

Williams, C. E., & Scott, J. T. (2005) *Concise handbook of management: A practitioner's approach.* London: Hawthorn Press.

SUGGESTED READING

Crossman, J., & Doshi, V. (2015). When not knowing is a virtue: A business ethics perspective. *Journal of Business Ethics, 131*(1), 1–8.

Francis, R. D., & Murfey, G. (2016). *Global business ethics: Responsible decision making in an international context.* London: Kogan Page.

Jackson, K. T. (2005). Towards authenticity: A Sartrean perspective on business ethics. *Journal of Business Ethics, 58,* 307–325.

Knox, S., Maklan, S., & French, P. (2005). Corporate social responsibility: Exploring stakeholder relationships and programme recording across leading FTSE organizations. *Journal of Business Ethics, Part 3, 61,* 7–28.

Maclagan, P. (2012). Conflicting obligations, moral dilemmas and the development of judgement through business ethics education. *Business Ethics: A European Review, 21,* 183–197.

Stango, M. (2006). Ethics, morals and integrity: Focus at the top. *Healthcare Financial Management, 60* 50–54.

Wempe, J. (2005). Ethical entrepreneurship and fair trade. *Journal of Business Ethics, 60,* 211–220.

Edited by Richa S. Tiwary, Ph.D., MLS

ETHICS IN ACCOUNTING

ABSTRACT

Accounting deals with the rules that govern the collecting, classifying, and summarizing of financial information about a given firm, and ethics is concerned with recording, reporting, and analyzing that information honestly, so that it reflects true market values. Ethics in accounting focuses on adhering to accurate and honest accounting practices, and scholars have identified a number of approaches and social norms that seek to explain how accountants make ethical decisions. Because employers and the public expect new accountants to already be trained in ethical behavior, the federal government and professional accounting organizations have accepted responsibility for setting guidelines for ethics in accounting.

OVERVIEW

The accounting profession depends on the ability of its client base and relevant stakeholders to trust the information that accountants provide about their firms. A series of scandals in the early twenty-first century focused global attention on the ethics of accounting and led to an increased emphasis on teaching ethics to accounting students. In the United States, a number of states now require that accounting students be trained in the ethics of accounting before they are licensed as certified public accountants (CPAs).

Once in the workplace, however, new accountants are faced with ethical decisions that may determine the course of their entire careers. Just as business executives depend on accountants to provide them with information about the financial health of their firms, governments depend on that information to produce information about the health of the economy as a whole. Accountants who do not behave ethically may find themselves facing criminal charges that lead to heavy fines and prison terms.

While *ethical behaviors* are closely related to *morals*, the two terms are not always synonymous. Morals govern personal rather than professional behavior (Mastracchio, Jiménez-Angueira, & Toth, 2015). The modern Occupy movement, which has been partially a response to corporate greed and unethical business behavior, has ignited a spark around the world with a grassroots movement dedicated to demanding more ethical behavior.

In the United States, there are 55 jurisdictions that license CPAs, and 35 of those jurisdictions require CPAs to either complete a stand-alone ethics course or prove ethical knowledge through an ethics examination. California, Illinois, Maryland, Texas, Indiana, and West Virginia require that CPAs present evidence of a stand-alone ethics course in order to be certified. California has gone further than any other state in promoting ethics in accounting, mandating ten units of ethics courses and requiring that at least three of those units be taken in accounting ethics. The American Institute of Certified Public Accountants has increased pressure on states to establish strict ethics accounting standards.

To explain ethical decision-making in accounting, scholars have identified such approaches as egoism, universalism, utilitarianism, and social norms that differ according to the goals involved in each, focusing variously on the interests of employers, society, and customs. The most common approach is utilitarianism, which considers consequences paramount to decision-making. In the late 1980s, scholars began focusing on cognitive-based models, paying close attention to psychological theories developed by Lawrence Kohlberg, who was the first to identify the stages of moral development.

Rest (1986) generated the Defining Issues Test (DIT), which depends on the concept of virtue for making ethical decisions. Rest's four models occur in sequence, beginning with the recognition that an ethical situation has occurred and considering possible actions and effects. Second, a desired course of action is decided on after examining all sides of the issue. Third, steps that must be taken to resolve the issue are identified. Last, the selected steps are put into practice. Martinov-Bennie and Mladenovic (2015) suggest that Rest's models do not pay sufficient attention to the moral intensity involved in decision-making in accounting.

Beginning in the 1990s and increasing significantly in the early years of the twenty-first century, the entire globe was plagued by a number of accounting scandals that shook the profession to

The Wall Street area from Brooklyn. The South Street Seaport is at the lower middle, a little to the right. (Courtesy of Hu Totya via Wikimedia Commons)

its core. Names of companies and individuals such as Adelphia, AIG, Bernie Madoff, Dynergy, Enron, Fannie Mae, Freddie Mac, Global Crossing, Rite Aid, Tyco, and WorldCom became as well known for their unethical behaviors as for the products and services they provided. Accounting students were required to study such scandals to learn how accounting frauds were perpetrated and the consequences suffered in each instance.

Some accounting scandals have come to light as the result of auditors discovering firms engaging in such practices as misrepresenting revenues or losses, but others are discovered by outside agencies, such as the Securities and Exchange Commission. Whistleblowers have also played a role in uncovering accounting sandals. Sherron Watkins was responsible for blowing the whistle on Enron, a giant energy company whose unethical practices bankrupted the company and led to a 24-year prison sentence for CEO Jeff Skilling. Former CEO Ken Lay died before he could begin serving time.

Cynthia Cooper opened the gate for the WorldCom scandal in which investors lost $180 billion. CEO Bernie Ebbers was sentenced to 25 years in prison after company auditors discovered fraud amounting to $3.8 billion. One of the first whistleblowers to receive national attention was James Alderson, a former CFO at North Valley Hospital. Alderson filed a lawsuit in 1993 under the False Claims Act (FCA) against HCA, the owner of North Valley Hospital, accusing them of defrauding the government of Medicare and Medicaid payments by keeping separate sets of books. The federal government joined Alderson's suit in 1998, and in 2001 HCA was forced to pay $745 million in civil damages, $95 million in criminal fines, and $881 to settle other charges.

In 2004, the collapse of the accounting firm Arthur Anderson after the public learned of frauds carried out by partners and managers resulted in a $457 million class action lawsuit and mounting public concern over ethics in accounting. David Costello, the president of the National Association of State Boards of Accountancy, and 160 charter members founded the NASBA Center for the Public Trust (CPT). In 2013, the group established the CPT Ethics Pilot Program, which provides online presentations, narrations, images, videos, and polls for use by teachers of

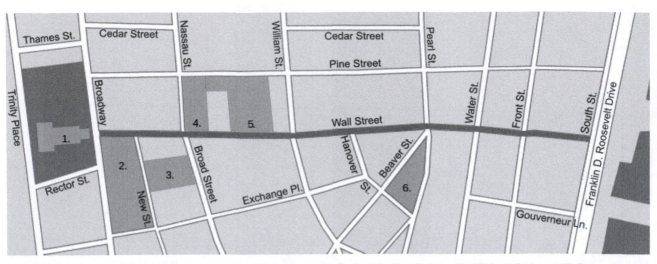

Map of Wall Street and the surrounding streets including: Trinity Church (1), Bank of New York Building (2), NY Stock Exchange (3), Federal Hall (4), Trump Building (5) and the Cocoa Exchange (6). (Courtesy of Hu Totya via Wikimedia Commons)

accounting certification programs. The CPT online certification program is an eight-hour course composed of separate sections, and students are required to take a test after completing each section. In order to pass, at least 80 percent of all questions must be answered correctly.

FURTHER INSIGHTS

The federal government has attempted to promote ethics in accounting through a series of laws. In 2002, Congress passed the Sarbanes-Oxley Act (SOX), which required American publicly traded companies to monitor accounting practices internally. Responsibility for honest reporting was assigned to CEOs and CFOs, who could face stiff punishment if convicted of unethical behaviors. SOX also established the Public Company Accounting Oversight Board to monitor ethics in auditing and accounting. The act banned auditors from being hired to provide non-auditing services to the companies they audit. SOX was not well received among American businesses, and it was dubbed "quack corporate governance" by its critics (Romano, 2005).

In 2010, Congress passed the Dodd-Frank Wall Street Reform and Consumer Protection Act, which significantly expanded the efforts made in SOX to ensure accountability of big business in the United States. Elements of Dodd-Frank included stricter standards for the accounting profession, more emphasis on peer reviews, and better methods for identifying

accounting fraud (Carlino, 2011). Increased attention meant that the pressure on accountants was increased even as firms demanded that auditing costs be reduced.

Recognizing the need, software developers responded by creating a plethora of applications for auditors that were designed to uncover unethical accounting behaviors and make the work of accountants easier. SOX has continued to be controversial, and Republicans and big business have attempted to mitigate what they see as interference in the market. In 2014, Congress passed the Jumpstart Our Business Startups Act, which allowed exemptions of new companies reporting revenues of less than $1 billion from the provisions of both Dodd-Frank and SOX.

In an effort to monitor itself, the accounting profession has created a number of state, national, and international organizations that attempt to establish guidelines for ethics in accounting. The United States has historically enforced accounting standards more stringent than those of other countries, but efforts to globalize accounting standards in the twenty-first century has led to some relaxing of those standards. The International Association for Accounting Education and Research (IAAER) was founded in 1984 to establish global standards for teaching professional ethics, and organizations such as the International Federation of Accountants (IFAC) continue to offer guidance for establishing ethical standards for accountants and auditors and for ensuring that accounting students are trained in making ethical decisions.

In 1986, the American Accounting Association's Committee on Future Structure, Content, and Scope of Accounting Education launched a campaign to improve ethics training in accounting programs in the United States. In 2008, NASBA announced that it was revising Rules 5-1 and 5-2 of the Uniform Accountancy Act to mandate that all accounting students take three semester hours of professional ethics classes.

In 2002, the American Institute of Certified Public Accountants began providing an Ethics Tree for accountants to use when determining the proper professional behavior, suggesting that accountants trust their instincts when discussing situations with management and treat all responses with "the necessary degree of professional skepticism" (AICPA, 2015). Accountants are encouraged to document all elements of the ethical situation, including questions asked and responses received in light of professional and legal standards. Based on the information as a whole, accountants are then advised to determine whether employment should continue and whether the situation needs to be reported to non-company accountants, regulatory agencies, banks, lending institutions, owners, investors, boards, and/or other stakeholders (AICPA, 2015).

ISSUES

The alarming number of high-profile accounting scandals led Wall Street to attempt to shift some of the blame for unethical behaviors to colleges and universities, insisting that they had failed to train accountants adequately in the ethics of the profession. In the 1960s and 1970s, most training programs for accountants had spent only limited time on teaching ethics, offering students a few case studies of firms that had violated ethics laws and been charged with violations. In 1979, however, the Association to Advance Collegiate Schools of Business (AACSB) added an ethics requirement for business majors. A decade later, the organization began mandating ethics training in accounting and demanded that ethics education be integrated across the business curriculum.

As new scandals erupted, more schools added ethics to the curriculum. In 1990, the Academy of Management's Social Studies Issues in Management section conducted a study of ethics training for accountants, finding that one in three schools accredited under the AACSB offered no stand-alone courses dedicated to the ethics of business and society (Martinov-Bennie & Mladenovic, 2015). Only half of the accredited schools had assigned full-time faculty members to teach ethics. In other schools, professors from others fields, particularly philosophy, taught ethics.

The debate over how ethics should be taught to accounting students has been intense, and researchers have devoted significant effort to analyzing efforts of colleges and universities to prepare new accountants to meet the demands of a profession that is in the global spotlight. Scholars suggest that ethics training should focus on the need for honesty, fairness, and justice as universal and inviolate concepts (Thomas, 2012). In a 2012 study, (Ethics and Accounting), Thomas found that education was a major factor in sensitizing accounting students to ethical questions. The study indicated that fourth-year students were more attuned to deliberate reasoning than first-year students were and that first-year accounting students were more aware of different levels of decision-making than were first-year business students.

A 2015 study by Martinov-Bennie and Mladenovic suggested that ethical sensitivity of accounting students was greatest when the teaching of ethics was integrated throughout the curriculum. They were surprised to find that the students who exhibited the most sophisticated levels of ethical judgments were those who had not been exposed to frameworks that discussed the various viewpoints on ethics in accounting. Some studies have revealed that student accountants who are repeatedly exposed to ethics are better equipped to make ethical decisions on the job and in their personal lives (Lau, 2010). Overall, studies have demonstrated that the best ethics training for accountants is both cumulative and integrative. However, benefits from a single course dedicated solely to ethics are considered highly significant. The emphasis on accounting in ethics has led to an overall finding that accounting students express less tolerance for unethical behavior on the job than either business majors or non-business majors.

Since 2004, the AACSB has suggested that all ethics courses cover business responsibility, ethical decision-making, ethics in leadership, and corporate government leadership (Martinov-Bennie & Mladenovic, 2015). In 2005, the education committee of NASBA began recommending that all accounting programs include three semester hours of accounting ethics and three semester hours of business ethics. The backlash forced NASBA to backtrack, reducing the recommendation to only three semester hours of ethics training that could be taught in a stand-alone course or integrated into the existing curriculum. Azusa Pacific University—a private evangelical Christian school located near Los Angeles, California—has gone further than most schools, establishing an endowed chair ($8.6 million) in ethical auditing within the Timothy Leung School of Accounting and providing a master's degree in ethical auditing. John Thornton was recruited from Washington State University to head up the program, which covers ethics from the ancient Greeks and the biblical period to modern philosophies of ethics. Methods for teaching ethics in college classrooms include written and video ethics cases, group learning, case studies, role-playing, film, and multimedia presentations (Thomas, 2012). These methods may be used in stand-alone ethics classes and incorporated into other accounting and business classes.

The increased emphasis on ethics in accounting has not completely stopped firms from engaging in illegal practices, but it has made it more likely that such practices will be made public. In 2005, Refco, a commodities trading company, was engaged in a scandal when it was reported that its CEO and chairman of the board had prevented auditors and investors from learning about $340 million in bad debts. Three years later, it was learned that Lehman Brothers had engaged in off-balance sheet accounting. The National Business Ethics Survey reported that between 2007 and 2013, incidences of unethical business behavior declined from 55 percent to 41 percent. However, more than one in four American firms is still believed to engage in some form of unethical behavior (Mastracchio, Jiménez-Angueira, & Toth, 2015).

TERMS & CONCEPTS

Dodd-Frank Wall Street Reform and Consumer Protection Act: Congressional act passed in 2010 that authorizes the federal government to engage in oversight of U.S. businesses in order to ensure transparency and accountability.

Egoism: Approach to accounting ethics in which the chief goals are maximizing the benefits of decision makers while minimizing costs of business operations.

Great recession: The worst economic crisis since the Great Depression, the Great Recession began in December 2007 after the collapse of the housing market, resulting in the loss of 7.5 million jobs and an unemployment rate of 10 percent. It was declared officially over in June 2009.

Occupy Wall Street: Social movement that began in 2011 on social media sites and spread throughout the developed world as individuals objected to rising poverty and increased corporate greed.

Sarbanes-Oxley Act (SOX): Controversial federal legislation passed in 2002 to increase accountability in business accounting. SOX also created the Public Company Accounting Oversight Board.

Social norms: Approach to accounting ethics based on the theories of American philosopher John Rawls that defines ethical behaviors according to accepted norms of justice and fairness.

Universalism: Approach to accounting ethics based on the theories of German philosopher Immanuel Kant that suggests that behaviors should be based not on consequences but on principles.

Utilitarianism: Approach to accounting ethics derived from the political theories of Utilitarians such as Jeremy Bentham that call for practices that promote the greatest societal good.

BIBLIOGRAPHY

American Institute of Certified Public Accountants. (2015). Ethics tree.

Carlino, B. (2011). The 21st century audit. *Accounting Today, 25*(4), 1–35.

Chawla, S. K., Khan, Z. U., Jackson, R. E., & Gray III, A. W. (2015). Evaluating ethics education for accounting students. *Management Accounting Quarterly, 16*(2), 16–25.

Lau, C. L. L. (2010). A step forward: Ethics education matters! *Journal of Business Ethics, 92*(4), 565–584.

Martinov-Bennie, N., & Mladenovic, R. (2015). Investigation of the impact of an ethical framework and an integrated ethics education on accounting students' ethical sensitivity and judgment. *Journal of Business Ethics, 127*(1), 189–203.

Mastracchio Jr., N. J., Jiménez-Angueira, C., & Toth, I. (2015). The state of ethics in business and the accounting profession. *CPA Journal, 85*(3), 48–52.

Meymandi, A. R., Rajabdoory, H., & Asoodeh, Z. (2015). The reasons of considering ethics in accounting job. *International Journal of Management, Accounting, and Economics, 2*(2), 136–143.

Rest, J. R. (1986). *Moral development: Advances in research and theory.* New York, NY: Praeger.

Romano, R. (2005). The Sarbanes-Oxley act and the making of quack corporate governance. *Yale Law Journal, 114,* 1521–1612.

Thomas, S. (2012). Ethics and accounting education. *Issues in Accounting Education, 27*(2), 399–418.

SUGGESTED READING

Chambers, D, Hermanson, D. K., & Payne, J. L. (2010). Did Sarbanes-Oxley lead to better financial reporting? *CPA Journal, 80*(9), 24–27.

Cooper, B. J., et al. (2008). Ethics education for accounting students: A toolkit approach. Accounting Education: *An International Journal, 17*(4), 405–430.

Gill, M. (2009). *Accountants' truth: Knowledge and ethics in the financial world.* New York, NY: Oxford University Press.

Goldberg, S., & Bettinghaus, B. Everyday ethics: Tougher than you think. *Strategic Finance, 97*(6), 46–53.

Stem, R. (2012). *Understanding moral obligation: Kant, Hegel, Kierkegaard.* Cambridge, UK: Cambridge University Press.

Essay by Elizabeth Rholetter Purdy, PhD

F

FINANCIAL AND ACCOUNTING COMPLIANCE

Accurate financial information is critical for decision making within the business world and governments alike. The absence of honest and accurate financial reporting to support sound financial decisions can cause economic calamities, as evidenced by the Great Depression and the business collapses of the early 2000's. In the United States, the SEC compels financial disclosure from companies that seek funds from the investing public. The generally accepted accounting principles (GAAP), established by a number of public and private organizations, provides the language in which those statements must be delivered. This article discusses the sources and history of US financial reporting law and the organizations responsible for establishing the GAAP. The article concludes with a brief discussion of the rise of an international accounting standard that seems poised to become the new standard; possibly replacing the GAAP.

OVERVIEW

A business's financial condition can be summarized by the major and familiar financial statements, including the balance sheet, income statement, and statement of cash flow. Those statements provide valuable information to management for internal company decisions and are important to parties outside the business such as lenders and investors. Businesses can be generally divided into two categories: public and private. Publicly traded companies are corporations whose stock is held by the public and openly traded as opposed to a privately owned or closely held corporation whose stock is not offered for public sale and is typically owned by a few individuals. Accurate financial information is, of course, valuable to every business but in the case of the publicly traded company, preparation and disclosure of financial statements are mandated by laws administered by the U.S. Securities and Exchange Commission

(SEC). Financial statements for external distribution are prepared according to guidelines referred to as the generally accepted accounting principles (GAAP). An independent body called the Financial Accounting Standards Board (FASB) takes the lead in determining and promoting those practices. With that general introduction, the remainder of this article discusses the governmental and private bodies that determine financial and accounting standards and rules relevant to the company that seeks investment from the public.

PUBLIC FINANCE LAW

Formation of the SEC

Following the great stock market crash of 1929, the Securities Exchange Act of 1934 created the SEC. Prior to 1929, there was little support for government regulation of the securities markets. In the post–World War I economic prosperity of the roaring twenties, many people turned to the stock markets to make their fortunes with little thought of the danger of investing in an unregulated market. It has been estimated that half of the $50 billion of new securities issued during that time became worthless. After the crash in 1929, many personal fortunes were lost and many banks, who also invested in the market, suffered heavy losses. As a result, depositors became concerned that their banks would not survive and withdrew their funds. This run on the banks caused many banks to close. The great depression followed, and the consensus in government was that confidence in the capital markets needed to be restored for the economy to recover.

In response, Congress held hearings to identify solutions. Based on their findings, they passed the Securities Act of 1933 (often called the "truth in securities law") and the Securities Exchange Act of 1934. The Securities Exchange Act of 1934 created the SEC and granted it broad authority over the securities

U.S. Securities and Exchange Commission headquarters in Washington, D.C. (Courtesy of Don ramey Logan via Wikimedia Commons)

industry. The essential purposes of these acts were twofold:

- First, they were enacted to compel companies who offered their securities for public sale to be honest about their business, the securities for sale, and the risks involved in investments.
- Second, the acts sought to ensure that people selling those securities—such as brokers, dealers, and exchanges—were treating investors justly and truthfully and that they put investors' interests in a prioritized position.

SEC Regulations

The SEC is headquartered in Washington, DC, and it is composed of five presidentially appointed commissioners, four divisions, and 18 offices. The SEC is charged with regulating the practice of selling securities (a document that indicates ownership, such as a stock certificate or bond) to the public. The laws that govern the securities are based on the idea that all investors, regardless of size, should have access to basic facts about a business or investment opportunity before they purchase that security and for the period during which they may hold that security.

Consequently, the SEC necessitates that public businesses reveal significant economic data to the public. All investors are, therefore, enabled to discover for themselves whether buying, selling, or holding a certain security is worthwhile. To ensure that investors and other interested parties have the information upon which they can base a sound judgment, financial reporting to the SEC must be timely, comprehensive, and accurate. Beyond the benefit to an individual investor, the SEC financial reporting requirements encourage economic growth because transparent and efficient capital markets facilitate capital formation.

The SEC also manages the most crucial players of the capital market (which includes securities markets, brokers and dealers, investment advisors, and mutual funds) to make sure that the important market information is disclosed.

Four Divisions of SEC

The SEC Division of Market Regulation creates and carries on the standards for just, organized, and effective markets, specifically through the regulation of brokers, dealers, stock exchanges, and other major players in the securities industry.

The Division of Investment Management manages the $15 trillion investment management industry by administering security law relevant to investment advisors and mutual funds.

The Division of Enforcement investigates likely breaches of the law and recommends civil action to the Commission, which brings civil enforcement lawsuits against individuals and companies for infractions such as insider trading, accounting fraud, and providing false or misleading information. Having only civil enforcement control, the division also cooperates with various criminal law enforcement agencies when appropriate.

The Division of Corporation Finance is relevant to the accounting profession and compliance. The division supervises the required business announcements of information to the public; both when a stock is initially offered for sale and then on a continued periodic basis. Required documents include registration statements for new securities, annual and quarterly reports, proxy matters given to stockholders prior to an annual meeting, annual reports to stockholders, paperwork about tender proposals, and filings related to mergers and acquisitions. The division reviews submissions, offers compliance assistance to companies, and recommends new rules to the SEC Commission. The division, in cooperation with SEC's Office of the Chief Accountant, monitors the accounting profession. The chief accountant is the principal advisor to the Commission on accounting and auditing matters and consults with accounting bodies that set standards including the FASB, the International Accounting Standards Board (IASB), the American Institute of Certified Public Accountants (AICPA) and the Public Company Accounting Oversight Board (PCAOB).

Additional SEC Governance

In addition to the Securities Act of 1933 and the Securities Exchange Act of 1934, the SEC enforces other laws related to the securities industry. The Trust Indenture Act of 1939 involves bonds, debentures, and notes intended for public sale. The Investment Company Act of 1940 controls the framework of businesses (namely mutual funds) that work closely with the contributions and trades of securities. The Investment Advisers Act of 1940 regulates investment advisors and requires registration and compliance with regulations designed to protect investors. More recently (in the wake of the well-publicized corporate scandals of the early 2000s, including the collapses of WorldCom and Enron and their accountants at Arthur Andersen), Congress passed the Sarbanes-Oxley Act of 2002. Sarbanes-Oxley made several reforms in order to improve shared responsibility and economic disclosure and battle corporate and accounting fraud. The act also created an independent nonprofit entity called the Public Company Accounting Oversight Board. The PCAOB oversees the auditors of public companies and has four main responsibilities, which include the following

- registering accounting firms that audit public companies trading in U.S. security markets
- inspecting registered accounting firms
- establishing quality control, ethics, and independent standards for registered public accounting firms
- investigating and disciplining registered accounting firms for violations of the specified laws and professional standards (PCAOB, 2007, p. 3)

Financial Accounting Standards Board

The FASB is a private sector independent organization that establishes standards for financial accounting and reporting. While the SEC has the authority under the Securities Exchange Act of 1934 to establish those standards, the SEC has historically relied on the private sector for those standards and particularly on FASB. FASB seeks to improve accounting standards by applying a number of principles. FASB seeks to

- make reports more useful by focusing on characteristics such as relevance, reliability, comparability, and consistency
- reflect changes in methods of doing business and the economic environment in current standards
- act quickly to address deficiencies in reporting with appropriate standards
- promote the convergence of international accounting standards
- improve understanding of the purposes and nature of financial reports

To promote the above aims, FASB develops broad accounting concepts and financial reporting standards. This framework of concepts and standards provides guidance in resolving accounting issues and guidance in preparing reports.

Federal Accounting Standards Advisory Board

The Federal Accounting Standards Advisory Board (FASAB) is a federal advisory committee that develops accounting standards and publicizes common and well-established accounting principles for federal government entities. The FASAB was established under the authority of the secretary of the treasury, the director of the Office of Management and Budget, and the comptroller general of the United States. The FASAB considers the economic and budgetary needs of governmental supervision groups and administrative agencies as well as the requirements of other users of economic information to develop rules that maximize the usefulness of the information. The FASAB board has ten members—four federal and six private sector members. After FASAB has completed its procedure for issuing concepts and standards, they are announced in the *Federal Register* and they become effective.

Hierarchy of Information

As with all law and regulatory frameworks, it is important to be aware of the hierarchy of a particular source of information. This is especially true when dealing with a subject like accounting. which applies to so many entities both public and private. Consequently, both the FASB, for the private sector, and the FASAB have a hierarchies of authority for GAAP interpretations as applied to federal agencies. The FASAB hierarchy gives an example of how those hierarchies are generally arranged and includes GAAP interpretations of the FASB, discussed above, and the American Institute of Certified Public Accountants (AICPA). The most authoritative pronouncement of the GAAP for federal bodies is the categories of officially established accounting principles:

- Category (a) consists of FASAB advisory board statements and FASB and AICPA pronouncements specifically interpreted as applicable to the federal government by FASAB.
- Category (b) consists of FASAB technical bulletins and those AICPA industry audit and accounting guides and statements of position that AIPCA has made applicable to the federal government and FASAB has cleared.
- Category (c) consists of the practice bulletins issued by the Accounting Standards Executive Committee of the AICPA made applicable to federal government and cleared by FASAB, in addition to Technical Releases of the FASAB Accounting and Auditing Committee.
- Finally, category (d) consists of implementation guides published by FASAB staff and widely recognized practices in the federal government (FASAB, 2007).

In the absence of guidance from these categories, a federal auditor may consider other accounting literature as appropriate under the circumstances.

The need for reliable financial disclosure became starkly apparent after the Great Depression. This need motivated the federal government to create the SEC in 1934 and pass the Sarbanes-Oxley Act (SOX) in 2002. The success of the SEC and other bodies that perform financial audits to protect the public and prevent fraud are dependent upon the reliability of the documents offered for disclosure. Reliability is dependent upon a coherent system of assembling and reporting financial data. That entire system, of course, is called the GAAP. The GAAP is a set of principles that when translated into complex rules and applied to a specific entity determine a particular result. GAAP interpretations are issued for the private sector (FASB), the public sector (FASAB), and for specific industries and practices.

The Emerging Issues Task Force

The private sector also has a similar four-category system that ranks the authoritative weight of accounting principles in which FASB and the AICPA figure prominently. The Emerging Issues Task Force (EITF), formed in 1984 by the FASB, is another entity that has bearing on GAAP interpretation. The EITF is a 12-member body composed primarily of members of public accounting firms, and it is designed to identify emerging issues and recommend positions before problems become widespread and entrenched. While the FASB is primarily concerned with private sector standards and the FASAB with federal entity reporting, the Governmental Accounting Standards Board (GASB) is concerned with the accounting and financial reporting standards for state and local governments. Consequently, practitioners seeking to apply permissible methods should be aware of the relevant and authoritative GAAP interpretations bearing on their particular task.

INSIGHTS

Financial Reporting in Global Business

Accounting and the resulting financial reports are relevant to all business operations of global importance. The International Accounting Standards Board (IASB), a London based nonprofit corporation (organized under the Laws of Delaware) develops international accounting standards called the International Financial Reporting Standards (IFRS). In 2005, public companies in the European Union began using the IFRS, and those standards have been adopted by some 70 other countries. In April 2005, the United States and the European Union agreed to accept both IFRS and GAAP. The process of making the GAAP and other national accounting standards (for example, those in Japan, China, and Canada) compatible with IFRS is called convergence. The IFRS are on the road to becoming the international language of accounting.

GAAP/IFRS Convergence

The GAAP is a rules-based system, while the IFRS is a principle-based system. The GAAP is composed of more than 2,000 separate pronouncements, all of which may be several hundred pages. Those pronouncements, as reviewed above, are issued by a number of different bodies. The IFRS is a principle-based system whose regulations fill approximately 2,000 pages. The difference could be thought of as the difference between telling a child to return home at a reasonable hour (principle based) and telling that child to be home at midnight but then listing exceptions that would allow a later arrival (rules based). The differences between the two systems may result in significantly different reports for the same company. However, because of continued convergence projects, those differences are shrinking. For example, while IFRS balance sheets must contain certain information, there is no requirement on how that information must be presented. There are several other differences and consistent with the convergence initiative, the IFRS may adopt some GAAP positions.

Convergence & the SEC

The SEC was initially supportive of the convergence project. SEC rules require that companies that issue securities in the United States provide a reconciliation of IFRS statements to GAAP. That reconciliation requirement was set to be eliminated by 2009, when the SEC would accept IFRS. Moreover, the SEC chairman, Christopher Cox, suggested that not all differences between U.S. GAAP and the IFRS would need to be reconciled before the SEC would accept IFRS-based financial reports (Gill, 2007). Nevertheless, the SEC repeatedly delayed adoption of the IFRS, still not satisfied that convergence had achieved an acceptable form. By 2012, all of the world's 10 largest economies were supportive of the IFRS and/or of convergence, but not one had fully adopted it.

CONCLUSION

Accurate financial information is critical for decision-making within the business world and governments alike. The absence of honest and accurate financial reporting to support sound financial decisions can cause economic calamities, as evidenced by the Great Depression and the business collapses of the early 2000s. In the United States, the SEC compels financial disclosure from companies that seek funds from the investing public. The GAAP, established by a number of public and private organizations, provides the language in which those statements must be delivered. However, with the apparent acceptance of the United States, our era of globalization has witnessed the rise of an international accounting standard that seems poised to become the new standard.

TERMS & CONCEPTS

Audit: An analysis performed by a trained accountant of a business's economic documents. The evaluation involves the observing of irregular practices, advice for improvements, and bookkeeping. Audits that employees themselves perform are called "internal audits," while independently performed audits by outside accountants are known as "independent audits."

Bonds: A document of debt that the government or a business issues as a means to guarantee repayment of the initial investment (including interest) prior to a specific due date.

Debentures: An unsecured bond issued by a civil or government corporation or agency and backed only by the credit standing of the issuer.

Federal Register: A daily newsletter published by the American government. The bulletin contains the hearings schedule for Congressional and federal agencies and the arrangements made public by the U.S. executive branch.

Note: A paper acknowledging a debt and promising payment; promissory note.

Proxy: A written permission that gives control and responsibility to another person so that that person can act on the signer's behalf (such as during a meeting of shareholders).

Tender offer: A proposal to purchase many shares in a certain business, generally at premium or above the market price.

BIBLIOGRAPHY

Ehoff Jr., C., & Fischer, D. (2013). Why the SEC is delaying adoption of international financial reporting standards. *International Business & Economics Research Journal, 12,* 223–227

Federal Accounting Standards Advisory Board. (2007). *FASAB facts 2007.* Washington, DC.

Gill, L. (2007). IFRS: Coming to America. *Journal of Accountancy, 203,* 70–73.

Holzmann, O., & Robinson, T. (2005). The hierarchy of GAAP. *Journal of Corporate Accounting & Finance (Wiley), 16,* 83–86.

Ibarra, V., & Suez-Sales, M. G. (2011). A comparison of the international financial reporting standards (IFRS) and generally accepted accounting principles (GAAP) for small and medium-sized entities (SMES) and compliances of some Asian countries to IFRS. *Journal of International Business Research,* 1035–62.

Kaya, D., & Pillhofer, J. A. (2013). PoteU of IFRS by the United States: A critical view. *Accounting Horizons, 27,* 271–299.

Nolke, A. (2005). Introduction to the special issue: The globalization of accounting standards. *Business & Politics, 7,* 1–7.

Public Company Accounting Oversight Board. (2007, May 1). *Strategic Plan 2007–2012.*

Walters, A., & Ramiah, V. (2017). Financial management or accounting: A theoretical analysis of the benefits and limitations of developing a 'true' financial management approach within government agencies in Australia. *Business and Financial Affairs, 6*(2).

SUGGESTED READING

A., D. (2007). US moves to accept IFRS accounting. *International Financial Law Review, 26,* 11.

Carlino, B. (2007). Who needs GAAP? *Accounting Today, 21,* 1–30.

Cooke, T. (1993). The impact of accounting principles on profits: The US versus Japan. *Accounting & Business Research, 23,* 460–476.

FASB takes a look. (2002). *Journal of Accountancy, 194,* 53.

Marlowe, J. (2007). Costs of compliance with generally accepted accounting standards. *Public Management (00333611), 89,* 17–20.

SEC may give U.S. issuers IFRS, GAAP choice. (2007). *California CPA, 75,* 8–10.

Smith, P. (2007). Convergence is 'some way off.' *Accountancy, 139*(1365), 8.

Willisch, M. (2007). The end of US Gaap? *International Financial Law Review, 26,* 12–13.

Essay by Seth M. Azria, J.D.

FUNDAMENTAL VS. TECHNICAL FINANCIAL ANALYSIS

ABSTRACT

This article will focus on the decision-making process for investing. There will be a special emphasis on comparing and contrasting fundamental and technical financial analysis. The success of the financial market is important to everyone across the world. If the market is not healthy, there is potential for crises. It has been suggested that most Americans do not know how to save or prepare for their future. As a result, many financial investment companies have approached employers as well as individuals in an attempt to educate the masses on the benefits of investing. When one is analyzing the financial market, he or she has the option of using one of two approaches. Fundamental and technical analyses are two types of analysis, but they have different approaches in terms of whether to trade or invest in financial markets.

OVERVIEW

The success of the financial market is important to everyone across the world. "We live in a world that is shaped by financial markets and we are profoundly affected by their operation. Our employment prospects, our financial security, our pensions, the stability of political systems and nature of the society we live in are all greatly influenced by the operations of these markets" (Fenton-O'Creevy, Nicholson, Soane, & Willman, 2005, p. 1–2). If the market is not healthy, there is potential for crises.

It has been suggested that most Americans do not know how to save or prepare for their future. As a result, many financial investment companies have approached employers as well as individuals in an attempt to educate the masses on the benefits of investing. Some of the tips that have been provided by organizations, such as the American Association of Individual Investors, include the following:

- Build and maintain a cash reserve to meet short-term emergencies and other liquidity needs.
- Develop an overall investment strategy even if it cannot be implemented immediately.
- Select mutual funds that fit into the overall investment strategy, then consider what the minimum initial investments are.
- Select a balanced fund for less aggressive investors or a broad base index fund for more aggressive investors. Build the portfolio after this initial investment has been completed.
- Review the percentage commitment to each stock market segment in order to determine when to add funds to the initial investment.
- Do not agonize over small deviations from the original allocation plan. Stay the course! (p. 1–2).

When one is analyzing the financial market, he or she has the option of using one of two approaches. Fundamental and technical analyses are two types of analysis, but they have different approaches in terms of whether to trade or invest in financial markets. Overall, the process focuses on how to select markets and tools in order to trade or invest and time when it is appropriate to open and close trades or investments to maximize returns.

Definitions: Technical Analysis vs. Fundamental Analysis

According to investorwords.com, technical analysis is defined as:

"A method in which to evaluate securities by relying on the assumption that market data (i.e., charts of price, volume, and open interest) may assist in predicting future (usually short-term) market trends. Unlike fundamental analysis, the intrinsic value of the security is not considered.

Technical analysts believe that they can accurately predict the future price of a stock by looking at its historical prices and other trading variables. Technical analysis makes the assumption that market psychology influences trading in a manner that allows an analyst to predict when a stock will rise or fall. For that reason, many technical analysts are also market timers. Market timers believe that technical analysis can be applied just as easily to the market as a whole as to an individual stock."

According to Investopedia.com, fundamental analysis is defined as:

"A method in which to evaluate a security by attempting to measure its intrinsic value by examining related economic, financial, and other qualitative and quantitative factors. Fundamental analysts study those things that may affect the security's value, including macroeconomic factors (i.e., the overall economy and industry conditions) and individually specific factors (i.e., financial condition and management of companies). For example, the goal of fundamental analysis is to identify a value that an investor can compare with the security's current price with the expectation of determining what position to take with that specific security."

Choosing an Approach

Which is better? Both types of analysts have been successful in the designated fields. Many studies have been undertaken to determine which approach is better and to delineate the merits of each approach (Kaouther, 2013). The "right" answer depends on what the investor is interested in. For example, a long-term investor looking for companies with a solid base, growth, and income potential may be interested in the fundamental approach. However, there have been scenarios where a long-term investor was not concerned about one company's basics because of plans to diversify in order to minimize risk, or where a short-term investor was waiting for investor sentiment to change. These types of investors would probably support the technical approach. Given the strengths of both approaches, many investors tend to find benefits from each type of analysis. Technical analysts can provide information on the broad market and its trends (macro level) but do not take into consideration the context of current economic and world events, which some consider to be a weakness of this approach (Field, 2013). Fundamental analysts, however, can assist an investor in determining whether an issue has the basics to meet the investor's needs (micro level). In order to get a glimpse of the "big picture," it may be beneficial to take the best from both approaches.

APPLICATION

Compare & Contrast
The question of which approach is better will probably never be answered given the explanation listed above. In addition, "there is little agreement on the supremacy of one approach because the success of a trader's system is so dependent on the individual characteristics of each trader" (Talati, 2002, p. 58). Let's explore the characteristics of both approaches.

VIEWPOINT

Capital Asset Pricing Model (CAPM)
In order to select investments for a portfolio, modern portfolio theory will use the capital asset pricing model ("What is modern...," 2007). The capital asset pricing model (CAPM) is utilized to calculate a theoretical price for a potential investment, and it is a linear relationship between the returns of the shares and the stock market returns over time. The model analyzes the risk and return trade-off of individual assets to market returns. It can be used to accomplish the following:

- Establish the desired equilibrium market price of a company's shares.
- Establish the cost of a company's equity, which takes into account the risk characteristics of a company's investments.

There will always be some type of risk associated with an investment portfolio. The degree of risk can fluctuate among industries as well as among companies. A portfolio's risk is divided into two categories: systematic and unsystematic risk. Systematic risk refers to investments that are naturally riskier than others are. Unsystematic risk is when the amount of risk can be minimized through diversification of the investments.

CAPM Assumptions
The CAPM operates on a set of assumptions such as the following:

- Investors are risk-averse individuals who maximize the expected utility of their end of period wealth, which implies that the model is a one period model.
- Investors have homogenous expectations about asset returns, which indicate that all of the investors perceive themselves to have the same opportunity sets.
- Asset returns are distributed by the normal distribution.
- A risk-free asset exists and investors may borrow or lend unlimited amounts of this asset at a constant rate, which is the risk-free rate.
- There are definite numbers of assets and their quantities are fixed within the one period model.
- All assets are perfectly divisible and priced in a perfectly competitive market.
- Asset markets are frictionless and information is costless and simultaneously available to all investors.
- There are no market imperfections such as taxes, regulations, or restrictions on short selling ("CAPM — ...," 2007)

In addition, the CAPM includes the following propositions:

- Investors in shares require a return in excess of the risk-free rate to compensate for the systematic risk.
- Investors should not require a premium for unsystematic risk because it can be diversified away by holding a wide portfolio of investments.
- Since systematic risk varies among companies, investors will require a higher return from shares in those companies where the systematic risk is greater.

The same propositions can be applied to capital investment by companies:

- Companies expect a return on a project to exceed the risk-free rate so that they can be compensated for the systematic risk.
- Unsystematic risk can be diversified away, which implies that a premium for unsystematic risk is not required.
- Companies should strive for a bigger return on projects when the systematic risk is greater.

Disadvantages of the CAPM

There are some disadvantages to the CAPM, which include the following:

- The model assumes that asset returns are normally distributed random variables. However, it has been observed that returns in equity and other markets are not normally distributed, which results in large swings in the market.
- The model assumes that the variance of returns is an adequate measurement of risk.
- The model does not appear to explain the variation in stock returns adequately.
- The model assumes that given a certain expected return, investors will prefer lower risk to higher risk.
- The model assumes that all investors have access to the same information and agree about the risk and expected return of all assets (Smith & Harvey, 2011).
- The model assumes that there are no taxes or transaction costs. However, this assumption may be relaxed with more complicated versions of the model.
- The market portfolio consists of all assets in all markets where each asset is weighted by its market capitalization.
- In theory, the market portfolio should include all types of assets that are held by anyone as an investment and people usually substitute a stock index as a proxy for the true market portfolio.
- Since CAPM prices a stock in terms of all stocks and bonds, it is really an arbitrage-pricing model, which throws no light on how a firm's beta is determined.

CONCLUSION

Financial markets can be seen as an economics term because it highlights how individuals buy and sell financial securities, commodities, and other items at low transaction costs and prices that reflect efficient markets. The overall objective of the process is to gather all of the sellers and put them in one place so that they can meet and interact with potential buyers. The goal is to create a process that will make it easy for the two groups to conduct business.

When one is analyzing the financial market, an investor has the option of using one of two approaches. Fundamental and technical analyses are two types of analysis, but they have different approaches in terms of whether to trade or invest in financial markets. Overall, the process focuses on how to select markets and tools to trade or invest and time when it is appropriate to open and close trades or investments to maximize returns.

Which is better? Both types of analysts have been successful in the designated fields. The "right" answer depends on what the investor is interested in. For example, a long-term investor looking for companies with a solid base, growth, and income potential may be interested in the fundamental approach. However, there have been scenarios where a long-term investor was not concerned about one company's basics because of plans to diversify to minimize risk or when a short term investor is waiting for investor sentiment to change. These types of investors would probably support the technical approach. Given the strengths of both approaches, many investors tend to find benefits from each type of analysis. Technical analysts can provide information on the broad market and its trends (macro level), whereas, fundamental analysts can assist an investor in determining whether an issue has the basics to meet the investor's needs (micro level). In order to get a glimpse of the "big picture," it may be beneficial to take the best from both approaches.

To select investments for a portfolio, modern portfolio theory will use the capital asset pricing model ("What is modern…," 2007). The capital asset pricing model (CAPM) is utilized to calculate a theoretical price for a potential investment, and it is a linear relationship between the returns of the shares and the stock market returns over time. The model analyzes the risk and return trade-off of individual assets to market returns. It can be used to establish the desired equilibrium market price of a company's shares and establish the cost of a company's equity, which takes into account the risk characteristics of a company's investments.

TERMS & CONCEPTS

Capital asset pricing model (CAPM): A model used in finance to determine a theoretically appropriate required rate of return (and, thus, the price if expected cash flows can be estimated) of an asset, if that asset is to be added to an already well-diversified portfolio, given that asset's non-diversifiable risk.

Compounding: Asserts that an investor can take a small amount of money and watch it grow into a substantial amount over time.

Day trading: The purchase and sale (or short sale and purchase) of the same security on the same day in a single account.

Financial markets: A market for the exchange of capital and credit, including the money markets and the capital markets.

Fundamental analysis: A method in which to evaluate a security by attempting to measure its intrinsic value by examining related economic, financial, and other qualitative and quantitative factors.

Investments: The act of investing; laying out money or capital in an enterprise with the expectation of profit.

Stock market: The business transacted at a stock exchange.

Technical analysis: A method in which to evaluate securities by relying on the assumption that market data (i.e., charts of price, volume, and open interest) may assist in predicting future (usually short-term) market trends.

Trading: Buying and selling securities or commodities on a short-term basis, hoping to make quick profits.

BIBLIOGRAPHY

American Association of Individual Investors (n.d.). *Investing basics: Investing questions that every successful investor should know how to answer.*

CAPM—Capital asset pricing model. (2007). *Value Based Management.net.*

Fenton-O'Creevy, M., Nicholson, N., Soane, E., & Willman, P. (2005). *Traders: Risks, decisions, and management in financial markets.* Oxford: Oxford University Press.

Field, N. (2013). Classic plays. *Money (14446219),* 70–72.

Fundamental analysis (n.d.).

Kaouther, F. (2013). Technical analysis on markets with memory. *Business & Economic Research (BER), 3,* 498–511.

Simons, H. L. (2015). Short-term rate expectations and markets. *Futures: News, Analysis & Strategies for Futures, Options & Derivatives Traders, 44*(5), 34–39.

Smith, A. L., & Harvey, T. W. (2011). Test of a theory: An empirical examination of the changing nature of investor behavior. *Journal of Management Policy & Practice, 12,* 49–68.

Talati, J. (2002, January). Fundamental vs. technical analysis. *Modern Trader.*

SUGGESTED READING

Gehrig, T., & Menkhoff, L. (2006). Extended evidence on the use of technical analysis in foreign exchange. *International Journal of Finance & Economics, 11,* 327–338.

Kapoor, J. R., Dlabay, L. R., & Hughes, R. J. (2016). *Business and personal finance.* New York: McGraw-Hill Education.

McDonald, M. (2007). Technical vs. fundamental analysis. *Equities, 55,* 100.

Phoa, W., Focardi, S., & Fabozzi, F. (2007). How do conflicting theories about financial markets coexist? *Journal of Post Keynesian Economics, 29,* 363–391.

The advantages of technical analysis. (2006, August 31). *Finweek,* 62.

Essay by Marie Gould

FUNDING NEW VENTURES

ABSTRACT

This article will focus on the different sources of funding for new ventures, especially small businesses. One of the greatest challenges for new ventures is the ability to secure capital that will allow the company to grow. There is no magic formula, and the management team will need to evaluate and assess which options are beneficial for the company. Each business will need to weigh the pros and cons of each option to determine what would be best. There are two options that these businesses may consider: debt financing and equity capital. The role of commercial banks, the Small Business Administration, angel investors, and venture capitalists will be introduced and discussed.

OVERVIEW

One of the greatest challenges for new ventures is the ability to secure capital for investments that will allow the company to grow. All projects will reach a point at which sufficient cash flow is necessary to attain the next level. It could be after a certain period or it could be because the venture is popular and the company is growing at a rapid rate due to demand. Regardless of the situation, the company's management team will need to determine when and how they will invest in efforts such as purchasing new equipment, hiring new staff, and putting more money into marketing initiatives. Raising money can be a difficult task if the company has not established a reputation or is still new.

When determining the amount of capital needed, the decision makers must analyze the situation and decide how much and what type of capital is required. Since the situation is not the same for all businesses, there is no magical formula. Some businesses may only need short-term financing for items such as salaries and inventory, while other businesses may need long-term financing for major items such as office space and equipment. Each business must develop a customized plan that will meet its unique needs.

Securing capital is a choice made after weighing the pros and cons of various options. There are three popular means of obtaining funding for new ventures: borrowing from financial institutions, partnering with venture capitalists, and selling equity/ownership in exchange for a share of the revenue (Goel & Hasan, 2004). All financing options can be classified into one of two categories: debt financing or equity capital.

Debt financing includes bank loans, personal and family contributions, and financing from agencies such as the Small Business Administration (SBA). Loans are often secured by some type of collateral in the company and are paid off over time with interest. On the other hand, venture capitalists and angel investors provide funding in the form of equity capital. Both are given ownership in the company in exchange for money. Pierce (2005) offers some advice that may be of assistance when assessing which option may be best for the company. Some of the tips include the following:

- A Small Business Administration (SBA) program may not be the best option if the company needs less than $50,000.
- Debt financing is usually cheaper and easier to find than equity capital. Debt financing requires that the borrower make monthly payments regardless of whether or not the business has a positive cash flow.
- While equity investors do not expect much, if any, return in the early business stages, they require information regarding a company's status. In addition, they expect the company to meet established goals.
- Most business types can usually acquire debt financing, but businesses with fast growth and high potential are usually the recipients of equity capital.
- Angel investors tend to invest money in companies that are within a 50-mile radius, and the amounts of funding tend to be in the range of $25,000 to $250,000. Angel investors may be friends, family, customers, suppliers, brokers, or competitors.
- It is difficult to secure venture capital funding, even in a good economy.

As the Cobb County Small Business Administration Loan Outreach Center opens, City of Austell Mayor Joe Jerkins confers with Small Business Administration Public Information Officer Michael Peacock, FEMA Intergovernmental Affairs Specialist Tom Hardy, FEMA Public Information Officer Noel Boxer, and Small Business Administration Public Information Officer Jack Camp. The Center provides help with completing loan applications and seeks to insure that every qualified individual and business receives help to recover from the storms and flooding which brought FEMA and partners here. (Courtesy of George Armstrong/FEMA)

APPLICATIONS

Two Options of Financing. Debt financing and equity capital options both require the business owner to complete detailed documentation prior to the award of financing. The owner should be prepared to produce quarterly balance sheets, background information on the company, and projections.

Debt Financing: Commercial Banks. If the company cannot finance the expansion through personal investments, the management team will need to develop a business plan that meets the criteria for potential lenders. Commercial banks may be the first choice, especially if the owner has a relationship with a specific lender. Since traditional lenders tend to be conservative, good rapport and an established relationship will be beneficial when applying for a loan. It is important for potential borrowers to understand the mindset of potential lenders. Most lenders tend to focus on five important factors when deciding whether to extend credit, and business owners need to be prepared to address them. The five factors are

- **Character**—What are your personal characteristics? Are you ethical and do you have a good reputation? Will you do everything possible to pay the loan back?
- **Capacity**—Will your business be able to generate sufficient cash flow to pay the loan back? Do you have access to other income?
- **Collateral**—Do you have collateral to cover the loan in the event that the venture does not perform well? Is there a qualified individual willing to cosign on the loan?
- **Conditions**—Have you researched the environment to see if there are any circumstances that could negatively impact your business (i.e., nature of product, competition)? How will you deal with these situations if they arise?
- **Capital**—What are you personally willing to invest in the venture? Most lenders are not willing to invest in ventures if you have not made a major investment in the future of the project. Why should they invest in the venture if you are not willing or able to?

Small Business Administration (SBA). If a commercial bank is not an option and the entity is a small business, the Small Business Administration (SBA) may be an alternative. The business must satisfy the agency's criteria and not be able to secure financing from other sources. The SBA is an independent agency of the federal government, and it is responsible for providing assistance to small businesses in the United States. The agency can offer four types of assistance: advocacy, management, procurement, and financial assistance. Financial assistance can be granted through the agency's investment programs, business loan programs, disaster loan programs, and bonding for contractors.

Business Loan Programs
There are three loan programs. The SBA sets the guidelines while other entities—such as lenders, community development organizations, and microlending institutions—make the loans to small businesses. In order to reduce the risk to these entities, the SBA will guarantee the loans. In reality, an SBA loan is a commercial loan with SBA requirements and guaranty.

Investment Programs
In 1958, Congress created a program for the group of privately owned and managed investment firms

recognized by the SBA as Small Business Investment Companies (SBICs) called the SBIC Program. SBICs partner with the government and use their own capital with funds borrowed at reduced rates to provide venture capital to small businesses.

Bonding Programs

According to the SBA, "the Surety Bond Guarantee (SBG) Program was developed to provide small and minority contractors with contracting opportunities for which they would not otherwise bid" (SBA, 2007). The SBA can guarantee bonds for contracts up to $6.5 million, covering bid, performance, and payment bonds for small contractors.

Equity Capital: Venture Capitalists. Venture capital is usually available for start-up companies with a product or idea that may be risky but has a high potential of yielding above-average profits. Funds are invested in ventures that have not been discovered. The money may come from wealthy individuals, government-sponsored Small Business Investment Corporations (SBICs), insurance companies, and corporations. It is more difficult to obtain financing from venture capitalists. A company must provide a formal proposal such as a business plan so that the venture capitalist may conduct a thorough evaluation of the company's records. Venture capitalists only approve a small percentage of the proposals that they receive, and they tend to favor innovative technological ventures.

Funding may be invested throughout the company's life cycle, with funding being provided at both the beginning and the later stages of growth. Venture capitalists may invest at different stages. Some firms may invest before the idea has been fully developed, while others may provide funding during the early stages of the company's life. However, there is a group of venture capitalists who specialize in assisting companies when they have reached the point at which the company needs financing in order to expand the business.

Angel Investors. Many firms receive some type of funding prior to seeking capital from venture capitalists. Angel investors have been identified as one source that entrepreneurs may reach out to for assistance (Gompers, 1995). Including angel investors in the early stages of financing could improve the chances of receiving venture capital financing. Madill, Haines, and Riding (2005) conducted a study with small businesses

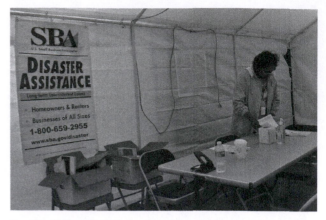

Jaqueline Swinger, Small Business Administration Representative, prepares for the next visitor for disaster assistance. FEMA played a vital role supporting State, Tribal and local governments as they responded to the impacts of remnants of Tropical Storm Lee in Hoosick Falls, N.Y. (Courtesy of Elissa Jun/FEMA)

and found that "57 percent of the firms that had received angel investor financing had also received financing from venture capitalists." Firms that did not receive angel investing in the early stages (approximately 10 percent of the firms in the study) did not obtain venture capital funding. It appears that angel investor financing is a significant factor in obtaining venture capital funding. Since obtaining venture capital tends to be difficult, businesses can benefit from the contacts and experience of angel investors in order to prepare for a venture capital application and evaluation. The intervention of an angel investor may make the company appear more attractive to the venture capitalists.

Regardless of how a company decides to finance the venture, it will have to make an agreement that is beneficial to the investors since they are the ones providing the money. Therefore, it is important to select a choice that benefits the business in the long run. Initial decisions may set the tone for future deals. Advani (2006) has provided some recommendations to consider when determining what will work best. These suggestions include the following:

- **Don't give pro rata rights to your first investors.** If your first investor is given pro rata rights, chances are your future investors will want the same agreement. It would be wise to balance the needs of your early investors to protect their stake in the company with how attractive the company will be to future investors.

- **Avoid giving too many people the right to be overly involved.** If too many people are involved, it could create a bureaucracy and make it difficult for decisions to be made in a timely manner. In addition, the daily tasks of a business may be prolonged due to the need for multiple authorization signatures.
- **Beware of any limits placed on management compensation.** Some investors may place a cap on the earning potential of senior management personnel. This type of action could create a problem with human resource needs such as attracting and hiring quality talent to run and grow the business.
- **Request a cure period.** Many investors will request representation for every legal agreement to protect themselves if the management of a company is not in compliance with laws, licenses, and regulations that govern the operation of the business. Although all parties may have good intentions, errors do occur. If a "cure period" is added to the financing agreement, the entrepreneur will have the opportunity to find a solution to the problem within a given period (i.e., two to four weeks).
- **Restrict your share restrictions.** Having unrestricted shares is often a good negotiating factor with future investors. Therefore, it would be wise to evaluate any requests to restrict the sale of shares owned by the founders or management team.

ISSUES

Making the Choice. In a perfect world, the business will be able to fund the venture. However, this is seldom the case. Most businesses will have to make a choice—will they incur debt or will they sell equity in the company? There are advantages and disadvantages for each type of source.

If the owner of a business decides to personally finance the venture, a loan or credit card financing may be a solution. There is an opportunity to secure competitive interest rates, and the terms of the loan are clear. Many owners have a desire to maintain control, and lenders are not a part of the company. They do not seek control and are only interested in businesses paying on time with interest. Although the owner maintains control of the business, there could be potential problems if the venture does not generate enough income to cover the basic cost of running the business and making the payments.

In order to avoid a "backlash of no cash," a business may determine that selling shares of equity would be the best way of securing working capital. This alternative could alleviate some of the stress associated with starting a new venture as well as provide the company an opportunity to grow at a quicker rate. However, the business will be required to give the investors some control and profits. Angel investors may want to take a role in the company, but venture capitalists will probably want to remain in the background as silent partners. If the venture is not successful, the investor loses. Therefore, angel investors and venture capitalists will probably require a higher return on investment than a conventional lender since the risks are greater.

CONCLUSION

There are many sources of capital for funding new ventures with potential. Securing capital for the venture requires the business to develop a business plan, forecast financial projections, and be knowledgeable about the sources of financial support.

"Given the importance of new business creation to global innovation and economic growth, an understanding of how people successfully obtain financing to pursue entrepreneurial opportunities is important" (Shane & Cable, p. 379). As the global economy becomes increasing integrated, the role of entrepreneurs will continue to be significant, and it will be important to make sure they are successful. One factor of success will be tied to the company's ability to finance its growth. Debt financing and venture capital have been identified as two options that a business can use to obtain financing. Entrepreneurs and small business owners will need to research and prepare the necessary documentation to secure financing from the various sources in these two options.

TERMS & CONCEPTS

Angel investors: Individuals that provides capital, contacts, and expertise to one or more start-up companies.

Capital: Usually measured in units of money, capital is referred to as tangible investment goods.

Commercial bank: Bank that takes deposits, makes loans, and offers additional related services; while accepting of individual business, commercial banks seek out business customers.

Debt financing: "When a firm raises money for working capital or capital expenditures by selling bonds, bills, or notes to individual and/or institutional investors. In return for lending the money, the individuals or institutions become creditors and receive a promise to repay principal and interest on the debt" (Schulman, 2007).

Equity: Funds provided to a business by the sale of stock.

Equity capital: Money invested in a business by owners, stockholders, or others who share in profits.

Financial institutions: An institution that places funds collected from the public in financial assets like deposits, loans, and bonds, rather than tangible property.

Investments: The procurement of a share in a financial vehicle so as to garner returns; simply, using money to make more money.

Nonprofit micro lenders: Lenders who offer small loans to people locked out of the banking system. The main purpose is to help start or expand small businesses that generate income.

Patient capital: Funding given without the expectation of short-term returns; long-term situation.

Pro rata rights: The investor is given the right to maintain ownership in the company through future investment rounds.

Share: Representation of a unit of monetary interest within a corporation, mutual fund, or limited partnership.

Small Business Administration: A federal agency that makes loans to small businesses.

Small Business Financial Exchange: A data repository, affiliated with Equifax, that collects loan, lease, line of credit, and credit card data to evaluate small business performance.

Start-up: A business venture in its earliest stage of development.

Venture: Often refers to a start-up or enterprise company that is associated with somewhat elevated levels of risk.

Venture capitalists: Investors that support start-up ventures or small businesses wishing to expand through the provision of capital; start-up ventures and small businesses are not traditionally given access to public funding.

BIBLIOGRAPHY

Advani, A. (2006, October 12). Raising money from informal investors. *Entrepreneur.com.*

Advani, A. (2006, November 10). Start-up financing trends for 2007. *Entrepreneur.com.*

Brush, C. G., Edelman, L. F., & Manolova, T. S. (2012). Ready for funding? Entrepreneurial ventures and the pursuit of angel financing. *Venture Capital, 14*(2/3), 111–129.

Colgren, D. (2014). The rise of crowdfunding: social media, big data, cloud technologies. *Strategic Finance, 96,* 56–57.

Edelhauser, K. (2007, April 11). Angel investing to grow in '07. *Entrepreneur.com.*

Forbes, M. (2013). The art of angel investing. *Forbes.* Forbes.com.

Gaynor, G., Morse, J., & Pevzner, M. (2015). The crowdfunding effect. *Strategic Finance, 97*(10), 34–39.

Goel, R. K., & Hasan, I. (2004). Funding new ventures: Some strategies for raising early finance. *Applied Financial Economics, 14,* 773–778.

Gompers, P. A. (1995). Optimal investment, monitoring, and the staging of venture capital. *Journal of Finance, 50,* 1461–1490.

Jonsson, S., & Lindbergh, J. (2013). The development of social capital and financing of entrepreneurial firms: From financial bootstrapping to bank funding. *Entrepreneurship: Theory & Practice, 37,* 661–686.

Key findings from the GEM financing report (2007).

Madill, J., Haines Jr., G., & Riding, A. (2005). The role of angels in technology SMEs: A link to venture capital. *Venture Capital, 7,* 107–129.

Mulcahy, D. (2016). Don't take money from VCs until you've asked 4 questions. *Harvard Business Review Digital Articles,* 2–5.

Pierce, C. (2005). How to prepare and present a successful business funding request.

Schulman, D. (2007). The sub prime continuum theory. *Localism.*

Shane, S., & Cable, D. (2002). Network ties, reputation, and the financing of new ventures. *Management Science, 48,* 364–381.

Small Business Administration. Finance start-up.

University of Maine Cooperative Extension, Bulletin # 3008. (n.d.) Capital Sources for Your Business.

Zachary, R., & Mishra, C. S. (2013). Research on angel investments: The intersection of equity investments and entrepreneurship. *Entrepreneurship Research Journal, 3,* 160–170.

SUGGESTED READING

Belleflamme, P., Lambert, T., & Schwienbacher, A. (2014). Crowdfunding: Tapping the right crowd. *Journal of Business Venturing, 29,* 585–609.

Bruno, A., & Tyebjee, T. (1985). The entrepreneur's search for capital. *Journal of Business Venturing, 1,* 61–75.

Churchill, N., & Lewis, V. (1986). Bank lending to new and growing enterprises. *Journal of Business Venturing, 1,* 193–207

Hall, J., & Hofer, C. (1993). Venture capitalists' decision criteria in new venture evaluation. *Journal of Business Venturing, 8,* 25–43.

Homburg, C., Hahn, A., Bornemann, T., Sander, P. (2014). The role of chief marketing officers for venture capital funding: Endowing new ventures with marketing legitimacy. *Journal of Marketing Research, 51*(5), 624–644.

Hustedde, R., & Pulver, G. (1992). Factors affecting equity capital acquisition: The demand side. *Journal of Business Venturing, 7,* 363–375.

Mollick, E. (2014). The dynamics of crowdfunding: An exploratory study. *Journal of Business Venturing, 29,* 1–16.

Neely, L., & Van Auken, H. (2012). An examination of small firm bootstrap financing and use of debt. *Journal of Developmental Entrepreneurship, 17.*

Phillips Erb, K. (2015). Debt, equity and startup money. *Forbes.com, 7.*

Essay by Marie Gould

G

GLOBAL FINANCE

Global finance is becoming a growing part of the financial world and the world of the investor. Global options for investing abound but require knowledge on the part of the investor and expertise on the part of the fund manager. Global finance allows emerging growth countries and economies to participate and access new markets and demand for new investments. However, the investor must weigh the cost and possible instability of global markets when investing. Portfolio diversification and strategy may suggest that a component of a well-rounded portfolio be global funds. But investors have no way of predicting the cultural and political shifts that may influence the stability of global funds. Other more secure investments may be needed to offset possible losses in global funds.

OVERVIEW

Global finance concerns the international financial system, financial institutions and instruments. Several international institutions regulate global financial markets. These include the World Bank, the International Money Fund, and the World Trade Organization. The prospect of investing in global instruments is attractive to some but worrisome to others. Tyson (2003) advised investors to be careful and often stay away from global investing. Tyson noted that the word *international* means the fund invests globally except in the United States. A fund with *worldwide* or *global* in its name includes the United States. Tyson gave two reasons for avoiding global fund investing—information and cost. He felt it was difficult for a fund manager to follow the action if it were occurring across the globe and much more difficult than following U.S. funds. Secondly, he felt that the costs associated with the operation and management of global funds would offset the yield and return an investor could anticipate.

Thinking globally means changing the view of what is important in global finance and who the primary players are. There was a time when the only markets that were deemed important were the United States and parts of Europe. The view then began to trend toward only the major industrialized nations. However, with improvements in technology and the desire of emerging growth countries to participate in global markets, the global finance landscape has changed. Poor and emerging economy countries are recognizing that they have valuable items to trade, such as natural resources and labor that were previously untapped. Harnessing those resources and participating in the global economy can change the status of an emerging country and its people.

Risks of Global Finance

Some issues related to global finance are the conditions in various underdeveloped and emerging countries. There can be uncertainty due to currency and political instability. There can also be war and military issues, poverty, and environmental and human rights issues. Some global funds can become undesirable based on the discovery of internal turmoil in the local economy. Funds can also face a backlash when information about such instability is uncovered.

Global finance is growing with the growth and expansion of multinational corporations. Many established corporations in the United States and Europe are looking for ways to expand their customer base and increase the demand for their products and services. Some are facing saturation in developed countries and are looking for opportunities in new areas. Mergers and acquisitions are also making companies bigger with multinational interests. Many fear that the "McDonaldization" or "Starbucktizing" of the world is not a good thing. This is because when multinational firms are investing in new economies, they will likely have influence over the activity, growth, and change that occurs.

Headquarters of the International Monetary Fund in Washington, D.C. (Courtesy of International Monetary Fund via Wikimedia Commons)

Banking & Globalization

The *Country Monitor* (2006, p. 5) noted the success of banks worldwide in reducing risk. The techniques used to do this included "statistical portfolio management, securitization, the sale of problem loans and derivatives hedging." These methods have helped banks to reduce risk and spread it around. Moody's rating service revised the way it rates banks. It contrived a five rating system from A to E to make the international ratings consistent across economies. The rating system is supposed to give investors a better idea of how credit worthy a bank is and what the true risk is in a certain economy. However, many experts believe that the rating system can only go so far, and in fact Moody's (as well as the other ratings agencies) came under sharp criticism after the 2008 global financial crisis when it was discovered that billions of dollars in bad debt, bundled into collateralized debt obligations, was given the highest rating—AAA (Fiderer, 2013).

Banks have experienced an influx of cash in the early twenty-first century, contributing to merger and acquisition activity. This new level of consolidation meant that mergers also began occurring across global borders. Citigroup led the way by making inroads into China, Taiwan, and Turkey (*Country Monitor*, 2006). Other changes in global banking have occurred in the asset makeup of banks. The economies of Russia and China with "less developed financial systems" tend to have a higher ratio of corporate loans than consumer loans whereas U.S. banks have

a 50:50 ratio. In 2013, China's banks were lending at a rate of 132 percent of GDP, and of that about 85 percent was to corporations (Dobbs, Leung, & Lund, 2013). The risk is lower when there are more consumer loans in the mix—spreading the risk around. With corporate loans, especially if those loans are largely to only a few institutions, the risk is greater (*Country Monitor*, 2006).

Role of Governments in Globalization

Dorn (2003) believed bad government policies are at fault for many global financial crises. Dorn (2003) provided examples of the Argentine government defaulting on debt in 2001 and the Brazilian crisis in 2002 as examples of how government can help devalue confidence in an economy. Dorn (2003) used these examples to indicate how important it is to find ways to deal with the crises of debt across the world combined with banking crises and currency crises. The International Monetary Fund (IMF) has stepped in to help countries in crisis but cannot remove the stigma that may remain on the credibility of investing in these regions with problems. Governments must cooperate with market forces to keep the flow of capital investment coming. In Europe, in the early days of the global financial crisis, Iceland partially nationalized its banks to prevent collapse, but it protected the deposits of Icelanders only; the large number of foreign depositors in the United Kingdom and the Netherlands were bailed out by their own governments, who expected reimbursement from Iceland but were instead rebuffed. Touryalai (2011) predicted long-term repercussions for Iceland from the global investment community. Refusing to impose austerity on its people to meet its credit obligations, Iceland's government instead provided mortgage relief and other measures. In contrast, Ireland, Portugal, Spain, Greece, and Italy struggled under huge debt burdens that ravaged their economies, and bailouts by the European Central Bank were conditioned on austerity measures that sparked massive protests. A fragile calm eventually ensued (though unemployment remained extremely high). By 2013, these nations were again issuing bonds (Fontevecchia, 2013). At the same time, Iceland's economy was recovered modestly, with growth in GDP and a steep drop in unemployment; the necessity of not remaining a pariah in the foreign investment market was obvious, and the government

World leaders at the 2010 G-20 summit in Seoul, South Korea, endorsed the Basal III standards for banking regulation. (Courtesy of Casa Rosada (Argentina Presidency of the Nation) via Wikimedia Commons)

was working toward satisfying foreign creditors and investors (Bremner & Valdimarsson, 2013). Worries remained, however, that in preserving institutions that had colossally failed, public debt had swollen to dangerous and unsustainable levels (Bilkic, Carreras Painter, & Gries, 2013).

Regard for Risk
A 1999 Federal Reserve Bank conference on "Bank Structure and Competition" (Brewer & Evanoff, 1999, para. 1) suggested ways to prevent global financial crises and ways to resolve them when they occur. Conference discussions pursued the causes of global financial crises finding that the integration of global markets increased the dependence countries have on one another; spreading the pain around. Excessive debt, herd mentality by investors and over speculation with a "boom-bust" mentality created a gambling like atmosphere among investors. Many investors rushed into new markets without regard for risk.

Disregarding risk is a classic mistake in an unknown investment environment. Crises occurred because the governments at the center of these financial investments did not back up the liabilities incurred by financial institutions. The reason investors engage in risky investments is high yield and protection from potential losses. Other conference participants blamed the IMF for bailing out failing financial institutions as a signal to financial institutions in other countries that they would also be helped if they wanted to find relief from financial liabilities. This "moral hazard" also fueled the savings and loan crisis in the United States since bailout was seen as a viable option (Brewer & Evanoff, 1999, para. 8). Not only are unnecessary risks taken when bailout is assured but market prices are distorted as well. Regulation is seen as a primary vehicle to prevent excessive risk-taking due to assurances of liability relief. The complexity of global finance can make it difficult for rating agencies and others to react to potential crises.

Some recommendations to avert future financial crises included restricting the IMF to bailout only if the affected country has a sound financial banking system. Sound systems would mean that private lenders would accept liability if the bank fails and foreign banks should be encouraged and allowed to compete fairly in their local markets to diversify the risk. Finally, investors would have to be compensated with a higher rate of return if failure occurs. These recommendations were felt to possibly curb the tendency for excessively risky behavior (Brewer & Evanoff, 1999). Conquering risk means regaining control and requires decision-making and careful calculation (Beck, 2002).

Global Challenges

Some of the challenges with global finance are cultural and political. There may be cultural and political influences on investments that can change the risk and value associated with the investment. These factors may be unknown, and it may be difficult to predict the result of cultural or political instability. Being some distance away from factors that influence investments can also give investors pause. There could be some language barriers and problems with interpretation, though many global funds have English-speaking and U.S. financial advisors.

It may be assumed that only emerging and developing countries have challenges with globalization and global finance. However, developed and highly industrialized nations must keep pace with changes to survive as emerging nations become stronger. The *Economist* (2006) reported on changes to the financial trading practices in London and its struggle to remain the capital of finance in England. Some of the changes have included investing in infrastructure, transforming formerly underutilized areas into booming economic centers, and changing trading methods. London was a worldwide center for finance in the 1960s and 1970s and became home for international banks in the 1980s but lost many brokers to New York because of stock market trading practices. London experienced a recession in the 1990s and weathered the storm of uncertainty with the euro as currency. London has followed the lead of the United States in beefing up regulatory policy to avoid financial collapses.

The integration of multiple financial systems is much more complex than it sounds. Clark (2005) found that previous attempts at understanding globalization emphasized the social aspects. Clark investigated global finance and money flow and noted that various systems are challenged by reality. The financial systems of the United States tend to be "market centered top-down systems regulated and controlled by" national and international institutions. European financial systems tend to be bottom-up systems that are loosely regulated. The argument for global financial systems calls for using the best practices of all systems (Clark, 2005, p. 101). Clark also called for research that is cross-functional along the disciplines of economics, geography, sociology, and finance.

Bank Stability

Ratings organizations like Moody's (Country Monitor, 2006, p. 5) have noted the improvement in the financial stability of banks. However, when considering global challenges, these ratings agencies look at "country risk, the regulatory environment, the stability of the financial system and the likelihood of government support." Country risk may include the capital inflow to an emerging economy and the stability of that inflow. Struggling governments may have no ability or desire to bail out a struggling financial institution. Debt in the United States continues to require substantial inflows and can influence interest rates in other nations. Some economies have regulatory entities that specifically look at ways to reduce risk. For example, the World Bank and European Union publish such guidelines.

Technology

Technology freed the flow of money during the dot-com era by sending money to the areas with the most innovation and productivity (Clark, 2005). Technology has done much to spur globalization and vice versa. A direct result of the increase in technology and financial markets being driven by technology is technological theft and terrorism. This new industry puts personal information about investors at risk. Investors who want to invest globally and online must heed warnings of scams and should deal with reputable entities regardless of the claims of high returns.

Time Zone Differences

Time zones can present challenges for global investors. One market may be active while another market is asleep. This presents challenges in tracking investments and making decisions about them. Freed (2006, p. 20) reported on a company called "Recerche"—a team of thirty analysts based in India who have high speed Internet access and tools for performing research on demand for global investment clients. Fund managers use services like this because analysts are literally working on investment issues while the fund manager sleeps.

Internal Security Threats

The *Computer Security Update* (2005) reported that for the first time there is an increase in internal security threats on financial institutions that now overtake external threats. Easy access to the Internet has made these attacks possible. Bogus e-mails and phishing scams are most popular. Financial institutions are engaging in awareness training for staff and information security strategies. A study of financial institution security officers noted that Europe, the Middle East, and Africa lead the way in adopting security standards and have information security strategies in place. Asian countries had the highest awareness level and commitment to training on these issues. Latin America and Caribbean countries had the lowest level of programming for managing privacy compliance. More than half of Canadians responding reported actual experience with security breaches. Along with the United States, Canada has committed adequate funding to address these issues (Computer Security, 2005).

Clark (2005, p. 105) compared the characteristics of global finance to the characteristics of the substance mercury. One characteristic is that mercury "runs together at speed." Global finance can do the same thing due to the ability to communicate instantly across the globe. Similarly, mercury "forms in pools." A distinct advantage of global finance is to shift pools of money to demand where it exists. Pooling transactions also reduces cost.

VIEWPOINTS

Benefits & Dangers of Global Investing

There can be benefits in investing globally. Investors can tap into profits and have alternatives to only investing domestically. At the same time, policies must exist to ensure risk is limited and that countries can share in the benefits of globalization. In no way can the individual investor alone participate in this policy making, nor can the investor predict the movement and changes in policy. The effect of policy cannot be determined in advance.

An understanding of globalization can also help investors determine how and where to invest. The International Monetary Fund (IMF) (2002, para. 13) found that there were four components of globalization including the following:

- trade
- capital movements
- movement of people
- spread of knowledge and technology

Trade

The percentage of trade by developing countries increased 19 percent from 1971 to 1999, with Asian countries benefiting from this trend primarily in the area of manufacturing. Accompanying this trend has been a change of opinion of these countries. In prior years, the countries were laughed at and assumed to produce inferior goods. Once the manufacturing techniques improved, some countries were seen as dangerous competitors and the source of many high-paying manufacturing jobs leaving the United States. Many have resigned themselves to the fact that the Japanese dominate automotive manufacturing and the Chinese dominate manufacturing of toys, electronics, and other consumer goods. Others have used these events as a rallying cry for a boycott of non-American made products or to push the government to intervene. The IMF supports government policy to retrain workers.

Capital Movements

Capital flow into developing companies has increased primarily due to expansion by multinational corporations. The migration of people for the purposes of better employment has primarily been concentrated to developed countries with limited movement back to developing countries to share knowledge and skill. Finally, investment in developing countries requires an increase in the local knowledge and technology. However, it is noted that poverty is not positively impacted by globalization. Instead, the rich countries continue to get richer while poor countries get poorer. Similarly, within countries the gap between rich and poor continues to increase.

Increased Portfolio Stability

One reason to invest globally is to reduce fluctuation in your portfolio. The reduction in fluctuation occurs because not every country's investment vehicle is going up or down at the same time as another country. In addition, only investing domestically can limit opportunities that may only exist in other countries. Finally, investments tend to act in cycles and investing outside of one's country can help the investor's portfolio by tapping into positive cycles of fast growth internationally that may not be taking place domestically. This action can reduce fluctuation in an investor's portfolio. Financial advice is important, especially with foreign investment. The investor should also be prepared for long-term investment and understand the overall equity returns or how domestic currency performs against foreign currency over the long haul (Khosrow & Salvatore, 1993).

Complexity

Some disadvantages to global investing include complexity. There may not be adequate information about investment practices or regulatory policies. Understanding tax liability may also be difficult. In developing countries, there is unlikely to be an organization like the Securities and Exchange Commission (SEC) providing regulatory guidance so some risk is inherent. Another information problem is that global investing may require getting information from other parts of the world that are not on the same schedule, and it may result in delays in getting updated financial statements or communicating with someone in real time (Khosrow & Salvatore, 1993).

Diversification

Jenks & Eckett (2002) believed that there were several advantages to global investing for the small investor, such as diversification as a risk amelioration strategy for investors. They suggest splitting a portfolio among various areas of the world, making sure different industries, asset types, and a mix of developing and emerging countries is selected. It is also suggested that investors become more familiar with risk terms and the meaning of volatility measures in order to better select a global investment. All types of risk, including political and regulatory risk, have to be balanced against any possible return on a global investment. Global investors should avoid investing in countries that have correlating stock relative to the investor's home country. Not following this advice could lead to losses and defeats the purpose of diversification. International markets may not have the sophistication of U.S. markets and the advantage to the U.S. investor is greater knowledge of how investments work applied to the international opportunity.

Crises & Regulatory Fallout

A constant danger in the global markets is that of a crisis and regulatory fallout and analysis of crises. Most crises are unforeseen events and have far-reaching consequences. Hoguet (2001) examined a 1999 global financial crisis caused by a default crisis in Russia, devaluation in Brazil, capital controls in Malaysia and the 1998 collapse of Long-Term Capital Management hedge fund. Hoguet (2001, p. 46) noted several reasons given by analysts for these crises, which included the following:

- shrinkage in bank lending
- macroeconomic policies in specific countries
- deficits as a percentage of gross domestic product
- excessive money supply growth
- "herd" behavior of investors
- IMF policies that adversely affected specific countries
- prosperous countries taking advantage of less prosperous ones
- "misallocation" of capital by corporate managers and lenders

Hoguet (2001, p. 47) felt that international equity investors and fund managers play a substantial role in "stabilizing the global economy." In addition, Hoguet believed that U.S. pension funds are the key because of their size (60% of the world's pension fund assets at $13+ trillion) and because more than "11% of these assets are invested in foreign equities." U.S. pension funds are expected to grow and can provide balance to corporate asset allocation. Hoguet (2001) accurately described increasing global investment as inevitable with the entry of China into the global economy. Hoguet (2001) suggested a number of policy guidelines to manage communication with emerging markets for investment. One of the most important ideas to communicate would be the international global finance guidelines as well as emphasizing the benefit of experienced U.S. fund managers. Hoguet (p.47) felt that the best reasons for increasing investments in emerging global markets are "diversification, return enhancement and a broader investment opportunity set." Hoguet's views are not unlike most others in the reasons to invest. The individual investor must create a portfolio that can withstand the volatility and potential for crisis that the global finance market offers.

CONCLUSION

Global investing is an opportunity for investors to capitalize on fast growth that takes place in other countries. It also provides a way to diversify a portfolio and guard against risk. However, just as in domestic investing, the investor will need to be armed with substantial knowledge about investing as well as knowledge about the possibilities in various regions throughout the world. Technology has made it easier to get information but the lure of high profits may cause investors to hurry into an investment without adequate preparation. The many dangers of global investing include unstable governments and currencies as well as the lack of country regulatory bodies that protect the investor. Novice investors should probably avoid risky global investments and stick with those that provide diversity in industry and region.

TERMS & CONCEPTS

Finance: The study of managing money.

Financial regulation: Rules that govern financial institutions.

Global: Pertaining to worldwide, including multiple countries around the world.

Globalization: Refers to the movement since the 1990s toward integration of worldwide markets. Technology has accelerated globalization.

International finance: The study of international economics, investment, and money transfer.

International monetary fund (IMF): An international organization located in Washington, DC, made up of 185 member countries. It monitors economic activity, advises on policy, and responds to financial crises.

Securities and Exchange Commission: The United States regulatory agency for the securities industry.

World Bank: An international organization providing advice and assistance to developing countries. The goal of the World Bank is to improve living conditions and reduce poverty worldwide.

BIBLIOGRAPHY

Beck, U. (2002). The terrorist threat. *Theory, Culture & Society, 19*, 39.

Bilkic, N. N., Carreras Painter, B. B., & Gries, T. T. (2013). Unsustainable sovereign debt-is the Euro crisis only the tip of the iceberg? *International Economics & Economic Policy, 10*, 1–45.

Bremner, B., & Valdimarsson, O. R. (2013). Beware of Icelanders bearing smiles. *Bloomberg Businessweek, (4329)*, 46–47.

Brewer III, E. & Evanoff, D. D. (1999, August). Global financial crises: Implications for banking and regulation. *Chicago Fed Letter.*

Capital city. (2006). *Economist, 381*(8500), 83–86.

Clark, G. L. (2005). Money flows like mercury: The geography of global finance. *Geografiska Annaler Series B: Human Geography, 87*, 99–112.

Dobbs, R., Leung, N., & Lund, S. (2013). China's rising stature in global finance. *Mckinsey Quarterly*, 26–31.

Dorn, J. A. (2003). International financial crises: What role for government? *CATO Journal, 23*, 1–9.

Fiderer, D. (2013). Moody's CEO Is Wrong, We Need Rating Agency Reform. *Asset Securitization Report, 13*, 7.

Freed, D. (2006). Research while you sleep. *Investment Dealers' Digest, 72*, 20–21.

The global finance function: Five focal points. (2013). *Journal of Accountancy, 216*, 20–21.

Grody, A. D. (2013). Risk adjusting the culture of global finance. *Journal of Risk Management in Financial Institutions, 6*, 178–180.

Hoguet, G. R., (2001). Forces for stabilization. *International Economy, 15*, 46–49.

How safe are the world's banks? (2006). *Country Monitor, 14*, 5.

Internal attacks surpassing external attacks at firms. (2005, August). *Computer Security Update*, 1–4.

International Monetary Fund. (2002, April 12). *Globalization: Threat or opportunity?*

Jenks, P. & Eckett, S. (2002). *The global-investor book of investing rules.* Upper Saddle River, NJ: Prentice Hall.

Khosrow F. & Salvatore, D. (1993). *Foreign exchange issues, capital markets & international banking in the 1990s.* Washington, DC: Taylor & Francis.

Touryalai, H. (2011). Iceland's stand against bailout repayment will hurt. *Forbes.com, 28.*

Tyson, E. (2003). *Personal finance for dummies.* Indianapolis: Wiley Publishing.

SUGGESTED READING

Kazemi, H. & Sohrabji, N. (2006). The role of the IMF on global financial institutions and markets. *International Advances in Economic Research, 12,* 141.

The politics of spending overseas. (2004). *Bank Technology News, 17,* 14.

SAS of N.C. revamps anti-launder product. (2006). *American Banker, 171,* 10.

Sohn, I. (2005). Asian financial cooperation: The problem of legitimacy in global financial governance. *Global Governance, 11,* 487–504.

The $350b outsourcing market. (2003). *Siliconindia, 7,* 15.

Essay by Marlanda English, Ph. D.

GLOBALIZATION AND INTERNATIONAL ACCOUNTING

This article focuses on international accounting. It provides a description and analysis of the principle international accounting standards as developed by the International Financial Reporting Standards Board. The push for a harmonization and convergence of international accounting and financial reporting methods and practices is addressed. The relationship between international accounting standards and economic globalization is explored. This article discusses the issues related to the United States' adoption of international accounting standards.

OVERVIEW

Accounting systems—which include accounting concepts, reporting practices, and principles—reflect the culture, philosophy, goals, and objectives of their users. Modern accounting systems are increasingly international in scope and standards. Economic globalization has created the demand for shared international accounting principles, standards, and practices. International accounting refers to accounting practices that cross national boundaries or are conducted in a location other than the firm's home country. International accounting encompasses "multinational enterprises, global movements to shape the direction of accounting, and comparative accounting requirements and practices" (Prather-Kinsey & Rueschhoff, 2004). The stakeholders of international accounting—including shareholders, corporations, and governments—require accurate and comparable economic data to make economic decisions and govern (Speidell & Bavishi, 1992). Comparable systems of transnational financial reporting facilitate international investment.

Globalization & the Harmonization of Accounting Practices

A lack of harmonization among national accounting laws characterized accounting practices in the twentieth century. Cultural and philosophical differences have historically been the norm in national accounting systems. Nations have based their accounting systems on culturally specific consolidation practices and long-term investments. Differences in accounting concepts, reporting practices, and principles remain common among nations. For example, the United States' Financial Accounting Standards Board promotes the United States generally accepted accounting principles (GAAP). Countries such as Japan and Canada, which conduct significant trade and investment with the United States, supplement their national accounting systems with GAAP. The European Union has mandated the adoption and use of International Financial Reporting Standards (IFRS). Diversity in international accounting practices challenges global markets and global trade. Significant differences in international accounting concepts, reporting practices, and principles compromise the ability of national businesses and industries to compete in international markets (Wells & Thompson, 1995). The lack of harmonization in international accounting practices is creating friction and roadblocks in the process of economic globalization.

Economic Globalization

Economic globalization results from political changes, new communication technology, and the end of financial barriers. The global economy is characterized by growth (in populations and in output and consumption per capita), interdependence of nations, and international management efforts. Indicators of global growth and interdependence include the huge increases in communication links, world output, international trade, and international investment since the 1970s. The global economy is built on global interdependence of economic flows linking the economies of the world. The global economy is characterized by economic sensitivity. National economic events in one region often have profound results for other regions and national economies. National economies exist not in isolation but in relationship and tension with other economies worldwide.

The global economy includes numerous economic phenomena and financial tools shared among all countries. The new global economy is characterized and controlled through global management or governance efforts. International organizations, both public and private, work to establish norms, standards, and requirements for international financial governance. These international organizations—including the International Accounting Standards Board (IASB), G-20, Financial Stability Forum, International Organization of Securities Commissions, Organisation for Economic Co-operation and Development (OECD), and the Basel Committee on Banking Supervision—develop and encourage implementation of economic standards, principles, best practices, and economic architecture (Preston, 1996).

Convergence

Increased international financial activity necessitates the alignment and harmonization of national accounting practices. In the twenty-first century, the main trend in international accounting is convergence and harmonization. In the field of international accounting, convergence refers to the standardization of national accounting standards. International accounting harmonization (IAH) is a goal shared by governments, international accounting organizations, and businesses. Accounting harmonization refers to the reduction of difference in accounting practices among countries. An international accounting harmonization system (IAH system) would create a common denominator for measuring, recording, and reporting business transactions, liabilities, and equities. The process of developing an IAH system will involve the selection of either fair value accounting (FVA) or historical cost accounting (HCA) as the shared common denominator for all international accounting practices (Barlev & Haddad, 2007).

The forces of globalization and global markets make international accounting standards necessary and advantageous for most countries. The harmonization of accounting concepts, reporting practices, and principles will allow for a level field of economic competition for all nations. The major international accounting organizations are working together with nations to build a framework for global financial reporting that is sensitive to the diversity of cultural environments worldwide. In addition, the new international accounting framework will be developed to respect differences in the following accounting values: professionalism, statutory control, uniformity, flexibility, optimism, and transparency (Marrero & Brinker, 2006).

The following section provides a description of the principle international accounting standards as developed by the International Accounting Standards Board. This section serves as a foundation for later discussion about the issues related to the United States' adoption and accommodation of international accounting standards.

APPLICATIONS

International Accounting Standards

The International Accounting Standards Board, known prior to 2001 as the International Accounting Standards Committee (IASC), is one of the main international organizations responsible for setting international standards for accounting and reporting practices. The International Accounting Standards Board uses a framework that defines terms used in financial accounting statements worldwide for the measurement of financial positions. The International Accounting Standards Board describes the terms *assets, liability, equity, income,* and *expenses* in the following ways:

- Assets refer to resources controlled by the entity as a result of past events and from which future economic benefits are expected to flow to the entity.
- Liabilities refer to present obligations of the entity arising from past events, the settlement of which is expected to result in an outflow from the entity of resources embodying economic benefits.
- Equity refers to the residual interest in the assets of the entity after deducting all of its liabilities.
- Income refers to the increases in economic benefits during the accounting period in the form of inflows or enhancements of assets or decreases of liabilities that result in increases in equity.
- Expenses refer to decreases in economic benefits during the accounting period in the form of outflows or depletions of assets or liabilities that result in decreases in equity ("Framework," 2008, p. 1–2).

International Financial Reporting Standards

The International Accounting Standards Board publishes and distributes its standards in reports under the name International Financial Reporting Standards (IFRS). Prior to 2001, the International Accounting Standards Committee (IASC) issued its reports under the name International Accounting Standards (IAS). The International Accounting Standards Board has honored and adopted the International Accounting Standards Committee's numerous International Accounting Standards. Nations committed to international financial activity are increasingly adopting International Financial Reporting Standards and International Accounting Standards. Common International Financial Reporting Standards include the following:

First-Time Adoption of International Financial Reporting Standards: The IFRS includes directives for the first-time adoption of its standards. In particular, the IFRS dictate the content and timing of a business entity's first IFRS financial statements.

Share-Based Payment: The IFRS includes directives and standards for three types of share-based payment transactions including, equity-settled share-based

payment transactions, cash-settled share-based payment transactions, and transactions in which a business entity acquires goods or services. Equity-settled share-based payment transactions refer to transactions in which the business entity receives goods or services in exchange for equity instruments. Cash-settled share-based payment transactions refer to transactions in which the entity acquires goods or services by incurring liabilities to the supplier of those goods or services. Transactions in which a business entity acquires goods or services refer to transactions in which the terms of the arrangement include options for payment in goods and services.

Business Combinations: The IFRS considers a business combination the conglomeration of separate entities or businesses into one reporting entity. The IFRS stipulates that business combinations be accounted for through the application of the purchase method.

Insurance Contracts: The IFRS defines an insurance contract to be a contract under which "one party accepts significant insurance risk from another party by agreeing to compensate the policyholder if a specified uncertain future event adversely affects the policyholder." Insurance contracts involve the insurer, the policyholder, and the insured event. Insurance contract disclosure is required to help stakeholders understand the amount in the financial statement that results from insurance contracts and the amount of future cash flows anticipated from insurance contracts.

Noncurrent Assets Held for Sale and Discontinued Operations: The IFRS considers a noncurrent asset held for sale to be an asset carrying an amount that that will be recovered principally through a sale transaction rather than through continued use. Noncurrent assets held for sale are required to be available and ready for immediate sale in their current condition. Business entities claiming that they have significant noncurrent assets held for sale must be actively marketing and publicizing these items for sale.

Exploration for and Evaluation of Mineral Resources: The IFRS considers exploration and evaluation expenditures to be expenditures that are "incurred by an entity in connection with the exploration for and evaluation of mineral resources before technical and commercial feasibility" of extracting mineral resources is able to be demonstrated.

Disclosures: According to the IFRS, disclosures are the financial instruments used to evaluate a business entity's financial position and performance. A business entity's disclosures must include information on the nature and extent of risks that it faces.

Operating Segments: The IRFS dictate how a business entity should report financial information about its operating segments and reportable segments. Operating segments refer to components of an entity "about which separate financial information is available that is evaluated regularly by the chief operating decision maker in deciding how to allocate resources and in assessing performance." Reportable segments refer to specific operating segments that meet specific needs or criteria.

Common International Accounting Standards include the following:

Presentation of Financial Statements: The IAS specify that annual financial statements must include a balance sheet, an income statement, a statement of changes in equity, and a cash flow statement.

Inventories: The IAS specify that inventories be evaluated using a first-in, first-out, or weighted average cost formula.

Cash Flow Statements: The IAS require business entities to issue cash flow statements with information about cash and cash equivalents. The IAS define cash flows as inflows and outflows of cash and cash equivalents. Cash includes cash on hand and demand deposits. Cash equivalents refer to short-term, liquid investments with a stable and known value.

Accounting Policies, Changes in Accounting Estimates and Errors: The IAS dictate procedures for accounting policies, changes in accounting, and prior period errors. Accounting policies refer to "the specific principles, bases, conventions, rules, and practices applied by an entity in preparing and presenting financial statements." Changes in

accounting estimates refer to adjustments of the carrying amount of an asset or a liability. Prior period errors refer to omissions and misstatements in a business entity's financial statements from one or more prior reporting periods. Errors include mathematical mistakes, accounting problems, oversights, and misrepresentations.

Income Taxes: The IAS control the accounting practices used for income taxes. Income taxes refer to all domestic and foreign taxes that are based on taxable profits. The IAS related to income taxes focus on recognition, measurement, and allocation. The IAS include very detailed instructions for the reporting of financial information about leases in financial statements.

Leases: The IAS separate leases into the two categories of operating leases and finance leases. An operating lease refers to a lease that does not transfer the risks and rewards associated with ownership. In contrast, a financial lease refers to a lease that transfers all the risks and rewards associated with ownership.

Revenue: The IAS consider revenue to be the "gross inflow of economic benefits during the period arising in the course of the ordinary activities of a business entity when those inflows result in increases in equity." The IAS specify that revenue must be evaluated and measured at the fair value of the item. Fair value refers to "the amount for which an asset could be exchanged or a liability settled."

Borrowing Costs: The IAS consider borrowing costs to be the interest and other costs incurred by an entity in connection with the borrowing of funds. The IAS specify that borrowing costs must be recognized and reported as an expense during the fiscal period in which they occur.

Interests in Joint Ventures: The IAS dictate the accounting practices involving interests in joint ventures. This standard applies to the accounting of joint venture assets, liabilities, income, and expenses. The IAS define joint ventures as a "contractual arrangement whereby two or more parties undertake an economic activity that is under joint control." There are three main types of joint ventures: jointly controlled operations, jointly controlled assets, and jointly controlled entities.

Earnings per Share: The IAS control how earnings per share are to be reported. The IAS apply to ordinary shares and potential ordinary shares. Ordinary shares refer to "an equity instrument that is subordinate to all other classes of equity instruments." Potential ordinary shares refer to financial instruments or other contracts that may entitle its holder to ordinary shares.

Investment Property: The IAS control the accounting practices applicable to investment property. Investment property refers to property held to earn rentals or capital appreciation. The IAS specify how investment property can be valued and derecognized.

In addition to the standards described above, the IAS provide accounting and reporting directions and specifications about numerous other topics and fields. Examples include agriculture; employee benefits; accounting for government grants; disclosure of government assistance; incorporating the changes in foreign exchange rates; property, plant and equipment; related party disclosures; reporting on retirement benefit plans; consolidated and separate financial statements; financial reporting in hyperinflationary economies; interim financial reporting; impairment of assets; contingent liabilities; contingent assets; intangible assets; and construction contracts.

Shared, harmonized, and comparable international accounting standards, as described above, are a necessary feature or tool of economic globalization. The pace of adoption of international accounting standards will vary among countries, as described in the next section, but the existence and growing relevance of international accounting standards will not.

ISSUES

The United States & International Accounting

The United States stands apart from most other industrialized countries in the pace of its adoption of shared international accounting standards. In 2002, the U.S. Financial Accounting Standards Board (FASB) and the International Accounting Standards Board (IASB) began the FASB/IASB convergence project with the signing of the Norwalk Agreement. The Norwalk Agreement, also referred to by the FASB and the IASB as a roadmap for convergence and a memorandum of understanding, is a pledge between the accounting organizations to work toward a shared set of global accounting standards. The FASB and IASB are working to develop converged standards on the following topics: business combinations, consolidations, revenue recognition, and postretirement benefits.

Since beginning their efforts in 2002, the FASB and IASB have developed updated international accounting standards called the International Financial Reporting Standards (IFRS). In 2005, the European Union mandated that businesses adopt the IRFS. The IRFS are replacing national accounting standards worldwide. In the United States, the GAAP dictates accounting standards and practices. Countries that do significant trade and investment with the United States often supplement their own national accounting practices with GAAP. In 2013 in the United States, the Securities and Exchange Commission (SEC) was still debating whether to replace the GAAP with the IRFS. The accounting industry in the United States would undergo a paradigm shift if or when the SEC allows U.S. businesses to satisfy accounting and reporting requirements through IFRS practices and reports.

Training & Education

The issue of training and education is slowing the United States' adoption of IFRS. For example, the majority of financial auditors in the United Sates do not currently have sufficient IFRS technical experience to audit companies reporting in IFRS. When the standards switch occurs, the certified public accountant (CPA) examination will have to be revised to include testing of items based on IFRS. Colleges and universities will need to train their professors and revise their curricula to begin to teach IFRS. Ultimately, when the United States fully adopts the IFRS, the country will have to transition with patience and significant aid to private industry. When the SEC mandates IFRS for U.S. registrants, the SEC will likely institute a multiyear period during which businesses and universities could educate their personnel about IFRS, integrate IFRS into the curriculum and licensing exams, and update their existing accounting systems (Gupta & Linthicum, 2007).

Policy Regimes

Ultimately, the issues associated with the United States' adoption of international accounting standards relate to larger issues of independence and governance. The United States must decide to what degree the nation will exchange national economic governance for global economic governance. The global economy is managed and coordinated by international organizations or policy regimes. According to Preston (1996), policy regimes refer to the "arrangements and understandings that facilitate international harmonization and coordination of economic, environmental, and political" affairs. As Preston writes, policy regimes tend to be cooperative, mutually beneficial alliances. There are four main types of international policy regimes:

- Global and comprehensive regimes refer to regimes that can "encompass the entire globe and any sphere of international activity."
- "Regional and associative regimes refer to agreements and understandings of less than global scope and with varying levels of comprehensiveness within their geographic limits."
- "Functional economic regimes refer to arrangements that might be global in geographic impact but with explicitly limited functional scope."
- "Environmental regimes refer to agreements involving natural resources" and the natural environment.

Major international policy regimes that manage and control the global economy include the United Nations, International Monetary Fund, World Trade Organization, the World Bank, and the Organisation for Economic Co-operation and Development. Regional policy regimes, such as NAFTA and the European Union, also have great control and influence over the global economy. Policy regimes are characterized by their scope, purpose, organizational form, decision and allocation modes, and strength.

- Scope refers to the "sphere of international economic or business activity covered by the regime."
- Purpose refers to the specific objectives intended.
- Organizational form refers to the institutional structure and membership.
- Decision and allocation modes refer to the role of voting or other group decision-making processes.
- Strength refers to the "extent to which members conform to the norms and guidelines of the regime" (Preston, 1996).

The United States will continue to negotiate its relationship to international accounting standards, policy regimes, and international governance as part of the nation's involvement in international economic activity and economic globalization.

CONCLUSION

In the final analysis, international accounting is a tool that allows for financial transactions, decision-making, and participation in global markets. International accounting standards reflect the cultures, philosophies, goals, and objectives of their users. In today's global economy, international accounting is becoming increasingly harmonized to accommodate and facilitate international financial activity.

TERMS & CONCEPTS

Accounting systems: An overall approach to accounting concepts, reporting practices, and principles.

Assets: Resources controlled by the entity as a result of past events and from which future economic benefits are expected to flow to the entity ("Framework," 2008, p. 1–2).

Convergence: Standardization of national accounting standards.

Disclosures: The financial instruments used to evaluate a business entity's financial position and performance.

Fair value: The amount for which an asset could be exchanged or a liability settled.

Harmonization: The reduction of difference in accounting differences among countries.

Equity: The residual interest in the assets of the entity after deducting all of its liabilities ("Framework," 2008, p. 1–2).

Expenses: Decreases in economic benefits during the accounting period in the form of outflows or depletions of assets or liabilities that result in decreases in equity ("Framework," 2008, p. 1–2).

Income: The increases in economic benefits during the accounting period in the form of inflows or enhancements of assets of decreases of liabilities that result in increases in equity ("Framework," 2008, p. 1–2).

International accounting: Accounting practices that cross national boundaries or are conducted in a location other than the firm's home country.

International Accounting Standards Board: The international organization responsible for setting international standards for accounting and reporting practices.

Liabilities: Present obligations of the entity arising from past events, the settlement of which is expected to result in an outflow from the entity of resources embodying economic benefits ("Framework," 2008, p. 1–2).

Policy regimes: The arrangements and understandings that facilitate international harmonization and coordination of economic, environmental, and political affairs (Preston, 1996).

BIBLIOGRAPHY

Barlev, B., & Haddad, J. (2007). Harmonization, comparability, and fair value accounting. *Journal of Accounting, Auditing & Finance, 22,* 493–509.

Beresford, D., Herz, R., Tweedie, D., & Heffes, E. (2006). The explosion of accounting standards. *Financial Executive, 22,* 16.

Chen, L., & Sami, H. (2013). The impact of firm characteristics on trading volume reaction to the earnings reconciliation from IFRS to U.S. GAAP. *Contemporary Accounting Research, 30,* 697–718.

Consolacion, F. (2007). The move towards convergence of accounting standards worldwide. *The Journal of the American Academy of Cambridge, 12,* 6.

Framework for the Preparation and Presentation of Financial Statements. (2008). Technical Summary.

Gupta, P., Linthicum, C., & Noland, T. (2007). The road to IFRS. *Strategic Finance, 88,* 29–33

Harris, P., Arnold, L., Kinkela, K., & Stahlin, W. (2013). A case study of the cash flow statement: US GAAP conversion to IFRS. *Global Conference on Business & Finance Proceedings, 8,* 8–13.

Herrmann, D., & Hague, I. (2006). Convergence: In search of the best. *Journal of Accountancy, 201,* 69–73.

Marrero, J., & Brinker Jr., T. (2007). Are accounting standards uniform? Recognizing cultural differences underlying global accounting standards. *Journal of Financial Service Professionals, 61,* 16–18.

Mueller, G. (1965). Whys and hows of international accounting. *Accounting Review, 40,* 386–394.

Prather-Kinsey, J. (2004). An analysis of international accounting research in U.S.—and non-U.S.-based academic accounting journals. *Journal of International Accounting Research, 3,* 63–81.

Preston, L. (1996). Global economy/global environment: Relationships and regimes. *EarthWorks.*

Speidell, L., & Bavishi, V. (1992). GAAP arbitrage: Valuation opportunities in international accounting standards. *Financial Analysts Journal, 48,* 58–66.

Standish, P. (2003). Evaluating national capacity for direct participation in international accounting harmonization: France as a test case. *Abacus, 39,* 186–210.

Wells, S., Thompson, J., & Phelps, R. (1995). Accounting differences: U.S. enterprises and international competition for capital. *Accounting Horizons, 9,* 29–39.

SUGGESTED READING

Cummings, J., & Chetkovich, M. (1978). World accounting enters a new era. *Journal of Accountancy, 145,* 52–61.

FASB and ASBJ discuss global convergence. (2007). *Strategic Finance, 89,* 19.

Fleming, P. (1991). The growing importance of international accounting standards. *Journal of Accountancy, 172,* 100–106.

Essay by Simone I. Flynn, Ph.D.

GOLD STANDARD

This article focuses on the gold standard. It provides a description and analysis of the pre-World War I gold standard and the post-World War I gold exchange standard. A historical overview of the United States' involvement in the international gold standard will be explored. The United States' current flat monetary system is discussed. The differences between fiat currency and gold currency are addressed. The relationship between the gold standard and exchange rate regimes is also described.

OVERVIEW

Currency, which refers to a medium that can be exchanged for goods and services, facilitates economic activities such as trade, accumulation of wealth, and purchase of goods and services. Two types of currencies predominated throughout the nineteenth and twentieth century: Fiat currencies and gold currencies.

- Fiat currency refers to a currency that serves as legal tender but is not redeemable for a specific commodity.
- Gold currency refers to a currency that is redeemable for a specific amount of gold.

Currencies linked to the price of gold characterized the global currency system throughout much of the nineteenth and twentieth centuries. The gold standard, which is no longer in use, was a complete, global currency system in which national currencies were redeemable for their value in gold. The gold standard emerged in England in 1821. England was the first country to formally adopt a gold standard as the foundation of their national currency. Germany adopted the gold standard in 1871. In the United States, the gold standard, which was used off and on throughout the nineteenth century, was not formally adopted until 1900 with the passage of the Gold Standard Act.

Metallic Currency Standards

The gold standard is a metallic currency standard. In a metallic currency standard, governments establish the value of their national currency in relation to the weight of a metal such as gold or silver. Citizens and nations do not always agree about which metal should be used as a metallic currency standard. In the United States, throughout the nineteenth century, stakeholders debated about the proper place of gold and silver as the economy's currency standard. Governments using the gold standard, or any metallic currency standard, constantly monitored and controlled the weight of metal used in the currency to ensure that the currency was not worth more as melted down bullion than as money in circulation. In the United States, throughout much of the nineteenth century, Congress defined the gold dollar as 24.74 grains of pure gold.

The following conditions are necessary for a metallic standard to operate effectively (Timberlake, 2007):

- The supply of common money that banks and individuals generate must be related to the quantity of monetary gold in government accounts.
- Market prices must be sensitive to changes in the quantity of money in circulation
- Gold must be allowed to flow freely throughout the economy.

There are three different types of gold standards associated with different goals, objectives, and periods in history:

- The traditional or fixed global gold standard, used from the early nineteenth century to 1914, was based on the premise that currency was always redeemable for its equivalent value in gold;
- The gold-bullion standard, used in Great Britain from 1925 to 1931, operated with a set quantity of gold in circulation;
- The gold-exchange standard, used from 1934-1971, operated under a scheme in which national currencies are convertible into the currency of a country tied to the gold standard.

The following section provides a description and analysis of the pre-World War I gold standard and the post-World War I gold-exchange standard. This section serves as a foundation for later discussion on the

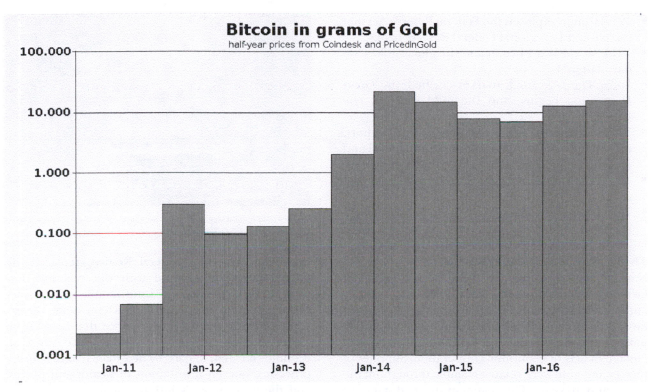

Bitcoin has many similarities to the gold standard. This graph shows Bitcoin in grams of Gold, from July 1, 2010 to July 1, 2016. (Courtesy of Sandegud via Wikimedia Commons)

connection between the gold standard and exchange rate regimes.

APPLICATIONS

The United States and the Gold Standard

The history of the U.S. economy is full of economic expansion and economic contraction. Following the American Revolution, the individual economies of the states were faltering, paper money had little value, and there was conflict between borrowers and lenders. The original thirteen states came together to draft the U.S. Constitution, in part, to stabilize and strengthen the U.S. economy. The U.S. Constitution established a bimetallic monetary standard for the United States. The U.S. Constitution gives the federal government the power to coin money, regulate the value, and fix the standards of weights and measures. The U.S. Constitution prohibits states from coining money, making bills of credit, or making anything but gold and silver coin legal for the payment of debts. The following timeline illustrates the evolution of the gold standard in the United States.

- 1792: Congress legalized gold and silver dollar coins.
- 1834: Congress changed the amount of gold in a gold dollar coin.
- 1853: Congress reduced the weight of gold and silver coins so that the coins would be worth more as money than bullion.
- 1862: Congress revoked the operational gold standard.
- 1863: Congress passed the National Currency Act that created a national banking system and the National Banking Act.
- 1873: Congress temporarily omitted the silver dollar from the list of authorized coins to be minted by the U.S. Mint.
- 1899: Congress passed the Gold Standard Act that established the gold dollar as the standard unit of value over silver.

- 1913: Congress passed the Federal Reserve Act that established 12 regional Federal Reserve banks.
- 1914: World War I began and the global gold standard faltered.
- 1929: The U.S. stock market crashed, the Great Depression begins, and the gold standard collapsed.
- 1933: President Roosevelt made gold export, without government license or permit, illegal and outlawed significant private gold ownership.
- 1945: The Bretton Woods currency system, known as the gold-exchange standard, was established.
- 1971: President Nixon ended the gold-exchange standard.

Under a gold bullion standard, paper notes are convertible at a preset, fixed rate with gold bullion. (Courtesy of Agnico-Eagle via Wikimedia Commons)

The Gold Standard During WWI

Nations embraced the gold standard as a means of facilitating capital mobility, trade, low inflation levels, and economic stability. The gold standard fell out of favor during World War I due to the hostility between nations and the unwillingness of multiple nations to engage in acts of economic cooperation. Supplies of money and gold were relatively stable throughout the gold standard years. The system of the gold standard gave national governments little freedom to develop monetary policy and prevented national treasuries from quickly increasing the amounts of money circulating in the economy. For example, the gold standard limited the U.S. Federal Reserve's ability to increase the money supply. As a result, national governments, under the gold standard, were limited in their ability to respond to changing economic and social situations in a country through the use of exchange rate policies. Monetary shocks and recessions were common under the gold standard. The issue of privatization of the economy was also an issue under the gold standard. Individuals could potentially influence the economy by purchasing significant amounts of gold. The gold standard established and controlled the economic relationship between the government and the people, limited the government's control in the economy by limiting the government's ability to make new monetary policy, and was considered a self-regulating entity of the economy.

The Gold Standard Following WWI

Following World War I, the gold standard faltered and collapsed. The U.S. Federal Reserve gradually abandoned the gold standard from World War I through the 1920s. The U.S. Federal Reserve replaced the operational gold standard with the real bill doctrine and the freedom to issue money as necessary (Timberlake, 2007). The Great Depression, the severe economic recession in America that lasted from 1930–1934, was caused by instability of the American economy created, in part, by new mass manufacturing processes, uneven distribution of wealth and profits, and the government's investment in new industries rather than agriculture. The Depression ended when President Franklin D. Roosevelt took office in 1933. Roosevelt's New Deal Campaign outlawed gold coins, set farm quotas, and established government work programs to generate confidence and money into the U.S. economy. In the 1930s, following the Great Depression, the U.S. government began a program and approach of mixed fiscal and monetary policies in an effort to produce sustained economic growth and stable prices (for goods, services, and natural resources).

The Gold-Exchange Standard Following WWII

Following World War II, the United States and 44 other nations came together at the Bretton Woods summit to address the problem of international economic instability. The Bretton Woods summit produced a system for international trade and financial activity. The International Monetary Fund (IMF) was established to oversee international rules and regulations governing international exchanges and the newly established international monetary system. The International Monetary Fund, founded in 1945, is an international organization of 185 member countries established to accomplish the following goals and objectives: Promote international monetary cooperation, exchange stability, and orderly exchange arrangements; foster economic growth and high levels of employment; and provide temporary financial assistance to countries in order to help ease balance of payments adjustment.

The Bretton Woods monetary system, put into practice in 1946, made the dollar into the world's currency. The Bretton Woods monetary system was called the gold exchange standard. The gold-exchange standard refers to the system in which governments could change their currencies into gold via the U.S. dollar. Under the Bretton Woods system, the United States pledged to exchange all dollars held by foreign countries into gold at the IMF-established exchange rate. The United States could function as the cornerstone of the new global gold exchange standard as the United States had most of the world's gold supply after WWI (75 percent of the world's monetary gold). The Bretton Woods monetary system was considered a success. All International Monetary Fund member nations quickly worked to define the value of their own national currencies in relation to the U.S. dollar.

Twentieth-Century Fiscal Policy

In the twentieth century, the U.S. government, which uses the tools of fiscal policy and monetary policy to achieve its economic and social goals, favored a limited or managed gold standard system. Fiscal policy refers to expenditures by federal, state, and local governments and to the taxes levied to support and fund the federal budget, aid the federal government's social policies, and promote overall economic growth and stability. Monetary policy is a tool used by the federal government to control the supply and availability of money in the economy. A managed gold exchange standard, as seen from 1945–1971, allowed the government to make monetary policy as needed.

The new global monetary system was a fixed or pegged exchange rate system in which currencies were pegged to the U.S. dollar. Under this currency system, $35 U.S. dollars equaled one ounce of gold. The Bretton Woods monetary system lasted until 1971 when the U.S. dollar could not support the fixed exchange rate. By 1971, foreign governments owned more dollars than the United States owned gold. President Nixon ended the practice of trading gold at the fixed price of $35 per ounce. In 1971, national currencies became independent of one another and subject to market forces. Following the end of the gold-exchange standard in 1971, national governments and international governance organizations continued to explore ways to create a global fixed or pegged exchange rate but abandoned those efforts in the mid-1980s.

In the United Sates today, the managed currency system has no ties to a metallic value. Gold, of any amount, is legal to own and trade. Gold is subject to the market forces of supply and demand. With the end of the gold standard in the United States came the increase in the role and power of the U.S. Federal Reserve and central bank to make monetary policy and control the business cycle. Most nations now operate with a form of managed currency or fiat currency system. Fiat currency refers to money that is given value by government fiat rather than by its metallic content. For example, during the Civil War, North and South financed war through the minting and use of fiat money that quickly lost its value after the Civil War.

The Role of Keynes in U.S. Fiscal Policy

U.S. fiscal policy of the twentieth century was strongly influenced by the economic theories of John Keynes, author of *The General Theory of Employment, Interest, and Money* (1936), that economic problems resulted from insufficient demand for goods and services in society-at-large. Economist John Keynes opposed the gold standard and worked to end the gold standard system in the United States. Keynes believed that the government had to be given the power to manage the business cycle. The gold standard did not give the federal government the discretion to make monetary and fiscal policy at will.

According to Keynesian economics, a vicious cycle results when people do not have sufficient income to buy everything the economy can produce, prices fall, and companies lose money and go bankrupt. Without government intervention, discretion, and management, Keynes said, this vicious cycle would bankrupt the economy. Keynes argued that government could stop economic decline, and promote economic growth, by increasing spending and by cutting taxes. Lastly, Keynesian economics accepted a government deficit as a necessary and acceptable consequence of strengthening the economy. Following the end of the gold standard in 1971, the U.S. government followed the Keynesian approach to economics (characterized by numerous tax cuts and increased spending to stimulate the economy) and, as a result, strengthened the U.S. economy and created a huge national deficit (Conte, 2001). Some Republican economic theorists continue to debate the negative consequences of abandoning the gold standard (Lipsky, 2012; Forbes, 2012).

ISSUES

The Gold Standard and Exchange Rate Regimes

The economy post-gold standard is regulated with exchange rates. The gold standard, which was in effect worldwide until 1971, was an example of a global fixed exchange rate. Following the collapse of the gold standard in 1971, the majority of global exchange rates are floating. National exchange rates are referred to as exchange rate regimes. Exchange rate regimes, also called currency institutional regime, refer to specific institutional structures designed to produce specific exchange rate outcomes. The main exchange rate regimes, including floating, fixed, and pegged, are characterized by different levels of control and produce different results. Exchange rate regimes are closely connected to international economic policy. The field of international economic policy debates the merits of different exchange rate regimes and international financial architecture. The field of international economic policy is working to identify viable international exchange rate regimes for a wide range of markets. The increase in global capital flows between the 1970s and 1990s has increased international trade, portfolio diversification, and risk-sharing. Countries invested in international trade are increasingly faced with the decision of whether or not to give up their nation's monetary-policy autonomy.

Types of Exchange Rate Regimes

The main exchange rate regimes, including floating, managed, and pegged, vary in their objectives and implementation (Tavlas, 2003):

- Floating exchange rate regimes have no commitment to a specific exchange-rate target. In floating exchange rate regimes, the exchange rate is determined by market supply and demand rather than macroeconomic policy. The U.S. dollar and the Euro tend to have floating exchange rates.

- Managed exchange rate regimes have no constant exchange rate target. Instead, policymakers tweak interest rates to raise or lower the exchange rate as needed. Managed exchange rate regime refers to scenarios in which the central bank intervenes in the currency market to achieve a variable currency target. Policymakers make these adjustments on a daily, weekly, or monthly basis to counteract misalignments in the economy. Misalignments refer to a sustained departure of the exchange rate from what policymakers perceive to be its equilibrium value.

- Pegged exchange rate regimes include a set exchange rate target. Policymakers use monetary policy to maintain the established exchange rate target. Examples of pegged exchange rate regimes include soft peg, adjustable peg, and crawling peg. Adjustable peg regimes tend to include infrequent large adjustments in response to perceived differences between the target exchange rate and the equilibrium rate. Crawling peg regimes operate with a target exchange rate zone rather than a single exchange rate target and tend to include frequent small adjustments to the exchange rate.

Strengths and Weaknesses of the Regimes

These three competing exchange rate regimes have different strengths and weaknesses (De Vita & Kyaw, 2011). Emerging market economies and long established market economies will choose their exchange rate regime based on various factors such as the different economic needs of citizens and government and established economic infrastructure (Russell, 2012). Both freely floating exchange rate regimes and managed floating exchange rate regimes experience depreciations. Depreciations refer to a loss in currency value. Stable fixed exchange rate regimes experience devaluations and revaluations. Devaluation refers to a loss of value forced by market or a purposeful policy action. Revaluation refers to increase of international value. All exchange rate regimes may experience currency crisis. Currency crisis refers to a rupture of fixed exchange rates with an unwilling devaluation or even the end of that regime in favor of a floating exchange rate (Piana, 2001). Ultimately, the gold standard united national currencies and stabilized national currencies but also slowed growth.

The end of the gold standard, and its global fixed exchange rate regime, has created opportunity for massive global economic growth.

CONCLUSION

The gold standard, which was in use as a global currency system until 1971, was a global currency system in which national currencies were redeemable for their value in gold. The gold standard was embraced as a means to prevent inflation and limit government's power to enact monetary policy at will. The gold standard structured currency relations for two hundred years. The collapse of the gold standard in 1971 produced economic opportunity. Strong capital flows, trade, and growth characterize the new post-gold standard global economy.

TERMS & CONCEPTS

Bretton Woods: The International meeting held in Bretton Woods, New Hampshire that established a fixed exchange rate backed by gold for all major currencies and established the International Monetary Fund.

Business cycle: A type of fluctuation found in the aggregate economic activity of nations that organize their work mainly in business enterprises.

Deficit: The amount of money which a government, company, or individual spends which exceeds its income.

Depression: A sustained economic recession.

Economic contraction: The downward phase of the business cycle.

Economic expansion: The upward phase of the business cycle.

Exchange rate regimes: Specific institutional structures designed to produce specific exchange rate outcomes.

Federal government: A form of government in which a group of states recognizes the sovereignty and leadership of a central authority while retaining certain powers of government.

Fiat currency: Currencies that serve as legal tender but are not redeemable for a specific commodity.

Fiscal policy: The expenditures by federal, state, and local governments and the taxes levied to finance these expenditures.

Gold currency: A currency that is redeemable for a specific amount of gold.

Inflation: The rate at which the general level of prices for goods and services is rising, and, subsequently, purchasing power is falling.

Monetary policy: A tool used by the federal government to control the supply and availability of money in the economy.

BIBLIOGRAPHY

Bohanon, C., Lynch, G., & Van Cott, T. (1985). A supply and demand exposition of the operation of a gold standard in a closed economy. *Journal of Economic Education, 16*, 16–26.

Abrams, B. (2007). Do fixed exchange rates fetter monetary policy? A credit view. *Eastern Economic Journal, 33*, 193–206.

Crabbe, L. (1989, June). The international gold standard and U.S. monetary policy from World War I to the New Deal. *The Federal Reserve Bulletin.* Retrieved October 16, 2007,

Conte, C. & Karr, A. (2001, February). An outline of the U.S. economy.

De Vita, G., & Kyaw, K. (2011). Does the choice of exchange rate regime affect the economic growth of developing countries? *Journal of Developing Areas, 45*, 135–153.

Forbes, S. (2012). Gold standard coming. *Forbes, 190*, 13–14.

Knafo, S. (2006). The gold standard and the origins of the modern international monetary system. *Review of International Political Economy, 13*, 78–102.

Lipsky, S. (2012, August 30). The gold standard goes mainstream. *Wall Street Journal - Eastern Edition.* p. A15.

Mitchell, D. (2000). Dismantling the cross of gold: Economic crises and U.S. monetary policy. *North American Journal of Economics Finance, 11*, 77.

Piana, V. (2001). Exchange rate. *The Economics Web Institute.*

Russell, J. (2012). Herding and the shifting determinants of exchange rate regime choice. *Applied Economics, 44,* 4187–4197.

Tavlas, G. (2003). The economics of exchange-rate regimes: A review essay. *World Economy, 26,* 1215.

Timberlake Jr., R. (2007). Gold standards and the real bills doctrine in U.S. monetary policy. *Independent Review, 11,* 325–354. R

SUGGESTED READING

Barro, R. (1979). Money and the price level under the gold standard. *Economic Journal, 89,* 13–33.

Clark, T. (1984). Violations of the gold points, 1890-1908. *Journal of Political Economy, 92,* 791.

Dowd, K. (1991). Financial instability in a 'directly convertible' gold standard. *Southern Economic Journal, 57,* 719.

Essay by Simone I. Flynn, Ph.D.

GOVERNMENTAL ACCOUNTING

Government entities use GASB (Government Accounting Standards Board) accounting standards for creation of their financial statements; for-profit businesses use FASB (Financial Accounting Standards Boards) standards. There are numerous reasons why governments need their own set of standards for financial reporting. This essay will discuss the main differences between government and for-profit business with regard to financial reporting and the need for differing standards. The differences include: Purpose, revenue generation, stakeholders, budgetary obligations and longevity. Public accountability is at the cornerstone of governmental reporting and as such has a strong influence on GASB standards (current and future). The GASB is under pressure on several fronts as it enters its third decade as an independent agency. Funding options for the GASB are being scrutinized, while opponents of the GASB question the need for the board at all. In particular, issues such as GASB recommendations on OPEB (Other Post & Employment Benefits), SEA (Service Efforts and Accomplishments), and the increasing involvement of the SEC (Securities and Exchange Commission) are topics that are being debated widely as the mission and role of the GASB is evaluated.

According to Marlowe (2007), "the GASB was founded in 1984 to bring cohesion to what was then a patchwork quilt of governmental accounting practices. Critics and advocates alike agree it has achieved that objective and, in the process, has improved the quality, transparency, and comparability of government financial information".

The GASB's mission is to be an independent standard-setting board for state and local governments and their financial statement users. While certain aspects of state sovereign power have been transferred to the federal Government, all other powers are retained by the states. The establishment of accounting principles is one such power–the standards were created by states and are a power retained by states.

The 2012 Census of Governments reported 90,056 local governments in the United States (U.S. Census Bureau, 2013). Expenditures by state and local governments are close to 20 percent of the total GDP (gross domestic product) of the United States. This percentage represents a significant portion of the American economy that is translated into vital services to the public, including education, public safety, transportation, social, and environmental and housing services (Government Accounting Standards Board, 2006).

According to the GASB (2006), "Systematic governmental financial reporting in the United States traces its beginnings to the last decade of the nineteenth century and early part of the twentieth century. At that time, the growth in the number and size of cities, coupled with corruption in municipalities, led to a demand for financial accountability. [There was a concern] that the then 'commercial accounting' was not entirely adequate for governments The lack of a profit motive is one important factor that affects financial reporting for governments; there is no need for governments to report on profit and loss" (p. 29).

The U.S. Treasury building in Washington, DC. The Washington Monument is in the background. (Courtesy of MeanieHyaena via Wikimedia Commons)

stakeholders to assess how well the resources, which their tax dollars are paying for, are being used.

Governments, usually, have greater longevity than businesses. Government entities operate in a noncompetitive environment and therefore are at less of a threat of liquidation or of going "out of business." Governments are put in place to deliver services over the long term with a consistent level of service and assurance that they will be available in the future.

How Do Existing Accounting and Financial Reporting Standards Reflect the Different Needs of Stakeholders?

Investors and creditors are stakeholders in all standard-setting organizations, whether business or governmental. The GASB has two other important information users of their financial reports: citizens (taxpayers) and their elected representatives who act on behalf of taxpayers. There are several key areas where governmental reporting is different from that of for-profit businesses. These areas are outlined below.

- Government revenue is from taxes or grants. A business sells goods or services to willing buyers.
- Government assets provide services (such as road construction). Business assets contribute to cash flow.
- The government uses fund accounting and budgetary reporting to meet public accountability needs.
- Accountability principals, rather than equity control, are used.
- Government treatment of pensions and other post-employment benefits is handled differently than in for-profits.

"Cities financed their operations through taxes, miscellaneous revenue, and borrowing for the purpose of raising sufficient amounts to meet total anticipated expenditures, including capital items. Early standard setters believed that financial reporting should show a government's fund surplus (or balance) that represents the resources currently available for expenditure. Many advocated financial reporting using funds, which would allow readers to assess whether an executive officer of a city had properly discharged his or her duties in accordance with legal requirements" (Government Accounting Standards Board, 2006, p. 29).

Why Are Separate Accounting and Financial Reporting Standards Essential for Governments?

The needs of those using government financial reports are different than those using for-profit financial statements. Because governments receive revenue through involuntary exchange (collection of taxes), governments must show accountability for the use of resources paid for by tax dollars. In a for-profit business, revenue is gained through voluntary exchange between willing buyers and sellers. The role of government financial reporting is to enable

The GASB has issued a number of new standards since it was formed in 1984. According to GASB literature, there are still "transactions" that do not have any GASB standards, which leaves gaps for stakeholders. The GASB is also aware of the changing environment in governmental accounting, and the increasing information needs of users and is working on meeting those needs for the future.

This article expands upon the differences between government and for-profit accounting standards to give the reader a better insight about the role and necessity of GASB standards.

Questions about whether GASB has outlasted its purpose are a current topic of debate, and there are supporters and opponents on both sides of the debate. Some of the issues and pressures that are being exerted on GASB by constituents, state governments, and outsiders are also discussed.

APPLICATIONS

Accounting Standards: Government versus Business

GASB published a white paper ("Why Governmental Accounting and Financial Reporting is – and should Be – Different," 2006) that provides an overview of the differences between governmental and business accounting principles. It is written in language that is clear and understandable. There is no question that the audience for governmental financial reports is different from that of business financial information. This article will report on the role GASB plays in helping state and local governments account for and report on their resources. Opposing views of the value of GASB standards will also be addressed.

Public Accountability

Public accountability is the guiding principal for all government entities as they provide their financial reports. Stakeholders should have easy access to information that shows them how public resources are acquired and used. Taxpayers should also know if current resources are sufficient to meet current needs (or if the burden will be shifted to future taxpayers). Taxpayers also want to know if services have improved from the previous year or deteriorated – and why.

Some questions that governments need to be able to answer to meet public accountability guidelines include the following (Government Accounting Standards Board, 2006):

- How and to what extent are resources devoted to specific services?
- What is the cost of providing those services?

- Is there compliance with spending authorities?
- Does the government have the ability to raise taxes to meet resource needs?
- Governments operate in noncompetitive environments and, as such, act as stewards of public resources. Governmental accounting does take into consideration nonfinancial reporting measures while businesses do not typically report nonfinancial information (for example, trade secrets), which could jeopardize competitiveness.

The following table shows a side-by-side comparison of the different needs of government versus business in accounting principles (Government Accounting Standards Board, 2006).

Government Business

1. Purpose – enhances and maintains wellbeing of citizens. 1. Purpose – in crease net earnings and income per share, wealth creation. 2. Revenue – involuntary through taxation. 2. Revenue – exchange transaction between buyer and seller. 3. Stakeholders obligation – provides proof of accomplishment of objectives and cost of service. 3. Stakeholders – in crease shareholder equity. 4. Budget – express public policy priorities – government management is accountable. 4. Budget – is controlled by management and considered proprietary. 5. Longevity – ongoing taxes and consistent need for services to in sure that entity will persist over time. 5. Longevity – business operates on principal of "going concern." Business can fail or merge.

Comprehensive Implementation Guides

The GASB is acutely aware of the changing nature and added complexity associated with governmental accounting standards. GASB has publicly stated that not all transactions have documented standards, and the board has updated its standards. To support constituents, GASB has become more responsive in issuing implementation guides for standards that it issues or alters. In the past, GASB issued individual implementation guides that covered only a specific standard. These guides were generally issued only after the standard had been adopted; they were essentially static documents (Shoulders & Freeman, 2007).

GASB publishes implementation guides that are meant to be a type of QA guide that reflects GASB staff's understanding of board intent. The value of the implementation guides is that they contain an expanded breadth of coverage and can be (and are) updated. The guides are drafted before the standard's release date and can be quickly edited and released. Comprehensive Implementation Guidelines are released periodically and incorporate related standards that have been updated and edited.

These implementation guides are becoming increasingly important for certified public accountants who are applying standards when doing audits for state and local governments. Because the content is updated far more frequently than past GASB guides, preparers now have the burden of staying current with the latest guidelines. The responsiveness of GASB to fast-changing accounting practices has been welcomed by users of the guides.

Cost of Compliance for GASB

New GASB standards are adding to the cost and complexity for states and localities to apply Generally Accepted Accounting Principles (GAAP). Local governments are obliged to follow standards and provide stakeholders the information that they need, but managers are also obliged to provide information that is cost-effective and consistent with local norms and standards (Marlowe, 2007).

According to Marlowe (2007), Many local governments do use various financial reporting principles collectively known as "non-GAAP" reporting. Non-GAAP reporting can take many forms, from simple cash-basis accounting where transactions are recognized when they occur (most people run their checkbooks this way), to more elaborate schemes that differ from GASB standards only on a single issue, like the previously mentioned infrastructure reporting. A local government's latitude on this issue is determined by applicable state statutes: fifteen states require full compliance with GASB standards, eleven states do not regulate local financial reporting at all, and the rest fall somewhere in between (p. 18).

States and municipalities have mixed feelings about the effects of non-GAAP reporting. It is widely felt that credit-rating agencies need GAAP-compliant reporting to compare government financials against one another. Another risk is that the bond market could demand higher borrowing costs to governments that are not GAAP compliant. "One study found that, all things equal, localities in states that require GAAP compliant local government financial statements pay about 20 basis points (0.20 percent) less to issue the exact same bonds as local governments in states that do not require GAAP. On a simple $25 million bond issue paid off over 25 years, that adds up to more than $1 million in interest savings over the life of the bonds" (Marlowe, 2007). Put in these terms, the findings suggest that GAAP reporting could save some governments lots of money.

GASB's role in setting governmental standards is growing as the pace of change in accounting practices quickens. GASB's issuance of new accounting standards (focusing on user-support implementation guidelines and increased market responsiveness) are all internally viewed as positive steps within the GASB. Outside the GASB, however, critics cite instances of the board overstepping its intended mandate, the added cost to municipalities of GAAP compliance, and unnecessary duplication of effort with some FASB standards.

ISSUES

The Future of GASB

Years after its inception, GASB faced significant public pressure that questioned if the board should continue to operate. The most vocal critic of the GASB was the Government Finance Officers Association (GFOA). The GFOA weighed in on several GASB policy initiatives to raise public awareness of governmental accounting issues. In particular the GFOA questioned the GASB project known as SEA (Service Efforts and Accomplishments). The state of Texas threatened not to comply with GASB policies regarding Other Post and Employment Benefits (OPEB) and GAAP accounting compliance. The SEC wanted to play a larger role in GASB policy-setting and raised questions about the independence of GASB as a policy-setting board. Nevertheless, GASB continued to issue new standards, including performance reporting. In 2013 a proposed economic-conditions reporting requirement, which would project cash flow over five years, sparked a counterproposal by GASB's parent, the Financial Accounting Foundation (FAF), which would rein in GASB's rule-setting process.

Service Efforts and Accomplishments (SEA)

The Service Efforts and Accomplishments (SEA) project is a voluntary proposal by GASB to help governments report on their managerial and organizational performance. GASB has long supported the need to evaluate the efficiency and economy of operations, and it considers performance reporting an important component of assessing how well governments manage and distribute public resources. While some constituents of GASB supported the inclusion of performance reporting on the GASB agenda, others were vehemently opposed.

In January, 2007, the GFOA reported that its executive board had strongly reaffirmed its long-standing position that performance measurement is beyond the scope of accounting and financial reporting, and that GASB involvement will impede rather than promote effective performance measurement in the public sector. GFOA called for the abolition of GASB, stating that GASB "is attempting more and more to find an accounting solution for every financial problem," even suggesting that the FASB should replace the GASB as the standards setter for state and local governments (Loyd &s Crawford, 2007, p. 2).

In February, 2007, GASB constituents voiced their opposition to having the GASB take any official action on the SEA reporting project. Opponents included the National Governor's Association, the Nation Conference of State Legislators, the U.S. Conference of Mayors, and the National League of Cities. Public expressions of dissatisfaction with GASB and its agenda items continued to plague the board.

According to Ackerman (2007), GFOA's outgoing president, Thomas J. Glaser, "ratcheted up GFOA's arguments that GASB has strayed well beyond its original mandate Some other vehicle would better meet the genuine needs of state and local government for accounting standards," he said. "On its face, we do not need one set of accounting standards for derivatives and pollution remediation in the private sector and another set of standards for state and local governments" (cited in Ackerman, 2007, p. 4).

Other Post-Employment Benefits (OPEB)

Post-employment benefits are defined as nonpension benefits such as healthcare benefits for retirees and their families and dental, life, and term insurance. Most governments "fund OPEB on a pay-as-you-go basis, paying an amount annually equal to the benefits distributed or claimed that year. They do not

prefund obligations as is the case with pension obligations" (Civic Federation, 2006, p. 3).

In 2004, GASB issued two guidelines – Statements 43 and 45 – that would mandate the detailed financial reporting of public-employee non-pension information. Previous to these statements, detailed financial information about employee nonpension benefits was not required. Statements 43 and 45 were phased in between 2005 and 2008.

It is important to differentiate between the types of retiree benefits. Pensions are often guaranteed by states, but OPEBs are actually considered to be part of an employee's compensation package earned in a given year. This compensation, however, would not be paid until after employment had ended, but the funding of current retirees benefits is part of the cost of providing public services today.

Governments typically report the cash outlay (cost) of what they pay in a given year, rather than the actual cost that is being earned by a current employee. The difference between the cash outlay and actual cost of benefits is quite significant. Since there were no reporting requirements before Statements 43 and 45, most governments were under-reporting the OPEB earned by employees in that year. GASB realized that this was not providing a complete picture of the full cost of public services to the public and therefore was not meeting accountability standards.

According to Grumet (2007), "Under GASB 45, state and local government entities are required to calculate and report a present-value dollar figure for the total cost of the OPEB obligations promised to employees in the future. They are not, however, required to set aside money to fund those benefits. In essence, GASB 45 would change a government entity's method of accounting for OPEB from 'pay-as-you-go – in which OPEB obligations are not recognized until actually paid to government employees once they retire – to an accrual method in which expenses are measured and recognized when they are promised" (p. 7).

The OPEB standard 45 requires that governments "account for and report the annual cost of OPEB and all outstanding obligations and commitments related to OPEB in the same way that they report pensions" (Civic Federation, 2006, p. 7).

Previously, "OPEB expenses are included [in] a government's general fund expenditures and spelled out in an audit note as the cost is expensed in the current year, reflecting the pay as you go nature of these expenses. Under the new guidelines, OPEB financial information will be produced using actuarial valuations performed in accordance with GASB standards" (Civic Federation, 2006, p. 7).

Overview of guidelines includes actuarial valuations:

- performed every two years for plans that administer OPEB for 200 or more plan members (active or retired).
- performed every three years for plans with fewer than 200 members

Some of the specific types of financial information that must be reported include

- other post-employment benefit assets and liabilities.
- unfunded accrued actuarial liabilities (UAAL). This is the excess of the unfunded actuarial liability over the actuarial value of assets.
- annual required contributions (ARC). This is the normal cost and the portion of the unfunded actuarial accrued liability of the employer for the period being reported.
- expenses, expenditures, and net obligations of the appropriate fund or funds.
- implicit rate subsidies for retirees. In health insurance plans where retirees and current employees are insured together as a group, premiums for retirees are lower than what they would be if retirees were insured separately (Civic Federation, 2006, p. 7).

GASB statements 43 and 45 have added significant overhead to many governments as they adopted these standards.

Other opposition to Statement 45 specifically addressed the role that GASB should play in setting this policy at all. "Some believe stakeholders need this information to decide if and how a jurisdiction should provide these benefits; others agree, but say that debate should be initiated by elected officials and not by accountants" (Marlowe, 2007, p. 18).

CONCLUSION

Questions abound regarding the future of GASB, its role in setting accounting standards, and the necessity of the board at all.

Specific points of SEC involvement that could result in potential influences on the state and local government accounting and reporting processes are

- regulation of the municipal securities market
- selection of FAF trustees

One other significant threat to the continuance of GASB is the lack of ongoing funding. The SEC relies on subsidies from its governing board (FAF). However, if funding needs to be secured from elsewhere, the threat to the board's independence in standard setting could also be jeopardized.

If the future of GASB and its oversight of governmental accounting are in question, the following questions provide a good starting point for future discussion and deliberation.

According to Loyd and Crawford (2007), the logical questions to ask are the following:

- If GASB does not continue as the independent standard setter for state and local government accounting and financial reporting principles, who will take on that responsibility and what effect will it have on government entities?
- Would the FASB be asked to take over the responsibility for local government accounting and financial reporting principles? If so, would FASB adopt existing GASB GAAP or defer to its accounting principles in place for for-profit and not-for-profit organizations?
- Would the SEC be ready to assume the responsibilities of setting government accounting standards or, at minimum, perform oversight of the standards setting process?
- What changes would the SEC make to existing GAAP?

TERMS & CONCEPTS

Accountability: Accountability is a government's responsibility to justify to its citizenry the raising of public revenues and to account for the use of those public resources (Government Accounting Standards Board, 2006).

Financial Accounting Foundation (FAF): The FAF is the oversight body for both the GASB and FASB.

Financial Accounting Standards Board (FASB): Designated by the SEC, the FASB is a nonprofit organization that develops accepted accounting principles (the GAAP) for the public interest.

Government Accounting Standards Board (GASB): The GASB is a private, nongovernmental organization with the mission to improve standards of state and local governmental accounting and financial reporting.

Government Financial Officers Association (GFOA): The GFOA is a professional association of finance officers in the United States and Canada that works to identify and promote sound, professional management practices in government.

Infrastructure: Infrastructure is long-lived capital assets that normally are stationary and can be preserved for a significantly greater number of years than most capital assets (Government Accounting Standards Board, 2006).

Operational accountability: Operational accountability is the responsibility of governments to report how they have met their operating objectives efficiently and effectively, using all resources available for that purpose, and whether they can continue to meet their future objectives (Government Accounting Standards Board, 2006).

Other post-employment benefits (OPEB): OPEBs are nonpension benefits such as health care benefits for retirees and their families and dental, life, and term insurance.

Service efforts accomplishments (SEA): SEAs are that which are reported to provide more complete information about a governmental entity's performance than can be provided by the traditional financial statements (Government Accounting Standards Board, 2006).

BIBLIOGRAPHY

Ackerman, A. (2007). NFMA to review GASB standards in wake of GFOA comments. Bond Buyer, 361(32670), 4.

DePaul, J. (2013). SP: Pensions face bumpy road, GASB changes will add volatility. Investment Management Mandate Pipeline, 7.

Government Accounting Standards Board. (2006; rev. 2013). Why governmental accounting and financial reporting is-and should be-different.

Grumet, L. (2007). The importance of financial transparency. *CPA Journal, 77*(6), 7–8.

Loyd, D., & Crawford, M. (2007). GASB's future as the independent standards setter for state and local governments. Governmental GAAP Update Service, 7(12), 1–5.

Marlowe, J. (2007). Costs of compliance with Generally Accepted 'Accounting Standards. Public Management (00333611), 89(7), 17–20.

Native American Finance Officers Association. (2007). GASB adds project on performance reporting.

Pounder, B. (2013). Post-implementation reviews of accounting standards. *Strategic Finance, 95*(2), 17–18.

Shoulders, C. & Freeman, R. (2007). Closing the gaps in GAAP. *Journal of Accountancy, 203*(6), 62–68.

The Civic Federation. (2006). Other post employment benefits.

United States Census Bureau. (2013). Government Organization Summary Report: 2012.

SUGGESTED READING

Cheney, G. (2007). GASB defines basic elements of gov't financial statements. *Accounting Today, 21*(14), 5.

Loyd, D., & Crawford, M. (2007). GASB issues statement No. 51, accounting and financial reporting for intangible assets. Governmental GAAP Update Service, 7(15), 1–3.

Roybark, H. M., Coffman, E. N., & Previts, G. J. (2012). The first quarter century of the GASB (1984–2009): A perspective on standard setting (part one). Abacus, 48(1), 1–30.

Solnik, C. (2007). CPA board sharpens focus on municipal accounting. Long Island Business News, 54(26), 3B–15B.

Essay by Carolyn Sprague, MLS

GROWTH OF NATIONS IN THE GLOBAL ECONOMY

This article will focus on the growth of nations in the global economy. The article will provide an overview of the two main national growth theories, including the neoclassical growth theory and new growth theory, and the concept of the global economy. The relationship between global governance and the growth of nations will be discussed. The issues related to human capital and technology as engines for growth of nations in the global economy will be introduced.

OVERVIEW

The growth of nations varies among regions, nations, and historical eras. Economic and political changes promote or depress the growth of nations depending on variables such as national leadership, political and economic stability, natural resources, international relations, and infrastructure. The current era of the global economy, a product of economic globalization, is creating strong, though variable, national economic growth and development worldwide (Jones, 2005).

The global economy is characterized by growth of nations, both in populations and in output and consumption per capita; interdependence of nations; and international management efforts. Indicators of global growth and interdependence include the huge increases in communication links, world output, international trade, and international investment since the 1970s. The global economy is built on global interdependence of economic flows linking the economies of the world. The global economy is characterized by economic sensitivity. National economic events in one region often have profound results for other regions and national economies. National economies exist not in isolation but in relationship and tension with other economies worldwide. The global economy includes numerous economic phenomena and financial tools shared between all countries. Examples include the price of gold, the price of oil, and the related worldwide movement of interest rates (Preston, 1996).

According to the World Bank, economic growth of nations refers to the quantitative change or expansion in a country's economy. The economic growth of a nation is measured as the percentage increase in its gross domestic product during one year. Economic growth occurs in two distinct ways. Economic growth of a nation occurs when a nation grows extensively by using more physical, natural, or human resources or intensively by using resources more efficiently or productively. According to the World Bank's approach to economic growth of nations, intensive economic growth of nations requires economic development (Glossary, 2007).

The new global economy is characterized and controlled through global management or governance efforts. International organizations, both public and private, work to establish norms, standards, and requirements for international financial governance. These international organizations—including the United Nations, the World Bank, the G-20, the Financial Stability Forum, the International Organization of Securities Commissions, the Organisation for Economic Co-operation and Development (OECD), and the Basel Committee on Banking Supervision—develop and encourage implementation of standards, principles, best practices, and economic architecture for worldwide use (Preston, 1996).

The following sections provide an overview of the main national growth theories and the global economy. These sections serve as foundation for later discussion of the relationship between global governance and the growth of nations. Issues related to the use of human capital and technology as engines for growth of nations in the global economy will be introduced.

Theories of Economic Growth of Nations

The economic growth of nations has been a topic of study by economists and political scientists since the nineteenth century. Economic growth of nations is considered by economists to be a natural result of market activity. Economists have long been interested in the relationship between income inequality and the economic growth of nations. Growth theories refer to the theories that explain the factors and relationships that promote the economic growth of nations. Economic growth theories incorporate variables representing the effects of production factors, public expenditure, and income distribution. The following factors influence the effect that income distribution has on growth: investment indivisibilities, incentives, credit market imperfections, macroeconomic imperfections, macroeconomic volatility, political economy aspects, and social effects (Alfranca & Galindo, 2003).

There are two main theories of the economic growth of nations: neoclassical growth theory and new growth theory.

- Neoclassical growth theory: Neoclassical growth theory, also referred to as the exogenous growth model, focuses on productivity growth. The neoclassical growth theory was the predominant economic growth theory from the nineteenth century to the mid-twentieth century. Exogenous growth refers to a change or variable that comes from outside the system. Technological progress and enhancement of a nation's human capital are the main factors influencing economic growth. Technology, increased human capital, savings, and capital accumulation are believed to promote technological development, more effective means of production, and economic growth. The neoclassical growth theory prioritizes the same factors and variables as neoclassical economics. The field of neoclassical economics emphasizes the belief that the market system will ensure a fair allocation of resources and income distribution. In addition, the market is believed to regulate demand and supply, allocation of production, and the optimization of social organization. Neoclassical economics, along with the neoclassical growth model, began in the nineteenth century in response to perceived weaknesses in classical economics (Brinkman, 2001).

- New growth theory: New growth theory, also referred to as the endogenous growth theory, began in the 1980s as a response to criticism of the neoclassical growth theory. Endogenous growth refers to a change or variable that comes from inside and is based on the idea that economic growth is created and sustained from within a country rather than through trade or other contact from outside the system. The new growth theory identifies the main endogenous factors leading to sustained growth of output per capita, including research and design, education, and human capital (Park, 2006).

United Nations headquarters in New York City with flags. (Courtesy of the Library of Congress)

These two theories vary in their arguments about what causes economic growth and what role technology plays in economic growth. There are three main criticisms of new growth theories: First, the new growth theory is criticized for a lack of conceptual clarity in its underlying assumptions. Second, the new growth theory is criticized for a lack of empirical relevancy. Third, the new growth theory is criticized for claiming to be a wholly new theory when it's closely tied to growth theories that came before. Economists debate the significance of this last criticism. The new growth theory claims to represent a total break from neoclassical theory but the continued focus on technology (whether exogenous or endogenous technology) and its relationship to economic growth, connects the two main growth theories in significant ways (Brinkman, 2001).

The World Bank headquarters building is located in Washington, D.C. (Courtesy of Library of Congress)

Criticism of the neoclassical growth theory focuses on the long-run productivity limitation created from exclusive focus on the addition of capital to a national economy. According to Mankiw (1995), the "neoclassical model predicts that different countries should have different levels of income per person, depending on the various parameters that determine" income levels (p. 282). The range of income levels among countries shows the magnitude of international differences is actually vast and variable. The neoclassical model also "predicts that each economy converges to its own steady state, which in turn is determined by its saving and population growth rates." Comparisons of the growth rates of rich and poor countries shows that the neoclassical model does not successfully predict the rate of convergence of all countries. Convergence refers to the tendency of poor economies to grow more rapidly than rich economies (Mankiw, 1995, p. 284).

Ultimately, sustained economic growth of a nation, as represented by enhanced productivity and growth, may require structural transformation within the nation. Economic growth, as reported by Brinkman (2001), may require creative destruction of an old system of institutions, modes of production, and relationships.

The Global Economy
The global economy is a product of economic globalization. Global markets are characterized by an increasing mobility in capital, research and design processes, production facilities, customers, and regulators. Global markets—created through socio-economic changes, political revolutions, and new Internet and communication technology—have no national borders. The modern trend of globalization, and resulting shifts from centralized to market economies in much of the world, has created opportunities for increased trade, investment, business partnerships, and access to once closed global markets.

Economic environments around the world are changing due to the forces of globalization. Globalization creates a turbulent global sociopolitical environment characterized by competing political actors, shifting power relations, and politically driven changes in national economies around the world. Business opportunities including international investments and joint ventures in the global economy are increasingly tied to trade pacts among nations, such as the North American Free Trade Agreement (NAFTA) among the United States, Canada, and Mexico; the Mercosur trade pact among Argentina, Uruguay, Brazil, and Paraguay; and the Asia-Pacific Economic Cooperation (APEC) trade zone. In addition, business opportunities are resulting from privatization worldwide. Nations are privatizing many state-owned industries and allowing foreign investors to purchase pieces of them through joint ventures or local operations in order to participate in these projects. Ultimately, the global economy is marked by change, innovation, and growth.

APPLICATIONS

Global Governance & the Growth of Nations
The growth of nations in the global economy is heavily influenced by international governance organizations that develop international policies, which effect business practices, profits, and the distribution of development aid to developing countries. International governance organizations, also called

policy regimes, are one of the main products of economic globalization. The increasing integration and interdependence created by international trade and product flows creates international markets and the need for international oversight and governance.

International governance, including political and economic governance, is one of the most significant trends of economic globalization. The global economy and the global environment are managed and coordinated by international organizations or policy regimes. Policy regimes refer to the arrangements and understandings that facilitate international harmonization and coordination of economic, environmental, and political affairs. Policy regimes tend to be cooperative, mutually beneficial alliances. There are four main types of international policy regimes. Global and comprehensive regimes refer to regimes that can encompass the entire globe and any sphere of international activity (Preston, 1995). Regional and associative regimes refer to agreements and understandings of less than global scope with varying levels of comprehensiveness within their geographic limits. Functional economic regimes refer to "arrangements that might be global in geographic impact but with explicitly limited functional scope. Environmental regimes refer to agreements involving natural resources and the natural environment" (Preston, 1995).

Major international policy regimes that manage and control the global economy and global environment include the United Nations, International Monetary Fund, World Trade Organization, the World Bank, and the Organisation for Economic Co-operation and Development. Regional policy regimes, such as NAFTA and the European Union, also have great control and influence over the global environment and global economy. Environmental regimes depend on compliance by all parties. The environment cannot be managed or tended to by one country and ignored by another. The responsibilities and effects of global environmental management are, by definition, global in nature.

Policy regimes are characterized by their scope, purpose, organizational form, decision and allocation modes, and strength. Scope refers to the sphere of international economic or business activity covered by the regime. Purpose refers to the specific objectives intended. Organizational form refers to the institutional structure and membership. Decision and allocation modes refer to the role of voting or other group decision-making processes and methods of distributing costs and benefits. Strength refers to the extent to which members conform to the norms and guidelines of the regime (Preston, 1996).

The following sections describe the work that two of the main policy regimes, the Organisation for Economic Co-operation and Development and the United Nations, do to promote the growth of nations in the global economy.

The Organisation for Economic Co-operation & Development

The Organisation for Economic Co-operation and Development (OECD), an international organization founded in 1961 including 35 member nations committed to democratic government and the market economy, promotes its *Principles of Corporate Governance* to nations around the world. The OECD principles, developed in 1999 and revised in 2015, serve as the international standard and reference for corporate governance practices. The OECD principles cover six main areas, including ensuring the basis for an effective corporate governance framework; the rights of shareholders; the equitable treatment of shareholders; the role of stakeholders in corporate governance; disclosure and transparency; and the responsibilities of the board.

The Organisation for Economic Co-operation and Development coordinates policy among industrialized countries and makes recommendations to less developed countries. OECD member nations—including Australia, Belgium, Canada, Czech Republic, Denmark, Finland, France, Germany, Greece, Hungary, Iceland, Ireland, Italy, Japan, Korea, Luxembourg, Mexico, the Netherlands, New Zealand, Norway, Poland, Portugal, Slovakia, Spain, Sweden, Switzerland, Turkey, the United Kingdom, and the United States—exchange economic data. The Organisation for Economic Co-operation and Development create unified economic policies to maximize the economic growth of member nations and help less developed nations develop more rapidly.

The Organisation for Economic Co-operation and Development monitors and analyzes the causes underlying differences in growth performance in OECD member nations. The Organisation for Economic Co-operation and Development identifies factors, institutions, and policies in the following categories that could enhance the growth of member nations:

Economic growth and development: The OECD works to reconcile the drive for the growth of nations with the need to achieve wider income.

Economic Growth and Productivity: The OECD regularly monitors the patterns of economic growth in member nations. The OECD assesses the output and productivity growth trends.

Human Capital: The OECD recognizes that human capital plays an important role in the process of economic growth. The OECD reviews policies that encourage investment in human capital.

Investment in and Financing of Learning: The OECD recognizes that learning, which is expensive to implement, is linked to economic progress and social cohesion in the global economy. The need for lifelong learning opportunities raises new and complex resource-allocation issues.

Micropolicies for Growth: The OECD, along with its Committee on Industry and Business Environment (CIBE), aims to identify effective micropolicies for stimulating growth through entrepreneurship and innovation.

Science and Technology Policy: The OECD, along with its Committee for Scientific and Technological Policy, contributes to the policy debates about the relationship between science and technology and sustainable growth.

Statistical Analysis of Science, Technology, and Industry: The OECD creates databases of statistics in the areas of science, technology, and industry. The databases are intended for international comparisons of member nation data.

The United Nations

The United Nations, a global association of governments facilitating cooperation in international law, security, economic development, and social equity founded in 1945, counts 193 nations as members. The United Nations has five regional commissions, in Africa, Asian and the Pacific, Europe, Latin America and the Caribbean, and Western Asia, which promote growth in nations around the world.

Africa: The Economic Commission for Africa (ECA) was established in 1958 to assist African nations to develop self-reliant socioeconomic systems. The ECA designs and implements economic and social policies to alleviate poverty; expands interregional trade and integrates Africa into the world economy; and enhances the capacity of states for growth and development.

Asia and the Pacific: The Economic and Social Commission for Asia and the Pacific (ESCAP) was established in 1947 to provide technical support to member governments for socioeconomic development through direct advisory services, information and training, sharing regional experiences, and intercountry networks.

Europe: The Economic Commission for Europe (ECE) was established in 1947 to promote a policy, financial, and regulatory environment conducive to economic growth, innovative development, and higher competitiveness for member nations.

Latin America and the Caribbean: The Economic Commission for Latin America and the Caribbean was established in 1948 to coordinate policies promoting economic development in Latin America and the Caribbean and to foster regional and international trade.

Western Asia: The Economic and Social Commission for Western Asia was established in 1973 to improve the economic and social situation and integration into the global economy of its member states.

The international governance organizations described above, the Organisation for Economic Co-operation and Development and the United Nations, base their development and economic growth efforts on the principles of the new growth theory (also referred to as endogenous growth theory). International governance organizations, a product of the global economy, promote development and growth in nations through the adoption of principles, tools, technologies, and aid from outside the nation rather than from within the nation (United Nations Regional Commissions, 2006).

ISSUES

Human Capital v. Technology

International governance and aid organizations that give support for economic growth and development in industrialized and developing countries operate based on implicit or explicit theories of growth. Economists debate whether technology or human capital is most responsible for promoting the growth of nations in the global economy. In practice, most international development and governance organizations promote growth of nations through investment in *both* technological support and human capital growth. Human resources or capital refers to the total quantity and quality of human effort available to produce goods and services. Investment in human capital is made by international governance and development organizations through training and education programs. Paradoxically, focus on promoting technological innovation and human capital may greatly enhance the likelihood of economic growth of a nation or may dissipate energy and resources for growth. Nations and their international supporters must decide their approach based on understanding of the variables that affect the growth of nations in the global economy.

CONCLUSION

In the final analysis, economic growth of nations in the global economy may be most important for the influence that growth of nations has on the standard of living and health for worldwide citizens. For example, the World Bank works to promote growth within nations that benefits people rather than simply creates corporate profit and opportunity. According to the World Bank, when economic growth is achieved by using more labor, it does not result in per capita income growth. In contrast, when economic growth is achieved through productive use of all resources, including labor, it results in higher per capita income. Ultimately, the approaches taken to promote economic growth and development profoundly influence the economic growth of nations and the quality of life for their citizens and residents.

TERMS & CONCEPTS

Convergence: The tendency of poor economies to grow more rapidly than rich economies.

Developing countries: Countries characterized by an underdeveloped industrial base, low per capita income, and widespread poverty.

Global economy: A model of economy characterized by growth of nations, both in populations and in output and consumption per capita; interdependence of nations; and international management efforts.

Globalization: A process of economic and cultural integration around the world caused by changes in technology, commerce, and politics.

Global markets: The economic markets of countries and regions open to foreign trade and investment.

Human capital: The utilization of human effort required to produce goods and services.

Markets: Social arrangements that allow buyers and sellers to carry out a voluntary exchange of goods and services.

Nations: Large aggregations of people sharing rules of law and an identity based on common racial, linguistic, historical, or cultural heritage; rarely act unilaterally.

Neoclassical growth theory: A growth model, also referred to as the exogenous growth model, which focuses on productivity growth.

New growth theory: A growth model, also referred to as the endogenous growth theory, which was developed in the 1980s in response to criticism of the neoclassical growth theory.

Organisation for Economic Co-operation and Development (OECD): An international organization founded in 1961 including thirty-five member nations committed to democratic government and the market economy.

Policy regimes: The arrangements and understandings that facilitate international harmonization and coordination of economic, environmental, and political affairs (Preston, 1995).

United Nations: A global association of governments founded in 1945 that facilitates cooperation in international law, security, economic development, and social equity.

World Bank: An international economic development assistance organization that was founded in 1944.

BIBLIOGRAPHY

Alfranca, O., & Galindo, M. (2003). Public expenditure, income distribution, and growth in OECD countries. *International Advances in Economic Research, 9,* 133–139.

Brinkman, R. (2001). The new growth theories: A cultural and social addendum. *The International Journal of Social Economics,* 28, 506–526.

Dougherty, C., & Jorgenson, D. (1996). International comparisons of the sources of economic growth. *American Economic Review, 86,* 25.

Glossary. (2007).

Jones, B., & Olken, B. (2005). Do leaders matter? National leadership and growth since World War II. *Quarterly Journal of Economics, 120,* 835–864.

Mankiw, N. (1995). The growth of nations. *Brookings Papers on Economic Activity, 6,* 25–29.

Park, C. (2006). The theory of economic growth: A "classical" perspective. *Science and Society,* 70, 558–562.

Preston, L. (1996). Global economy/global environment: relationships and regimes. *EarthWorks.*

Skonhoft, A. (1997). Technological diffusion and growth among nations: The two stages of catching up. *Metroeconomica, 48,* 177.

The United Nations Regional Commissions. (2006). The United Nations.

SUGGESTED READING

Hanushek, E., & Kimko, D. (2000). Schooling, labor-force quality, and the growth of nations. *American Economic Review, 90,* 1184–1208.

Nelson, R. (1997). How new is new growth theory? *Challenge, 40,* 29–58.

Rima, I. (2004). Increasing returns, new growth theory, and the classicals. *Journal of Post Keynesian Economics, 27,* 171–184.

Wälde, K. (2005). Endogenous growth cycles. *International Economic Review, 46,* 867–894.

Essay by Simone I. Flynn, Ph.D.

H

HISTORY AND PROCESSES OF THE STOCK MARKET

This article describes the concept of a stock market and outlines its historical development and its role (in a capitalist economy) in raising finances for corporations to expand. Different exchanges in the United States and around the world as well as the rapid development of the system of stock trading are also discussed. The process whereby a corporation first issues shares to the public through an IPO and then how those shares are later traded on the secondary market is explained. Specifically, the increased role of technology, the diminished role of traditional stockbrokers, and how the stock market industry has moved well into a new era of computerized screen-based trading is reviewed.

OVERVIEW

The stock market is an organized system for the trading of securities. A security is a type of financial asset issued by a corporation and represents a legal interest in that corporation that can be transferred from owner to owner. The stock market acts as a means for owners, or investors, to quickly buy or sell their stocks, or shares. Traditionally, U.S. stock markets, also known as equity markets, have focused almost exclusively on the publicly listed equity securities of U.S.-based corporations and have traded them through a floor based broker system. However, over the last decade, stock markets, traditionally based around a set handful of specific stock exchanges, have also introduced trading in a huge variety of new securities, such as bonds, derivatives, exchange traded funds (ETFs), options, and even commodities. There has also been a dramatic move away from the old face-to-face method of trading securities and toward electronic automated trading. Additionally, the reach of the U.S. stock market has expanded globally to include the trading of securities issued by foreign corporations between not only U.S.-based buyers and sellers, but also foreign investors as

well. Different stock markets throughout the United States and around the world now aggressively compete for business from corporate issuers. Major Asian and European corporate issuers are just as likely to list their shares in New York as in Tokyo or London.

History

Historically, the stock market was based at a fixed physical location. While the New York Stock Exchange (NYSE) based in New York City is by far the largest in the United States, there are also a large number of smaller regional exchanges. These regional exchanges are located in Boston, Cincinnati, Chicago, Los Angeles, Miami, Philadelphia, Salt Lake City, San Francisco, and Spokane. The largest over-the-counter stock market, where stocks are traded electronically through a computer network rather than at a physical exchange, is the NASDAQ (National Association of Securities Dealers Automated Quotation system). NASDAQ had gained prominence in the late 1990s because a bulk of the companies listed were in the telecom, technology, or media sectors (TMT)—which all experienced huge price appreciation. The prices of NASDAQ stocks peaked in 2001 and then entered into a steady, sharp decline. The decline in prices resulted in huge investor losses and a number of new government initiatives regulating the operations of stock markets and regulating how corporations disclose financial information and communicate with their shareholders.

Internationally, all major industrialized nations also have stock markets. Outside of the United States, the world's largest stock markets are located in London, Paris, Tokyo, Hong Kong, and Toronto. The major over-the-counter market in Europe was the European Association of Securities Dealers Automated Quotation system (EASDAQ), which is now a part of the New York-based NASDAQ. While some international exchanges have a centralized location, more are moving toward screen-based systems

A view from the south of Paternoster Square in London, England from the top viewing deck of St. Paul's Cathedral. Paternoster Square, City of London, England – the new home of the London Stock Exchange and next door to St. Paul's Cathedral. (Courtesy of Gren via Wikimedia Commons)

widely viewed as a barometer of the economy, where huge fortunes could be made—or lost. The stock market crash of 1929, in fact, marked a sort of unofficial beginning to the Great Depression. The crash also marked a turning point from an era where the federal government did as little as possible to interfere with the markets to a new era where the stock market has become one of the most heavily regulated institutions in the national economy. Today, U.S. federal securities laws require the registration of stock exchanges and of all securities that are listed for sale to the public. A security must be registered with the U.S. Securities and Exchange Commission (SEC) and be approved for listing by a registered stock exchange before it can be traded. All stock exchanges have their own listing standards concerning the type of security listed and any possible restrictions on the investors who trade in it as well as requirements for continuing disclosure of financial information by the issuer.

The golden era of the stock market, which arguably may never be repeated for a generation or more, occurred from 1996 to 2001. Trading margins expanded and the market for initial public offerings (IPOs) soared in volume. IPO volumes rose from $29.9 billion in 1995 to more than $61.8 billion in 1999 (Hintz & Tang, 2003). Institutional equities headcount, the number of people employed in the equity divisions of Wall Street financial institutions, expanded rapidly. The equity business grew its sales and trading activities as well as its research coverage. Institutional equity earnings peaked in 1999, with the return on equity (ROE) attained by Wall Street firms averaging more than 40 percent (Hintz & Tang, 2003). For the first time, many ordinary U.S. households began to individually pick and buy stocks—as opposed to merely investing in mutual funds selected by their financial advisor. The equity culture was finally established in the American psyche. In 2000, as the TMT boom wound down, equity IPO volumes fell 30 percent year-over-year between 2000 and 2001

where a physical presence at the exchange is not required. Today, the distinction is rapidly becoming blurred and intertwined between a centralized stock market and a national screen-based system as there has been a wave of consolidations and alliances among different exchanges. The landscape of the stock markets and the ways in which they operate are rapidly changing and still very much in progress.

Since the New York Stock Exchange (NYSE) is the world's largest market for publicly listed equity securities, activities on NYSE, whether in terms of daily prices or in terms of how the exchange actually functions, are felt by other stock markets around the globe. The NYSE can trace its roots back to 1792, when traders met on a sidewalk on Wall Street in New York City. It officially adopted the name of New York Stock Exchange in 1863. Since 1868, membership—represented by a "seat," which gives the right to trade securities on the exchange—could be acquired through purchasing a seat from other members. Since 1953, the number of seats has been limited to 1,366.

By the 1920s, the stock market had progressed so rapidly in terms of both daily trading volume and the number of companies listed that it became and another 47 percent between 2001 and 2002 (Hintz & Tang, 2003). More importantly, prices, particularly for the TMT heavy NASDAQ, suffered a dramatic drop and wiped hundreds of billions of dollars in wealth out of the personal savings of the same ordinary households that first began buying stock just a few years earlier.

Technology Squeezes Pricing

Today, the stock market is back in full force as a major, albeit declining, profit center for Wall Street firms as well as a huge center of attention for the investing public at large. Even major media conglomerates generate a significant share of their advertising revenue by reporting on the minute-to-minute developments in the market. NYSE seats are now sold for some $3.5 million each and have

The New York Stock Exchange. (Courtesy of Wikimedia Commons)

been sold for as much as $4 million. Daily trading volume on the NYSE, which was limited to about 100 million shares daily in the early 1980s, routinely topped 4 billion per day in 2008 (New York Stock Exchange) but by 2013 averaged about 3 billion per day (Mandaro, 2013). More than half of this trading is executed not by individual investors picking up the phone and placing an order but through automated systems known as algorithmic trading, also referred to as program trading. Program trading is the generic name given to various trading strategies defined as the simultaneous purchase or sale of a group of stocks based on a mathematical set of rules. The NYSE defines program trading as the purchase or sale of at least fifteen stocks with the value of the trade exceeding $1 million. Program trading accounted for approximately 9.9 percent of total NYSE volume in 1989, rose to 18 percent in 2001 and to 27 percent in 2002, and it had been as high as 40 percent of total volume by 2003 (Hiliman, 2004). Program trading has substantially increased daily trading volumes on the stock markets, which is widely perceived as beneficial for investors. However, at the same time, program trading has dramatically increased volatility where 1 percent or 2 percent daily price movements are far more common today than in decades past. (Hiliman, 2004).

Virtually every significant player in the stock market has heavily invested in program trading technology to help make trading more cost efficient and to help formulate complex trading strategies. Large mutual fund companies managing trillions of dollars in assets with multiple portfolio managers have found program trading to be an easy way to reduce execution charges and "stretch" the budgets they allocate toward stock trading commissions during weak business cycles.

Perhaps the most significant development for both the NYSE as well as the global industry of trading stocks occurred in April 2007, when NYSE formally completed the acquisition of Euronext, a European screen-based equity trading system spanning the continent. Then in 2013, NYSE Euronext was itself purchased by Intercontinental Exchange (ICE) (Kierman & Bunge, 2013). These acquisitions formally signified that the stock market was no longer a localized market composed of individual brokers meeting face to face to trade securities by verbally agreeing to a price. Instead, the stock market is increasingly a globalized electronic system based on an advanced real-time technology platform encompassing investors and equities from around the world. The exact roles that human beings will play in operating this giant financial cyber world, other than simply maintaining the machines, still remains to be fully determined.

Electronic trading and price discovery through an electronic system, rather than the traditional floor based face-to-face verbal interaction, is perhaps the most significant issue facing the stock market for the next decade as it directly affects investor protection in terms of accessing the best possible price. Pricing is a highly contentious issue for many constituents in the stock market industry. A price of a stock in the market is expressed as either a bid price or a sell price. A bid price is what a broker will pay to acquire a stock. An ask price is what the broker will expect in return for selling a stock. The bid-ask spread is the difference between the two. A wide bid-ask spread signifies that there is a large difference between the two prices. A tight spread signifies that there is a small, or narrow, difference.

Under the old floor based method of trading, prices were expressed in fractions of a dollar where the smallest movement was one-eighth of a point, or 12.5 cents. A typical bid-ask spread could easily be half a point, half a dollar, or more. In absolute terms, the difference between the bid-ask price could run as high as 1 percent, 2 percent, or even more of the stock's price. Decimalization, first introduced in 2001, lead to prices being expressed in hundredths of a dollar, or decimals. The price is now usually expressed in basis points, which is one one-hundredth of a cent.

For example, under the old fraction system, a bid-ask spread for a share of XYZ corporation might be 50 1/2 to 50 3/4. That is, an investor would have to pay 50 3/4 dollars, or $50.75 to buy the stock. If the investor already owned it, he or she would receive 50 1/2, or $50.50 if he or she sold it. Under the decimal system, this bid-ask spread has been considerably tightened, particularly for stocks that trade in large volumes. A typical bid-ask spread might be as tight as 50.49999 to 50.50001. The difference between these two is merely two basis points. The distinction between fraction based trading and decimal based trading may seem insignificant when dealing with a few hundred shares, but considering the billion-plus daily share trading volume in the United States representing trillions of dollars, the difference is enormous.

Apart from the trading of stocks that takes place on the floor of an exchange, the last few decades have seen the birth and explosive growth of a parallel market in electronic communication networks (ECNs), which use supercomputers to match huge buy-sell orders from institutional buyers and sellers in a manner of milliseconds. ECNs actually compete fiercely for trading volume with the established exchanges, such as NYSE and NASDAQ.

Electronic trading is fraught with controversy. On one side, fully transparent pricing made possible through electronic trading systems and the ensuing tight bid-ask spreads are highly beneficial to the investor community. On the other hand, with the rapid implementation of electronic trading, the broker-dealer community is faced with diminishing profits and inevitable job losses. In fact, on the day that John A. Thain—chief executive officer of the New York Stock Exchange Group, the corporate owner of the NYSE—stood on the balcony overlooking the old trading floor and formally announced the completion of the acquisition of Euronext, the world's largest electronic stock trading system, he was greeted with a chorus of boos from NYSE traders because of the substantial job cuts that resulted from NYSE's aggressive implementation of electronic trading systems.

Financing the Private Sector

Stock markets play a vital role in free market economic systems by enabling corporations to raise capital in order to expand. Through raising finance from the U.S. stock market, corporations were able to rapidly grow and industrialize the national economy in the nineteenth and twentieth centuries. Because the process of raising capital from the public may expose investors to losses, the stock market is one of the most heavily regulated parts of the entire economy. Starting from the Panic of 1837, the government began a steady century-long process on implementing tougher laws on how exactly corporations are allowed to raise money from the investing public as well as laws on to disclosing information about their financial results. The stock market crash of 1929 led to the creation of the Securities and Exchange Commission (SEC), which is now the leading governmental regulatory agency overseeing public security markets in the United States.

Corporations raise finance through selling shares in the stock market, usually with the help of an investment bank. The investment bank advises the corporation on the exact means of how to sell the securities and deals with issues such as filing documentation with the appropriate regulatory authorities, finding potential investors who may be interested in purchasing shares, and eventually stetting a price for the shares, which are sold in an initial public offering (IPO) in a primary market. In this market, corporations directly receive all the proceeds of the initial stock sales. Then, the securities can be bought and sold on the secondary market. The company does not usually become involved in the secondary trading of its stock, though, from time to time, it may repurchase shares or offer new shares. Stock exchanges essentially function as secondary markets. By providing investors with the assurance and reliability of being able to trade shares at a later date, the exchanges support the performance of the primary markets and thus the entire capital raising process of corporations. This arrangement makes it easier and more cost effective for corporations to capitalize building and expanding their businesses.

While corporations do not directly benefit from sales on the secondary market, corporate managers closely monitor the organization's stock price in secondary markets. This is because the price of a company's stock in the secondary market influences the amount of funds that can be raised in the future. If expansion funds are needed, additional stock can be issued in the primary market. For smaller, new companies, issue of stock on the primary market, and then the later success of the stock on the secondary market, is an essential means to fund their growth as they may have only limited access to debt financing and then only at costly rates of interest. A successful IPO and strong future share price in the aftermarket should ensure continued funding for new investment. An IPO met with lackluster investor interest or declining prices in the secondary market will make future capital raising for the company more challenging.

Managers of all corporations, from the newest to the largest global multinationals, are also keenly interested in the activities of their stocks in the secondary market since the managers usually hold a large number of shares for their personal benefit as well as a large number of stock options—that is, the right to buy more shares at a specific price. Effectively, secondary markets determine the wealth of the corporation's owners—the stockholders. If the price rises, then the owners are happy with management and will perhaps even award management with more salary and more stock options. If the price falls, shareholders may then find fault with management and possibly try to force changes in management structure. The stock market acts as the center of exchange of information about more than merely the pricing of stocks. The very first place to look to see how newly released information will affect the future of a company, for better or for worse, is the movement of the company's share price on the stock market.

VIEWPOINTS

Apart from the rising of new capital for business expansion and the trading of shares in the secondary market, stock markets also act as a means to influence and improve corporate governance. Economic activity and gross national product is primarily determined by the activities of public corporations. Public corporations are owned by stockholders, who are effectively represented by corporate management. Over the last few decades, and intensifying with the scandals in 2001 and 2002 involving such corporations as WorldCom and Enron, stock markets have been at the leading edge of protecting shareholder rights, insuring transparency of financial information, and attempting to improve standards of corporate governance. In fact, it is stock exchange authorities rather than any federal or state regulatory entities that now conduct most investigations into violations of insider trading rules and take action to ensure that listed corporates adhere to requirements for public disclosure of financial results.

Investor protection, which became a hot topic following the TMT meltdown post-2000, will also continue to be of major interest to policy makers. While brokers and investors alike are satisfied when stock prices rise, the generally increased levels of market volatility will mean that there will be many instances when investors—from private individuals to state pension plans and insurance companies—suffer major losses. On October 19, 1987, the stock market posted its largest one-day percentage decline ever when the Dow Jones Industrial Average fell 508 points, a drop of more than 22 percent in a single day. Prior to the crash of 1987, the largest single-day drop in the stock market occurred on October 29, 1929, when the market fell by about 13 percent (New York Stock Exchange). The largest point drop occurred on September 29, 2008, when the market lost 777 points with a percentage change of only 6.98. While drops of this magnitude are rare, today it not uncommon for stock prices to rise or fall by 3 percent or more in a single week. Managing the effects of stock market volatility is an important area within the growing field of financial risk management—which only came of age in Wall Street after the multibillion-dollar losses caused by the collapse of a major hedge fund, Long-Term Capital Management (LTCM), in October 1998.

On the technology front, the ultimate question of how exactly the equity markets will function—or more specifically what role, if any, traditional voice brokers will play—is far from resolved. As a business model, the institutional equities business is in trouble. One needs to look no further than the 2008 collapse of Lehman Brothers, which at the time of its bankruptcy filing was the fourth largest investment bank in the United States, for evidence of this decline (Maiden, 2013). The profitability of equity trading for major Wall Street firms, as measured by the ROE of their equity divisions, has fallen from approximately 40 percent at the peak of the TMT boom of 1999 and 2000 to 5 percent in 2006. The growth of program trading, decimalization, the decline of NASDAQ profitability, and the growth of ECNs have reduced realized commissions per share by 34 percent since 1999 and are expected to further narrow commissions by 4 percent in 2007 (Hintz & Tang, 2003). With narrowing margins in its core business, Wall Street equity market participants have embraced the same strategic initiative—improving their business mix and building scale to improve profitability. Unfortunately, these steps might not be sufficient to change the inevitability of purely automated, electronic-based trading not just in the United States but globally as well. Persistently falling bid-ask spreads and squeezed profit margins will lead to a war of attrition as Wall Street competes over equity trade flow in the coming years, which will continue to depress employment levels—from brokers and salesmen to research analysts and operations staff (Preston, 2012).

Effectively, the stock market has now become a business of scale: technology, size, narrow bid-ask spreads of tiny fractions of basis points, and speed of processing as measured by milliseconds rather than minutes will determine the road ahead. In such a business of scale and speed, only a few players with strong institutional equity client lists and an ability to invest $100 million or more each year in continuing technology will succeed in making the transition to the new size-based model of the stock market. Only the largest global firms on Wall Street are certain to remain market share leaders and retain their position as major stock market participants in the next five years.

TERMS & CONCEPTS

Bid-ask spread: The difference between the price that a broker offers to buy a stock (bid price) and the price a broker offers to sell it (ask).

Broker-dealer: A broker acts as an intermediary between a buyer and seller of a stock. A dealer buys or sells stock from his or her own account. The term *broker* is often used interchangeably with the concept of broker-dealer.

Electronic communication network (ECN): A private independent computer system that enables the matching of huge numbers of buy-sell orders for stocks in milliseconds.

Equities: A term used interchangeably with the concept of stock. Specifically, the equity portion of a corporation represents all assets of a corporation less all liabilities. Equity owners are effectively the owners of the corporation.

Initial public offering (IPO): The very first time that a company issues shares to the public at large for purchase.

Liquidity: Term used to describe trading volume. Liquid markets are those where a large number of shares can be easily bought or sold. Illiquid markets are those where it would be difficult to trade in large number of shares.

NASDAQ: National Association of Securities Dealers Automated Quotation system

Price discovery: The process of finding the best possible price at which to trade a stock. For the buyer of a stock, this is the lowest price available. Conversely, for the seller, it is the highest price.

Program trading: Also known as algorithmic trading. A trading system whereby orders to buy or sell shares are calculated and automatically executed by a computer system based on a complex set of mathematical rules.

Return on equity (ROE): A measure of profitability used by corporations to assess the success, or failure, of their individual business units. Equity in this case is measured by the value of the assets of that business unit less its liabilities.

Secondary market: The trading of all shares except those that are first issued during an IPO.

Stock exchange: The physical venue or the exact platform where stock trading actually takes place. Major exchanges include the New York Stock Exchange, NASDAQ, and the former American Stock Exchange (AMEX). Increasingly, exchanges are moving away from physical venues toward computer systems, which may be scattered in different locations.

Technology-media-telecom (TMT): A generic phrase used to refer to a broad group of stocks that appreciated in price rapidly during the dot-com era of the late 1990s. The era officially ended in March 2001 with the peak in the value of NASDAQ.

Transparency: Term used to describe the degree to which corporate management discloses fair and accurate information about their company's performance to the investing public. Also describes the availability of fair and accurate information about the prices of securities. Setting for the investing public at large the exact price of a stock is one of the fundamental purposes of a stock market.

Volatility: The degree to which stock prices fluctuate. High volatility, or vol, implies that prices are moving upward or downward quickly relative to historic averages.

BIBLIOGRAPHY

Bresiger, G. (2004). The conflicts of regulators. *Traders Magazine, 17*, 70–71.

Hiliman, R. (2004). Securities markets: Opportunities exist to enhance investor confidence and improve listing program oversight: GAO-04–75. *GAO Reports, 1*.

Hillman, R. J. (2005). Securities markets: Decimal pricing has contributed to lower trading costs and a more challenging trading environment: GAO-05–535. *GAO Reports, 1*.

Hintz, B., & Tang, K. L. (2003). U.S. brokerage: Institutional equities at a crossroads. *White Book—U.S. Brokerage: Institutional Equities at a Crossroads*, 1–20.

Keim, D. B., & Madhavan, A. (2000). The relation between stock market movements and NYSE seat prices. *Journal of Finance, 55*, 2817.

Kelly, K. (2001). NYSE and NASDAQ discuss trading each other's stocks. *Wall Street Journal—Eastern Edition, 238*, C1.

Kierman, K., & Bunge, J. (2013, June 4). NYSE investors ok sale to ICE. *Wall Street Journal—Eastern Edition*, C3.

Li, K. (2002). What explains the growth of global equity markets? *Canadian Investment Review, 15*, 23.

Maiden, B. (2013). 1,831 days later. *Compliance Reporter*, 3.

Mandaro, L. (2013, July 16). *NYSE volume at lowest of year, and that's saying something.*

Mendelson, M. (1974). Abstract—The stock market: Some considerations of its future structure. *Journal of Financial & Quantitative Analysis, 9*, 829.

Preston, A. (2012). You eat what you kill. *New Statesman, 141*(5125), 22–35.

SUGGESTED READING

Lee, C. J. (1987). Fundamental analysis and the stock market. *Journal of Business Finance & Accounting, 14*, 131–141.

Malkiel, B. G. (2003). The efficient market hypothesis and its critics. *Journal of Economic Perspectives, 17*, 59-82.

Mutual funds and the U.S. equity market. (2000). *Federal Reserve Bulletin, 86*, 797.

Reilly, F. K. (1972). Evidence regarding a segmented stock market. *Journal of Finance, 27*, 607.

Sill, D. K. (1993, Jan./Feb.). Predicting stock-market volatility. *Business Review (Federal Reserve Bank of Philadelphia)*, 15.

Edited by Richa S. Tiwary, Ph.D., MLS

INCOME DISTRIBUTION

A focal point of common interest among social scientists, policy makers, and economists is whether the middle class is disappearing given the evidence of a widening gap between the rich and the poor on socioeconomic status. Income distribution is a topic in economics that warrants further attention. One of the formidable challenges in this field is to achieve an equitable, or more equal, distribution of income, in the absence of parameters that define exactly what degree of inequality is acceptable. Furthermore, consensus may be difficult to attain until there is an agreement on which underlying factors determine a worker's wages. A philosophical divide runs deep as one group of economists subscribes to the view that a self-regulating labor market determines wages and an opposing group holds the view that labor unions and other organizations create market imperfections and therefore a need for governmental interventions. Putting those philosophical foundations aside, there are some important tools available to analysts as they seek to understand and describe in a quantifiable manner trends and international comparisons with respect to income distribution. The Lorenz curve expresses the relationship of a percentage of income to a percentage of households, and the Gini coefficient accompanies the curve as a measure of the degree of income equality. Although those tools have some limitations, this essay provides some methods and statistics that readers can use to compare Europe and the United States and examine domestic trends. The primary purpose of this essay is to provide readers with basic information for initiating and pursuing their own inquiries and for achieving a better understanding of income distribution and redistributive policy complexities.

OVERVIEW

Undergraduate students in economics courses learn quite early about poverty levels and income dispersions. Most undergraduate textbooks and courses introduce the notion of an equitable distribution of income alongside a few other goals for a nation's economy. Absent is a consensus on what precisely defines an equitable income distribution for any given country; a common interpretation is that equity improves with a movement toward equality over time and/or when one country exhibits a distribution closer to equality relative to other countries. Eventually, that basic information paves the way for learning how government policies attempt to redistribute income and provide relief to the poor.

Let us begin by considering some facts about income distribution. In 2002, 50 percent of the total income in the United States went to the richest 20 percent of households, and 3 percent went to the poorest 20 percent; keep in mind that households differ in size and those differences lead some analysts to focus instead on individuals. Furthermore, income inequality in the United States has grown since the 1960s. In 1967, 44 percent of income went to the richest fifth of households, and 4 percent went to the poorest fifth. A comparison of those two years reflected a growing inequality and suggested that the middle class might be falling to the wayside as the richest got richer and the poorest poorer. A further comparison of the years 1979 and 2007 shows that the top 1 percent of earners experience income growth of 275 percent, whereas the bottom 20 percent of earners saw household income growth of only 18 percent (Serwer, 2013). Frequently, income distribution of a given country becomes a major topic in discussions about the socioeconomic welfare of its citizens.

Income distribution essentially provides a reference point for comparing welfare and poverty across nations and over time. Casting issues of justice and fairness aside for the moment, one of the reasons many scholars and students find this topic appealing and/or fascinating is the challenges associated with securing a more equitable, or ideal, distribution of income while stopping far short of arguing for equality in the distribution of income. Consistent with that line of reasoning, Horn (1993) prefers to interpret perfect equality as a benchmark, knowing it is perhaps the best target available until scholars and policy makers establish a socially acceptable normal level of income equality.

It is uncertain whether a normative measure will ever become a reality. Nonetheless, there exists a real need for readers to become familiar with two types of income distribution:

- personal distribution
- functional distribution

Personal distribution explains that individual abilities, characteristics, and preferences and possibly discriminatory hiring practices determine income. Functional distribution describes income as a payment to resource owners. Each resource receives income in the form of a payment for its use in production as follows: Labor receives wages, capital receives interest, land receives rent, and the business owner or entrepreneur who assembles those resources receives profit. This essay's primary interest resides with the personal distribution, but a basic model depicting the flows of money and quantities and referencing these functionalities appears later.

Additional complexities make their way into the analysis as one enters the issue of whether an equal distribution of income removes incentives for entrepreneurs. Those individuals assemble the resources necessary in producing goods and services. In the absence of those incentives and presumably fewer producers, consumers may find themselves facing fewer choices, smaller quantities, and higher prices in the marketplace. Some downstream consequences of those outcomes include fewer workers, higher unemployment rates, and lower incomes. As the reader might guess, the topic can become quite complex, especially when philosophies on income determination and redistribution are brought into the mix.

A natural extension of this topic delivers readers onto a discussion of methods for redistributing income after they get a better sense of whether income distributions are equitable or inequitable. As its major focal point, this essay avoids many complexities by limiting its breadth and depth. Consequently, the reader will receive practical guidance on measuring and interpreting income distributions in addition to brief coverage of some economic perspectives. We will return later in this essay to a discussion of whether wages are the result of this concept, market structure, or a combination of both. In addition, this essay offers some key explanations for income inequality, and it presents a common measure that helps analysts to assess the degree of inequality in the distribution of income. Discussions of those components follow the next section, which outlines some economic concepts that facilitate mastery of the income distribution topic.

Conceptual Foundations: Markets, Employments, & Incomes

Economics as a field of study contains two divisions. Macroeconomics is the branch that focuses on the economy as a whole, and microeconomics examines the interactions between firm actions and consumer behaviors as they pursue exchanges in a market. Physical quantities of resources, goods, services, and monetary payments flow between consumers and households as they interact through their marketplace transactions.

There are two sectors (households and businesses) and two markets (goods and resources) that comprise the circular flow model. Readers are encouraged to consult their textbooks for a graphical presentation of the model. It depicts the business sector using resources such as labor, land, and capital to produce goods and services for the household sector. Each receives a physical quantity of something and issues money in payment. Respectively, businesses pay wages, rent, and interest as they acquire those resources. Households are the source of those quantities, and they purchase goods and services, issuing dollars from their personal incomes in exchange for an item.

Supply & Demand

Both markets contain a demand component and a supply component. In the goods market, a household demands quantities of items and pays the price for each item bought; businesses supply those quantities and receive revenues from each item sold. In the resource market, specifically the labor market, households supply quantities of labor and receive incomes in payment for those quantities; businesses demand quantities of labor and pay wages for them. More precisely, consumers are willing and able to purchase a specific amount at any given price according to a demand schedule that records various combinations of prices and quantities. Likewise, businesses are willing and able to provide a specific amount at any given price according to a supply schedule. Curves or lines in a graph, which are available elsewhere, display those schedules.

Whether one examines the resource market or the goods market, a direct relationship exists between price and quantity according to the Law of Supply; that is, large quantities will be supplied at high prices and small quantities at low prices. An inverse relationship exists between price and quantity according to the Law of Demand; in other words, large quantities will be in demand at low prices and small quantities at high prices. The intersection of the supply curve and the demand curve is the point of equilibrium for price and quantity, which establishes the market price.

Equilibrium Adjustments

Sometimes there are distortions or imperfections in the market that affect price. Occasionally, quantity demanded is higher or lower than quantity supplied resulting in prices temporarily above or below the market price. Usually, the price will adjust tending toward an equilibrium point. However, government may intervene by establishing a price control that is higher or lower than the market would dictate when left alone; the minimum wage, for example, is a price for labor that is set above the equilibrium price in the labor market. In this instance, actual wages paid to employees must be greater than the market wage.

Another distortion arises from the ability of an individual or a group to exert pressure on market prices for goods or resources. For example, the employer in a one-company town may hire workers at a low rate of pay. An opposite example is the case of a labor union that restricts the supply of labor through apprenticeship programs or a licensure process effectively increasing the price of labor. By altering the price for labor, these market imperfections often determine the amount of employment, output, and income. In brief, market structures can determine what payments employees receive from their employers.

Labor Income

Persons receive labor income from their gainful employments. However, personal income is the result from adding labor income, asset income, and transfer payments and subtracting taxes (Arnold, 2005). The last two items result from government actions, but the first two result primarily from individual actions and sometimes family history. Asset income accrues from savings accounts, inheritances, and other types of investments, which is really what economists refer to as wealth. Income is a flow variable and wealth is a stock variable. One can view it as the accumulation of savings, income, or assets over time, whether it originates from an individual or another member of the household in which the individual resides.

Household Income

Household income is the sum of personal income from all those individuals who reside at the same address, with some slight modifications beyond the scope of this paper. The reader should keep in mind that household income will be larger than personal income for obvious reasons and that it adds some amount of distortion and complexity to income distribution analyses. The distribution of household incomes varies significantly in aggregate and more so when one examines along the dimensions (education level, race, gender, and age).

Variations in Income Distribution

Variations in income distribution according to age exist, in part, because some households are poor for long periods of time and some only temporarily. In terms of the latter, it is reasonable to expect young households to earn a low income as they enter the early career phase. Consequently, analysts need to recognize the effect of age on income distribution. As one might suspect, labor income at the individual level also varies along the aforementioned dimensions.

On the one hand, some economists subscribe to the view that worker's wages are a consequence of their abilities and productivities. On the other hand, some hold the view that market characteristics influence product availability, and workers find themselves in jobs receiving a wage determined largely by market forces. A key difference between these two perspectives appears to center on the determinants of income and on whether a worker's wage is a consequence of individual characteristics or market factors. The next section summarizes those two perspectives.

Economic Perspectives on Income Determination

Payments to workers are determined in several ways. One view is that structures and organizations operating within the labor market can and do exert an influence on wage rate determination. Another view draws from the concepts of marginal benefit and marginal cost, which weighs heavily in economics especially among some labor market economists. Furthermore, they assert that labor markets, like other markets, are self-regulating in the absence of structural or other artificial distortions. The marginal revenue product of labor doctrine holds that the hourly wage rate a worker receives is equal to the additional revenue that worker generates during one hour of work in producing a good or service.

In terms of the whole production process, labor is often a resource that has supplements from land and capital resources. Resource prices, of which wages are one, reflect demand and supply factors. By extension, production activities create a demand for labor, and workers comprise the supply of labor. In addition, the quality and content of that supply varies because individual workers differ in many ways. Each person is unique, and his or her abilities determine his or her value as a human resource in the labor market.

Without making any distinction here with respect to worker classifications (managerial, clerical, etc.), wage rates simply reflect the worker's abilities, and earnings are the mathematical product of effective wage rates multiplied by the hours employed. Wages and incomes are different because workers are different. Accordingly, income inequality is primarily a result of differences among workers in their abilities and in their education and training levels. In essence, individual ability is the primary factor whether individuals or households place low or high in the income strata.

Up to this point, this section emphasized a view that wages and incomes are determined largely in a labor market that operates freely and is self-regulating. In contrast, another view holds that governments and organizations intervene in the labor market. Those interventions attempt to craft wage rates that are usually higher than the market would determine if left alone. Minimum wage laws are one example and labor union contracts are another example of methods of wage determination that fall outside the marginal revenue product doctrine. In addition, wages are likely to be different according to geographic location; for example, rural areas may have a sole employer around which villages of workers reside. In summary, wages are determined both by market and by artificial forces. It is clear that wages effect incomes, and income distributions are relatively easy to discern through some common applications for analysis.

APPLICATIONS

The Lorenz curve is a graph of the income distribution, which expresses the relationship of a percentage of income to a percentage of households. The Gini coefficient is used in conjunction with the curve as a measure of the degree of income equality. The Gini coefficient was developed by the Italian statistician Corrado Gini and published in his 1912 paper titled "Variability and Mutability" after its translation in English. Another form of that measure is the Gini index, which is the Gini coefficient expressed as a percentage multiplied by 100. The next section covers these measures and the curve in greater detail.

ANALYSES OF INCOME DISTRIBUTIONS: LORENZ CURVES & GINI COEFFICIENTS

The Lorenz Curve

Common presentations of the distribution of money income in graphical form contain a Lorenz curve, which illustrates the total cumulative percentage of income that goes to each cumulative percentage of households. Its frame is a square-shaped by design. The horizontal, or bottom side, of the square shows the cumulative percentage of population, which ranges from 0 to 100, as one follows that axis from left to right. Bearing the same range, following the vertical axis, from bottom to top, of the square, the left side shows the cumulative percentage of income.

The reader should note that the Lorenz curve receives significant amounts of criticism, in part because it suggests that a proven relationship exists between income distribution and social welfare. Nonetheless, readers should keep in mind that it is a useful tool for depicting changes over time within a county, differences at a specific time between countries, or some combination of the two. In the case of an equal distribution of income, the curve would actually take the form of a straight line that slopes upward to the right as a diagonal within a square; for example, 25 percent of a country's population earns 25 percent of a country's total income, 50 percent

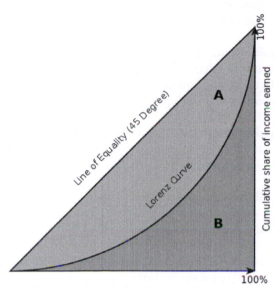

Cumulative share of people from lowest to highest incomes

(Gini coefficient diagram, based on the version by Bluemoose/BenFrantz-Dale.) You can think of the horizontal axis as percent of people and the vertical axis as the percent of income those people receive. Therefore the Lorenz curves always start and end at the same places, where 0% of people make 0% of the country's income and 100% of people make 100% of the total income. Inequality is implied when the curve is below the 45-degree line: At the left, the percentage of people is higher than the percent of income they receive (i.e. 10% of the people getting 5% of the total income); at the right, the percent of income received rises more than the percent of people receiving it. The area above the Lorenz curve – marked "A" – is shaded differently from the area below the curve – marked "B". This simplifies the mathematical explanation of the gini coefficient, which is A/(A+B) (Courtesy of Reidpath via Wikimedia Commons)

earns 50 percent, and so forth. In reality, the distribution of income is unequal, making the Lorenz curve concave; for example, 50 percent of the total population earns less than 50 percent of total income.

Gini Coefficients

The size of the area between the actual income distribution curve and the diagonal equality line is a component for calculating a useful metric. Basically, the Gini coefficient is defined as a ratio of the area between that straight line and the convex curve present within a Lorenz curve diagram. The Gini ratio is a measure of the dispersion of the income distribution. Estimating the ratio involves dividing the area between the Lorenz curve and the diagonal by the entire area below the diagonal. Its numeric value ranges between 0 for income equality and 1 for inequality;

the latter would occur if one person earns all the income. Avoiding all those calculations, readers of this essay need to know that the formula takes into account an approximate number of earners in each income class and that the mathematical product is widely useful in income analysis.

Income Distribution Comparisons

Analyses of income distribution are possible whether one compares the world to a nation or a country to a country at a specific point in time or examines a trend within a specific country. Comparisons are also available in terms of a population's health status, education level, and age group. Recent research on income inequality in the United States suggests a growing divide in the socioeconomic status between college graduates and others. Research publications also report that the disparities in health status by educational achievement grew from 1982 to 2004—more among older adults than among younger adults. One conclusion is that the trend of growth in health status disparities among older adults reflects disparities in economic resources, health promotion behaviors, health service access, or other factors that vary widely even among or within highly developed countries.

Worldwide Gini Coefficients

While most European nations tend to exhibit Gini coefficients between 0.24 and 0.36, the United States' Gini coefficient is above 0.40, which provides further evidence that the United States is experiencing greater inequality in its distribution of income than other developed countries. Although this metric can help quantify differences in welfare and compensation, readers should bear in mind that Gini coefficients may be inappropriate for comparing small and large countries on political dimensions. Nonetheless, the metric can help describe the distribution of income at the global level in addition to inter- and intracontinental levels.

It is estimated that the Gini coefficients for the entire world range between 0.56 and 0.66. Some recent research points to movement toward a more equitable distribution of global income, noting that inequality declined during the period between 1980 and 2000. Among their explanations for that significant decline is above-average income growth in highly populated developing regions including China and South Asia, where 40 percent of the world's inhabitants reside. They conclude this trend toward greater equality in the distribution of income is likely to continue into the near future as poor counties enter progressive phases in the economic maturation process.

Redistribution of Income

After learning statistics about income distribution and methods for measuring it, this essay winds down by informing readers that income redistribution is equal in importance to income levels and distributions. Greater equality in the distribution of income can occur through government policies that aim to provide relief to the poor. Transfer payments, in their most generic form, consist of payments to individuals unrelated to their production or an exchange of goods and services, favorable tax treatments, food stamps, subsidized housing, medical assistance, and Social Security benefits. As examples of methods used by governments to redistribute income, the explicit purpose of these efforts is to transfer income from the richer groups to the poorer groups. When considering the recent trends in income distribution within the United States, the effectiveness of income redistribution policies remains open for further investigation guided by applications of the Lorenz curve and the Gini metrics.

CONCLUSION

A lot of work remains in terms of the goal to establish an equitable, or more equal, distribution of incomes. One can begin to imagine what lies ahead in light of recent trends in the United States that provide evidence of a widening division between the rich and poor. The underlying causes of that divide are elusive at best, but the jury is out as to whether the middle class of income recipients, as opposed to the upper echelons, are bearing a disproportionate burden of caring for the lower-income classes. In conclusion, this essay attempts to provide the reader with a foundation on which to launch those and related inquiries. Hopefully, the reader gained a better sense of the complexities of income distribution and redistribution along with the advantages and disadvantages of using Gini coefficients as a measure of income inequality.

TERMS & CONCEPTS

Demand: The amount of a good or service an individual consumer or a group of consumers wants at a given price.

Demand schedule: The actual quantities that consumers are willing and able to purchase at various prices.

Equilibrium: The price and quantity associated with the intersection of the demand and supply curves, reflecting alignments among consumers and producers on an item's price and quantity.

Equilibrium price: The price at which demand and supply curves intersect, reflecting an agreement among consumers and producers.

Equilibrium quantity: The quantity at which demand and supply curves intersect, reflecting an agreement among consumers and producers.

Gini coefficient: The ratio that results from dividing the area between income equality and the Lorenz curve by the area underneath the diagonal line representing income equality.

Gini index: The Gini coefficient multiplied by 100.

Income inequality: An arbitrary degree to which an actual income distribution deviates from equality.

Labor market: Consists of the demand for and supply of workers and equilibrium wage rate.

Law of demand: Specifies the inverse or negative relationship that exists between an item's demand quantity and its price; quantity and price move in opposite directions.

Law of supply: Specifies the direct or positive relationship that exists between an item's demand quantity and its price; quantity and price move in same direction.

Lorenz curve: A line graph illustrating the actual distribution of income across a given population.

Marginal revenue: The contribution to total revenue from the sale of one additional item.

Market: A virtual space where consumers and producers interact while exchanging a specific item in accordance with their demand and supply schedules.

Market failure: The results stemming from imperfect or unavailable information for consumer and producer decisions; from an individual or group hold and bring a disproportionate amount of influence into a market transaction; and/or from an imposition of costs on or harm to third parties and those outside the exchange or transaction.

Output: The quantity of items or services produced by a firm or group of firms in a market.

Price: The amount of money that is required to obtain an item.

Price controls: Prevent prices from rising above or falling below a specific dollar amount.

Producers: Firms that supply or provide goods or services desired by consumers.

Quantity demanded: The amount of goods or services that consumers desire at given prices.

Quantity supplied: The amount of goods or services that suppliers are willing and able to produce at given prices.

Resource market: Consists of the demand for and the supply of labor, land, capital, and their equilibrium respective payments in the form of wages, rent, and interest.

Revenue: The proceeds from the sale of an item; the mathematical product of quantity of item sold times the price of item.

Supply: The amount of a good or service an individual producer or a group of producers will provide at a given price.

Supply schedule: The actual quantities that producers are willing and able to purchase at various prices.

Transfer payment: A payment from a governmental entity for the benefit of low-income persons and households.

BIBLIOGRAPHY

Armour, P., Burkhauser, R. V., & Larrimore, J. (2014). Levels and trends in U.S. income and its distribution: A crosswalk from market income towards a comprehensive Haig-Simons income approach. *Southern Economic Journal, 81*, 271–293.

Arnold, R. A. (2005). *Economics* (7th ed.). Mason, OH: Thomson South-Western.

Assous, M., & Dutt, A. (2013). Growth and income distribution with the dynamics of power in labour and goods markets. *Cambridge Journal of Economics, 37*, 1407–1430.

Colvin, G. (2013). America's 400 richest: Not a club but a collective (really!). *Fortune, 167*, 51.

Dagsvik, J., Jia, Z., Vatne, B., & Zhu, W. (2013). Is the Pareto-Lévy law a good representation of income distributions? *Empirical Economics, 44*, 719–737.

Guell, R. C. (2007). *Issues in economics today* (3rd ed.). Boston, MA: McGraw-Hill Irwin.

Horn, R. V. (1993). *Statistical Indicators for the economic and social sciences*. Cambridge, UK: Cambridge University Press.

McConnell, C. R., & Brue, S. L. (2008). *Economics* (17th ed.). Boston, MA: McGraw-Hill Irwin.

Serwer, A. (2013). The income gap. *Fortune, 168*, 10.

SUGGESTED READING

Danziger, S., Haveman, R., & Plotnick, R. (1981). How income transfer programs affect work, savings, and the income distribution: A critical review. *Journal of Economic Literature*, XIX, 975–1028.

Firebaugh, G., & Goesling, B. (2004). Accounting for the recent decline in global income inequality. *American Journal of Sociology, 110*, 283–312.

Goesling, B. (2006). Getting rich: America's new rich and how they got that way. *Administrative Science Quarterly, 51*, 314–316.

Goesling, B. (2007). The rising significance of education for health? *Social Forces, 85*, 1621–1644.

Kleiber, C. (2013). On moment indeterminacy of the Benini income distribution. *Statistical Papers, 54*, 1121–1130.

Liebman, J. B. (1998). The impact of the earned income tax credit on incentives and income distribution. In J. M. Poterba (Ed.), *Tax policy and the economy 12.* Cambridge, MA: MIT Press, 1998.

Rector, R., & Hederman, R. (2004). Two Americas: One rich, one poor? Understanding income inequality in the United States.

Essay by Steven R. Hoagland, PhD

INCOME TAX ACCOUNTING

This article focuses on how net operating losses and valuation allowances have an effect on income taxes. In addition, there is a discussion on income tax disclosures. Finally, the article compares and contrasts GAAP and tax code, especially as the two views affect nonprofit organizations. A net operating loss occurs when the annual deductions are greater than the taxable income for the year. Studies show that change in the current period income is a significant determinant of changes in valuation allowance. Changes in valuation allowance have a negative impact on changes in current income.

OVERVIEW

This article highlights some of the events that affect income taxes. Two of these events are net operating losses and valuation allowances. Each of these events is discussed in detail so that the reader has an understanding of the impact each of the two events has on income taxes.

Net Operating Losses

When does a net operating loss (NOL) occur? A net operating loss occurs when the annual deductions are greater than the taxable income for the year. Also, there is a net operating loss when the taxable income is negative. There are a number of reasons why a net operating loss is reported. For example, it could be due to deductions from a business, the cost of renting property, and casualty and theft losses. In most cases, net operating loss occurs as a result of a business operating in the red. The business may have a year in which the expenses incurred exceed the revenue that has been generated. This is very common, especially for new businesses during the first couple of years.

Claiming a Net Operating Loss

The year that the NOL occurs is called the NOL year. However, the loss may be carried forward or back to another tax year and applied against the taxable income for that given year. The deduction for net operating loss can be claimed by individuals, estates, and trusts. Unfortunately, partnerships and

S corporations usually cannot claim a net operating loss. However, partners and shareholders of partnerships and corporations can take their individual shares of business income and deductions into account when calculating their individual net operating losses (Hagen)

Deductions Not Included in Declaring Net Operation Loss

In order to claim a net operating loss on an income tax return, one must calculate the amount that can be taken as a deduction to be applied against the taxable income from another year. According to Hagen (n.d.), one must evaluate which deductions can or cannot be included in the net operating losses. Some of the deductions not included in net operating losses are as follows:

- Personal exemptions
- Section 1202 exclusion of 50 percent of gains from the sale or exchange of qualified small business stock. One must add back any gain that was excluded when calculating the net operating loss.
- The excess of nonbusiness capital losses over nonbusiness capital gains (does not include the Section 1202 exclusion). There is a limit on the amount of business capital losses that can be included when calculating the net operating loss. The limit can be calculated as the total nonbusiness capital gains in excess of the nonbusiness capital losses and excess nonbusiness deductions as well as the total business capital gains once the Section 1202 exclusions have been added back.
- Deductions that are not connected to the business or the owner's employment. Examples of this type of deduction include alimony paid, contributions to an IRA or self-employed retirement plan, and the standard deduction if the individual does not itemize. If itemization occurs, some of the deductions are taken into account in calculating a net operating loss while others are not. The net operating loss calculation includes casualty and theft losses, state income taxes on business profits, and employee business expenses.

The Internal Revenue Service Building, located in the center of the Federal Triangle complex in Washington, D.C. (Courtesy of Library of Congress)

Deductions Included in Declaring Net Operation Loss
The income tax preparer must keep in mind that there are limits for certain categories, and one cannot use all tax deductions when calculating the net operating costs. Some of the deductions that are included in the net operating loss consist of the following:

- Moving expenses
- Employee business expenses can be claimed as an itemized deduction. These include work-related travel and entertainment expenses, education expenses, uniforms, tools, and union dues
- Casualty and theft losses, on either business or nonbusiness property
- Deduction for one-half of the self-employment tax
- Deduction for self-employed health insurance
- State income tax on profits from the business
- Rental losses
- Loss on the sale or exchange of real or depreciable business property
- The owner's share of a loss from a partnership or S corporation
- Ordinary loss on the sale or exchange of stock in a small business corporation or a small business investment company

- The portion of an investment in a pension or annuity plan that is not recovered and is claimed on the final income tax return

Sole proprietors and independent contractors will have a net operating loss if their business expenses exceed their revenues. It should also be noted that there are some business deductions for NOL purposes that may not be connected with the business. These deductions include expenses connected with one's employment and certain other losses, such as casualty and theft losses.

If a net operating loss has been calculated in the current year, the income tax preparer may carry this loss back to the two preceding years and apply the loss against the taxable income for those years. This action will allow the individual to receive a refund of previous income tax that has been paid. The two years mentioned above are referred to as the carry back period. If there is a situation in which there are still net operating losses remaining after it has been carried back two years, the taxpayer can carry the remaining NOL forward. The taxpayer may carry forward any remaining NOL balance up to 20 years after the NOL year. This period is referred to as the carry forward period.

Valuation Allowances

The Statement of Financial Accounting Standards (SFAS) No. 109 mandates that all organizations are to establish valuation allowances if there is a possibility that their deferred tax assets will not be realized (Financial Accounting Standards Board, 1992). Some of the main points of the standard include the following:

- Recognition of deferred tax assets for all temporary differences that are tax deductible in the future and the more likely than not provision in valuation of such assets (Schatzberg & Sevcik, 1994).
- Discretion to assess the possibility of deferred tax assets occurring. For example, organizations may use estimates such as future profitability and the availability of tax planning strategies.

Colley (2012), however, states that "deferred taxes do not represent assets and liabilities as defined by accounting standards."

Earnings Management

Organizations have the discretion to manage earning through a variety of accruals such as depreciation and allowance for questionable accounts (McNichols & Wilson, 1988). Some of the motives for earnings management include earnings smoothing, accounting numbers-based incentives in bonus plans, and debt covenants (Watts & Zimmerman, 1986). Some scholars have written on the topic of earnings management in order to provide support for motives such as asset sales and allowance for doubtful accounts (Bartov, 1993; McNichols & Wilson, 1988). The above-mentioned studies highlight how income from a specific accounting accrual is related in a systematic way to earnings management motives. Other scholars (Ali & Kuman, 1994) consider interaction effects when researching earnings management. Their studies assert that the relationship between the motives for earnings management and discretionary accruals may in turn depend on the amount of income generated by the discretionary accrual.

Sources of Income & Valuation Allowances

The guidelines provided by SFAS No. 109 need to be addressed in order to test earnings management as it relates to valuation allowance. These guidelines evaluate four sources of income in establishing the level of valuations allowances. The four sources are future taxable differences that reverse in time, history of profitability, expected future profitability, and tax planning strategies. Changes in these sources are considered in conjunction with changes in the current period. However, it does not include the change in the valuation allowance. It has been shown that changes in the current period income are a key factor to changes in valuation allowance. Studies show that change in the current period income is a significant determinant of changes in valuation allowance. Changes in valuation allowance have a negative impact on changes in current income. For example, when current year income increases (decreases), valuation allowances decrease (increase).

Sources of Income & Deferred Tax Assets

There are four sources of taxable income outlined in SFAS No. 109 that correlate to deferred tax assets. Two of the sources are future reversals of taxable temporary differences and income in previous carry back years. Both are objective and verifiable. The other two sources (future taxable income and tax planning strategies) are subjective. The standard emphasizes the need to consider both positive and negative evidence in evaluating the value of deferred tax assets. Some examples of positive evidence are sales backlogs, existing contracts, and unrealized holding gains that will produce taxable income. Some examples of negative evidence are history of losses, anticipated losses, and any unsettled circumstances that could reduce income.

Determining Need for a Valuation Analysis

Deferred tax assets are the deferred tax consequences that can be attributed to deductible temporary differences and carry forwards. After the deferred tax asset has been measured using the appropriate tax rates and provisions of the enacted tax law, one should assess the need for a valuation allowance. A valuation allowance is needed when there is a high probability (more than 50 percent) that some or all of a deferred tax asset will not be realized. Realization of a deferred tax asset is dependent on whether there will be sufficient future taxable income of the appropriate character (e.g., ordinary income, capital gain income) in the period during which deductible temporary differences reverse or within the carry back and carry forward periods available under the tax law.

Sources of Taxable Income for Tax Benefits

When attempting to show how positive findings can reverse the impact of negative findings, a key factor could be the future taxable income that has a significant value within the carry back and carry forward periods available under the tax law. The following sources of taxable income may be available under the tax law to realize a portion or all of a tax benefit for deductible temporary differences and carry forwards:

- Future reversals of existing taxable temporary differences
- Taxable income in prior carry back year(s) if carry back is permitted under the tax law
- Tax planning strategies
- Future taxable income exclusive of reversing temporary differences and carry forwards

APPLICATION

Generally Accepted Accounting Principles (GAAP) Versus Tax Code

There are a few differences between the GAAP and tax code, especially as they relate to nonprofit organizations. Before those differences are discussed, some of the general issues will be mentioned. For example, there are several differences between the two views when looking at revenue recognition, the matching principle, and revenue from municipal bonds.

What are the differences in a nonprofit environment?

According to Miller (n.d.), a San Francisco consultant, "nonprofits, being tax exempt, are creatures of the tax code. GAAP requires that professional judgment be exercised to avoid misleading financial statements that technically conform but distort nonetheless" (par. 2). Some of the differences in a nonprofit environment are in the areas of government awards, cost-sharing arrangements, gifts of property or service, prepaid fund-raising costs, and fair market value on investments.

VIEWPOINT

State Corporate Tax Disclosure

Some tax professionals and policy makers reviewing the state corporate income tax believe there is a problem with it. "The share of corporate profits in the U.S. collected by state governments via the corporate income tax has fallen sharply in the past quarter century" (Wilson, 2006, p.1). Mazerov (n.d.) reported that there is data that suggests the following:

- The share of tax revenue supplied by this tax in the 45 states that levy it fell from more than 10 percent in the late 1970s to less than 9 percent in the late 1980s to less than 7 percent in 2008.
- The effective rate at which states tax corporate profits fell from 6.9 percent in the 1981–85 period to 5.4 percent in 1991–95 to 4.8 percent in 2001–05.
- Many state-specific studies have found that most corporations filing income tax returns paid the minimum corporate tax even in years in which the economy was growing strongly. In the wake of the 2008 financial crisis, cash-strapped states began to look for politically tolerable ways to raise revenues. Led by Illinois in 2010, state corporate tax rates edged up, ranking the United States second (behind Japan) among OECD countries with the highest statutory (combined federal and state) corporate tax rate at 39.2 percent (Bedell, 2011).

Benefits of Corporate Tax Disclosure

Although there is continuous debate surrounding this information, many in the business community believe that there are organizations that are taking advantage of the provisions of corporate income tax laws that have been enacted (i.e., tax incentives for businesses that make major investments in the state). However, the policy makers and advocates disagree. This group of individuals believes that corporate tax incentives are not cost-effective at stimulating economic development. Mazerov (n.d.) believes that this debate will not be able to reach closure until the states mandate public disclosure of the amount of corporate income tax that specific corporations pay to specific states. He believes that this type of change would do the following:

- Help show policy makers and the public whether the corporate income tax is structured in a way that ensures all corporations doing business in the state are paying their fair share of tax. Because of the large number of variables that affect a corporation's tax liability, it is difficult for nonexperts to understand the impact of states' tax policy choices. Examples of how these policies actually affect the tax liability of identifiable corporations could be an asset in assisting policy makers and advocates to comprehend the effectiveness and fairness of a state's corporate tax policies.

- Shed light on the effectiveness of tax policies designed to promote economic development. A number of states have enacted corporate tax incentives and/or tax cuts with the aim of creating jobs or encouraging investment in the state. Without the information provided by company-specific tax disclosure, it is difficult to analyze the effectiveness of such policies.

- Stimulate any needed reform of the state's corporate income tax system. Despite the significant drop in state corporate income taxes prior to the 2008 financial crisis, very few states have enacted meaningful reforms to address this problem. Efforts against this tax shelter have been successful in a number of states, primarily because the public has learned the names of specific well-known corporations that have exploited this shelter. Similarly, corporate tax disclosure could inspire tax reform efforts by encouraging public and policy maker interest in these issues.

In short, corporate tax disclosure would help clarify the real-world outcomes of a state's corporate tax laws and policies and facilitate reforms if needed.

CONCLUSION

This article highlights some of the events that affect income taxes. Two of these events are net operating losses and valuation allowances. A net operating loss occurs when the annual deductions are greater than the taxable income for the year. The year that the NOL occurs is called the NOL year. In order to claim a net operating loss on the income tax return, one must calculate the amount that can be taken as a deduction to be applied against the taxable income from another year.

The Statement of Financial Accounting Standards (SFAS) No. 109 mandates that all organizations are to establish valuation allowances if there is a possibility that their deferred tax assets will not be realized (Financial Accounting Standards Board, 1992). Some of the highlight points of the standard include recognition of deferred tax assets "for all temporary differences that are tax deductible in the future, and the more likely than not provision in valuation of such assets" (Hirst & Sevcik, 1996), and discretion to assess the possibility of deferred tax assets occurring.

The guidelines provided by SFAS No. 109 need to be addressed in order to test earnings management as it relates to valuation allowance. These guidelines evaluate four sources of income in establishing the level of valuations allowances. The four sources are future taxable differences that reverse in time, history of profitability, expected future profitability, and tax planning strategies.

There are four sources of taxable income outlined in SFAS No. 109 that correlate to deferred tax assets. Two of the sources are future reversals of taxable temporary differences and income in previous carry back years. Both are objective and verifiable. The other two sources, future taxable income and tax planning strategies, are subjective.

Some tax professionals and policy makers have been reviewing the state corporate income tax and believe there is a problem with it. "The share of corporate profits in the U.S. collected by state governments via the corporate income tax has fallen sharply in the past quarter century" (Wilson, 2006, p. 1). Although there is continuous debate surrounding this information, many in the business community believe that there are organizations that are taking advantage of the provisions of corporate income tax laws that have been enacted (i.e., tax incentives for businesses that make major investments in the state). However, the policy makers and advocates disagree. This group of individuals believes that corporate tax incentives are not cost-effective at stimulating economic development.

TERMS & CONCEPTS

Carry back: A technique for receiving a refund of back taxes by applying a deduction or credit from a current year to a prior year.

Carry forward: A technique for applying a loss or credit from the current year to a future year.

Generally Accepted Accounting Principles (GAAP): A set of widely accepted accounting standards set by the FASB and used to standardize financial accounting of public companies.

Income taxes: A tax levied on net personal or business income.

Independent contractor: A person or business who performs services for another person under an express or implied agreement and who is not subject to the other's control, or right to control, the manner and means of performing the services; not as an employee.

Net operating losses: Occur when a company's deductions are more than its income for the year.

Sole proprietor: A business owned and operated by one individual.

Tax code: Includes all federal tax laws. Originally written in 1939, and thoroughly revised in 1954.

Valuation allowances: Actual income tax paid divided by net taxable income before taxes; expressed as a percentage.

BIBLIOGRAPHY

Ali, A., & Kumar, K. (1994), The magnitudes of financial statement effects and accounting choice: The case of the adoption of SFAS 87. *Journal of Accounting and Economics, 18,* 89–114.

Bartov, E. (1993). The timing of asset sales and earnings manipulations. *Accounting Review, 68,* 840–855.

Bedell, D. (2011). Cash-poor states eye corporate tax hikes. *Global Finance, 25,* 7.

Colley, R., Rue, J., Valencia, A., & Volkan, A. (2012). Accounting for deferred taxes: Time for a change. *Journal of Business & Economics Research, 10,* 149–156.

Cornia, G., Edmiston, K., Sjoquist, D., & Wallace, S. (2005). The disappearing state corporate income tax. *National Tax Journal, 58,* 115–138.

Cowan, M. J. (2012). A GAAP critic's guide to corporate income taxes. *Tax Lawyer, 66,* 209–259.

Financial Accounting Standards Board (1992). Statement of financial accounting standards No. 109.

Hagen, K. (2007). Net operating losses and U.S. income taxes. Associated Content.

Mazerov, M. (n.d.) State corporate tax disclosure: The next step in corporate tax reform.

McNichols, M., & Wilson, G. (1988). Evidence of earnings management from the provision for bad debts. *Journal of Accounting Research, 26,* 1–31.

Schatzberg, J., & Sevcik, G. (1994). A multiperiod model and experimental evidence of independence and "lowballing." *Contemporary Accounting Research, 11,* 137–174.

GAAP versus tax (2006). The Nonprofit Times.

Watts, R., & Zimmerman, J. (1986). *Positive accounting theory.* New Jersey: Prentice-Hall.

Wilson, D. (2006). The mystery of falling state corporate income taxes. *FRBSF Economic Letter,* 2006, 1–3.

SUGGESTED READING

Bujaki, M., & McConomy, B. (2007). Income tax accounting policy choice: Exposure draft responses and the early adoption decision by Canadian companies. *Accounting Perspectives, 6,* 21–53.

Reinstein, A., & Lander, G. (2006). Accounting for income tax uncertainties: A step towards financial transparency. *Real Estate Review, 35,* 37–43.

Wong, N. (2005). Determinants of the accounting change for income tax. *Journal of Business Finance & Accounting, 32*(5/6), 1171–1196.

Essay by Marie Gould

INFORMATION SYSTEMS AUDITING

This article examines the purposes of information systems (IS) auditing, the methods that are used to perform IS audits, and the types of findings that IS auditors include in audit reports. The article explains the five different types of audits performed on information systems: development, application, computer operations, management, and technology. Control Objectives for Information and Related Technology (COBIT) are explained, and the use of COBIT in the audit process is examined. To illustrate the types of findings that IS auditors present to audit sponsors, the results of a General Accountability Office (GAO) audit of multiple U.S. government agencies are presented. The development and dissemination of the IS auditing standards by Information Systems Audit and Control

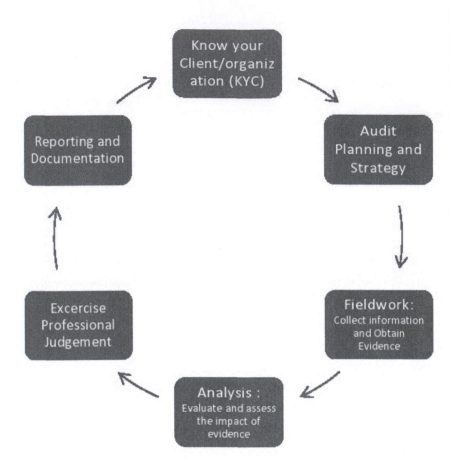

During a development audit, system designers and auditors work together to ensure that the application being developed has adequate controls and security.

An application review is a process during which auditors, often with assistance from designers, review that adequate controls exist to assure proper levels of security.

An operations audit focuses on information systems operations environment to assess the overall control of the environment.

A management audit concentrates on the management practices of an IS organization and is designed to assess how well controls of the IS environment are designed, implemented, and monitored.

A technology audit is designed to review a specific technology used in the processing of business data in order to assess how well information systems controls are implemented for the technology.

Some typical stages in the audit process are portrayed here. (Courtesy of Agasthya 1992 via Wikimedia Commons)

Association (ISACA) are reviewed along with the IS auditor's code of ethics.

OVERVIEW

The function of an information systems (IS) audit is to review management controls applicable to the security, integrity, reliability, and effective utilization of information systems. An IS audit of an existing application or system often includes tests of transactions and outputs in order to provide reasonable assurance that security standards and controls are properly designed and implemented (Morris & Pushkin, 1995). There are several types of audits performed on information systems including:

Development Audits

During a development audit, auditors participate in projects before and during implementation to ensure that adequate controls and security are built into the system. There are two steps in the development audit. The first round of work is done before an application program is put into use in an organization (pre-implementation). The second round of work is done after the application program is in use (post-implementation). The first audit process examines security plans and documentation among other things. The second round of audit work examines the conversion of data from old systems to new systems and checks for integrity and validity. Weaknesses identified in either phase of the audit are reported to managers responsible for the application program ("IS Auditing Guideline," 2001).

Application Reviews

An application review is designed to "ensure that controls exist to provide a reasonable assurance that transactions are complete, valid, recorded accurately, and in a timely manner." Many auditors use computer-assisted audit techniques (CAATs) to perform a reconciliation of control totals, review outputs of the application, or perform a review of the logic, parameters, or other characteristics of the application. There are several CAATs available for use by auditors ("IS auditing guideline,"1998). Audit expert systems "can be used to assist IS auditors in the decision-making process by automating the knowledge of experts in the field. This technique includes automated risk analysis, system software, and control objectives software packages" ("IT Standards, Guideline and Tools," 2009).

Operations Audits

An operations audit focuses on an information system's operations environment in order to assess the overall control of the environment. Auditors examine operations policies and procedures for adequacy and compliance with appropriate laws, regulations, or standards. A review of implemented policies and procedures is conducted to assure that all the resources required for implementation are available and in place. Auditors also test to determine whether personnel consistently follow policies and procedures.

Management Audits

A management audit concentrates on the management practices of an IS organization and is designed to assess how controls of the systems environment are implemented and monitored. Auditors can use a variety of approaches when examining IS management practices and many rely on the IT Governance Institute's (ITGI) Control Objectives for Information and Related Technology (COBIT) as a guide to widely adopted best practices. The COBIT framework has been structured into 34 IT processes clustering interrelated life-cycle activities or interrelated discrete tasks. IS management audits based on the COBIT *IT Assurance Guide* minimize the impact of opinions dominating audit conclusions. COBIT is based on numerous standards and best practices documents that were published by standards organizations around the world, including Europe, Canada, Australia, Japan, and the United States ("COBIT Mapping," 2007).

Technology Audits

A technology audit is designed to review a specific technology used in the processing of business data in order to assess how well an information system's controls are implemented for the technology. This could include specific types or models of file servers, security tools, or network equipment. Auditors examine how the technology is used, deployed, and configured to determine whether appropriate standards and practices are applied for the environment.

APPLICATIONS

What IS Auditors Find from an Audit

One of the largest IS auditing organizations in the world is the U.S. Government Accountability Office (GAO), which is an independent, nonpartisan agency that works for Congress. The GAO is often called the "congressional watchdog" because it investigates how the federal government spends taxpayer dollars. The GAO gathers information to help Congress determine how well executive branch agencies are doing their jobs. The GAO supports the U.S. Congress's oversight of government agencies by doing the following:

- performing evaluations of government agencies and programs to determine how well they are working
- performing audits of government agency operations to determine whether federal funds are being spent properly
- performing investigations of alleged illegal or improper activities of government agencies
- researching, developing, and issuing opinions and decisions on legal matters

Fraud Susceptibility

The GAO has been conducting IS audits of U.S. government agency information systems for decades. The findings of a GAO audit provide examples and insight into what IS auditors may find during an audit. In one multiple agency audit, the GAO found that the weaknesses that the audit revealed increased the risks that many federal government operations are exposed to, including potential fraud, intentional as well as unintentional misuse, and possible disruption from a wide array of events. The Department of the Treasury, for example, was vulnerable to fraud and, with the hundreds of billions of dollars that the federal government pays and collects each month, could easily be jeopardized. The audits also showed that as the Department of Defense was continuously relying on more and more computer systems, there was a corresponding increase in the vulnerability of several military functions that support the war-fighting capability of the United States and its allies ("Serious and widespread weaknesses," 2000).

Access to Information

The GAO audits further indicated that the information security weaknesses that were found during the audits of federal agencies put vast amounts of very confidential data at risk. This included personal and tax data as well as proprietary business information. One very serious case was in 1999, when a Social Security Administration employee gained unauthorized access to computer systems that held the files of social security recipients. The employee used this unauthorized access to obtain information and make inappropriate disclosures.

In numerous cases the GAO audits showed federal agencies had very weak computer security controls in place on a wide range of computer systems and applications software. Some audit findings were very basic and showed that several aspects security planning and implementation were inadequate. Additional audit findings addressed complex security problems including ineffective physical and logical access controls as well as ineffective software change controls.

Access controls were evaluated at all 24 of the agencies covered in this particular audit, and significant weaknesses were reported. The GAO found that agencies had not implemented effective user account and password management practices to reduce the risk that accounts could be used to gain unauthorized system access. One problem that auditors encountered on a widespread basis was very poor control over user accounts on computer systems, and many accounts were still active even though the person with the account no longer worked at the agency. Numerous contractors and former employees still had access to computers and could still read, modify, copy, or delete data ("Serious and widespread weaknesses," 2000).

Application Software Development & Change Controls

The GAO identified weaknesses in application software development and change controls in 19 of the 21 agencies where such controls were evaluated. Problems found during the audits ranged from undisciplined testing procedures that could not really ensure that software used by the agencies operated as it was intended to operate. In some agencies, auditors found that policies and procedures designed to protect software program libraries maintained by the agency were not adequate to address that important security need ("Serious and widespread weaknesses," 2000).

Segregation of Duties

Segregation of duties is important to maintain security in both the private and public sector. The design of jobs and functions in managing computer systems is generally done in a manner that keeps employees from having end-to-end control over a process involving financial management. Auditors found many weaknesses in how agencies were managing segregation of duties. One of the most common issues the auditors encountered was that computer programmers and operators were authorized to perform a wide scope of tasks and responsibilities. The auditors contended that, under the job structure, the computer programmers and operators could independently modify, circumvent, and disable system security features. Auditors pointed out cases where staff with procurement responsibilities had system access privileges that enabled them to personally request, approve, and record the receipt of purchased items. This enabled those staff to purchase equipment and process paperwork without anybody else knowing it and could result in theft or misappropriation of equipment and supplies ("Serious and widespread weaknesses," 2000).

Operating System Software Controls

Auditors found problems with operating system software controls in most of the agencies. The most typical problem was that access to computer systems and operating systems was not restricted in a manner that could keep computer staff from disabling or circumventing controls. This included the ability to change data in the system audit log. Auditors contended that this lack of control could allow computer personnel to perform a variety of inappropriate and unauthorized actions. In the event that staff did do something to systems that they wanted to hide, they had the ability to delete related segments of the audit log, which means that their actions would be very difficult to detect ("Serious and widespread weaknesses," 2000).

Service Continuity Controls

Auditors also examined service continuity controls and found the controls to be inadequate in most agencies. The auditors typically found that service continuity plans were often incomplete and could not be used to ensure continuity. The missing element in most plans had to do with a complete and up-to-date inventory of operations and supporting resources and priorities were not properly set for recovery of systems and data. In addition, the auditors found that disaster recovery plans had not been tested and thus computer staff in the agencies had not gone through the proper steps to identify the weaknesses in the plans.

The auditors concluded that there was a wide variety of causes for the security and control procedures and processes in the agencies being as weak as they were. However, the roots of these problems were that the agencies were not adhering to existing security program management standards and techniques. The ongoing trends may also show that government agencies do not have an adequate program of internal IS auditing procedures in place. Ongoing IS audits are a means of detecting problems and supporting continuous process improvement ("Serious and widespread," 2000).

ISSUES

Setting Standards for Auditing

As corporations grow in both size and value, investors and investment advisors rely heavily on the reliability of financial and operational information provided by companies. It is also important because of the public's investment and the public's trust that not-for-profits, nongovernment organizations, and government agencies have reliable financial and operational disclosure. The audit process is one way to help assure the accuracy of information corporate managers,

investors, policy makers, and regulators rely upon in their decision-making processes (Janvrin & Jeffrey, 2007).

Globalization has led to more complex corporate structures that face more complex accounting challenges and thus more complex audit challenges. The need for international auditing standards is now more important because the health of global corporations is more important to the economic well-being of most nations. The frequency of international investment is also on the rise and thus the use of a common set of international standards auditing can provide clear benefits to investors, regulators, and audit firms. To help achieve stronger international standards for auditing, the International Auditing and Assurance Standards Board (IAASB) was founded as a standard-setting body designated by, and operating under, the auspices of the International Federation of Accountants ("IFAC History," 2007).

Information Systems Audit & Control Association

IS auditing requires both knowledge of audit methods and an in-depth understanding of information technology, applications software, and the processes by which both are managed in an organization. There must also be a common set of standards and methods applied to IS audits and the Information Systems Audit and Control Association (ISACA) has taken on the role of developing and advancing globally applicable IS audit standards.

These standards developed or recommended by ISACA provide a baseline of mandatory requirements for IS auditing and reporting. These standards and practices are the minimum level of audit performance that is required to achieve the professional responsibilities documented in the ISACA Code of Professional Ethics. The standards also communicate to corporate managers and the business and government world in general of how professional IS auditors conduct audit work. The various IS auditing procedures documented by ISACA give auditors and others very detailed information on how an organization and individuals can be in compliance with the body of IS auditing standards ("IFAC History," (2007). As corporate governance becomes more complex the ISACA audit standards and the ISACA Code of Professional Ethics provide boards of directors with a critical tool to examine and mitigate risk to which their organization is exposed (Holm & Laursen, 2007).

COBIT

COBIT has become widely accepted around the world as a set of detailed control techniques for the IS management environment. It is used by IS managers as well as IS auditors as a framework for IS management as well as IS auditing (Violino, 2006). The framework and techniques provided by COBIT are used as a baseline in information security and management and encompass a wide variety of best practices and standards from several countries (Ali Pabrai, 2005). The COBIT framework is divided into several sections, which are aligned with IT management process. These are control objectives and control practices and management guidelines. The management guidelines provide metrics that allow auditors and managers alike to assess performance of IS in business terms and help to identify control gaps and strategies for improvement ("COBIT Mapping," 2007; Lainhart IV, 2001).

Engagement Letters & Charter Audits

IS auditors may be required to perform audits of information systems that are designed and governed by varying standards. The applicable standards will be determined by the type of organization being audited and may be different for publicly traded companies, government agencies, nongovernment organizations, or even for privately held companies (O'Donnell & Rechtman, 2005).

An IS auditor generally works with the guidance of an engagement letter or audit charter. These documents set out the scope of an audit and provide high-level statements of what the audit team will examine during the audit process. The engagement letter, or scope of audit, is most often mutually agreed upon by the auditors and the parties responsible for the information systems being audited. The charter provides the authority for the IS audit and gives auditors access to appropriate information and resources to effectively and efficiently complete the audit. IS auditors also retain the working files, documents, and audit evidences obtained during the course of the audit and can use the material as the basis of reference in case of any issues or contradictions.

Auditor Code of Conduct

Accounts and accounting firms and auditors have faced considerable criticism during the last decade. There have been several crises of confidence as some of the world's largest companies have fallen under the weight of misrepresented financial statements and misunderstood risks. There were many warning signs that such a crisis was coming and that ethics were waning (Pearson, 1995). ISACA has been addressing the issue of ethics for IS auditing. *IS Auditing Guideline: Responsibility, Authority and Accountability* from ISACA provides a basic outline of the acceptable code of conduct for IS auditors and the companies that employee the IS auditor. Highlights from a long list of ethical standards include the following:

- Auditors should be honest and sincere in their approach to their audit work.
- Auditors should maintain an independent position and appearance from the firms they audit.
- Auditors should abide by their respective codes of professional ethics.
- Auditors should conduct all audits in accordance with appropriate standards and practices.
- Auditors should comply with all applicable regulatory and legal requirements in the situations where they conduct audits.
- Auditors should be adequately trained to conduct their audit assignments.
- All audit staff assigned to an IS audit should be appropriately supervised.
- Auditors should always collect and properly handle audit evidence that supports their conclusions.
- Auditors should always assure that their audit evidence is adequately and properly stored and is retrievable if required.
- Auditors should always respect the confidentiality of information obtained from clients.
- Auditors should not make misstatements or ambiguous statements.
- Auditors should always be honest about any instance in which there is a loss of independence ("IS auditing guideline," 2005).

CONCLUSION

There are several different types of audits performed on information systems including development, application, computer operations, management, and technology audits. Auditors can use a variety of approaches when examining IS management practices, and many rely on the IT Governance Institute's (ITGI) Control Objectives for Information and Related Technology (COBIT) as a guide to widely adopted best practices. The COBIT framework has been structured into 34 IT processes clustering interrelated life-cycle activities or interrelated discrete tasks. COBIT is based on numerous standards and best practices documents that were published by standards organizations around the world, including Europe, Canada, Australia, Japan, and the United States ("COBIT Mapping," 2007).

The GAO has been conducting IS audits of U.S. government agency information systems for several decades. The findings of a GAO audit provide examples and insight into what IS auditors may find during an audit. In one multiple agency audit, the GAO found that the weaknesses that the audit revealed increased the risks that many federal government operations are exposed to, including potential fraud, intentional as well as unintentional misuse, and possible disruption from a wide array of events.

Globalization has led to more complex corporate structures that face more complex accounting challenges and thus more complex audit challenges. The need for international auditing standards is now more important because the health of global corporations is more important to the economic well-being of most nations. As corporations grow in both size and value, investors and investment advisors rely heavily on the reliability of financial and operational information provided by companies.

TERMS & CONCEPTS

Access controls: Mechanisms or processes that limit or detect inappropriate or unauthorized access to computer applications or data.

Application review: An audit process designed to evaluate whether appropriate controls are in place so that an application completely performs all steps in a program and that those steps results in valid transactions.

Application software development and change controls: Mechanisms or processes that prevent unauthorized applications software programs or modifications to applications software from being implemented.

Development audit: An audit process that is conducted while an application is under development or being implemented to ensure that adequate controls and security are built into the system and that any concerns are addressed before the system is completed.

Management audit: An audit process that concentrates on the management practices of an IS organization that is designed to assess how controls of the IS environment are implemented and monitored.

Operations audit: An audit process that focuses on the information system's operations environment in order to assess the overall control of the environment.

Segregation of duties: A process of splitting duties among IT and other staff that assures that one individual does not control all of the major aspects of a process or operation that would enable him or her to implement unauthorized activities or achieve unauthorized access to assets or records.

Service continuity controls: Mechanisms or processes that guide IT staff in implementing measures to maintain uninterrupted service and protect sensitive data during unexpected events such as natural disasters.

System software controls: Mechanisms or processes to limit and monitor access to applications programs or sensitive data related to computer systems operation.

Technology audit: An audit process designed to review a specific technology used in the processing of business data in order to assess how well information system controls are implemented for the technology.

BIBLIOGRAPHY

Ali Pabrai, U. (2005). The CobiT security baseline. *Certification Magazine, 7,* 28–29.

COBIT Mapping: Overview of international IT guidance (2nd ed.). (2007).

Grabski, S. V., Leech, S. A., & Schmidt, P. J. (2011). A review of ERP research: A future agenda for accounting information systems. *Journal of Information Systems, 25,* 37–78.

Holm, C., & Laursen, P. (2007). Risk and control developments in corporate governance: Changing the role of the external auditor? *Corporate Governance: An International Review, 15,* 322–333.

IFAC history in brief. (2007).

IS Auditing Guideline Application Systems Review Document G14. (2001). Information Systems Audit and Control Association (ISACA).

IS auditing guideline use of computer-assisted audit techniques (CAATs) document G3. (1998). Information Systems Audit and Control Association (ISACA).

IS auditing guideline responsibility, authority and accountability document G34. (2005). Information Systems Audit and Control Association (ISACA).

IT standards, guidelines, and tools and techniques for audit and assurance and control professionals. (2009). Information Systems Audit and Control Association (ISACA).

Janvrin, D., & Jeffrey, C. (2007, September). An investigation of auditor perceptions about subsequent events and factors that influence this audit task. *Accounting Horizons, 21,* 295–312.

Lainhart IV, J. (2001). An IT assurance framework for the future. *Ohio CPA Journal, 60,* 19.

Morris, B., & Pushkin, A. (1995). Determinants of information systems audit involvement in EDI systems development. *Journal of Information Systems, 9,* 111–128.

O'Donnell, J., & Rechtman, Y. (2005). Navigating the standards for information technology controls. *CPA Journal, 75,* 64–69.

Pearson, M. (1995). Doing the right thing. *Journal of Accountancy, 179,* 82–86.

Serious and widespread weaknesses persist at federal agencies. (2000). *United States General Accounting Office (GAO) Report to the Chairman, Subcommittee on Government Management, Information and Technology, Committee on Government Reform, House of Representatives.*

Violino, B. (2006). Sorting the standards. *Computerworld, 40,* 46–47.

Wright, M., & Capps, I. J. (2012). Auditor independence and internal information systems audit quality. *Business Studies Journal,* 463–83.

SUGGESTED READING

Bertine, H., Faynberg, I., & Lu, H. (2003). Overview of data and telecommunications security standardization efforts in ISO, IEC, ITU, and IETF. *Bell Labs Technical Journal, 8,* 203–229.

Carnaghan, C. (2000). Discussion of an analysis of the group dynamics surrounding internal control assessment in information systems audit and assurance domains. *Journal of Information Systems, 14,* 117.

Leech, T. (2000). Discussion of an analysis of the group dynamics surrounding internal control assessment in information systems audit and assurance domains. *Journal of Information Systems, 14,* 123.

O'Donnell, E., Arnold, V., & Sutton, S. (2000). An analysis of the group dynamics surrounding internal control assessment in information systems audit and assurance domains. *Journal of Information Systems, 14,* 97.

O'Donnell, E., Arnold, V., & Sutton, S. (2000). Reply to discussion of an analysis of the group dynamics surrounding internal control assessment in information systems audit and assurance domains. *Journal of Information Systems, 14,* 127.

Pierce, E. (2004). Assessing data quality with control matrices. *Communications of the ACM, 47,* 82–86.

Schneider, G. (1995). Discussion of determinants of information systems audit involvement in EDI systems development. *Journal of Information Systems, 9,* 129–132.

Essay by Michael Erbschloe, MA

INTERNATIONAL CORPORATE FINANCE

This article focuses on how multinational corporations decide on whether or not to enter foreign markets and evaluate their performance once they have entered the markets. One of the main questions that the financial team will ask when contemplating whether or not it should go into foreign operations is "what are the benefits?" In order to evaluate its risk-return profile, the multinational corporation

Toyota is one of the world's largest multinational corporations with their headquarters in Toyota City, Japan. (Courtesy of Chris 73 via Wikimedia Commons)

will review imperfections in the various markets for goods and services, factors of production, and financial assets that can be created. Two long-run investment and financing options (i.e., international capital budgeting and direct foreign investments) are explored, and the results from a study conducted on how to measure overseas financial performance are reviewed.

OVERVIEW

One of the focal points for many multinational corporations is to have the ability to perform financial transactions outside of the United States. It is important for these corporations to have the ability to participate in the international trade process. Financial managers of multinational corporations must be aware of the financial techniques involved in the international trade process. Three basic needs of import-export financing are guarantee against the risk of a business deal being incomplete, security against foreign exchange dangers, and a way of financing the transactions involved (Eiteman & Stonehill, 1979). Some of the key banking services that are needed include letters of credit, wire transfers, collections, and foreign exchange (Teller Sense, 2003). It is

important for organizations to have the ability to wire deposits in a timely manner, have the credibility for banks to provide a letter of credit on its behalf, and collect payments quickly and easily.

"Although the original decision to undertake operations in a particular foreign country may be determined in practice by a mix of strategic, behavioral, and economic decisions, the specific project and all reinvestment decisions should be justified by traditional financial analysis" (Eiteman & Stonehill, 1979, p. 264). One of the main questions that the financial team will ask when contemplating whether or not it should go into foreign operations is "what are the benefits?" In order to evaluate its risk-return profile, the multinational corporation will review imperfections in the various markets for goods and services, factors of production, and financial assets that can be created (Eiteman & Stonehill, 1979).

APPLICATION

Long-Run Investment & Financing
Two key areas of long-term investments and financing are international capital budgeting and direct foreign investments. Although many large multinational corporations with international sales have been the focus of many capital budgeting studies, direct foreign investments are just as important when a multinational corporation is reviewing its long-run investment and financing options. Direct foreign investments deal with market imperfections and behavioral factors that may entice a multinational corporation to invest in a foreign country on a long-term or permanent basis. International capital budgeting applies contemporary finance theory and special research into international operations to considerations of techniques by which foreign investment decisions should be made (Eiteman & Stonehill, 1979).

International Capital Budgeting
"Capital budgeting is a financial analysis tool that applies quantitative analysis to support strong management decisions" (Bearing Point, n.d.). Capital budgeting seeks to provide a simple way for the finance department to see the "big picture" of the benefits, costs, and risks for a corporation planning to make short-term and/or long-term investments. Unfortunately, many of the leading methods have

experienced problems, especially when an organization is using a standardized template. Examples of potential problems include the following:

- The benefits, costs, and risks associated with an investment tend to be different based on the type of industry (i.e., technology versus agricultural).
- A corporation may highlight the end results of the return on investment model and the assumptions that support the results versus a balanced analysis of benefits, costs, and risks.

If an organization does not account for the above-mentioned scenarios, there is a possibility for the results to be skewed, which would make the data unusable. This type of error could hinder a project from getting approved. Therefore, it is critical for financial analysts to have a more effective and efficient technique to use. BearingPoint (n.d.) identified several leading practices that organizations are using in order to avoid reporting faulty information. The theme in all of the techniques is that capital budgeting is not the only factor considered. Other quantifiable factors are utilized in order to see the big picture.

- **Consider the nature of the request.** The type of benefit obtained by the investment will determine the nature of the request. Therefore, it may be beneficial to classify the benefit types into categories such as strategic, quantifiable, and intangible.
- **All benefits are not created equal.** Benefits should be classified correctly in order to properly analyze. There are two types of benefits—hard and soft. Hard benefits affect the profit and loss statement directly, but soft benefits do not have the same affect.
- **Quantify risk. Make sure that the risks are properly evaluated.** In most cases, risks are neglected. Also, it would be a good idea to build a risk factor into whatever model is utilized.
- **Be realistic about benefit periods.** Make sure that the expectations are realistic. In the past, corporations have created unrealistic goals for the benefits period by anticipating benefits to come too early and reusing models that reflect the depreciation period for the capital asset.

Although the same theoretical framework applies, capital budgeting analysis of a foreign product can be

more complex than the domestic products. Eiteman and Stonehill (1979) identified eight potential complications for the international capital budgeting process. Potential problems included the following:

- There is a need to distinguish between project cash flows and parent cash flows.
- Financing and remittance of funds to the parent company need to be absolutely identified due to the conflicting tax systems, constraints on financial flows, local norms, and changes in financial markets and institutions.
- Differential rates of national inflation can be important in changing competitive positions and cash flows over time.
- Foreign exchange rate changes that are not matched by differential national inflation rates may alter the value of cash flows from affiliate to parent and vice versa.
- Segmented worldwide capital markets may initiate a chance for financial gain or could cause even more financial losses.
- Terminal value is hard to evaluate due to possible divergent market values of a project to potential buyers from the host, parent, or third countries.
- Political risks may drastically reduce the value of a foreign investment.

Direct Foreign Investment
Investment decisions must be made for both foreign and domestic endeavors. However, the process is more complex when evaluating foreign investment decisions. Foreign investments are usually made with a more complicated set of strategic, behavioral, and economic considerations. In addition, the evaluation phase tends to be longer and more costly and results in less information on which to evaluate opportunities. Financial assessments of initial financial overseas investments that use the ordinary discounted cash flow technique are not considered as reliable as domestic investments because of larger perceptions based on corporate, political, and foreign exchange risks.

Strategic Considerations for Foreign Investments
Hogue (1967) was the first to introduce the concept that the motivation of multinational corporations is based on four types of strategic consideration when making decisions on direct foreign investments. The

four types are market seekers, raw-material seekers, production-efficiency seekers, and knowledge seekers.

- Market seekers have a desire to produce in foreign markets in order to satisfy local demand or to export to markets outside of their home market.
- Raw-material seekers focus on extracting raw materials wherever they can be found. They will either export their findings or process them for sale in the host country.
- Production-efficiency seekers produce in countries where one or more of the factors of production are underpriced relative to their productivity.
- Knowledge seekers operate in foreign countries in order to gain access to technology or managerial experience. It should be noted that the four types of strategic considerations are mutually exclusive.

Methods for Multinational Investing
Given the complexities experienced by most multinational corporations when evaluating foreign investments, researchers in the field have indicated a need for a better way to evaluate the investments. One proposal was to establish operational foreign investment criteria that are consistent with the behavioral theory of the corporation. Stonehill and Nathanson (1968) conducted a survey to see what methods were utilized by organizations when making multinational financing investments. The researchers used *Fortune*'s list and selected 219 American firms and 100 foreign firms. The results of their research revealed that most foreign and domestic investment alternatives use the same capital budgeting procedures; there was a difference in the way that organizations viewed foreign income; over 64 percent of the organizations did not vary cost or capital for foreign investments; nearly all of the organizations indicated that they made allowances for risk; and nearly all of the organizations consolidated majority owned foreign subsidiaries with domestic divisions.

Oblak and Helm (1980) conducted a similar study to see if there had been any significant changes since the study conducted by Stonehill and Nathanson. Their survey was sent to 226 Fortune 500 organizations which operated wholly owned subsidiaries in 12 or more foreign countries. There was a 26 percent response rate, and the capital budgets of the respondent firms ranged from $10 million to $2 billion annually with a median of $200 million. The results of the survey indicated that multinational corporations conducted more detailed analyses of their foreign projects. Compared to the results found by Stonehill and Nathanson in 1966, Oblak and Helm reported that a higher percentage of multinational corporations used discounted cash flow methods and adjusted for risk in foreign project evaluations. However, the corporations had not made a significant change in the way in which they measured the returns from foreign projects or in the determination of the appropriate discount rate.

VIEWPOINT

Overseas Financial Performance
International business strategy provides corporations the opportunity to expand and manage business operations in many locations across the world. Many organizations are weighing the pros and cons of starting operations overseas. However, it is imperative that the decision makers identify opportunities, explore resources, and assess core competencies before implementing a plan to move forward. These three factors may provide a foundation for many corporations as they implement an international strategy. According to Hoskisson, Hitt, and Ireland (2003), each factor should be evaluated when determining whether or not to move forward.

"In today's international environment of economic uncertainty and volatile markets, financial executives face a number of unique and challenging problems when seeking to evaluate the financial performance of operations outside of their home country" (Persen and Lessig, 1979, p. 5). Persen and Lessig (1979) conducted a study in order to identify and evaluate the methods and procedures that tend to be used by leading multinational corporations as they attempt to find answers to these problems. The study addressed specific ways in which overseas operations are evaluated, especially financial performance. It was found that most multinationals use more than one criterion when measuring the results of their operations. Some of the most common performance standards included sales unit growth, growth in earnings from operations, earnings from operations after tax, and three efficiency indicators (earnings from operations after tax return on net operating assets; earnings from operations after return on investment; and free cash flow rate of return on investment).

Three of the topics from the study that will be discussed in this article include principle evaluation techniques, foreign exchange considerations, and other external financial considerations.

Principle Evaluation Techniques — According to the survey, the top four measurements were operating budget comparisons, contribution to earnings per share, return on investment, and contribution to corporate cash flow. Operating budget comparisons was ranked as the number one choice among the respondents. It was found that large multinational corporations favored the "contribution to earnings per share" technique more so than smaller firms. It was found that the "return on investment" technique's popularity was growing as a leading measurement base. Oil and metal corporations tended to utilize the contribution to corporate cash flow technique.

Foreign Exchange Considerations — One of the areas in the evaluation process that tended to be ignored was how the multinational corporations dealt with results that are denominated in currencies other than the one used by the American parent company. "Most US companies doing a substantial volume of business overseas have been operating abroad for a number of years, and thus the matter of changing foreign exchange rates is nothing new. With the onset of more volatile fluctuations in recent years and new accounting developments (i.e., Financial Accounting Standards Board's statement on translation accounting), this area has assumed a greater significance" (Persen & Lessig, 1979, pp. 87–88). Most multinationals will deal with this issue in one of two ways. First, there may be the local company perspective. This perspective places emphasis on how well the local company performs in its own (foreign) environment and its own currency. The second approach is the parent company perspective. The emphasis is placed on how well the local unit is performing in terms of its contribution to the overall corporation in the parent's currency.

Other External Financial Considerations — Although inflation was identified as the most significant external financial consideration, there were other concerns listed. Some of these areas included political instability, other government regulations, labor unions, differences in tax regulations, different accounting standards, language barriers, cultural differences, industrial democracy, and communications facilities. The survey asked the respondents what they considered to be the main difference between evaluating the financial performance of domestic and overseas operations. Although there were a variety of responses, most fell into five categories that could be broken down into two basic groups. One group dealt with the variety of currencies and inflation rates, and the other group dealt with the financial atmosphere and local government regulations. The five categories reported were differences in currencies' exchange rate flux; translation of currencies; variances in inflation rates; variation in financial and economic conditions; and multiplicity of government regulations and controls.

CONCLUSION

One of the focal points for many multinational corporations is to have the ability to perform financial transactions outside of the United States. It is important for these corporations to have the ability to participate in the international trade process. Some of the key banking services that are needed include letters of credit, wire transfers, collections, and foreign exchange (Teller Sense, 2003). It is important for organizations to have the ability to wire deposits in a timely manner, have the credibility for banks to provide a letter of credit on their behalf, and collect payments quickly and easily.

"Although the original decision to undertake operations in a particular foreign country may be determined in practice by a mix of strategic, behavioral, and economic decisions, the specific project and all reinvestment decisions should be justified by traditional financial analysis" (Eiteman and Stonehill, 1979, p. 264). One of the main questions that the financial team will ask when contemplating whether or not it should go into foreign operations is "what are the benefits?" In order to evaluate its risk-return profile, the multinational corporation will review imperfections in the various markets for goods and services, factors of production, and financial assets that can be created (Eiteman & Stonehill, 1979).

"In today's international environment of economic uncertainty and volatile markets, financial executives face a number of unique and challenging problems when seeking to evaluate the financial performance of operations outside of their home country" (Persen & Lessig, 1979, p. 5). Persen and Lessig (1979) conducted a study in order to identify and evaluate the methods and procedures that tend to be used by leading multinational corporations as they attempt to find answers to these problems. The study addressed specific ways in which overseas operations are evaluated, especially financial performance. Three of the topics discussed in this article are principle evaluation techniques, foreign exchange considerations, and other external financial considerations.

As more financial institutions begin to participate in the global economic system, process improvement has led to the reduction of communication and information costs as a result of technology (Baldwin & Martin, 1999). "One variable that has been used in the international finance literature to proxy information costs is the (geographical) distance between two markets" (Buch, 2005, p. 787). Many have attempted to determine if there is a correlation between international asset holding and distance. Unfortunately, there has not been much research on the effect of distance on international financial relationships over time. Although researchers (Portes & Rey, 2001) have found that some investors have a preference for doing business in surrounding markets with substantial business cycle correlations, Petersen and Rajan (2002) reported that there has been an increase in the business being conducted between banks and their credit buyers. What is important is the fact that international banking is a key factor in the way organizations, such as multinationals, conduct their business.

TERMS & CONCEPTS

Capital budgeting: The process of weighing the cash flows with rates of return to determine what types of long-term projects are worth investing in.

Direct foreign investment (DFI): A corporation in one country that makes a financial and physical investment in the creation of a factory in a different country.

Discounted cash flow techniques: A tool and method used to analyze and evaluate the income capitalization approach to value.

International business operations: When projects are located in host countries other than the home country of the multinational corporation.

International capital budgeting: The process of running a company in order to produce value for those who own shares of the stock.

International strategy: An organization's attempt to instill value in its company by relocating some of its core competencies to overseas markets where there is higher need for such competencies.

Multinational corporation (MNC): A corporation that has its facilities and other assets in at least one country other than its home country.

BIBLIOGRAPHY

Aliber, R. (1979). *Exchange risk and corporate international finance.* London: The MacMillan Press.

Baldwin, R., & Martin, P. (1999). Two waves of globalization: Superficial similarities, fundamental differences. In H. Siebert (ed.), *Globalization and Labor,* Tubingen: Mohr Siebeck.

BearingPoint (n.d.). Improve your capital budget techniques.

Brealey, R. A., Cooper, I. A., & Kaplanis, E. (2012). International propagation of the credit crisis: Lessons for bank regulation. *Journal of Applied Corporate Finance, 24,* 36–45.

Buch, C. (2005). Distance and international banking. *Review of International Economics, 12,* 787–804.

Eiteman, D., & Stonehill, A. (1979). *Multinational business finance,* (2nd ed.). Reading, MA: Addison-Wesley Publishing Company.

Hogue, W. (1967, December 29). The foreign investment decision-making process. *Association for Education in International Business Proceedings.*

Hoskisson, R., Hitt, M., & Ireland, R. (2003, January). International strategy.

Lucey, B. M. (2012, March). Perspectives on international and corporate finance. *Journal of Banking & Finance,* 625.

Matoussi, H., & Jardak, M. (2012). International corporate governance and finance: Legal, cultural and political explanations. *International Journal of Accounting, 47,* 1–43.

Oblak, D., & Helm, R., Jr. (1980). Survey and analysis of capital budgeting methods used by multinationals. *Financial Management (1972), 9,* 37–41.

Persen, W., & Lessig, V. (1979). *Evaluating the financial performance of overseas operations.* New York: Financial Executives Research Foundation.

Petersen, M., & Rajan, R. (2002). Does distance still matter? The information revolution in small business lending. *Journal of Finance, 57,* 2533–2570.

Portes, R., & Rey, H. (2001). The determinants of cross-border equity flows. Center for International and Development Economics Research, University of California, Department of Economics, Berkeley, CA.

Stonehill, A., & Nathanson, L. (1968). Capital budgeting and the multinational corporation. *California Management Review, 10,* 39–54.

SUGGESTED READING
Bliss, C., Clark, P., Oppenheimer, P., Tyson, L., & Williamson, J. (1981). Exchange risk and corporate international finance/The financing procedures of British foreign trade/money in international exchange. *Journal of International Economics, 11,* 123–129

Dince, R. (1980). Exchange risk and corporate international finance (Book Review). *Southern Economic Journal, 47,* 247–249.

Rugman, A. (1980). Internalization theory and corporate international finance. *California Management Review, 23,* 73–80.

Essay by Marie Gould

INTERNATIONAL FINANCIAL ACCOUNTING

The establishment of international financial accounting standards has proven critical in a worldwide economy that is increasingly eschewing national borders in order to conduct global commercial enterprise. Such standards provide uniformity in practice from industry to industry and region to region, an important characteristic in a world that is becoming more interconnected. This paper will explore the ways uniformity may be created among financial accounting practices, outlining the global standards that have been established in this arena and the areas in which those standards are applicable. The reader will glean a more comprehensive understanding of the benefits and intricacies of international financial accounting practices.

OVERVIEW

The famed American writer and humorist James Thurber was once called into his bank to speak with the manager about his account, which was overdrawn. After some discussion, Thurber confessed that he did not keep a record of the checks he paid. Confused, the bank manager asked Thurber if he knew how much money was in his account. Thurber simply responded, "I thought that was your business" (Anecdotage.com).

There are countless methodologies by which businesses manage their books; thankfully, the majority of these methods are not nearly as lax as the system employed by Thurber. In fact, financial accounting is one of the most important aspects of a successful business, providing a detailed report on the true fiscal status of the company.

Adding to the diversity of financial accounting is the twenty-first-century global economy. Over the last several decades, aided by state-of-the-art technology such as the Internet and cellular telecommunications, businesses from virtually every industry have made connections around the globe. This new environment seems to thrive outside of the traditional purview of the nation-state, locating a lack of uniformity among accounting practices.

This paper will explore the ways uniformity may be created among financial accounting practices, outlining the global standards that have been established in this arena and the areas in which those standards are applicable. The reader will glean a more comprehensive understanding of the benefits and intricacies of international financial accounting practices.

Accounting Organization & Uniformity in Europe

In the mid-eighteenth century, the Industrial Revolution brought a new era of development, as advances in agriculture, transportation, and manufacturing technology helped increase production and the speed by which the products of that output

This portrait shows Pacioli standing behind a table and wearing the habit of a member of the Franciscan order. He draws a construction on a board, the edge of which bears the name Euclides. His left hand rests upon a page of an open book. Upon the table rest the instruments of a mathematician: a sponge, a protractor, a pen, a case, a piece of chalk, and compasses. In the right corner of the table there is a dodecahedron resting upon a book bearing Pacioli's initials. An rhombicuboctahedron (a convex solid consisting of 18 squares and 8 triangles) suspends at the left of the painting. (Courtesy of Jacopo de' Barbari via Wikimedia Commons)

could be delivered. As these industries continuously and quickly evolved, so too did their marketability. However, although the Industrial Revolution began in Europe in the mid- to late-1700s, the field of accounting did not see full development until the latter years of the era, when that marketability led to the formation of publicly shared joint stock companies.

Prior to the mid-1850s, the field of accounting was limited to bankruptcy work; the creation of detailed reports of the failings of businesses so that assets could be distributed and debts paid. In 1856, however, the British government introduced what was known as "the Companies Act," which helped increase the power and relevance of accountancy companies while establishing regulations for those in business and stock trading to follow in uniform fashion. Provision 69 of that act mandated that boards of directors keep "true accounts" of stock trades, profits, expenses,

credits, and liabilities (Joint Stock Companies Act, 1856).

By the time the Companies Act became law, organizations comprised of accounting firms and professionals began taking shape, primarily in Edinburgh and Glasgow, Scotland. In 1870, the landscape changed significantly, however, when the first local accounting societies formed in England. Within two years, those groups joined together to form a national body, the Institute of Accountants in England. At the same time, another group, the Society of Accountants, also came into being. Other groups, most notably the Chartered Institutes of England and Wales (ICAEW) and the Chartered Institutes of Scotland (ICAS), would join them soon after (MacDonald, 1995).

Although accounting and bookkeeping had been prevalent throughout history, the formal practice of accounting was largely specific to individual businesses and certain political systems. Even as accounting associations began to jell in Europe by the late nineteenth century, accounting as a collective industry still had not formally taken shape. One exception was Argentina, which in 1886 legally recognized the profession of accountant, applying government standard qualifications to those individuals who sought to enter the field (Brown, et al., 1905). Argentina stood out, however, as accounting remained fragmented in industrialized countries. The ICAEW was one of the few organizations of accounting professionals that worked to create some regional connectivity and even industry standards.

Prior to World War I, the ICAEW led the charge to create recognition for the industry under the law. The war, however, rendered moot the debate over the dozens of bills filed to that end. In the meantime, commerce continued to expand, and international trade crossed borders, continents, and oceans. In 1966, the efforts initiated by the ICAEW were reinitiated, as a proposal was offered to create an international study group comprised of that organization, the American Institute of Certified Public Accountants, and the Canadian Institute of Chartered Accountants. The study group, which was finally approved a year later, began to offer a number of position papers and research materials, many of which would later become the standards of international financial accounting.

International Financial Accounting Standards

In 1973, the push for international financial accounting standards was furthered with the establishment of the International Accounting Standards Committee (IASC). For 27 years, that organization crafted a wide range of standards that were designed to reverse the countless variations of the practice of accounting. In 2001, the IASC was replaced with the International Accounting Standards Board (IASB). During that time, the standards that were introduced by the IASC and its successors were becoming increasingly popular throughout the industry. In 2000, the U.S. Securities and Exchange Commission endorsed the acceptability of establishing international accounting standards (Institute of Chartered Accountants, 2009). The central vehicle for delivery of such standards would be the International Financial Reporting Standards (IFRS), which are a series of benchmarks crafted by the IASB that create universally accepted public company financial statements.

The establishment of international financial accounting standards has proven critical in a worldwide economy that is increasingly eschewing national borders in order to conduct global commercial enterprise. It provides uniformity in practice from industry to industry and region to region; an important characteristic in a world that is becoming more interconnected. Many areas of international financial accounting have been updated and rendered in-tune with accounting practices around the world.

FURTHER INSIGHTS

In the Interest of Transparency

The rationale behind the establishment of uniform international financial accounting standards is to foster transparency in business profiles. Previously, accounting was focused on assessing the fiscal health of a company for the purposes of offsetting debt and/or bankruptcy. However, since the advent of the

James Thurber, half-length portrait, seated, facing right, lighting cigarette. (Courtesy of Library of Congress)

publicly traded company and the joint stock venture, accounting is seen as a vital tool in creating a full illustration of a company's strengths and weaknesses that could be easily reviewed by would-be investors from all over the world.

Income Statements

One of the first areas of attention in this regard is the income statement. An income statement is, in essence, a report on the financial operational health of the company. It is a review of a business's performance over a certain period of time. This document reviews revenues and weighs them against expenses, creating a clear assessment of whether the company is operating at a profit or a loss. By establishing this profile, investors are given a useful tool in understanding the profitability of the company.

Balance Sheets

Another important document for the purposes of international financial accounting is the balance sheet. A balance sheet is similar to an income statement, identifying revenues received and taking into account expenses. The difference between the two reports is timing—whereas an income statement measures a company's profitability over a certain period of time, such as a month, quarter, or year, a balance sheet is more of an immediate snapshot, taken at a specific time. Balance sheets are useful for providing an immediate illustration of the status of a company instead of analyzing trends that may have been reversed with alternate financial planning.

Balance sheets and income statements are of great use in the twenty-first-century global economy. As more and more companies are developing in the current landscape, they are relying on foreign-based capital to fund their enterprises. Likewise, American investors are getting involved in international securities markets for the same reason—to help develop potentially profitable businesses in the global environment. The potential returns on investment are, to be sure, speculative, but the data provided in income statements and balance sheets prove invaluable to better understanding the status of the company.

In fact, such information is considered vital for the integrity of the market as well, providing accurate information about publicly traded businesses. In 1988, the U.S. Securities and Exchange Commission (SEC) recognized this fact, calling upon regulators to develop uniform standards of reporting, stating that "all securities regulators should work together diligently to create sound international regulatory frameworks that will enhance the vitality of capital markets" (cited in "SEC concept release," 2000). In that statement, the SEC endorsed the work of the IASC in this endeavor.

Cash Flow Statements

Another important aspect of accounting is the cash flow statement. Cash flow statements are reports that delineate how changes in balance sheets and income statements affect a company's available cash and assets. A cash flow statement is arguably one of the most sensitive documents produced by a company, as it demonstrates a company's ability to cover its bills, repay debts, and pay employee salaries. Simply put, a cash flow statement provides clear data for external and internal shareholders and investors to evaluate whether that company is financially sound.

Because of the sensitivity of the cash flow statement, many companies have opted to keep such reports close to the vest. Local and national accounting standards on the subject have varied with regard to requiring companies to include cash flow statements in their annual reports, enabling those who wish to keep such information private protected from any unintended access to their records.

Then again, the promise of new sources of capital and/or other forms of investment from sources around the world has led some systems to consider (if not mandate) cash flow reporting as part of a financial report. In some European countries, for example, the idea of creating a system in which cash flow statements are included in overall financial reports was initially met with some skepticism at the end of the twentieth century. However, a 2000 study of the European Union's largest member, Germany, revealed two major points: capital market forces motivate voluntary cash flow statement reporting and the development of international accounting standards facilitates the development and distribution of universally accepted cash flow statements (Leuz, 2000).

The development of international financial accounting standards for cash flow statements, balance sheets, and income statements has facilitated the increased connectivity of businesses to capital and investment sources in the global economy. Accounting continues to diversify along these uniform lines. This paper will next review some of the areas under discussion for future standardization and how that uniformity will benefit business.

From Country-Specific to Global

Over the last 35 years, the push for uniform international accounting standards has largely transformed the accounting landscape from one that is fractured and country-specific to one that is universal. This development stems predominantly from potential gains from capital sources in the international system. However, the system was still limited by national boundaries and government systems. The global economy, which does not necessarily recognize national borders, is helping modify the international political system so that it may continue to develop.

In Europe, for example, the consistently integrating European Union recognized in 2005 that in order to foster openness in commerce, it must adopt uniform standards. As a result, a rule was issued that most publicly traded European Union–based companies must use the standardized systems of the IFRS

(Hines, 2007). Such policies are reflective of the popularity of IFRS—although specific accounting practices indubitably differ from system to system, the flexible, general application of standards is seen as a way to open doors for business and the international community as a whole.

There have been latent concerns, however, that a standardized international financial accounting system may not benefit a given economic and commercial environment. A 2009 study revealed that despite the increased integration of American and European accounting standards (and the aforementioned endorsement by the SEC of the endeavors of IFRS), there remains a wide gulf on a number of issue areas that have created barriers for further adoptions of IASB standards. In fact, the study revealed, the United States, by virtue of the fact that its preeminence in international business has fostered a demand for unparalleled transparency in accounting. As such, the US accounting system is one of the more comprehensive environments in the world—the adoption of further IFRS standards might actually weaken a comparatively strong American accounting system ("Mind the GAAP," 2009).

Nevertheless, the IASB continues to work on standardization projects on a number of fronts. In some cases, the effort is based on the recent global recession of 2007–2009, which prompted the IASB to develop standardization projects on a number of areas that are considered contributing factors to the recession. Such projects include credit risk in liability measurement, fair value measurement, and hedging. Other projects are geared toward employment benefits reporting, income taxes, leases, and rate regulations (IASB, 2009). These efforts are representative of an IASB effort to stave off future recessions, address a number of political and economic issues, and create greater connectivity among countries around the world.

Like the rest of the globalizing economy, international financial accounting remains in a state of evolution. This evolution is due in part to the conditions and trends of each system and in part to the conditions of the international environment.

CONCLUSIONS

In 1494, a Franciscan monk named Luca Pacioli wrote a book on mathematics. The piece might have disappeared into literary history if not for a chapter he wrote on the practical use of mathematics in business. He wrote that three factors would make a businessman successful:

- sufficient cash or credit
- an accounting system to show his status
- a bookkeeper to manage that system (LaMoine, 2004)

Pacioli's recipe for a strong business would become the basis for modern accounting, a practice that depends on detailed information in order to ensure a true portrait of a business is created.

For centuries, the field of accounting was focused on businesses that were suffering from poor financial health. However, in the modern economy, accounting has evolved into a vehicle by which business may be conducted. In fact, the global business environment offers operational and burgeoning enterprises greater potential resources for capital investment, mergers, and partnerships.

International financial accounting is therefore dedicated to creating comprehensive illustrations of a company's health so that investors and potential partners may demonstrate willingness to work with them. Then again, in the international setting, how those portraits are created has traditionally varied from nation to nation.

Because such diversity in financial reports can create confusion, the effort that began in the early twentieth century to foster accounting standards has seen considerable support. This paper has provided a detailed analysis not only of the various aspects of international financial accounting but also of how those types of reports and information have increasingly become standardized in the interest of taking advantage of the global economy. It is likely that, as the field of accounting continues to seek new elements by which a company's financial health may be assessed, the manner by which such elements are reported will be given careful consideration for international standardization.

TERMS & CONCEPTS

Balance sheet: A financial report that covers revenues versus expenses at a given time.

Cash flow statement: A report that delineates how changes in balance sheets and income statements affect a company's available cash and assets.

Income statement: A financial report in which revenues are weighed against expenses over a certain period.

BIBLIOGRAPHY

Brown, R., Ed. (1905). *A history of accounting and accountants.* Edinburgh: T.C. & E.C. Jack.

Hines, T. (2007). International financial report standards: A guide for sources for international accounting standards. *Journal of Business and Finance Librarianship, 12,* 3–26.

Institute of Chartered Accountants in England and Wales. (2009). *Knowledge guide to international accounting standards.*

Joint Stock Companies Act 1856. (1856).

Lemoine, J. (2004, September 7). History of accounting.

Lin, J., & Fink, P. (2013). International financial reporting standards: Are they right for the United States? *Journal of Global Business Issues, 7,* 59–67.

Leuz, C. (2000). The development of voluntary cash flow statements in Germany and the influence of international reporting standards. *Scmalenbach Business Review, 52,* 182–207.

MacDonald, K. M. (1995). *The sociology of the professions.* Thousand Oaks, CA: SAGE.

Nour, A., AbuSabha, S., Al Kubeise, A., & Nour, M. (2013). The fundamental issues with financial derivatives within the framework of international accounting standard no. and their relative responsibility for the current global financial crisis. *Journal of Business Studies Quarterly, 4,* 173–222.

Pounder, B. (2013). Have we lost our ability to improve financial reporting? *Strategic Finance, 95,* 16–18.

SEC concept release: International accounting standards. (2000). International Series 1215, Release 33-7801, 34-42430.

Mind the GAAP: Analyzing the proposed switch to international accounting standards. (2009, April 1). *Knowledge@Wharton.*

SUGGESTED READING

Cain, M. (2008). FASB and IASB propose a complete change to financial reporting. *RMA Journal, 90,* 84–88.

Cortesi, A., Montani, E., & Tettamanzi, P. (2008). Family business in Italy: An empirical study on the effects of the transition from the Italian to the international accounting standards. *World of Accounting Science, 1,* 219–236.

Rozycka, G. (2000). Financial reporting: International accounting solutions. *Accountancy, 126*(1284), 113.

Spengel, C. (2003). International accounting standards, tax accounting and effective levels of company tax burdens in the European Union. *European Taxation, 43*(7/8), 253–266.

The treatment in the income statement of unusual items and changes in accounting estimates and accounting policies. (1976). *Accountancy, 87,* 82–86.

Wallace, R., & Choudury, M. (1997). Cash flow statements: An international comparison of regulatory positions. *International Journal of Accounting, 32,* 1–22.

Essay by Michael P. Auerbach, MA

INTERNET SECURITY

ABSTRACT

The Internet has revolutionized the way that many companies do business. However, Internet use is not without its risks. Cybercrime has been on the rise, and its potential consequences can be disastrous for both the individual and the organizational victim. Internet security is an increasing problem, and there are a number of types of computer crimes to which an organization may be susceptible if sufficient security measures are not in place. However, an enterprise can make cybercrime more difficult and thereby become a less desirable target. In the end, it is important to remember that no computer that is connected to the Internet is completely secure. However, for many businesses, not using the Internet is poor corporate strategy. Therefore, Internet security must be taken into account in the enterprise's strategic plan, and sufficient resources must be given to maximize the system's security.

OVERVIEW

The Internet has become an integral part of the industrialized world of the twenty-first century. One can communicate with friends and family almost instantaneously through e-mail and pass along text messages as well as documents, photographs, and audio/video clips. The Internet also provides an inexpensive way to connect people together at short or long distances for voice conversations and even allows people to see each other while talking. One can shop and compare costs and features of products or can gather information to better understand a medical condition or another topic of interest. One can book hotel rooms as well as airline tickets. Banking, grocery shopping, and purchasing sports and theater tickets can all be done online. The proliferation of information on the Internet

Sailors analyze, detect and defensively respond to unauthorized activity within U.S. Navy information systems and computer networks. (Courtesy of Mass Communications Specialist 1st Class Corey Lewis, U.S. Navy via Wikimedia Commons)

makes it possible to research and compare similar products and features and obtain the best price available on electronics, furniture, books, and more in minutes, rather than in hours or days, from the comfort of one's own home.

The Internet has not just made life easier for the individual. These same features make it popular with businesses eager to keep up in the global marketplace and have revolutionized the way that many companies do business. Sometimes organizations use local area networks that link multiple local computers to one another and to various peripheral devices, metropolitan area networks that link computers over citywide distances at higher speeds than local area networks, or wide area networks that link multiple computers that are widely dispersed and use high-speed, long-distance communications networks or satellites to transmit and receive data. However, many companies also use the Internet to do business on a wider scale. The Internet has contributed to the modern trend toward globalization so that businesses no longer operate only locally or nationally but internationally as well.

Security Risk. Although the Internet has expanded the capabilities of many businesses, its use is not

without risk. Without adequate safeguards in place, networked computers are open to attacks not only from within the company but also from external hackers. Breaches of security can affect the validity of data and conclusions and the reliability of processes and harm not only the organization's reputation and ability to do business but also the customer's security and safety. Hackers can access sensitive information or alter or corrupt software programs so that they produce invalid results or so that the system becomes unreliable and unusable. The impact of security breaches on the customer can range from false charges on credit cards to unauthorized access to sensitive information or even identity theft of the individuals whose data are contained in the databases. Complete identities comprising birth dates, social security numbers, and credit card and bank account numbers are being increasingly targeted by hackers since they are worth so much more. In 2013, it was reported that individual credit card numbers were worth between $4 and $8, whereas complete identities were worth between $25 and $40 to the cybercriminal. For just under $300, a cybercriminal could purchase the stolen credentials for a bank account ("Report on Commodities Value in the Cyber Criminal Underground Market," 2013).

Research in the early 2000s found that the time between the announcement of a software vulnerability and the time that attack is made on that vulnerability could be as little as 16.5 hours, and security teams are preparing for a time when new threats emerge with little or no warning. This means that organizations need to quickly address vulnerability issues and correct them in a timely fashion. Although this may seem like an occasional problem, there were a reported 5,225 vulnerabilities in 2012 alone, which was a 26 percent increase from the year before (Lemos, 2013).

Cybercrime. Cybercrime has been on the rise, and the potential consequences can be disastrous for both the individual and the organizational victim. Attacks on e-commerce sites are on the rise exponentially, with a report of 16 percent in 2004 over 4 percent the previous year. Between 2010 and 2011, e-commerce sites saw a 153 percent increase in attacks during the winter holiday season (Lee, 2012). The estimated annual cost to the global economy from cybercrime is more than $400 billion (Center for Strategic and International Studies, 2014). A report by the Center for Strategic and International Studies stated that approximately 800 million individuals had their personal information stolen worldwide in 2013 (Center for Strategic and International Studies, 2014). In addition, adware—a software application that displays advertising banners while the program is running—has become more problematic. Adware frequently includes additional code called spyware that tracks users' personal information and distributes it to third parties without the individuals' knowledge or permission. Adware is also used to deliver malicious codes to other computers.

In 2014, the data breach that occurred at Sony Pictures Entertainment provoked further national debate over the vulnerability of data on the Internet when the theft of confidential employee and company information was used by hackers as a form of potentially violent blackmail. The hackers released internal emails, passwords, and insurance and medical files of employees. While initial reports were blaming North Korea for the cyberattack, some experts suggested that it may have originated inside Sony.

Computer Viruses. Organizations' computer systems and networks can also be vulnerable to external attack by computer viruses. These programs or pieces of code are loaded onto the computer without the user's knowledge and against the user's wishes and alter the way that the computer operates or modifies the data or programs that are stored on the computer. Simple viruses can be self-replicating bits of code that use up a computer's memory or otherwise disable a computer; more complex viruses can transmit themselves across networks and bypass security systems to infect other computers or systems, corrupting or erasing programs or data. Computer viruses can be loaded into the computer intentionally by hackers and indirectly through the receipt of infected e-mail or attachments.

Although responses to cybercrime are becoming more sophisticated, so are the cybercriminals. The *Journal of Accountancy* reported an increasing collaboration between cybercriminals resulting in a 29 percent increase in computers affected by malicious bots in the last half of 2006. Indeed, as the use of the Internet and e-commerce increases, so does cybercrime, including risk from industrial spies, foreign governments, competitors, and even legitimate business partners. In a 2012 Ponemon Institute report on cybercrime, more than 90 percent of the organizations in the report had experienced loss of sensitive or confidential documents and data over the preceding twelve-month period (Kendler). Despite these statistics, however, it is not practical for most companies to stop using the Internet. Without the Internet, it would become extremely difficult, if not impossible, to be competitive in the global marketplace. Similarly, customers have come to expect that organizations have a presence on the Internet, including a website and e-mail capabilities. Use of the Internet is a risk that most companies have to take. The problem is to minimize the risks associated with doing so.

Types of Computer Crime: Unauthorized Entry. There are a number of types of computer crimes to which an enterprise may be susceptible if sufficient security measures are not in place. One general category of computer crime involves the unauthorized entry of a criminal into the company's computer system. For example, in piggybacking, a criminal uses the codes or passwords of an authorized user to gain illegal access to the system. Another type of computer crime in this category is illegal access to the system through entry by a trapdoor. Trapdoors are prohibited, unknown entry points into a program or network that allow criminals to gain access to the system.

Intentional Damage. A second general category of computer crime includes intentional damage to the system's data. Data leakage is the intentional erasure or removal of files, or even entire databases, from a system without leaving any trace that they have been removed or even that they existed. This type of cybercrime can result in cost to the enterprise in the recovery of the data as well as from loss of goodwill from customers due to errors resulting from the data loss. Customers can also be harmed from data leakage if receipts or credits are not correctly posted to their accounts. The enterprise's communications networks can be harmed through zapping, the process of damaging or erasing data and information, causing problems for both the enterprise and the customer. Another type of intentional damage to the system's data is scavenging, which is searching through the physical trash can in the computer center or the electronic trash can in the computer to find discarded data or other information about the system's programs or processes. Zapping typically occurs as a result of a cybercriminal bypassing the enterprise's security systems.

Stealing or Capturing Data. A third category of computer crime comprises attempts to steal or capture data in the enterprise's systems. Eavesdropping is the use of electronic surveillance devices to either listen to or capture the content of electronic transmissions. Wiretapping is the use of any device to electronically capture data during transmission or to listen to conversations that take place over the network. Both wireless transmissions and those that occur over copper wire are susceptible to wiretapping. Cybercrime does not necessarily involve the capture or manipulation of large amounts of data, however. Small amounts of the enterprise's data can be captured or rerouted through salami attacks, or data slicing. This crime uses software to capture small amounts of financial transactions and redirect them to a hidden account. Because the amounts ("slices") are so small, they typically are not noticed. Over time, however, a large volume of small losses can yield a significant amount of lost money for the enterprise and its customers.

Sabotage. Stealing money or capturing data and information are not the only purposes of cybercrime, however. Sometimes the point is merely to sabotage the enterprise's computer systems. One of the ways that this is done is through logic bombs: programs designed to sabotage data, programs, or processes. These programs execute when certain conditions exist in the system. A similar type of program is the time bomb, which monitors the computer's internal calendar and executes on a specific date. Trojan horses are programs that appear to be harmless applications but that cause damage once they are loaded into the computer.

APPLICATIONS

Defense in Depth. Defense in depth is a strategy used to reach a level of information assurance (IA) and information security. It utilizes the capabilities of current technology and follows approved procedures to guard against and monitor intrusions on an information technology (IT) system. Security measures that are incorporated into a defense-in-depth plan are multilayered in design and are intended to thwart an attack and simultaneously slow down its force and speed to allow for the detection of and response to it.

Defense in depth was originally a military strategy that made use of multiple lines of defense to reduce the strength of an attack rather than prevent or immediately advance against it. Its first recorded use was by ancient Roman armies, and the tactic is used by modern armies worldwide.

Over the centuries, the strategy of defense in depth evolved to apply to several nonmilitary environments such as engineering and fire prevention. In addition, defense-in-depth principles are used to provide protection of electronically networked settings. The most current and effective technology, information, and procedures are applied to three main components of the multitiered defense strategy as it relates to computer network protection: people, technology, and operations.

For an IT defense-in-depth policy to be effective, senior-level management must be committed to establishing, implementing, and monitoring the system. This is done primarily through a well-defined awareness of perceived threats on the system and then ensuring that effective procedures, policies, technology, and personnel are involved in monitoring and operating the system. For example, senior management is usually responsible for researching and acquiring security technology and then training necessary personnel in its use.

A defense-in-depth system should contain the most up-to-date information protection technology available. Just as military use of defense-in-depth tactics slows an attack in order to ultimately protect against it, the same is true in computer network settings. One method is to defend a system at multiple points and locations, such as at the network and infrastructure levels as well as at the data transmission stage, and by controlling access to hosts and servers.

Another method used in slowing an attack on an IT system is through the use of multiple layers of defenses in order to create redundancy and to provide additional lines of defense in case one security measure fails. In terms of layering, the goal is to provide a different and more challenging obstacle to defeat at each layer, which will offer additional opportunities to detect the intrusion and identify the aggressor. Installing firewalls at both the outer and the inner boundaries of a network is an example of redundancy and layering.

The primary focus of the operations facet of a defense-in-depth strategy for information security is on the activities that ensure the effectiveness and efficiency of the strategy. For example, virus updates, security patches, and access lists are completed on time; security assessments are routinely completed; and threats are monitored and responded to.

Cybercrime Prevention. Internet security is not only a continuing problem but also an evolving and increasing one. Yet, many companies do not have adequate Internet security measures in place. To help businesses thwart cybercriminals operating over the Internet, several steps are recommended. First, before deciding to use the Internet for business purposes, organizations should articulate how they intend to use the Internet (e.g., e-commerce; marketing website; communication with business partners, customers, and suppliers, etc.). Once this information is articulated, the company should next assess what risks are associated with each of the uses. Risks are the quantifiable likelihood that a financial investment will result in loss for the investor. A high-risk investment is associated with both a higher probability of loss and a possibility of greater return on

investment. Risk assessment is the process of determining the potential loss and probability of loss of the organization's objectives.

In doing risk assessment, the organization needs to take into account the probability of various types of cyberattacks and the cost to the organization if these attacks occur. Potential costs could result from computer downtime, loss of data, loss of reputation in the marketplace, or even law suits in reaction to preventable theft of identity or other information. A number of risks can occur as a result of cybercrime, including destruction of data, interference with business operations, modification or replacement of data, unauthorized altering of data, unauthorized downloading of data, unauthorized transactions, and unauthorized disclosure of proprietary or sensitive information. In some situations, the potential damage from these risks is less important than in others. For example, it is less likely that a hacker would be interested in breaking into the computer system at a coffee shop than into the system at a bank. The potential rewards from data in the latter—including not only the ability to move money but also the ability to steal identities—is much more tempting for the thief and damaging for the organization than from the former. When deciding how to use the Internet, the organization needs to do a cost/benefits tradeoff analysis to determine whether the proposed use will be more beneficial to the company than the potential damage that could occur due to cybercrime.

Controls for Reducing the Threat of Cybercrime. There are a number of ways that an enterprise can help make cybercrime more difficult. It has been observed that today's savvy hackers can get into most computer systems. Therefore, one of the keys to reducing cybercrime is to make it difficult to break in, thereby creating a less attractive target. There are six sets of controls to help reduce the threat of cybercrime.

User Identification & Authentication. User identification typically includes the use of user names and passwords. However, these simple tools can be very easy for a cybercriminal to break. Passwords can be made harder to break by various techniques, including requiring longer character strings, including numbers as well as letters, making them case sensitive, and requiring that they be changed at regular intervals (e.g., monthly). For enterprises where security is paramount, a smart card system can be put in place. Smart cards are a more efficient method for user authentication, control integrity, and maintain confidentiality. These credit card–sized cards contain a microprocessor that can store 10 to 20 public key certificates. These are used as part of an encryption system that uses public keys that are known to everyone and private keys that are known only to the recipient of the message. In this system, the sender of a message uses the receiver's public key to encrypt the message; the receiver uses his/her private key to decrypt it. The right public key has to be used to encrypt messages, and only the matching private key is able to decrypt them. It is virtually impossible to deduce the private key from knowledge of the public key alone. Smart cards can also be used to generate one-time-use passwords that require network authentication. The use of smart cards is expected to increase in the future since it requires both the card and a personal identification number known only to the cardholder. Access is impossible without both pieces.

Firewalls. Another set of controls for Internet security are authorization controls. Firewalls are special-purpose software programs or pieces of computer hardware that are designed to prevent unauthorized access to or from a private network and that are often used to prevent unauthorized access to a private network from the Internet. The firewall is located at the network gateway server and examines incoming messages to determine their origin, destination, purpose, contents, and attachments. Based on this information, the decision is made whether or not to forward the message to the intended recipient. Firewalls are useful for protecting against intruders. However, they often filter out executable programs or attachments of excessive length on the assumption that they may contain harmful contents.

Low-Tech Security Mechanisms. Not every security mechanism is high-tech, however. Accountability mechanisms that can be used to boost Internet security include audit mechanisms and logs that record Internet use. Such mechanisms can be used as an audit trail if a breach of security occurs. Internet use policies can also provide guidelines for how to maintain security when using the Internet. In addition to controls to help increase Internet security, the enterprise should also have a contingency plan for how to recover functioning as quickly and seamlessly as possible in the case of a breach of security. In the end, it is important to remember that no computer that is connected to the Internet is completely secure. However, for many businesses, not using the Internet is poor corporate strategy. Therefore, Internet security must be taken into account in the enterprise's strategic plan and sufficient resources must be given to maximize the system's security.

TERMS & CONCEPTS

Cybercrime: A criminal act dealing with computers and networks or a traditional crime conducted over the Internet. Cybercrimes include fraud, identity theft, hacking, and unauthorized acquisition of data and information.

E-commerce: E-commerce (i.e., electronic commerce) is the process of buying and selling goods or services via electronic and computer systems.

Encryption: The translation of data transmitted over a network into a secret code. Encrypted files can be read only through the use of a key or password. The two primary methods of encryption are asymmetric, or public-key encryption, and symmetric encryption.

Enterprise: Any organization that is designed for commercial purposes.

Firewall: A special-purpose software program or piece of computer hardware that is meant to prevent unauthorized access to or from a private network while allowing authorized communications.

Hacker: Although the term is used by some to refer to any clever programmer, it has come to be used specifically to refer to an individual who attempts to break into a computer system.

Network: A set of computers that are electronically linked together.

Risk: The quantifiable likelihood that a financial investment will result in loss for the investor. Higher risk is associated with both a greater probability of loss and a possibility of greater return on investment.

Security: The process of safeguarding and protecting the data, hardware, software, and processes of a business's information technology assets.

Server: The computer system that hosts a network and provides essential services to the other computers in the network (e.g., a web server powers web pages). The term *server* can also refer to the software running on the server computer.

Strategy: A strategy is a comprehensive plan of action aimed at helping an organization realize its goals. A good business strategy is based on a meticulous analysis of empirical data that include information on market trends, consumer demand, competitor capabilities, and the organization's resources and abilities.

Virus: In computer science, a virus is a program or minute piece of code that is loaded onto the computer without the user's knowledge and against the user's wishes and that alters the way that the computer operates or that modifies the data or programs that are stored on the computer. Simple viruses can be self-replicating bits of code that use up a computer's memory or otherwise disable a computer; more complex viruses can transmit themselves across networks and bypass security systems to infect other computers or systems.

BIBLIOGRAPHY

Bailey, T., Miglio, A. D., & Richter, W. (2014). The rising strategic risks of cyberattacks. *Mckinsey Quarterly, 2*, 17–22.

Center for Strategic and International Studies. (2014, June). Net losses: Estimating the global cost of cybercrime: Economic impact of cybercrime II.

Collaborative fraud networks on the rise. (2007). *Journal of Accountancy, 203*, 17.

Filshtinskiy, S. (2013). Cybercrime, cyberweapons, cyber wars: Is there too much of it in the air? *Communications of the ACM, 56*, 28–30.

Kendler, P. B. (2013, February). Securing systems in financial institutions: Recommendations for preventing and responding to IT security threats. *Wall Street Technology.*

Kerner, S. (2013). Cybercrime costs continue to rise: Study. *Eweek, 2.*

Lee, J. (2012, October 29). Prolexic study offers e-commerce website strategies to combat holiday DDoS attacks.

Lemos, R. (2013, February 11). Software vulnerabilities rise again after 5-year decline. *eWeek.*

Lucas, H. C., Jr. (2005). *Information technology: Strategic decision making for managers.* New York: John Wiley and Sons.

Mcguire, B. L. (2000). What your business should know about Internet security. *Strategic Finance, 82*, 50–54.

Report on commodities value in the cybercriminal underground market. (2013, November 25). *Securtiy Affairs.*

Roenker, R. (2016). Prioritizing cybersecurity. *Lane Report, 31*(12), 21–26.

Senn, J. A. (2004). *Information technology: Principles, practices, opportunities* (3rd ed.). Upper Saddle River, NJ: Pearson/Prentice Hall.

Tehrani, P., Manap, N., & Taji, H. (2013). Cyberterrorism challenges: The need for a global response to a multijurisdictional crime. *Computer Law & Security Review, 29*, 207–215.

The Internet is a well-worn channel, yet security issues remain. (2004). *ABA Banking Journal, 96*, 73.

Wisniewski, M. (2014). Giant web vulnerability brings indirect risk to digital banking. *American Banker 179*, 2.

SUGGESTED READING

Britton, K. (2016). Handling privacy and security in the Internet of things. *Journal of Internet Law, 19*(10), 3–7.

Engebretson, D. (2004). The beginnings: Beyond the PC. *Distributing & Marketing, 34*, 74–76.

Iannarelli, J. (2015). *Information governance and security: Protecting and managing your company's proprietary information.* Waltham, MA: Elsevier.

Kamens, M. (2007). Making user access policies work for you. *Network World, 24*, 33.

Kissell, J. (2014). How to make two-factor authentication less of a pain. *Macworld, 31*, 82.

McLean, S. (2013). Beware the botnets: Cybersecurity is a board level issue. *Intellectual Property & Technology Law Journal, 35*, 22–27.

McPherson, D. (2007). IP network security: Progress, not perfection. *Business Communications Review, 37*, 54–58.

Menon, S., & Siew, T. (2012). Key challenges in tackling economic and cybercrimes: Creating a multilateral platform for international cooperation. *Journal of Money Laundering Control, 15*, 243–256.

Essay by Ruth A. Wienclaw, PhD

ISSUES IN INTERNATIONAL BANKING

This article focuses on the international banking supervision system and how the Bank for International Settlements and the Basel Committee on Banking Supervision relate to it. The establishment of the Basel Committee was a significant point in the history of international banking supervision. The Basel Committee has made two major contributions since its inception.

OVERVIEW

"The present international, regional, and national rules on banking supervision are strongly permeated by a high degree of fluidity directly descendent both from the revolution of principles and techniques steering the global financial markets, and from the connected difficulty of the nation states to face the new technological challenges" (Ortino, 2004, p. 715). Policy makers, experts, and scholars will need to analyze and evaluate the level of fluidity when attempting to implement policies and regulations to govern global financial markets. The changes in information technology have challenged the European states by requiring them to evaluate the political and economic systems that they have in place.

International Banking Supervision
According to Ortino (2004), there are two specific features of the institutional order as it relates to banking supervision at an international level.

- First of all, national legislators are responsible for setting up the legal norms and developing the foundation for the proper power structure and procedures.
- Second, the powers of the banking supervision authorities are assigned by the banking sector.

These features are encouraging banking supervision authorities to work together as well as with supervisory authorities in other financial sectors.

Basel Committee on Banking Supervision
One entity that works at the international level is the Basel Committee on Banking Supervision. This entity was set up in December 1974 by the central bank governors of the Group of Ten (G-10) nations and meets four times a year. The membership includes representation from countries such as Belgium, Canada, France, Germany, Italy, Japan, the Netherlands, Sweden, Switzerland, the United Kingdom, and the United States. The countries meet in order to consult on economic, monetary, and financial matters. The purpose of the committee is to discuss how to handle supervisory problems, such as global financial crises. Although the committee coordinates the supervisory responsibilities among the national authorities and monitors the effectiveness of supervision of banks' activities, it does not have formal status as an international organization (Ortino, 2004). However, the establishment of the Basel Committee was a significant point in the history of international banking supervision.

G-10
In 1999, there was a section that was added to the Gramm-Leach-Blilely Act, which broadened the range of activities that banking institutions in the United States could participate in, especially those institutions that elected to become financial holding companies. Although this was a significant step, financial institutions in the United States still had a narrower range than most of the other countries that were members of the G-10 group. What are some of the differences among some of the countries?

As a rule, most G-10 countries have allowed their banks to provide a full range of securities market activities (i.e., underwriting, brokering, and dealing) versus performing the transactions through a subsidiary. Also, there are a few G-10 countries that will allow a full range of insurance activities. However, the main restrictions tend not to be on the types of insurance activities. Rather, many of the restrictions tend to focus on where the activities are performed (i.e., some of the activities are required to be performed via a subsidiary). In addition, there are also restrictions on real estate activities for banks based on the range of activities, whether or not the activities are performed at a subsidiary or bank, or both. Nolle (2003) provided research that compared which G-10 country banks were allowed to own nonfinancial firms and which nonfinancial firms were allowed

Basel Committee on Banking Supervision's headquarters is located in Basel, Switzerland. (Courtesy of Taxiarchos228 via Wikimedia Commons)

to own banks. The results showed that most G-10 country banks were allowed to own nonfinancial firms, and nonfinancial firms were allowed to own banks. However, the United States is one of the countries that has greater restrictions on having a mixture of the above-mentioned combination of activities. Japan was the only country to have a greater level of restrictiveness than the United States.

G-10 Supervisory Systems & Their Effects

"The United States' supervisory system has the most complex structure in the G-10, and in several key respects its banking supervisory structure puts it among the minority of G-10 countries. However, in one key respect—the funding of bank supervision as practiced by the OCC—the U.S. is similar to the majority of G-10 countries" (Nolle, 2003, par. 10). Nolle's report (2003) showed that nine of the 11 G-10 countries assign banking supervision to a single authority. The United States and Germany were the only two countries that had more than one federal level bank supervisor. In addition, the United States is one of four G-10 countries that assigns bank supervisory responsibility to the central bank. The majority

of G-10 countries' bank supervisory authorities have responsibilities beyond the banking industry, either for securities firms, insurance firms, or both.

The type of supervision is important because the type of funding received could have an effect on how bank supervisors make decisions, especially if there is an opportunity for some type of political influence. For example, supervisory agencies that receive funding from the institutions they supervise may have less pressure to pursue a political agenda than supervisory agencies that are dependent on general government revenues (Nolle, 2003). Nolle's report showed that the United States tends to have a hands-on approach in performing the bank supervision role. It tends to conduct on-site exams on an annual basis and has a good ratio of total supervisory organization staff to the number of banks as well as a good ratio of banking system assets to the banking system. The United States' ratio of banking assets per supervisory staff member is the lowest among the G-10 countries. This finding indicates that there is a significant amount of coverage on the banking system activities on a per-staff-member basis. With the exception of Italy, all of the G-10 countries require an external audit as part of the bank supervision role. However, the United States does not require external auditors to report bank misconduct to the supervisory authorities, but there is a commitment to the external auditing process.

Basel Committee Contributions

The Basel Committee has made two major contributions since its inception.

The first contribution occurred in 1975 when the committee took a lead role in making sure that countries share responsibilities when making international banking transactions. The Basel Concordat was an agreement that established the foundation for this process. The first stipulation was that the parent and host authorities shared responsibility for the supervision of the foreign banking establishments. The second stipulation stated that the host authorities had primary responsibility for supervision of liquidity. The third stipulation indicated that the solvency of foreign branches and subsidiaries was the primary responsibility of the home authority of the parent and the host authority.

The second major contribution was a standard that would assist in adequately measuring a bank's capital and establishing minimum capital standards.

APPLICATION

Bank for International Settlements

The Bank for International Settlements is responsible for promoting monetary and financial stability. This organization meets on a bimonthly basis to discuss monetary and financial matters. The organization is composed of four major committees, including the Basel Committee on Banking Supervision, the Committee on the Global Financial System, the Committee on Payments and Market Systems and the Markets Committee. In addition, there are several independent organizations involved in the international cooperation in the area of financial stability, and these organizations have their secretariats at the Bank for International Settlements. These organizations are the Financial Stability Forum, the International Association of Insurance Supervisors, and the International Association of Deposit Insurers.

The Basel Committee on Banking Supervision will be discussed in greater detail during the next section of the paper. The Committee on the Global Financial System is responsible for monitoring developments in global financial markets for the central bank governors of the G-10 countries. The Committee on Payments and Market Systems serves as a forum for central banks to monitor and analyze developments in domestic payment, settlement, and clearing systems as well as in cross-border and multicurrency settlement schemes.

The Markets Committee was established in 1962 following the initiation of the Gold Pool. When the Gold Pool arrangements collapsed in 1968, members continued to meet at the BIS in order to exchange views. However, the focus has shifted toward coverage of recent developments in foreign exchange and related financial markets, an exchange of views on possible future trends, and consideration of the short-term implications of particular current events for the functioning of these markets.

VIEWPOINT

Basel Committee on Banking Supervision

The Basel Committee on Banking Supervision provides an avenue for the banking industry to discuss banking supervisory matters. The overall objective of this entity is to increase knowledge and understanding of key supervisory issues and improve the quality of banking supervision worldwide. In order to achieve this objective, the organization seeks to exchange information on national supervisory issues, approaches, and techniques and promote a common understanding around the world (Bank for International Settlements, n.d.). Stefan Ingves, Governor, Sveriges Riksbank, is the current chairman of the committee. The committee's secretariat is located at the Bank for International Settlements in Basel, Switzerland, and it is staffed by professional supervisors from member institutions.

Basel II

In January 1999, the Basel Committee proposed a new concept, which became known as Basel II. However, it was a work in progress and additional proposals for consultation occurred in January 2001 and April 2003. The final version of the Basel II accord was distributed in June 2004. The foundation of Basel II relies on three pillars, which are minimum capital requirements, supervisory review, and market discipline (Riskglossary.com).

Basel II tends to retain the definition of bank capital and the market risk provisions that were a part of the 1996 amendment. However, there is a replacement of how credit risk is treated as well as the requirement of capital for operational risks. The basic capital requirement for banks can be calculated as:

Based on the level of market risk allowed under the 1996 amendment, banks have options to determine how they will value their credit risk and market risk. For credit risk, they may select a standardized approach, a foundation internal rating–based approach, and/or an advanced internal rating–based approach. As far as operational risk, they may choose a basic indicator approach, a standardized approach, and/or an internal measurement approach.

Mixed Acceptance of Basel II

Although Basel II became effective in December 2006, it was not as widely embraced as the first Basel. The purpose of Basel II was to achieve the European regulators' objectives of addressing shortcomings in the original accord's treatment of credit risk, incorporating operational risk and harmonizing capital requirements for banks and securities firms. Although banks in Europe applied Basel II, regulators in the United States did not embrace it. While they shared the same goal of addressing shortcomings in the original accord's treatment of credit risk, there was a belief that the existing bank supervision in the United States already addresses operational risk. In addition, harmonization had never been a priority for US regulators. Their perception was that Basel II was more relevant for international banking activities. Therefore, only 10 of the largest banks in the United States initially applied Basel II.

Basel II was slow to be adopted because of its complexity and the difficulty of implementing it (Samuels, 2013). In the wake of the 2008 global financial crisis, Basel III addressed many of the shortcomings of Basel II. Basel III attempts to increase bank liquidity and reduce bank leverage. In the United States, the Final Rule—a U.S. version of Basel III's liquidity coverage ratio (LCR)—was proposed by the Federal Reserve Board. The Final Rule would apply to U.S. financial institutions and significant foreign banks with U.S. subsidiaries and would require banks to hold more capital (How US Basel III rules, 2013).

Committee Reorganization

The committee reorganized in October 2006 and is being operated by four main subcommittees. These subcommittees are the At present, there appears to be 5 subcommittees: Policy Development Group, Supervision and Implementation Group, Macroprudential Supervision Group, Accounting Experts Group, and Basel Consultative Group. (Bank for International Settlements, n.d.).

The Accord Implementation Group (AIG)—The purpose of this group was to share information and promote consistency in the implementation of Basel II. Although the AIG provided a forum for members to discuss how they intended to implement Basel II, the purpose of the subcommittee was not to mandate uniformity of application of the revised framework. There were three subgroups in this subcommittee, and they shared information and discussed specific issues related to Basel II implementation. The group was superceded by the Standards Implementation Group.

The three subgroups were the Validation Subgroup, the Operational Risk Subgroup, and the Trading Book Subgroup. The Validation Subgroup

was chaired by Maarten Gelderman, the head of quantitative risk management at the Netherlands Bank, and the subgroup was charged with exploring issues related to the validation systems used to generate the rating and parameters that serve as inputs into the internal ratings–based approaches to credit risk. The Operational Risk Subgroup was chaired by Kevin Bailey, deputy comptroller, Office of the Comptroller of the Currency in the United States, and the subgroup was responsible for addressing issues related primarily to the banks' implementation of advanced measurement approaches for operational risk. The final subgroup, Trading Book, was cochaired by Norah Berger, associate director of the Board of Governors of the Federal Reserve System in the United States, and Thomas McGowan, assistant director of the Securities and Exchange Commission in the United States. This subgroup dealt with issues that were related to the implementation of the recommendations in the committee's July 2005 paper entitled "The Application of Basel II to Trading Activities and the Treatment of Double Default Effects." Another function of this subgroup was to develop principles that would provide a treatment for default risk in the trading book.

The Standards Implementation Group (SIG)—The purpose of the group is to assist in implementing the accords. There are four main subcommittees: the Operational Risk Subgroup, the Task Force on Colleges, the Task Force on Remuneration, and the Standards Monitoring Procedures Task Force.

The Policy Development Group — This subgroup replaced the committee's former Capital Task Force and has the objective of assisting the committee with identifying and reviewing emerging supervisory issues. In addition, the subgroup proposes and develops policies to promote a sound banking system and high supervisory standards. There are five working groups that report to this subgroup: the Risk Management and Modeling Group, the Research Task Force, the Trading Book Group, the Liquidity Group, the Definition of Capital Group, the Cross-Border Bank Resolution Group, and the Capital Monitoring Group.

The Accounting Task Force — This subgroup has been charged with ensuring that the international accounting and auditing standards and practices promote sound risk management at financial institutions, support market discipline through transparency, and reinforce the safety and soundness of the banking system. There are three working groups, which consist of the Conceptual Framework Issues Subgroup, the Financial Instruments Practices Subgroup, and the Audit Subgroup.

The Basel Consultative Group (BCG) — This subgroup replaced the International Liaison Group, which in turn replaced the former Core Principles Liaison Group, and is charged with facilitating engagement between banking supervisors among member and non-member countries.

CONCLUSION

According to Ortino (2004), there are two specific features of the institutional order as it relates to banking supervision at an international level. First of all, national legislators are responsible for setting up the legal norms and developing the foundation for the proper power structure and procedures. Second, the powers of the banking supervision authorities are assigned by the banking sector. These features are encouraging banking supervision authorities to work together as well as with supervisory authorities in other financial sectors.

In 1999, there was a section that was added to the Gramm-Leach-Blilely Act, which broadened the range of activities that banking institutions in the United States could participate in, especially those institutions that elected to become financial holding companies. Although this was a significant step, financial institutions in the United States still had a narrower range than most of the other countries that were members of the G-10 group.

The Bank for International Settlements is responsible for promoting monetary and financial stability. This organization meets on a bimonthly basis to discuss monetary and financial matters. The organization is composed of four major committees, including the Basel Committee on Banking Supervision, the Committee on the Global Financial System, the Committee on Payment and Market Infrastructures, and the Markets Committee. In addition, there are several independent organizations involved in international cooperation in the area of financial stability, and these organizations have their secretariats at the Bank for International Settlements. These organizations are the Financial Stability Forum, the International Association of Insurance Supervisors, and the International Association of Deposit Insurers.

In January 1999, the Basel Committee proposed a new concept, which became known as Basel II. However, it was a work in progress and additional proposals for consultation occurred in January 2001 and April 2003. The final version of the Basel II accord was distributed in June 2004. The foundation of Basel II relies on three pillars, which are minimum capital requirements, supervisory review, and market discipline (Riskglossary.com). The accord was slow to be adopted, however, because of its complexity and the difficulty of implementing it (Samuels, 2013). In the wake of the 2008 global financial crisis, Basel III addressed many of the shortcomings of Basel II. Basel III attempts to increase bank liquidity and reduce bank leverage. In the United States, the Final Rule—a U.S. version of Basel III's liquidity coverage ratio (LCR)—was proposed by the Federal Reserve Board. The Final Rule would apply to U.S. financial institutions and significant foreign banks with U.S. subsidiaries and would require banks to hold more capital (How US Basel III rules, 2013).

TERMS & CONCEPTS

Bank for International Settlements: Serves the world's central banks as well as other official monetary institutions and nations. The bank does not take deposits from or offer financial services to individuals or corporations.

Basel Committee on Banking Supervision: An institution created by the central bank governors of the Group of Ten (G-10) nations. It was created in 1974 and meets regularly four times a year.

G-10 Group: The Group of Ten is made up of 11 industrial countries (Belgium, Canada, France, Germany, Italy, Japan, the Netherlands, Sweden, Switzerland, the United Kingdom, and the United States), which consult and cooperate on economic, monetary, and financial matters. The ministers of finance and central bank governors of the Group of Ten usually meet once a year in connection with the autumn meetings of the Interim Committee of the International Monetary Fund. The deputies of the Group of Ten meet as needed, but usually between two and four times a year. Ad hoc committees and working parties of the Group of Ten are set up as needed.

Gramm-Leach-Blilely Act: A federal law enacted in the United States to control the ways that financial institutions deal with the private information of individuals. The act consists of three sections: the Financial Privacy Rule, which regulates the collection and disclosure of private financial information; the Safeguards Rule, which stipulates that financial institutions must implement security programs to protect such information; and the Pretexting provisions, which prohibit the practice of pretexting (accessing private information using false pretenses). The act also requires financial institutions to give customers written privacy notices that explain their information-sharing practices.

Market risk: Exposure to the uncertain market value of a portfolio.

Operational risk: Risk of loss resulting from inadequate or failed internal processes, people, and systems or from external events.

BIBLIOGRAPHY

Abdel-Baki, M. A. (2012). The impact of Basel III on emerging economies. *Global Economy Journal, 12.*

Bank for International Settlements (n.d.). About the Basel Committee.

Bank for International Settlements (n.d.). Monetary and financial stability.

Guégan, D., & Hassani, B. K. (2013). Operational risk: A Basel II + + step before Basel III. *Journal of Risk Management in Financial Institutions, 6,* 37–53.

How US Basel III rules could impact non-US banks. (2013). *International Financial Law Review, 32,* 77.

Meyerson, L. A., McGinn, S. E., & Chorazak, M. (2013). Basel oversight committee endorses revised liquidity standards and extends fully phased-in compliance to 2019. *Banking Law Journal, 130,* 217–225.

Nolle, D. (2003, June). Bank supervision in the U.S. and the G-10: Implications for Basel II.

Ortino, S. (2004). International and cross-border cooperation among banking supervisors: The role of the European central bank. *European Business Law Review, 15,* 715–734.

Petersen, M. A., Maruping, J. B., Mukuddem-Petersen, J. J., & Hlatshwayo, L. P. (2013). A Basel perspective on bank leverage. *Applied Financial Economics, 23,* 1361–1369.

Riskglossary.com (n.d.). Basel committee on banking supervision.

Samuels, S. (2013). Why markets do not trust Basel II internal ratings–based approach: What can be done about it? *Journal of Risk Management in Financial Institutions, 6,* 10–22.

Schwerter, S. (2011). Basel III's ability to mitigate systemic risk. *Journal of Financial Regulation & Compliance, 19,* 337–354.

Triana, P. (2013, September 6). Global banks are undercapitalized. Is that so wrong? *American Banker, 178,* 20.

SUGGESTED READING

Borak, D. (2013, January 8). Qualified Praise for Easing of Basel Rules. *American Banker, 178,* 1–3.

Cornford, A. (2007). Trade, investment and competition in international banking. *Journal of Banking Regulation, 8,* 195–197.

Haines, C. (2007). Global banking and national regulation: A conference summary. *Chicago Fed Letter,* 1–4.

Natter, R. (2007). Ensure that U.S. rules mesh with foreign ones. *American Banker, 172,* 11.

Sloan, S. (2007). Basel issues spur S&P to form its own standards. *American Banker, 172,* 20.

Essay by Marie Gould

IT MANAGEMENT APPLICATIONS

It is the job of managers to attempt to control processes and functions within the organization and to make strategic decisions concerning its future. With the explosion of information that has occurred over the past few decades, this means that managers need to be able to process and analyze massive amounts of data. Information technology offers managers a number of tools to support them in their decision making and planning processes as well as in their administrative and organizational tasks. Management information systems are information technology systems that are used to help managers effectively manage the organization as a whole or manage structured problems, processes, functions, or departments within the organization. Decision support systems are information technology systems that are used in unique, complex situations in which a decision needs to be made.

Every day, managers are required to make countless decisions in an attempt to control processes and functions. Many of these decisions can affect the effectiveness and efficiency of the organization as well as its profitability. Processes that malfunction or schedules that slip even in the smallest way can snowball, affecting other parts of the project or organization. It is the manager's job to keep this from happening and to make decisions about how best to keep the projects and processes on track so that the organization can continue to perform at a high level.

In today's organizations, this means that the manager needs to be able to process and analyze massive amounts of data—facts, figures, or details—in order to make the best decision possible. In addition, according to systems theory, the organization comprises multiple subsystems, and the functioning of each affects both the functioning of the others and the organization as a whole. On a practical level, this means that the decisions a manager makes often affect not only the function, department, or specific process or personnel about which the decision was made but also the whole interconnected chain. For example, the manager of the engineering department may be faced with the decision about how to best deploy his/her personnel on the various projects being undertaken by the organization. If the engineering manager makes the deployment decision based on which project manager complains the loudest, the other projects may not have sufficient personnel to do the engineering tasks on their projects. Because of this fact, the other projects may experience schedule slippages or end up with less-than-optimal engineering designs for their products. Either consequence could mean penalties imposed by the customer for late delivery or the product not meeting specifications as well as longer-term consequences of the business losing its reputation in the industry and not being able to win new work. Therefore, it is essential that managers make the best decisions possible.

Use of Management Information Systems

With the advances in computer technology that have occurred over the past decades, information technology is able to offer managers a number of tools to support them in their decision-making and planning processes as well as in their administrative and organizational tasks. Management information systems are information technology systems that are used to help managers effectively manage the organization as a whole or manage structured problems, processes, functions, or departments within the organization. For example, the manager of a bookstore needs to know what inventory is on hand both in the store and at the distributor, what books have been sold during given time periods, and what books customers have requested. She/he also needs to receive this information in usable form (e.g., with a user-friendly interface that allows searching of the various databases) and be able to use these data to place orders to replenish stock and meet current and anticipated customer demands. The manager also needs to know what the buying trends of the store's clientele are and what the trends are in new books and be able to forecast specific titles that should be purchased and stocked as well as whether or not the bookstore should change the emphasis in the types of books that it carries. The manager also needs to know how much money was received each day, including whether the receipts were by cash, check, house account, or credit card, and relay this information to corporate headquarters. If the receipts do not balance at the end of the day, the manager needs to discover where the discrepancies lie and balance the accounts. The manager also needs to be able to schedule personnel so that all shifts are covered with sufficient personnel, including sales associates and receivers, taking into consideration the various needs of the employees (e.g., days off during the week, maximum number of hours to be worked during the week, requests for leave or vacation time, shift preferences). The manager can be aided in all these tasks and more through information technology.

Resources for an Effective Management Information System

As illustrated in Figure 1, a good management information system uses several types of resources. The physical system of the organization includes the facilities, equipment, and personnel necessary to produce the business's products or services. Internal data are gathered throughout the physical system, stored in the database, and processed by the information-processing resources. These resources comprise the server, workstations, application programs, and information technology personnel. The information technology system together is used to analyze the data and summarize it in ways that the managers and executives can use and understand. These individuals use this information to make decisions about the operations of the organization. There are two other sources of information that need to be taken into account by decision makers. These are information gathered from the environment in which the organization operates (e.g., political realities, business intelligence, economic trends). This information can also be fed into the management information system and used in decision-making. Not all data can be processed by the information technology system, however. As illustrated in the figure, there are additional internal data (e.g., word of mouth, observation) that are important in managerial decision-making processes that can only be factored in by the manager. The management information system alone cannot make decisions. It is only a tool to be used by the manager.

Data Retrieval & Processing

Management information systems can support managers in their tasks by retrieving and processing data received during transactions and presenting it to managers in formats that they can use in their operations and decision-making capacities. Management information systems use data captured and stored during transactions (e.g., what books have been sold, what books have been received, how many transactions have been made and in what amounts). Management information systems synthesize and summarize this information and present them to the manager in a usable form rather than giving him/her raw data. This is done through various screen or print reports designed into the system or through special reports designed by the manager to meet the special needs of the store or situation.

Monitoring & Evaluation

Management information systems can also support managers in monitoring and evaluating situations (e.g., whether or not the new line of children's books

is doing well) and making decisions concerning what actions should be taken (e.g., what types of books people are special ordering and do these show a trend that should be taken into account for the store's normal line of books). In addition, management information systems support managers in making recurring decisions (e.g., how to schedule employees, what books should be ordered).

Operations Control

Information technology can also help managers control the operations within the organization. With the use of information technology systems, organizations can process large numbers of transactions efficiently. However, these systems can be vulnerable in a number of areas. Operating systems can have errors in coding or can be penetrated by computer criminals. Applications programs can have errors that not only affect the server but also replicate over the client computers as well. Proprietary or sensitive data on the server can be breached by internal or external sources. If any component in the system goes down, the entire system or network can go down. These and other issues need to be addressed if the system is to be of reliable aid to the manager in operating and controlling the organization and its processes.

Tools to Aid in Decision-Making

In addition to helping managers run the day-to-day operations of the business through the support of management information systems, information technology can aid managers in their tasks by giving them the tools to support them in making decisions. One of the major tasks of the managerial job description is to make decisions that affect the health and effectiveness of the operation. Although some of these decisions are straightforward or have few alternatives, many are not. To help management make such complex decisions, one of the tools of information technology is the decision support system. These management tools are interactive computer-based systems that help managers and others make decisions regarding operations of the organization.

Decision support systems are used in unique, complex situations in which a decision needs to be made. These tools help decision makers better understand the issues underlying the situation and to make decisions in unstructured situations when the extent to which certain variables that influence the activity or outcome are not initially clear or only part of the information is available in advance. Unstructured questions require decision support systems to be flexible so that the impact of various variables and conditions can be tested and the analysis be returned to the user in a form that is useful for the specific situation. Typically, finding the answer to unstructured problems also requires an iterative process: the answers to the questions are not ends in themselves but raise other questions for consideration that need to be run through the decision support system.

Decision support systems provide the information and structure that decision makers need to make a rational decision by creating a quantitative model of the situation and processing data to show the impact of the variables under consideration on the outcomes.

Frequently, decision support systems require the processing of data from multiple files and databases. Decision support systems are used to help decision makers answer questions concerning conditions under which an outcome might occur, what might happen if the value of a variable changes, or how many potential customers have certain characteristics.

Expert Systems

Another type of information technology application that is used by managers is the expert system. These systems often include the application of artificial intelligence to help managers make decisions. Artificial intelligence is a branch of computer science concerned with the development of software that allows computers to perform activities normally considered to require human intelligence. Artificial intelligence applications can be used in the development of expert systems that allow computers to help managers make the kind of complex, real-world decisions with which they are faced every day. Expert systems are useful in decision-making for medical diagnosis, manufacturing quality control, and financial planning.

Top executives tend to take a more global view of the organization than middle managers. In addition, top-level managers are more concerned with the systems approach and need to know how decisions made regarding one part of the organization affect other parts of the organization as well. Executive support systems take these needs into account. To support top-level managers in such decision-making

processes, executive support systems allow executives to look not only at the organization as a system itself but also at the organization as part of a larger system as well. Executive support systems permit scanning of data and information on both internal activities as well as the external business environment.

Executive Information Systems

Executive information systems are data-driven decision support systems designed to support executive decision making. This type of information technology application presents information about the activities of the company and the industry and offers quick, concise updates of business performance for top executives. Executive information systems have powerful processing capabilities in order to summarize and present data in a format appropriate to executive decision-making.

Most top-level managers who use executive information systems find them to be helpful in supporting them in their decision-making processes. This is partially because these systems have relatively simple user interfaces to support the way that most top-level managers work, and they can be used for a wide range of purposes. In addition, since executives tend to look at things from a higher level than do many analysts, executive support systems highlight significant data and present information in summary form rather than giving the user all the details and supporting data, although users are allowed access to these data if desired. This feature allows the user to go down several levels to acquire the data necessary to make a well-informed decision.

APPLICATIONS

Khoong and Ku (1994) describe the total service concept project (TSC) of the Information Technology Institute of Singapore. The purpose of this information technology project was to achieve a comprehensive suite of generic but robust tools to support management decision-making of service operations and resources. The system was designed around state-of-the-art operations research and management science models to support decision-making in operations management—those areas of management that are concerned with productivity, quality, and cost in the operations function (i.e., activities necessary to transform inputs such as business transactions and information into outputs such as completed transactions) as well as strategic planning for the organization. The TSC framework focuses on the management of service operations and resources, with an emphasis on manpower and service management. The TSC comprises four products: service design and analysis, manpower establishment planning, service resource management, and service activity management. The TSC project is applicable to a wide variety of organizations including service organizations in general and organizations requiring direct customer contact. These tools were made to be useful for airports, hospitals, transportation companies, fast-food chains, banks, hotels, supermarkets, and public services organizations as well as for the organization of large events such as sporting matches, trade fairs, and conventions.

Service Design & Analysis

The service design and analysis component supports strategic decision-making for service configuration. This component can be used to perform service analysis to determine whether there will be a customer demand for a given service and to predict what the level of customer demand will be. In addition, the service analysis component allows the user to analyze the effects of various service levels on customers. The service location module is used to determine appropriate locations for service facilities using the criterion of cost optimization in service provision. The service layout module helps managers determine the appropriate layout for service facilities to optimize costs related to the flow of operations and materials within the facility. The final module of the service design and analysis component is service packaging, which helps configure types or grades of services to be provided and predict the effect of these on customer satisfaction.

Manpower Establishment

The manpower establishment planning component is used to support analyses regarding manpower resource management within the organization. This component comprises both descriptive manpower establishment planning and normative manpower establishment planning. The descriptive module is used to analyze data concerning the state of manpower establishment, including forecasting, waste analysis, labor market analysis, and career planning.

The normative module focuses on developing courses of action to improve the manpower establishment. These functions include considerations of staff movement, succession planning, job/task assignment, performance management, recruitment, and training.

Service Resource Management

The service resource management component of the TSC is concerned with the efficient management of key management and other resources within a service organization. This component has two modules. The resource deployment module is used by managers to help plan how best to allocate service resources including manpower, facilities, and equipment to specific tasks over time. This module includes considerations of on-order deployment (i.e., when orders for service are placed in advance), on-call deployment (i.e., when orders come in on an ad hoc basis), and on-wait deployment (i.e., when service resources operate continually in the background without disturbing resource deployment). In addition, the service resource management component has a manpower rostering module that helps schedule employees for each shift, including consideration of days off and shift types.

Service Activity Management

The service activity management component of the TSC helps managers effectively plan the deployment and use of shared resources that are needed for multiple activities. This component includes a project management function to help managers schedule project activities. It also includes an event management function to help managers schedule activities in large organized events, including optimal sequencing of events within resource constraints as well as the preferences of both the customers and the people involved in the events. This component also has a module to help manage time and resources in the provision of personalized services. This module includes appointment scheduling and meeting scheduling sub-functions. Finally, the service activity management component has a timetabling module to help managers allocate resources to parallel activities over time with consideration of competition for limited time, facilities, instructors, and students. This module also includes tools for course scheduling and test scheduling.

TERMS & CONCEPTS

Artificial intelligence (AI): The branch of computer science concerned with the development of software that allows computers to perform activities normally considered to require human intelligence. Artificial intelligence applications include the development of expert systems that allow computers to make complex, real-world decisions; the programming of computers to understand natural human languages; the development of neural networks that reproduce the physical connections occurring in animal brains; and the development of computers that react to visual, auditory, and other sensory stimuli (i.e., robotics).

Client computer: A computer that accesses information stored on a server.

Decision support system (DSS): A computer-based information system that helps managers make decisions about semi-structured and unstructured problems. Decision support systems can be used by individuals or groups and can be standalone or integrated systems or web-based.

Executive information system: A data-driven decision support system designed to support executive decision-making by presenting information about the activities of the company and the industry.

Expert system: A decision support system that utilizes artificial intelligence technology to evaluate a situation and suggest an appropriate course of action.

Information technology (IT): The use of computers, communications networks, and knowledge in the creation, storage, and dispersal of data and information. Information technology comprises a wide range of items and abilities for use in the creation, storage, and distribution of information.

Manager: A person whose job is to facilitate the process of efficiently and effectively accomplishing work through the coordination and supervision of others.

Management information system (MIS): A business information technology (IT) system that is used to help managers effectively manage the organization as a whole or manage structured problems, processes, functions, or departments within the organization.

Operations management: Those areas of management that are concerned with productivity, quality, and cost in the operations function (i.e., activities necessary to transform inputs such as business transactions and information into outputs such as completed transactions) as well as strategic planning for the organization.

Operations research: An analytical method of problem-solving and decision-making in which problems are broken down into basic components and solved using mathematical analysis.

Service sector: In essence, the service sector includes those industries and businesses that provide services rather than tangible products for individual consumers, businesses, or a combination of the two. These can include physical, mental, or aesthetic activities (e.g., legal services, entertainment, auto repair) or the transformation of something through such an activity (e.g., hair cutting, education, management consulting).

Server: The computer that hosts a network and provides services to the other computers in the network (e.g., web pages). The term *server* is also used to refer to the software running on the server computer.

Systems theory: A cornerstone of organizational behavior theory that assumes that the organization comprises multiple subsystems and that the functioning of each affects both the functioning of the others and the organization as a whole.

BIBLIOGRAPHY

Drnevich, P. L., & Croson, D. C. (2013). Information technology and business-level strategy: Toward an integrated theoretical perspective. *MIS Quarterly, 37*(2), 483–509

Li; C., Peters, G. F., Richardson, V. J., & Weidenmier Watson, M. (2012). The consequences of information technology control weaknesses on management information systems: The case of

Sarbanes-Oxley internal control reports. *MIS Quarterly, 36*(1), 179–204.

Lucas, H. C., Jr. (2005). *Information technology: Strategic decision-making for managers.* New York: John Wiley and Sons.

McLeod, R., Jr. (1986). *Management information systems* (3rd ed.). Chicago: Science Research Associates.

Pritchard, S. (2013). Business applications and data analytics make companies lean. *Computer Weekly,* 22–24.

Senn, J. A. (2004). *Information technology: Principles, practices, opportunities* (3rd ed.). Upper Saddle River, NJ: Pearson/Prentice Hall.

Sprague, C. (2014). 21st century IT applications. *Research Starters Business.*

Vieira da Cunha, J. (2013). A dramaturgical model of the production of performance data. *MIS Quarterly, 37*(3), 723–748.

SUGGESTED READING

Harrysson, M., Metayer, E., & Sarrazin, H. (2012). How "social intelligence" can guide decisions. *Mckinsey Quarterly,* (4), 81–89.

Khoong, C. M., & Ku, Y. W. (1994). The TSC project: A strategic R&D initiative in operations management. *International Journal of Operations & Production Management, 14*(8), 35–46.

Marco, D. (2005). CIOs and metadata management, part 2. *DM Review, 15*(8), 60–65.

Molina-Azorin, J. F. (2012). Mixed methods research in strategic management: Impact and applications. *Organizational Research Methods, 15*(1), 33–56.

O'Brien, J. A., & Marakas, G. M. (2011). *Management information systems* (10th ed.). New York, NY: McGraw-Hill/Irwin.

Spangler, T. (2004). Putting tasks on the fast track. *Baseline,* (37), 68–75.

Essay by Ruth A. Wienclaw, PhD

L

LAW OF PROPERTY

This article will explain the broad areas that are covered by the law of property. The overview provides an introduction to the concepts and principles of law that govern estates in land, land conveyancing, and security interests in real property. In addition, factors that affect the use of land are discussed, including nuisance regulations, zoning regulations, and the government's exercise of its eminent domain and regulatory takings powers. To help illustrate how the law of property applies to many common real estate transactions, a discussion of landlord-tenant relationships, the use and exploitation of natural resources, and instances in which one person may gain rights in another's land is included. The following sections will explain these concepts in more detail.

OVERVIEW

The law of property can be divided into two distinctive fields—real property and personal property. Real property is immovable, but personal property is movable. Thus, the law of real property governs laws regarding land and anything affixed to it as well as ownership and security interests in real estate, whereas the law of personal property includes anything that is not real property, such as clothing, automobiles, financial instruments, or other personal assets. However, while real property and personal property are generally distinctive areas, there are a few areas where there is a fine line distinction between the two. For instance, crops that grow organically on the ground are considered real property, while crops that are planted by humans are considered personal property.

This article primarily focuses on the law of real property. When people discuss the law of property, they are typically referring to the law of real property. The laws governing real property are extensive because there are many different aspects of real property. The primary fields included in the law of real property are estates in land, conveyancing land, and security interests in real estate. In addition, significant factors can affect the right to use and enjoy property, such as nuisance regulations, zoning regulations, and the right of the government to exercise its eminent domain or regulatory takings power. Also, the law of property plays an important role in many common matters involving real estate transactions, such as establishing and regulating landlord-tenant relationships and the use and exploitation of natural resources. Finally, property law also governs the areas of adverse possession and easements, which come into play when one person gains rights in land that belongs to another person. These major areas of the law of property will be discussed in more detail below.

Estates in Land

The law of real property is an area of law that has been greatly colored and shaped by both culture and the concept of land ownership over the centuries of history. Some cultures, such as the Anglo-Saxons of Great Britain or Native Americans that migrated and settled throughout North America, have viewed real property largely as communal property. In these cultures, members built communal structures where the entire community gathered to eat, celebrate, govern, or take shelter from the environment or raiding armies. While individual families may have constructed temporary forms of individual housing, these cultures were often nomadic and thus they viewed their relationship to the land as fluid and a function of necessity. They worked and ate from the land where they lived and when necessity dictated that they relocate, they moved to a new area and settled on land that was conducive to their needs. Other non-nomadic cultures took a different view of land ownership and developed the concept of individual rights in plots of land. Still other cultures viewed the land as belonging to a king, ruler, or patriarch of a region or to the aristocratic class that possessed sufficient wealth to own and maintain large plots of land.

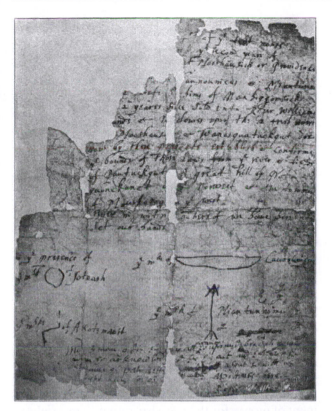

The original 1636 Indian deed creating the State of Rhode Island signed by Native American Chief Canonicus to Roger Williams. (Courtesy of Wikipedia)

In addition to these various concepts of land ownership, the law of property that took shape in the United States was greatly influenced by the feudal institutions of England and Europe. Although feudalism took many forms, particularly during the Middle Ages, its basic structure included a lord, who was an aristocrat or a noble entitled to land ownership; vassals, whom the lord charged with managing sections of the land; and peasants, who actually worked the land. As this system became increasingly complicated and social classes became less stratified, the structure of feudalism faded into the system of estates in land that now govern ownership interests in real property in the United States. The following section provides a more in-depth explanation of the concept of estates in land.

Common Forms of Estates in Land

Under the system of feudalism, one person could be entitled to manage land as if he owned the land, though the property was actually owned by another individual. This concept separated land ownership from land possession. Over the years, various estates in land developed that defined the various rights to ownership and possession of land that were commonly used. Today, the basic form of interest in real property that gives the holder the right to both own and possess the land is known as a present possessory estate. For instance, a fee simple, which is how property is commonly held today and represents absolute ownership in property, is a form of a present possessory estate. However, another form of a present possessory estate is a life estate, which entitles the holder to present possession of land for the life of one or more persons, though the land reverts to the ownership and possession of another at the end of the person's life by whom the life estate is defined. For instance, Landowner A could convey property to Individual B for her life, with the estate reverting back to Landowner A upon Individual B's death.

In addition to a present possessory estate, another type of estate in land is a future interest. A future interest entitles its holder to the right or possibility of possession of an estate in land in the future. For instance, Landowner A may convey property to Individual B on the condition that the land not be used for specified purposes, and if the land is so used, its ownership will revert to Individual C. Thus, while a future interest is a legally protected right in property, there is no guarantee that the estate will become possessory because the land will not convert to Individual C unless Individual B violates the conditions of the conveyance set by Landowner A. While there are other types of estates in land, present possessory estates and future interests are the most common forms of land ownership and possession.

Ownership of Estates in Land

Estates in land may be held individually or concurrently by several people. If an estate is held concurrently, all of the owners have the right to use and possess the land. For instance, one common form of a concurrent estate is a joint tenancy. "When two or more people own property as joint tenants and one owner dies, the other owners automatically gain ownership of the deceased owner's share. For example, if a brother and sister own a house as joint tenants and the brother dies, the sister automatically becomes full owner" ("Joint tenancy," 2007). This form of land ownership is often used because of its automatic right of survivorship. No will is required to transfer the property because ownership automatically vests in the surviving joint tenant, and this feature eliminates the time and expense of probate. Another type of concurrent estate is known as tenancy by the entirety. This estate generally arises presumptively in any property that is conveyed to a husband and wife. Under a tenancy by the entirety, the husband and wife each have an undivided interest in the entire estate and a right of survivorship in the property. Thus, "both spouses have the right to enjoy the entire property, and when one spouse dies, the surviving spouse gets title to the property" ("Tenancy by entirety," 2007).

Conveyancing Land

Conveyancing is the name given to the process of transferring ownership of land from one person to another. There are three stages involved in the process of land conveyance. The first stage includes the time after an agreement in principle is reached between a buyer and a seller but before the seller and buyer are bound by contract to proceed with the transaction. This may involve settling certain questions about condition of the property or financing terms. The second stage occurs after the contract has been signed but before the transaction has closed and property ownership actually transfers. Issues involving the condition of the property, repairs, and financing also arise during this stage. Once the transaction has closed, the third stage involves the registration and completion of any documents that have been prepared relating to the transfer of ownership and recording these documents with the appropriate state or county office.

While these basic stages describe the process of the transfer of land ownership, there are a number of important points in this process during which disputes and legal questions commonly arise. The following sections will describe these issues in more detail.

Land Sale Contracts

Most transfers of land must be preceded by a contract of sale. The contract must generally be in writing, contain the signatures of the parties, and set out the essential terms of the transaction including the names of the parties, an identifiable description of the property, and the price of the property. In most jurisdictions, once the contract is signed, the doctrine of

Castles were a traditional symbol of a feudal society. This is the Orava Castle in Slovakia. (Courtesy of Wojsyl via Wikimedia Commons)

equitable conversion arises, which holds that the purchaser of real property becomes the equitable owner of title to the property and is bound to complete the purchase of the land at the closing. The seller retains legal title of the property until the closing, but the seller's interest in the property is considered personal property. Thus, the seller is entitled only to the payment of money for the property rather than a right to possess the property.

This doctrine is important in terms of determining who bears the risk of loss of property after the contract is signed but before ownership of the property has transferred. Under the doctrine of equitable conversion, the risk of loss is transferred from the seller to the buyer when the contract is signed. This means that after the contract is signed, the buyer is locked into the agreed-upon price even if the property is damaged or destroyed. Most buyers purchase insurance to protect their interest in the property and to mitigate their risk of loss. Also, buyers and sellers can determine their own terms by stipulating in the contract who will bear the risk of loss in the event the property suffers damage.

Marketable Title

Every land sale contract contains an implied warranty that the seller of the property will provide marketable title to the property at closing. Marketable title means that the buyer may take the title of the property with reasonable assurance that there are no issues or defects in the chain of title that will present an unreasonable risk of litigation after closing. The implied warranty of marketable title protects buyers from "purchasing a lawsuit."

Some of the defects that could prevent a seller from obtaining marketable title include encumbrances on the chain of title, such as mortgages, liens, or unpaid taxes on the property. Also, if a property has some condition that has caused an existing violation of a zoning ordinance, this would render the title unmarketable. However, the mere presence of a zoning restriction that governs or includes the property would not make the title unmarketable without an actual violation of the zoning ordinance.

Even if there is a defect in the title that renders it unmarketable at the time the contract is signed, the buyer and seller may still move forward with their agreement to complete their transaction on the specified closing date. This is because sellers typically have until the date of closing to cure any title defects. Thus, if two weeks before the scheduled closing, a buyer discovers a zoning violation on the property or learns that the seller has obtained a second mortgage on the property, the buyer may not rescind the contract at that time. The seller has until the day of closing to resolve any issues that may cloud the marketability of the title. In addition, the seller may use the proceeds of the sale of the property to clear any mortgages that remain on the property. However, if the seller does not provide marketable title at closing or the seller knows the title is not marketable, the remedies to the buyer at that time include recision of the contract, monetary damages, or the right to bring a lawsuit to quiet title or resolve any questions of ownership in the property. If, prior to closing, the seller is unaware that the title is unmarketable but the buyer learns of a defect in the title, the buyer must notify the seller that the title is unmarketable and give the seller a reasonable amount of time to cure the defect.

Deeds
Once the closing occurs, the land sale contract merges with the deed, which essentially extinguishes the contract along with its implied warranty of marketability. Thus, after the closing, the buyer must look to the deed for any covenants that expressly warrant defects in the title. The deed is the document that actually transfers title to an interest in real property. To be effective, a deed must comply with certain formalities. For instance, it must be in writing and signed by the seller or grantor of the property and should

identify the property and the parties to the transaction. The description of the property does not have to be as precise as the property description in a land sale contract, but it should not leave any doubt as to the property to be conveyed. A deed that is forged or obtained by deceit will be considered void, and the deed will be set aside by the court, even if a buyer has already purchased the property. However, if a deed was executed by a minor or obtained by certain types of fraud, the deed will be considered voidable, and a court will set it aside only if the property has not been purchased by a party who was unaware of the defects in the deed.

Today, there are three basic types of deeds that are used to convey most property interests—general warranty, special warranty, and quitclaim deeds. These types of deeds differ in the extent to which they protect buyers by charging the seller of the property with certain responsibilities regarding the condition and habitability of the property. The general warranty deed generally contains a series of covenants that provide the buyer with certain assurances regarding the property. These covenants include the covenant of seisin, which ensures that the property is the grantor's to convey; the covenant of right to convey, stating that the grantor has the authority to transfer the property; and the covenant against encumbrances, which provides that there is no encumbrance or defect in the title. These three covenants can be breached only at the time of the closing. In addition, general warranty deeds also commonly include a covenant for quiet enjoyment, which provides that no third party has a lawful claim to the title, and a covenant of warranty, wherein the seller agrees to defend the buyer against a third party's claim to any interest in the property. If included in the general warranty deed, the covenant for further assurances provides that the grantor will take the steps necessary to perfect title to the property. The covenants of quiet enjoyment, warranty, and further assurances can be breached only if the grantor's possession of the property is violated.

The special warranty deed is a special type of deed in which the grantor guarantees the title against defects only arising during the period of his or her ownership of the property and not against defects that existed before that time. A quitclaim deed releases the grantor from any interest that he or she held in the property and provides the grantee no warranties or protections regarding the title or condition of the property. The parties to a contract may decide what type of deed they will use to transfer ownership in the property. However, buyers in particular must pay close attention to the type of deed that will be used and any protections it may or may not offer. Any covenants, or lack thereof, that are included in a deed are typically reflected in the price of the property in that the more assurances a grantor makes, the higher the sales price.

Recording Acts

After the closing and the actual transfer of property occurs, every state has enacted legislation that requires the purchaser to file a record of the transaction, generally with the county recorder or recorder of deeds, to provide constructive notice of the change in ownership or interest of a particular property. These statutes are known as recording acts. Recording acts generally require that all deeds, mortgages, and certain types of leases be recorded. Recording acts help maintain an official record of the chain of title of ownership so that any person may research the chain of title to any piece of property to determine the extent of the interests and ownership in that property. This protects a subsequent bona fide purchaser, or a person who pays value for property and who has no notice of any prior ownership interests in it, from purchasing land only to learn later that a third party still maintains an ownership interest in the property.

There are three common types of recording acts that provide different types of protections for bona fide subsequent purchasers of property. However, the burden is on the party filing under the recording act to ensure that the transaction is covered by the statute and that the proper documents are filed in a timely manner. The recording acts are typically known as race, race-notice, and notice statutes. Under a pure race statute, the person who records first wins, even if the recorder had notice of a prior unrecorded conveyance. This means that if Landowner A conveys land to Individual B, and two weeks later conveys the same property to Individual C, Individual C will take title to the property if she records before Individual B, even if she knew that Landowner A had previously conveyed the property to Individual B. A race-notice type of act operates in the same way as the race statute but only if the first recorder had no notice of any prior unrecorded conveyance.

Under a notice type of recording act, a subsequent bona fide purchaser would win over a prior purchaser who failed to record so long as the second purchaser had no knowledge of the prior conveyance at the time the purchase was made. For instance, if the first purchaser failed to record his or her deed at the time the second purchase is made, and the second purchaser files her deed after the conveyance, she would win in a dispute over the ownership of the property.

Security Interests in Real Estate

There are several different types of security interests in real estate. A security interest gives a creditor the right to take all or part of a property that has been offered as security if the purchaser defaults on a loan. Thus, when a customer seeks to borrow funds from a bank or credit union to purchase a home, the customer agrees to make regular payments of principal and interest and gives the bank or credit union a mortgage until the loan is paid in full. Thus, if the purchaser defaults on the loan, the creditor has the right to initiate foreclosure proceedings in an attempt to recoup the balance of the outstanding debt. The mortgage lien is the bank's or credit union's security interest, and it is recorded in the title documents in public land records according to the state's recording act. Once the mortgage is paid in full, the lien is removed and title remains in the homeowner's name. The most common types of security interests in real estate are mortgages, deeds of trust, installment land contracts, and sale-leasebacks. These security interests will be explained in more detail below.

Mortgages

A mortgage is a legal document that a purchaser gives to a lender that provides the lender with an interest in the property to secure the repayment of the debt, and the mortgage is evidenced by a mortgage note. Once the debt has been repaid, a satisfaction of mortgage is recorded with the recorder of deeds in the county where the mortgage is located. Each state has enacted laws and statutes that govern property rights to land located within its borders. Mortgages must be executed according to the laws of the state in which the property is located and must fulfill certain formalities, such as describing the real estate, including the signatures of all owners of the property, and containing an official seal of a notary public, if necessary. The mortgage note establishes the borrower's promise to repay the debt. In addition, it describes the terms of the transaction, such as the amount of the debt, the interest rate, the amount of monthly payments, the due date, and any other terms, such as any prepayment penalties.

The law has developed over time in relation to the legal effect of mortgages. Years ago, under the prevailing common law, if a borrower failed to pay a mortgage debt in full or make timely monthly payments, the lender could foreclose on the property, leaving the borrower with a complete loss of title, regardless of how long payments had been made up to that point. However, courts eventually began to seek a more equitable remedy for debtors who have made payments on a property but have run into financial hardship. One such equitable remedy allows such debtors to regain title under certain circumstances after a default by paying the remainder of the debt in full plus interest and other costs. Today, almost all states have enacted statutes that regulate the mortgage lending industry, and many of these statutes allow debtors to redeem the property within a specified period of time after they have fallen behind on payments.

However, if the borrower defaults on the mortgage note and is unable to meet any redemption options, lenders have the right to foreclose on the property. Because foreclosure can result in financial losses for both the lender and the borrower, lenders are often willing to work with debtors to help create payment options during periods of financial hardship. In spite of this, if a lender does move forward with foreclosure proceedings, the real estate is generally sold, often by a county official, at a public foreclosure sale. When the real estate is sold at a foreclosure sale, the lender is most commonly the purchaser of the property. If the bid at the foreclosure sale is less than the debtor still owes on the property, the lender may be granted a deficiency judgment for the balance of the debt, even if the bid represents the property's fair market value. Thus, a deficiency judgment permits a lender with the right to seize any other assets or income a debtor may own to collect the balance of the outstanding debt. This process has often been criticized by consumer rights organizations.

Another option, which arose as an alternative to foreclosure during the real estate downturn of the early twenty-first century, is the short sale. As real estate values declined sharply, many homeowners found their mortgages "upside down"—that is, they owed more than the home was worth. Mortgage defaults became so common that banks began offering alternatives to foreclosure, including allowing the property to be sold "short," or below the amount owed. This solution circumvented the lengthy foreclosure process while preventing the property from falling into an abandoned condition (Sheridan, 2011).

Deeds of Trust

A deed of trust is another type of security interest in real estate that involves three parties—the debtor, the lender, and the trustee. The way a deed of trust operates is that the debtor gives a deed of trust to a trustee—a third party who holds the title in trust until the lien is paid in full. If the debtor defaults, the lender instructs the trustee to foreclose the deed of trust and sell the property in a foreclosure sale. The trustee may be a third party that is associated with the lender, or, in some instances, a neutral third party. Depending upon the state, either attorneys or insurance companies provide trustee service. The deed of trust is recorded in public records and is canceled when the debt is paid.

The country is equally divided into states that utilize mortgages and those that utilize deeds of trust as security instruments. Mortgages and deeds of trust are similar and essentially serve the same purpose. However, there are a few important differences between these two forms of security interests, primarily relating to the foreclosure process in the event of a default. With a mortgage, if a borrower fails to make monthly payments or meet other conditions of the loan, "the lender must typically bring a court action in order to foreclose on the property. With a deed of trust, if the homeowner does not pay the loan, the foreclosure process is usually much faster and less complicated than the formal court foreclosure process" because the trustee has the power to sell the house if the borrower defaults on the loan ("Deeds of trust?" 2007). The lender simply gives the trustee proof of the delinquency and asks the trustee to initiate foreclosure proceedings. The trustee must proceed with the foreclosure according to the state's laws, but the process bypasses the court system, which makes the foreclosure process considerably faster and less expensive for lenders.

Installment Land Contracts

"An installment land contract is an agreement between a buyer and seller whereby the seller finances the sale price of the property on an installment method and retains legal title until the obligation is paid in full" ("Installment land contracts," 2007). Thus, the installment purchaser obtains legal title only after the entire contract price has been fully paid. Installment land contracts are less common than mortgages or deeds of trust but are sometimes used in place of those other security interests.

When an installment land contract is used, the parties agree to the terms of the contract but do not actually transfer a deed or title to the property as in a closing. Instead, the installment land contract enables the buyer to use, possess, and enjoy the property as long as he or she makes timely payments. The installment land contract is recorded according to the state's recording act immediately after execution of the agreement, but the deed is not recorded and title does not pass until the balance is fully or substantially paid.

Installment land contracts are most often used in slow markets, during periods of higher interest rates, or when a borrower is unable to qualify for more conventional forms of financing. The installment loan contract is attractive for buyers in that they are able to obtain property without having to qualify for a loan or pay closing costs, and these contracts often require a lower down payment than a typical mortgage requirement. Sellers, too, often find installment loan contracts a solid option because sellers are permitted to hold legal title and the deed to the property while the buyer is making payments. However, sellers must continue to use caution because even though they hold legal title and have the ability to foreclose on a property if the buyer defaults, the process of foreclosure and the legal fees that may be involved could be expensive and time-consuming. Thus, installment land contracts are still used with caution.

Sale-Leasebacks

In a sale-leaseback transaction, a property owner sells property to a buyer for cash and then leases the property back from the buyer over an extended period of time. Businesses have increasingly begun to use sale-leaseback financing options for their commercial property because the sale of the property allows the company to gain a significant influx of equity, which the company can use for other purposes or invest back into the business while taking advantage of the tax write-offs that are permissible with leased property. The tax consequences of a sale-leaseback differ from conventional loans in that businesses may generally write off the full payment of a lease obligation rather than only the interest payment. Because real estate sale-leaseback transactions have become an increasingly popular form of financing, some companies have begun to offer sale-leaseback transactions for equipment as well (Sabatini, 2013).

Community Land Trusts

Community land trusts (CLTs) are nonprofit landowners who lease properties for use as farms or homes. Lessees may build (and own) the structures on the land, but the landowner is responsible for paying taxes on the land. The concept was developed in the 1970s as a way of assisting young farmers who could not otherwise afford the necessary land. It was later used in urban settings to make housing more affordable and protect tenants from rising real estate values. The unintended consequences of underfunded public services in areas with many CLTs results where nonprofits enjoy tax exempt status. (Bagdol, 2013).

Factors Affecting the Use of Land

Even though a property owner may have paid for her land in full and own title to the property outright, she does not necessarily have unmitigated rights to use and enjoy the land however she sees fit. As society becomes more populous and the sprawl of urban areas begins to extend into once rural regions, land use is increasingly being regulated by multiple layers of governance. The federal government has certain powers pertaining to regulating land use. In addition, state, county, and even local agencies and governing bodies may enact regulations that restrict how landowners may use their property. The following sections will explain some of the significant factors that affect the use of land.

Nuisance Regulations

A nuisance is an unreasonable interference with another person's use and enjoyment of his or her property. There are two types of nuisance: private or public. A private nuisance occurs when there is an interference with another's private property rights. A public nuisance is an interference with the general public's rights. For instance, if odors from a manufacturing plant are offensive to a nearby neighbor, the nuisance is considered private because only the individual property owner is harmed. However, if the odors affected schoolchildren, neighborhoods, and businesses in the vicinity, the nuisance is public because it interferes with health, safety, or comfort of the general public.

Because the activities that may or may not constitute a nuisance are relative or impossible to define in advance, courts must weigh each instance in which nuisance is alleged on a case-by-case basis to determine whether a nuisance has actually occurred. In reaching a decision, courts use a balancing test to weigh various competing factors that affect both parties, such as the extent of the harm, the nature of the harm, the social utility of the activity, the suitability of the activity relative to the character of the locale, and the burden of halting the activity.

When property owners allege nuisance in a lawsuit, they almost always seek injunctive relief, which is a request that the nuisance activity be stopped or mitigated. Further, property owners may seek monetary damages to compensate for any bodily harm or loss of property value as a result of the nuisance activity. In order for the courts to award complaining property owners with injunctive relief, the interference with their property must be substantial and ongoing. This is because if the alleged nuisance stems from a business operation, injunctive relief may require that the company halt its entire business operations. Thus, in constructing a suitable form of relief, courts will attempt to balance the relative hardships to both of the parties involved in the action and craft a decision that attempts to minimize the economic impact on parties on both sides of the dispute.

Zoning Regulations

Under a state's police power, each state is permitted to enact statutes to reasonably control the use of land in ways that are designed to protect the health, safety, morals, and welfare of its citizens. However, the due process and equal protection clauses of the Fourteenth Amendment to the U.S. Constitution provide individuals with federal rights and protections that limit the actions that states can take. Cities and counties can exercise zoning power only if a state enabling act authorizes such actions.

Zoning provides state and local government bodies with the ability to control the physical development of land and to limit the uses of land within their jurisdiction. Zoning laws typically classify areas according to their predominate use, such as residential, industrial, recreational, or commercial areas. Once an area has been zoned for a particular use, activities that do not conform to the prescribed use of the area may be restricted or highly limited. Besides restricting the uses that can be made of land and buildings, zoning laws may also limit the dimensional requirements for lots and for buildings on property located within specified areas and regulate the extraction of natural resources from land within the zoned areas.

While zoning ordinances may be enacted to regulate certain land uses and business activities, zoning boards may permit certain exceptions to the zoning regulations. For instance, a nonconforming use is a use of land that violates the current zoning ordinances but that existed at the time the zoning act was passed. A nonconforming use may be grandfathered into the zoning requirements so that it becomes a legal violation of the current zoning ordinances or a certain amount of time may be allotted for the nonconforming use to be corrected. Another exception to zoning ordinances is a variance, which is a departure from zoning requirements that is permitted by the zoning board for a particular purpose. For instance, a homeowner who wants to make a change to his home that is not permitted under current zoning requirements may request that the zoning board grant him a variance so that he may lawfully make the desired changes to his home.

Eminent Domain & Regulatory Takings

Eminent domain refers to the power of a state to appropriate property for a public use. While a state may exercise its eminent domain power for the benefit of the public, the Fifth Amendment to the U.S. Constitution requires that private property may not be taken for public use without just compensation being paid to the property owner. Just compensation has generally been defined to mean the fair market value of the property at the time that the property was appropriated. Although only the state has eminent domain powers, it may occasionally delegate these powers to certain public and private companies, such as utilities providers, so that these companies can use eminent domain powers to run telephone, electric, water, or gas lines over private property. The process of taking land under eminent domain powers is known as a condemnation proceeding.

Another way that the government can affect the use of land is when it passes regulations that limit or erode the value of private property. When the government regulates property so that it no longer has any economic value, such regulatory actions constitute a regulatory taking, and the owner is entitled to just compensation. If a regulation leaves property with only limited economic value, a court uses a balancing test to determine whether a taking has occurred by weighing factors such as the social objectives of the regulation, the diminution in value of the property, and the property owner's reasonable expectations for use of the property.

APPLICATIONS

Law of Property in Common Real Estate Transactions

Most people have exposure to the law of property at several points in their lives. Many people rent apartments and forge landlord-tenant relationships. Others buy homes or purchase land to develop for a range of purposes. When a person buys land, he or she has the responsibility to stay abreast of the condition of his or her property and to take action to correct any improper uses of the property. If a property owner fails to do so over an extended period of time, he or she may lose rights to complete use and possession of the property, as third parties may develop rights to the land. The following sections will explain these common real estate transactions in more detail.

Landlord-Tenant Relationships

Landlord-tenant law governs the rental of commercial and residential property. Landlord-tenant law is regulated by state statutes, common law, and the terms of an individual lease. Landlord-tenant relationships are created when a person leases property from the property owner. The leasehold is actually an estate in land that gives the lessee, known as the tenant, a present possessory interest in the premises with the property owner, known as the landlord, retaining a future interest in the property at the end of the lease. The tenancy may be for a set period of time, such as for one year; for an indefinite period of time, as in a month-to-month lease; for a terminable period that ends at any time by either party;

or until a landlord takes steps to evict a tenant who has remained in possession of the premises after the expiration of the lease.

The landlord-tenant agreement, which is embodied in a lease, may eliminate or limit these rights. However, a fundamental component of any lease is the implied covenant of quiet enjoyment. This covenant ensures the tenant that her possession of the property will not be disturbed by someone with a superior legal title to the premises, including the landlord. This means that the tenant may use and enjoy the property according to the terms of the lease with no expectation that a third person may enter or use the property without her permission. The covenant of quiet enjoyment may be breached by an actual eviction or a constructive eviction, as when the landlord causes the premises to become so uninhabitable that the tenant is forced to leave the property.

A constructive eviction can occur when governing housing codes are violated by another tenant or by the condition of the property. Housing codes were established to ensure that residential rental units are habitable when they are rented and remain habitable during the tenancy. Depending on the state, housing code violations may lead to administrative action by a state agency against the landlord or to the tenant being allowed to withhold rent until the violation is cured. If a tenant breaches the terms of a lease, summary eviction statutes commonly allow a landlord to quickly evict the tenant. However, federal law prohibits discrimination in housing and the rental units.

Use & Exploitation of Natural Resources

Although natural resources are a part of the landscape, their use and value is not necessarily assumed when a buyer purchases land that contains or is adjacent to these resources. In general, an owner of real property has the exclusive right to use and possess the surface and soil of his property and the airspace above it up to a certain extent. A property owner's ability to use the water that exists on or runs through his property depends on whether it is groundwater, surface water, or a watercourse, such as a stream, river, or lake. For ground or percolated water in wells, about a dozen eastern states hold that the owner of the overlying land can take any amount of the water and use it for any purpose. About half of the remaining states follow a similar doctrine but allow a property owner to export the water only if it does not harm the interests of other landowners with rights in the water. Most western states follow doctrines that determine ownership of the water either by ownership of overlying land or by being the first to make beneficial use of the water.

For surface waters such as rainfall and seepage, half of the states follow the theory that owners may not alter the natural flow of the water's drainage patterns, while the other states hold that an owner may erect structures to channel the water away from his or her property. Similarly, two major doctrines divide watercourse rights. Under one doctrine, the owners of the property that border the watercourse own the water. The other doctrine holds that the order in priority of beneficial use determines rights to the water, and a right can be lost if the use of the water is abandoned.

Property owners have a right to the airspace above their property, but the airspace is finite. Airplanes are able to fly in airspace regulated by the federal government, though property owners may have the right to be free of excessive noise. Also, property owners have rights to the lateral support of their property in its natural state and to the subjacent, or underground, support of their property.

Rights in the Land of Another

A property owner has the responsibility to know the extent of his or her property and to take steps to eliminate any threat to his or her possession and enjoyment of her land. Thus, if a person trespasses, a property owner may take the necessary actions to evict the trespasser. However, if the trespasser continues to cross and use the property of another beyond the time established for the statute of limitations for trespass without the property owner taking steps to evict the trespasser, the trespasser may acquire title to the property by adverse possession.

In order to satisfy all of the elements of adverse possession, the use and possession of the land must be sufficiently open and notorious so that the owner has notice of the trespass, and the land use must be without the owner's permission. In addition, the trespasser must actually occupy the land for a continuous period of time throughout the statutory period. If these elements exist until the statute of limitations for trespass expires, title to the property will vest in the trespasser.

While adverse possession occurs when a trespasser acquires title to land through continuous

occupation of it, there are several non-possessory interests in land that create a right for one person to use the land of another without gaining title to the property. For instance, an easement provides its holder with the right to use a tract of land belonging to someone else for a specified purpose, such as to cross land to gain access to a road or to lay utility wires. A license permits a person to enter another person's property for a specific purpose, such as when a repairman is hired to fix a broken dishwasher. Profits are written documents that grant one person the right to take certain natural resources from another person's land. Finally, real covenants are promises concerning the use of land and are either affirmative, meaning a person promises to do something, such as pave the driveway, or negative, meaning a person promises not to take a certain action, such as promising not to develop land for industrial use. Real covenants run with the land at law, which means that subsequent owners may be able to enforce them or be obligated to honor them.

CONCLUSION

Property law is the area of law that governs the various forms of ownership and interests in real property. The law of property has been developed through the common law legal system, and the roots of its concepts date back hundreds and thousands of years. Some of the most familiar aspects of the law of real property include issues involving landlord and tenant relationships, possessing ownership of an estate in land, and granting a security interest in real property through a mortgage or deed of trust. However, the law of real property also covers many other areas, such as rights to natural resources, obtaining rights in the land of another, or zoning and nuisance regulations. While there are some federal laws and regulations that govern the law of property, the legal and regulatory framework of the law of property is primarily composed of state laws, regulations, and statutes. The law of property essentially reflects the predominant views that a culture and community have toward land, land ownership, and the exploitation of natural resources. Thus, property laws continue to develop according to the needs of individuals and communities, particularly in urban environments where property ownership and use is at a premium.

Terms & Concepts

Assignment: The distribution of legal rights (such as lease time) from an individual to another individual.

Bailment: Legal situation in which property is given by someone who harbors exclusive control of it to someone else in order to ensure that the property is reasonably cared for and protected.

Binder: Serves as a summary of the contractual agreement between a buyer and a seller.

Closing: Pertaining to real estate, the time at which the deed is given to the buyer, the title is handed over, and the costs are paid—the final interaction between a buyer and seller.

Contract: Legal agreement detailing the offer and acceptance consented to by two or more parties; often required to be in writing.

Damages: Upon determination of a wrongful act, the monetary compensation given to the harmed.

Deed: Legal description of a property and its boundaries; final step in a sale involves the deed being exchanged for the agreed-upon price.

Easement: Allows individuals access to another individual's property; in order to run pipes or phone lines, utility companies often hold easements.

Encumbrance: Any claim or restriction on a property's title.

Estate: All the property a person owns.

Fixture: Most frequently those items which are attached to a property and are included in a sale; includes ceiling lights, awnings, window shades, and doorknobs.

Foreclosure: When a borrower cannot repay a loan and the lender seeks to sell the property.

Grantor: Individual that creates a trust.

Implied warrant of habitability: In most states, the law that requires landlords to ensure safe and habitable premises for tenants; essential services and cleanliness can be included.

Joint tenancy: "When two or more people own property as joint tenants and one owner dies, the other owners automatically gain ownership of the deceased owner's share. For example, if a brother and sister own a house as joint tenants and the brother dies, the sister automatically becomes full owner" ("Joint tenancy," 2007).

Lien: A claim against someone's property that ensures receipt of payment; a mortgage is an example of a lien.

Partition: Court-ordered division of property; occurs in situations of joint tenancy that have been disrupted by a dispute.

Quitclaim deed: Deed that transfers an owner's rights to a buyer without guaranteeing that there aren't other outside claims on the property.

Real property: Term referring to a piece of land and all of those things that are a part of it; houses are real property while couches and other similar furnishings are not.

Title: Ownership of property.

Bibliography

Bagdol, A. (2013). Property taxes and community land trusts: A middle ground. *Texas Law Review, 91,* 939–959.

Bowie, I. (2005). The law of land. *Lawyer, 19,* 25.

Deed of trust? (2007). What are these other terms I keep hearing?

Depoorter, B. W., & Parisi, F. (2003). Fragmentation of property rights: A functional interpretation of the law of servitudes. In *Working Papers-Yale School of Management's Legal Scholarship Network,* 1–41.

Installment land contracts. (2007). Classroom.

Joint tenancy. (2007). Useful information: Glossary.

Luxton, P. (2002, May). Business property. In *Journal of Business Law,* 304.

Lyons, J. (2002). Basic principles of property law (book). *International Journal of Commerce & Management, 12,* 126.

McClurg, A. (1998). Conquering renters' blues. *ABA Journal, 84,* 14.

Priest, C. (2006). Creating an American property law: Alienability and its limits in American history. *Harvard Law Review, 120*, 386–459.

Reid, K. (2003). Vassals no more: Feudalism and post-feudalism in Scotland. *European Review of Private Law, 11*, 282–300.

Robertson, D. (2006). Cultural expectations of homeownership. Explaining changing legal definitions of flat 'ownership' within Britain. *Housing Studies, 21*, 35–52.

Sabatini, G. (2013). Sale-leaseback—Corporate real estate as a long-term source of financing. *Site Selection, 58*, 190–196.

Sheridan, T. (2011). Short on results. *Mortgage Banking, 71*, 42–47.

Tenancy by entirety. (2007). Useful information: Glossary.

Suggested Reading

Combs, M. (2006). Cui bono? The 1870 British Married Women's Property Act, bargaining power, and the distribution of resources within marriage. *Feminist Economics, 12*(1/2), 51–83.

De la Cruz Skerrett, J. (2006). Condominiums and home owners associations. *Caribbean Business, 34*, 10–11.

Forbes, S. (1991). A note on teaching the time value of money. *Financial Practice & Education, 1*, 91.

Essay by Heather Newton, JD

Liability Risk Management

ABSTRACT

Society must balance the interests of business and the injuries that flow from it. The law attempts to strike that balance by allowing the injured to recover and by giving businesses an incentive to prevent injury. To minimize the risks of legal liability, businesses or individuals must first understand the nature and source of legal liability within their particular field of endeavor. With that knowledge, steps can be taken to eliminate known risks, reduce the effects of possible risks, and prepare for the chance of unforeseeable or uncontrollable risks. This essay provides an overview of risk factors generally faced by businesses and methods to control them.

OVERVIEW

Liability risk management is a concept with specific application to a variety of settings. For a general introduction, it is helpful to begin with clear definitions of the terms to frame the discussion. Liability is a legal obligation that is enforceable by a civil remedy or criminal punishment. A risk is the chance of injury, damage, or loss (Garner, 1999). Management is the act of handling or controlling. Generally, liability risk management is an activity that controls the chances of incurring legal obligations for injury, damage, or loss. The range of risk any particular organization may face varies according to its industry and to its position within that industry. A business may incur liability to individuals within the organization. For example, federal employment discrimination laws give employees the right to sue and recover from employers that violate those laws. Employers must also comply with certain standards that mandate safety and fairness in the workplace. Managers may attempt to minimize risk through accounting strategies and diversification to help absorb shocks caused by lawsuits (Gormley & Matsa, 2011). The most effective way to avoid such liabilities, however, is to prevent the happening of events that may cause claims or lawsuits. With positive control of their environment, businesses can eliminate or minimize their exposure to internally generated liabilities. Commanding positive control of the work environment entails training, education, and other programs and systems designed to enable employees and management to act appropriately with respect to each other.

For this discussion, liability risks are unintended or unexpected legal obligations that an organization may incur to an individual or entity outside the organization and that arise from conduct in which a business must engage. A business must carry on its business, and its activities carry a degree of risk. Some activities may be safer than others, but the chance of injury does not disappear; things can go wrong in ways never imagined. To minimize such risks, an organization should understand how risks may arise and then take active steps to eliminate the factors that may contribute to unexpected or unwanted legal obligations. Specific events that can cause liability are too numerous to list. However, as a general matter, troublesome legal obligations, in the form of lawsuits, arise from the law of torts. A tort is a civil wrong for which a remedy may be obtained. Defamation and interference with business relations are examples of torts, but the centerpiece of the tort system is negligence. Negligence is a cause of action whereby an injured person may recover from a responsible party if he or she can show that another party breached its duty of care and that the breach caused his or her injury. A standard of care is the minimum level of care (e.g., precaution, expertise) that a business must exercise in the course of its dealings to protect others from injury. If a business fails to meet that standard, the business is said to have breached its duty of care, and the legal mechanism, or cause of action, which allows the injured person to recover is called negligence.

Every business, and indeed every person, has a permanent responsibility to meet its duty of care at all times, and every activity has a corresponding standard of care. For example, a construction company builds a bridge with grade A steel, which is the same steel it had always used without incident. The bridge buckles and collapses during an especially cold winter. Some people are killed, and others are injured. It is later determined that grade A-1 steel would have held up. Is the construction company liable to the people for injuries? Did it fail to meet its standard of care by not using A-1 steel? Maybe and maybe not, but the company would be likely to find out because the injured will seek a remedy, and the construction company would almost certainly be sued—and maybe even bankrupted—as a result. For another example, imagine that morning commuters are crowding into a train from the platform as the train's doors begin to close in anticipation of departure. A man who arrived a few seconds too late is determined to be on that train. He tries to squeeze between the doors with some help from the train workers and by doing so drops a package onto the tracks. The package contains fireworks that begin to go off and cause a clock, hanging from a column on the other end of the platform, to shake lose. The clock falls on a woman waiting for the next train and

Judge Learned Hand, half-length portrait, seated at desk, facing left. (Courtesy of Library of Congress)

causes her injury. Is the railroad liable to the woman for her injuries? These circumstances are based on a famous case decided by the highest court in New York State. In that case, the railroad was not liable, and the court announced a famous and much-debated rule that limited liability to foreseeable plaintiffs. The results of litigation over injuries are all around us. Have you seen a coffee cup warn that its contents are hot? (Wild west judgments, 1996)

The appropriate level of reasonable precaution required by the law varies with the circumstances and according to the parties involved. For example the standard of care is determined differently for professionals (lawyers, doctors, architects, etc.), grocery store clerks, and hotel owners. A standard can also evolve over time to adapt to society; the same conduct that may have been acceptable in the past may incur legal liability at some point in the future. Situations tend to be unique, and whether any particular precaution should have been taken requires close examination of the facts in light of similar cases previously decided. A general formula, called the

"Hand Formula," named after Judge Learned Hand, can help determine which precautions should be taken under a business's duty of care. The formula is represented by $B \& < P \times L$. B is the cost or burden on the company of taking a precaution that would avoid a foreseeable injury. P is the increase in the probability of loss if B is not done, and L is the probable magnitude of loss. If the cost of taking a precaution B is less than the benefit of the precaution to the consumer, calculated by $P \times L$, the company should take the precaution, and if not, then negligence is suggested. The "Hand Formula" is helpful as a tool to understand the obligations that a business could face. Clearly, enormously costly initiatives to eliminate a minor injury are generally not required, but inexpensive actions that would prevent great injury are generally always required (Owens, 2005).

Strict products liability is of particular concern for businesses that sell or produce products (cars, drain cleaners, frozen dinners, perfumes, airplanes, etc.). Depending on the case, an injured party can recover based on negligence or strict liability. Strict liability is often preferable because an injured party does not have to prove that an offending company, usually a manufacturer or retailer, was at fault or negligent. The injured party needs only to prove that the product was defective. Products can have manufacturing defects, design defects, or inadequate warnings. Manufacturing defects are unintended flaws in production. Design defects are unnecessarily risky designs that reasonably could have been avoided. Warning defects are those injuries that could have been avoided with reasonable access to information.

Contracts are an integral part of any business and a potential area where businesses can incur unwanted liability. Contracts are voluntary exchanges of promises by parties that are enforceable as legal obligations. Parties are free to negotiate the terms, or promises, that make up the contract. Contracts can be written, oral, or implied by the conduct of the parties. Oral contracts, which are enforceable in many situations, and contracts that arise by conduct often lack a clear definition of the performance required by the promises. As a result, they are subject to misunderstandings and disagreement. When the parties can't agree, some binding authority, like a court or an arbitration board, must decide. As a result, parties to an oral or implied contract may end up with a deal they did not intend in addition to the expense and aggravation of presenting their case to a court.

There appears to be a popular belief that a contract is a signed writing and only a signed writing. This is false. A contract is a legal obligation formed by an agreement; a signed writing is a common form. There is some truth to the common notion in that there is a legal rule, intended to prevent fraud, that requires certain contracts to be in writing to be enforceable, but that rule has exceptions and is not universal. The writing is not the contract; it is a description of the agreement. If the writing fails to adequately describe the obligations formed by the exchange of promises or attempts to impose illegal or inappropriate obligations, it may be changed or not enforced as decided by a court of law that can cause unexpected liability. This understanding underscores the importance of using due care when obligations are committed to paper and that obligations may arise without a writing and from outside a writing. A businessperson seeking to limit potential exposure to liability should understand the fundamental nature of contracts. Otherwise, a person may unintentionally incur an enforceable legal obligation in the course of doing business.

Written contracts are best for a business trying to control potential liability. With some degree of care, the written contract goes a long way to avoid unexpected liability. Writing, or drafting, clear and precise contracts is a part of any comprehensive effort to minimize unexpected liability. Accordingly, the writing should describe the expectations and obligations of each party under the contract clearly and fully and address as many contingencies as possible. The terms of the contract may include provisions related to the risk of loss or impose the duty to carry insurance to cover particular risks. It may include a clause that determines damages or a dispute resolution method in the event of breach. The contract may spell out the order of performance of the parties and the time and method for payment. There are a number of clauses that can be included in contracts to apportion risk and help ensure that the parties get only the liability, and therefore benefit, of what they bargained for. Where the contract fails to address a particular matter or the parties disagree about what the agreement was, the courts will decide, and the expense and aggravation of unexpected liability will again surface.

Liability can take many forms. The word *liability* has many variations, but those directly relevant to negligence include *vicarious liability*, or liability for a supervisor based on the conduct of a subordinate; *enterprise liability*, or liability for all members of an industry determined according to their market share; and *joint and several liability*, where each codefendant is responsible for the entire obligation even though he or she may not have caused all the injury. Liability can attach to an employer based on conduct by an employee, perhaps 200 miles away. Liability has been imposed on companies simply because they were part of a particular industry that caused harm even though that company may not have caused injury. If a party is liable for 35 percent of a million-dollar verdict, that party may pay the entire sum and would be forced to go after the other responsible parties for the difference. Businesses must continue to operate in the face of perpetual risk; therefore businesses would be wise to take steps to minimize the chance that somehow and in some way, they will be liable for someone's injury.

The standard of care relies on words that invite argument—*reasonably* and *foreseeably*—and make it difficult to determine with precision whether a particular behavior will incur liability. However, that does not mean that businesses are powerless to protect themselves from unwanted liability. The legal profession is an important component of liability risk management for businesses and individuals. People tend to call lawyers after trouble arises; as a method to control liability, this reactionary use of the legal profession is not ideal. Prior to an injury, a lawyer could have advised the business to take reasonable precautions that may have prevented the injury or at least limited the business's liability for that injury. A contract could have been written slightly differently, or a warning sign could have been put in a particular place, or any number of seemingly slight factual variations to a casual observer could have made a large legal difference. When a business has a continuing relationship with legal counsel—many businesses have in-house or general counsel—it can often avoid or limit liability that arises from common business by engaging legal advice on the best practices for doing business in its industry. For example, counsel for a manufacturer may advise to alter a warning on a particular product because a similar warning had been held inadequate by a court.

The government provides an important source of liability risk protection with particular business organization laws. Imagine that a person starts a business and operates it as a sole proprietor, or two or more people get together and carry on as a general partnership. If someone dies because a patio the business built collapsed and a court decides that the business was at fault, a judgment against the business is awarded, and the business is responsible. If the business is bankrupt, the owners themselves are personally liable for judgment. This means that the owners' houses, cars, savings accounts, and other assets are all up for the taking in order to cover the damages. Sole proprietorships and general partnerships have unlimited liability; legally, the business and the person or people are the same thing. State governments, however, provide an alternative business form that has limited liability; legally, the business is separate from the owners. The two most popular entities are the corporation and the limited liability company (LLC). A relatively simple and inexpensive filing will form either entity, and when coupled with certain administrative practices, the entity will limit the liability of the owners to the amount they had invested. Generally, a judgment against an LLC or corporation is collectable against only the assets of that LLC or corporation. In the above example, the judgment may take everything that the business has, but the owner's or owners' personal assets would typically be safe. Hereafter, limited liability entity (LLE) refers to corporations, LLCs, and other limited liability forms that may be available under state law.

The LLE controls the chances of liability by compartmentalizing the effect of liability to parties associated with the entity. For the individual who starts a business, the LLE contains the legal liability to the business, which leaves personal assets aside. This same concept applies to businesses as well because businesses may start and own other businesses. A company may set up and own several different LLEs, each of which owns certain operations or particular assets. In that way, potential legal obligations that could threaten the entire organization are contained to only those assets committed to a particular LLE. For example, consider a cab company that has a fleet of 50 cabs. The company may set up an LLE for each cab. If an accident were to occur, the company could be spared from paying the insurance policy for every cab. This would allow the entire company to be insulated from liability. This principle also applies to real estate. Companies with various real estate holdings and operations may own a separate LLC for each building. These, of course, are only examples of a general concept and are not necessarily effective in every given case. These ownership structures are very complicated and involve significant consideration of relevant law by experienced professionals before they can be used.

Despite the best efforts of businesspersons and their legal counsel, events occur and accidents happen, so it is often wise to purchase insurance. Generally, insurance is an agreement by which one party assumes a risk faced by another party in return for a premium. An insurance policy is a document detailing such an agreement. Insurance policies cover a wide variety of risks; some of the common types purchased by or for individuals are life insurance and health insurance. Fire insurance covers losses by fire to specific property, and casualty insurance covers legal liability for accidents, property damage, etc. Together, they provide comprehensive coverage for real property and specified personal property like boats, cars and planes. These types of insurance are called "first party insurance" because the triggering event for coverage is loss to the insured property (Dobbyn, 2003).

The most prevalent type of insurance, and the type most relevant to this discussion, is third-party liability insurance. The triggering event is not loss to the insured's property but liability of the insured for damage to another or another's property. Commercial general liability (CGL) policies are a common form of liability insurance purchased by businesses. CGL policies typically cover a broad spectrum of risks, from customer injuries to libel and slander suits. The basic agreement is that the insurance company will pay the amount, up to the agreed maximum, that the insured became legally obligated to pay as damages. Under such a policy, the insurer is said to have the duty to indemnify the insured. The word indemnity refers generally to an insurance relationship and simply means that one party must make good on the losses of another party. In addition to the duty to indemnify, an insurance policy will typically put on the insurance company the duty to defend any lawsuit that arises from a covered event. The duty to defend may also apply to potentially fraudulent or frivolous actions brought by a third party because the allegations in true would be covered under the policy. Liability insurance also comes in several forms to cover the great many events that can potentially cause injury, including professional malpractice

insurance used by doctors, lawyers, and other professionals to cover the possibility of claims that arise from their practice.

In the first decades of the 2000s, experts have begun stressing the necessity for businesses to obtain some form of cyber coverage because of the universal dependence upon computers and the Internet. As of 2015, most businesses maintained websites (including social media pages) and stored records as well as employee information on computer networks. Therefore, they are exposed to both third-party and first-party liability. If a business does not properly safeguard the confidential or private information stored on its network or an offense is committed electronically, the company may have to pay to defend against individual allegations. Additionally, if a business's network is hacked, the company may suffer first-party losses to restore the system, notify persons affected, manage the crisis, and heighten security measures (O'Rourke, 2014).

CONCLUSION

Society must balance the interests of business and the injuries that flow from it. The law attempts to strike that balance by allowing the injured to recover and by giving businesses an incentive to prevent injury. To minimize the risks of legal liability, businesses or individuals must first understand the nature and source of legal liability within their particular field of endeavor. With that knowledge, steps can be taken to eliminate known risks, reduce the effects of possible risks, and prepare for the chance of unforeseeable or uncontrollable risks.

TERMS & CONCEPTS

Breach: A violation of a legal obligation.

Contract: An agreement between two or more parties that creates legally enforceable obligations.

Corporation: A business form provided by state law that creates a separate legal identity for a business that limits liability for corporation owners to the amount they have invested in the corporation.

Foreseeable: The quality of being reasonably anticipatable; relates to liability in tort in that a foreseeable injury is a more likely case liability than a non-foreseeable injury.

Commercial general liability (CGL): Type of insurance policy purchased by businesses to cover a broad spectrum of risk arising from liability to a third party.

"Hand formula": General formula described by Judge Learned Hand used to determine whether particular conduct was negligent. Breach of a duty of care is indicated where the possibility of injuries times the severity of injury is more than the cost of preventing the injury.

In-House or General Counsel: Attorneys that advise businesses on a continual basis with respect to general legal matters associated with their business. If those attorneys are employees of the firm they are called "In-House." Such general practice attorneys often coordinate efforts with specialist attorneys should the need arise.

Insurance: An agreement by which one party assumes a risk faced by another party in return for a premium; an insurance policy is a document detailing such an agreement.

General Partnerships: A business structure that requires no filing with the government and that arises when two or more people carry on business for profit. Partners have unlimited liability for partnership obligations. See also, *Sole proprietor*.

Limited Liability Company (LLC): A business form provided by state law that creates a separate legal identity for a business that limits liability for corporation owners to the amount they have invested in the corporation.

Negligence: A type of tort whereby an injured plaintiff can recover from another if the plaintiff can prove that the other party breached a duty of care owed to that plaintiff and the breach caused the injury.

Sole Proprietorships: A business structure that requires no filing with the government and that arises when someone carries on business for profit. Sole proprietorships have unlimited liability for business obligations.

Strict liability: Liability that does not depend on negligence or intent to harm; is based on absolute duty to make something safe.

Tort: A civil wrong for which a remedy may be obtained, including negligence.

BIBLIOGRAPHY

Aro, H., & Pennanen, T. (2017). Liability-driven investment in longevity risk management. *Optimal Financial Decision Making under Uncertainty*, 121–136.

Garner, B. (Ed.) (1999). *Black's law dictionary* (7th ed.). St. Paul, MN: West Publishing.

Gormley, T. A., & Matsa, D. A. (2011). Growing out of trouble? Corporate responses to liability risk. *Review of Financial Studies, 24,* 2781–2821.

Hadlock, C. J., & Sonti, R. (2012). Financial strength and product market competition: evidence from asbestos litigation. *Journal of Financial & Quantitative Analysis, 47,* 179–211.

Dobbyn, J. F. (2003). *Insurance law in a nutshell.* St. Paul, MN: West Publishing.

Owen D. G., & Phillips, G. G. (2005). *Products liability in a nutshell.* St. Paul, MN: West Publishing.

O'Rourke, J. (2014). Internet liability. *Smart Business Philadelphia, 8*(5), 18.

Van der Smissen, B. (1990). *Legal liability and risk management for public and private entities.* Cincinnati, OH: Anderson Publishing.

U.S. Congress, Congressional Budget Office. (2003). *The economics of U.S. tort liability: A primer.* Washington, DC: U.S. Government Printing Office.

The 'wild west' judgments. (1996). *International Insurance Monitor, 49,* 17.

SUGGESTED READING

Inwood, J. (2003). Liability risk management. *Caterer & Hotelkeeper, 192*(4296), 48.

Fiscus, P. (2002). Hope for the best prepare for the worst. *Pharmaceutical Executive, 22,* 22.

Corlosquet-Habart, M., Gehin, W., Janssen, J., & Manca, R. (2015). *Asset and liability management for banks and insurance companies.* Hoboken, NJ: Wiley.

Cuddihy, T. (2000). Environmental liability risk management for the 21st century. *Geneva Papers on Risk & Insurance—Issues & Practice, 25,* 128.

Swartz, T. (2006). LLC, S-Corp or sole proprietor? *Professional Remodeler, 10,* 8–12.

Essay by Seth M. Azria, JD

LOSS DISTRIBUTIONS

A very small portion of events generates the majority (about two-thirds) of all financial losses. This essay devotes a larger amount of its text to distributions than it does to losses. Specifically, it directs most of its attention to the normal probability distribution. That distribution introduces the target readership, which is undergraduate college students, to basic elements in statistical analyses and prepares them for inquiries into sophisticated loss estimation processes. Toward that end, this essay demonstrates the relevance and importance of mastering undergraduate courses in statistics, economics, and finance. Another aim of this essay is to enhance the ability of college students, financial analysts, and prospective actuaries to evaluate each alternative model they may engage in for estimating future payments and loss distributions. With an overarching challenge related to calculating the appropriate dollar amount of a balance sheet reserve, the literature review finds a variety of publications concerned with defining the nature of risk management itself and with refining methods of loss estimation. A basic challenge stems from the need to specify with some certainty a single point estimate for the distribution of future payments and to attach an interval that expresses some degree of uncertainty about its variability. Certainty and uncertainty are natural components of estimation processes and statistical analyses.

OVERVIEW

One percent of all finance-related events create about two-thirds of all financial losses, according to a recent report. What does this say, if anything, about the risk of loss for insurance, banking, or other organizations? Any attempt to answer this and similar questions needs to start by acknowledging the critical roles of financial institutions in regional, national, and global economies. Effective management of risk, therefore, will contribute to the success of financial institutions and other sectors of an economy.

Transactions between a seller and a buyer certainly require some form of bank involvement. In terms of the range of possibilities, one can imagine some economic consequences from a failure by the banking system to assess and manage its potential for loss. Estimation of that exposure may involve assessing whether any loss will occur, the frequency at which a loss will occur, and/or the amount of a loss beyond an expected value. Several articles tend to favor a comprehensive approach taking into account all those considerations. Authors of some key publications address many challenges in their endeavors to develop models of risk that can harness the compound nature of loss frequency and severity.

Some of those challenges arise from the need to separate expected losses from unexpected losses because of their natural inclusion in the distribution of future payments. Portraying risk as the difference between expected and unexpected losses presents the opportunity to delineate operations management and operational risk management. A broad scan of recent publications on the topic of loss distributions brought many issues to the forefront. A summary report, which was presented at a 2005 meeting of the Casualty Actuarial Society, calls attention to the following items: the lack of common definitions on key terms among risk managers; the problematic nature of the "range of reasonable estimates" approach to reserve creation; and the value of adopting a more objective method by which to estimate the "distribution of future payments" for property and casualty losses.

On a much lighter note, recent commercials by a major insurance company seem to portray risk in a most effective manner as they succinctly inform television viewers of the pervasive and nocturnal nature of risk. Nevertheless, risk of loss is indeed a serious matter for a countless number of professionals whether they serve in the insurance or the banking field. Around the world, banking supervisors are also working collaboratively to integrate regulations and a superlative set of practices and methodologies pertinent to the risk management arena. The fruits of their labors are evident in the recent series of regulatory frameworks many refer to as Basel I & II; the first was released in 1988 and the second in 2004. In short, those regulations challenge banks to measure and manage their risks against a common set of standards and to create and advance a global culture of risk awareness.

A shift in culture usually requires time, and more often than not, its realization evolves through new recruits and the fresh perspectives they bring to the field and the workplace. Emergence of that culture suggests that current, as well as prospective, bank staff and bank supervisors will need to pursue additional opportunities for education and training in risk management. Whether one is a seasoned bank professional or an undergraduate business or mathematics major in college, a number of international certificate programs are now available to those who can demonstrate a basic knowledge of statistics and who seek a deeper understanding of banking risk as set forth by the Basel Committee on Banking Supervision.

Including references to a small yet critical portion of the larger Basel framework and intermingling examples from banking and casualty insurance, this essay directs attention to the interrelationship between loss probability distributions and liability reserve estimations. More precisely, the purpose of this essay is to convey various aspects of how statistical analysis, probability distributions, and model development serve as key tools and objective methods for estimating the amount of resources that organizations need to set aside in order to mitigate their potential losses. In essence, some banking regulations seem to call for the formation and the implementation of valid and reliable methods with which to estimate with better precision the amount of those financial reserves.

APPLICATIONS

This essay is about loss distributions, but it devotes a larger amount of its text to distributions than it does to losses. Specifically, it directs attention to the normal probability distribution because it introduces the reader to basic elements in statistical analyses, and it serves as a reference point for sophisticated estimation processes. As readers progress though this essay toward a discussion of the tools available for estimation purposes, it seems that the nature of risk in the financial domain is a good place to start.

Types of Risk

In general, the three types of risk bankers usually face are credit risk, market risk, and operational risk.

- Credit risk refers to the probability that a borrower will default on a bank loan. Banks exercise a significant amount of control over this risk by con-

ducting reviews of applicant credit scores, income history, and the like.
- Market risk is largely a function of current and anticipated economic states over which banks have minimal control. The author of this essay found a list of operational risks in all reports that cite the work of the Basel committee.
- Operational risk seems to be an area in which banks have the greatest control and the largest exposure so it receives more attention in this essay than the other types do.

In an effort to cover operational risks, regulatory agents expect banks to set aside funds from internal sources and/or to acquire insurance coverage. By taking these actions, they are demonstrating good faith efforts to stabilize economies and to comply with regulations governing risk capital requirements. In other words, bankers are responsible for gathering enough resources to accommodate the likelihood of a potentially hefty loss. The reader should also note that some banking officials devote more attention to unexpected losses than expected losses. Most importantly, banking supervisors and examiners expect to find valid and reliable statistical models and procedures for estimating the amount of capital reserves.

Quantitative skills are obviously critical for developing models of expected profitability and loss risk. Actuaries are the professionals who develop those models and who demonstrate admirable levels of understanding and appreciation for quantitative methods of inquiry. At a minimum, their work involves conducting price and risk analyses before contract execution, validating model assumptions and variables in collaboration with various counterparts, and understanding probabilistic and statistical concepts and rationale perhaps first introduced to them in an undergraduate level statistics course. In addition, actuaries focus their attention on loss distributions using a variety of methodologies through which many authors suggest they need an all-inclusive method to be the most effective.

The literature review for this essay points to opportunities for other important refinements. For instance, there is real need for a formal everlasting distinction between operations management and operational risk management. O'Brien (2007) suggests that the difference between those two functional areas corresponds to the difference between expected and unexpected losses. By extension, a comparable interpretation suggests that operations management personnel focus their energies and resources on the subject of expected losses whereas operational risk management personnel focus on unexpected losses.

Challenges & Perspectives in Loss Estimation

While some scholars concern themselves with the previously discussed refinements, others examine the capacities and methods of financial professionals to estimate the appropriate amount of capital to be set aside for covering an unexpected loss. One complication among many is that a low risk of loss translates into a small amount of capital reserves, thereby making financial resources available for other purposes.

Dutta & Perry (2007) and other authors point out that bank regulations advance the capital reserve as a method to mitigate risks. They also advance the notion of integrating loss frequency and loss severity into a single model for risk assessment. More importantly, their comprehensive analysis highlights the significance of examining the fit between probability distributions and loss data. Most of the literature reviewed by the author of this essay makes it clear that risk managers both today and into the future need to understand the various types of probability distributions, the shapes of those distributions, and the basics in their construction.

Hayne and associates (2005) draw some attention to the work of accountants that appears to be at odds with the work of actuaries. Evidently, what some accountants consider appropriate for inclusion as a reserve on the financial statements or books frequently drives what actuaries methodically assess as a probable risk. One interpretation is that drive needs to occur in reverse because so much more is at stake when given the apparent sequence. Nonetheless, as a backup or recourse measure, prospective reconciliation can occur when actuaries examine the likelihood that future payments differ from the book amount and calculate the expected financial consequences of the booked number. Hayne and associates (2005) conclude that book value determination processes of those in the accounting profession stand to gain a lot from the leadership and wisdom of those in the actuarial profession.

Casting issues of appropriateness aside for the moment, let us move deeper into the domain of actuaries and statisticians while highlighting the absence of a single vocabulary.

Statistical Dimensions of Loss Distributions

An underlying problem stems from the need to specify with some certainty a single point estimate of the distribution of future payments when a range is more appropriate given the inherent existence of uncertainty about contemplating future status. Whether one employs phrases such as "the range of reasonable estimates" or the "distribution of future payments" there is a statistical concept universal in its scope, application, and/or definition. In general, the concept draws heavily from statistics terms, including the mean and the standard deviation.

Readers need to keep those statistical terms in mind as they progress through this essay as well as their undergraduate course work. Those terms provide a foundation for the distribution of probabilities. A probability distribution describes a range of possible outcomes. Furthermore, objective models for estimating those ranges of distribution are readily available. Moreover, there are two requirements for a probability distribution. First, the sum of the probabilities of all events within the sample space must equal one. Second, the probability of each event in the sample space must be between zero and one. The sample space, by definition, is the set of all possible outcomes from a probability experiment.

A variable is a characteristic or an attribute that can assume different values. A random variable is a variable specifically associated with a probability distribution. The value of a random variable is determined by chance. Let us pause for a moment, before moving into a discussion of the types of probability distributions, to recognize that variables may be discrete or continuous. Discrete variables such as the die and the coin have countable values. In contrast, continuous variables are variables that can assume all values in between any two given values. Continuous random variables provide data that are measurable as opposed to countable. By extension, these properties determine whether the probability distribution is continuous or discrete.

Calculations of the mean, the variance, and the standard deviation for a probability distribution differ from those for samples. As a first step, the former calculation involves recording the outcomes of an infinite number of samples randomly drawn from a population in constructing the probability distribution. The second step is to multiply each possible outcome by its probability and then add all the products. That resultant mean of the random variable describes the theoretical average, which is called the expected value. That average or expected value is a good start, but we need more information that informs us about the spread of values within the probability distribution. For guidance on how to calculate the variance and the standard deviation, the author of this essay refers readers to textbooks for statistics courses such as Bluman (2003) and others.

A summary statistic of the distribution is a specific value that conveys some information about the entire distribution. The mean along with the mode and the median are summary statistics known as measures of central tendency. As was discussed above, the mean is the average or expected value. The mode is the most likely value, and the median is the middle value. The median is also the 50th percentile because one-half of all possible values are above it, and the other half of all possible values are below it. In addition, the 25th percentile is the point halfway between the lowest value and the median, and the 75th percentile is the point halfway between the highest value and the median. Furthermore, one-half of possible values reside between the 25th percentile and 75th percentile, which by definition is the interquartile range (IQR).

Relevance of Normal Probability Distribution
With some certainty, analysts know that the mean or the expected value will occur somewhere within the IQR. Certainty and uncertainty, as natural components of estimation processes, play an important role in statistical analyses. Hayne and associates (2005) inform us of three sources of uncertainty. Roughly speaking, process uncertainty arises from attempts to predict the outcomes of a roll of die; parameter uncertainty arises from attempts to claim the mean or the standard deviation in a sample will be equal to that of the population; and model uncertainty arises from attempts to recognize future patterns as an extension of past patterns. All these uncertainties exert undue influence on the work of analysts. Recognizing them when estimating loss values and ranges may be most effective when communicated in terms of their association with a probability distribution. In brief, analysts need to form ranges and convey the degree of confidence that the mean lies within the estimated interval; more on confidence intervals will follow a brief discussion of two major types of probability distributions.

Binomial and normal probability distributions are relevant to understanding and articulating loss distributions. On the one hand, the binomial distribution contains all the probabilities for each of two possible outcomes. Comprising this distribution are events that actually have only two outcomes, such as success or failure; it is permissible to collapse other events with more than two outcomes into two categories. On the other hand, the normal distribution contains all the probabilities for an infinite number of possible outcomes. Many continuous variables are normally distributed. The normal distribution is bell shaped.

When the mean, mode, and median assume the same numeric values, one can be certain that the normal distribution is symmetrical in its shape and appearance. The symmetry can encompass those bell shapes with a short height and wide base to those with a tall height and narrow base. Likewise, the top-middle portion of the normal or bell-shaped probability distribution is higher in some instances than other instances. Furthermore, movement away from that middle segment to the right or to the left toward the outer fringes of the base takes one into the area known as the tail of the distribution. Measures of variation describe the area between the outer fringes with reference to the middle section. The range, the variance, and the standard deviation are measures of dispersion that indicate the relative horizontal distance between the outside edges of the bell and the mean.

The normal distribution can also be asymmetrical in shape. In the case of asymmetry, there will be different values among the mean, the median, and the mode. That inequality is observable in normal distributions that are left skewed, wherein the mean is less than the median, and both are less than the mode. It is also observable in those that are right skewed, wherein the mean is greater than the median, and both are greater than the mode. Approximately 60 to 70 percent of bank operational losses arise from a few large events according to O'Brien (2007). This evidence suggests a left-skewed distribution because the largest probability or area under the normal curve appears in the left side of the distribution.

Among the several properties of a normal distribution, the total area under the normal distribution curve is equal to one and separation of the area expressed in terms of standard deviations. Approximately 68 percent of the area is within one standard deviation of the mean; 95 percent is within 2 standard deviations; and 99 percent is within three standard deviations. Looking at these segments from a different angle, using the three standard deviation approach, 99 percent of the probability values reside within three standard deviations from the mean and so on. Conversely, approximately 1 percent of the values occupy the tails; one-half of it is in the right-hand tail and one-half of it is in the left-hand tail.

These segments are very useful whether one refers to the range of reasonable estimates, the distribution of future payments, or the distribution of losses. Utilization of these deviations and the area they represent allow the analyst to make statements about his or her confidence in the estimate. For example, the normal distribution informs us that 95 percent of the possible values are within 2 standard deviations of the mean—that is, two standard deviations below the mean and two standard deviations above the mean. By extension, the actuary is able to form a statement such as "the mean true loss will likely be somewhere within that range 95 percent of the time." In other words, an opportunity exists to include on the balance sheet the dollar value of a potential liability greater than or less than the calculated mean. If one subscribes to the convention of conservative estimation—thereby overstating expenses and liabilities and understating revenues and assets when permissible—then the book value would equate to the highest possible amount, which is two standard deviations above the mean.

With the information from O'Brien (2007) with respect to a left-skewed loss distribution, the amount may be smaller than it sounds because few values will exist in the upper tail area. The area in the tail of the curve is an important consideration receiving brief mention here but is otherwise beyond the scope of this essay. Readers should keep in mind that the area under the normal distribution curve is often also separated into columns of varying width to suit specific inquiries. In general, each column of the area represents a specific amount of probability.

A literature review will produce references to the vertical height of the normal distribution. In fact, several articles on loss distribution refer to the vertical dimension or thickness of its tails. The probability density function for a given value of variable is the height of the curve as opposed to the size of an area. It is a measure of the vertical distance between the tail portion of the curve and the horizontal axis.

This wraps up the presentation of key characteristics of the normal distribution, as we head toward conclusion of this essay. The normal distribution is one among many types of probability distributions. Analyses of the risk of loss suggest that there is a need to incorporate multiple probability distributions. At the most basic level, the binomial distribution can accommodate the probability of a claim filing and/or whether it will exceed a specific amount. At a more complex level, probability distributions other than the normal probability distribution may be required to handle combinations such as loss frequency and loss severity because some analysts may be unwilling to assume that losses follow a normal distribution. Readers who are comfortable with the normal probability distribution are better equipped to examine alternative forms. Their cursory review of some recent works will most likely find conclusions that losses follow the chi-square, the lognormal, and other advanced distributions.

CONCLUSION

Some recent reports assert that the actuarial profession needs a single all-inclusive method for estimating the distribution of future payments for property and casualty liabilities. The primary aim of this essay is to enhance an analyst's ability to evaluate each alternative model he or she may engage in for estimating future payments and loss distributions. The essay covered a few applications of the concepts and the methods found in a recent scan of the literature. Readers who desire more breadth and depth are encouraged to consult academic journals and trade publications. Certainly, a reader will find a diverse array of information that will challenge and satisfy the needs of that individual. Some articles will be more helpful and comprehensive than others.

TERMS & CONCEPTS

Binomial distribution: The outcomes and probabilities of an event in which there are only two possible outcomes, such as success or failure.

Credit risk: The risk of nonpayment by a borrower to a banker/creditor.

Expected value: The population mean when derived by taking several random samples from a population.

Interquartile range: The range of values between the 25th percentile and the 75th percentile or the 1st quartile and the 3rd quartile.

Market risk: The risk to bankers of unfavorable fluctuations in the domestic and international financial sectors of an economic market.

Mean: The sum of values divided by the total number of values.

Median: The midpoint of a data array; the same number of values are above it as are below it.

Mode: The value that occurs most often in a data set.

Normal distribution: A continuous, usually symmetric bell-shaped distribution of a variable.

Operational risk: The risk to financial institutions of fraud, failure, or incompetence in its operations; see definitions provided by Basel Committee on Banking Supervision.

Probability density function: The vertical position of a probability distribution that determines the thickness of the tail segment of a distribution curve.

Probability distribution: The values a random variable can assume and the corresponding probabilities of those values.

Random variable: A variable with values determined by chance.

Sample space: The sample of all possible outcomes of a probability event.

BIBLIOGRAPHY

Bernardi, M., Maruotti, A., & Petrella, L. (2012). Skew mixture models for loss distributions: A Bayesian approach. *Insurance: Mathematics & Economics, 51*(3), 617–623.

Bluman, A. G. (2003). *Elementary statistics* (2nd ed.). Boston: McGraw-Hill Higher Education.

Brazauskas, V., & Kleefeld, A. (2011). Folded and log-folded-t distributions as models for insurance loss data. *Scandinavian Actuarial Journal, 2011*(1), 59–74.

Gzyl, H. (2011). Determining the total loss distribution from the moments of the exponential of the compound loss. *Journal of Operational Risk, 6*(3), 3–13.

Hayne, R., Khury, C., Pulis, R., Leise, J., Kumar, R., Sanders, D., et al. (2005, Fall). The analysis and estimation of loss & ALAE variability: A Summary report.

O'Brien, P. (2007, October 30). Operations management vs operational risk management.

Ramaswamy, S. (2005). Simulated credit loss distribution. *Journal of Portfolio Management, 31*(4), 91–99.

SUGGESTED READING

Dimakos, X., & Aas, K. (2004). Integrated risk modeling. *Statistical Modeling: An International Journal, 4*(4), 265–277.

Neil, M., Fenton, N., & Tailor, M. (2005). Using Bayesian networks to model expected and unexpected operational losses. *Risk Analysis: An International Journal, 25*(4), 963–972.

Merton, R. C. (1974). On the pricing of corporate debt: The risk structure of interest rates. *Journal of Finance, 29*(2), 449–470.

Peters, G., & Terauds, V. (n.d.). Quantifying bank operational risk.

Essay by Steven R. Hoagland, PhD

M

MONEY, BANKING, AND THE ECONOMY

Banks and the monies they administer play an invaluable role in local, regional, national, and even international economic systems. Indeed, money is the driving force behind an economy. How it is managed and distributed within a given system is often the most pivotal issue facing developing as well as developed economies. In light of this fact, it is important to understand what money is and the role it plays. This paper will cast a more comprehensive light on the fundamental purposes of these two concepts and how money and banks positively and adversely impact an economy.

OVERVIEW

At the end of the American Revolution, the fledgling United States immediately found itself in deep debt. There was no common currency, as the states printed their own money after the failure of the first American national money, the "continental." Without such resources, it was feared that the United States would fail to develop a stable economy after the departure of the British.

The new secretary of the Treasury, Alexander Hamilton, looked to create what so many other countries had installed within their own governments—a central bank. The bank would be responsible for issuing currency and would fund the states' debt. However, Hamilton did not limit his vision to these parameters. He saw the key to economic development in the new country to be the establishment of new businesses. His brainchild, the First Bank of the United States, would be not only the earliest incarnation of what would eventually become the Federal Reserve but also a major commercial bank in a country largely bereft of them ("A history of," 2009).

As the example of the first federal financial institution in the US demonstrates, banks and the monies they administer play an invaluable role in local, regional, national, and even international economic systems. This paper will cast a more comprehensive light on the fundamental purposes of these two concepts and how money and banks positively and adversely impact an economy.

Money

Abraham Lincoln once commented on the need for the government to create, issue, and circulate money that will satisfy its own spending needs as well as maximize the buying power of the consumers. By bringing such principles to bear, he is reported to have said, "Money will cease to be master and become the servant of humanity."

Indeed, money is the driving force behind an economy. How it is managed and distributed within a system is often the most pivotal issue facing developing as well as developed economies. In light of this fact, it is important to understand what money is and the role it plays.

FURTHER INSIGHTS

In general terms, money is manifest in two forms. The first is a commodity, which is a physical currency that can be exchanged for goods and services. Commodities may be coins or paper monies as long as they are interchangeable with other products of equal value. However, commodities may also be food products, grains, and precious metals. Commodities may be exchanged in the open marketplace or within a commodities exchange (InvestorWords. com, 2009). The second is fiat money. Although fiat money may appear in the form of currency as well, it has no value other than that which is assigned to it by those who printed or produced it (Hummel, 2008).

Commodities and fiat money have long played important roles in economies around the globe. In light of this fact, it is important to expound on the principles, benefits, and shortcomings of each of these forms of money.

Commodities

Put simply, commodities are physical items that are exchanged on the open market. Gold and silver are among the most well-known commodities, but equally important as commodities are items such as wheat, soy, crude oil, and steel. Throughout history, commodities have been exchanged for money in the marketplace. Chicago, for example, became a central market for the exchange of wheat between farmers and purchasers.

By the mid-nineteenth century, commodities markets had become more complex; in addition to the open exchange, the practice of speculation became more widespread. This practice involves an investor predicting the price of the exchange of commodities based on futures contracts (an arrangement between buyers and sellers for the future delivery of commodities) and trading on the market based on his or her assessment of the profitability of such contracts ("A brief history," 2009).

Today, futures trading has become a vast and highly profitable form of commodities exchange. The world's largest market for futures exchanges is the New York Mercantile Exchange (also known as NYMEX), which has been in operation since 1874 and represents trading of a myriad of commodities, from precious metals to foodstuffs to uranium. As an example of the breadth of NYMEX's own operations, the exchange has a port through which hundreds of thousands of transactions take place each day in 400 commodities markets (NYMEX.com, 2009). Although none are as large as NYMEX, there are countless, similarly constructed exchanges in operation around the world.

Futures trading offers the potential for enormous profitability, which accounts for the tremendous volume of trading being conducted. However, there are risks involved with such activity. Commodities such as wheat, oil, and other resources are subject to changes in conditions that may affect their price, often in dramatic fashion. A cold weather spell might cause an immediate drop in prices for Florida-grown oranges. Similarly, a terrorist attack on a pipeline might immediately send oil prices skyward. The futures trader banks on such fluctuations, looking to reap the benefits of a sizable differential in the agreed-upon price of a given futures contract. However, when the negative event takes place, the same trader stands to lose significantly. While he

Alexander Hamilton statue in front of the Treasury Building in Washington, D.C. (Courtesy of Library of Congress)

or she may take steps to mitigate a loss, there is no guarantee that he or she will lose not only the initial margin but also the entire amount in the account (National Futures Association, 2009).

Commodities remain a robust monetary form in terms of exchange. However, it is not the only form of money that is employed in great volume around the globe.

Fiat Money

Of course, most nations in the world do not rely on physical commodities like gold or silver to exchange products and services to back their currencies. Such forms of money like the U.S. dollar, the British pound, and the Japanese yen, for example, are known as fiat money, which is a token that is intrinsically worthless but is assigned value by its government.

Fiat money is not backed by another commodity, which contributes to its lack of value. Rather, it acquires its worth based on the confidence the consumers have in it. Governments may assign its worth, but they are not expected to back such currency

New York Mercantile Exchange. (Courtesy of Shiny Things via Wikimedia Commons)

was significant and long-term, requiring bonds and taxes to be issued to help pay down what was owed (Mitchell, 1903).

The United States was able to pay down the debt over the course of the next two decades. The country was further able to avoid inflation and price instability of the dollar by once again attaching a gold value to its worth, a trend that lasted until World War I. During that conflict, the United States and other countries reintroduced fiat money, as their needs necessitated the creation of more paper than there was gold to which it could be attached. Again, the United States and many of its allies avoided instability when the guns fell silent, as the industrialized world established the "gold standard," intrinsically linking the U.S. dollar and the British pound to every other national currency, backed by the price of gold. The start of the Great Depression brought an end to the gold standard, as nations en masse attempted to sell their pounds and dollars for gold, ending the gold standard and causing the reissue of fiat money around the world ("Fiat Money History," 2009). The Depression only exacerbated the situation, as fiat money was the only currency available in a collapsed economic environment.

Fiat money does have its strengths and value, particularly during times when gold and other commodities are not in great volume or at top value. As stated earlier, however, this strength and value comes from perception. As one study suggests, the amount of backing a particular currency enjoys stems from its stability and durability in the face of regulation. According to Quint and Shubik, "The use of government money is intimately related to reputation, taxation, legal enforcement, and to the control over production and public goods in a modern society … Trust in government money is implicitly assumed" (2009, p. 6).

Based on the relative strength of the fiat monies (mostly in industrialized countries), a different form of commerce emerged from the demise of the gold standard: currency exchange. Once again, the difference between two or more currencies in terms of value is based on reputation and consumer backing rather than a given commodity. The exchange of currency is dependent on the comprehensive information that exists about its strength and the speed by which that information is transferred. It is understandable, therefore, that fiat currency exchange has

when that value experiences negative conditions. The lack of depth in confidence in fiat money stems from the fact that such currencies are usually introduced during times of debt and/or financial crisis.

U.S. history provides an excellent example of the use of fiat money and the effect its unpredictable backing can have on an economy. During the Civil War years, the enormous cost of the military effort led the government, which had previously pegged U.S. currency to gold, to create currency redeemable by gold at a future, unspecified date. In 1862, it began printing "greenbacks" in this vein. This currency was made possible by a congressional act, which passed overwhelmingly and with President Lincoln's backing, and the Treasury Department, which borrowed about $900 million against U.S. credit in order to give some strength to the greenbacks. Fortunately, the greenbacks program was short-lived, as the paper was discontinued after only one year—the debt created by a slimmed-down appropriation of greenbacks become increasingly the norm in international finance (as opposed to commodities exchange), given the fact that information is transferred between parties exponentially faster today than it was only a decade ago (Araujo & Camargo, 2006). Such speed and comprehensiveness work to the benefit of fiat money's stability, value, and exchange.

Exchanges

The exchange of commodities and currency is a fundamental underpinning of a stable economy. In fact, some argue that although the markets on which monies and goods are exchanged are subject to daily and long-term volatility and government policy that addresses such volatility is often equally inconsistent, stable, sound currency is the most effective and reliable element in ensuring fiscal and economic health (LeBaron, Deemer & Ungewitter, 2009).

The global recession that began in 2008 provides evidence of this hypothesis. As stock markets underwent near-collapses during the course of a year, housing markets bottomed out, and credit debt skyrocketed, people around the world began to take account of their finances in a manner reminiscent of tactics used during the Great Depression. The mantra heard in virtually every household seemed to be "security over risk." Central to that policy was ensuring that the individual's money was "stashed" in a place or places that were safe from the tumult of the recession.

Money Markets

One such "hiding place" was the money market. Money markets are exchanges involving short-term debt securities, commercial paper, Treasury bills, and other monetary investments. As such, they are not typically seen as either high-yield or high-risk. Money markets have long been a component of mutual funds, 401(k) plans, and other investment portfolios, serving as a repository for the investor's "loose change." They generally yield a small sum, usually about two percent, but at the same time, they very rarely lose money for the investor. Because of this low-risk, low-yield approach, investors typically saw little need for heavy involvement in money markets.

This perception changed in 2008. When people began losing money on the stock markets, and as more people were losing their jobs, money markets became an important way to protect an individual's

money. The U.S. federal government seemingly acknowledged this trend when, in late 2008, a key money market lost principal. The government intervened almost immediately with a rescue plan that helped right the market. Even as economists and the media reported signs of economic recovery in the spring of 2009, advisors still advocated strongly for wary investors to put their cash in money markets rather than on the stock market (Max, 2009).

With uncertainty prevailing in a global economic system that may soon recover from a powerful recession, investors are still clinging to their most important asset—money. Interestingly, this investor attention to money markets (Americans alone hold an estimated $13 trillion in money markets) may play a role in helping sluggish stock markets gain more investors. Central banks like the Federal Reserve, in an effort to catalyze the purchase of stocks, have during the recession lowered interest rates. It is their hope that such policies will entice previous investors to return to the fold, forgoing the minimal yields of money markets for the more potentially profitable stock markets ("Searching for value," 2009).

Banks & Banking

Money, whether in the form of a commodity or fiat, relies on some sort of backing to give it value. In the seventeenth century, as European nations became more numerous and offered their own currencies, some of the earliest banks were the central institutions where the myriad of currencies that were being exchanged could be reconciled for their values. Because of their proven ability to identify the value of money, banks over time became seen as the chief savings institutions of a given country as well as the place in which a person could entrust his or her money (Scott, 1981).

Of course, banks have not always achieved success in the long run. The bank panics and great financial tumult that accompanied the Great Depression provide an example of the conditions in which banks suffered. Still, as industrialized countries developed their own financial systems, banks have evolved along with these systems. Today, banks are manifest in several ways. Retail banks, for example, provide a range of basic services to consumers, such as mortgages, auto loans, and other lending services in addition to checking and savings deposit accounts. Investment banks offer companies the ability to raise income through bonds and stock issuances and also provide assistance in mergers and acquisitions. Central banks, such as the Federal Reserve and similar institutions, conduct monetary policy, regulate the activities of financial organizations, and even provide financial services like loans.

Banks rely on deposits in order to generate their own money. An individual may deposit his or her paycheck into an account, expecting to receive a modest 1 percent in interest. The bank in turn uses that money and the deposits of other consumers (known as capital) to support its other activities (such as issuing loans and mortgages). If a mortgage loan includes a 5 percent rate, and the 1 percent in interest is paid out to the account holder each year, the remaining 4 percent stays in the bank. This system is thus dependent on the ability of loan recipients to repay their debts. When they fail to do so, the bank's ability to cover its endeavors becomes compromised (Chua, 2009).

Bank Failures

Banks have evolved alongside consumer and commercial enterprise. Unfortunately, this means that when economic downturns take place, banks become entwined in them as well. The recession that began in 2008 provides an excellent example of this connection. As stocks began to tumble and the economy entered a recession, the situation was worsened by the faltering of banks. Early in 2008, federal regulators expressed concern that hundreds of banks, from the smallest local banks to large, international institutions, would fail because of consumer failure to repay subprime and construction loans (Isidore, 2008). Such a collapse in the banking industry echoed the late 1980s, when more than 200 banks folded under the savings and loan scandal, a number unequalled since the Great Depression.

That fear would ultimately prove valid, as 252 banks fell victim to the economy by the end of 2008 and the first quarter of 2009. Much of the precipitous fall of American banks was attributed to losses on loans, credit, and other assets. The Federal Deposit Insurance Corporation (FDIC), which backs American banking institutions, reported in early 2009 that banks paid $69.3 billion to cover potential losses, an amount that more than doubled from 2008 (Gordon, 2009).

Banks play an integral role in the distribution and management of money owned not only by individual consumers but also by commercial enterprises, nonprofit organizations, and the government. Because of that central positioning, they are closely tied to both the successes and failures consumers experience in the management of their own money.

CONCLUSIONS

Because of the scarcity of money for so many and the amount of customer money that is managed by banks, the concepts of money and banking generate considerable cynicism among the general public. However, money and banking have been woven into the fabric of American society since the birth of the country at the end of the eighteenth century.

This paper has cast a light on the varying forms in which money, one of the most precious of nonnatural resources, becomes manifest. Commodities, such as gold and silver, have an intrinsic value attached to them based on the scarcity or abundance of them at a given time. Fiat money, on the other hand, has no value beyond the initial endorsement by a government—its long-term strength depends on word of mouth among those who are dealing in money.

Throughout the history of money management, banks have played an important role in the distribution and generation of individual and commercial money. In essence, banking institutions are at the center of any given monetary system, intrinsically linked between the consumer and his or her money. This unique position means that banks are subject to the same ebb and flow that consumers and their money experience.

The links among the three have become even stronger in the twentieth century, as modern technologies and systems continue to build global networks capable of rapid information transmission. Despite the system-wide errors that helped begin and perpetuate the Great Depression and other financial crises (such as the global recessions of the early twenty-first century), there has been little call for any shift in policy that breaks the fundamental relationship between money and the banks that manage it.

TERMS & CONCEPTS

Capital: Cash or goods used to generate revenue through investments.

Central bank: Government agency that issues monetary policy, controls money supply and interest rates, and provides guidelines for other institutions.

Commodities: Physical items, materials, and natural resources that are exchanged on the open market.

Fiat money: A token that is intrinsically worthless but is assigned value by the government.

Futures trading: The practice of investing in contracts between two parties who will exchange monies at a future date.

Greenbacks: American Civil War–era fiat money used to fund the war effort.

Money market: Exchange that involves short-term debt securities, commercial paper, Treasury bills, and other monetary investments.

BIBLIOGRAPHY

A history of central banking in the United States. (2009). The Federal Reserve Bank of Minneapolis.

Araujo, L., & Camargo, L. (2006). Information, learning, and the stability of fiat money. *Journal of Monetary Economics, 53,* 1571–1591.

Commodity. (2009). *Dictionary.*

Fiat money history in the US. (2009).

Gordon, M. (2009, February 26). US banks post first quarterly loss since 1990. *The Huffington Post.*

Hummel, W. F. (2008). Money basics. *Money: What it is how it works.*

Isidore, C. (2008, March 3). New recession worry: Bank failures. *Recession Watch 2008.*

LeBaron, D., Deemer, W., & Ungewitter, M. (2009). A way forward. *Journal of Wealth Management, 12,* 10–16.

Matsuoka, T., & Watanabe, M. (2017). Banking panics and liquidity in a monetary economy. *Tinbergen Institute Discussion Paper,* 17-091/VII.

Max, S. (2009). 5 things to know about … stashing your cash. *Money, 38,* 28.

National Futures Association. (2009). Understanding (and managing) the risks of futures trading.

Part 1: A brief history. (2009). *A Short Course Introducing Commodity Markets & Futures Trading.*

Quint, T., & Shubik, M. (2009). Multistage models of monetary exchange: An elementary discussion of commodity money, fiat money and credit, part 4. *ICFAI Journal of Monetary Economics, 7,* 6–67.

Scott, W. A. (1981). *Money and banking.* Ayer Publishing.

Searching for value. (2009). *The Economist, 390*(8624), 85.

SUGGESTED READING

Barba, R. (2009). Bankers' banks: Not like Silverton, but challenged. *American Banker, 174,* 5–6.

Duffy, F. (2008). *Monetary theory. Monetary Theory — Research Starters Business.* 1–9.

Keegan, D. (2009). Options strategy. *Futures, 38,* 18.

Otellini, P. (2009). Billion-dollar bets on the future. *Directors and Boards, 33,* 25.

Plosser, C. I. (2009). Improving financial stability. *Vital Speeches of the Day, 75,* 281–285.

Takemori, S., & Savtchenko, L. (2008). Monetary regimes and inflationary expectations. *Japanese Economy, 35,* 3–21

Essay by Michael P. Auerbach, MA

N

Nonprofit Accounting

This essay reviews the accounting standards that are used by nonprofit organizations (NPOs) to meet their financial reporting requirements. There are two bodies that issue standards for nonprofits: The Financial Accounting Standards Board (FASB) and the Office of Management and Budget (OMB). The American Institute of Certified Public Accountants (AICPA) also has oversight in auditing of NPOs. Nonprofits are similar to the government in that their mission is to provide services for the public good. Nonprofit organizations are not in business to make money but to provide services with revenue from private donations or federal awards. Because nonprofits receive money through donations, gifts, or grants, they are highly accountable to their constituents to show value from their programs and services. Nonprofits vary in size and may or may not have paid staff or access to professional managers or financial advisors. Because of the nature of revenue streams for nonprofits (grants, gifts, and memberships), special accounting procedures and financial statements are required, especially if the NPO receives federal money. This essay describes the general requirements for NPO accounting and financial reporting as well as the unique requirements for NPO financial statements. Future trends related to the funding, growth, and management of NPOs are reviewed.

NPOs are not in business to make a profit; they are funded through donations or government awards, and they are in existence to provide services for the common good. NPO stakeholders (particularly donors and volunteers) want certainty that resources are being used wisely to provide services to constituents. Operational costs must be reasonable, and fiscal and ethical accountability are also an expectation. Donors and awarding agencies expect NPOs to spend funds and not save them for the future. Annual expenditures for NPOs should end up very close to revenues (Elmerraji, 2007).

NPOs have been existence in the United States, in one form or another, for more than 200 years, and they continue to serve as important social service providers within our economy today.

Growth of Organizations for the Public Good

There has always been a strong feeling in the United States that there is a private responsibility to support the public good. The first charitable entities in the United States were charitable trusts and community trusts. The first foundations were formed in the late nineteenth century. By World War I, public-private partnerships had been formed to support public endeavors through private support or fun-draising. After World War I, New Deal programs and initiatives such as Social Security and unemployment insurance were being created to fill the growing social need. In the 1930s, taxes were increased for individuals and business, and this proved an incentive for many wealthy individuals and businesses to give money to organizations. With the start of World War II, there was a drop in government support for social welfare programs, and nonprofits began to fill the void.

The two decades after World War II saw a continued increase in government funding to nonprofits. The so-called "Great Society" programs came about in the 1960s, including Medicare, Medicaid, and training and employment programs. In the 1970s, the U.S. government began to shift grant money toward nonprofits as a means to support an even greater number of social programs. By the 1980s, the U.S. government was actively encouraging the growth of nonprofits as government support shifted from education and income assistance to health care, housing, and pension programs. Nonprofits began to primarily focus on the provision of social services to the middle class while for-profit organizations also began to provide services to the same population. There has been a steady increase in demand for social welfare programs since the 1980s when government support increased. The increased demand for services increased competition between nonprofit and for-profit organizations, and nonprofits began to look to private funding sources to remain competitive (Bourgeois, 2003).

The Future of Nonprofit Organizations

From 1997 to 2007, there was an 88 percent increase in the number of foundations that were formed (Husock, 2007, p. 20). Philanthropy (money available) was expected to reach $6 trillion by 2050, with much of the funding coming from baby boomer wealth. Wealthy retirees pouring money into philanthropic endeavors had been largely responsible for the "augmentation of government services" by nonprofits and helped to increase the overall number of nonprofits by 67 percent from 1999 to 2007 (Husock, 2007). In 2007, private charitable giving reached an all-time high. The recession that began that year, however, caused a dramatic pull back of both individual and corporate philanthropic gifts. Private giving went from $344.5 billion in 2007 to $293.8 billion in 2009, with modest gains between 2010 and 2012. Living donors saw a decrease of 11 percent from the 2007 high. Retirees conserved their savings, which had been hit hard by the stock market crash and a string of corporate failures, and professionals expressed job insecurities and lower earnings. In 2013, charitable giving was not expected to rise to its prerecession level until 2018 (GivingUSA, 2013).

Financial & Stakeholder Management

The need for financial accountability and reporting is ever increasing for nonprofits as the sources of funding increase. Nonprofits must be accountable for financial and management reporting of government grants and contracts, as well as to the public for in-kind donations and gifts. Nonprofit entities often have numerous stakeholders that carry varied expectations regarding the mission and vision of the organization.

Nonprofit stakeholders can include any of the following groups (Balser & McClusky, 2005):

- funders/donors
- government officials
- volunteers
- clients
- executive director/staff
- boards of directors

A view of the front of the Bill and Melinda Gates Foundation building in Seattle, Washington. The Gates Foundation is one of the nation's wealthiest nonprofit organizations. (Courtesy of Adbar via Wikimedia Commons)

The management of stakeholder relationships is critical to organizational effectiveness in nonprofits where balancing "social" expectations can be as critical to the health and longevity of the entity as financial management is. This essay discusses specific financial reporting requirements that need to be met for stakeholders (namely governmental and accounting stakeholders). The federal requirements for the managing, administering, and financial reporting of awards will be outlined. The future role of NPOs in providing social services, the need for internal audits and professional management, and oversight are discussed.

APPLICATIONS

NPO Financial Reporting

NPO financial statements are easily interpreted by individuals who are familiar with for-profit financial statements. There are, however, a few significant differences between nonprofit and for-profit accounting. Regardless of the size of an NPO, it is advisable to have access to a financial advisor who is familiar with NPO accounting principles; advisors may be volunteers, staff, financial advisors, or accountants.

It is imperative to keep in mind that economic data for nonprofit organizations is interpreted differently from financial statements that are for profit. According to "What a Difference Nonprofits Make: A Guide to Accounting Procedures," 1990:

"Meaningful evaluations and comparisons of nonprofit performance almost always prove difficult and complex. While the profitability of two businesses can easily be calculated, it is much harder to compare the effectiveness of two counseling centers to see which is doing a better job of helping the mentally ill. Without the standard of profitability, it is also difficult to compare the job performance of non-profit staff and managers" (Alliance for Nonprofit Management, 2004).

Fund Accounting

NPOs often use "fund accounting" procedures to group money (and sometimes the associated financial data) into individual funds. For example, an NPO may have an established general fund or one or more special funds. Money in a general fund may be used for maintenance, day-to-day operations, and wages. A special fund is set up with restrictions and associated internal controls and is designated for separate activities (e.g., an acquisition fund). Fund accounting provides a way for organizations to have a clear idea of what resources are available for specific tasks or programs. In some cases, funds must be treated, legally, as separate accounting entities and may be required by law to have separate financial statements for each fund. Fund accounting is used in both governmental and NPO accounting and, as such, is critical to understand when looking at an NPO financial statement.

Financial Accounting Standards Board (FASB) Nonprofit Requirements

FASB116

The FASB has issued two sets of guidelines for NPOs with regard to accounting standards. FASB116 outlines how nonprofit organizations should handle contributions made to an organization. Contributions to an NPO may include monetary gifts, services, and historical artifacts. Due to the nature and diversity of what is defined as a "contribution," FASB116 provides guidance for reporting contributions.

FASB116 — Accounting for Contributions Received and Contributions Made provides the following guidelines as they apply to NPOs:

- Unconditional pledges must be recorded in accounting records. Contributions must be recognized as revenue in the period in which they are received and at fair market value.
- NPOs must account for contributions of most goods, such as property and equipment. Exemp-

tions can be made for gifts of art and items in museum collections as outlined in the guidelines.
- NPOs must distinguish between the three types of assets that are outlined in FASB117 below (unrestricted, temporarily restricted, and permanently restricted assets). NPOs must also record and track all donor-imposed restrictions.
- Volunteer time must be recorded if it results in the making or embellishment of non-economic advantages (e.g., renovation of a building, special professional skills, or craftsmen) (FASB, 2003).

FASB117

FASB117 outlines the requirements for creating a general external financial statement for a nonprofit organization. The guidelines have been created to promote consistency and comparability for NPO financial statements. By requiring NPOs to create financial statements using FASB117 guidelines, NPOs may also increase the relevancy and understandability of their financial reporting mechanisms (Financial Standards Accounting Board [FASB], 2003).

Nonprofits don't publish comprehensive annual financial reports CAFRs (governments do). Instead, nonprofit reports will typically just be called a "report of consolidated financial statements." In any event, the statements for governmental and nonprofit companies are alike in format and fashion.

- The statement of financial position (balance sheet) is a snapshot of the health of the NPO on a given date. Like a typical balance sheet, it records the organization's assets and liabilities and net assets (assets-liabilities). The NPO statement of financial position also requires that assets be categorized as unrestricted, temporarily restricted, or permanently restricted assets.
- The statement of activities (income statement) provides a summary of financial activity over time. This statement shows how an organization's net assets (unrestricted, temporarily restricted, and permanently restricted assets) have changed or changed in relation to each other.
- The statement of cash flow documents information about cash receipts and disbursements—it shows an organization's "cash position" (Elmeraji, 2007).

"The three financial statements are used together to project and analyze the fiscal health of an organization. Many states and funding organizations require nonprofits to provide these financial statements to address questions about their financial activities. The financial statements may also be used to compile a formal audited statement, prepared by a certified public accountant, that complies with FASB standards" (Bourgeois, 2003, p. 9).

Office of Management & Budget Guidelines for Nonprofits

The Office of Management and Budget (OMB) has issued three sets of standard guidelines (circulars) for use by NPOs in the administration and reporting of certain activities. The three areas outlined by OMB circulars include the following:

Circular A-110 is titled Uniform Administrative Requirements for Grants and Other Agreements with Institutions of Higher Education, Hospitals, and Other Non-Profit Organizations. This document provides comprehensive guidance for the administration of federal grants by NPOs.

OMB Circular A-122 is titled Cost Principals for Non-Profit Organizations. This document deals with how to designate and report the different types of costs associated with the administration of federal awards.

Circular A-133 is titled: Audits of States, Local Governments, and Non-Profit Organizations. This document outlines the requirements of awarding agencies, award recipients, and auditors.

OMB A-110

OMB Circular A-110 is titled Uniform Administrative Requirements for Grants and Other Agreements with Institutions of Higher Education, Hospitals, and Other Non-Profit Organizations. "This circular sets forth standards for obtaining consistency and uniformity among Federal agencies in the administration of grants to and agreements with institutions of higher education, hospitals, and other non-profit organizations" (OMB, 1999, 1.). Grant recipients and sub-recipients are obligated to follow the provisions of this document. Primary grant recipients often hire subcontractors to fulfill some part of the service agreement—the money that is used to fund the subcontractor is called "pass through" money. Nonetheless, subcontractors must also use A-133 to administer and track their portion of the award-funded project. Circular A-110 is a very detailed

document that outlines all the guidelines for recipients to administer awards. The guidelines spell out how to do "business" with federal awarding agencies. The major requirements of A-110 are as follows:

- pre-award policies
- post-award requirements
- financial program management
- property standards
- procurement standards
- reports and records
- termination and enforcement
- after-award requirements

OMB A-122

OMB Circular A-122 is titled Cost Principals for Non-Profit Organizations. This circular applies to nonprofits—excluding colleges and universities. Circular A-122 helps federal agencies determine the costs of work done by nonprofits. The costs as defined by the circular apply to pricing, administration, and settlements of contracts. The same guidelines apply to subcontractors or sub-grants that may be under the original grant award.

According to Circular A-122, the agency (federal) that is responsible for program administration will implement the provisions outlined in the circular. This circular outlines basic guidelines for grant recipients in determining what direct and indirect costs can be paid from federal money. Organizations receiving the grants are required to designate a liaison or agency representative who can work with federal agencies in determining allowable costs. Circular A-122 provides very detailed guidelines for grant recipients to help what costs may be paid out of federal grant money. The provision for determining "indirect costs" is the most complicated section of the circular and leaves the most to interpretation. Circular A-122 outlines the following:

- Prior approval must be secured in advance before costs of questionable nature can be paid out of grant.
- The total cost of direct and allowable costs.
- Factors affecting allowable costs.
- Reasonable costs.
- Direct costs.
- Indirect costs.

OMB A-133

The Office of Management and Budget's (OMB) Circular A-133 is titled Audits of States, Local Governments, and Nonprofit Organizations. Circular A-133 must be completed by recipients of federal awards (grants) of $500,000 or more. A-133 outlines guidelines and responsibilities for award recipients, auditors, and awarding agencies as well as audit report requirements.

Circular A-133 "establishes the standards in order to obtain consistency and uniformity among federal agencies for the audit of states, local governments, and not-for-profit organizations expending federal awards" (AICPA, 2005, "Purpose of this tool").

Award recipient responsibilities under OMB Circular A-133 are to

- maintain internal controls to meet compliance standards;
- identify all grant programs by Catalog of Federal Domestic Assistance (CFDA) number and title, awarding agency, and year of award;
- ensure that the OMB 133 audit is filed with appropriate federal agency;
- follow up on all compliance issues and make appropriate corrective actions; and
- sign off on audit forms (AICPA, 2005, "Requirements and Responsibilities").

Auditor responsibilities under OMB Circular A-133 are to

- plan and conduct the audit in accordance with GAAS (generally accepted auditing standards) and GAGAS (generally accepted government auditing standards);
- determine whether the organization-wide and federal award financial statements are presented fairly in accordance with GAAS and GAGAS;
- complete report and audit of expenditures;
- list all internal controls;
- monitor recipient's compliance with laws, regulations, and agreements (compliance testing); and
- follow up on previous audits (AICPA, 2005, "Requirements and Responsibilities").

The awarding agency responsibilities under OMB Circular A-133 are to

- ensure that audits are filed on time and are complete;

- provide technical assistance to auditors and recipients;
- issue management decisions on audits within six months of filing date; and
- ensure that recipients review audit findings and take corrective actions (AICPA, 2005, "Requirements and Responsibilities").

The last requirement in filing Circular A-133 is to file an auditor's report which requires that auditor to

- ensure financial statements and expenditures are presented in accordance with generally accepted accounting principles;
- outline the status of award recipient's internal controls;
- state that the recipient complied with all laws;
- list all programs that were audited; and
- make a statement about the level of risk of the "recipient" in administering the federal award (AICPA, 2005, "Requirements and Responsibilities").

ISSUES

Public Trust of Nonprofit Branding

Nonprofit scholars and managers generally recognize that "nonprofits need the public's trust for legitimacy, for effectiveness, and for non-financial as well as financial support" (Bryce, 2007, p. 112). Nonprofits have been spared the mud-raking that many for-profits corporations have suffered due to high-profile corporate accounting scandals, but nonprofits must be prepared for greater public scrutiny in the future.

The fallout of financial mismanagement is not only a risk in the for-profit world but also a concern for nonprofits. While for-profit businesses have typically been held to higher "accountability" standards by investors and corporate boards, nonprofits are now realizing that they must raise the bar in accounting for their assets. Maintaining and documenting sound financial accounting principles is one of the best ways for NPOs to maintain public confidence. The social contract implies that money will be used for public good. The "reciprocity of expectations" is that "we" as donors and taxpayers, expect that NPOs will have the resources, manpower, and information to use our money better than we could (Bryce, 2007).

Loss of reputation or "brand" can also cause great financial hardship to an organization. Relationship marketing is a term that is typically associated with customers and businesses, but it can also be applied to the relationship between donors and NPOs. There is a social contract between an individual and the NPO that she or he supports. The contract can actually be described as a transaction (nonprofit-public) because of the exchange of money for services.

Other components of the nonprofit-public transactions are (Bryce, 2007)

- contracting, particularly for charitable services;
- promising commitment exclusively to a public service mission;
- soliciting and receiving tax exemption and deductible donations in exchange for performance of the promised mission;
- employing the organization's social capital for the public's benefit; and
- exercising custody over assets for the promised public purpose.

Revenues & Custody of Assets

The two most important earnings transactions for nonprofits are program-related revenues, such as government contracts and tuition or hospital fees for individuals (which account for 72 percent of all revenues of 501(c)s, the largest group of nonprofits), and donations or contributions (accounting for another 22 percent) (Bryce, 2007). Governance and financial management are the means by which nonprofits hold and operate in the disbursement of social assets. Custodial trust implies care of assets and sound decision-making around preserving, accumulating, and growing assets. Much of NPO decision-making is discretionary and therefore is increasingly subject to public scrutiny and governmental oversight. NPOs can gain donor confidence and increase credibility by enlisting professional accountants or financial experts to help with oversight of their accounting functions.

Oversight by Auditors

NPOs are subject to increasing financial scrutiny and oversight from governmental agencies and the public. An audit by a CPA can be a very valuable exercise in identifying and preventing noncompliance and financial accounting mistakes (unintentional or fraudulent). Three of the most common deficiencies found by auditors of nonprofits are

- insufficient staffing of accounting or finance departments;
- weak internal communication regarding revenue, grants, and contracts; and
- deficient application of internal controls.

Any one of the above mentioned issues can be very costly to an NPO in terms of noncompliance, loss of confidence, and fraudulent activities. Auditors cite the need to maintain low operating costs as one reason why accounting individuals may be performing multiple duties at an NPO. Insufficient staffing of critical financial roles can lead to errors and misapplication of funds. A financial expert on staff or under contract may prove invaluable to reducing risk and providing the needed "check and balance" of accounts. Poor internal communication can lead to noncompliance of regulations and incorrect expenditures of restricted funds and can even put future grants and funds in jeopardy, particularly if mistakes are made public.

Implementing internal controls in an NPO does not have to be a costly or time-consuming task. While many large NPOs have staff accountants and oversight boards, smaller NPOs can tighten controls with existing staff and a contract accountant. The overall goal is to control the reliability of the organization's financial information. This can be accomplished by conducting regular reviews of budgets and forecasting revenues and expenses. Documenting policies and procedures and making them readily available to staff, along with improved internal communications, is another simple way to avert potential compliance and financial reporting problems before they are identified in an audit.

CONCLUSION

The FASB and OMB provide numerous written guidelines to help NPOs administer federal grants and complete required reporting. General FASB guidelines in completing financial statements benefit all NPOs—even small organizations that don't typically administer federal awards. While the guidelines are specific and comprehensive, they are also complex and time consuming to complete for many NPOs with limited staff.

Successful compliance in the administration and reporting of federal awards is only part of the task for NPOs. Successful documentation, administration, and reporting of outcomes to federal agencies don't necessarily indicate overall success or acceptable performance of an NPO in meeting its program objectives. It can be added that federal administration of social programs is difficult to assess from a success standpoint as well. In many cases, money is spent, but overall performance objectives are difficult to quantify. "Would service organizations that relied on private donations—whether from individuals or foundations or both—prove more accountable for their performance than their public or publicly funded counterparts?" (Husock, 2007, p. 20).

It has been documented that nonprofit organizations were very successful in the administration and oversight of social programs prior to the U.S. government becoming involved with funding. Individual citizens contributed largely to community support and social welfare programs before widespread support by the federal government became the norm. Futurists believe that social entrepreneurship will continue to expand as capable individuals retire from for-profit ventures and bring large amounts of personal capital to NPOs.

George Overholser of the Nonprofit Finance Fund has observed that "generally accepted accounting procedures for nonprofits do not distinguish between an investment meant to help an organization develop a new program and a grant meant to support an existing, effective program. In contrast, in the private for-profit sector, private venture capital and equity investments are clearly distinguished from revenue realized through the sale of a successful product" (Husock, 2007, p. 22).

Perhaps the nonprofit of the future will operate more like a for-profit entity in managing its assets and finances. Overholser continues by suggesting "a quasi–stock market in which so-called venture philanthropists might put their funds at risk to support a social entrepreneur's new idea and, if the idea proves successful, might be reimbursed—with interest—by a group of philanthropists less interested in taking risks than in supporting a successful program and helping it expand. Such a philanthropic 'market' would require refined measures of effectiveness, as judged not by service providers themselves but by neutral outsiders—the equivalent of bond rating

agencies, which examine financial sustainability, or Underwriters Laboratories, which vouch for the safety of products" (Husock, 2007, p. 22).

Robert Steel, a former undersecretary for domestic finance and a former vice chairman of Goldman Sachs, has developed a list of the attributes of a nonprofit he would judge ready for investors. A nonprofit must

- demonstrate that it has a clear purpose ("mission") and a succinct approach ("business model") to fulfill it;
- show both good management and good governance (e.g., an active board);
- provide measurements showing its work leads to good outcomes; and
- demonstrate what he calls "interest and enthusiasm for reporting regularly" on its progress.

These are similar, in Steel's view, to the attributes that an investment bank looks for in its "due diligence" for a private, for-profit firm (Husock, 2007, p. 22). Accounting and financial management of NPOs will continue with oversight from the federal government for the foreseeable future. However, as privately funded NPOs begin to surpass the number that are supported by federal funds, a shift in the ways and means of accounting for NPO assets is likely to change. Accountability by NPOs will remain a priority for constituents that provide funding. Mandatory auditing of NPOs will likely become a requirement for organizations as scope of service and funding increases.

TERMS & CONCEPTS

Audit: The analysis of the accounting archives and internal data of a company that helps to form an opinion about the organization's economic position.

The American Institute of Certified Public Accountants (AICPA): The nationwide professional organization for all certified public accountants (CPAs).

Fund accounting: Government and nonprofit companies are not concerned with acquiring financial status, but they do use a form of accounting system known as "fund accounting." Fund accounting groups economic data and transfers the information into accounts with like goals and purposes.

GAAS: Generally accepted auditing standards.

GAGAS: Generally accepted government auditing standards.

FASB116: "Accounting for contributions received and contributions made. Generally requires the recording of contributions and pledges received at their fair market value at the time of receipt" (Bourgeois, 2003, p. 26).

FASB117: "Financial statements of not-for-profit organizations. Establishes standardized financial statements for most non-profit organizations" (Bourgeois, 2003, p. 42).

Nonprofit: Corporation, trust, or association that operates primarily for scientific, educational, service, or charitable capacity in the public interest. The goal is not to make a profit but to use proceeds to maintain, improve, or expand operations.

OMB Circular A-110: "Uniform administrative requirements for grants and other agreements with institutions of higher education, hospitals, and other nonprofit organizations" (OMB, 1999, 3.).

OMB Circular A-122: Cost principles for nonprofit organizations.

OMB Circular A-133: Audits of states, local governments, and nonprofit organizations.

The Office of Management and Budget (OMB): This office is responsible for providing expert advice to people in senior White House positions. The advice can span a variety of topics, such as federal policy, legislature, national budget, and management.

Public-private partnerships: The sharing of responsibility by the government and private sectors in the designing, planning, financing, and operating of projects.

Social welfare programs: Often referred to as public charities, these programs have historically been funded by the government and deal with educational, cultural, or medical programs.

Unconditional pledge: Refers to a pledge that does not rely on an unforeseen event, like a matching grant from another donor.

BIBLIOGRAPHY

Abraham, A. (2006). Financial management in the nonprofit sector: A mission-based approach to ratio analysis in membership organizations. *Journal of American Academy of Business, Cambridge, 10*(1), 212–217.

Balser, D., & McClusky, J. (2005). Managing stakeholder relationships and nonprofit organization effectiveness. *Nonprofit Management & Leadership, 15*(3), 295–315.

Bottiglieri, W. A., Kroleski, S. L., & Conway, K. (2011). The regulation of non-profit organizations. *Journal of Business & Economics Research, 9*(9), 51–60.

Bourgeois, K. (2003). Nonprofit financial statements. Master's Thesis.

Bryce, H. (2007). The public's trust in nonprofit organizations: The role of relationship marketing and management. *California Management Review, 49*(4), 112–131.

Elmerraji, J. (2007, May 25). Navigating government and nonprofit financial statements. Investopedia.

Financial Accounting Standards Board. (2003). Accounting for contributions received and contributions made.

Financial Accounting Standards Board. (2003). Financial statements of not-for-profit organizations.

Husock, H. (2007). Stock market for nonprofits. *Society, 44*(3), 16–23.

Kelley, C., & Anderson, S. (2006). Advising nonprofit organizations. *CPA Journal, 76*(8), 20–26.

Kuna, S., & Nadiv, R. (2013). Organizational development dilemmas in nonprofit organizations in difficult economic time. *Organization Development Journal, 31*(2), 62–71.

Robinson, J. H. (2006). Monitoring your organization's financial health-A CEO's guide. Society for Nonprofit Organizations.

Single audits circular no. A-133: Audits of states, local governments, and non-profit organizations. (2005). In *The AICPA audit committee toolkit.* New York, NY: American Institute of Certified Public Accountants.

Study: Half of U.S. charitable organizations report an uptick in fundraising during 2011. (2012). *Nonprofit Business Advisor,* (272), 8.

Tightening NPOs' controls and procedures. (2006). *Practicing CPA, 30*(5), 6.

United States Office of Management and Budget. (1999). Circular A-110.

What are the differences between nonprofit and for-profit accounting? (2004). Alliance for Nonprofit Management.

Yetman, M. H., & Yetman, R. J. (2012). The effects of governance on the accuracy of charitable expenses reported by nonprofit organizations. *Contemporary Accounting Research, 29*(3), 738–767.

SUGGESTED READING

Helmig, B., Jegers, M., & Lapsley, I. (2004). Challenges in managing nonprofit organizations: A research overview. *Voluntas, 15*(2), 101–116.

Jegers, M., & Lapsley, I. (2003). Foreword: The 21st century challenge: managing charitable entities as business enterprises. *Financial Accountability & Management, 19*(3), 205–207.

Owen, J. (2004) Nonprofits without audit committees. Society for Nonprofit Organizations.

Panepento, P. (2007). Rising costs put pressure on charity budgets. *Chronicle of Philanthropy, 19*(16), 48.

Sarbanes-Oxley prompts nonprofits to take action. (2005). *Association Management, 57*(6), 22.

Essay by Carolyn Sprague, MLS

P

PRINCIPLES OF MACROECONOMICS

This article examines macroeconomic principles that are commonly taught in college courses. The various schools of macroeconomic thought are presented and the growing use of macroeconomic research in the public policy-making process is examined. Key government agencies that create and disseminate macroeconomic data are reviewed along with some of the types of data or indicators that the agencies provide. In addition, the expanding list of think tanks and organizations which create macroeconomic data or research are reviewed along with their history, goals, and funding sources. The importance of understanding the philosophy or political agenda behind the research in the policy-making process is also explained.

When discussing the principles of macroeconomics, it is important to remember that there is more than one school of thought in economics. Some of the important strains of economics are Austrian, Classical, Neoclassical Economics (NCE), Original Institutional Economics (OIE), Marxian, Schumpeterian, Keynesian, and Monetarism (Underwood, 2004). Each of these theoretical orientations approaches the study of economics differently and each has its own basis from which to develop principles. Thus, a central and universally agreed upon set of principles of macroeconomics is difficult. It is also noteworthy to mention that at the undergraduate level there is a bias towards Keynesian macroeconomics (Butos, 2006).

There is some debate as to the most important concepts to be taught in a macroeconomics course and perhaps even what constitutes principles of macroeconomics (Kennedy, 2000) (Taylor, 1997). It is important that material covered in a principles of macroeconomics course is simple enough to understand and consistent with the modern economy. It is also important that the material is relevant to contemporary economic policy and strategy evaluation (Taylor, 2000).

Mankiw's Principles of Macroeconomics

To assist in teaching economics and simplify the teaching of the many complex ideas in the academic discipline, Professor N. Gregoery Mankiw, author of one of the most popular textbooks, presents the principles of macroeconomics. Mankiw (1998) organizes concepts and begins a discussion of ideas regarding human behavior (including decision making and interaction) and the organization of economies. These principles were developed through the observation and analysis of human and social behavior. Mankiw's 10 principles are (1998):

- decision making
- people face tradeoffs
- the cost of something is what you give up to have it
- rational people think at the margin
- people respond to initiatives

Human interaction:

- Trade can make everybody better off.
- Markets are usually a good way to organize economic activity.
- Governments can sometimes improve market outcomes.

The Economy as a whole:

- A country's standard of living depends on its ability to produce goods and services.
- Prices rise when the government prints too much money (inflation).
- Society faces short-term tradeoff between inflation and unemployment.

Macroeconomic Analysis

Macroeconomic analysis is a data intensive discipline. One approach to examining and testing economic theories and principles is to examine the major

Professor N. Gregory Mankiw (Courtesy of Wikimedia Commons)

- Gross domestic product (GDP) price index, which is designed to measure "the prices paid for goods and services produced by an economy" ("GDP," 2009). The index is created from several other measures including "the prices of personal consumption expenditures, gross private domestic investment, and net exports of goods and services" ("GDP," 2009).
- Gross domestic product (GDP)-by-industry accounts. This data shows the contribution of each private industry and government to the Nation's gross domestic product (GDP) ("GDP," 2009).

The Conference Board

In 1995 Bureau of Economic Analysis of the Department of Commerce decided to contract with a private organization to produce and disseminate monthly cyclical indicators. These included leading economic indicators and the composite leading index. The Conference Board was selected to provide the official composite leading, coincident, and lagging indexes. The board also maintains the Business Cycle Indicators database, which has more than 250 economic series and publishes Business Cycle Indicators reports. The data series in the U.S. BCI dataset cover a wide range of topics including employment and unemployment, personal income and industrial production, interest rates and money supply, and consumer price indexes ("Why and when…," 2009).

The Conference Board is a not-for-profit organization located in New York City. The board assesses economic trends, makes economics-based forecasts, and publishes analysis and indices. The Conference Board was established in 1916 and views itself as a network of thousands of business leaders from around the world and as an independent source of unbiased information and analysis. The board has established a global presence with relationships in Asia, Europe, India, and the Middle East ("History of the conference board," 2009).

The Leading Economic Indicators (LEI) report is released monthly, usually in the third week of the month. The Business Cycle Indicators (BCI) monthly report not only highlights the leading index and indicators but also provides additional data series and historical graphs. The Conference Board also publishes the Consumer Confidence Index, which is based on the Consumer Confidence Survey which

components of an economy and the forces which impact that economy. This examination is undertaken by measuring economic activity or creating indices. Various governments and institutions around the world have worked to develop economic indices over the last several decades ("Informing our nation," 2004). The European Union (EU), the United Nations (UN), and the Organization for Economics Cooperation and Development (OECD), all use indicators to measure economic conditions and performance.

The Bureau of Economic Analysis

In the United States there are several federal government agencies that provide data that helps to explain or analyze the condition of the economy. The Bureau of Economic Analysis (BEA), an agency of the Department of Commerce, is charged with producing economic statistics to help government and business decision-makers understand the state of the economy. The BEA collects data from numerous sources, conducts research, and provides an analysis of econmic data ("About BEA," 2009). Some of the many indicators that are of interest to economists, policymakers, and corporate executives are:

- Gross domestic product (GDP), which is the market value of all of the goods and services produce in an economy during the time that is being measured.

polls a representative sample of 5,000 households in the United States.

Other Sources of Economic Indicators

Another agency that is a major contributor of economic data is the U.S. Census Bureau. Economic statistics include information on retail and wholesale trade, construction activity, industrial output, capital expenditures, e-commerce sales, and foreign trade ("How to Find the Latest Business Data," 2009). Other agencies that create economic indicators include the Office of Federal Housing Enterprise Oversight (OFHEO), which publishes quarterly house price indexes for single-family detached homes ("House Price Index," 2009). In addition, the U.S. Small Business Administration (SBA) produces statistics and analysis that show economic conditions of small businesses ("Research and Statistics," 2009).

APPLICATIONS

Applying Macroeconomics to Policy & Strategy

The Great Depression had a profound impact on individual citizens, small and large businesses, and governments at all levels. In 1933, the unemployment rate reached 25 percent in the United States and the real GDP fell 31 percent below its 1929 level (Mankiw, 2006). In 2008 the economic crisis toppled Wall Street firms, banks, mortgage companies, and automobile manufactures. It also and sent millions of people to the unemployment lines (Reinganum, 2009). This type of crisis clearly shows that the economy cannot go unmanaged, and it is important that public policies which relate to the economy are well thought and properly executed.

There is a role in the policymaking process for macroeconomics and economists (Perry, 1984). Since the mid-twentieth century, the United States and other countries have implemented a wide variety of public policy initiatives that were ground in macroeconomic principles or theories. These policies have impacted central banking, inflation management, monetary policy, and taxation practices (Chari & Kehoe, 2006). There have also been policies that have changed the wealth and status of social groups (Seguino & Grown, 2006).

Macroeconomics as a discipline focuses on the study of trends or events that impact an entire economy. This can include the study of what impacts

The Brookings Institute in Washington, D.C. (Courtesy of Gryffindor via Wikimedia Commons)

the gross domestic product (GDP), total spending in a specific sector, global trade and national deficits, or the impact of interest rates on a wide array of economic conditions and activities. Economists also study topics concerning the societal distributions of resources including land, raw materials, and means of production of goods, and the delivery of services. Economists also research a wide variety of business and social issues including energy costs, inflation, interest rates, exchange rates, taxation, and unemployment levels.

When communicating the results of macroeconomic research, it is important to present economic concepts and statistical data in an understandable and meaningful format. Providing analyses that includes reports with tables and charts to present their research results is a central part of an economist's activity.

Many economists specialize in a particular area of study. Industrial economists, for example, focus on the market structure of specific industries. International economists mostly focus on global financial markets, exchange rates, and the effects of trade policies and tariffs. A labor economist primarily focuses on studying the supply and demand for labor and trends in wages and benefits.

In 2006, there were about 15,000 economists employed in the United States. About half of them were employed by government agencies at the state and federal level. Non-government organizations (NGOs) such as the World Bank, the International

Monetary Fund, and the World Trade Organization, also employ economists. In addition, many economists work for research or consulting firms, financial service organizations, or private corporations. It is not unusual for an economist to supplement a full-time job in the public sector or academia with part-time consulting activities.

Economists employed in the public sector or by NGOs are most often concerned with public policy that either impacts the economy or policies that can succeed or fail depending on economic conditions. Economists that work for private corporations focus on analyzing economic conditions or trends that may impact the performance of their company as well as government policies and legislation that could hinder or aid in the growth of their company (Bureau of Labor Statistics, 2008).

Macroeconomics & Public Policy in the Coming Decades

Both macroeconomists and public policy makers have their work cut out for them during the coming decades. In 2013, the U.S. federal government faced a dramatic unsustainable growth in debt. This debt growth posed a number of risks, including a declining GDP that would eventually impact the living standards of almost all Americans. Rising inflation and higher interest rates were also concerns, as was the difficulty of attracting foreign investment. In addition to these concerns, which had lingered (though had not materialized) since 2008, the federal government anticipated the demands on the federal budget of entitlement programs such as Medicare and Social Security that would expand considerably with the aging and retirement of the "baby boomers." ("The nation's long-term…," 2008).

If the federal deficit problems and an aging population were not enough to baffle both policy-makers and economists, then add the fact that most Americans are deficit spenders. Until 2008, the typical American household spent more than its annual income by depleting past savings, selling off assets, or borrowing money ("National saving," 2006), particularly in the form of credit card debt and home equity loans. The financial crisis curtailed this behavior and savings rates jumped (Chamley, 2012). Meanwhile, the value of pension plans suffered greatly during the downturn of 2008; having lost more than $2 trillion in value (Weller, 2009). The underfunding and even total loss of defined benefit plans remained one of the most intractable problems resulting from the financial crisis (Blitzstein, 2013). The bottom line for many workers in the United States is that they may need to work past their expected retirement age.

Applying macroeconomics to public policy is a complex problem. Policy designers must understand macroeconomic principles and be able to use them to draft policies. Then the U.S. Congress must understand the value of the policy to the overall economy and pass legislation that remains consistent with the intent of the draft policy. This is not an easy process. A wide range of groups will lobby congressional representatives and Senators to bend the policy in a direction that can help their causes. Once the legislation is passed, the executive branch will have responsibility to implement the policy or program designed to impact macroeconomic trends. Basically, the good that applying a macroeconomic principle could bring can easily be erased through this complex political process.

ISSUE

The Institutionalization of Macroeconomics

Macroeconomic principles and concepts are used by a variety of organizations in their efforts to influence the outcome of the public policy process and the legislative process that drives policy making. These organizations range from blatant lobbying efforts to sophisticated and well-respected research organizations. Clearly, macroeconomic principles and analysis have become tools in the arsenal of many organizations that strive to influence the outcome of policymaking in democratic societies.

When weighing the value of macroeconomic research presented by these organizations, it is important to consider the source of the research as well as the motivation or political bent of the organization itself. Research can be made to look good and be presented in a very convincing manner. However, that does not make it good research. In addition, just because a researcher is educated in macroeconomic does not make him or her objective or unbiased. Some of the better-established organizations that provide macroeconomics research are detailed below.

Economic Policy Institute

The Economic Policy Institute (EPI) is a nonprofit think tank founded in 1986 and headquartered in Washington D.C. The institute strives to include the interests of low-income and middle-income workers and their families in the formulation of economic policy. The EPI has a very impressive group of founders, many of who have held high-level policy positions or prestigious university positions. The majority of funding (about 53 percent) comes from foundation grants and another 29 percent comes from labor unions. Other sources of funds include individuals, corporations, and other organizations.

The EPI conducts a wide variety of original independent research covering issues of concern for workers such as trends in wages and incomes, retirement security, and healthcare. Other research focuses on economic development strategies, world trade, and global competitiveness. EPI research is published in books, special briefs, and educational materials. EPI utilizes the research to brief policymakers as well as to provide technical support to activists and community organizations. Material is also disseminated to media outlets ("About the Economic Policy Institute," 2009).

The Stanford Institute for Economic Policy Research

The Stanford Institute for Economic Policy Research (SIEPR) is a nonpartisan policy research organization that was established to advise policymakers and the public on the economic impact of public policies. The goal of SIEPR is to improve long-term economic policy. SIEPR scholars have worked on a wide variety of projects including analyzing the impact of welfare reform in California, improvements in federal government budget policy, the fuel efficiency of automobiles, and energy policy in the United States. SIEPR accepts funding from individuals as well as corporations ("About SIEPR," 2009).

The American Enterprise Institute for Public Policy Research

The American Enterprise Institute for Public Policy Research (AEI) is a not-for-profit institution with a focus on government, politics, economics, and social welfare. The institute, founded in 1943, stresses a nonpartisan perspective and position but asserts that it is in favor of limited government, private enterprise, individual liberty and responsibility, vigilant and effective defense and foreign policies, political accountability, and open debate ("AEI's organization and purposes," 2009). Research activities are

divided into three major categories: Economic Policy Studies, Social and Political Studies, and Defense and Foreign Policy Studies. Funding for AEI comes from corporations, foundations, and individuals and by investment earnings from an internal endowment. AEI does not accept contract research projects and seldom accepts government grants ("AEI's organization and purposes," 2009).

The Urban Institute

The Urban Institute, founded in the mid-1960s, focuses its efforts on fostering sound public policy and effective government. Issues researched include economic policy and taxation, work and income, retirement, education, and crime. The research in the area of economics includes federal and state budgets and fiscal policy, income and wealth distribution, poverty, tax distribution, and social programs ("About UI," 2009).

The Brookings Institution

The Brookings Institution, a nonprofit organization based in Washington, D.C., conducts independent research designed to improve the economic welfare of Americans. Brookings publishes books, papers, and articles and sends its researchers to testify before congressional committees. Brookings stresses quality, independence, and impact. Founded in 1916, the institute has contributed to the establishment of the United Nations, design of the Marshall Plan, and creation of the Congressional Budget Office. Brookings receives funds through an endowment as well as contributions from foundations, corporations and private individuals. ("About Brookings," 2009).

American Institute for Economic Research

American Institute for Economic Research (AIER), founded in 1933, also stresses nonpartisanship and independence in its economic research efforts. AIER gets its funding primarily from annual member's fees, the sale of its publications, and tax-deductible contributions. The institute also owns an investment advisory organization, American Investment Services, Inc., and profits from that subsidiary help fund the institute. Publications include a twice-monthly research report covering current economic events and the Economic Bulletin that provides in-depth coverage of economics ("About AIER," 2009).

The Economic Cycle Research Institute

The Economic Cycle Research Institute (ECRI) examines sequences in market-oriented economies, growth, employment and inflation. ECRI lays claims to expertise in cyclical investigation and cyclical forecasting to predict the timing of cyclical turns. This includes a broad array of cycle indexes. ECRI's funding comes from subscribers to their forecasting services ("About ECRI," 2009).

The Asia Economic Institute

The Asia Economic Institute (AEI), founded in 1999, focuses on developing discussion between figures in Asian economics with the goal of providing information about and acting as a source of knowledge about the economic markets of Asia. AEI is not accepting support through government funds or political contributions ("About Us, The Asia Economic Institute," 2009).

The Korea Economic Institute

The Korea Economic Institute (KEI) focuses on broadening the understanding among Americans about developments in Korea by providing information and analysis. Publications include a two-volume set entitled "On Korea," which is a compilation of academic papers that the institute commissioned. KEI is a not-for-profit, educational organization that is closely affiliated with the Korea Institute for International Economic Policy that is funded by the South Korean government ("Welcome to the Korea Economic Institute (KEI)," 2009).

The Montreal Economic Institute

The Montreal Economic Institute (MEI), established in 1999, stresses independence and non-partisan research on public policy issues. The MEI's goal is to develop and propose original and innovative public policies. The MEI studies markets in order to understand the mechanisms and institutions that promote long-term prosperity. The MEI is supported by Montreal-area entrepreneurs, academics, and economists and does not accept any government funding ("Who Are We?," 2009).

CONCLUSION

Although textbooks may focus on or present principles of macroeconomics, it is important to recognize that there is more than one school of economic thought. The viewpoints expressed by the economists and analytical approaches of these competitive schools should be considered before accepting any one set of macroeconomic principles as doctrine.

Macroeconomic principles and research are now used by a wide variety of government agencies, private corporations, non-profit organizations, and individuals to help guide policy, strategy, and decision-making. There have certainly been successful applications of macroeconomics to policy development, but the legislative process is both complex and political. This means that even a policy that starts with a pure application of macroeconomics it can be influenced and altered by modifications, amendments, or changes in the committee legislative voting processes.

There is now a macroeconomic marketplace where principles and concepts are funded, sold, and leveraged by a variety of organizations. These think-tank organizations are motivated by their desire to influence legislative outcomes. When assessing the validity of macroeconomic research presented by these organizations, it is important to consider the overall goals of the organization, its track record, and its funding sources.

TERMS & CONCEPTS

Gross domestic product (GDP): The market value of all the goods and services produced in an economy during a specified period of time.

Gross domestic product (GDP) price endex: Index designed to measure the prices paid for the goods and services produced by an economy. The index is created from several other measures including the prices of personal consumption expenditures, gross private domestic investment, and net exports of goods and services.

Gross domestic product (GDP)-by-industry accounts: This data shows the contribution of each private industry and government to the nation's gross domestic product (GDP) ("GDP," 2009).

Monetary policies: Government policies that control, shape, or impact how a nation's money supply and exchange with other currencies is managed.

National deficits: The amount of money that a national government spends that is beyond the revenue collected by the government through taxes, fees, tariffs, or other sources.

BIBLIOGRAPHY

About AIER. (2009).

About BEA. (2009).

About Brookings. (2009).

About ECRI. (2009).

About SIEPR. (2009).

About the Economic Policy Institute. (2009).

About UI. (2009).

About Us. (2209)

About Us. (2009).

AEI's organization and purposes. (2009).

Blitzstein, D.S. (2013). Restructuring occupational pension plans in crisis: a US labor-management case study. *Rotman International Journal of Pension Management, 6*(1), 12–19.

Bureau of Labor Statistics, U.S. Department of Labor. (2008-09). *Occupational Outlook Handbook*, 2008-09 edition, economists.

Butos, W. (2006). Money, prices, and capital: An Austrian approach to macroeconomics. *Quarterly Journal of Austrian Economics, 9*(4), 5–19.

Chari, V., & Kehoe, P. (2006). Modern macroeconomics in practice: How theory is shaping policy. *Journal of Economic Perspectives, 20*(4), 3–28.

"GDP." (2009). Bureau of economic analysis glossary.

History of the conference board. (2009).

House Price Index. (2009). The Office of Federal Housing Enterprise Oversight (OFHEO).

How to Find the Latest Business Data. (2009)

Informing our nation: Improving how to understand and assess the USA's position and progress. (2004).

Kennedy, P. (2000). Eight reasons why real versus nominal interest rates is the most important concept in macroeconomics principles courses. (2000). *American Economic Review, 90*(2), 81.

Mankiw, N. (2006). The macroeconomist as scientist and engineer. *Journal of Economic Perspectives, 20*(4), 29–46.

Mankiw, Greogry N. (1998). *Principles of economics.* Fort Worth, TX: The Dryden Press.

National saving: Current saving decisions have profound implications for our nation's future well-being. (April 6, 2006). GAO Testimony Before the Subcommittee on Long-term Growth and Debt Reduction, Committee on Finance, United States Senate.

Perry, G. (1984). Reflections on macroeconomics. *American Economic Review, 74*(2), 401.

Reinganum, M. (2009). Setting national priorities: Financial challenges facing the Obama administration. *Financial Analysts Journal, 65*(2), 1–4.

Research and Statistics. (2009). The United States Small Business Administration, Office of Economic Research.

Seguino, S., & Grown, C. (2006). Gender equity and globalization: Macroeconomic policy for developing countries. *Journal of International Development, 18*(8), 1081–1104.

Taylor, J. (1997). A core of practical macroeconomics. *Choices: The Magazine of Food, Farm & Resource Issues,* 10.

Taylor, J. (2000). Teaching modern macroeconomics at the principles level. *American Economic Review, 90*(2), 90–95.

The nation's long-term fiscal outlook. (2008, September).

Underwood, D. (2004). Principles of macroeconomics: Toward a multiparadigmatic approach. *Journal of Economic Issues, 38*(2), 571–581.

Welcome to the Korea Economic Institute (KEI). (2009). The Korea Economic Institute.

Weller, C. (2009). What now? Benefits & Compensation Digest, 46(4), 24-29.

Who Are We?, (2009). The Montreal Economic Institute (MEI).

Why and when did The Conference Board become the source for the Business Cycle Indicators? (2009). Frequently asked questions & answers.

SUGGESTED READING

Bennett, D., Padgham, G., McCarty, C., & Carter, M. (2007). Teaching principles of economics: Internet vs. traditional classroom instruction. Journal of Economics & Economic Education Research, 8(1), 21-31.

Boskin, M. (1986). Some thoughts on teaching principles of macroeconomics. *Journal of Economic Education, 17*(4), 283–287.

Chamley, C. (2012). A paradox of thrift in general equilibrium without forward markets. *Journal of the European Economic Association, 10*(6), 1215–1235.

Collard, F., & Dellas, H. (2008). Monetary policy and inflation in the 70s. *Journal of Money, Credit & Banking, 40*(8), 1765–1781.

Du, R., & Kamakura, W. (2008). Where did all that money go? Understanding how consumers allocate their consumption budget. *Journal of Marketing, 72*(6), 109–131.

Lee, D. (1992). Internationalizing the principles of economics course: A survey of textbooks. *Journal of Economic Education, 23*(1), 79–88.

Levinson, M. (2009). The economic collapse. *Dissent* (00123846), *56*(1), 61–66.

Markowitz, H. (2009). Proposals concerning the current financial crisis. *Financial Analysts Journal, 65*(1), 25–27.

Montiel, P.J. (2011). On macroeconomic reforms and macro- economic resiliency: Lessons from the Great Recession. *Modern Economy, 2*(4), 528–537.

Philips, T., & Muralidhar, A. (2008). Saving social security: A better approach. *Financial Analysts Journal, 64*(6), 62–73.

The principles of macroeconomics at the millennium. (2000). *American Economic Review, 90*(2), 85–90.

Essay by Michael Erbschloe

PRINCIPLES OF MICROECONOMICS

Economics is a subject that provides guidance on how to reconcile unlimited wants and limited resources. In general, it involves applying the concept of trade-offs within a context where decisions occur through marginal analysis. As they engage themselves in this framework, students will encounter questions regarding the content, purposes, and processes of production in a market-based economy. Some will find answers to those questions as they ponder models of demand and supply. Those models are merely tools with which we can simplify reality and attain a better understanding of the nature of demand and supply. Readers will find discussions on how their purchases are sensitive to income, satisfaction, and prices. They will also learn how their employments generate revenue and profits while their employers respond to consumer wants and needs, seize or miss opportunities, and deal with market constraints. In addition, readers will gain additional insights into the relevance of microeconomics to areas such as labor markets, government regulations, market failures, public goods, and international trade.

OVERVIEW

We can think of economics as a study of reconciliations between unlimited wants and limited resources. Reconciliation is an attempt to find some middle ground in problem-solving. The economic problem arises due to resource scarcity, and it prompts individuals to make rational choices from amongst all the alternative solutions. Each and every choice involves a sacrifice because it is very difficult, if not impossible, to avoid trade-offs.

The value of the foregone alternative is, by definition, an opportunity cost. In essence, finding solutions to the economic problem of scarcity involves minimizing opportunity costs. Trade-offs sometimes take the form of sacrifices that are linear in their relationship, which translate into the correspondence of a benefit with some given or constant amount of cost. However, economists tend to view the equation as one that involves increasing amounts of cost taking the form of a curvilinear relationship.

Whether opportunity costs are constant or increasing, their illustration is most effective when one attempts to consider all the possible choice combinations. A study of economics introduces students to many models, some of which focus on consumers and others on producers. It is best to think of graphs and models as tools that simplify reality. With a view toward a nation's ability to produce two items, say goods X and Y, there are numerous combinations of X and Y possible but the production of more X essentially translates into the production of less Y and vice versa.

APPLICATIONS

Economics, in general, involves applying the opportunity cost concept to decisions made at the margin. In other words, how a change in one variable results in a change in another variable. As an introduction to the orientation of economics toward marginal analysis, the production possibilities frontier is a model that portrays all those combinations that a country's entire economy can produce. It is a macroeconomic concept, which effectively conveys the interdependencies among scarcity, choices, and trade-offs. Nonetheless, this essay is on microeconomics. The difference between those economic divisions resides in their scope. Macroeconomics is a study of economics using models of the whole economy whereas microeconomics is a study of the behaviors of consumers and producers as they interact in models we can refer to as a market.

Foundations of Microeconomics

Students in economics courses may find these three questions in their textbooks and possibly their exams: What will be produced? For whom will it produced? How will it be produced? Furthermore, studies in microeconomics usually begin by acknowledging a set of assumptions.

- First is the ceteris paribus (translation means all else is held constant) assumption.
- The second assumption is that consumers and producers behave as rational agents who have access to full, perfect information relevant to their decisions.
- Another assumption is that those agents engage in transactions through which no individual or group brings an inordinate amount of influence to an exchange decision.
- The fourth and last assumption is that an exchange between a buyer and a seller yields benefits and/or costs for them only, thereby omitting or ignoring the private exchange's relevance to larger society. A theme in economics is that individuals pursuing their own self-interests promote societal betterment.

Problems unrelated to scarcity arise in the marketplace when any of the last three assumptions become unrealistic or fail to hold true. Policy analysts and economists refer to that situation as a market failure. Its occurrence may establish a rationale for governmental intervention including the formation and the implementation of public policies; market failure will be revisited toward the end of this essay.

A call for governmental policies or interventions suggests that something should occur in order to alleviate a problem. That call would fit the classification of normative economics, which is one of two types of economic analysis. The other type is positive economics, which occurs when analysts deal strictly with data or facts centering their attention on whether that information is accurate. For example, individuals are more likely to agree on matters regarding the accuracy of data than they are on matters regarding what ought to occur in response to their interpretations of the data. In sum, differences exist in the content of a statement containing the word *is* versus others containing the words *ought* or *should*. Macroeconomics is more normative than microeconomics due primarily to its orientation toward policies promoting economic growth, employment, and price stability.

Students will receive information on a variety of distinctions, some more subtle than other, and concepts in an economics course. The fallacy of composition concept is one. It occurs when an analyst is errant in forming the conclusion that what is true for an individual is also true for a group. In addition, there is a distinction between correlation and causation. Economic theory and models utilize causation in the sense that a change in an independent variable causes a change in a dependent variable; for example, many economists agree that consumer's demand for an item causes firms to supply it. Analysts define correlation as the presence of a statistical association between variables in the absence of a theoretical basis that specifies a change in one variable causes a change in another; for example, studies show that the number of babies born under a full moon is statistically and significantly higher than a new moon. Yet we are confident that one does not cause the other because the moon is always present regardless of its illumination phase.

The aforementioned set of clarifications, distinctions, and assumptions provide a foundation with which readers can form a better, yet terse, understanding of the way economists view the world. In the exposition ahead, readers will also gain a better sense of microeconomic theory, and they will receive suggestions that purport to reinforce their learning. This condensed essay of microeconomics may require readers to consult textbooks and other sources for additional details, examples, and cases due to their deliberate omission for the sake of brevity. The remainder of this essay represents an attempt to apply the worldview as introduced above.

The foundation of economics emphasizes consumers and demand as integral components. With regard to the consumer or demand side, students learn very early in their coursework that an inverse relationship exists between price and quantity demanded in accordance with the law of demand. Relatively speaking, smaller amounts are in demand at higher prices and vice versa. On the producer or supply side, they learn that a positive relationship exists between price and quantity supplied according to the law of supply.

Demand & Supply Models

Models contain a set of relationships and those relationships use lines and curves for illustrative purposes. However, graphs are a known stumbling block for many students so their omission from this essay serves to expedite learning. Although this author attempts to describe what an economics student might see on a graph, there are points within this essay when students will benefit by referring to graphs in an economics textbook; those by Arnold (2011), McConnell & Brue (2012), Guell (2007), and other economists will suffice. When the need arises, readers are encouraged to consult those sources as they read this essay. All said, when viewing a two-dimensional graph showing the demand and supply curves in the market for any given item, viewers would notice that its price appears on the vertical axis and its quantity appears on the horizontal axis.

Equilibrium

Equilibrium price and quantity occur where quantity demanded equals quantity supplied or where the downward-sloping demand curve intersects the upward sloping supply curve. On the one hand, a surplus occurs at a price above equilibrium. It is the result of the quantity supplied being greater than the quantity demanded. On the other hand, a shortage occurs at a price below equilibrium. It results from the quantity demanded exceeding the quantity supplied. In order to move price and the situation toward equilibrium, two forms of movement may occur on the graph: a movement along the curve and a shift in the curve. Students frequently confuse those two forms. To keep them clear, students need to remember that a change in price initiates movement

along the curve whereas a change in a determinant initiates a shift in the curve. In addition, the curve illustrates the relationship between the axis variables, thus any change in them will result in movement along the curve.

An equilibrium point is static at one instance, but it is also dynamic in nature by virtue of a curve shift that results in a different intersection of the demand and supply curve. New intersections and new equilibrium prices and quantities often result from any inward or outward curve shift. The demand curve will shift in accordance with a change in a determinant and so will the supply curve. In the pages ahead, readers will gain valuable insights into studying microeconomic concepts and learning how to apply them successfully.

Curve Shifts

Five determinants exist each for demand and for supply and any change in them will prompt the curve to shift. Increases or decreases in demand or supply occur in accordance with a change in a determinant. A rightward, outward, or upward shift in the demand curve is an increase in demand whereas an opposite shift is a decrease in demand. By extension, an increase (decrease) in demand means consumers will purchase a larger (smaller) quantity of an item at any given price. A rightward, downward, or outward shift in the supply curve is as an increase in supply whereas an opposite shift is a decrease in supply. Likewise, an increase (decrease) in supply means producers will supply a larger (smaller) quantity of an item at any given price. In contrast to curve shifts, any movement along a demand curve or a supply curve is respectively a change in quantity demanded or quantity supplied to which there is a corresponding change in price. The list of five determinants for demand and those for supply is as follows:

Demand & Supply Schedules

Correspondence between prices and quantities is revealed through demand and supply schedules. Construction of these schedules occurs at two levels of aggregation. Compilations of a market-level demand schedule and supply schedule originate with individual-level schedules. All individuals who buy or sell an item constitute the market for that item. Individual demand schedules represent the quantities each consumer is willing and able to purchase at each price. The summation of quantities from those individual demand schedules across each price becomes the market demand schedule. In comparison, market supply schedules represent the sum of quantities that individual producers are willing and able to sell at each price as long as the market price makes it is feasible for them to do so.

Origins & Extensions of Demand: Consumers' Income, Satisfaction, & Sensitivities

Marginal Utility

In terms of those individual-level demand schedules, the ability to purchase an item is a function of a consumer's income and the willingness to purchase is a function of the satisfaction that originates from the item's consumption. In other words, consumers maximize their utility subject to their budget constraints. Utility is another word for the satisfaction an individual receives when consuming the item. Marginal utility then, by definition, is the additional unit of satisfaction from consuming an additional amount of the item. However, marginal utility increases but it becomes smaller with additional amounts until a point is reached at which it is zero. Afterwards, marginal utility then becomes negative and it decreases at an increasing rate as a consumer begins to regret overindulgence. This pattern illustrates the diminishing marginal utility concept. One example of this concept is how the feeding frenzy that accompanies a buffet-style meal often results in regrets as the diner attempts to get the most out of each dollar spent.

Income constraints, marginal utility, and item prices jointly influence a consumer's purchase plans. Income and item price are primary factors in determining how much the consumer will purchase. With a simplifying assumption that only two items are available for purchase, it is useful to ponder for a moment what combination of them is attainable for a given amount of income and is desirable for achieving an equal amount of utility. Consumer equilibrium is, by definition, a point at which the marginal utility per dollar spent is equal across all items under consideration. Consequently, item prices are an important element of demand.

Elasticity

Consumer sensitivity to price changes may be more important and worthy of elaboration at this juncture. The price elasticity of demand allows us to determine precisely in percentage terms how purchases respond to changes in price. Calculations of the elasticity coefficient involve division of the percentage change in quantity demanded by the percentage change in price. Percent change is the observed difference between two points, namely the starting point and the endpoint, divided by the value at the starting point. In the broadest sense, we can think about and talk about elasticity of a specific item at its extremes along a demand spectrum. The demand for an item is either elastic, inelastic, or unitary elastic when the respective coefficient as an absolute term is greater than one, less than one, or equal to one.

Guell (2007, p. 41) summarizes a few studies on the price elasticity of demand for gasoline as follows: A 10 percent increase in its price will result in a decrease of less than 3 percent in quantities purchased. This result tells us that the price elasticity of demand coefficient, in absolute terms, is 0.03. Furthermore, omission of the negative sign is appropriate because we know there is an inverse relationship between price and quantity demanded. Moreover, price elasticities are a function of a few factors.

Elasticity depends on a set of factors known as the determinants of elasticity.

- First, it depends on how much time consumers have to adjust to a price change; for example, the amount of gasoline in their vehicle's tank and the remoteness of their geographic location jointly influence whether they can afford to shop for cheaper gasoline.
- Second, elasticity is also determined by the number and relative availability of items considered to be viable alternatives or substitutes for any given item.
- Third, the set includes whether an item is something that a consumer needs and wants (a necessity like food, clothing, or shelter) or something that a consumer wants but perhaps doesn't need (a luxury like jewelry, cruises, or electronic gadgets).
- The fourth factor is the portion of the consumer's budget spent on the item.

The coefficient of elasticity is different than, but has some relation to, the slope of a straight line. The slope formula calls for dividing the rise by the run or, in other words, the change in the vertical direction by the associated change in the horizontal direction. Another important distinction between elasticity and slope is that the slope is the same along a straight line at any given point on the line, but its elasticity varies. Conversely, the slope varies along a curved line at any point on the line, but its elasticity is the same.

Three regions of elasticity exist along the demand line. The upper segment of the line is where demand is elastic. The lower segment is where it is inelastic. The segment in the middle is where demand is unitary elastic. Because price elasticity of demand describes how sensitive consumer purchases are in relation to changes in price, those segments serve as reminders that consumers are more sensitive to changes in price for high-priced items than they are for low-priced items. The relevance of these regions to firms selling items appears near the end of this section, but we turn our attention away from price elasticity for now, considering two other demand elasticity concepts.

Demand Coefficients
Some instructors spend a considerable amount of time with their students comparing apples to oranges. Those comparisons are highly appropriate when examining the cross elasticity of demand concept. One might begin by asking the question: What happens to the purchases of oranges when there is an increase in the price of apples? In more precise terms, we need to attach the word *percentage* to the changes in price and in quantity. Coefficients for cross elasticity of demand will reveal whether consumers switch between apples and oranges and/or whether they eat them in some combination. These fruits are likely to be substitutes, but it is possible that some consume them in combinations as complements; an example of the latter would be hot dogs and hot dog buns. If the coefficient for the cross elasticity of demand is a positive number, we can conclude with some certainty that apples and oranges are indeed substitutes; for instance, the percentage increases in price and in quantity move in the same direction. On the other hand, if the coefficient is a negative number, we can be certain that they are complements; for instance, the percentage increases move in opposite directions.

We can also ascertain whether an apple, an orange, or some other item is a normal good or an inferior good. Examinations of the percentage change in item purchase quantities with respect to the

percentage change in consumer income will reveal whether the income elasticity of demand coefficient is positive or negative. If the coefficient is positive, then we can conclude that the item is a normal good; for example, an increase in income may generate an increase in apple consumption. In other words, the normal case is that higher incomes generate additional purchases and larger quantities. If it is negative, then we can conclude that the apple is an inferior good.

Price Elasticity
These three elasticities of demand are important considerations for both consumers and producers, but price elasticity of demand is probably the most relevant to a seller's decision with regard to prices. As one might guess, most firms would prefer to sell only those items for which demand is inelastic. Consequently, firm revenue, which by definition is the mathematical product of price times quantity sold, from those sales would increase in concert with price rises but only up to a point. As prices move higher along the demand curve and begin to enter the upper region, consumers become more sensitive to price changes and then they begin to reduce their purchases of the item. Purchase quantities fall faster than prices rise resulting in decreases in a consumer's total expenditures and a firm's total revenues.

Unabated price increases or decreases eventually move past the point at which demand is unitary elastic (for instance, where the price elasticity of demand coefficient in absolute terms is exactly equal to 1.00). The total revenue test directs attention to the danger of constant increases in an item's price and to the appeal of constant decreases in an item's price. In brief, upward movements in price through the middle region of the demand line tend to decrease seller's total revenues and consumer's total expenditures whereas downward movements tend to increase them. The next section diverts attention away from consumers and the demand side of the model toward producers and the supply side of the model.

Origins & Extensions of Supply: Producers' Revenue, Profits, & Constraints
Most firms face constraints including competition, market price, and cost functions. The relationship between market prices and producer costs is critical. It influences whether the production of an item

will occur at all and in an efficient and profitable manner. Business owners expect to earn profits and their firms will incur a variety of costs in their production of goods and services.

Total costs are the sum of fixed and variable costs. Fixed costs are those that exist even without any production. Furthermore, they are constant, as they do not vary with the scale of production. Some examples of fixed costs include monthly installments paid for machinery, buildings, and land. Variable costs are those that vary with production. Some examples of variable costs include wages, materials, and supplies.

The allocation of costs across larger scales of production results in a variety of cost curve shapes. Graphs depicting these functions show cost on the vertical axis and quantity on the horizontal axis. Average total cost and average variable cost form important U-shaped curves. Their calculation involves dividing them by the production quantity. The lowest points on those curves are significant. At those points is where the marginal cost curve, which is J-shaped, intersects them. Marginal cost is the change in total costs that arise from producing one additional unit.

As firms produce and sell items, they receive a price for each one sold. Total revenue is the mathematical product of price times the quantity sold at each price. Marginal revenue is the change in total revenue that arises from selling one additional unit. A key relationship exists where marginal revenue equals marginal cost and where these two curves intersect. That intersection determines the profit-maximizing amount of output. Most, if not all, firms attempt to produce that amount because of their profit-maximizing behaviors.

Rules of Production

Two rules of production determine whether a firm will continue its operation as a viable economic entity. First, they must produce at the profit-maximizing output. Second, they must receive a price that is equal to or greater than average variable cost. Moreover, the price at which an item sells must cover average variable costs, and it should cover average fixed costs. In other words, firms must cover their variable inputs, labor costs for instance, in the near term and make payments on their plants and machinery as part of their operations. Furthermore, they must operate at or above the shutdown point, which is where the marginal cost curve intersects the average variable

cost curve and at the latter's lowest point. In essence, firms will only supply a good or service over time if the item's price is above the shutdown point.

Another key reference point is the break-even point. It occurs where the marginal cost curve intersects the average total cost curve and at the latter's lowest point. The break-even point also marks the location at which those costs are equal and the firm earns a normal profit. The term may be misleading to some as it suggests the absence of profit; it is noteworthy that a major difference exists here between accounting and economics. Profits are part of the cost of doing business given the opportunity cost concept, which is the value the owner attaches to the best foregone alternative. In essence, the firm owner expects to earn a specific minimum level of profit in order to remain in the current business. Therefore, to remain in the business, a firm owner or an entrepreneur will receive a rate of profit considered normal for the market in which he or she conducts business operations. A real need exists to sell items at a market price that covers average total costs. Otherwise, the owner will consider producing other items, operations, and markets whenever exit and entry are feasible.

Market Structure

Depending on competitiveness and structures of the markets in which they operate, some firms can influence the market price and others merely accept the market price for their outputs. Market structure reflects the firm's ability to make the price or to take the price. Structures at the extreme ends of a continuum refer to the presence or the absence of competition in a market for a specific output or item. The bookends of that continuum are perfect competition and monopoly, or imperfect, competition. Two other market structures exist between those ends, namely monopolistic competition and oligopoly, but student comprehension is highly likely when thinking only in terms of the structural extremes for now.

One way to differentiate between those structural ends is to examine price in relation to marginal revenue as it appears in a table or a graph. Price is equal to marginal revenue in competitive market structures, and it is greater than marginal revenue in monopolistic market structures. Although graphs can become quite confusing with each new addition of a line or curve, keep in mind that the marginal revenue line is horizontal in perfectly competitive market structures, and it is downward sloping in monopolistic structures.

In addition to whether firms are price makers or price takers, market structure descriptors often include the number of sellers and buyers, the ease at which firms can enter or exit a market, and the level of profit. One example of product produced in a perfectly competitive market structure is agriculture. In this instance, there are numerous buyers and sellers of an agricultural product such as corn. Consequently, corn farmers take the price dictated by the market and almost anyone can obtain enough resources to grow corn. An example of a product produced in a monopolistic market structure is a computer operating system. In this instance, there are numerous buyers of the system but only one seller. Consequently, system developers make the price, as they are the only producer, and virtually no one can obtain the resources needed to develop the operating systems software. Furthermore, monopolists produce lower quantities than perfect competitors do, and they charge higher prices as a result. Moreover, those prices are much higher than the break-even point, which means monopolists and other imperfectly competitive firms earn profits greater than the normal level.

Economic profit results when prices are higher than average total cost, which usually invites entry into the market. However, entry into the market for software is virtually impossible for a producer mostly due to legal constraints such as licenses and patents. If firm entry into a market is viable, then it is likely that an increase in supply will result; forcing prices down toward and possibly lower than the normal profit level. That erosion of profits effectively induces firm exit; decreasing supply, increasing price, and generating higher profits, etc. At this point, we shift our attention toward other applications of microeconomics beginning with regulations designed to infuse competition into noncompetitive situations and market environments.

Other Applications: Antitrust, International Trade, Resource Markets, & Failures

Several antitrust laws exist for controlling economic behaviors and monopolistic inclinations. They deserve brief mention here in an effort to provide a comprehensive view regarding the applicability of microeconomics to a number of areas. For instance, an industrial organization course expands upon topics such as structure, conduct, and performance, which are instrumental in examining potential market power when firms propose to merge. An international trade course, which spans microeconomics and macroeconomics and integrates normal and positive economics, examines policies that affect the prices and the quantities of items on a global scale and it expands upon the production possibilities frontier and opportunity costs. As we move toward conclusion, this last section of the essay provides a foundation for further and deeper inquiry into those areas.

Resource Markets

Up to this point, the essay emphasizes product markets along with the demand and supply model and its respective variables and relationships. As we move into the final pages, attention moves away from product markets toward market failures and resource markets. Resource markets, by definition, are where the factors of production—such as land, labor, and capital—are available for employment in the production of goods and services. Payments for those factors are as follows: land receives rent; labor receives wages; and capital receives interest.

Labor receives payments derived naturally from the demand for goods and services or artificially from the specifications by organizations or legislation. Federal, state, and local governments may create a labor market wage rate through passage of minimum wage laws. Many economists believe those laws raise wages above the market equilibrium point, thereby generating a surplus of labor, which translates into unemployment for some workers or reducing the number of hours of work for others. Labor unions also can dictate what wage rate its members will receive in payment for their services. In short, they hold the capacity to restrict the supply of labor through training, certification, and other types of programs, but argue that those programs instill worker quality and productivity and therefore boost the demand for unionized labor. These programs effectively create barriers to entry in terms of the labor market, but such barriers also exist in the product market as described earlier in this essay.

Market Failure

By way of a review, entry barriers and economic profit suggest the presence of market power. They may also represent the existence of an inordinate amount of influence in the marketplace that tends to favor one party over another in the exchange of products. That influence means that there is a violation of one or more of assumptions listed earlier in this essay. Economists contend that markets are failing when they exhibit characteristics contrary to that set of assumptions. In response to a market failure, government can intervene in a number of ways, including its implementation of price controls. Those controls are of two types, namely price ceilings and price floors. In an effort to protect an industry subject to intense competition, such as dairy farming, a price floor prevents the price from falling below a specified amount; for example, a minimum price for a gallon of milk or a pound of cheese. In an effort to emulate a competitive situation, a price ceiling will prevent the price from rising above a specific amount; for example, the rate for a unit of electricity or natural gas.

A market failure can also prompt governmental actions to protect the physical environment. Market systems also fail when a third party suffers costs imposed by an exchange between two parties, which by definition is a negative externality. Similarly, a market failure occurs when a third party receives benefits in the absence of a direct cost, which by definition is a positive externality; in such a case, an imposition of a tax on beneficiaries is a possibility. Obviously, a more serious problem exists regarding the former. At any rate, externalities provide a rationale for governmental intervention in a market-based economy.

Public Goods

Sometimes the provision of goods and services is most appropriate for delivery through government agencies as opposed to private firms. For instance, public safety services like police and fire protection and national defense are available to consumers regardless of their ability to pay. Furthermore, it is impractical to exclude some citizens from receiving the benefits of defense or protection even though they may not pay directly for the services. Moreover, one person's consumption of those services does not detract from another's consumption. Public goods exhibit those non-exclusionary and non-rival characteristics, which set them apart from private types of goods and services. In a free-enterprise market-based system, for example, the price for a good or service typically excludes those who do not pay for it.

CONCLUSION

As the reader can see, microeconomics covers a lot of ground given its focus on markets and the integral roles of producers, consumers, and organizations. In conclusion, this essay attempts to convey a vast array of concepts, models, and views that undergraduate students will encounter in a study of microeconomics. In closing, this essay opens the possibility of guiding readers toward deeper inquiries into a broad field, and it aims to prepare them for that challenge.

Terms & Concepts

Consumer equilibrium: When the marginal utility per dollar spent for one item equals that for all other items.

Demand: The amount of a good or service an individual consumer or a group of consumers wants at a given price.

Demand schedule: The actual quantities that consumers are willing and able to purchase at various prices.

Elasticity: The sensitivity of consumer purchases to changes in price or income; a coefficient of elasticity results from dividing the percentage change in quantity demanded by the percentage change in price or in income.

Equilibrium: The price and quantity associated with the intersection of the demand and supply curve reflecting alignments among consumers and producers on an item's price and quantity.

Law of demand: Specifies the inverse or negative relationship that exists between an item's demand quantity and its price; quantity and price move in opposite directions.

Law of supply: Specifies the direct or positive relationship that exists between an item's demand quantity and its price; quantity and price move in the same direction.

Marginal revenue: The contribution to total revenue from the sale of one additional item.

Marginal utility: The additional satisfaction an individual receives from the consumption of one additional amount of an item.

Market: A virtual space where consumers and producers interact while exchanging a specific item in accordance with their demand and supply schedules.

Market failure: The results stemming from imperfect or unavailable information for consumer and producer decisions; from an individual or group holding and bringing a disproportionate amount of influence into a market transaction; and/or from an imposition of costs on or harm to third parties and those outside the exchange or transaction.

Price controls: Prevent prices from rising above or falling below a specific dollar amount.

Producers: Firms that supply or provide goods or services desired by consumers.

Quantity demanded: The amount of goods or services that consumers desire at given prices.

Quantity supplied: The amount of goods or services that suppliers are willing and able to produce at given prices.

Public goods: A good or service for which exclusion from nonpayment is unlikely and for which consumption among individuals is independent or without rivalry; deliveries and provisions are usually accomplished through governmental agencies or nonprofit organizations.

Resource market: Consists of the demand for and the supply of labor, land, and capital and their equilibrium respective payments in the form of wages, rent, and interest.

Revenue: The proceeds from the sale of an item; the mathematical product of quantity of items sold times the price of item.

Supply: The amount of a good or service an individual producer or a group of producers will provide at a given price.

Supply schedule: The actual quantities that producers are willing and able to sell at various prices.

BIBLIOGRAPHY

Arnold, R. A. (2011). *Economics* (10th ed.) Mason, OH: Thomson South-Western.

Comanescu, A., & Marinescu, C. (2012). Food paradox—a microeconomic concept. *Economics, Management & Financial Markets, 7,* 473–482.

Guell, R. C. (2007). *Issues in economics today* (3rd ed.). Boston, MA: McGraw-Hill Irwin.

Kamiru, J. G. (2013). The pedagogy of belief and doubt in principles of microeconomics: In quest for a market solution for human organs. *Journal of International Business & Economics, 13,* 167–174.

McConnell, C. R., & Brue, S. L. (2012). *Economics* (19th ed.). New York: McGraw-Hill Irwin.

SUGGESTED READING

Cohn, E., Cohn, S., Balch, D., & Bradley Jr., J. (2004). The relationship between student attitudes toward graphs and performance in economics. *American Economist, 48,* 41–52.

Colander, D. (2005). What economists teach and what economists do. *Journal of Economic Education, 36,* 249–260.

Hill, R., & Myatt, A. (2007). Overemphasis on perfectly competitive markets in microeconomics principles textbooks. *Journal of Economic Education, 38,* 58–76.

Pashigian, B., & Self, J. (2007). Teaching microeconomics in wonderland. *Journal of Economic Education, 38,* 44–57.

Pressman, S. (2011). Microeconomics after Keynes: Post Keynesian economics and public policy. *American Journal of Economics & Sociology, 70,* 511–539.

Pyne, D. (2007). Does the choice of introductory microeconomics textbook matter? *Journal of Economic Education, 38,* 279–296.

Saunders, P. (1991). The third edition of the test of understanding in college economics. *American Economic Review, 81,* 32.

Watts, M., & Lynch, G. (1989). The principles courses revisited. *American Economic Review, 79,* 236.

Essay by Steven R. Hoagland, Ph.D.

PRINCIPLES OF TAXATION

This article examines the basic principles of taxation and how the current tax structure in the United Sates was first initiated. Five categories of taxes are reviewed, including income tax, property tax, sales tax, import tariffs, and social program taxes. Tobacco and alcohol taxes are used to illustrate how policy makers attempt to promote social and behavioral changes, and this article reviews how successful these efforts have been. The evolution of e-commerce and Internet transaction taxes are also examined.

OVERVIEW

Taxation is a method for governments to raise the funds necessary to pay for operations, capital building projects, and social programs. Some form of tax or another can be traced back to well over 3,000 years ago ("A Short History of Taxation," 2008). Taxes have also been levied to meet increases in demand for revenue and during World War I in the United States, Congress raised taxes to help pay for the cost of the war (Tausig, 1917). The cost for a tax administration system is carried by both the governments that levy taxes and by taxpayers who must maintain records of taxable activities and file their taxes with the taxing entity ("Tax Policy: Summary," 2005).

Types of Taxation
There are several forms of taxation that fall into five major categories:

- income taxes
- property taxes
- consumption (sales) taxes
- fees, duties, and tariffs
- specialized taxes

Income Taxes
Taxes on income are levied against individuals and corporations on income they derive from a wide variety of sources. Governments have used income taxes to generate revenue to pay for government operations. In the United States, the income tax was first used to help pay for the cost of the Civil War ("Story of the Income Tax," 1944). During the 1800s, several state and local governments also started taxing income in a variety of ways (Kinsman, 1909). Income is earned from numerous sources, including sale of goods or services, interest on bank accounts or bonds, sale of assets, and sale of stocks, to name just a few. These sources of income can be taxed at different rates depending on the policies of the taxing entity.

Property Taxes
Federal governments charge property taxes on real estate holdings, business assets and equipment, and personal property owned by private citizens. State and local governments also levy property taxes on real estate holdings, business assets and equipment, and personal property owned by private citizens (Hale, 1985). Property tax has become the primary source of revenue for most local governments and provides more revenue than income taxes or sales taxes. In most states, property taxes are collected on all property with the exception of that owned by religious and charitable organizations or property owned by government entities. If property owners do not pay property taxes, then the taxing government places a lien on the property. The past due property taxes must be paid before title of the property can be transferred and, in cases where large sums of overdue taxes are owed, the government can seize the property and sell it to raise the owed taxes (Fisher, 1997).

Consumption (Sales) Taxes
Taxes on economic activities are often referred to as consumption taxes, which are levied on the purchase of goods and services. Governments have used consumption taxes for centuries ("A Short History of Taxation," 2008). In the United States, the first consumption tax was levied in 1791 on distilled spirits ("The Story of Federal Taxation," 1936). Since then, most states have instituted some form of sales taxes when property, goods, or services are purveyed or transferred (Watts, 1938). The general sales tax became popular at the state level in the 1930s. In most transactions, sales tax is collected by businesses and then submitted to the state departments of revenue on a periodic basis (Cornia, et al., 2000). Currently, there are more than 7,000 government entities in the United States that levy some type of sales tax (Haas, 2004).

Social Security, established by President Roosevelt, is a popular government program. Here an AFSCME supporter holds a sign over his head - Hands Off Our Social Security. This photo was taken at a rally in Senate Park, Washington DC, on Feb. 12, 2013. (Courtesy of Djembayz via Wikimedia Commons)

Fees, Duties & Tariffs

Taxes on the international movement of many products are often referred to as customs fees, duties, or tariffs ("A Short History of Taxation," 2008). The

United States first started collecting duties on imported goods in 1789, when the Customs Service was established. The country then needed money to pay for the formation of the new government ("A Continuing Tradition..," 2009). Prior to the implementation and maturation of the income tax programs in the United States, import duties accounted for one of the largest sources of income for the government. More than $25 billion per year was collected on imported items in the early twenty-first century ("International Trade," 2006).

Specialized Program Taxes

Finally, there are specialized taxes that have been instituted to pay for government programs. The social security system in the United States is one of the largest programs for which a specific tax is levied. President Franklin D. Roosevelt started this system as a result of the Great Depression of the 1920s and 1930s (Martin & Weaver, 2005). The program provides retirement benefits for the elderly and a wide variety of benefits for disabled people ("Social Security Act of 1935," 2009). The Social Security Act also established Medicare, which is the largest health insurance program in the United States ("Medicare," 2008). Although popular among benefit recipients, it has long been known that social security systems in several countries will face fiscal strains in the future as the number of workers paying their social security taxes declines compared to the number of people receiving benefits (Börsch-Supan, 1991).

Tax Collection

At the national level in the United States, the Internal Revenue Service (IRS) is responsible for collecting taxes based on income. The IRS was established under President Abraham Lincoln in 1862 to collect taxes to help pay for the Civil War. Ratified in 1913, the 16th Amendment to the Constitution gave Congress the authority to pass laws that permanently created the federal income tax ("Brief History of IRS," 2009). The IRS is currently organized into several major divisions that focus on tax administration activities ("At-a-Glance," 2009).

In 2008, the IRS processed more than 230 million tax returns ("Tax Stats," 2008), and in 2005, American taxpayers paid more than $2 trillion per year in federal taxes ("Summary of Estimates," 2005). In addition, there are more than $300 billion in taxes that are due to the federal government every year that are not paid. This unpaid amount is often referred to as the tax gap ("Reducing the Tax Gap," 2005).

The collection of state taxes is most often managed by the states' Departments of Revenue. A similar structure is also found in counties across the United States. The organization of state and local revenue collection functions depends on the types of taxes that are being collected. As with the federal government, tax monies collected by the tax administration agency are turned over to the treasury department or a function of that government entity.

APPLICATIONS

Taxes & Social Policy

Taxation is not just a means of raising money to pay for wars or government operations. Taxation has evolved into a method of implementing social policy and has been used to influence business practices as well as individual behavior (Berliant & Rothstein, 2003).

Several tax laws in the United States are designed to either provide rewards or penalties for the way corporations or individuals behave. One such tax policy is known as the negative income tax, which simultaneously helps to support poor families while providing an incentive for heads of households to work in paying jobs (Moffitt, 2003). In both of these cases, tax policy is addressing the disparate distribution of wealth and resources in modern societies (Steinmo, 2003).

The social and political debate about the design of the tax system and the purpose and effectiveness of various taxes is endless. The principles behind tax policies can be very complex as well as riddled with bias ("Understanding the Tax Reform Debate," 2005). In the United States, there are opposing forces that attempt to influence tax policy for their advantage or in line with philosophical or political points of view. Corporations, of course, attempt to influence policy makers that they should not pay high taxes or they work to pressure local governments to reduce corporate property taxes. Republicans and Democrats are often opposed in their views on tax policy, as are religious conservatives and social liberals (Peele, 2005). There are also various noneconomic social factors that influence

President Franklin D. Roosevelt (Courtesy of Library of Congress)

taxpayers' viewpoints about the fairness of tax laws (Ackert, Martinez-Vasquez, & Rider, 2004).

Several theories have been put forth as to how and why humans consume addictive substances. Likewise, there are conflicting theories about the relationship between the cost of consuming addictive substances and patterns of consumption. Some of these theories have been adopted by individuals, social agencies, and government policy makers in efforts to use economics as a deterrent to the consumption of addictive substances. They believe that if taxes are increased on legalized addictive substances, people will consume less of these substances. As a result, numerous tax laws have been passed to heavily tax tobacco and alcohol (Andersson, Bask, & Melkersson, 2006).

Tobacco Taxes for Revenue & Health Reform

Tobacco taxes have historically been a very good source of revenue for local, state, and federal governments. However, since the United States surgeon general's report on the harmful health effects of tobacco use was released in 1964, governments have been steadily increasing tobacco taxes to reduce smoking and to offset the negative impact of tobacco-related illness on health care costs (Meier & Licari, 1997). The public sentiment toward tobacco has shifted since the 1964 surgeon general's report, but not without considerable debate and lobbying efforts by those supporting tobacco and those opposing tobacco (Givel, 2006).

The goal of the World Health Organization (WHO) has been to get countries around the world to address tobacco usage and the health problems that result. WHO supported the Framework Convention on Tobacco Control (FCTC), an agreement among the 192 member countries of WHO designed to decrease tobacco use. WHO has presented evidence that countries that have increased the tobacco tax, supported public awareness programs on the hazards of smoking, and placed restrictions on where people can smoke have succeeded in reducing tobacco use (Chaloupka, et al., 2003).

Although taxes on cigarettes vary from country to country, they generally comprise 30 to 50 percent of the cost of cigarettes. Policy makers have hoped that higher taxes on cigarettes would deter people from smoking by increasing their personal smoking costs (Hoang Van, et al., 2006). There is, however, debate as to the long-term effectiveness of higher taxes to reduce tobacco consumption. Since these efforts have been in place for less than two decades, it may be difficult to determine if higher tobacco taxes will actually reduce consumption (Sugarman, 2003).

Alcohol Taxes for Revenue & Health Reform

Over the last several decades, many health officials and law enforcement agencies have taken the position that alcohol causes considerable health and social problems. Like higher tobacco taxes, the effectiveness of higher alcohol taxes for the purpose of decreasing consumption is heavily debated ("Alcohol Tax," 1987). In fact, distilled spirits were among the first items to have a consumption tax in the United States ("The Story of Federal Taxation," 1936). When the impact of the rise and fall of alcohol prices on consumption have been studied, no clear relationships between price and consumption could be found. It also seems that national cultures affect the consumption patterns more than price (Mäkel, Bloomfield, et al., 2008).

Even though the debate over whether higher alcohol taxes, and thus high alcohol prices, will deter consumption seems to be unsettled, there is still the debate about the economic effect of higher alcohol taxes. Producers of alcoholic beverages as well as purveyors of alcoholic beverages such as liquor stores, bars, and restaurants want to protect their economic interest. They do not want consumption to decrease because it will negatively impact their sales and their profits (Cook, 1982; Giesbrecht, et al., 2004).

Alcohol taxes have also been turned into a competitive tool for adjoining jurisdictions at the state, county, and local level. The government entities that restrict alcohol consumption or heavily tax alcohol consumption are frequently bordered or are in close proximity to other communities or states that use liberalized consumption laws and lower taxes to attract consumers (Rinaldi, 2007). In this situation, tax policy is being used to influence consumptive behavior from two different directions. One side wants to reduce consumption, while the other side wants to increase consumption and gain tax revenues from the direct sales of alcohol as well as other products or services that may be consumed along with alcohol.

ISSUES

Taxation in the Internet Age

The Internet has created a tax debate at the local, state, national, and international levels. The primary issue is the collection of sales tax on e-commerce transactions that occur across international borders and state lines. There are also debates about charging taxes for Internet access services as well as web-based services provided by a variety of pay-per-use websites (Haas, 2004; Stanton, 2007). In an effort to promote e-commerce and the growth of the Internet, the U.S. Congress passed the Internet Tax Freedom Act (ITFA), which expired in 2003, theoretically leaving states and other jurisdictions free to pursue their own sales tax issues (Haas, 2004). However, the taxation of Internet access services met with intense opposition and was again delayed by congressional action (Schroeder, 2007).

At the heart of the debate over Internet taxes is the taxation of sales across state lines in the United States. In 1992, the U.S. Supreme Court decided in *Quill Corp. v. North Dakota* that sellers could not be required to collect sales or use taxes for transactions unless they had physical sales locations within that state. Government entities that collect sales taxes have been opposed to this proposition, even though buyers are often legally required to submit the sales tax that is due to the state voluntarily (Vadum, 2000).

As the amount of such uncollected sales tax grew into the billions of dollars, various government associations started to lobby aggressively to gain access to those tax dollars ("Alliance," 1999). Although it has been difficult to estimate lost tax dollars because of Internet sales, local governments remained steadfast in their desire and their efforts to tax Internet transactions (Meisler, 1998; Miller, 2004). Meanwhile, free market advocates remained active in their efforts to block governments from collecting taxes on Internet transactions and ensure that taxing entities did not attempt to charge higher tax rates for Internet transactions (Ponnuru, 2000).

Another challenge that taxing entities face is how to collect taxes from Internet sales in a manner that is cost effective. Whatever the processes a taxing entity uses to administer its tax system, the administrative costs should not exceed the amount of taxes that are collected (Goolsbee & Zittrain, 1999). The burden on the taxpayer also needs to be considered and requiring Internet sellers to send numerous checks and sales records to different taxing entities could become rather burdensome for them as well (Lukas, 2001).

To simplify the process of collecting taxes on Internet sales, government entities banded together on the Streamlined Sales and Use Tax Agreement (SSUTA). The agreement is designed to establish a uniform process that would ease the collection of taxes by government entities and hopefully provide greater ease for sellers in paying the taxes that are due (De Rugy, 2002; Feinschreiber & Kent, 2003). The SSUTA went into effect in 2005 ("Streamlined," 2005), and within three years, one thousand sellers were voluntarily collecting sales tax on remote sales (Blackston, 2008).

In 2008, the SSUTA continued the debate on how to tax digital products and determined that digital products should not be taxed as tangible personal property, though member states were left free to tax digital products in other manners (Harris & Kulwicki, 2008).

As state budgets shriveled during the 2008–2009 recession and lingering financial downturn, the issue was revisited by Congress, and the Marketplace Fairness Act was passed in 2013. The act at last provided a framework for state taxation of Internet commerce by allowing states to require Internet sellers doing annual business of more than $1 million to collect and remit sales taxes to the states in which sales originate, thus overriding the standing legal objection that the seller must also have a presence in the state in which the sale originates. Internet retailers had objected that the logistics of sorting out remittances to the states, which vary widely in their sales tax laws, was too onerous. The act dealt with this objection by restricting the requirement to states that abide by the SSUTA (Yang, 2013). Brick-and-mortar retailers applauded the act for leveling the playing field, at least somewhat (Adams, 2013).

CONCLUSION

Taxation is virtually universal among all countries, states, and local governments. The five major types of taxes are also used to some extent in industrialized countries around the world. In terms of revenue for government operations, income taxes and property taxes yield the largest amounts of revenue. In addition, specialized taxes, such as those that support the social security system in the United States, are designed to make such programs self-sufficient.

Although taxation is commonly accepted, policies on what to tax and how much to tax are always being debated. When social policy is executed through the taxation process, the debate about taxes can be even more heated. In the case of tobacco and alcohol taxes, policy makers and anti-tobacco and anti-alcohol advocates are now in agreement that these items should be taxed heavily. The impact of higher taxes on the consumption of addictive substances has yet to be proven. That is with the exception that higher taxes can yield more revenue for taxing entities. The desired shifts in social behavior, on the other hand, may be temporarily effective, but it is too soon to tell if they will have the desired affect in the long term.

The Internet has created new debates about taxes and has presented policy makers and taxing entities with new challenges. At the federal level, government policy has been favoring the economic growth that has resulted from e-commerce and other digital services and products. At the local and state level, the perception has been that those taxing entities were losing out on revenue. The battle over Internet taxes and digital property taxes is far from over, and it will likely be many years before taxation practices can actually catch up to the new digital age.

TERMS & CONCEPTS

The Great Depression: The global economic collapse that started after World War I and was accelerated by the stock market crashes of the late 1920s. Government intervention was required for economic recovery, and numerous social programs and government policies designed to stabilize the economy were enacted.

Negative income tax: A tax system designed to incentivize lower income people to work by providing tax rebates for earned income and that structures tax credits in a manner that supports the continued economic productivity of the individual.

Social policy: Laws, regulations, and methods by which a government attempts to reengineer society and control or change the behavior of individuals or corporations.

Social security: A government program that provides benefits to selected classes of recipients based on government policy, required participation or the individual, and eligibility under program regulations.

Tax administration: The organization, personnel, facilities, and technology that a government entity needs to collect taxes and the maintaining of records, analyzing of income, and submitting of tax payments by taxpayers.

Taxing entity: The national, state, county, or local government entity that has the authority to levy a tax.

BIBLIOGRAPHY

Ackert, L., Martinez-Vasquez, J., & Rider, M. (2004). Tax policy design in the presence of social preferences: Some experimental evidence. *Working Paper Series (Federal Reserve Bank of Atlanta), 2004*, 1–33.

Adams, M. (2013). Online sales tax could pump up retail values. *Real Estate Finance & Investment*, 23.

Alcohol tax policy reform. (1987). *American Journal of Public Health, 77*, 106–111.

Alliance of counties calls for net taxes. (1999). *Journal of Internet Law, 3*, 26.

Andersson, L., Bask, M., & Melkersson, M. (2006). Economic man and the consumption of addictive goods: The case of two goods. *Substance Use & Misuse, 41*, 453–466.

At-a-glance: IRS divisions and principal offices. (2009).

Berliant, M., & Rothstein, P. (2003). Possibility, impossibility, and history in the origins of the marriage tax. *National Tax Journal, 56*, 303–317.

Blackston, M. (2008). Closing the online tax loophole. *State Legislatures, 34*, 24–25.

Börsch-Supan, A. (1991). Aging population: Problems and policy options in the US and Germany. *Economic Policy, 6*, 103–139.

Brief history of IRS. (2009).

Chaloupka, F., Jha, P., Corrao, M., Silva, V., Ross, H., Ciecierski, C., et al. (2003). Global efforts for reducing the burden of smoking. *Disease Management & Health Outcomes, 11*, 647–661.

A continuing tradition of 220 years of service to the nation. (2009).

Cook, P. (1982). Alcohol taxes as a public health measure. *British Journal of Addiction, 77*, 245–250.

Cornia, G., Edmiston, K., Sheffrin, S., Sexton, T., Sjoquist, D., & Zorn, C. (2000). An analysis of the feasibility of implementing a single rate sales tax. *National Tax Journal, 53*, 1327–1350.

De Rugy, V. (2002). State bureaucrats plot higher Internet taxes. *Human Events, 58*, 10.

Feinschreiber, R., & Kent, M. (2003). Understanding the streamlined sales and use tax agreement. *Corporate Business Taxation Monthly, 4*, 21.

Fisher, G. (1997). Some lessons from the history of the property tax. (Cover story). *Assessment Journal, 4*, 40.

Giesbrecht, N., Greenfield, T., Anglin, L., & Johnson, S. (2004). Changing the price of alcohol in the United States: Perspectives from the alcohol industry, public health, and research. *Contemporary Drug Problems, 31*, 711–736.

Givel, M. (2006). Punctuated equilibrium in limbo: The tobacco lobby and U.S. state policymaking from 1990 to 2003. *Policy Studies Journal, 34*, 405–418.

Goolsbee, A., & Zittrain, J. (1999). Evaluating the costs and benefits of taxing Internet commerce. *National Tax Journal, 52*, 413–428.

Hale, D. (1985). The evolution of the property tax: A study of the relation between public finance and political theory. *Journal of Politics, 47*, 382.

Haas, A. (2004). Internet taxation: The battle begins! *Journal of State Taxation, 23*, 43–50.

Harris, S., & Kulwicki, L. (2008). Update on streamlined sales and use tax agreement: Taxation of digital products. *Corporate Business Taxation Monthly, 9*, 13–38.

Hoang Van, K., Ross, H., Levy, D., Nguyen Thac, M., & Vu Thi Bich, N. (2006). The effect of imposing a higher, uniform tobacco tax in Vietnam. *Health Research Policy & Systems, 4*, 6–16.

International trade: Customs' revised bonding policy reduces risk of uncollected duties, but concerns about uneven implementation and effects remain. (2006). *Report to the Chairman, Committee on Ways and Means, House of Representatives.*

Kinsman, D. (1909). The present period of income tax activity in the American states. *Quarterly Journal of Economics, 23*, 296–306.

Lewit, E. (1989). U.S. tobacco taxes: Behavioral effects and policy implications. *British Journal of Addiction, 84*, 1217–1134.

Lukas, A. (2001). Should Internet sales be taxed? *USA Today Magazine, 129*(2668), 14.

Mäkel, P., Bloomfield, K., Gustafsson, N., Huhtanen, P., & Room, R. (2008). Changes in volume of drinking after changes in alcohol taxes and travellers' allowances: Results from a panel study. *Addiction, 103*, 181–191.

Martin, P., & Weaver, D. (2005). Social Security: A program and policy history. *Social Security Bulletin, 66*, 1–15.

Medicare: Thousands of Medicare Part B providers abuse the federal tax system. (2008). *Testimony before the Permanent Subcommittee on Investigations, Committee on Homeland Security and Governmental Affairs, U.S. Senate.*

Meier, K., & Licari, M. (1997). The effect of cigarette taxes on cigarette consumption, 1955 through 1994. *American Journal of Public Health, 87*, 1126–1130.

Meisler, D. (1998). Let taxes trail sales from stores to Web, groups urge. *Bond Buyer, 325*(30471), 1.

Miller, M. (2004). Technology and politics: The choices for 2004. *PC Magazine, 23*, 7–8.

Moffitt, R. (2003). The negative income tax and the evolution of U.S. welfare policy. *Journal of Economic Perspectives, 17*, 119–140.

Peele, G. (2005). Electoral politics, ideology and American social policy. *Social Policy & Administration, 39*, 150–165.

Ponnuru, R. (2000). The tax man cometh. *National Review, 52*, 44–46.

Rinaldi, G. (2007). The use of economic tools to develop a consensus on alcohol policies within and between jurisdictions. *Contemporary Drug Problems, 34*, 729–751.

Schroeder, P. (2007). Bush signs into law seven-year extension of ban on Internet taxes. *Bond Buyer, 362*(32746), 6.

A short history of taxation. (2008, October). *New Internationalist,* 16–17.

Stanton, L. (2007). Despite progress in state-industry talks, issues remain in Internet tax debate. *Telecommunications Reports, 73*, 8–9.

Steinmo, S. (2003). The evolution of policy ideas: Tax policy in the 20th century. *British Journal of Politics & International Relations, 5*, 206–236.

The story of federal taxation in American history. (1936). *Congressional Digest, 15*, 135–137.

Story of the income tax. (1944). *Congressional Digest, 23*, 260–262.

Streamlined sales tax agreement goes into effect. (2005). *State Legislatures, 31*, 5.

Sugarman, S. (2003). A balanced tobacco control policy. *American Journal of Public Health, 93*, 416–418.

Table 2: Numbers of Returns Filed by Type of Return Fiscal Years 2007 and 2008. (2008).

Tausig, F. (1917). The War Tax Act of 1917. *Quarterly Journal of Economics, 32*, 1–37.

Tax policy: Summary of estimates of the costs of the federal tax system. (2005, August). *Report to Congressional Requesters.*

Understanding the tax reform debate: Background, criteria, and questions: GAO-05-1009S. (2005). *GAO Reports,* 1.

United States Congress. (1935). Social Security Act of 1935.

Vadum, M. (2000). Cox: Congress won't expand state sales tax powers for Internet. *Bond Buyer, 331*(30816), 5.

Walker, D. (2005, April 14). Reducing the tax gap can contribute to fiscal sustainability but will require a variety of strategies. *Testimony before the Committee on Finance, U. S. Senate.*

Watts, D. (1938). History and development of the sales tax. *Congressional Digest, 17*, 265–267.

Yang, J.S. (2013). The impact of the Marketplace Fairness Act of 2013 on internet commerce taxation. *Journal of State Taxation, 32*, 13–45.

SUGGESTED READING

Alexander, A. (2000). The tax policy regime in American politics, 1941-1951. *Congress & the Presidency, 27*, 59.

Banthin, C. (2004). Cheap smokes: State and federal responses to tobacco tax evasion over the Internet. *Health Matrix: Journal of Law Medicine, 14*, 325–356.

Boyd, R., & Seldon, B. (1991). Revenue and land-use effects of proposed changes in sin taxes: A general equilibrium perspective. *Land Economics, 67*, 365.

Buehler, A. (1931). The general sales tax in the fiscal system. *Harvard Business Review, 9*, 348–359.

Cahoon, C., & Brown, W. (1973). The interstate tax dilemma—A proposed solution. *National Tax Journal, 26*, 187–197.

Conway, K. (1997). Labor supply, taxes, and government spending: A microeconometric analysis. *Review of Economics & Statistics, 79*, 50–67.

Cornick, P. (1959). The property tax and housing. *American Journal of Economics & Sociology, 19*, 17–25.

Elliott, G. (2005). Imported works of art face higher taxes. *Accountancy, 135*(1340), 112.

Fortune, J. (1972). Excise taxes, tariffs and imports. *Applied Economics, 4*, 197.

Furman, J. (2008). Health reform through tax reform: A primer. *Health Affairs, 27*, 622–632.

Garner, C. (2005). Consumption taxes: Macroeconomic effects and policy issues. *Economic Review (01612387), 90*, 5–29.

Gemmell, N., & Morrissey, O. (2005). Distribution and poverty impacts of tax structure reform in developing countries: How little we know. *Development Policy Review, 23*, 131–144.

Greenhut, M., & Norman, G. (1986). Spatial pricing with a general cost function: The effects of taxes on imports. *International Economic Review, 27*, 761.

Irwin, D. (1998). Changes in U.S. tariffs: The role of import prices and commercial policies. *American Economic Review, 88*, 1015.

Jeske, K., & Kitao, S. (2005). Health insurance and tax policy. *Working Paper Series (Federal Reserve Bank of Atlanta), 2005*, 1–27.

Koski, A., Sirén, R., Vuori, E., & Poikolainen, K. (2007). Alcohol tax cuts and increase in alcohol-positive sudden deaths—A time-series intervention analysis. *Addiction, 102*, 362–368.

Maroney, J., Rupert, T., & Wartick, M. (2002). The perceived fairness of taxing social security benefits: The effect of explanations based on different dimensions of tax equity. *Journal of the American Taxation Association, 24*, 79–92.

Martinez, M. (1997). Don't tax you, don't tax me, tax the fella behind the tree: Partisan and turnout effects on tax policy. *Social Science Quarterly (University of Texas Press), 78*, 895–906.

McNulty, J. (2000). Flat tax, consumption tax, consumption-type income tax proposals in the United States: A tax policy discussion of fundamental tax reform. *California Law Review, 88*, 2095.

Mieszkowski, P. (1966). The comparative efficiency of tariffs and other tax-subsidy schemes as a means of obtaining revenue or protecting domestic production. *Journal of Political Economy, 74*, 587.

Moore, M. (1996). Death and tobacco taxes. *RAND Journal of Economics, 27*, 415–428.

Rivlin, A. (1989). The continuing search for a popular tax. *American Economic Review, 79*, 113.

Rolph, E. (1950). Equity versus efficiency in federal tax policy. *American Economic Review, 40*, 391.

Snavely, K. (1988). Innovations in state tax administration. *Public Administration Review, 48*, 903–910.

A statement of tax concepts to be used as a basis for teaching income taxation. (1969). *Accounting Review, 44*, 1–18.

Stone, E. (2005). Adhering to the old line: Uncovering the history and political function of the unrelated business income tax. *Emory Law Journal, 54*, 1475–1556.

Thorson, D. (1965). An analysis of the sources of continued controversy over the tax treatment of family income. *National Tax Journal, 18*, 113–132.

Tin-Chun, L. (2006). The impact of corporation income tax policy on investment expenditures: A United States survey. *International Journal of Management, 23*, 412–418.

Weinrobe, M. (1971). Corporate taxes and the United States balance of trade. *National Tax Journal, 24*, 79–86.

Yeates, N. (2005). The General Agreement on Trade in Services (GATS): What's in it for Social Security? *International Social Security Review, 58*, 3–22.

Essay by Michael Erbschloe, M.A.

PROPERTY AND LIABILITY INSURANCE

This article will provide an overview of property and liability insurance. The article will explain the nature of an insurance contract and important concepts relating to property and liability insurance. These concepts include the coverage commonly provided by homeowners' and business owners' property insurance policies and the basis for the premiums charged by insurers to cover property under an insurance policy. Also, an explanation of liability insurance is provided along with information about the most common type of liability insurance—commercial general liability insurance—and exemptions that are typical in these policies. Other issues that frequently arise in conjunction with property and liability insurance, such as subrogation, reinsurance, and bad faith causes of action, also are described. This article provides an explanation of some of the factors that affect insurance rates and policies, such as insurance regulation, risk, and insurable interests. Finally, the issues that commonly arise relating to the liability of insurers, such as the procedures that policyholders must follow to file claims, the defenses that insurers typically use to dispute claims, and the measure of recovery that is used to assess claims and determine the proceeds paid by insurers in response to those claims, are explained.

OVERVIEW

Insurance is essentially a way to manage risk and protect assets against potential financial loss. In exchange for a fee, known as a premium, risk is transferred from one entity to another. There are many different types of insurance, and each one type provides coverage for different assets. For instance, life insurance provides a monetary benefit to a decedent's family upon the death of the insured; automobile insurance covers legal liability claims against a driver and any loss of or damage to the insured's vehicle itself; property insurance provides protection against risks to property arising from natural disasters or criminal activity; and liability insurance covers legal claims that are brought by third parties against the insured. Each type of insurance differs in the scope of coverage it provides, the premiums that are charged, and the procedures that are required for

policyholders to maintain coverage, file claims, and receive payments.

Property and liability insurance are both common forms of insurance. Property insurance is often sold by insurers in tandem with other types of insurance. For instance, when people purchase a home, they generally buy a homeowner's insurance policy that covers damage to the home and property and the replacement value of the owner's belongings. The owner or management of a company may purchase a business owner's policy that will cover damage or loss to the property. Liability insurance is routinely purchased by businesses to cover any liability from damages or losses owed to a third party that arise from conduct relating to its business activities or its agents or employees. The following sections provide a more detailed explanation of property and liability insurance policies.

Basic Concepts in Property & Liability Insurance

Insurance is a unique form of contract, known as a policy, between an individual or entity and an insurer, whereby the policyholder pays the insurer regular installments, called premiums, and in return receives financial protection or reimbursement against losses from the insurer. The insurance company pools the premium payments of its policyholders along with other income-generating assets to create a reserve fund from which payments are made. Insurance companies assess the risks involved in insuring various assets against loss or damage and use this information to determine whether to underwrite insurance policies and to develop appropriate rates for premiums and coverage limits for claims. Property and liability insurance policies are commonly purchased by individuals and businesses to protect their most valuable assets. The following sections provide further detail about these two types of insurance policies.

Nature of Insurance

An insurance policy is generally characterized by distribution of risk among a substantial number of members through an insurer engaged primarily in the business of insurance. Risk distribution acts to mitigate the onus of an individual or a business entity single-handedly bearing the full consequences

Hurricane Irma moved through parts of Florida in December of 2017. Blue tarps cover the roof of this damaged home. (Courtesy of Liz Roll/FEMA News Photo)

of a misfortune. Most individuals and businesses do not have sufficient cash reserves on hand to cover significant losses to their property or to pay substantial damages in the event of a lawsuit. However, most of these same individuals and businesses can afford to make reasonable monthly, quarterly, or even annual payments to an insurer that will in turn pay these significant costs when they arise.

Insurers use statistics and the law of averages to determine when it is economically feasible to underwrite insurance policies. When insurers underwrite an insurance policy, the insurance company assumes the risks of the occurrence of any of the events it lists in the policy, which is a contract of insurance wherein the term, coverage, premiums, and deductibles of the contract are listed in writing. Insurers fix the premium rates that policy members pay by predicting the number and size of losses during the period of the insurance policy and then spreading these costs evenly among its members. Although payments on a claim, or a request for reimbursement from an insurance company when the insured has suffered a loss that is covered under an insurance policy, can be substantial, they may not occur very frequently. Thus, insurance companies are able to build their cash reserves by collecting premium payments from a substantial number of policyholders and only paying claims for losses that are relatively infrequent.

The process whereby insurers allocate prospective risks among many members to minimize the economic liability for any one member is what distinguishes an insurance policy from a traditional contract. In most contracts, one party is willing to assume the liability of another only for some consideration. For instance, a surety (a person or organization that promises in writing to pay the debt of another in the event of default) generally accepts this responsibility only upon receipt of payment or some other type of consideration. However, in an insurance contract, the insurer promises to cover an economic loss that falls within the scope of a policy held by any of its policyholders. Thus, the one-to-one nature of the exchange of liability for consideration in traditional contracts is diffused among many members in insurance contracts.

Finally, insurance policies differ from traditional contracts in that they are written by an insurer that is primarily in the business of insurance. There are other types of contracts that have the common elements of distribution of risk among a sizeable group of participants, such as warranty contracts that cover certain types of merchandise such as household appliances. However, these appliance manufacturers are not primarily in the business of insurance, and the purpose of the risk distribution in these contracts is merely to obtain an amount of immediate income to defray the potential future expense of rendering services on the appliances.

Property Insurance
Property insurance provides protection against most risks to property, such as damages resulting from fire, theft, or weather events. Specialized forms of property insurance may be sold to cover specific types of damage, such as fires, floods, or earthquakes. Property insurance is often packaged with other types of insurance and sold as homeowner's insurance or a business owner's policy.

Homeowner's Insurance
Homeowner's insurance typically includes a number of sections. These sections define the terms and scope of insurance coverage relating to different assets. For instance, a homeowner's insurance policy may include sections that specify the policy's coverage for the main dwelling, other structures on the property, the owner's personal property, the loss of use of the property, and any liabilities arising from loss or damage to the property, such as the personal liability of the owner and coverage for medical payments.

The portions of the policy that cover the dwelling and any additional structures on the property state the coverage limits in the case of damage or total loss to these structures. If there is a total loss, the amount paid is based on the policy limit of the insurance contract and the type of coverage provided. For instance, structures other than the main dwelling house, like garages, sheds, or guest houses, are usually covered at 10 percent of the limit set for the main dwelling. In other words, if an insurance contract provides $500,000 coverage for the main dwelling, it will likely provide up to $50,000 coverage for the other structures. If landscaped property that includes trees and other shrubbery is protected against loss or damage by the policy, the coverage is generally about 5 percent of the dwelling limit. Finally, most property insurance policies cover personal belongings, such as jewelry, artwork, furniture, computers, and other similar items, and many include coverage for third party liability, which protects property owners against personal liability if somebody is injured while on their property.

Business Owner's Policy

Insurance companies that sell business insurance typically offer policies that bundle property and liability protections into one package. These packages are known as business owner's policies (BOPs). BOPs include three types of coverage:

Property insurance for buildings and contents owned by the company.

Business interruption insurance, which covers the loss of income due to any catastrophe that disrupts the operation of the business so as to cause no income.

Any additional expenses that businesses may incur while operating out of a temporary location due to damage or loss of its office space or facilities until the original property is restored or rebuilt.

Finally, BOPs generally offer liability protection, which covers legal responsibilities arising from harms that a business or its employees cause to another. These responsibilities can be the result of a business doing something or failing to do something in its business operations that causes bodily injury or property damage to another. For instance, a BOP may provide coverage for liabilities stemming from defective products or faulty services rendered by an employee. It is important to distinguish BOPs from other types of insurance that businesses may purchase to cover specific aspects of their operations. BOPs, for example, do not provide coverage for automobiles, workers' compensation claims, or health and disability benefits. These are generally covered through other types of insurance.

Premiums

Insurance companies determine the amount of premiums that they charge policyholders based on the statistical frequency of major risks to a home or business, such as through fire or theft. Property insurance premiums are set by considering several factors, such as the type of building structure, the presence or absence of safety measures, and the proximity of the property to potentially dangerous hazards. Once an insurance company has established a baseline premium, the individual policies it offers can be easily adjusted to allow each insurer to purchase additional types of insurance or greater amounts of coverage for additional assets. Some states have set caps on certain types of insurance rates, whereby premiums may not be charged above the limits established by state law.

Liability Insurance

One of the most prevalent types of insurance today is third-party liability insurance. Liability insurance differs from first-party insurance, such as life or property insurance, in that liability insurance covers the liability of the insured for damage caused to a third party rather than a loss to the insured's own property. While liability insurance provides important protections, its coverage is not universal. The damages or tort liabilities that it protects against are generally carefully specified in the policy, and if liabilities arise from an occurrence or accident that is not covered by the policy, the individual or business charged with causing the damage may be personally responsible for those costs.

Comprehensive General Liability Insurance

The most common type of third-party liability insurance in use today is the commercial general liability (CGL) policy, also known as comprehensive general liability insurance. The basic CGL insurance policy provides coverage up to the face amount of the policy for bodily injury and property damage that the insured becomes legally obligated to pay, including harm caused to intangible property, such as a company's goodwill or reputation. In addition, many CGL policies provide coverage for damages arising from any personal injury suits filed by a customer or from libel or slander suits filed by a competitor. However, like most forms of liability insurance, to cover legal responsibilities resulting from bodily injury or property damage, most CGL policies require that the injury results from an occurrence or accident that is defined in the policy.

Exclusions

Liability insurance policies, including CGL policies, frequently have exclusions that limit the coverage provided by the policy. Any activities, errors, or omissions that the insurance company will not cover or that are beyond the insurer's interest are referred to as exclusions and are specified in a separate section of the policy. Common exclusions include any fraudulent, criminal, malicious, or dishonest acts committed by the insured that result in the incurrence of damages or a lawsuit.

In addition, one notable exclusion in CGL policies is the work product exclusion. This exclusion generally precludes coverage for property damage to the insured's products or to a third party's property caused by work done by or on behalf of the insured or for claims that the insured's product or completed work was not completed according the claimant's expectation. This exclusion has been redefined by the courts and the insurance industry over the years, but in 1973 the insurance industry specified that the work product exclusion would eliminate coverage in any case in which a defective product damages another part of the insured's work, even if the insured's work was performed by a subcontractor or another entity working on behalf of the insured. This revision has since been upheld by the courts and continues to be included in many CGL policies today.

COMMON ISSUES IN INSURANCE LAW

Insurable Interests

While insurance provides a means of protecting an insured against a financial loss, insurance is not meant to provide the insured with a net profit after he or she has received a payment for a claim. Insurance companies prevent overpayments by requiring that policyholders have an insurable interest in the asset they are seeking to insure. An insurable interest exists when loss or damage would cause the insured to suffer a measurable financial loss. For example, if a dwelling is damaged by fire, the value of the property has been reduced. A measurable financial loss thus occurs whether the homeowner pays to have the house rebuilt or sells it at a reduced price.

Further, with regard to property insurance, the insurable interest must exist both at the time the insurance is purchased and at the time a loss occurs. Thus, the homeowner must own the home when he or she buys a homeowner's policy to insure it, and he or she must also be the owner at the time the home experiences any damage or loss for which he or she will file a claim against the insurance policy.

Subrogation

Subrogation occurs when one person or business entity assumes the legal rights of a person for whom expenses or a debt has been paid. In the insurance industry, subrogation occurs when an insurance company pays a policyholder for injuries and losses he or she sustained that are covered by the policy, assumes the policyholder's right to sue for damages, and then sues the party that injured the policyholder to collect the damages originally due the policyholder. Subrogated rights arise in the insurer by operation of law, which means they arise regardless of whether they are provided for in the insurance contract or in any transactions between the insured and a third party. They apply to all causes of action the insured may have against the third party with regard to the loss concerned, whether the cause of action arises from a tort or contract claim.

Because property insurance covers assets whose value is most easily determined, which is generally based upon an assessment of fair market value, subrogation almost always applies in these policies. In terms of liability insurance, insurers are generally able to either assume any rights of the insured against a third party in order to recover any money the insurer has paid to the insured or to seek recovery from the insured of any sums it has paid to the insured that have resulted in the insured being overcompensated, such as if an insurer paid a claim in full and the insured also recovered damages from the third party for the same injury.

Reinsurance

Insurance policies are essentially a form of risk management. Individuals and businesses buy insurance policies to minimize their exposure to substantial losses, and insurance companies set premiums based on the likelihood of a covered event actually occurring. While insurance companies carefully assess their risks before deciding whether to underwrite policies, insurers sometimes decide to minimize their own exposure to liability on their outstanding policies by taking out liability insurance with another insurance company, called a reinsurer. For instance, if an economic downturn threatens to result in significant business reversals or if the possibility of excessive losses under its existing policies brings its own solvency into question, an insurer may bolster its financial position by insuring its own potential liabilities with another insurance company. This allows an insurer to seek indemnification, or compensation from another for a loss paid, from the reinsurer for some of the money it pays on claims filed by its policyholders.

Reinsurance is an important aspect of the insurance process because it allows insurers greater capacity to underwrite policies and lends a measure of financial stability to the insurance industry by spreading the risks faced by any one insurer over a much larger base. With the exception of mutual insurance companies, which generally do not have the authority to reinsure, any insurer authorized to issue original insurance may also take steps to enter into reinsurance contracts. However, there are some insurers that exclusively underwrite reinsurance policies.

When a reinsurance policy is drafted, it can provide that the reinsurer will indemnify the insurer for the full amount of any liability incurred on a policy up to the limits of the reinsurance contract, or it can provide that the reinsurer will indemnify the insurer for only a specific proportion of any such liability. The amount of indemnification that the insurer may seek depends on any limits or regulations set by state law. In some states, insurers are prohibited from reinsuring their total risk on any policy and thus must retain some risk on their current liabilities. Today reinsurance is a global industry.

Factors Affecting Property & Liability Insurance

Insurance companies are in the business of providing financial coverage to policyholders for events that would likely be economically catastrophic without the protections offered by insurance policies. Because the stakes in these claims can be high, the insurance industry is regulated by court decisions and statutes enacted by state legislatures and administrative agencies. While these regulations serve to ensure that the insurance industry is free from fraudulent or abusive practices, insurers must also protect their financial viability by constantly evaluating whether the assumption of certain risks could expose them to liabilities that could cripple their ability to survive. In order to receive a payment based on the financial coverage provided in an insurance policy, the beneficiaries of the proceeds of an insurance policy must be found to have an insurable interest, or an interest in the property that is insured, in order for a claim to be valid. These factors that affect property and liability insurance policies are explained further in the following sections.

Insurance Regulation

Regulation of the business of insurance emanates from three primary sources—the courts, state legislatures, and state regulatory agencies. Courts regulate insurers when they render decisions on the scope of coverage of an individual insurance policy or deliver rulings that define the permissible activities that insurers may take in underwriting policies or investigating claims. State legislatures also regulate the insurance industry, and all states have enacted legislation relating to insurers primarily in three ways. First, many states have set controls on the rates insurers may charge for policies in order to ensure that the rates are not inadequate, excessive, or discriminatory. Second, states have enacted legislation to prevent unfair practices by insurance companies toward their insureds and competitive insurance companies. Finally, states have created procedures to aid in the prevention of insolvency of insurers so that the assets of the insured are protected.

At the federal level, Congress passed the McCarran-Ferguson Act of 1945. It mandates that state law governs the regulation of insurance and that no congressional act can invalidate any state law, unless the federal law specifically relates to insurance. Thus, a federal law that does not specifically regulate the business of insurance cannot preempt a state law related to insurance regulation. Under the McCarran-Ferguson Act, state departments of insurance are primarily responsible for overseeing the operations of insurance companies and protecting policyholders from insurer insolvency and bad faith on the part of insurers. To accomplish this, state insurance agencies have established policies that regulate the licensure of insurers and their agents, enforcement of state laws regarding the insurance industry, and oversight of the professional conduct of insurers.

Risk

Historically, under the American system of jurisprudence, the financial consequences of any economic loss that occurred and that was not covered by insurance would be borne by one of three individuals. First, the person suffering the misfortune may bear the economic loss. Second, under the common law, any person who negligently or deliberately caused the misfortune to occur could be compelled to bear the economic loss. Finally, state or federal statues may require a party to bear the loss, such as an employer under workmen's compensation statutes.

While there is no way to reassign the emotional or psychological losses that accompany any misfortune, insurance contracts distribute the risk of economic loss among as many members as possible. By paying a premium into a general fund out of which payment will be made for a defined economic loss, "each member contributes to a small degree toward compensation for the losses suffered by any member of the group. The member has no way of knowing in advance whether he will receive in compensation more than he contributes or whether he will merely be paying for the losses of others in the group; but his primary goal is to exchange the potentially devastating consequences of facing a loss alone for the opportunity to pay a fixed amount into the fund, knowing that that amount is the maximum he will lose on account of the particular type of risk insured against" (Dobbyn, 2003, pp. 2–4).

In the context of businesses insuring against losses to merchandise and other property, the premium paid into the fund is considered a cost of doing business and is computed into the prices charged to the public for their products or services. In this way, the distribution of risk is spread even more widely through the entire community of businesses and consumers.

Bad Faith Causes of Action

In a further effort to protect the interests of insureds in their dealings with insurance companies, the majority of state courts have fashioned a cause of action known as a "bad faith cause of action." The basis of this cause of action is the doctrine of good faith and fair dealing, which holds that all parties to a contract must act in such a way that the other party to the contract is not hindered from reaping the benefits of the contract. Although the doctrine has historically been a central tenet in contract law, in the context of insurance policies, courts have chosen to apply it solely as the foundation for a cause of action by insureds against insurers. The doctrine of good faith and fair dealing exists as a covenant, or a legally binding arrangement between parties, that arises by implication and is enforceable even if it is not reduced to writing in a contract.

APPLICATIONS

Understanding the Scope of Property & Liability Insurance

Before an insurer is required to pay a claim filed by a policyholder, there must first be a judgment or determination that the claim falls within the coverage provided by the insurance policy and that the insurance policy is valid and binding. Once these questions are resolved and a determination is made that the insurer must pay the claim, the insurance company then becomes liable to the insured for the amount of the claim. To test the merits of any claim, insurance companies require that claims be filed according to specific procedures that enable the insurer to collect the information necessary to determine the scope of the damage or liability and to assess whether the loss falls within the provisions of the insured's policy. If the insurer discovers any information that mitigates or invalidates a claim, the insurer may raise certain defenses to dispute the claim. Also, insurance companies may limit their exposure to certain risks by including limitations or exceptions to the scope of the coverage a policy provides. These issues are discussed in more detail in the following sections.

Procedure for Filing Claims

Insurance policies commonly contain specific provisions requiring the insured to comply with certain requirements as conditions to the payment of proceeds. If a policyholder fails to follow these procedures, the insurer may have a defense against payment of the claim. These procedures allow the insurance company to collect and document all of the information it will need to test the merits of an individual claim.

One procedure that almost all insurers require is for the insured to provide the insurer with notice of a loss immediately after it occurs. This procedure allows the insurer to gather information while the damage is fresh and to take the necessary steps to prevent further loss to the property. Insurance policies also typically require, as a condition to recovery of proceeds, that within a certain period after the loss, such as 30 to 60 days, the insured file with the insurer a proof of loss, which is a sworn statement that includes a recital of the facts and circumstances surrounding the nature and extent of the loss and that is put in writing and signed by the insured. Insurance policies also typically include a period of limitation, or a designated period of time within which the insured must notify the insurer of a loss; if the insured does not notify the insurer within this period, the insurer will not be required to take action or pay any claim filed after this date.

In property insurance policies, if the insurer and insured cannot agree to the value of the property that has been damaged or lost, these policies generally include procedures that allow each party to select an appraiser to determine the value of the property. These two appraisers will work together to reach an agreed-upon value, and if they cannot agree, they may select an umpire who will facilitate the discussions to reach a final determination of the property's value. Finally, property insurance policies commonly exclude payment for any damage to the property that occurs after the initial damage and that is a result of the failure of the insured to take appropriate action to prevent further loss to the property.

Liability insurance policies commonly require that the insured cooperate and assist in the investigation and defense of any claim that is filed against the insured and that is covered under the policy. This cooperation may include requirements such as avoiding engaging in settlements with the third party, attending all court hearings, furnishing all information necessary for drafting legal documents, and supplying any additional evidence that may surface during the investigation.

Defenses of Insurer

Insurers are entitled to raise defenses to support their determination that an insured is not entitled to some or all of the value of an insurance policy's coverage. Some of these defenses are related to activities of the insured, such as concealment or misrepresentations regarding the facts or circumstances of any loss or damage to an insured interest. Other defenses stem from the terms of the insurance contract, such as any conditions, warranties, or exceptions to coverage that are specified in the policy. The following sections provide further explanations of these defenses.

Concealment

Any individual or business that seeks to purchase an insurance policy is obligated to disclose to the insurer all material facts relating to the interest to be insured. Material facts are facts that would influence the insurer in making a final decision regarding whether to issue an insurance policy or the premium levels that will be set for an individual policy. If the insured provides an answer to the insurer that is misleading and the insurer relies on incorrect information in issuing the policy or setting the premiums, the policy may be avoided on the grounds of concealment. However, any information on the application that is obviously missing or incomplete will not be grounds for voiding a policy. Only if an incomplete answer appears to be complete will it result in voidance.

However, the insured only has a duty to disclose facts that relate to the matter being insured and not merely fears or concerns that the insured may have about the subject matter of the policy. There is also no requirement that the insured disclose facts that the insurer already knows or that relate to a risk excluded from coverage by the policy.

Misrepresentations

A representation is any oral or written statement that is expressly made or implied by the insured to the insurer and that forms at least part of the basis on which the insurer decides to issue an insurance policy. According to Dobbyn (2003), "If a representation of the insured is untrue or misleading, and is material to the risk and is relied upon by the insurer in issuing the policy at the specified premium, the insurer can use this misrepresentation as grounds for avoidance of the policy" or as a defense to payment of proceeds under the policy (p. 188).

Further, a majority of courts have held that if these factors have occurred, the insurer may raise a defense, and it is immaterial whether the insured made the misrepresentation innocently, or with no intent to defraud insurer. A minority of courts, however, have held that unless the misrepresentation was made with deliberate intent to deceive the insurer, the insurer may not avoid the contract, even though the representation included material facts that were false.

Warranties & Conditions

In an insurance policy, a warranty is essentially a promise by the insured party that all statements made relevant to the validity of the insurance contract are true. Insurance contracts require the insured to make certain warranties. An insurer is within its rights to cancel a policy and refuse to pay claims if an insured's warranty is found to be untrue. To qualify as a condition or warranty, the statement must be specifically included in the contract, and the contract must clearly show that the parties intended for the rights of the insured and insurer to depend on the truth of the statement.

As with misrepresentations, the effect of a misstatement of a warranty or condition may depend on the intent of the insured in making the statement. To date, many state legislatures have enacted laws providing that a misrepresented warranty will not result in the cancellation of an insurance policy unless the misrepresentation was fraudulent or increased the risks covered by the policy.

Limitations on Coverage

Insurers frequently include clauses that impose specific exceptions or limitations on the coverage provided by an insurance policy. Such limitations may apply to terms such as the subject matter of the policy, the types of harms the policy will insure, the duration of the policy, or the amount of proceeds payable by the insurer.

The major difference between a limitation on coverage and a warranty or condition is that if a warranty or condition is breached, not only does the insurer have a defense against payment of proceeds, but the policy itself is voidable. On the other hand, an occurrence that falls outside of coverage because of a limitation or exception simply means that the insurer is not liable for any loss because of that occurrence and provides no basis for the insurer to avoid the policy.

MEASURE OF RECOVERY

Property Insurance

In most cases, an insurance policy includes specific information about both the amount of proceeds that the insurer will pay should a covered event occur and the procedures that the insured must follow to recover the payment. For instance, most property insurance policies provide for payment of an amount up the "actual cash value" of the property at the time of loss. If the property covered by a policy consists of items that are readily replaceable, such as books, furniture, or business equipment, the actual cash value is the market value of the property.

If the property is unique and therefore not readily replaceable, such as a home, garage, or shed, the measure of recovery for these structures is generally based upon their fair market value. Homeowner's insurance policies also generally cover all of the personal property included in the home. However, most insurance companies now offer guaranteed replacement cost coverage, which pays to repair or replace damaged homes without a deduction for depreciation or a dollar limit. Thus, if an older home is damaged in a fire, replacement coverage will pay the full cost of rebuilding the home and replacing its possessions. Without replacement coverage, the homeowner would receive only the actual cash value of the home, or the replacement cost minus depreciation. Unless a homeowner's policy specifies that property is covered for its replacement value, the coverage is generally only for actual cash value. Replacement coverage generally raises the rates of a homeowner's premium from 10 to 15 percent.

Liability Insurance

Liability insurance was originated to protect the insured against liability claims brought by third parties. In particular, liability insurance was founded to protect employers against losses stemming from liability to employees for work-related injuries. However, because the original purpose of these policies was to indemnify employers, or compensate them for their costs paid to injured employees, a third party who also sustained an injury could not bring a direct action against the insurer to sue for damages, even after obtaining a judgment against the employer. In the years that followed, states enacted legislation that allowed injured third parties with a cause of action against the insured the statues of a type of third-party beneficiary of the liability policy. Today the scope of coverage and the measure of recovery of many types of liability policies continues to be reshaped as courts and legislatures examine reform measures that will affect the damages that injured parties may collect from the insured as well as the insurer's liabilities to both the insured and injured third parties.

Tort Immunity

Finally, one area that has come under increased scrutiny by consumers, legislatures, and insurers is the area of tort immunity. When a tortfeasor, or a person who either intentionally or through negligence commits a tort or a civil wrong, is immune from suit, a liability insurance policy may address the issue in one of three ways. First, a policy may be silent on the issue of tort immunity. In this case, it is generally left to the insurance company to decide whether to attempt to exercise this immunity. Second, the policy might reserve to the insured the right to determine whether tort immunity will be exercised. This type of clause has been criticized on the grounds that it gives the insured unrestrained ability to favor certain interests and that it seems to invite fraud. Third, the policy may totally forbid the insurance company from exercising a right to tort immunity. This type of provision has generally been held valid by courts. Thus, a person who is injured by a tortfeasor immune from suit must look to the terms of the governing liability insurance policy for the possibility of recovery.

CONCLUSION

Insurance offers important protections for both individuals and businesses. While people cannot predict the advent or nature of misfortunes, unfortunate events do occur. Whether caused by an accident, an economic downturn, or a third party's intentional act, situations can arise that, without some form of protection, would financially devastate an individual or business enterprise. Insurance serves to fill that gap. Insurance companies collect premiums, regular payments from individuals and businesses, and in return provide financial assistance to policyholders if a covered event occurs. Thus, in the business world, insurance provides a measure of security and business efficiency in that it eliminates a great deal of risk and uncertainty.

Some forms of insurance, such as property insurance, can even serve as a basis for credit in that businesses are not likely to be able to obtain loans from lenders if the property will not be insured against loss. Also, insurance enables businesses and

individuals to save money for future investments that will enhance their net worth or profit margin because insurance policies protect them against many types of losses. For instance, property insurance protects homes and business offices from loss or damage, while liability insurance provides coverage for any liability that may arise due to damage to a third party. Without these forms of insurance, many homeowners and businesses would be at risk of facing bankruptcy in the event of any significant claim against them.

However, an insurance policy is a form of a contract. Thus, to be binding, certain procedures must be followed in the creation of the policy that protect the interests of both the insurer and the insured. Even after a policy is signed, disputes may arise about the interests that are insured, the events that are covered, and the extent of the coverage that is provided. Policyholders are able to raise disputes to challenge an insurer's denial of a claim or the sufficiency of any payments or settlements. Insurers may raise defenses to support their payments or denials of claims. Out of these competing interests, an entire body of insurance law has developed to help insurers and policyholders settle or resolve their disputes and continues to be shaped by courts and legislatures today.

TERMS & CONCEPTS

Absolute assignment: An irrevocable transfer of all ownership rights under an insurance policy from the owner to another person.

Chose in action: A right of action for the possession of personal property that may be assigned from one insured to another.

Claimant: A person who claims or asserts a right or an interest.

Common disaster: A disaster in which more than one person loses his or her life.

Counterclaim: A claim presented by the defendant in an action and growing out of the transaction or contract on which the plaintiff's action is based.

Defendant: The person against whom an action or suit is brought.

Disclaimer: The refusal or renunciation of an interest, right, claim, or power; also, the document in which the renunciation is expressed.

Grace period: A period provided by an insurer of usually 31 days after the premium due date, during which a premium still may be paid, without jeopardizing the policy coverage.

Insured: The person on whose life an insurance policy is issued.

Lapsed policy: A policy terminated because of nonpayment of premiums.

Policy: The printed document issued to the insured by the insurer detailing the terms of the contract.

Premium: The payment due, usually monthly or annually, for an insurance policy.

Rider: A special policy provision or group of provisions that is added to a policy to expand or reduce the benefits payable.

Warranty: A statement or condition relating to a fact or an action to be taken in relation to a contract that must be true or that must be taken in exactly the manner stated or the contract will be void.

BIBLIOGRAPHY

Bradford, M. (2006). Guidance leaves lasting impression. *Business Insurance, 40*, 52–54.

Dingler, W. (2007). Mind the gap in liability coverage. *Pennsylvania CPA Journal, 77*, 21.

Dobbyn, J. (2003). *Insurance law in a nutshell* (4th ed.). Thomson/West. 2–4.

Dodell, L. (2006). Occurrence form gives eternity of coverage. *National Underwriter / Property & Casualty Risk & Benefits Management, 110*, 14.

Glick, P. (2012). Protecting your business. *Smart Business Philadelphia, 6*, 12.

Glick, R. (2006). GE cannot group asbestos claims to increase insurers' liability. *Insurance Advocate, 118*, 10–11.

Grace, M.F., & Leverty, J. (2010). Political cost incentives for managing the property-liability insurer loss reserve. *Journal of Accounting Research, 48*, 21–49.

Guthrie, C., & Rachlinski, J. (2006). Insurers, illusions of judgment & litigation. *Vanderbilt Law Review, 59*, 2016–2049.

Klinedinst, T. (2007). Private business owners: Why an outside board, why D&O insurance? *Production Machining, 7*, 24–26.

McGreevy, S. (2007). Why insurers aren't paying, and you are. *Contractor Magazine, 54*, 44–57.

Nelson, L., Morrisey, M., & Kilgore, M. (2007). Damages caps in medical malpractice cases. *Milbank Quarterly, 85*, 259–286.

Schmautz, M., & Lampenius, N. (2013). Deriving the minimal amount of risk capital for property-liability insurance companies utilizing asset liability management. *Journal of Risk, 15*, 35–55.

SUGGESTED READING

Hood, J., & Acc-Nikmehr, N. (2006). Local authorities and the financing of the employers' liability risk. *Public Money & Management, 26*, 243–250.

McCoy, J. (2006). You, your lawyer and the insurer. *LP/Gas, 66*, 14.

O'Connor, N. (2007). Discharging static. *Insurance & Technology, 32*, 20.

Essay by Heather Newton, JD

R

ROLE OF INTERNATIONAL FINANCIAL MARKETS

This article focuses on different aspects of the international financial market. There are many influences on international financial markets, and the article will provide an exploration of the role of international banking, the euro, hedge funds, and moral hazards within international financial markets. *Financial markets* could be defined in two ways, and there are different categories of financial markets.

OVERVIEW

Money is power. A former Treasury Department official has stated that the most significant conflicts countering terrorism following 9/11 took place in the buildings and boardrooms of economic corporations (Taylor, 2007). Taylor, in an interview with USINFO, stated that he believes that "financial issues should be treated jointly with the two other pillars of international relations, military and political" (Anders, n.d.). According to Taylor (2007), finances are a crucial factor in foreign policy. Let's step back and look at the foundation of financial markets and then tie the concept to its role in a global economy.

Financial markets could be defined in two ways. The term could refer to organizations that facilitate the trade of financial products, or it can refer to the interaction between buyers and sellers to trade financial products. Many who study the economic field will utilize both definitions, but finance scholars tend to apply the second meaning most often. Economic markets have the potential to be both domestic and foreign.

Financial markets can be explored on an economic basis because it focuses on how individuals purchase and sell financial security, assets, and other forms of capital with cheap transaction fees and prices that symbolize the efficiency of the markets. The overall objective of a financial market is to gather all the sellers and put them in one place where they can meet and interact with potential buyers. The goal is to create a process that will make it easy for the two groups to conduct business.

When looking at the concept of financial markets from a finance perspective, one could view financial markets as a way to facilitate the process of raising capital, transferring risk, and conducting international trade. The overall objective is to provide an opportunity for those who want capital to interact with those who have capital. In most cases, a borrower will issue a copy of the purchase to the lender agreeing to pay back the finances in full. These receipts are known as securities and are able to be purchased or sold. Lenders expect to be compensated for lending the money. Their compensation tends to be in the form of interest or dividends.

There are different categories of financial markets, including the following:

Capital markets. Capital markets are comprised of primary and secondary markets and are considered a critical factor in American capitalism. Recently established securities are purchased and sold in the primary market, and investors sell their securities in the secondary markets. Companies rely on these markets to raise the funds needed to purchase the equipment required to run a business; conduct research and development; and assist in securing other items needed for the operations of the company.

Stock markets. In order to raise a large amount of cash at one time, public corporations will sell shares of ownership to investors. Investors gain profits when the corporations increase their earnings. Many view the Dow Jones Industrial Average as the stock market, but it is one of many components. Two other components are the Dow Jones Transportation Average and the Dow Jones Utilities Average. Stocks are traded on world exchanges such as the New York Stock Exchange and NASDAQ.

Bond markets. Bonds are the opposite of stocks. Usually when stocks go up, bonds go down. The forms of bonds include Treasury bonds, corporate bonds, and municipal bonds. Each bond has a crucial influence on mortgage interest rates.

Commodity markets. These facilitate the trading of raw or primary commodities. The commodities are traded on regulated commodities exchanges. According to Amadeo (n.d.), "the most important commodity to the American economy is oil, and its price is determined in the commodities futures market. Futures are a way to pay for something today that is delivered tomorrow, which helps to remove some of the volatility in the American economy. However, futures also increase the trader's leverage by allowing him to borrow the money to purchase the commodity. This can have a huge impact on the stock market, and the American economy, if the trader guesses wrong" (Amadeo, n.d., "What are commodities").

Money markets. These provide short-term debt financing and investment. The money market is the international financial market for temporary borrowing and lending. Money markets allow for short-term liquid financing for the international economic system. In most financial markets, borrowers tend to repay their debts after about a year of lending, in most cases. Money markets use "paper" as their instruments in short-term financing.

Derivatives markets. These provide tools for the administration of economic risk.

Futures markets. These offer standardized contracts for exchanging products in the future.

Insurance markets. These facilitate the redistribution of different risks.

Foreign exchange markets. These facilitate the trading of international exchange.

Hedge fund markets. "Recently, hedge funds have increased in popularity due to their supposed higher returns for high-end investors. Since hedge funds invest heavily in futures, some have argued that they have decreased the volatility of the stock market and therefore the U.S. economy. However, in 1997, the world's largest hedge fund at the time, Long Term Capital Management, practically brought down the U.S. economy"

—(Amadeo, n.d., "What are hedge funds").

APPLICATION

Influences on International Financial Markets

There are many influences on international financial markets. This section will discuss three of them: The euro, moral hazard, and hedge funds.

The Euro

"Economic and monetary union (EMU) prompted some speculation as to the future international role of the new European currency" (Detken & Hartmann, 2002). Many had speculated that the euro would challenge the dollar's dominance as the number one currency in the world while others were skeptical that the euro would last. "The emergence of one currency as a medium of exchange in currency trading is an important dimension of a currency's role in international financial markets, and is related to a currency's trading volume and trading costs" (Detken & Hartmann, 1998, p. 564). Detken and Hartmann (2002) found that the euro's role is similar to the deutschemark before EMU and features a prominent position in spot trading in the Nordic and other Central European nations. The euro was severely tested during the eurozone crisis, as first Greece and then Italy sank under economic pressures and required financial assistance from stronger EU members. Fields & Vernengo (2013) contended that despite predictions of euro supremacy, the dollar would remain the hegemonic international currency for the foreseeable future.

Moral Hazard

Moral hazard in international financial markets has received considerable attention in the past years. Moral hazard refers to "the possibility that the provision of insurance, by diminishing the incentives to prevent a particular outcome, may actually lead to a rise in the incident of that outcome" (Kamin, 2004, p. 26). Many believe that efforts to stall financial crises were unsuccessful and moral hazard has developed as a result of when the IMF started to offer large funding packages to emerging market countries.

Multinational corporations (MNCs) are looking for growth opportunities, and they are finding them in emerging markets. According to a study of multinational corporations, "two thirds of the respondents believed investment in emerging markets is likely to continue to grow, with three quarters claiming to be actively investing in Central and Eastern Europe" (Credit Control, 2005, p. 43). Antoine van Agtmael, a senior executive at World Bank Group, was the first person to use the term "emerging markets" (Jana, 2007). Many of the new ventures can be found in developing countries such as Brazil, Russia, India, and China, which are known as the BRIC economies. The combined GDP of the BRIC countries in 2012 was close to $14 trillion, almost equal to the annual GDP of the United States (Van Agtmael, 2012). The significance of emerging markets has reached a point where corporations have recognized their influence on the corporations' bottom line. For example, Coca-Cola expected the BRIC countries to contribute 41 percent to its soft drink growth in 2008 (Chakravarty, 2004). Ford Motors predicts that the emerging markets (i.e., Asian countries) will contribute 80 percent to its automotive sales growth (Ford Motor, 2003). Emerging markets have become an important source of revenue.

The Altradius survey reported that the highest percentage of respondents from the multinational corporations was investing as follows: 74 percent invested in Central and Eastern Europe, 43 percent invested in China, and 35 percent invested in India and Southeast Asia. The countries that received the most funding in Central and Eastern Europe include Poland (60 percent), Czech Republic (46 percent), and Russia (percent) followed by other EU accession countries. In Southeast Asia, India was the top choice followed by Malaysia, Thailand, and Indonesia ("Survey reveals major risks," 2005, ¶ 11).

With the growth of investment in these emerging markets, there is a pressure to determine whether or not the right thing is being done when offering financial packages. Kamin (2004) wrote a paper and provided evidence on "whether anticipations of IMF assistance by investors have distorted the price and quantity of private capital being offered to emerging market countries" (Kamin, 2004, p. 53). He sought to find out whether IMF programs had an effect on creditor moral hazard. His research begins by establishing the point that before the Mexican crisis, investors did not expect bailout packages to be awarded to

countries struggling financially. As a result, one can assume that the pre-1995 period represents a period where there was no moral hazard.

Kamin's second step was to compare "recent measures of spreads and capital flows to emerging market countries with those prevailing in the pre-1995 period. He found some evidence indicating that credit was very easy to obtain during the mid-1996 through mid-1998 period" (Kamin, 2004, p. 24). However, this practice did not last long. The final step was to determine whether or not countries that were designated to receive a large sum of IMF funding had easier access to credit than countries who were not in the same financial situation. Kamin concluded that moral hazard did not correlate with distortions in the international capital markets. It is notable, however, that Brazil, China, and India were almost alone among major economies to experience growth during the global financial crisis, while Iceland, Ireland, Portugal, Greece, Italy, and Spain struggled with implosions in their financial institutions and economies. The UK and Netherlands bore the cost of Iceland's largest bank default, bailing out their own nationals who had invested in the Icelandic bank and going unreimbursed by Icelanders who refused to repay the two larger governments for the failure of a "bad bank" (Touryalai, 2011). By 2010 the European Central Bank was arranging rescues for banks in Ireland and Portugal (Richards & Sinclair, 2010). Bailouts for Greece, Italy, and Spain were already on the horizon (Tora, 2012). Though Touryalai predicted in *Forbes* that Iceland would rue its revolt, Greenstein reported in the same magazine in 2013 that Iceland was the only troubled economy in Europe to have landed softly (Greenstein, 2013).

Hedge Funds

Hedge funds have become popular over the last years due to their ability to take both short (sold) and long (bought) positions (Lubochinsky, Fitzgerald, & McGinty, 2002). In other words, positions are "market neutral" but with leverage (Edwards, 1999). The funds are well received because they have the ability to utilize "active management skills to earn positive returns on capital regardless of the market direction" (Lubochinsky, Fitzgerald, & McGinty, 2002, p. 33).

Most hedge funds have two distinct features. First, the funds have to be what is called absolute return funds. The goal is not to acquire additional returns over a prescribed benchmark but to acquire the proper absolute returns for the risk that is involved. The other aspect is the funds' use of leverage. The level of leverage used by hedge funds tends to vary. There are three main mechanisms that hedge funds can use to leverage new asset positions. They are (Lobochinsky, Fitzgerald, & McGinty, 2002):

- Traditional margin loans extended by prime brokers to their clients.
- Fixed income hedge funds that extensively use repurchase agreements.
- The use of all types of derivative positions including future contracts, total return swaps, and options.

VIEWPOINT

The Role of International Banking

One of the focal points for many multinational corporations is to have the ability to perform financial transactions outside the United States. These corporations have identified a need to participate in the international trade process. "The burgeoning impact of technology, the globalization of trade, and the general trends towards political and regulatory liberalization is highlighted by the emergence and growth of the multinational bank (MNB)" (Moshirian, Sadeh, & Zein, 2004, p. 351). Some of the key banking services that are needed include letters of credit, wire transfers, collections, and foreign exchange (Teller Sense, 2003). It is important for organizations to have the ability to wire deposits in a timely manner, have the credibility for banks to provide a letter of credit on their behalf, and collect payments quickly and easily.

"The establishment of multinational banks across national boundaries, together with the increasing importance of other international capital mechanisms has meant that the growth of a given economy is no longer constrained by its ability to maintain surplus capital above its own gross national expenditure" (Moshirian, Sadeh, & Zein, 2004, p. 351). In March of 2004, the International Banking Federation was established when the banking associations from Europe, the United States, Australia, and Canada united. The headquarters for the group was London. The purpose of this consortium was to provide an international forum to address issues such as legislation, regulations, and other matters that affected the countries and the global banking system. One of the main objectives of the group was to accentuate the efficiency of the banking industry's reaction to national and international affairs (Teller Vision, 2004).

One issue that this group may discuss is the ability for the market to absorb shocks in times of financial crises such as the crash of 1987, the Asian crisis of 1997, and the Russian crisis of 1998. One of the effects of globalization in the financial industry is that the banking sectors across the world have become interdependent across borders (Elyasiani & Mansur, 2003). Given the fact that the banking systems in different countries are not the same in structure and regulatory constraints, it is important that the international financial community is responsible and collaborates on what type of plan should be in place for the global financial market. Organizations such as the International Banking Federation need to develop a plan of action to address these types of events so that the members are not adversely affected when a crisis happens. They are responsible for minimizing the risk of the occurrence of a domino effect.

CONCLUSION

A former Treasury Department official has stated that some of the most significant battles opposing terrorism after 9/11 have occurred in the workrooms and boardrooms of economic companies (Taylor, 2007). There are many influences on the international financial markets, and the article will provide an exploration of the role of international banking, the euro, hedge funds, and moral hazards in international financial markets. Financial markets could be defined in two ways, and there are different categories of financial markets.

Detken & Hartmann's (2002) study found the following:

- The euro dominated spot interbank trading in the Nordic countries and several Central and Eastern European countries.
- In Denmark and Norway, the euro share increased to 83 percent and 93 percent, respectively, compared to 1998; in Sweden it almost remained constant at around 80 percent.

- Large euro shares between 80 percent and 98 percent existed in the Czech Republic, Hungary, the Slovak Republic, and Slovenia, with a fundamental change in Hungary from a dollar-dominated market in 1998 to a euro-dominated market in 2001.
- The dollar continued to dominate in regions such as Asia, the Middle East, and North and Latin America (Detken & Hartmann, 2002, p. 564).

Lobochinsky, Fitzgerald, & McGinty (2002) conducted a study of hedge funds and arrived at the following conclusions:

- During the period of 1990–2000, the performance of a composite hedge fund index showed a significant superior risk-return profile to traditional asset categories such as equities and bonds.
- Greater diversification benefits could be obtained by introducing individual hedge fund styles rather than via the composite index. In this case, arbitrage and relative value strategies played a specific role.
- Even a small addition of hedge fund investments to a traditional asset mix produced consistent return benefits at all levels of risk (p. 53).

TERMS & CONCEPTS

Euro: The single currency for Europeans.

Hedge funds: Funds that take short (or sold) positions in the securities as well as the long (or bought) positions. Funds aiming to utilize active management abilities to receive positive returns on capital despite the direction in which the market heads.

International banking: Banking transactions crossing national boundaries.

International Banking Federation: A consortium of banking institutions from Europe, the United States, Australia, and Canada charged with addressing financial service issues on a national and international level.

Financial markets: A market for the trading of capital and credit, such as money and capital markets.

Letters of credit (LOCs): Documents issued by banks in the event that a customer wants to purchase goods from an overseas supplier. The supplier is guaranteed

being paid because the bank's credit sponsors the customer.

Moral hazard: The prospect that being insured from risk might promote a different behavior than would be expected if it were completely exposed to the risk.

Wire transfers: Wire transfers are forms of transferring and moving money from one individual or corporation to another. A customer can usually purchase, sell, or wire transfer any form of currency in forty-eight hours or less.

BIBLIOGRAPHY

Ahmed, S., Coulibaly, B., & Zlate, A. (2017). International financial spillovers to emerging market economies: How important are economic fundamentals? *Journal of International Money and Finance, 76*, 133–152.

Anders, J. (2007, January). Financial warriors stand guard over global markets.

Amadeo, K. (n.d.) An introduction to the financial markets.

Detken, C., & Hartmann, P. (2002). Features of the euro's role in international financial markets. *Economic Policy, 17*, 554–569.

Edwards, F. (1999). Hedge funds and the collapse of long term capital management. *Journal of Economic Perspective, 13*, 189–210.

Elyasiani, E., & Mansur, I. (2003). International spillover of risk and return among major banking institutions: A bivariate GARCH model. *Journal of Accounting, Auditing & Finance, 18*, 303–330.

Fields, D., & Vernengo, M. (2013). Hegemonic currencies during the crisis: The dollar versus the euro in a Cartalist perspective. *Review of International Political Economy, 20*, 740–759.

Hartmann, P. (1998). *Currency competition and foreign exchange markets: The dollar, the yen and the euro.* Cambridge, MA: Cambridge University Press.

International banking federation established. (2004). *Teller Vision, (1321)*, 5–6.

Kamin, S. (2004). Identifying the role of moral hazard in international financial markets. *International Finance, 7*, 25–59.

Lubochinsky, C., Fitzgerald, M., & McGinty, L. (2002). The role of hedge funds in international financial markets. *Banca Monte dei Paschi di Siena SpA, 31*, 33–57.

Moshirian, F., Sadeh, I., & Zein, J. (2004). International financial services: Determinants of banks' foreign assets held by non-banks. *Journal of International Financial Markets, Institutions and Money, 14,* 351-365.

Richards, J., & Sinclair, R. (2010). Europe mobilises rescue bonds as ECB escalates buying barrage. *Euroweek, (1183),* 63.

Survey reveals major risks involved in trading with emergent markets. (2005). *Credit Control Journal.*

Taylor, J. (2007). *Global financial warriors: The untold story of international finance in the post 9/11 world.* New York: W.W. Norton.

Tora, B. (2012). Groundhog Day. *Money Marketing,* 18.

Touryalai, H. (2011). Iceland's stand against bailout repayment will hurt. *Forbes.com,* 28.

The world of international banking. (2003, April 1). *Teller Sense,* 1–7.

SUGGESTED READING

Bordo, M., & Murshid, A. (2006). Globalization and changing patterns in the international transmission of shocks in financial markets. *Journal of International Money & Finance, 25,* 655–674.

Claessens, S., & Schmukler, S. (2007). International financial integration through equity markets: Which firms from which countries go global? *Journal of International Money & Finance, 26,* 788–813.

Lin, A., & Swanson, P. (2004). International equity flows and developing markets: The Asian financial market crisis revisited. *Journal of International Financial Markets, Institutions & Money, 14,* 55.

Essay by Marie Gould

S

STATISTICAL APPLICATIONS IN ACCOUNTING

This article focuses on how statistical sampling techniques are utilized in the field of accounting. Techniques such as auditing sampling are discussed. The role of the American Institute of Certified Public Accountants in the development of guidelines for this approach is highlighted. In addition, there is a historical overview of how statistical techniques were introduced into the field of accounting.

OVERVIEW

Many have argued that statistics is important to the field of accounting. The tools of statistics can assist accountants with more effectively performing their job. In addition, "there is definite evidence in accounting periodicals of an increasing interest in the use of statistics, especially statistical sampling techniques, in accounting" (McGurr, 1960, p. 60). Many scholars have recognized that the two fields can yield creative results when they are combined. As a result, there was considerable interest in relating statistical methods to accounting, auditing, and management control during the postwar years (Trueblood & Cooper, 1955). Fan & Zhang (2012) show that statistical reporting is key to quality accounting practices.

Methods for Combining Statistics & Accounting
Trueblood (1953) provided some foundational principles for guiding and organizing research in this area. Based on his report, the principles were as follows:

- Collaboration between the two disciplines is crucial to the success of the partnership between the two fields. The accountant must be willing to work closely with the statistician when stating and defining accounting problems and objectives. The statistician is responsible for understanding the accountant's point of view in order to develop a joint development of technique. Both individuals must gain an understanding of the other's field in order to develop the basis for a common language.
- Statistical techniques that are used in other areas cannot be blindly accepted for accounting. There is a belief that time will be saved when existing statistical methods can be applied directly. However, it should be noted that there may be certain accounting problems that require new statistical techniques to be developed in order to solve them.
- Satisfactorily operating accounting techniques should not be supplanted by statistical procedures for the sake of change only. An increase in the use of accounting, auditing, or management control techniques is the criterion for suggesting integration of present or new statistical techniques in the accounting field.

Further Study on Statistical & Accounting Integration
According to Trueblood and Cooper (1955), the Pittsburgh group found that many of the published statistical applications did not conform to the above-mentioned principles. As a result, this group decided to conduct its own studies to support the principles that were discussed earlier. Some of these studies included the following:

- Internal accounting procedures and management control problems.
- In a small specialty steel-manufacturing corporation, quality control charts were developed as a way to investigate performance variances on a daily basis. This experiment also produced practical procedures involving statistical correlation techniques to evaluate the consistency of cost standards.
- A LIFO price index based on statistical sampling was developed to yield reductions in cost, higher-quality results, and simplification of administrative problems. It was found that the data could be used for other managerial initiatives, such as

The offices of the American Institute of Certified Public Accountants (AICPA) at Palladian Office Park (220 Leigh Farm Road) in Durham, North Carolina. (Courtesy of Ildar Sagdejev via Wikimedia Commons)

price index purposes. Some of these correlative initiatives included forecasting, establishing cost of sales determinants, and calculation of interim inventory turnover rates.

- Auditing cases.
- The aging of accounts receivable in department stores. The sampling procedures developed for aging purposes are directed toward both the control and audit processes.
- A statistical application was made to the evaluation of the recorded book value of inventory. The evaluation was completed by statistical analyses of adjustments to records developed from past cycle counts.
- An audit application had been made in relation to physical tests of bulk inventories for internal and external audit purposes. Two significant findings of this experiment were that the external auditor decided that his sample should be increased versus decreased and statistical sampling cannot yield significant protection to the auditor in fraud detection without large samples.

Audit Sampling Technique

The American Institute of Certified Public Accountants' (AICPA) auditing standards board (ASB) had formed a task force to develop and implement an audit sampling policy for using the sampling techniques as described in Statement on Auditing Standards (SAS) number 39, Audit Sampling (Journal of Accountancy, 1983). The policy became effective for any examination of financial statements for periods ending on or after June 25, 1983. However, when a meeting was held in April 1983, the ASB recommended that the AICPA provide additional guidance to practitioners for implementing the provisions. The task force's response was to create a question and answer (Q&A) list with the five most frequently asked questions by practitioners.

In 1992, the Audit Sampling and Analytical Techniques Committee of the New York State Society of CPAs conducted a survey of New York accounting firms. According to Hitzig (1995), the purpose of the survey was to obtain information regarding the use of audit sampling based on SAS No. 39, Audit Sampling. The main interest was to determine the level of use of the audit sampling technique by local accounting firms. A survey had been conducted in 1984 by the Audit Testing Techniques Subcommittee of the AICPA. However, it did not address the use of sampling in practice.

APPLICATION

Statistical Sampling

"To meet their clients' needs in an environment of heightened competition and runaway inflation, many auditors are turning to scientifically supported methods of planning, executing and evaluating audit procedures to obtain evidential matter. Statistical sampling is one such method" (Akresh & Zuber, 1981, p. 50). There are many ways that an accountant can set up a statistical sampling. Hitzig (2004) provided a model that worked on the premise that one could set up a statistical sampling by defining the population, frame, and sampling unit.

The Population

The population is the set of all accounts or transactions that the auditor wishes to use in order to arrive at the conclusion. The first step in the process is to define the test objective. Once the test objective has been determined, the auditor should define the population. The steps are in this order so that the auditor can draw a sample based on the specific test objective.

The Frame

Once the testing has been completed, the auditor must attribute the results to the items versus the population since auditors do not select a sample directly from the population. This representation is referred to as the frame. The frame provides the auditor with a foundation for identifying items to be included in a sample.

In most cases, the accounting population is presented in the form of a list (i.e., payroll file, accounts receivable detail). This list (or frame) tends to streamline and simplify the sample selection process. However, the population's sampling frame does not have to be a list. Sometimes, the physical locations provided by floor plans or other population identifiers can be used as frames. Also, there may be an occasion when the auditor has to create an appropriate frame when one is not available. Regardless of whether or not a list is used, the selection of a frame is usually based on convenience and accessibility. Most convenient frames are computer data files. If these files are used, there is an opportunity to integrate them with an application of computer-assisted audit techniques and data retrieval.

There are some circumstances where auditors have to be on alert to make sure that they do not encounter any problems with their samplings. Hitzig (2004) provided some examples:

Over-specified frames. If there are units in the frame that do not contain members of the population, they are not applicable to the conclusion that the auditor wishes to draw. These units would be considered irrelevant.

Under-specified or incomplete frames. As the auditor makes plans to collect a sample, he/she must ensure that every item in the population is also in the frame. If a frame is not complete, there is a probability of some significant members of the population not being included in the sample. If this type of action were to occur, there is a violation of AU 350's requirement for representativeness, which requires that every item in the

population under examination must have a chance of being selected. If a frame is incomplete, there is an opportunity for biased estimates of the population value that is under examination. This statement is true especially if the auditor is not careful to distinguish between the size of the population and the size of the frame on which the selection of the sample was performed.

The Sampling Unit

A population is composed of basic units that are clustered into sampling units. The sampling unit is determined by the auditor's choice of frame. The item that the auditor conducts the examination on is referred to as the sampling unit, and the sampling unit is vouched or traced. The examination can be conducted by inspection, observation, or confirmation.

Auditors tend to make the statistical sampling procedures flexible. If the selection and evaluation are performed properly, there is a high probability that there will not be any questions regarding validity due to technical issues. For example, if the total recorded amount of the sampling units equals the total recorded amount of the population under examination, the technical information has been confirmed. Therefore, it is valid.

How are sampling units selected? Auditors have different preferences. However, listed below are some common trends in the field.

Accounts. Accounts are the preferred method of sampling unit, especially if dealing with consumer accounts (i.e., credit cards). Using this approach will allow the auditor to directly confirm the net balance in any designated account. However, there may be problems if an auditor attempts to confirm account balances on commercial accounts. Therefore, commercial accounts tend to be maintained on vouchers payable systems.

Open invoices. If an organization has a file of open invoices that can be directly accessed, open invoices would be the preferred method. Since the open invoices consist only of debits to the accounts receivable, the auditor will need to apply a separate test procedure for credits to accounts.

Since many organizations document their purchases in a vouchers payable system, they have found that it is easier to confirm individual invoices versus account balances. This choice of sampling unit may be applied with either equal probability (i.e., simple random sampling) or with probability proportional to size (i.e., dollar-unit sampling).

Invoice line items. Dollar-unit sampling enables an auditor to choose an invoice line item as the sampling unit. This approach is referred to as subsampling (Leslie, Teitlebaum, & Anderson, 1980). In this scenario, a computer program identifies the invoice and the dollar within the invoice in which the selected line item is located. The auditor is responsible for manually identifying the line item by footing the invoice until the selected item is found. The auditor has to vouch only that item and every other selected line item in the sample. In dollar-unit sampling, the auditor projects the results associated with the selected line items by using the total book value of the frame as the representation of the frame size.

VIEWPOINT

Audit Sampling
As mentioned earlier, SAS No. 39 was adopted in 1981. Since that time, accounting firms have adapted their policies and procedures to the requirements listed in SAS No. 39. Although SAP No. 54 only included statistical sampling, SAS No. 39 includes statistical and non-statistical audit sampling. The four key requirements that are related to audit sampling include the following:

- A sample should be selected in such a way so it may be representative of the population from which it is selected.
- Errors disclosed in a sample should be projected to the population, thus yielding an estimate of the total amount of error in the population.
- The auditor should consider sampling risk, which is the risk a sample will result in an incorrect audit decision.
- The auditor should consider tolerable error, which is the auditor's specification of the largest error that may exist in the sampled population without causing the financial statements to be materially misstated.

Audit sampling did not become popular until the 1970s when many of the large accounting firms decided to invest in the development and delivery of statistical sampling policies and support. Kenneth Stringer, chairman of the Statistical Sampling Subcommittee of the AICPA, and Herbert Arkin, a professor of statistics at Baruch College and a consultant to two Big Eight firms and the IRS, were two of the pioneers in this effort. Stringer used SAP No. 54 to introduce the concept of audit sampling to the accounting field while Arkin wrote the first book on statistical techniques for auditing, and it was geared toward practitioners in the profession.

Decline in Statistical Sampling
Unfortunately, the use of statistical sampling as a methodology for audit testing experienced a drastic decline in the 1980s. Many have speculated as to why this decline occurred. Some have implied that the decline was a result of the changed nature of internal control work, which affected the way many firms organize their audit procedures. Some firms, especially those among the Big Six, had reduced or eliminated tests of transactions as a test of controls. The main reason for this change was attributed to the viewpoint that a transaction test provides little or no information as to the performance of control procedures over a routine data process.

Another reason for the decline in statistical sampling was attributed to SAS No. 39. The AICPA's audit guide defines non-statistical sampling as "any sampling procedure that does not measure the sampling risk." Therefore, random selection and non-statistical evaluation were considered acceptable under GAAS, which gave equal status under GAAS to both non-statistical and statistical sampling. As a result, many auditors elected the non-statistical approaches since they were easier to apply.

At the Financial Executives International (FEI) peer-to-peer forum in 2013, however, participants were in agreement that detailed reporting at the unit level was significantly less useful than higher-level statistical aggregation reports, which facilitated analysis and enabled management decisions. An understanding of profitability was more easily gained when business divisions and lines within those divisions could be grouped and identified by markets, products, operations, and so on, especially when a contribution margin reporting approach was used.

CONCLUSION

Many have argued that statistics is important to the field of accounting. The tools can assist accountants with being more effective on their job. In addition, "there is definite evidence in accounting periodicals of an increasing interest in the use of statistics, especially statistical sampling techniques, in accounting" (McGurr, 1960, p. 60). Many scholars have recognized that the two fields can yield creative results when they are combined.

There has been much debate among practitioners as to whether or not statistical sampling is useful. There are two main concerns that are mentioned when conversations about the topic are discussed. The first concern deals with the perception of practitioners. Some believe that statistical sampling is not useful in their practice because "it replaces the auditor's judgment with mechanical procedures and because it is difficult to understand and apply" (Akresh & Zuber, 1981, p. 50). The second concern deals with educating practitioners on statistical sampling. According to Akresh and Zuber (1981), some auditors have found it useful to seek the guidance of a statistical sampling specialist. These researchers indicated that some ways of obtaining a specialist include the following:

- obtaining the help of a professor from a local university on a consulting basis
- hiring an auditor experienced in statistical sampling
- developing an internal specialist
- participating in a professional group (p. 53)

The American Institute of Certified Public Accountants' (AICPA) auditing standards board (ASB) had formed a task force to develop and implement an audit sampling policy for using the sampling techniques as described in Statement on Auditing Standards (SAS) No. 39, Audit Sampling (Journal of Accountancy, 1983). The policy became effective for any examination of financial statements for periods ending on or after June 25, 1983. However, when a meeting was held in April 1983, the ASB recommended that the AICPA provide additional guidance to practitioners for implementing the provisions. The task force's response was to create a question and answer (Q&A) list with the five most frequently asked questions by practitioners.

SAS 39 mandates that sample items be selected based on their ability to be representative of the population. In order to ensure that this directive is applied, auditors must understand what populations, frames, and samplings are. If the auditor has an understanding of these terms and how they relate to a test of details of an account or a class of transactions, the auditor can properly execute an audit test of details and draw valid, defensible conclusions. Although audit sampling is slowly returning as the basis for the most rigorous test procedure available to an auditor, there is a need to reeducate auditors in the basics of sampling (Hitzig, 2004).

TERMS & CONCEPTS

American Institute of Certified Public Accountants: A professional association for CPAs providing guidance to members on accounting techniques and standards.

Audit sampling: The application of audit procedures to less than 100 percent of the items within a population to obtain audit evidence about a particular characteristic of the population.

Dollar unit sampling: A method that uses a combined-attributes-and-variables method of statistical inference. It can be used simultaneously for both variables and attributes sampling. It differs from most sampling techniques in that the sampling units are defined as individual dollars rather than as physical units (such as inventory items). The procedures are performed on the individual accounts or inventory items containing the dollars selected.

Simple random sampling: A sample in which the population is first divided into strata (classes of elements). Within each stratum, each element has an equal chance of being chosen for the sample.

Statistical correlation technique: In probability theory and statistics, correlation, also called correlation coefficient, is a numeric measure of the strength of linear relationship between two random variables.

Statistical sampling technique: A method of selecting a portion of a population, by means of mathematical calculations and probabilities, for the purpose of making scientifically and mathematically sound inferences regarding the characteristics of the entire population.

Statement on auditing standard: Guidelines used to establish standards and provide guidance on the design and selection of an audit sample and the evaluation of the sample results.

BIBLIOGRAPHY

Akresh, A., & Zuber, G. (1981). Exploring statistical sampling. *Journal of Accountancy, 151,* 50–56.

Audit sampling task force to aid applying SAS no. 39. (1983). *Journal of Accountancy, 156,* 12–14.

Fan, Q., & Zhang, X. (2012). Accounting conservatism, aggregation, and information quality. *Contemporary Accounting Research, 29,* 38–56.

Hitzig, N. (1995). Audit sampling: A survey of current practice. *CPA Journal, 65,* 54–57.

Hitzig, N. (2004). Elements of sampling: The population, the frame, and the sampling unit. *CPA Journal, 74,* 30–33.

Leslie, D., Teitlebaum, A., & Anderson, R. (1980). *Dollar unit sampling: A practical guide for auditors.* London: Pitman.

McGurr, F. (1960). The integration of statistics and accounting. *The Accounting Review, 35,* 60–63.

Najarian, G. (2013). What's the 'best' approach to profitability management reporting? *Financial Executive, 29,* 67.

Trueblood, R. (1953, October). The use of statistics in accounting control. *The New York Certified Public Accountant,* 619–626.

Trueblood, R., & Cooper, W. (1955). Research and practice in statistical applications to accounting, auditing, and management control. *The Accounting Review, 30,* 221–229.

SUGGESTED READING

Finley, D. (1989). Decision theory analysis of audit discovery sampling. *Contemporary Accounting Research, 5,* 692–719.

Hall, T., Hunton, J., & Pierce, B. (2002). Sampling practices of auditors in public accounting, industry, and government. *Accounting Horizons, 16,* 125–136.

Power, M. (1992). From common sense to expertise: Reflections on the prehistory of audit sampling. *Accounting, Organizations & Society, 17,* 37–62.

Essay by Marie Gould

STOCK MARKETS

This essay offers a broad description of the United States' (US) and international stock markets, the interplay and globalization of these financial spheres, and ultimately the relationship between the U.S. economy and the stock market. To develop a better understanding of the complexities of the market, the article weaves into context events of the famous stock market crash and the resulting regulatory safeguards in place today. The essay is easily understood by those new to the world of financial markets and provides a springboard for exploration into the complex and sometimes risky world of financial markets.

OVERVIEW

For the reader, a 30,000-foot view of the financial investment field for corporations, investors, brokers, and managers—the stock market—follows. Scores of businesses start small, as one- or two-person enterprises; with continued growth, the successful develop into a partnership, and in due course, a full-fledged corporation is born. Corporations need short-term money to maintain accessible inventory and capital; they usually accomplish this by borrowing directly from banks. When a corporation needs longer-term financing, funds can be obtained by selling off portions of the business in the form of common or preferred stocks. These same stocks attract investors, who often trust their monies to large securities firms or dealers who specialize in investing. The expectation is that the professionals working for the firm will handle the investor's money well, with many years of expertise guiding their decisions. The stock market is the trading field for exchanges worldwide.

APPLICATIONS

Defining "The Markets"

The stock market takes two forms: a virtual (electronic) marketplace and the other a true, physical marketplace. The market, put simply, is the venue that facilitates the selling and trading of securities (primarily bonds and common stock); the employees are known as "stockbrokers." The brick-and-mortar stock exchange on Wall Street, USA, brings to mind images of tumultuous crowds of traders and investors shouting orders to sell or buy—the classic picture of rapid decision-making based on indicators, gut instinct, or computer-directed trading recommendations. The U.S. market consists of stock exchanges, the vehicles by which securities are bought and sold. The size of the U.S. stock market, in today's dollars, is $51 trillion. The short list of what comprises "the stock market" includes stock exchanges, commodities, bonds and other exchanges, a few of which are listed below:

The floor of the New York Stock Exchange. (Courtesy of Kevin Hutchinson via Wikimedia Commons)

- The New York Stock Exchange
- The Dow Jones Industrial Average
- NASDAQ (National Association of Securities Dealers Automated Quotations system)
- OTCBB (Over-the-Counter Bulletin Board)
- Pink Sheets

U.S. Stock Exchanges

- The New York Stock Exchange (NYSE), nicknamed "The Big Board," is the oldest and largest dollar volume bidding market for stocks in the United States. The NYSE, situated on Wall Street, obtained its first publicly traded company in 1792. Public trading of the over 2,700 securities on the NYSE is driven by supply and demand, an economic challenge of changing equilibrium driven by sellers and purchasers in an auction-like environment. In 2008 the NYSE acquired the American Stock Exchange (AMEX), the second-largest stock exchange in the United States (Amex members approve buyout, 2008).
- The Dow Jones Averages are stock market indices that express the U.S. economy in three distinct sectors: industry, transportation, and utilities. The averages are calculated from a compilation of data from thirty companies in these sectors.

- The NASDAQ is the largest electronic stock-bidding market in the United States. There is growing preference for electronic exchanges because this mode increases competition while offering equal access for large and small investors alike. The NASDAQ Composite is a listing of stocks and their composite values; it represents a tool characterizing its component stocks, all of which have some common characteristic. For example, component grouping may be those trading on the same exchange market, being participants in the same industry, or having similar market capitalizations (the calculated value of a company). The NASDAQ is considered an indicator of stock performance in technology and growth companies—those whose rate of growth significantly exceeds that of the average in their field.

- OTCBB stands for the Over-the-Counter (OTC) Bulletin Board, a structure that provides an electronic quote system for numerous over-the-counter securities not listed on the national or the NASDAQ exchange. The OTCBB provides brokers with real-time quotes, last-sale prices, and

Tokoya Stock Exchange. (Courtesy of Fg2 via Wikimedia Commons)

volume information. Anyone who subscribes to the system can use the OTCBB to look up prices or enter quotes. Like the larger, more familiar exchanges, eligibility rules for the OTCBB require SEC registration of current financial reports.

- Pink Sheet Stocks are over-the-counter trading securities that are not large enough to be listed on the bigger exchanges. These smaller company stocks are primarily high risk, considered some of the most speculative investments. The Pink Sheets are, quite literally, a daily pink-colored publication of the "bid and ask" prices of thousands of over-the-counter stocks for companies who are smaller in asset size and have lower share prices.

International Stock Market Exchanges (Non-U.S.)

International stock exchanges, far too numerous to list here, include the London Stock Exchange, the Bourse de Paris, the Tokyo Stock Exchange, and the Hong Kong Stock Exchange. Globalization is pushing stock exchanges around the globe to combine and buy stakes in one another to meet clients' demands. Today's investor wants are simple: investors want to trade stocks of companies located anywhere in the world at a fast pace, across various classes of assets, for a cheap price. Globalizing exchange transactions

saves costs in this industry since the largest single expense is building the technology to operate trading platforms (Werdigier, 2007).

History & the Regulation of the Stock Market under Pressure

The catastrophic stock market crash of 1929 ended the prosperity of the era and brought upon the United States a disaster never to be forgotten. Reasons for the crash remain uncertain, though the most solid theory speculates that investors rapidly selling their stocks for profit led to unrest and a groundswell of anxious people following suit. The businesses that relied on investors' money began to fail; vast numbers of people lost their jobs as a result. Without jobs, people withdrew money from their checking and savings accounts out of fear for their very survival. The banks simply could not meet the demands for monies, having invested much of the depositors' cash into the spiraling stock market, so many of the financial institutions failed right alongside other weakening companies. The entire economy began a treacherous downward spiral, ultimately leading to the Great Depression. Speculation that the stock market crash of 1929 was caused by a lack of formal rules and regulations led to Franklin Delano Roosevelt's urging of Congress to pass the Securities Act of 1933 and the Securities Exchange Act of 1934. These two legislative acts led to strict regulation of how new stocks were issued and how stocks were to be traded. Today any company that sells stock (corporations) must register with the Securities and Exchange Commission (SEC), which provides investors with the assurance of a much more stable market.

Fears of Market Crash Assuaged

In October 1987, apprehension was mounting as stock prices declined precipitously. The market had been doing so well for so long; few were surprised when the decline began. By the time the Dow Jones average had dropped more than 500 points on October 19, panic ensued; the day was dubbed "Black Monday." Yet, a full stock market crash was never realized, a credit to Congress's proactive 1934 legislation. Today strict barriers to deception are enforced; for example; firms are required to submit proof to the SEC of how much money they have on loan to customers in relation to their cash reserves. Scrutiny of every report submitted assures that firms have enough cash on hand to continue operations for a specified amount of time, thereby protecting the customers' financial well-being.

Other safeguards exist, including "Regulation T," which requires that purchasing of stocks on credit is permitted only when the investor deposits at least 50 percent of the market value of the stock with the broker (Dalton, 2001). In the 1920s, the market was taught a lesson a little too late by a dangerous precedent that allowed purchase of stocks with a mere few dollars on deposit. Additional legislation brought forth the Glass-Steagall Act of 1930, which provided regulatory controls in defining commercial versus investment banks. The act disallowed financial intermediaries (investment banks) that advise clients on mergers and acquisitions to function as commercial banks (whose main business functions are taking deposits and making loans for commercial or consumer purposes).

"The Glass-Steagall Act was enacted to remedy the speculative abuses that infected commercial banking prior to the collapse of the stock market and the financial panic of 1929–1933. Many banks, especially national banks, not only invested heavily in speculative securities but entered the business of investment banking in the traditional sense of the term by buying original issues for public resale. Apart from the special problems confined to affiliation, three well-defined evils were found to flow from the combination of investment and commercial banking" (Benston, 1990).

Glass-Steagall was repealed in 1999 and there followed a period of acquisitions that once again married commercial and investment banks. After the string of bank failures beginning in 2007 and the prolonged and global financial crisis that followed, critics called for a return of Glass-Steagall. Many economists noted that under Glass-Steagall there had been no big-bank failures (Glass-Steagall: Repeal the repeal?, 2013). Opposition by financial institutions, however, remained strong.

Impact of Globalization: October 1987 & 2007

Globalization has led to real-time communication and Internet access worldwide; the market continues to grow more and more virtual every day. There are few today unable to participate in the market because of access restraints. Market money virtually transfers from one continent to another with the click of a computer. Because of the high-tech linkages that existed, it was no surprise that the international markets felt panic alongside their U.S. counterpart on Black Monday in 1987. Japanese, British, German, and Swiss markets tumbled in synchrony with the U.S. market drop. Reliance on computer-managed stock portfolios did not protect money managers who were counting on the electronic programs to respond safely and appropriately to these kinds of rapid changes. When the electronic system failed, it was clear that no one knew where the stocks were headed. Portfolio managers learned there was no replacement, electronic or otherwise, for experienced human decision-making.

DISCOURSE

The Stock Market's Relation to the U.S. Economy
The stock market fluctuates up and down, sometimes from benign causes, sometimes for more troublesome reasons. Risk-averse investors, particularly the less experienced, are apt to act rashly, selling off stocks for fear of corollary economic downturns. Prudent investors must understand that a direct correlation between market downturns and the economy cannot and should not be assumed. "Wall Street is not Main Street. Its fluctuations may demonstrate economic health and distress, but often does not. It can be reacting to evidence of rapid, broadly shared economic growth—or the prospect of such growth—and in those cases, it should elicit a cheer from us all. But it also can be reacting to higher corporate profits that come not from increased productivity or growth but directly out of wages, benefits, higher prices or a variety of cost-saving, corner-cutting measures that don't make the median American's life any better. Sometimes, the market is just reacting to shortsighted business practices that supercharge earnings, but only temporarily—as in the case of the housing boom. Or it can go up because of simple irrational exuberance that is reversed with the next morning's trading—or the next year's crash. The market's fluctuations may not say much about the economy, they may not be as simplistically positive or negative as they seem at first glance, and they may not signal durable trends. They must be treated with care. The media, however, don't have a whole lot of time to treat them with care. In an age of 24-hour financial channels and daily business broadsheets, the allure of an easily comprehensible

number that comes out every few seconds and can serve as the subject for further commentary is hugely seductive. Increasingly, the stock tickers serve the same purpose in economic reporting that poll numbers serve for political scribes: They provide constant, reportable data that can be used to draw broad conclusions about the subject as a whole—but at a cost of accuracy, random fluctuations and significant separation from the issue at hand" (Klein, 2007).

Opportunity Present in a Tumultuous Market

For the stout of heart, menacing market downturns present an opportunity to gain, especially as others panic and sell. Impressions from Gene Marcial of *Business Week* offer sage advice for the investor in August of 2007. "This latest round of panic selling presents steeled investors with a unique buying opportunity. Let's be realistic and get a grip. If I were an investor with ample resources, or a money manager who feels besieged by the market's latest tantrum, I would go shopping—for stocks. Not just any stock. I would buy the market's top losers on Thursday, Aug.9, when the Dow Jones industrial average plummeted 387 points, or 2.8%, to 13,270.65. And now we have the subprime mortgage woes. If you buy these loss leaders now, you will see them in the big-winners list next year, if not sooner. My point is the stock market should be seen for what it really is: a market of opportunity. If you take such a perspective, you will never panic, whatever is causing people to rush for the exits. That is the herd mentality at work. Be prepared for the market to exhibit extreme behavior. A market that is plunging is an opportunity to buy the stocks you know are solid. When the market is scoring record highs, as it did earlier this year, take profits to build up a reserve fund" (Marcial, 2007). Proactive financial advisors know that bear markets are inevitable; counseling their investors to diversify mitigates the impact when the market starts to drop and alleviates some anxiety of their clients.

Capitalizing at the Right Time

The markets have a way of adjusting to fears when exchanges show clear and continued signs of a bear approaching. The reader can find dozens of sources in the literature cautioning against over-anticipation and reactivity to a market downturn. Financial performance uncertainty can cause panic and a flawed belief that the market is following a path to recession. But, anytime there is fear, there are those who capitalize on risk—willing to take advantage and win from others' uncertainty. Advice following the summer of 2007 roller-coaster ride from *Business Week Online*: "Until a trend is clear, expect the market to continue to swing wildly as investors place bets on their fears, real or imagined, of a U.S. recession" (Steverman, 2007).

Jason Kirby, of *MacLean's*, recently highlighted a risk-taking company whose objective is to capitalize on the debts of struggling companies. "Stock markets the world over have been in freefall. Four years of optimism have suddenly given way to fear. Finally, things are starting to look up for Toronto money manager Alex Jurshevski. Jurshevski is CEO of Recovery Partners, an investment firm he launched in 2005 to pursue the risky strategy of buying portfolios of underperforming corporate loans from banks in North America and Europe. By snatching up the debt of struggling companies, he aims to take over the businesses, turn their fortunes around, and re-sell them. It's a precarious strategy, akin, he says, to safely catching a falling knife, but it's one that promises huge returns. Jurshevski is part of a relatively small but vital niche of the business world that thrives on the trials and tribulations of other companies" (Kirby, 2007, ¶1).

Housing & Mortgage Loan Struggles

In autumn of 2007, housing market downturns continued to dominate the media, sparking fears in the economy and the nation. *Electronic News* reported,

> "Technology stocks were not at all immune as the U.S. stock market took a plunge upon opening this morning, with fears of a potential crisis in the credit markets spurring steep declines in stock prices worldwide. After the opening bell this morning, the Dow Jones Industrial Average quickly plummeted by more than 212 points to hit 13,057.86 just after 10:30 a.m. ET. At around the same time, the NASDAQ market, on which the majority of tech stocks are traded, fell to 2,503.16—two percent below the previous day's close and down a whopping 8.1 percent from the index's status less than a month ago. Financial analysts say that larger effects of the long-struggling housing market are a major cause

behind the widespread plummet. 'What began with rising delinquencies on U.S. home mortgages to risky borrowers months ago has evolved into a worldwide flight from risk by investors,' according to a *Wall Street Journal* report. "The ripple effects have… knocked dozens of lenders out of business, battered an already weak housing market and fueled weeks of stock-market turmoil. Marking the severity of the situation, the United States Federal Reserve issued a statement saying that it would provide "reserves as necessary" in an attempt to help stabilize and reassure the volatile market. On Friday, the Fed said it would accept $19 billion, and then another $16 billion, in mortgage backed securities to provide liquidity to the market; earlier, on Thursday, the Fed injected $24 billion in temporary reserves to the U.S. banking system. Similarly, banks around the world, including the European Central Bank and the Bank of Japan, injected funds this week into their own respective stock markets; according to the Associated Press, this week's events have marked the first time such banks have worked together to add liquidity to the markets since the aftermath of the September 11 attacks in 2001" (Taylor, 2007, ¶1–3).

The crash that began in 2007 did not bottom out until March 9, 2009. The crash was not confined to U.S. stock markets but was repeated in markets around the world during the six months following the initial American crash. Market losses between 2007 and 2008 totaled $21 trillion worldwide (Meric, Lentz, Smeltz, & Meric, 2012). On May 6, 2010, the Dow Jones Industrial Average lost 998 points when high-frequency traders, a new phenomenon of the digital age, began a frenzied game of "hot potato," trading stocks downward in reaction to a single large trader's sell order. The market recovered somewhat before closing as it became apparent that something aberrant had occurred (Madhavan, 2012). In August 2011 nervous investors began to move investments from stocks to safer instruments as ratings agencies threatened to downgrade the U.S. credit rating and Europe struggled to cope with failing economies within the Eurozone. In what was termed a "correction," stock

markets plunged as they opened around the world. As the political situations were resolved, investors once again looked to stocks for the gains they had come to expect. By November 2013, the Dow Jones Industrial Average had surged above the 16,000 mark.

CONCLUSION

A complex system, the stock market grows more multifaceted every day. As the world grows flatter; real-time transactions across the globe make for quick decisions and even quicker response times. The reader of this essay now understands more clearly the need for thoughtful decision-making; the benefit of rigorous education; and understanding market changes. Reactivity to changes in the market is risky behavior unless preceded by a thorough review and understanding of forces causing the variation. Trends are more predictive than short-term bursts of volatility; consultation with an investment specialist combined with knowledge of the companies in which one has invested can provide a balanced perspective and prudent management of valuable assets.

TERMS & CONCEPTS

Bear market: A prolonged period in which investment prices fall.

Globalization: A term used to express the growing interdependence of people around the world in the realms of society, communication, economy, and culture.

Great depression: A worldwide economic downturn; in the United States, the depression was associated with the stock market crash of 1929 (October 29, aka Black Tuesday).

Growth companies: Firms whose business generates considerable positive cash flows, which increase at faster rates than the economy at large.

Investment company/firm: A financial entity that sells stock shares to individuals and invests in securities issued by other companies.

Investment vehicle: Generally, any method used to invest.

NASDAQ: The largest electronic stock-bidding market in the United States.

New York Stock Exchange: Nicknamed "The Big Board," the oldest and largest dollar volume bidding market for stocks in the United States.

Primary market: Part of the capital markets that issues new securities.

Recession: A decline in general business/economic activity continuing over a period of time.

Secondary market: Market for trading securities that have already been issued.

Security: An exchangeable, replaceable, negotiable instrument used to represent financial value. Securities are broadly categorized into debt (loan) and equity (ownership) securities. Examples are bonds and common stock respectively.

Security and Exchange Commission: U.S. government agency that enforces federal securities laws and regulates the stock market.

Stock market: A market for the buying and selling of stocks, such as the NASDAQ or Dow Jones Industrial exchanges.

BIBLIOGRAPHY

Amex members approve buyout by NYSE Euronext. (2008). *FOI: Future & Options Intelligence, (1325),* 7.

Antonakakis, N., & Scharler, J. (2012). Volatility, information and stock market crashes. *Journal of Advanced Studies in Finance, 3,* 49–67.

Bar-Yosef, S., & Prencipe, A. (2013). The impact of corporate governance and earnings management on stock market liquidity in a highly concentrated ownership capital market. *Journal of Accounting, Auditing & Finance, 28,* 292–316.

Benston, G. (1990). The separation of commercial and investment banking. The Glass-Steagall Act revisited and reconsidered. *Department of Banking and Finance, City University Business School, London.*

Clary, I. (2007). Consolidation of exchanges could be N.Y.'s trump card. *Pensions & Investments, 35,* 30. Retrieved September 23, 2007, from EBSCO Online Database Business Source Premier.

DeLarosiere, J., & Nielsen, S. (2017). Information uncertainty and volatility in financial stock markets: Commodity price fluctuations and business cycles. *Premier Reference Source.*

Kirby, J. (2007). Let the feasting begin. *Maclean's, 120,* 30–31. Retrieved September 30, 2007, from EBSCO Online Database Academic Search Premier.

Madhavan, A. (2012). Exchange-traded funds, market structure, and the flash crash. *Financial Analysts Journal, 68,* 20–35.

Marcial, G. (2007, September 13). After the drop, it's time to stock-shop. *Business Week Online, 3.* Retrieved September 27, 2007, from EBSCO Online Database Academic Search Premier

Meric, G., Lentz, C., Smeltz, W., & Meric, I. (2012). International evidence on market linkages after the 2008 stock market crash. *International Journal of Business & Finance Research (IJBFR), 6,* 45–57.

Naoui, K. (2011). Intrinsic bubbles in the American Stock Exchange: The case of the S&P 500 Index. *International Journal of Economics & Finance, 3,* 124–132.

Sloan, A. (2007). These days, the Dow's big swing don't mean a thing. *Washington Post.*

Steverman, B. (2007, September 7). The street's recession fears. *Business Week Online, 29.*

Taylor, C. (2007). Tech stocks tumble as credit fears cause tailspin in worldwide stock markets. *Electronic News* (10616624), *52,* 3.

Thredgold, J. (2007). Self correcting. *Enterprise/Salt Lake City, 36,* 9–19. Retrieved September 27, 2007, from EBSCO Online Database Regional Business News.

Werdigier, J. (2007). NASDAQ is selling its London stock exchange stake. *International Herald Tribune.* Retrieved September 27, 2007.

SUGGESTED READING

Dalton, J. (2001). *How the stock market works* (3rd ed.). New York Institute of Finance, Prentice Hall Press.

Sivy, M. (2007). Is it safe yet? *Money, 36,* 59–62. Retrieved September 30, 2007, from EBSCO Online Database Business Source Complete.

Werlin, P. (2007). Bear necessity. *Bank Investment Consultant, 15,* 41–42. Retrieved September 30, 2007, from EBSCO Online Database Business Source Premier.

Essay by Nancy Devenger

T

21ST CENTURY IT APPLICATIONS

This article will examine several emerging software applications that will have a larger role in information technology (IT)/business applications for the twenty-first century. The areas of discussion in this article include software applications that are being developed to serve niche or vertical markets and applications that address the issues of disaster recovery/data backup and content security. IT applications that are currently under development exhibit a specificity that has not previously been seen in the business software marketplace. Generic applications that can be used interchangeably by a variety of industries will become more the exception than the rule as new IT applications target the needs of specific vertical markets. As new applications evolve to meet changing industry needs, partnerships, and opportunities that help connect and enhance these markets are evolving as well. Vertical markets are often subject to government regulation, compliance initiatives, and stringent data security requirements. The applications that are being developed to serve these markets must be flexible and scalable to allow for future customization. Protection of company data is a critical issue for organizations today. Business applications are being developed that provide enhanced data backup and content security and are also addressing the need for qualified users to have access to critical business information when it is needed.

OVERVIEW

Generic information technology applications for business have become standard tools for today's knowledge workers. Almost without exception, today's employees have access to email, spreadsheets, and contact management databases that were not as widely available in previous years. The last quarter of the twentieth century heralded not only the era of the desktop computer, but also the standard software that allowed for the creation and distribution of digital content. Generic software solutions enabled major corporations and small businesses alike to deploy standard solutions that allowed for interoperability and collaboration.

The first decade of the twenty-first century revealed major shifts in the ways that companies were seeking to use software applications. Most companies still have a need for generic and widely used applications for document creation and financial analysis. Companies are increasingly demanding specialized applications that allow for optimized business operations. Too many organizations defaulted to using spreadsheets for tracking projects and critical information when a database is really a more appropriate tool. Interoperability now requires that businesses interact with customers and suppliers through supply chain integration, which requires more sophisticated custom applications for data sharing.

Industries such as healthcare, financial services, and government agencies now require custom applications that speak to the kind of business they are in. Additionally, each interface between a company's internal and external applications and supply chain links may require the implementation of custom applications or solutions. The developing symbiosis within organizations (application to application) or outside of organizations (supply chain sourcing to customer) is currently determining the trends in the development of highly customizable and specialized software applications that are already emerging in today's market.

Closely related to the software applications that serve today's organizations are the issues that surround the protection of the data that is necessary to run an organization's business applications. Two areas of data security are often closely scrutinized from the applications standpoint: data protection and data security. Data protection has to do with ensuring that company data and information is replicated (backed up) in the event of a natural or manmade disaster. Data security applications involve protecting internal intellectual property and pre-mium content. Defense in- depth is an information protection strategy that utilizes the capabilities of current technology and follows approved procedures to guard against and monitor intrusions on an IT system. Security measures that are incorporated into a defense-in-depth plan are multi-layered in design and are intended to thwart an attack and to simulta-neously slow down its force and speed to allow for the detection of and response to it.

APPLICATIONS

The Emergence of Vertical Markets

Industry consolidation and aggressive market com-petition are driving the emergence of software appli-cations to support vertical markets. Vertical markets focus on serving clients in very specific industries such as pharmaceuticals, healthcare, banking, and retail. Vertical industries are finding that managing relationships with customers is often as important as the service that is provided to the customer.

Examples of relationship mapping are:

- a vendor relationship with a company's product development department
- a service (online banking) and a customer's access to information
- employees (sales associate) and shared clients (overall customer database rather than one spe-cific client)

Data sharing between employees, customers, and part-ners is critical to agile response in the marketplace where "customer management is a strategic initiative" (Gold, 2007). The capture of internal knowledge (tacit knowledge) ensures that information about a specific customer or client is not lost even if client turnover happens. Financial services organizations have been early adopters of technology that caters to their spe-cific customer base. A generic CRM (customer rela-tionship management) database may not allow for the capture of information that the industry requires. A rapidly shifting customer base doesn't eliminate the need to capture specific information that will help to enhance the customer experience. Shared connec-tions and relationship mapping between clients and service providers have now become as important as the service provided to the customer.

The customization of software applications such as customer relationship management (CRM) applica-tions gives a company an advantage in managing cus-tomer information in ways that were never possible before. According to Gold (2007), a "recent study by Forrester Research Inc., a Cambridge, Mass.-based think tank, 60 percent of senior executives at 176 companies surveyed felt that improving the customer experience was 'critical.' Relationship intelligence, and all of the contacts and relationships that com-pany professionals have in the marketplace, gives you the ability to really leverage that information to put together much more focused and targeted business development and marketing initiatives" (p. 5). The current company professionals want to know more about their customer and want to have a record of sales and relationships so that if a salesperson leaves, the knowledge doesn't leave with them (Gold, 2007).

Software applications under development to serve vertical markets and market segments will have ro-bust capability to manage data about customers, services, and vendors. In increasingly competitive markets, the management of key relationships and enhanced customer service are seen as strategic dif-ferentiators for business.

Data Recovery Applications

Another emerging trend for twenty-first century soft-ware applications deals with the issue of how com-panies will protect their critical data and processes in the face of natural and manmade disasters. The interruption of business is of critical concern to many organizations today. Power outages, severe weather, earthquakes, or terrorist attacks are all vi-able threats that could interrupt business operations. Lack of preparedness and the poor responses that were so well documented following the terrorist at-tacks of September 11, 2001, and Hurricane Katrina have left many companies wondering how before a disaster (large or small) may strike. The loss of key data and business interruption are only part of the concern; documented cases show that many com-panies were not able to continue operations after a disaster struck. Many companies have some type of disaster preparedness plan in place though it is often only specific to a company's IT assets. Loss of access to data now poses a serious risk not only to a com-pany but also to every facet of a business that is linked to that business. Twenty years ago, loss of data would have impacted the internal processes of an organization almost exclusively; today data loss and business disruption has the potential to interrupt an entire supply chain.

Continuous data protection (CDP), also called continuous backup, illustrates how companies are seeking to protect internal data in the event of disaster. Remote datacenters house back-up data for many companies and ensure the risk is distributed geographically (decentralized). Companies are aware of the need to store data at widely dispersed locations in the event of a wide-impact disaster; backups stored on site can be lost during disasters. Previously, most organizations did their own manual backup of critical business data to tape. Tape backup generally happened once every twenty-four hours, which left companies at risk of losing data that had not been captured since the last backup.

Companies often outsource the continuous backup of the most critical data, ensuring that little or no information is lost. Today, instant or real time access to back-up data is a necessity. Users cannot afford to wait hours or days to access data backups. The National Weather Service has been able to shorten its data restoration process from hours to minutes by implementing a web-based portable backup system. The system allows any user with an Internet connection to access backed up data almost instantaneously (Valverde, 2006).

Data backup and recovery was once the sole responsibility of the IT department. Business Continuity Plans (BCPs) have evolved as a collaboration between IT, HR (human resources), and facilities. BCPs outline not only the policies and procedures for disaster recovery, but they also ensure that business issues and IT issues are aligned. In the era of corporate mergers, many companies are upgrading infrastructure and are taking the opportunity to look at crisis management planning at the same time. Continuity planning and the applications and processes associated with the plans are emerging as pivotal IT/business issues for this century.

Content Security

The value of an organization's internal knowledge and data cannot be underestimated in today's information economy. The backup and protection of a company's knowledge assets has been discussed in terms of a business continuity plan in the face of a potential disaster. Companies also face internal and external threats that pose risks to the security of intellectual property and proprietary data. The rapid digitization of corporate knowledge (including email) has put companies at great risk for data loss. Digital data's high portability and the ease at which it can be copied and shared have now made the loss of critical data a real concern for many organizations. Most organizations have instituted sophisticated security software and restricted access to prevent unauthorized access to internal data. Ponemon Institute reports that in 2012, 94 percent of the healthcare organizations that were surveyed experienced at least one data breach in the previous two years, and more than five data breaches were experienced by 45 percent of the organizations surveyed. It was estimated that data breaches in the healthcare industry could be costing an average of $7 billion annually, with an average cost of $1.2 million per organization.

Data risks among the healthcare industry have been estimated by the following percentages (ID Experts, 2012):

- 46 percent equipment failure
- 42 percent employee error
- 33 percent malicious
- t technology failure

Additionally, Ponemon's 2014 Cost of Data Breach: Global Analysis revealed that the average cost of a data breach to a given company, regardless of industry, was $3.5 million—a 15 percent jump from the previous year's report, showing that data breaches are becoming more expensive for organizations. Outbound content security applications are being rapidly explored by companies to address the data that is lost through employee error. Pattern matching in contextual searching is commonly used to identify sensitive data such as social security and credit card numbers in outgoing data; the application is similar to spam blockers that block incoming junk mail. Organizations typically restrict sensitive internal data to certain employees; often this still means that thousands of employees and partners have access to sensitive data. Gruman (2007) writes that, "at BCD Travel, a corporate travel service, nearly 80 percent of its 10,000 employees work in call centers and thus have legitimate access to sensitive customer information" (Gruman, 2007).

According to Miller (2007), corporate data is typically found in three states, all of which pose risks to data loss.

- data in motion (heading out by email)
- data in rest (resides on internal drives or at the printer)
- data in use (employees moving data via USB on laptop)

Companies are actively seeking ways to block confidential company information such as product specifications, payroll, or salary information. Organizations also face litigation risks for the inappropriate use of company resources if sensitive data is leaked; a business reputation can be damaged severely by data security losses, thefts, or breaches. Companies are aware of the risk of restricting the transfer of information inside and outside of an organization. Restricting outgoing information could potentially hurt customer service and inter business collaboration. Content blocking that is too restrictive can result in a great number of false positives, situations where information that is to be legitimately passed out is not allowed to do so. One alternative is to quarantine at-risk content for review. However, given the potential volume of content that is transferred digitally on a daily basis, the volume of quarantined content could be huge and quickly overwhelm the quarantine system.

At this point, it is obvious that content security applications are only part of the solution to protecting a company's internal data from loss or inappropriate use. Employee education and the implementation of a comprehensive security policy will go a long way in protecting internal data. Content security is like many other strategic business issues facing organizations today. Sophisticated rules need to be written into software applications to make them "smarter," but the applications are only part of the answer. A collaborative undertaking by IT, HR, and corporate legal teams is essential for the design and communication related to both automated (application) solutions and the documented policies that are put in place to address content security issues.

ISSUES

Vertical Markets

Software applications that serve specific vertical markets offer tremendous opportunity to customize tools to meet specific industry needs. Many companies are no longer interested in fitting their business needs into a generic set of tools. Within a given industry or segment, there's simply too much opportunity to create a superior customized solution that exceeds rather than meets business needs.

One of the greatest opportunities for fast-growing verticals, such as healthcare and financial services, is the implementation of wireless technology. These markets are so competitive, that having access to the right application that provides the right data is essential for success in the marketplace. As one marketing executive stated, "Those markets (healthcare and financial services) are highly competitive, often dealing with commoditized products and constantly changing rates and programs. They employ sales reps with six-figure salaries, who are constantly in front of customers and need information at their fingertips" (Alleven, 2006, p. 34).

Other issues that need to be addressed in the development of vertical software applications are:

- GRC (governance, risk, and compliance)
- compliance with security for HIPAA privacy rules (ensuring that sensitive medical information is protected)
- identity management (allowing only authorized users access to data)
- risk management
- data encryption
- security of data in motion (mobile data transfer).

Still another area of customization and support that will be required for successful deployment of application for vertical markets is in the area of middleware interpretation (DeFelice, 2007). Middleware, or bridge, applications will be built in vertical markets to help connect integral parts of these systems.

Brenda Brinkley's company Epiphany, which "developed vertical products on top of NetSuite's applications," concentrated on a few core areas to serve, such as "electronic systems contractors, audiovisual companies, and the commercial flooring industry." Epiphany designs products and services that help other companies manage business processes such as invoicing, accounting, and project management. Epiphany's middleware applications and services are an example of the opportunity that is available for business applications in serving the exploding area of vertical market applications. The concept of "channel partners" for vertical industries is a popular one today where specificity and segmentation of markets has created opportunities for applications developers to create applications that interface with larger business applications (DeFelice, 2007, p. 4).

Data Recovery Applications

Storage requirements will be one of the issues related to the support of future applications associated with data and disaster recovery applications. Storage of data will need to be designed in a scalable manner to ensure that future growth can be accommodated. More and more companies will outsource data backup as a way to free-up internal resources, disperse risk of data loss, and ensure that data is secure at its remote location and while it is en-route to or from the users/organizations.

The service that the National Weather Service selected, enables automated, daily backups of critical data residing on multiple platforms ranging from HPUX, Linux and Sun Solaris servers to Windows XP and Windows 2003 systems. In one step, data is automatically encrypted, backed up and vaulted in remote, fault-tolerant data centers . . . The online backup and recovery system enables password protection and 256-bit AES in-flight and at-rest encryption for added security in both data transfer and storage. These features enable the NWS to address the security aspects of regulatory requirements, and also to more easily implement data retention policies (Valverde, 2006, pp. 23–24).

Other issues that organizations will deal with have to do with allowing employees access to data through VPNs in case of emergency. In many cases, IT infrastructure is largely untested and the capability of networks to handle large numbers of remote workers (home to office data and voice transmission) is in question. Many organizations are likely to find out the hard way that their organizations are ill prepared to deal with potential disasters. Many companies have put plans in place to deal with possible flu pandemics and other scenarios that may keep employees from going to work.

Content Security Applications

Numerous issues will confront the IT industry as it seeks to build future applications to protect data content. The protection of a company's intellectual property is invaluable in many industries today. Patents, trademarks, and trade secrets represent some of an organization's most valuable assets. The innovative output of an organization's workforce needs to be accessible to the right audience, while carefully guarded against others.

Outbound Content Management

Outbound content management tools are becoming more specialized over time. Typical filtering applications come with a set of standard templates, but companies will increasingly put time and effort into customizing the filters. An analysis of the contents of servers and databases will reveal the type of at-risk data. Company-specific information analysis will allow for the development of sophisticated concept filters that can customize the filtering templates. The risk for data loss for companies is high. One estimate states that 21 percent of a company's IP (intellectual property) resides in email. With statistics like these and the associated risks, it is no wonder that some companies are hiring subject matter experts or linguists to help write the content filtering rules to protect their organization's internal content (Gruman, 2007).

Protecting Premium Content

The development of digital television and alternative delivery platforms has led to a whole new business model, based on the premise of having superior content as the differentiating factor. The value and in some cases the cost of the content skyrocketed and for the first time there was a fundamental need for operators to protect their content in order to protect their revenue streams (Devreese, 2007). The delivery of unauthorized content via the web cuts into profits from DVD sales and other content delivery systems that were once more traditional. Defining a baseline level of security for content is important, as are the designs of flexible systems that will allow for changing requirements over time. The need to ensure that content is kept secure has a huge impact on the design of the video on demand systems as these applications are being designed and built.

CONCLUSION

This article has covered just a few of the IT applications that are being developed to meet the business needs of the twenty-first century organization. Software applications that serve niche markets will continue to be developed and deployed as more industries seek custom business solutions for their markets. Channel partners will help enhance niche markets with value added service and expertise in specific subject areas to aid in the deployment, support, and training associated with new business applications. Relationship management will continue to define business strategy in the coming decade as competition for and retention of customers becomes more of a focus for industry and, in turn, customers will come to expect superior service.

Part of the customer service experience will be the assurance of round-the-clock access to applications, accounts, and processes such as online banking with little tolerance for business interruption. In an effort to assure that business processes and supply chains are always accessible to customers, applications that ensure data backup and security of core systems will be given more focus by business. Likewise, companies are focusing on disaster preparedness planning as a way to ensure that critical company data is preserved, which will mitigate the risk of business interruption.

As companies seek out custom applications that enhance products and services to their customers, access to key business information and premium content will be closely monitored. Superior business applications need access to secure, timely, appropriate data and content to deliver on key business processes, products and initiatives.

TERMS & CONCEPTS

Channel partners: In computer and Internet marketing, a channel is a middleman between a product creator and the marketplace-related to VAR.

Concept filters: Refer to the business rules or terms that are built into data filters (keywords, terms-similar technology use for email spam filters).

Continuity plans: Also business continuance or business continuity. The processes and procedures an organization utilizes for essential functions to continue during and after a disaster.

Data encryption: A means of securing data by translation of data into a secret code. One must have access to a key or password to decrypt a protected file.

Identity management: From an IT standpoint, this refers to the management of an individual user's credentials when accessing an online system. Identity management allows for control of user access to specific applications or resources.

Independent software vendor: Generally refers to a company that specializes in making or selling software for niche markets such as healthcare or financial services.

Partnership relationship management (PRM): A business strategy used to improve communication between companies and their channel partners.

Premium content: Content that is paid for by a user.

Relationship intelligence: The concept that there is strategic value in managing customer relationships to enhance business opportunities. Superior service is seen as a key differentiation in highly competitive markets.

Risk management: The activity that identifies or recognizes risk, the assessment of the risk and strategies that will help to manage risk.

Supplier connectivity: Maintains effective communications with a network of suppliers to maximize order fulfillment operations.

Tacit knowledge: The knowledge that people carry in their heads. Increasingly, companies wish to capture this knowledge (often about customers/processes) and make it accessible through a customer relationship database or knowledge management system.

Value-added reseller (VAR): A company that adds features to an existing product. The product may then be sold to an end-user as an integrated product. The value may come from professional services that offer customization and training.

Vertical market application: software with specific requirements used in a single, narrowly defined market, such as software that helps doctors manage patient records, insurance billing, etc.

BIBLIOGRAPHY

Alleven, M. (2006). Demand in verticals on the rise. *Wireless Week, 12* (19), 34–34.

Brooks, J. (2011). Self-service IT. *Eweek, 28* (3), 6.

Burgert, P. (2007). Cost savings drive suppliers to plug into Web, networking. *American Metal Market, 115* (19), 17–17.

Dolbeck, A. (2007). Valuation of the e-commerce and internet industry. *Weekly Corporate Growth Report,* (1430), 1–12.

DeFelice, A. (2007). Finding focus. *Accounting Technology, 23* (5), 4.

Devreese, T. (2007, Mar/Apr.). Quick, call security: Someone's after our content! *IBE: International Broadcast Engineer,* 44–45.

Eddy, N. (2013). Network security remains a blind spot for businesses. *Eweek,* 7.

Gold, L. (2007). CRM booms, but not at CPA firms. *Accounting Today, 21* (11), 5–30.

Gruman, G. (2007). No exits. *CIO, 20* (13), 25–28.

Hoffman, W. (2007). Electronics goes, well, electronic. *Traffic World, 271* (6), 16–16.

ID Experts. (2012, December 6). Ponemon study reveals ninety-four percent of hospitals surveyed suffered data breaches. *Data Breach Press.*

McKenna, B. (2013). Shift in focus sees large companies beginning to gather in the cloud. *Computer Weekly,* 6–7.

Miller, R. (2007). Plugging information leaks. *EContent, 30* (1), 26–30.

Setia, P., Setia, M., Krishnan, R., & Sambamurthy, V. (2011). The effects of the assimilation and use of it applications on financial performance in health-care organizations. *Journal Of The Association For Information Systems, 12* (3), 274–298.

Valverde, M. (2006, August). Safeguarding critical data. *Scientific Computing, 23* (9), 22–24.

Weiss, T. R. (2013). Google seeks patent for process to scour documents for illegal conduct. *Eweek,* 4.

SUGGESTED READING

DeFelice, A. (2007). Software for rent. *Accounting Technology, 23,* 37–41.

Caruso, D. (2006). It's all about the architecture. *Manufacturing Business Technology, 24,* 28–30.

Ellis, L., Saret, J., & Weed, P. (2012). When company IT is 'consumerized'. *Mckinsey Quarterly,* 29.

Lin, W. T., & Chuang, C. (2013). Investigating and comparing the dynamic patterns of the business value of information technology over time. *European Journal of Operational Research, 228,* 249–261

McAdams, J. (2007). A sentry who is one step ahead. *Computerworld, 41,* 44–44.

Sun retools back-up and recovery process. (2007). *Manufacturing Business Technology, 25,* 54.

Winkler, T. J., & Brown, C. V. (2013). Horizontal allocation of decision rights for on-premise applications and software-as-a-service. *Journal Of Management Information Systems, 30,* 13–48.

Essay by Carolyn Sprague, MLS

TAX ADMINISTRATION

Tax administration entails the application of tax laws and regulations. This component of government is manifested on three general levels — national, state and municipal — in most national systems. The area of tax administration has evolved considerably over the millennia as commerce has developed. Along with this development have arisen a number of issues. In addition to providing an overview of the evolution of taxation and the management thereof, this paper will examine such issues in two general thematic areas.

OVERVIEW

President Lyndon Johnson once commented on the public's popular opinion of taxes. "In 1790," he said, "the nation which had fought a revolution against taxation without representation discovered that some of its citizens weren't much happier about taxation with representation." Indeed, most people find much to disdain about taxes, particularly since so much of life — owning a home and/or a car, shopping or dining out and, of course, worker salaries — is subject to taxation from local, regional. or national-level government.

Still, most people will argue that taxes are necessary for the maintenance of critical government programs, such as road repairs, school operations, public assistance programs and national defense. Naturally, much political debate has ensued over the extent and degrees to which taxes should be levied in a given political system. Battles in this arena are constantly fought in legislative circles, brought to an end by the passage of tax legislation into law. Once such legislation becomes law, however, the politics is separated while the new policy is implemented and enforced.

Tax administration entails the application of tax laws and regulations. This component of government is manifest on three general levels — national, state and municipal — in a given national system. This paper will provide an illustration of how tax administration has evolved as well as the issues that coincide with that development and application in the twenty-first-century economy.

President Obama signing the Patient Protection and Affordable Care Act on March 23, 2010. (Courtesy of Pete Souza via Wikimedia Commons)

Taxation Through History

Taxation is a practice that has been conducted for millennia. In ancient Egypt, pharaohs sent "scribes" to collect taxes on cooking oil, ensuring that the pharaohs' subjects were not exceeding recommended amounts and seeking punishment for those who skirted the laws by using other cooking sources. In early Greece, taxes were imposed universally on citizens to help fund war efforts — when a war was won, the tax would be refunded to the citizens using the spoils of the conflict.

The Roman emperor Caesar Augustus is widely viewed as one of the earliest and most effective tax strategists, able not only to impose a complex system of taxation for the diverse Roman citizenry but an administrative network by which the tax would be collected. The Roman Empire's tax administration system, which would reach across the Empire's domain as far as what are now the British Isles, would become the inspiration for European taxation systems.

As the British Empire grew in its own right, its own territories would become subject to the taxes of the crown — this "taxation without representation" eventually contributed heavily to the American Revolution. After the British were repelled at the end of the Revolution, American leaders implemented taxes to both help the fledgling country pay its war debts and build its government institutions. The American model of taxation would include the first-of-its-kind income tax, implemented during the Civil War era ("A History," 2009).

The examples of ancient Egypt, Greece, Rome, Western Europe, and the United States underscore two important points about taxation. First, the need of societies to generate revenues from the citizenry which will be used to fund government endeavors and programs. Second, as the myriad of civilizations has evolved and diversified internally over the last several millennia, so too has the manner by which taxation is administered. Concurrently, the issues surrounding tax administration have become equally diverse during this development.

FURTHER INSIGHTS

A Confrontational Relationship

It may be said that the imposition of taxes occasionally creates an adversarial relationship between the government and the private citizens. In the United States, few residents anticipate April 15, for that date is the deadline for reporting federal and state income tax — an often arduous and complex task, particularly for those who are not familiar with accounting and cannot afford the services of a certified public accountant (CPA). Once taxes are filed, many people dread the possibility of an audit, which is usually initiated when discrepancies in personal income tax returns are detected.

In light of the consumer's ingrained desire to protect as much of his or her income as possible, the goal

Ronald Reagan meets with Jack Abramoff and Grover Norquist in connection with the College Republican National Committee in 1981. In 2006 Jack Abramoff, lobbyist, was found guilty of conspiracy, tax evasion and corruption of public officials in three different courts in a wide-ranging investigation. He is now serving 70 months and was fined $24.7 million. (Courtesy of Karl Schumacher via Wikimedia Commons)

is to minimize one's adjusted gross income (AGI), which is an assessment of a taxpayer's liability based on the aggregate of all income sources, less expenses. By diverting some of their income into tax-free retirement accounts and carefully calculating all business expenses, taxpayers are able to avoid higher tax liability. Unfortunately, minimizing tax liability is often perceived as a daunting and expensive (especially when one must call upon the services of a CPA) task that may exacerbate the often negative attitudes the public has toward government tax administration.

Efforts to Improve Relations

To the end of alleviating the stress that creates a confrontational relationship between taxpayers and the government, many political systems are implementing reforms and improving services. Governments that create opportunities for taxpayers to file returns online using user-friendly software (including ProSystem fx Tax, Lacerte, UltraTax CS, TaxACT, and TurboTax) for example, may see more on-time filings with fewer calls for audits because of the relative simplicity and guiding hand of the software. Consumer stress may also be ameliorated by the quick turnaround time within which refunds checks are received.

In some cases, government tax agencies are going even farther to reach out to customers. In the United States and Norway, for example, tax agencies are not only utilizing modernized information technologies — they are training employees to change their attitudes about taxpayers. Rather than looking at taxpayers as subjects to the tax administration system, employees are learning to treat them as customers, worthy of respect and courtesy (Aberbach & Christensen, 2005). Results of an American Customer Service Index (ACSI) survey published in 2013, however, showed that IRS's website has "consistently ranked below the average" in customer satisfaction compared to websites from other federal agencies and many sectors of the private economy, including banks, Internet retailers, and Internet brokerage firms (GAO Reports, 2013). Despite such shortcomings, however, both the United States and Norwegian governments anticipate that adopting consumer-oriented attitudes will help break down barriers between tax agencies and the public.

In times of economic hardship and declining tax revenues, however, that relationship may return to an adversarial and even politically polarizing status. During the tail end of the global recession that began in 2007, for example, President Barack Obama and the Democrat-controlled House and Senate introduced sweeping legislation designed to reform the nation's health care system. (The Patient Protection and Affordable Care Act was subsequently enacted in 2010.) With the federal deficit skyrocketing, the legislation's advocates looked for other revenue sources. One such source was a proposed 40 percent tax on high-cost medical plans (Reuters, 2009). This proposal, considered an important piece of that legislation, immediately met with strong opposition from within Congress and from the public, who saw the measure as an unnecessary burden placed on the current health care system.

Tax Evasion

It comes as no surprise then that there are some who seek to avoid paying their taxes altogether. Although it is difficult to determine the amount of outstanding revenues owed to the government due to privacy laws, it is estimated that 21 percent of U.S. individual tax returns went unpaid in 2008, causing a loss of about $300 billion nationwide (Cauchon, 2009). Because businesses pay a considerably larger share of the tax base, business tax scofflaws (those who refuse to pay taxes), are usually the biggest targets of revenue collections agencies. In times of economic recession or stagnation, the significant loss of tax revenues from evaders can throw entire state budgets far out of balance.

Governments generally take two approaches to this problem. The first is a hard-line approach — if they know who owes large sums of tax monies agencies may identify them in the media and/or initiate prosecutorial measures against them. The other approach is "tax amnesty," a program by which businesses that are considered tax scofflaws may avoid prosecution and high fines by simply approaching their respective revenue collections agencies and paying what they owe. States and local governments often employ this tactic, and the results are often significant. In 2003, Arizona offered a 45-day amnesty program with the expectation of generating $25 million in revenues to offset a budget shortfall. At the end of the period, the state revealed that it had exceeded its goal, generating about $73 million. Even with administrative expenses for the program totaling $75,000 and the fact that $22 million of that $73 million was expected to be generated through audits and other activities, the net of about $51 million was considered a major success (Peterson & Nakamura, 2004).

The relationship between taxpayers and taxation agencies is as an important part of tax administration. In times of budget shortfalls and economic stagnation, the gulf between the two parties often becomes wider, which can result in fewer revenues and a continued adversarial relationship. It is for this reason that many governments see the need to reach out to taxpayers as well as reform bureaucratic systems to help bridge that gulf.

The relationship between agencies and taxpayers is not the only issue that arises regarding tax administration. The fact that not all tax systems apply charges in an equitable fashion causes considerable confusion among taxpayers and government agencies alike.

Uniformity and Disconnect

As stated earlier in this paper, the practice of tax administration has evolved into a vast and complex series of systems and networks, some of which are interconnected but others of which are independent. This myriad of schemes often causes confusion among taxpayers and governments alike. It is to this issue that this paper will next turn attention.

In general, nation-states define taxation systems that link national, regional/state and local governments. These linkages ensure clarity and uniformity in the law, at least in terms of tax reporting. For example, a citizen of the United States sees a percentage of his or her salary withheld by an employer for federal income taxes and another portion withheld for state income taxes. When April 15 arrives, the taxpayer will often deliver with his or her state income tax return a copy of his or her federal return. Similarly, an individual who purchases a home must pay local property taxes as well as state sales taxes and, but may also be able to apply federal tax breaks and credits to the purchase.

Issues do arise, however, with regard to tax administration when disconnects between the various levels and types of taxation become manifest. One of the areas in which this issue is particularly visible is Internet-based sales. When two or more separate tax systems are utilized for the purposes of Internet sales questions arise as to which rate should be applied. Consumers naturally gravitate toward vendors who offer the least expensive products and items, and Internet stores and sites tend to offer low rates for one major reason — the taxes applied to the sales of such products tend to be lower than those found in a local store (if there are any sales taxes included in the purchase at all). In the United States, some states are able to track their residents' out of state purchases in order to collect local sales taxes, but those efforts are time-consuming and often cost-prohibitive. The problem is that although sales taxes on such commerce are in place, consumers must voluntarily report their sales but seldom do so within thousands of American tax administration agencies.

ISSUE

Collecting Internet Sales Tax

The case of Internet taxation provides an interesting example of the challenges facing tax administration agencies. As the Internet continues to grow and generate worldwide commerce, how to collect taxes on such commerce remains a revenue conundrum in light of the diversity of tax agencies in operation.

There are two general approaches to taxing Internet sales. The first is a sales tax, which many states require for in-state sellers to collect upon the sale of goods and services in the same state. Sales taxes are percentages applied based on the price or value of the item sold. Second, and concurrent with the sales tax is the use tax, which is a tax levied on the use of a good or product within the government's jurisdiction, regardless of where it was purchased.

In both of these cases, however, the ability to collect sales taxes on Internet purchases is hampered by an inability to find applicable cases from which to collect. Although the sales tax laws have been presumed to apply to online purchases, questions have lingered for years. Taxing sales that take place in other states, such as mail order purchases, has long been the subject of debate in the U.S. In 1998, the passage of the Internet Tax Freedom Act (ITFA) provided important clarity on this front pertaining to remote sales, but it works against the tax administration agencies. In essence, the ITFA established that the Internet seller was not required to collect taxes from the buyer if the seller does not have a physical store in the jurisdiction. Furthermore, if the seller outsources sales to other companies in a given jurisdiction, that seller is not required to collect taxes from the seller (Reddick & Cogburn, 2007).

The lack of regulation on Internet purchases has caused states like Texas, which houses an Amazon.com distribution facility, to allegedly lose millions of dollars in uncollected revenue even as U.S. states appeal to the federal government to change the laws (Elkind & Burke, 2013).

A more viable approach for states is to create a uniform sales tax, which is a tax rate that is applicable outside of the state by state tax system. Uniform sales taxes are widely considered the most optimal of applicable taxes for Internet sales by those who seek tax revenues for depleted budgets, but the will to fully impose such a tax has not yet come to bear (Swisher, 2001). While Internet marketplaces like eBay (which in 2008 reported $8.5 billion in sales) seem to be tempting targets for revenue-minded tax administrators, in reality, the complexity of the Internet marketplace has made it extremely challenging for monitors to gauge the specific tax rates that might apply to such transactions. eBay, for example, involves not just inter-state transactions but international sales as well (Barlow, 2009).

Adding to the lack of action in this arena is the fear that state and federal pursuit of Internet sales taxation will hurt Internet commerce, one of the most important forms of business in the 21st century global economy (Barlow, 2009). States are also concerned with the probability of reciprocation — that if one state enforces its sales taxes on purchases conducted by its residents in another state, that second state may enforce its own sales taxes, in essence creating a zero-sum gain while expending the resources for the endeavor.

In the European Union (EU), the issue of Internet sales taxation is somewhat different. The EU has already implemented its own regional Internet tax — a value-added tax (VAT). A VAT is an indirect tax, in which a tax is imposed on each stage of production from the point of production to the time of purchase. In the EU, the VAT on online purchasing is about 20 percent. At the present stage, the question of taxation for the EU is not whether or not to impose a tax on online sales, it is whether or not to expand it to the growing inventory of Internet services, such as downloaded music and other services, many of which are based outside of the EU (Brown, 2000). In the United States, for example, there is not one single institution for tax collections but literally thousands, from the federal government to municipal governments — to apply a tax on American online companies would mean finding a way to track such sales, which are seemingly innumerable.

CONCLUSION

The area of tax administration has evolved considerably over the millennia in which commerce has developed. Along with this development have arisen a number of issues. In addition to providing an overview of the evolution of taxation and the management thereof, this paper has examined such issues in two general thematic areas.

First, the application of taxes and tax laws has created a polarizing relationship between taxpayers and the government. This relationship has fostered a desire among law-abiding taxpayers to minimize their tax liability, but has also spurred those who would break the law to hide their assets from the government. Governments are looking to improve this relationship, both in the interest of enticing taxpayers to continue paying their taxes and to collect much-needed revenues during times of economic uncertainty.

Second, the emergence of the Internet as one of the most important commercial vehicles in economic history has raised debates over how to tax the sales it produces. As the example of the EU has provided, even with such taxes in place and operation, its continued growth means ongoing debate on the extent to which it may be taxed. Indeed, the evolution of tax administration as a whole continues, sometimes a step behind that of commercial development but close nonetheless.

TERMS & CONCEPTS

Adjusted gross income (AGI): An assessment of a taxpayer's liability based on the aggregate of all income sources, less the expenses that person pays.

Internet Trade Freedom Act (ITFA): A 1998 U.S. law that clarifies tax statutes governing Internet sales.

Tax amnesty: A tax administration program whereby delinquent taxpayers and business may pay their liabilities without additional penalties or prosecution for tax evasion.

Uniform sales tax: A sales tax rate that is applicable outside of the state-to-state tax system.

Use tax: A tax levied on the use of a good or product within the government's jurisdiction, regardless of where it was purchased.

Value added tax (VAT): Also known as an indirect tax; a tax that is imposed on each stage of production from the point of production to the time of purchase.

BIBLIOGRAPHY

Aberbach, J. & Christensen, T. (2005). The challenges of modernizing tax administration: Putting the public first in a coercive public organization. *Conference Papers — American Political Science Association, 2005 Annual Meeting*, 1–3.

Barlow, T. (2009, September 8). EBay: Internet sales tax hurts businesses. *Daily Finance*.

Bonner, P. (2012). 2012 tax software survey. *Journal of Accountancy, 214*, 23–27.

Brown, D. (2007). European net tax unwelcome. *Inter@ctive Week*, 7, 66.

Cauchon, D. (2008, April 17). Big names owe big-time on taxes. *USA Today*.

Elkind, P., & Burke, D. (2013). Amazon's (not so secret) war on taxes. *Fortune, 167*, 76.

Keen, M., Slemrod, J. (2017). Optimal tax administration. *Journal of Public Economics, (152)*, 133–142.

Peterson, D.F. & Nakamura, K. (2004). State amnesty programs: The advantages and disadvantages.

Reddick, C. & Coggburn, J. (2007). E-commerce and the future of the state sales tax system: Critical issues and policy recommendations. *International Journal of Public Administration, 30*, 1021–1043.

Smith, D. (2009, October 7). Opposition to insurance tax grows in House.

Swisher, K. (2001, April 9). E-tailers faced death; now can they handle taxes? *Wall Street Journal — Eastern Edition, 237*, B1.

A history of taxation. (1999).

Taxation quotes. (2009).

Taxpayers' rating of IRS's website is below average and oversight entities recommend enhancements. (2013). *GAO Reports*, 15–17.

SUGGESTED READING

Brock, E. (2006). Tax program seeks uniform collection. *American City and County, 121*, 16–20.

Gleckman, H. (2000, March 27). The great Internet tax debate. *BusinessWeek, (3674)*, 228–236.

Kiser, E. & Kane, J. (2001). Revolution and state structure: The bureaucratization of tax administration in early modern England and France. *American Journal of Sociology, 107*, 183–223.

LeFevre, E. (1935). When in doubt, tax twice. *Saturday Evening Post, 207*, 27–88.

Powell, D. (2004). Access denied: Federal preemption of state internet access taxes. *Conference Papers — Midwestern Political Science Association*, 1–26.

The case for flat taxes. (2005). *The Economist, 375* (8422), 59–61.

Essay by Michael P. Auerbach, M.A.

TAX IMPACT ON DECISIONS

This essay examines the issues surrounding corporate tax liability and the impact that corporate tax rates have on business decisions. Tax liability can be defined as the total amount of taxes that a business or corporation is required to pay as a percentage of its profits. Tax liability is a manageable expense and can vary depending upon the jurisdiction levying the tax. Allowances and deductions set forth in federal and state tax codes provide a means for corporations to reduce the amount of their gross profits and therefore reduce their tax liability. Tax directors in corporations are responsible for reducing the effective tax rate (ETR) for their organizations while ensuring high compliance standards for financial reporting. Tax directors are also tasked with defining overall tax risk strategies for their organizations; as well as with educating key organizational employees about the implications of decision-making and the effects on tax liability. Corporate business units need to partner with tax managers to insure that applicable allowances and deductions are captured to help reduce a company's ETR. This essay will also discuss the trend followed by corporations in creating overall tax management planning and risk assessment and the importance of understanding ETRs between competitors within given industries. An overview of the tax allowances available for "green business strategies" will be discussed along with the competitive nature of global tax rates as an incentive to lure corporate investment to different jurisdictions.

OVERVIEW

Businesses make many decisions regarding their tax liability. Tax liability represents one of the largest, if not the largest, expense items on corporate income statements (Murray, 2006).

The Internal Revenue Code (IRC)

Corporations and businesses are subject to the codes outlined in the Internal Revenue Code (IRC), which outlines the domestic tax code for U.S. companies. Most corporations pay taxes as C-corporations, but there are other designations in the tax code

for non-profit companies and those operating as S-corporations. The designation of a corporation can have a big impact on the amount of taxes paid by a corporation.

The IRC refers generally to the IRC of 1986, which includes statutory tax law for the U.S. The IRC is organized topically, and broken into many hierarchical sections — the term that is used to describe the organization of the statutes is "codified." There have been many changes to the U.S. tax code over the years. The following timeline shows the major revisions to the cod:.

- 1874 — First codification of the tax code was undertaken; prior to 1874, the codes were generally unorganized acts that had been passed by Congress.
- 1939 — U.S. tax laws first codified as an integral part of the U.S. Code.
- 1954 — IRC was greatly reorganized and expanded by Congress and replaced the 1939 code.
- 1986 — with the passage of the Tax Reform Act, the IRC was renamed Internal Revenue Act of 1986. Numerous amendments to the code were added.

The IRC in use today is essentially the 1986 code, which contained many amendments to the 1954 version. Since 1986, there have been many changes to the IRC and there are renewed calls by legislators and the public to "reform" the overly complex and onerous tax code. Since the last overhaul of the U.S. tax code, there have been many amendments and additions to the code. Many critics claim that the tax code has become overly complex and unwieldy.

The topic of tax reform is discussed in the issue section of this essay and includes not only current topics regarding tax reform, but also discusses some of the topics that have come up since the last formal tax change in 1986.

Tax Risk Management

Tax risk management is a finance function and as such has been receiving increasing attention since corporate failures of the early 2000s. Along with corporate risk management, tax risk management has been given more scrutiny by corporate boards and executives. The current business climate exhibits increased shareholder interest and activism around all risk. Corporate taxpayer behavior is now a political issue in the eyes of many. Companies that don't pay their fair share of taxes are seen as lacking in integrity. Not complying with tax laws and underpaying corporate taxes can result in "reputational risk" (Johnson, 2006).

When creating a task risk management strategy, clear discussion and communication are critical. The basic components of a proactive task risk management structure include the purpose, principles, business and the group, tax authorities, government and procedures ("Creating a tax risk management strategy for a multinational," 2013).

A number of stakeholders care about a company's tax liability and the associated risks. Most corporations today must manage the following groups from an overall business standpoint, and from the perspective of tax liability.

- The Public: Expects responsible, ethical behavior as part of an overall corporate social responsibility policy. A subset of this group might include customers and staff.
- The Government: Needs tax revenue and companies are good sources of revenue. Companies that make a big profit but pay little in taxes are not favored. The government might encourage public/customer/staff backlash against a company that is not paying its fair share.
- Tax Authorities: Seek to maximize the amount of tax oversight. Companies already see an increase in audit activity related to compliance. Shareholders concerned about a company's reputation might look favorable upon increased oversight as proof that their organization is paying its fair share.
- Shareholders: Will increasingly want board involvement in tax planning. There's a definite acknowledgement that companies need to do a better job of forecasting effective tax rates. Tax management is being thought of as a more strategic function that is much more than number crunching (Johnson, 2006).

Tax Planning as a Business Strategy

U.S. corporate tax directors make sure that they always know their own corporate tax rate, that of their competitors and the average in their particular industry ("A new age of tax planning," n.d.) A review of Effective Tax Rates (ETR) by industry has revealed that various methods are used to reduce tax costs. If a tax manager researchers a given industry and finds a wide range of ETRs within that industry, this would indicate that there's an opportunity for additional tax planning as a means to reduce the ETR. Given the fact that a single % point reduction in an ETR could be worth a million dollars, there is significant incentive to reduce a company's ETR.

It is important for corporations to stay on top of their ETR to remain competitive within their industry. Companies that proactively and aggressively manage their ETR can potentially save millions of dollars in tax liability. Over the past decade, tax competition has emerged as a global trend. The United States once boasted one of the most competitive corporate tax rates in the world and corporations were attracted to set up operations in America. During the past two decades, many other countries have reduced their corporate tax rate to attract foreign companies. Today, the United States has one of the highest corporate tax rates of industrialized nations and stands to lose its advantage as the place to locate a corporation's operational headquarters. The implications of falling global corporate tax rates are discussed in more detail later in this essay.

APPLICATIONS

Tax Risk Assessment

If you ask tax directors about their main current challenges, their responses always include lowering effective tax rates (ETRs) while preserving high compliance standards ("A new age of tax planning," n.d.).

In general, risks associated with tax planning are similar to other types of corporate risk. Risks surrounding tax planning include:

- Complying with the law — not just filing correctly, but assurance that all tax laws are being followed.
- Tax reporting — Sarbanes-Oxley has only increased the awareness of having internal controls and having transparency in reporting.

- Integration of tax planning with business planning — new products, markets and business can create tax obligations resulting in missed tax planning opportunities. Tax planning cannot be a stand-alone event; it must be part of corporate decision making ("A new age of tax planning," n.d.).

- Management of taxes as a cost — taxes are a manageable cost for corporations. Most companies have some control over the ETR and could reduce their tax liability given more support. The downside here may be that when a company reduces its tax liability- the company may be seen as not paying its fair share of taxes.

- Reputational risk — corporate executives do not want to wake up and see their company's tax planning mistakes plastered on the financial newspaper pages ("A new age of tax planning," n.d.).

Strategic Partnership with Business

Many good tax plans have become ineffective due to minor changes in the practices of the front line operations ("A new age of tax planning," n.d.).

In corporations today, there is a deliberate effort to integrate functional business units within the overall strategic planning initiatives of the organization. Organizations have done a good job of linking corporate finance functions to specific organizational functions or initiatives. Because corporations have control over their tax liability, there is increased emphasis on tax planning. Tax planning is no longer just the responsibility of the corporate finance department; managers and others who make decisions on capital expenditures need to be aware of tax implications. While it may not make sense to make line mangers into tax experts, many finance departments are seeing the value in educating employees about the tax implications of their decision-making.

> "It wouldn't be so bad if the rest of the business had tax relief on the mind. But, not unnaturally, managers at the sharp end are more concerned with making commercial decisions than with the intricacies of the tax implications of them" (Bartram, 2005).

CFOs are aware that their organization may be missing qualified claims on capital allowances. Taking advantage of and finding qualified allowances is one of the best ways for an organization to lower its effective tax rate. Aggressive tax planning can really help a company wipe tax liability off the books (Bartram, 2005). CFOs understand that they can't make everyone into a tax expert, but there are ways to heighten the awareness of tax liability amongst personnel. Basic education about the tax implications related to expenditure and other decision-making is the best way to start.

Green Initiatives

"Green initiatives" are a hot topic at corporations today. Corporations that put environmental responsibility in the public eye are looked upon with favor as being responsible corporate citizens. "Green" practices enhance performance and increase shareholder value by optimizing the corporate tax position (Werthheim, 2007). Companies can benefit from reduced tax liability by taking advantage of tax incentives that support eco-friendly practices. The enormous amount of press that is devoted to environmental issues is being used as a branding opportunity for corporations, while the incentives are becoming an integral part of tax planning for corporations.

Today's "clean and green" business practices are being encouraged at the federal and state level with significant tax credits and incentives. There are numerous benefits to a company from a financial standpoint; corporations can (Wertheim, 2007):

- produce permanent savings through credits
- obtain special grants from construction and rehab projects
- hold onto their cash longer
- enhance partnerships through shared knowledge opportunities

Numerous tax incentives in the federal tax code are available for corporations looking to implement eco-friendly practices. The costs associated with many of the outlined expenditures are significant as are the potential tax credits to organizations. The past few years have seen an explosion in the amount of press that has been given to issues of energy conservation and sustainability. Corporate America has been anxious to jump on the "do the right thing" band wagon in the wake of so much negative public relations news in the not too distant past. Companies take advantage of a double win when they lower their tax liability and get high corporate responsibility ratings by embracing green business. Some of the most common tax incentives available to business are outlined below (Chirstian, 2007):

- Energy conservation through new equipment purchases (heating, cooling, ventilation).
- New building construction or renovations-using energy efficiency materials or recycled products.
- Water and air pollution control practices or cleanup of polluted areas.
- Alternative energy supplies for buildings (solar, geo-thermal).
- Alternative fuel supplies for automobiles and fleets.

One may expect to see a continued emphasis given to incentives for green initiatives as energy prices rise, and public demand for corporate responsibility rises. The good news for many corporations is that there are tax incentives to encourage green practices and the savings is a great way to reduce tax liability.

ISSUES

Tax Reform

Tax reform is a perennially hot topic for legislators and corporate boards. Globalization of world economies and markets has impacted corporate tax rates in profound ways. In global markets, capital moves easily across borders and there is fierce competition by many countries to attract business. "Tax competition" has become a common strategy employed by countries to attract corporations with the lure and promise of reduced corporate tax rates. Consider the following statistics from the European Union (EU) (Mitchell, 2007):

- In 2007, seven EU nations cut their corporate tax rate.
- Between 2002 and 2007, 16 EU nations have cut their corporate tax rate.
- Between 1995 and 2007, 24 EU nations have cut their corporate tax rates.

These statistics reflect a corporate "tax cutting binge" in the EU, however, the corporate tax rates are also falling across the globe. The following countries have cut their corporate tax rate in recent years or plan to cut their rate in the near future: Australia, New Zealand, Canada, Singapore, and Russia.

America hasn't always been in its current position as having a very high corporate tax rate. The Tax Reform Act of 1986 under the Regan Administration cut the corporate tax rate from 46 percent to 34 percent and was credited with significantly improving the U.S.'s competitive position. By the late 1980s, there was a trend among other nations to cut corporate tax rates as the U.S. had done in 1986; this was a sure sign that tax competition was heating up. In the United States, the corporate tax rate rose 1 percentage point to its current level of 35 percent during the Clinton administration; when combined with state-level corporate taxes, the statutory U.S. corporate tax rate is estimated to 40 percent. Put into perspective, the U.S. rate of 40 percent was on average, as of 2007, 16 percent points higher than most EU corporate tax rates (Mitchell, 2007).

Until the early 1990s, the combined state and federal statutory corporate tax rate kept up with the rate in other developed nations. But since then, rates in other Organisation for Economic Cooperation and Development (OECD) member nations have "fallen sharply, making the U.S. an outlier" (Desai, 2012). However, despite having one of the highest corporate tax rates, the U.S. now collects less in corporate tax revenue, as a percentage of GDP, than most of the other OECD nations (Desai, 2012).

Corporate Tax Burden

The statutory or official federal taxation rate is just one measure of the actual corporate tax burden. Other measures include:

- effective tax rate may be higher or lower than statutory rates depending upon government rules surrounding receipts, depreciation and other deductions
- compliance around tax laws is time consuming and expensive as companies struggle to comply with complex tax code across many countries

The United States also had the dubious distinction of being cited as the 107th nation out of 117 in terms of tax efficiency according to rankings published in 2007 by the Cato Institute. Put another way, only 10 other nations were documented as having a more inefficient tax structure than the United States. Contributing to the inefficiency in administration of the U.S. tax code was the fact that of 175 nations, the United States had the fifth longest tax code (Mitchell, 2007). The U.S. tax code is notorious for being overly complex and unwieldy.

More recently, in 2012, Markie and Shackelford analyzed publicly available financial statement information for 11,602 public corporations from 82 countries from 1988–2009 in an attempt to isolate the impact of domicile on corporate taxes. They found that the country in which the parent of a multinational is located, and to a lesser extent its subsidiaries are located, "substantially affects its worldwide effective tax rate (ETR)." Japanese firms always face the highest ETRs, the authors concluded. U.S. multinationals are among the highest taxed, and multinationals based in tax havens face the lowest taxes. And although ETRs have been falling over the last two decades, Markie and Shackelford wrote, "the ordinal rank from high-tax countries to low-fax countries has changed little."

The IRC has been described as "ever expanding and incredibly arcane" by critics who cite that federal tax rules and regulations have more than doubled since the 1970s. Consider some of these statistics from 2000, and assume that the problems have only worsened (Stinton, 2000):

- The federal tax code in 2000 consisted of 46,000 pages.
- The chief source of federal tax complexity is related to the income tax levied on individuals and businesses.
- The compliance burden associated with filing a federal income tax return (for a business with assets under $1 million) is three times larger than the tax burden (taxes paid).
- There is a major tax law change, on average, every 18 months.

"The U.S. corporate tax system is an anachronism that discourages growth and undermines job creation. High tax rates are driving jobs and investment abroad" (Mitchell, 2007, ¶2).

"America generally does a good job at attracting capital because of its stable currency, dynamic economy, favorable tax rules for individual foreign investors, and lower overall burden of government. But the corporate tax system is one area that needs radical improvement, one where lawmakers can learn lessons from Europe" (Mitchell, 2007, p.2).

Global Competition of Corporate Tax Rates
A 2007 KPMG Survey of global corporate tax rates outlines statutory tax rates for 92 countries. According to the survey, the trend toward lower corporate tax rates continued in 2007 but there were signs that the fall in rates is slowing. There is even some speculation that corporate tax rates may have reached a natural low point (Hickey, 2007). 2007 showed that the most pronounced reduction of corporate tax rates was in the European Union—as had been the case in 2006. Collectively, rates for EU member states fell as tax competition gained momentum amongst EU member states themselves. In 2006, "Europe looks distinctly more attractive than either Asian-Pacific or Latin America" for locating business in "tax friendly" jurisdictions ("KPMG's corporate tax rate survey," 2006).

With tax competition equalizing tax rates across the globe, countries have to resort to incentives other than a low corporate tax rate to attract and maintain business investments. According to the KPMG survey, "business friendliness" is becoming a key differentiator when rating a potential tax environment ("KPMG's corporate tax rate survey," 2006).

Statutory or Headline Tax Rates must be evaluated with caution when determining the overall "corporate tax burden" of a particular jurisdiction. The following factors could significantly change (increase or decrease) a country's statutory tax rate:

- Indirect taxes, which include Value Added Tax (VAT) or Goods and Services Tax (GST).
- Other financial inducements for domestic investment.
- The sophistication.

Increasing Importance of Indirect Taxes
KPMG Corporate and Indirect Tax Rate 2007 Commentary was the first to include specific information about indirect tax rates and their impact in contributing to business friendly environments. For this discussion, indirect taxes include: VAT and GST tax rates and trends. As corporate tax rates have fallen

and equalized the importance of indirect taxes as revenue, gathering strategies have increased. Trends appear to be to reduce corporate tax rates and make up for the revenue shortfalls with increased indirect taxes. It is clear that most countries that have cut their corporate tax rates have not been able to make up for the deficit with an expanded tax base. Attracting new investment is only one part of the equation; keeping investment is also a measure of success. There's no doubt that countries are resorting to more sophisticated methods of attracting and keeping investment as corporate tax rates become more equalized.

It is now common for countries to advertise their VAT/GST rates in an effort to attract businesses. Because of the "huge numbers of special rates and exceptions which many countries apply to their indirect tax regimes" it's not possible to draw many specific conclusions about the impact of advertised indirect taxes on business attraction (Hickey, 2007).

"The link between higher indirect taxes and higher prices is obvious to anyone who buys goods and services, but the link between lower corporate tax rates and increased inward investment, with the increased employment and infrastructure development it can bring, is less well understood" (Hickey, 2007, ¶9). The benefits of cutting corporate tax rates are difficult to communicate to voters. The impact of indirect taxes is obvious to voters in higher prices. Thus, the challenge remains for countries to keep corporate tax rates competitive to attract business investment, but use creative strategies to make up for decreased revenue. The reliance on indirect taxes is a trend that KPMG researchers see continuing into the future. Indirect taxes have the added benefit of providing a steady stream of revenue throughout the year, even with the added burden of tracking and compliance of this revenue stream.

TERMS & CONCEPTS

Codified: To arrange something into a systematic code (e.g. laws).

Effective tax rate (ETR): The effective tax rate is an average quantitative measure of an individual's income tax rate or of a corporation's pre-tax profits tax rate.

Headline: The publicly disclosed or advertised tax rate (statutory rate) that may be influenced by other factors such as indirect taxes or other hidden costs.

Indirect taxes: A fee levied by a government on a product, income, or activity in order to finance government programs. Taxes are either direct (charged directly on individual or corporate income) or indirect (added to the price of a good or service).

Internal Revenue Code (IRC): The Internal Revenue Code (IRC) of 1986 is the major regulatory entity of U.S. tax law. The IRC is organized topically and includes laws covering the income tax, payroll taxes, gift taxes, estate taxes, and statutory excise taxes. It is Title 26 of the United States Code (USC), and is also known as theInternal Revenue title.

Federal tax code: Aka Internal Revenue Code-Title 26.

Strategic tax review: Strategic tax review is a comprehensive review of an individual's tax position encompassing federal, international, and state taxes.

Statutory tax rate: A statutory tax rate is the legally imposed taxation rate for a certain tax grouping. For example an income tax might have multiple statutory rates that depend on income levels while a sales tax might have one consistent statutory rate.

Tax risk management: Refers to the linking of tax management practices and strategic corporate initiatives. Organizations must link tax decisions with business practices and capital expenditures.

Tax reform: Refers to the ongoing debate about how to reduce the expense and complexity of administrating the U.S. Federal Tax Code (for individuals and businesses).

BIBLIOGRAPHY

A new age of tax planning (n.d.) Deloitte & Touche, LLP.

Are you seeking ways to lower your tax rates? (n.d.) Deloitte & Touche, LLP.

Bartram, P. (2005, October). Making allowances. *Financial Director*, 22–24.

Creating a tax risk management strategy for a multinational. (2013). *International Tax Review, 24*, 26.

Desai, M.A. (2012). A better way to tax U.S. businesses. *Harvard Business Review, 90* (7/8), 134–139.

Johnston, A. (2006, November). The explosion of tax risk. *International Tax Review,* 24–26.

Hickey, L. (2007) KPMG corporate and indirect tax rate 2007. Commentary KMPG.com.

KPMG's corporate tax rate survey 2006. (2006). KPMG.com.

Markie, K.S., & Shackelford, D.A. (2012). Cross-country comparisons of corporate income taxes. *National Tax Journal, 65,* 493–527.

Mitchell, D. (2007). Corporate taxes: America is falling behind. *Cato Institute.*

Murray, D. (2006). Optimizing the business benefits from technology acquisitions. *Financial Executive, 22,* 36–41.

Stinton, P. (2000). Tax code still too complex. *San Francisco Chronicle.*

Understanding tax reform: A guide to 21st century alternatives. (2005). AICPA.

Wertheim, N. (2007). Going green, staying green. Deloitte & Touche, LLP.

SUGGESTED READING

President's Advisory Panel on Federal Tax Reform. (2005). Final report — November 1, 2005.

Stein, D. (2005). Shopping for tax rates. *Financial Planning, 35,* 83–84.

Walsh, M. (2006). Ireland climbs rankings of holding company locations. *International Tax Review, 17,* 70–72.

Wolk, M. (2006). Why the tax system keeps getting more complex. *MSN.com.*

Essay by Carolyn Sprague, MLS

TAX PLANNING AND PREPARATION

Tax planning helps a taxpayer find his or her way through a maze of paperwork and tax codes. There are a number of resources available to help taxpayers prepare their annual reports to local, state, and federal revenue agencies. By exploring these aspects of tax planning and preparation, the reader will better understand both the planning schemes and the environments of tax policy and reporting. A synopsis of the number of ways tax planning may take place in the course of preparing an income tax return is provided.

OVERVIEW

The iconic economist John Maynard Keynes once quipped, "The avoidance of taxes is the only intellectual pursuit that carries any reward."

Paradoxically, taxes are simultaneously one of the most loathed and most invaluable components of any political system. They are despised in popular circles because they draw away from our personal incomes, add cost to the goods and services we buy, and are imposed on our personal belongings such as cars and property. At the same time, taxes fund local, state, and federal coffers, which are in turn drawn upon to pay for schools and roadway repairs, social services, and national security. One of the contributing factors to the public's distrust of taxation is the amount of paperwork, details, and bureaucracy that any American filing a tax return must endure throughout the process. Tax planning helps a taxpayer find his or her way through this maze of paperwork.

Indeed, there are a number of resources in use to help taxpayers prepare their annual reports to local, state, and federal revenue agencies. By exploring these aspects of tax planning, the reader will better understand both the planning schemes and the environments of tax policy and reporting.

Very few industrialized countries operate without heavy reliance on tax revenues. Oman, for example, levies no income tax on its residents, but that revenue is compensated by a significant tax on businesses, particularly those in the oil industry. Without taxes, countries simply cannot operate unless an alternative form of revenue is located. Roads, education, social services, national security, and other government operations depend on taxation.

While the value of tax revenues cannot be discounted, most people lament the taxes taken from personal income or assessed on the purchase of a candy bar. Indeed, taxes seem to be imposed on every aspect of life—income, business, home ownership, retail, lodging, restaurants, alcohol, fuel, and personal property are among the various forms of taxation that are in place on the federal, state, and local levels in the United States. Many other countries have a similar, diverse collection of taxes, often at even higher rates.

In light of the myriad of taxes that are prevalent in the United States, reporting them to the federal and state governments is often an arduous affair for the uninitiated as well as those who understand it thoroughly. For this reason, a sizable percentage of the population turns to certified public accountants to assemble their returns. According to Harris Interactive, 47 percent of American men and 33 percent of women turn to computer software that helps them walk through each aspect of their returns step by step. The minority of people either prepare their taxes themselves, using paper forms, or turn to family members and friends to help file their taxes for them (Harris Interactive, 2006). While taxation is a fact of life for hardworking Americans, it is also a common fact that of the 91 percent of Americans paying their taxes, about 37 percent of them do not take steps to minimize their liability.

Reducing Tax Liability

Central to the issue of tax planning and preparation is the need for individuals to generate yearly tax reports that are accurate and incur the least amount of tax liability. Since people who earn more income pay more in taxes, the first way for individuals to reduce their tax liability is by reducing their income. Of course, they need not take a pay cut from their jobs in order to do so. Tax liability is determined by assessing the individual's adjusted gross income (AGI), which is the aggregate of all income sources less any adjustments to income. If an individual, rather than applying all income to a deposit account, invests part of his or her income in a 401(k) or similar retirement account, that modification signals a reduction in taxable income. Similarly, a taxpayer who reports deductions to account for student loan payments, alimony, or

John Maynard Keynes (Courtesy of National Portrait Gallery via Wikimedia Commons)

other expenses is also documenting an adjustment in income, thereby reducing tax liability (Perez, 2009).

Another important vehicle for reducing AGI is the deduction. There are a myriad of deductions an individual may report on his or her tax return, each of which must be itemized. In general terms, the IRS allows 11 types of deductions:

- automobile registration fees
- real estate expenses
- charitable contributions
- investment expenses
- taxes
- casualty and theft losses
- job-related books and publications
- professional organization and government dues and fees
- education and research
- business use of an individual's home computer and Internet service
- job search expenses (Robson, 2009)

In addition to deductions and adjustments, taxpayers may also see their tax liability decrease by taking advantage of available tax credits. There are a number of such credits, including incentives offered for a dependent's college education and another to encourage parents to adopt. For lower- and middle-income taxpayers, there is the earned income tax credit (EITC), which is designed to help those people who have full-time jobs but are not making very much in salary. The EITC helps qualified taxpayers reduce their tax liability and even see a refund despite receiving a relatively low paycheck (Internal Revenue Service, 2009).

Another vehicle for reduction of an individual taxpayer's tax liability is by increasing the withholding amount in that person's paycheck (Financial Web, 2009). Withholding is usually established when an individual begins his or her employment, but the modification can be made at any point thereafter. Increased withholding will result in a reduction in income but can also help generate a larger refund after April 15.

The greatest challenge for a taxpayer who is filing a return is to know about and take advantage of the myriad of vehicles that can help reduce tax liability by reducing one's AGI. This issue is the central point of tax planning—taxpayers would prefer to avoid losing tax refund monies by exploring every available resource.

FURTHER INSIGHTS

Do It Yourself

Most people are not tax professionals. As such, the notion of filing an individual tax return that takes into account the extreme complexity of relevant tax laws is often intimidating. Then again, there are advantages that many Americans see to preparing their own tax returns. About 45 percent of Americans file their own taxes. The rationale is threefold. First, many taxpayers see this avenue (as opposed to using an accountant or other tax service) as cost-effective. A tax preparation service may charge between $125 and $450 depending on the complexity of the return. These charges can negate a taxpayer's expected refund.

The second reason is a matter of convenience. An individual who files his or her own tax return does not need to set up an appointment, travel to a consultant's office, and spend an hour or more either in a waiting room or at the accountant's desk while awaiting preparation. Instead, he or she may prepare the return at a time or place at his or her convenience.

Third, many consumers consider a tax return an important document that helps them understand their own finances. By becoming familiar with the myriad of deductions, adjustments, and vehicles for AGI reduction, the taxpayer may better appreciate not only his or her tax liability but how he or she manages personal and business expenses.

Tax Software & E-Filing

Tax software became widely available in the 1990s and early twenty-first century, and has made personal tax filing even simpler for individual taxpayers and small business owners. A wide range of software systems has been introduced to the marketplace to enable the taxpayer to simply file online. All that individuals must do is either download the software from a company's website or visit one of many stores that sell such software. These programs are designed to help the taxpayer in every step of the return-development process, using clear and simple guidance language. This software is relatively inexpensive and easy to use, particularly for those whose income tax returns are simple. Business returns that involve a great deal of itemized deductions may prove frustratingly complex even with tax software.

An added benefit of electronic tax return filing (also called "e-filing") is the time involved between filing and receipt of the refund check. Whereas working with an accountant or simply sending in paper versions of the return may take weeks or more for processing, taxpayers who e-file may receive a refund check within 10 days (Wilburn, 2007). Furthermore, in light of the ongoing public concern of identity theft in the new global economy, taxpayers who e-file may take solace in the tight security this software provides them as they file their returns.

Those who are concerned with environmental protection also enjoy the fact that e-filing virtually eliminates the amount of paper involved with filing taxes. This fact has also taken root in state and federal revenue agencies, which have increasingly and actively encouraged taxpayers to use e-filing software to prepare and submit their returns.

In 2004, for example, 4.2 million Californians e-filed their taxes three weeks before the April 15 deadline. In that state, e-filing increased 69 percent over the course of a year, causing a drop of 40 percent in the use of government paper. Additionally, the cost of processing paper returns in California was $1—the lack of paper returns saved California's government millions of dollars ("State tax e-filing," 2004).

Thus, for a growing number of individuals, filing returns themselves has become more popular. However, there are still conditions in which help may be needed.

Getting Help with Tax Planning: CPAs

The common practice of filing one's own returns owes much of its momentum to the increased prevalence and user friendliness of online filing software. This has proven particularly useful for taxpayers with simple returns. However, there are situations in which taxpayer returns are considered better handled by a certified public accountant (CPA) or similar professional.

One benefit is the amount of experience a CPA brings to the tax-planning process. While tax-planning and tax-return software is becoming more and more in tune with tax laws governing deductions and other aspects of AGI reduction, it is still a common perception that certified public accounts are more likely to find a higher number of tax breaks when performing a taxpayer's return. In fact, some studies indicate that CPAs are typically more aggressive in terms of locating relevant tax cuts for their clients than other tax preparers, such as lawyers (Dunn, 1986).

Another situation in which a certified public accountant often proves more useful is one of complexity. Indeed, the average taxpayer may have a relatively simple return to file—one that reports income, a few deductions and adjustments, and perhaps income generated from market investments. However, in many cases, such as for businesses and multistate returns, more complex filings are to be expected. Although such returns may be filed using "do it yourself" software, the intricacies of these types of returns may be too daunting for inexperienced taxpayers to perform by themselves. Those who do draft their returns in this arena are often

well-advised to take the draft to a CPA to ensure that no mistakes were made and no deductions, tax breaks, or adjustments were missed.

The familiarity of CPAs with the abundance of available tax deductions and adjustments helps the taxpayer, particularly in cases when the return is being filed close to the deadline. Many taxpayers, private and business alike, do not review their tax information (including organizing receipts, reviewing the previous year's returns, and researching updated benefits) until close to April 15. The short window they give themselves means that comprehensive reviews of such information may not be conducted in the interest of time. Small business owners, for example, may miss important deductions on travel, meals, and entertainment, which could help reduce significantly the amount of taxes actually owed (Lynott, 2006). While a last-minute return can cause hasty tax preparation, an accountant's familiarity and experience with both long-standing and new deductions may help the taxpayer craft a more accurate return.

Taxpayers who turn to CPAs place a great deal of trust in them. If a taxpayer files his own returns, he alone must assume responsibility for any mistakes on the documents. However, a CPA bears some responsibility for any return he prepares and can be held accountable for any missteps and improper entries. The Internal Revenue Service carefully monitors the records of CPAs. If any CPA inserts erroneous data into a return, the IRS will often take pause to review not just that return but any others that the accountant prepared as well. In fact, such reviews may include holding a taxpayer's refund check pending a review of the tax return (Boyles & Feldman, 1988).

The use of certified public accountants has developed into a matter of taxpayer preference. Until recently, CPAs and tax attorneys represented the dominant entity by which tax filings were prepared. Over the last two decades, the development of online software has led many to eschew the CPA and file without help. Then again, the CPA remains a valuable resource for those who have complex returns, who do not understand the intricacies of their personal income taxes, and/or are constrained by the limits of the looming filing deadline.

CONCLUSIONS

In the 1980s, congressional leaders pushed for a simplification of the U.S. tax code. The system, proponents argued, was far too daunting for the average taxpayer to understand. A bipartisan compromise was ultimately reached by the mid-1980s but not until after a long period of rancorous debate and sifting through countless proposals. One congressman, Republican Delbert Latta of Ohio, took the floor and held aloft a thick document and said, "I hold in my hand 1,379 pages of tax simplification" (Anecdotage. com, 2009).

Naturally, the fact that taxation draws money away from an individual's regular income is the biggest reason why taxes are one of the most maligned aspects of life in the modern world, even though most people understand that taxes keep government and its services operating. Adding to the negative image people have of taxes is the fact that their application is usually complex, especially for the layman.

In order to protect his or her income, a taxpayer will usually seek to minimize the amount of taxable assets by reducing the elements that, in the aggregate, comprise his or her tax liability.

Each year, individuals who are planning their income tax returns will seek out the most effective ways by which they may reduce their adjusted gross incomes. In some cases, individuals may manage the planning and filing processes themselves, particularly if the returns are simple in nature. Such situations have been more common over the last few years in light of new tax-planning software. Then again, the certified public accountant, long the authority in terms of knowledge of tax policy, remains relevant, particularly among those with complex returns or a lack of in-depth knowledge of the myriad of liability-reducing options. As this essay has demonstrated, consulting with an accountant or simply filing a return without help, as well as what options to apply on those returns, is a matter of individual choice.

TERMS & CONCEPTS

Adjusted gross income (AGI): The aggregate of all income sources less any adjustments to income such as deductions.

Earned income tax credit (EITC): Helps qualified taxpayers reduce their tax liability and even see a refund despite receiving a relatively low paycheck.

E-filing: A manner of filing an income tax return using computer software and e-mailing that return to the government.

Tax liability: The amount of taxes for which a given individual or company is responsible.

BIBLIOGRAPHY

Aalberts, R. J., Biggart, T. B., & Harden, J. (2013). Tax and financial planning for same-sex couples in light of Windsor. *Journal of Financial Service Professionals, 67,* 64–74.

Anecdotage.com. (2009). Tax code.

Boyles III, J. V. & Feldman, D. L. (1988). Defensive strategies for CPAs tax practices. *Journal of Accounting Practices, 166,* 162–168.

Brinker, T. M. (2013). Identifying key American Taxpayer Relief Act and Health Care Reform changes in year-end tax planning. *Journal of Financial Service Professionals, 67,* 12–15.

Dunn, D. (1986, April 21). CPAs score the highest on April 15. *BusinessWeek 2943.*

Harris Interactive, Inc. (2006, March 20). Two in five Americans filing taxes doing nothing to minimize tax liability.

Internal Revenue Service. (2009). EITC for individuals.

Lynott, W. J. (2006). 13 ways to cut income tax bill now. *Ophthalmology Times, 31,* 122.

Perez, W. (2009). Tax planning basics: 3 ways to reduce your taxes.

Reducing your tax liability: The basics. (2009).

Robson, R. (2008, February 8). Finance/Taxes: List of tax deductions. *Ezine Articles.*

Soled, J. A. (2012). Comparative negligence defense in tax return preparation malpractice actions. *CPA Journal, 82,* 58–60.

State tax e-filing becoming more popular. (2004, March 26).

Wilburn, D. (2007). Make filing less taxing. *NEA Today, 25,* 48.

Suggested Reading

Blazek, J. (2004). Tax planning and compliance for tax-exempt organizations: Rules, checklists, procedures (4th ed.) [Book Review]. *Chronicle of Philanthropy, 17*, 64.

Clements, J. (2004, April 14). Tax cuts aren't forever: four strategies to lower your tab in the years ahead. *Wall Street Journal—Eastern Edition, 243.*

Hoffman, E. (2004, November 1). Time to do your tax checkup. *BusinessWeek, (3906),* 110.

Novack, J. (2005). Tax planning in the dark. *Forbes, 176,* 210–214.

Raskolnikov, A. (2008). Relational tax planning under risk-based rules. *University of Pennsylvania Law Review, 156,* 1181–1262.

Wiener, L. (1999). No vacation from taxes. *US News and World Report, 127,* 62.

Essay by Michael P. Auerbach, MA

Taxes and Business Strategy

This paper will take an in-depth look at how businesses develop their strategies relative to taxation. Specifically, the essay will look at several key areas of business activity, how companies' liability is impacted as a result of such activity, and how they may plan their respective tax returns in a way that serves the best interests of the business by incurring the least impact on profit. Discussion of internal operations tax strategies and more complex tax situations is presented.

OVERVIEW

There are few elements of life in modern industrial society more popularly unpopular than taxation. Governments impose taxes on income, property, retail sales, restaurant patronage, and commerce. In the United States, one of the targets of most citizens' vitriol is the agency responsible for collecting taxes—the Internal Revenue Service (IRS). Taxes are typically levied on the basis of commercial transactions—an individual receives compensation for working at a factory, while the owner is taxed because his or her factory generates profits. Out of this application of taxes to nearly every aspect of life, an unknown author once quipped, "A fine is a tax for doing something wrong … a tax is a fine for doing something right."

Still, although they do so begrudgingly, most taxpayers acknowledge the fact that taxes are used to fund government programs and projects at the federal, state, and local levels. From police, schools, and roadway repair to national security, international trade, and support of the elderly, taxes play an integral role in society. As such, taxes are largely viewed as a necessary evil.

This reluctant acceptance of taxes does not mean, however, that individuals and businesses alike will not seek to minimize their tax liability. The effort to find ways to avoid paying excessive taxes is at the core of tax planning. Individual taxpayers, for example, will ideally look at ways to modify their adjusted gross income, one of the main areas targeted by taxation agencies, so that as much of their financial assets as possible are fragmented into non-taxable funds (such as retirement accounts and 401(k) programs) or offset by tax credits.

Businesses must also seek to reduce their tax liability "footprints," taking into account their employee expenses, new tax laws and regulations, and any existing tax credits and exemptions for which they may be eligible. This paper will take an in-depth look at how businesses develop their own strategies relative to taxation. Specifically, the essay will look at several key areas of business activity, how companies' liability is impacted as a result of such activity, and how they plan their respective tax returns in a way that serves the best interests of the business.

Doing Business in the Twenty-First-Century Economy

The fundamentals of conducting business in the twenty-first century are in many ways not dissimilar from those of commercial enterprises of the latter twentieth century and earlier eras. Business exists to meet the demands of the customer. In order to sell its product or service to the consumer, the company will market it, helping spread the word about the value of the product, tapping into and taking advantage of various networking opportunities in order to present the product to as many consumers as possible. As demand for the company's goods increases, the company hires additional personnel to conduct internal operations (such as human resources and accounting), public relations, sales, and marketing.

Of course, the landscapes involved with commerce have changed considerably. In the late 1980s, for example, the American financial system was in relative disrepair while the rest of the economy was experiencing sluggish growth. Meanwhile, Japan's technological industries gave that country's economy an extraordinary boost. By the late 1990s, the U.S. economy, revived by the explosion of information technology and financial services, recaptured the lead from Japan in terms of prominence in the international economy ("The 21st Century," 1998). In fact, the development of a new international economy in only the last few decades represents a major evolution in the way business is now conducted, attributed in no small part to the development of new information technologies and Internet commerce.

The economy of the twenty-first century is global. Many transactions are conducted via the Internet, which means that companies that seek to be competitive in this marketplace must expand and diversify their operations to account for increased business opportunities. Large and small businesses alike may act similarly in this regard—they may expand their staffs, develop web-based commercial platforms, and link with other companies to fortify their positioning in the market.

Because of this evolution, businesses must also adjust their tax-planning endeavors in order to account for recently imposed and/or heretofore irrelevant tax laws and regulations. There are many examples of taxation issues facing businesses in this new environment.

APPLICATIONS

Internal Operations

When developing a tax strategy, a business, like any other taxpayer, will seek to minimize its taxable income. This pursuit does not literally mean cutting staff and other assets; rather, it means that by taking a full account of all expenses and taking advantage of all tax exemptions and credits, a company may see a reduction in its tax liability.

Reducing Tax Liability

There are a number of steps businesses may take toward this end. In one area, internal operations, the company seeks to reduce its liability by increasing expenses. Businesses all require office supplies and office machines (such as copy paper and computers). These items qualify as business expenses, which may be used to offset tax liability. In other words, businesses often seek to purchase equipment as well as basic office supplies in large quantities. The rationale is simple—if a company purchases all of the items it needs in a given tax year, then that company will also see a reduction in the amount of taxes it owes. Similarly, tax advisers recommend that businesses that are nearing the end of the year should make sure that all of their bills for that year are paid before December 31; any bills paid in the next year are applied to the following year's tax bill.

Write-offs

In addition, it is important for businesses to take account of any expenses or investments that for whatever reason fail to bring a return. Companies may purchase shares of another company or purchase computer systems or otherwise acquire systems and products that are designed to benefit the business's operations. If the investment fails to generate that return, its purchase may be considered a "write-off"—listed on a tax return as a deduction from the company's overall tax liability. While companies seek to avoid such types of purchases and investments, they may offset the losses via tax reporting. Careful monitoring of write-offs may help a company recoup losses caused by that expense and at the same time reduce the company's overall tax bill.

Employee Income Tax

One of the most important elements of a business tax strategy is addressing payroll. Employee income is, after all, subject to taxation, and businesses are required to withhold a percentage of full-time employee salary for state and federal taxes. In order to help organize these funds, companies often create a separate fund for the purposes of paying state and federal income taxes. For some of these companies, however, the presence of a payroll tax fund is a tempting resource from which to draw when business is slow, and if that fund is drained when it is time to submit income taxes, the company must scramble to find those owed monies or risk stiff fines.

In this arena, tax experts recommend that businesses organize well in advance of impending deadlines, budgeting for at least 10 percent of each employee's salary to be paid to the state and governments. In order to avoid the temptation of dipping into a company's payroll tax fund, businesses are encouraged to use computerized payment systems, such as the federal government's Electronic Federal Tax Payment System (EFTPS), so that payments are made automatically and not withdrawn from the payroll tax fund. Others simply never handle payroll, deferring instead to an external payroll and/or accounting service to manage this aspect of a company's operations (Rozbruch, 2009).

Internal Audits

Payroll is also one of the most audited aspects of a company's tax report. In 2004, the IRS saw more than $43 billion in enforcement revenue (money collected as a result of audits and collections activity). The main source of such audit revenues was payroll. With payroll activities firmly in the crosshairs of revenue collection agencies, most businesses, whether small, medium, or large in size, are strongly encouraged by tax experts to conduct internal audits well in advance of tax time. By doing so, these companies may account for any discrepancies in income reporting. Internal audits are not easy—they may take months to conduct—but may help a business avoid a far more painful government audit ("Follow these strategies," 2005).

Internal operations such as the ones described above comprise an arena in which many companies (and in particular, small businesses) minimize their tax liability. By organization and careful strategizing, businesses may avoid painful audits and fines. Still, in the twenty-first-century global economy, there are many businesses for which taxation is a much more complex issue.

Complex Tax Situations

The fundamentals of business today are not dissimilar from the basic tenets of business that have been practiced for millennia. Businesses provide goods and services based on customer demand. However, the environment in which business is conducted has changed considerably, especially in the last few decades. An ever-growing segment of the business population uses the Internet as an invaluable marketing tool to draw customers from broader regions, including other states and even other countries. Interstate and international commerce is common in the twenty-first century—not just for large multinational corporations but for small businesses as well.

While the global economy brings enormous potential for business development and ultimately, profit generation, it also presents a challenge for businesses in terms of taxes. Indeed, while the global economy has taken shape in spite of state and international borders, governments remain invariably bound by them. Regional trade and commerce organizations have become increasingly prevalent in the United States and in other countries, led by one of the most comprehensive multinational integrations, the European Union. However, tax codes generally remain compartmentalized and specific to the regions they serve.

Taxes between States

In the United States, taxes vary from state to state, both in terms of rate and application. For example, a person could purchase a cup of coffee in Connecticut and pay a few cents more than he or she would in New Hampshire or Massachusetts but for different reasons: Massachusetts applies a 6.25 percent sales tax, while Connecticut imposes a 6.35 percent tax and New Hampshire does not have a sales tax at all (Sales Tax Institute, 2009).

One of the most complex areas of assessing the application of taxes in other states and countries is payroll. Companies that operate regional or satellite offices and branches in other states and countries must take into account the income tax regulations and rates applied in the area in which they operate. Many large and/or multinational corporations are able to effectively address this issue by creating or establishing payroll groups (organizations dedicated to managing local employee payrolls), which are fully versed in the tax laws applied to the business. Payroll groups are able to simply shift employees from group to group with all the proper tax protocols in order. Other companies, however, do not have the resources to create or hire such groups—they must operate on a site-to-site basis.

Taxes between Countries

This issue is particularly complicated when dealing in multinational situations. Businesses seeking to conduct operations in another country must glean a full understanding of that country's income tax withholding rules. For example, U.S. and British citizens working abroad are subject to laws that require employers to withhold employee taxes in their home countries. However, companies with workers whose homes are in countries without such exemption laws to other locations where those laws are also nonexistent may be forced to withhold payroll taxes for both countries (Moore, 2005). In light of this fact, employers must be extremely vigilant of in-country rules governing employee income tax liability.

As the payroll example demonstrates, taxes on business operations in multiple states or countries present sizable challenges for companies in terms of strategy. Companies that conduct business in other states or countries must keep careful records and a watchful eye on the tax rates and laws of those regions as well as the expenses and revenues generated from those areas. A company's business strategy must follow two general objectives. The first is to extensively assess the company's activity in a given state. By conducting this analysis, a business may effectively establish its taxable income subject to apportionment (the distribution of taxes among various jurisdictions in which the company operates). Doing so will both help paint an accurate illustration of a company's tax liability while assisting planners in structuring the company's overall operational strategy. The second objective is to minimize the tax costs. Such an endeavor involves a total analysis, however, instead of a segment-by-segment assessment. Companies with multistate or multinational activities must weigh the various tax codes and rates in each system in order to determine whether taxes saved in one state or country are not offset by higher tax rates in other systems (Healy & Schadewald, 2009).

As businesses vary in size, industry, and operations, so too do the systems by which they pay and withhold taxes. In some cases, the company's tax-reporting system is simple—the business may be small in terms of staff and client base as well as service area. In cases that involve multistate or international business, however, taxation policies to which companies must adhere become more complex and, as a result, business strategies related thereto must be detailed and observant of that complexity.

CONCLUSIONS

Albert Einstein once complained that "the hardest thing in the world to understand is the income tax," a comment that was quickly seized upon by prominent congressman and senator Warren Magnuson (D-Washington): "If Einstein and the agents of the Internal Revenue Service cannot understand the Tax Code, then the ordinary taxpayers of the US are entitled to a little help" (cited in Goodman, 2007).

For the uninitiated citizen with simple tax-reporting responsibilities, understanding the complexities of tax policy and administration is often a daunting task. For small businesses, the task is sometimes even more challenging, and for large businesses, that complexity is compounded. Regardless of the unfavorable nature of this undertaking, countless people, business owners, and managers alike must take stock of their tax liability and develop strategies to minimize that liability. Businesses must take care when developing their strategies toward minimizing liability. All businesses must carefully monitor their internal operations, accounting for expenses and write-offs, as well as assessing payroll. By doing so, the company may also help glean a better understanding of ways it might adjust its operations to contain costs and create better efficiencies in addition to minimizing tax liability.

In the global economy of the twenty-first century, the broader scope of potential clients and customers in neighboring states and across national borders has added a considerable degree of complexity to the development of a business's tax strategy. Multijurisdictional taxation requires that companies pay extra attention to the income and sales tax requirements of the areas in which they conduct business. In many cases, these businesses must either dedicate a larger sum of their budgets to local taxation analysis or acquire the services of external vendors to do so.

Whether the company is large or small and the client base is local or international, the fundamental necessity of business tax strategy remains careful vigilance. Without a comprehensive and up-to-date understanding of a company's tax requirements in the market in which it operates, a lack of attention to detail may significantly impact the health and sustainability of that company.

TERMS & CONCEPTS

Apportionment: The distribution of taxes among various jurisdictions in which the company operates.

Electronic Federal Tax Payment System (EFTPS): An automatic federal payroll tax withholding system.

Multinational corporation: A corporation based in one country but with operations in other countries.

Payroll tax fund: Organization dedicated to managing local employee payrolls.

Tax liability: The amount of taxes owed.

Write-off; An investment that fails to generate a return that is cited on a tax return as a deduction.

BIBLIOGRAPHY

Follow these strategies to avoid an IRS audit in your payroll department. (2005). *Payroll Manager's Report, 5*, 1–7.

Garbarino, C. (2011). Aggressive tax strategies and corporate tax governance: an institutional approach. *European Company & Financial Law Review, 8*, 277–304.

Goodman, T., Ed. (2007). *The Forbes Book of Business Quotations.* New York: Black Dog Publishing.

Healy, J., & Schadewald, M. (2008). *Multistate Corporate Taxation 2009: CPE Course.* Chicago: CCH Publishers.

Klassen, K. J., & Laplante, S. (2012). The effect of foreign reinvestment and financial reporting incentives on cross-jurisdictional income shifting. *Contemporary Accounting Research, 29*, 928–955.

Moore, R. (2005). International payrolls. *International Tax Review, 16*, 57–60.

Quotations about taxes. (2009).

Rozbruch, M. (2009, August 17). Is IRS enforcement of small business delinquent payroll tax problems treasonous?

Connecticut governor allows budget bill to become law without signature—includes rate decrease and amnesty program. (2009). *Hot News Update.*

The 21st century economy (Cover story). (1998). *Business Week,* (3593), 58–59.

SUGGESTED READING

Barrett, J. (2009). 2009 mid-year tax planning. *Business West, 26*, 30–34.

Leverich, J. (2005). Developing a better business tax strategy. *Enterprise/Salt Lake City, 34*, 9.

Mayover, S. (1989). The Coopers and Lybrand guide to business tax strategies and planning. *Library Journal, 114.*

Mitrusi, A., & Poterba, J. (2000). The distribution of payroll and income tax burdens, 1979–2009. *National Tax Journal, 53*, 765–795.

Young, R. (1980). Taxation ... multistate corporations. *American Bar Association Journal, 66*, 780.

Essay by Michael P. Auerbach, MA

THE GLOBAL FINANCIAL CRISIS OF 2007–2010

ABSTRACT

Because of the numerous causes of this event, the U.S. recession and subsequent global financial crisis that began in 2007 has generated a great deal of academic and political interest in understanding its nature and how its repetition may be avoided in the future. This paper will cast a light on the roots of the 2007–2010 global financial crisis, its impacts, and the tools employed to bring it to a close.

OVERVIEW

Adherents to the familiar George Santayana axiom, "Those who ignore history are condemned to repeat it" would find validation in the history of recessions in the United States. One of the worst recessions in U.S. history took place when a land speculation bubble (an uncorrelated increase in prices) began to rapidly collapse upon itself. Banks, fearful of insolvency, suspended certain transactions, sending the economy into a severe recession that lasted for a year. This recession was at the time the worst recession the United States had ever experienced. More important, it was one of the first recessions in U.S. history, commencing in 1797, less than 10 years after the Constitution was ratified.

The "Panic of 1797," as it was known, would be succeeded by dozens of recessions over the course of the following two centuries. This list includes what most historians deem the worst recession in US history: the Great Depression of the 1930s. The first decade of the twenty-first century began with a severe recession, exacerbated by the horrific terrorist attacks on the World Trade Center and the Pentagon in 2001. Only a few years after that recession came to an end and the economy grew again, another recession began. This period, which began in 2007, resembled the Panic of 1797 in many ways, although its severity and global impact most commonly drew comparisons to the Great Depression.

There are those who believe that the global recession of 2007–2010 and the subsequent crisis it created came unexpectedly, while others claim to have seen the warning signs more than a year before it began. Because of the numerous causes of this event, global financial crisis that began in 2007 has generated a great deal of academic and political interest in understanding its nature and how its repetition may be avoided in the future. This paper will cast a light on the roots of the 2007–2010 global financial crisis, its impacts, and the tools employed to bring it to a close.

The Housing Bubble. Similar to the Panic of 1797, the roots of the global financial crisis of 2007–2010 can be found in real estate. After the United States began reemerging from the 2001–2004 recession, housing prices began to show unusual upward mobility. Political leaders and other observers, however, were clouded by the apparent good news surrounding home ownership—more homes purchased meant more jobs and more consumer spending. Then again, the rise in housing prices could not be correlated to any other area of growth. In fact, many economists argued that what was occurring was not a sign of economic growth but a housing bubble

(an unexpected and temporary inflation in housing prices) that was doomed to burst and contract. In 2005, that possibility became reality, as a number of key markets saw housing prices decline. Then-chair of the Federal Reserve Bank (the Fed) Alan Greenspan acknowledged that the market, in some areas, was becoming "frothy," but said that a housing bubble was unlikely (Freeman, 2005).

By 2006, Greenspan's comments were largely discredited. In fact, many began to turn on the Fed, suggesting that that institution's recommendation that interest rates stay at record low levels (a policy that began in the late 1990s) started a housing boom. Home purchases were promoted by the government as contributors to individual wealth and retirement plans. The Fed even made mortgage interest rates tax-deductible, another incentive for homeowners to buy homes and make renovations thereto (Kohn Bryant, 2010). Home ownership increased with the government's message to Americans that the more real estate they owned, the greater their wealth would be.

The Community Reinvestment Act and Subprime Lending. The increased number of home purchases that occurred was also attributable to another trend. Lending institutions had begun to sell subprime mortgages to a growing number of homeowners. Subprime mortgages are housing loans that are offered to people with low incomes and/or poor credit. Subprime mortgages have been in existence since the 1990s, although the government strongly encouraged banks to provide affordable loans to low-income and debt-ridden residents since the 1970s, when the government passed the Community Reinvestment Act (CRA) to prevent discrimination among mortgage programs (Brook, 2008). The CRA gave rise to the government's push for lending institutions to have available mortgages that the poor could afford. Subprime lending was ardently backed by the government, including the mortgage security giants Fannie Mae and Freddie Mac. Still, in light of the fact that subprime lending involves providing individual loans of hundreds of thousands of dollars to people already saddled with debt and/or poor credit, there is an obvious risk attached to the practice. Still, the government, Fannie Mae, and Freddie Mac forged ahead with the subprime lending campaign (Brook, 2008).

Because the government was actively promoting subprime lending (and apparently looking the other way on predatory lending), lending institutions became focused on securing high volumes of such mortgages. Major financial institutions, like AIG and Merrill Lynch, worked diligently to compete for this business by acquiring smaller lenders with reputations for subprime lending (Dickey, 2010). These lenders were paid not based on the quality of the mortgages but by volume, and major institutions took account of this volume and the profits it yielded. Indeed, subprime lending presented great potential returns in the short term.

By 2007, it became clear that the risks associated with subprime mortgages were very real. A stagnant economy meant more people were making less and starting to realize that they were unable to meet their financial commitments. The Fed, which is supposed to protect banks through regulation, went instead with the tide, supporting the subprime industry and the dangers they represented. In fact, the Fed did not require financial institutions to set aside the adequate amount of money to offset potential losses—this regulatory requirement was woefully outdated (Appelbaum & Cho, 2009). Meanwhile, the Fed signed off on acquisitions of subprime lenders made by Citigroup and Wachovia, two major financial institutions with global connections. Banks also sought to offset the risks by selling high-risk loans in pools on the markets. Over time, banks began to realize that the housing market was becoming sour, and their losses were starting to pile up.

FURTHER INSIGHTS

The Crisis Goes Global. The overwhelming losses affecting U.S.-based financial institutions sent shockwaves around the world. Financial giant Lehman Brothers went bankrupt in September 2008 and AIG teetered on the brink as well. High-risk mortgages were folded into other pension, mutual, money market, and other funds in order to mitigate those dangers. Investors from all over the world were unwittingly made participants in the subprime industry; when the risks came to fruition, investors worldwide experienced losses. In fact, because few understood that the subprime lending industry was so vast and integrated into the securitized market, some investors actually invested more of their money than they had

through leveraging; their faith in the marketplace was based on ignorance of the presence of toxic subprime mortgages.

The growing global crisis was exacerbated by the fact that, in the midst of the collapse of Wall Street's biggest figures, short-term lending and capital was nearly halved. New loans to large borrowers fell by 47 percent in the last quarter of 2008 compared to the previous quarter. Lending actually sloughed by 79 percent compared to the height of the "credit boom," which had peaked in 2007 (Ivashina & Scharfstein, 2010). Banks, particularly those that were dependent on credit rather than deposit accounts, were becoming less likely to lend to expanding businesses. On the global stage, monetary policy was extremely loose. Monetary policy that was used in the United States to boost consumption after the "dot com" bubble burst during the early twenty-first century led to a large number of trade imbalances with emerging market economies such as China (Mohan, 2009). These emerging economies were also threatened by the instability in the United States and Europe, as a large proportion of their income is derived from goods and services provided to Western countries, which now had less money to spend on them.

Lack of Communication. If the U.S. Federal Reserve did little to curtail the growth of the subprime mortgage issue, the Fed's peers on the international stage did little to halt the crisis as it spread overseas. The International Monetary Fund, the World Trade Organization, and networks of regulatory agencies all fell short on efforts to address the growing crisis. Some argue that the failure of these international organizations and networks (as well as the U.S. financial regulatory system) was not based on an ignorance of the scope of the subprime issue but rather due to a lack of global connectivity between these regulatory bodies (Zaring, 2010). Unlike the markets, these groups were not interconnected prior to the period in which subprime lending developed into a juggernaut. Without the ability to recognize the roots of the growing problem and fashion an adequate response, the regulatory organizations of the global economy could not intervene quickly enough to contain the crisis.

The American financial crisis spread quickly to other international markets. One month after the Lehman Brothers collapse in 2008, the European

Central Bank spent approximately 771 billion to provide emergency liquidity to European banks in order to slow the growing crisis. However, fears on the European markets continued to rise—banks began offering much higher interest rates based on distrust in market stability (Teply, Cernohorska & Cernohorska, 2010). The fact that international lenders were pulling back on credit meant that the financial crisis that had begun in the United States was now a global issue—one that threatened the stability of some of the world's most integrated market systems.

Conditions in Europe. The globalization of the financial crisis occurred while the European Union (EU) was already in a vulnerable position. Countries such as Greece, Italy, Ireland, and the Baltic states, by joining the EU and suddenly experiencing the low-interest rates that accompanied the Euro, began to consume in large quantity. Spain, for example, built more homes in 2006 than Germany, France, and Great Britain combined. The former Soviet nations in the Baltics saw a 15 percent growth rate—a rate that was built not on economic growth but on credit ("The financial crisis," 2008).

One of the most glaring and potentially devastating situations during the tail end of this crisis was centered in Greece. For years leading up to the crisis, that country had taken advantage of low Euro-based interest rates and engaged in a spending policy that resulted in a condition of severe debt. In 2009, the crisis continued to topple banks from Europe to Asia. Incoming Prime Minister George Papandreou assumed office to discover that the severe debt Greece suffered had been woefully understated and that it was in fact three times higher than previously thought ("Credit Crisis," 2010). Papandreou announced his commitment to reducing the country's debt—a move that was made to placate the European Union as well as Greek voters. His government pushed for a hard-line austerity plan, slashing public services as well as other large portions of the Greek budget. In return, he sought help from the EU—a request that the International Monetary Fund and the EU begrudgingly voted to approve, authorizing 110 billion in aid to that country. Throughout the EU and the rest of the international community, however, fears remained that, if Greece defaulted on its debt in an already tumultuous global economy, it could have devastating impact on the markets (Parker, 2010).

Such a situation would send ripples from Europe around the globe and could return the international economy to a state of recession. Greece defaulted on its debt obligation in the summer of 2015, but the country accepted increased austerity measures in October 2015 in order to receive an additional $2.3 billion in bailout funds in order to pay off its international loans. However, the EU has taken measures to limit financial contagion if Greece should leave the Eurozone, reducing the potential negative impact of the Greek debt crisis on the global financial system.

Intervention and Avoiding Recurrence. One of the most significant developments fostered by the global financial crisis of 2007–2010 was the reversal of policy regarding government's role in private industry. During the 1990s, the government had stayed largely away from direct involvement on Wall Street. As stated earlier, the Fed (and indeed the entire federal government) did nothing to mitigate subprime lending; in fact, it was actively promoted.

However, when the crisis reached global proportions, the administrations of Republican George W. Bush and Democrat Barack Obama both saw the need to inject an enormous sum of money into the financial industry to prop up flagging financial institutions. The Troubled Asset Relief Program (TARP) of 2008, for example, appropriated $700 billion of taxpayer money to "bail out" those financial institutions that, because of their connections to global markets, were deemed too big to be allowed to fail. While there were previous stimulus efforts in recent decades, TARP and other government-sponsored industry investments had strings attached. These bills came with regulatory changes, business policy requirements, and other rules that dictated how recipients should operate in order to prevent future such crises (Moulton & Wise, 2010).

In 2010, the U.S. Congress passed a series of major reforms to the country's financial system. The bill, called the Dodd-Frank Wall Street Reform and Consumer Protection Act, added several new rules regarding credit approval and lending practices, risk mitigation, and fees. The law also created several new oversight programs, including the introduction of a new bureau within the Federal Reserve charged with consumer financial products, such as mortgages and credit cards (Jackson, 2010). The new law was significant for its major reversal of policy, from a laissez-faire approach to the financial markets to one in which the government more heavily regulated virtually every type of investment and at every level of risk.

The severe contraction that began in 2007 and continued until 2010 had a significant impact worldwide. Though measures such as TARP were able to help financial corporations mitigate the damages caused by the subprime crisis, the federal government's slowness to action, followed by a similar reaction by international regulatory agencies and organizations meant that recovery was a slow process. Some forecast a continued, though shallower, decline in lending ("United States banking sector outlook," 2010). Unemployment rates remained high in the United States and throughout much of the world for years. Although recovery persisted, it was weak, and many feared a "double dip." The Eurozone, particularly, continued to struggle over the four years following the end of the recession, facing persistently high unemployment rates, the threat of deflation, and stagnating economic growth rates. The long-term impact of the crisis of 2007–2010 remains uncertain, as reforms had scarcely been imposed before calls to repeal at least some measures began. The breadth, causes, and responses of the global crisis will be the focus of analysts and arguments for the foreseeable future. However, the financial crisis did underscore the dominance of the financial sector in U.S. politics and has signaled an erosion of U.S. financial and economic power and influence worldwide.

VIEWPOINTS

Will Reform Work? Although these reforms are significant, some believe they are likely to fall short unless policymakers target risk on every level—from the risk managers in private businesses to the taxpayers themselves. It has been argued that the policymakers were both active supporters of the creative risk-taking that was associated with subprime lending as well as absorbing losses during crises (Kane, 2010). While the reforms add a layer of regulatory oversight, the government previously had a watchdog in place, the Fed, before the crisis took shape. According to some critics of the measure, the law simply looked to enforce the same faulty system of laws that allowed the crisis to unfold (Bozzo, 2010). Unless all parties, including the federal government and the investors themselves, adopt a more cautious approach regarding risk, reform measures such as these may not be effective enough to prevent further crises.

In the United States and elsewhere, many of the worst economic periods were worsened by the inaction of government leadership. It may be argued that this inaction was largely due to the political unpopularity of government intervening in the free market. This assertion is given validity in particular in light of the most recent economic crisis. After the major recession and economic slowdown of 2001–2004, the government continued its campaign of stressing affordable home ownership, even for those who might not be able to afford such real estate over the long term. The glut of home purchases created a housing bubble that many chose to disregard. It also created toxic subprime mortgages that spread throughout the increasingly global marketplace.

An interesting aspect of the global crisis of 2007–2010 was not necessarily that the government failed to intervene when the crisis first began. In fact, one of the most egregious issues was the fact that there were actually safeguards in place designed to prevent a widespread crisis. As shown here, the Fed had regulations in place designed to mitigate risk and warn lenders against the dangers of subprime lending. Unfortunately, the federal government's endorsement of the subprime industry started a lucrative wave of home purchases that neither the United States nor international government watchdogs sought to curtail.

CONCLUSION

The three-year financial crisis that completed the first decade of the twenty-first century was one of the worst economic periods in modern history. It is notable particularly because it showed the interconnectedness of the global economy. It is likely that, had key financial institutions not received billions of dollars in emergency aid, the crisis would have been far more devastating on the international stage. Nevertheless, there are lessons to be learned based on this crisis—historical concepts that, if not assessed, could force future elements of the global economy to repeat them.

TERMS & CONCEPTS

Community Reinvestment Act (CRA): A 1970s law passed to prevent discrimination in mortgage lending for home ownership.

Federal Reserve Bank (Fed): The agency charged with regulating banks and financial institutions in the United States.

Housing bubble: An uncorrelated increase in the price of residential real estate that becomes unsustainable and can even result in negative equity for the homeowner.

Subprime mortgage: Housing loan offered to residents with low incomes and/or debt issues.

Troubled Asset Relief Program (TARP): A law passed in 2008 to fund emergency aid for failing financial institutions and other industries as a result of an economic crisis.

BIBLIOGRAPHY

Anand Tularam, G., & Subramanian, B. (2013). Modeling of financial crises: a critical analysis of models leading to the global financial crisis. *Global Journal of Business Research (GJBR)*, 7, 101–124.

Appelbaum, B. & Cho, D. (2009, December 21). Fed's approach to regulation left banks exposed to crisis. *The Washington Post.* A1.

Bozzo, A. (2010, June 10). Financial reform bill's core element has lots of critics. *CNBC.*

Brook, Y. (2008, July 18). The government did it. *Forbes.*

Credit crisis — the essentials. (2010, July 12). *The New York Times.*

Dickey, R. (2010, May 12). Dissecting the global meltdown. *The Philadelphia Inquirer.*

Fahlenbrach, R., Prilmeier, R., & Stulz, R.M. (2012). This time is the same: Using bank performance in 1998 to explain bank performance during the recent financial crisis. *Journal of Finance, 67,* 2139–2185.

The financial crisis in Europe. (2008, October 13). *STRATFOR Global Intelligence.*

Fox, J. (2013). What we've learned from the financial crisis. *Harvard Business Review, 91,* 94–101.

Freeman, M. (2005, June 21). Report: Housing market at risk. *San Diego Union- Tribune.*

Ivashina, V. & Scharfstein, D. (2010). Bank lending the financial crisis of 2008. *Journal of Financial Economics, 97,* 319–338.

Jackson, J. (2010, June 25). Wall Street reform: A summary of what's in the bill. *CBS News/Politics.*

Johnston, C. W. (2013). Will the new banking regulations prevent the next U.S. financial crisis? *Journal of International Finance & Economics, 13,* 43–48.

Kohn, J. & Bryant, S. (2010, March). Modeling the US housing bubble: An econometric analysis. *Research in Business Economics Journal, 2,* 1–14.

Lahmiri, S., Uddin, G., Bekiros, S. Nonlinear dynamics of equity, currency and commodity markets in the aftermath of the global financial crisis. *Chaos, Solitons, & Fractals, 103,* 342 – 346.

Lupo-Pasini, F., & Buckley, R. P. (2015). Global systemic risk and international regulatory coordination: Squaring sovereignty and financial stability. *American University International Law Review, 30* (4), 665–741.

Lynch, D. (2010, April 8). Greenspan says, 'I was wrong 30% of the time'. *USA Today.*

Martin, F. (2014, October). The "new mediocre"— and why the Eurozone may be sliding back into recession. *New Statesman, 143* (5232), 35.

Mir, M. A. (2013). Global financial crisis and Indian economy: Causes and consequences. *Annamalai International Journal of Business Studies Research, 5,* 7–24.

Mohan, R. (2009, April 23). Global financial crisis— causes, impact, policy responses and lessons. 7th Annual India Business Forum Conference.

Moulton, S. & Wise, C. (2010). Shifting boundaries between the public and private sectors: Implications from the economic crisis. *Public Administration Review, 70,* 349–360.

Parker, R. (2010). Athens: The first domino? *The Nation, 290,* 5–8.

Singala, S., & Kumar, N. (2012). The global financial crises with a focus on the European sovereign debt crisis. *ASCI Journal of Management, 42,* 20–36.

Teply, P., Cernohorska, L. & Cernohorska, J. (2010). Key economic policy lessons from the 2008 financial crisis. *Anadolu University Journal of Social Sciences, 10,* 123–133.

United States banking sector outlook. (2010). United States *Commercial Banking Report Q3* 2010, 17–19.

Warren, M. (2016). The global financial crisis and US housing policy. *Journal of Business Retail Management Research, 10* (2), 105–110.

Zaring, D. (2010). International institutional performance in crisis. *Chicago Journal of International Law, 10,* 475–504.

SUGGESTED READING

Berkaert, G., Ehrmann, M., Fratzscher, M., & Mehl, A. (2014). The global crisis and equity market contagion. *Journal of Finance, 69* (6), 2597–2649.

Demyanyk, Y. & Hasan, I. (2010). Financial crises and bank failures: A review of prediction methods. *Omega, 38*, 315–324.

Hart, N. (2010). Macroeconomic theory and the global economic recession. *International Bureau of Business Research, 10*, 205–214.

Lewis, V., Kay, K., Kelso, C. & Larson, J. (2010). Was the 2008 financial crisis caused by a lack of corporate ethics? *Global Journal of Business Research, 4*, 77–84.

Malliaris, A. G., Shaw, L., & Shefrin, H. (Eds.). (2016). *The global financial crisis and its aftermath: Hidden factors in the meltdown.* New York, NY: Oxford University Press.

Matthews, C. (2014, October). The case for a global recession in 2015. *Fortune.*

Morici, P. (2010, May 12). Outside view: Trade deficit. *UPI Emerging Threats.*

On the issues: Financial reforms. (2010, July 20). *The (Vancouver, WA) Columbian.*

Essay by Michael P. Auerbach

THE U.S. FINANCIAL CRISIS OF 2007–2010

ABSTRACT

Scholars, economists, and leaders continue to compare the 2007–2010 recession to the Great Depression of the 1930s. It is clear that the 2007–2010 financial crisis had a profound impact on a number of key industrial sectors as well as individual consumers. This paper will provide an overview of the root causes of the financial crisis and discuss the efforts to foster a long-term recovery.

OVERVIEW

Not long after the start of the Great Depression, famed economist John Maynard Keynes was asked by a reporter whether any event like it had occurred before. "Yes," he answered, "it was called the Dark Ages, and it lasted 400 years." While the Great Depression did not last nearly as long as the Dark Ages, it did have an indelible impact on American history. The Depression changed the relationship between the government and the free market, leading President Franklin D. Roosevelt to adopt Keynes's ideal of government intervention in a time of crisis. It also forced upon Americans the notion of self-subsistence, as all family members sought work wherever it could be found, regardless of the location of a job or its suitability, in order to survive and rebuild from the economic collapse.

The Great Depression remains one of the most significant events in modern U.S. history. Since it came to an end during World War II, political leaders in the decades that followed took great steps to implement measures to protect against a recurrence. Entrepreneurs also took great pains to safeguard their businesses in the event of another Depression. Even those whose lives are more than two generations removed from the Depression look back on it in fear, comparing any economic downturn to that devastating period.

In 2007, the global economy began to suffer a series of events that led to a staggering economic recession that many dubbed the worst economic period since the Depression. This recession brought corporate and financial industry giants to the brink of failure, resulting in millions of job layoffs and foreclosures for countless businesses and homeowners. While scholars, economists, and leaders continue to compare this recession with the Great Depression, it is clear that the relatively short recession of 2007–2010 had a profound impact on a number of key industrial sectors as well as consumers themselves. This paper will look at the root causes of the financial crisis and discuss the efforts to foster a long-term recovery.

FURTHER INSIGHTS

Depression or Recession? The Great Depression was indeed one of the most significant periods of economic stagnation in modern history. Between 1929 and 1933, the gross domestic product (GDP) of the United States declined by 30 percent. In the view of many, there were many smaller depressions that took place before the Wall Street collapse of 1929. Within this school of economic thought, a depression was simply a period in which a downturn in economic

Alan Greenspan, chair of the US Federal Reserve, testifies before the House Senate Economic Committee, Washington, D.C. in 2005. (Courtesy of Library of Congress)

activity occurred. However, the Great Depression was an iconic event, so widespread and devastating that many felt it simply deserved its place in history—any "smaller depression" that occurred after this period would therefore be dubbed a "recession" (Moffat, 2010). More concretely, however, some economists have defined a depression as a period in which a country's GDP declines by more than 10 percent or a period of contracting GDP that lasts for more than three years.

There is very little universal agreement on the difference between a recession and a depression. A common definition of a recession is a period in which a country's GDP is in a period of decline over two or more consecutive quarters, although this definition is considered somewhat simplistic, as it does not consider unemployment rates or consumer confidence. What is agreed upon is that the Great Depression, in light of its severity, is typically the benchmark by which subsequent recessions are gauged (Moffat, 2010).

By 2007, the state and the national economies had largely returned to a state of reasonable growth after several years of stagnancy that lasted between 2001 and 2004. However, a number of factors that went largely unnoticed or ignored during this recovery helped lay the groundwork for another recession, one that would draw comparisons to the most significant recession in modern history. During the global financial crisis of 2007–2010, the GDP of the United States shrank by 0.3 percent in 2008 and by 3.1 percent in 2009, qualifying it as a recession but not as a depression.

The Housing Bubble. In the spring of 2005, the chair of the U.S. Federal Reserve, Alan Greenspan—whose nearly 20 years in the position gave him significant credibility among political leaders—acknowledged that there was a change in the housing landscape. However, he stopped short of saying there was cause for concern, saying instead that some housing markets had become "frothy" (Freeman, 2005). Others, however, expressed concern that this "froth" was in fact a housing bubble.

A housing bubble in essence is an unexpected increase in the valuations of residential real estate until they reach unsustainable levels. Housing bubbles typically lead to a point at which home values exceed incomes and employment growth, in addition to other economic factors. When a housing bubble "deflates"—a process that is typically gradual and not explosive—it can even result in negative equity for the homeowner (a mortgage debt that exceeds the value of the property).

The roots of this housing bubble extend back to a 2001–2004 recession and recovery period. The Federal Reserve ("the Fed") recommended that interest rates remain low in order to stimulate spending, as most consumers opted to minimize spending until the crisis was over. Some observers argue that these rates should have been increased after a short period, rather than held low for several years.

Subprime Lending. While the low interest rates almost certainly played a role in spurring home buying, it is believed that a major culprit was subprime lending. This practice entailed offering fixed-rate mortgages to individuals who could afford monthly payments but had poor credit histories. Because it offered growth to the housing industry, subprime lending was even endorsed by the government-backed Fannie Mae and Freddie Mac, the two corporations charged with purchasing and securitizing mortgages for lending institutions (Lynch, 2010). This approach satisfied many political leaders, who were under pressure (and who therefore applied pressure to the relevant agencies) to enable low-income Americans to purchase homes.

As subprime lending became more and more popular in 2004, the housing bubble began to grow. Lenders offered interest-only mortgages and other creative packages to entice lower-income people to buy homes. They also loosened their credit standards, which further broadened the market. Lenders, according to one real estate analyst, became more concerned with the quantity rather than quality of the mortgages they secured (Burry, 2010). To lower the risks, the lenders would then sell them on Wall Street as mortgage-backed securities. Meanwhile, the government (including Alan Greenspan and Fed officials) openly encouraged Americans to take advantage of record-low interest rates and buy a home. Such pronounced endorsements sent buyers to legitimate lenders, but it fostered increased cases of mortgage fraud as well (Burry, 2010).

In 2008, the housing bubble began to collapse upon itself. Homeowners, many of whom were coerced into thinking they could afford their mortgages, could not keep up with monthly payments or increases due to adjustable rate mortgages, especially as the economy began to slow. In Florida, a state with a traditionally vibrant real estate market, more than one-fifth of the state's mortgages were either 90 or more days behind in payment or were in foreclosure in 2009. The state's population dropped by 57,000 people (it normally grew by 200,000 to 400,000 people annually), and fewer state tax revenues sent the state budget into a $3.5 billion deficit ("Paradise," 2010, p. 5). According to RealtyTrac's Midyear 200 Metropolitan Foreclosure Market Report, for the first half of 2010, Miami recorded the highest number of foreclosures out of the top metro cities in the country, with 94,466 properties filing (Harmon, 2010).

The collapse of the housing bubble had an enormous impact on the American economy. It created record numbers of foreclosures, increased unemployment, and tore at the fabric of state infrastructures. It also created chaos in the heart of the business world—the financial sector.

The Collapse of the Financial Industry. The fact that subprime lending was so widespread was exacerbated by the fact that a large number of major financial institutions were heavily invested in the practice, and that the Fed, which regulates many of those major lenders, did not intervene. Speaking to a 2007 Fed conference in Chicago, Greenspan's successor, Ben Bernanke, told attendees that subprime lending did not pose a risk to the country's major financial institutions. However, five of the ten major institutions heavily invested in subprime lending were banks that

Federal Reserve Chairman Ben Bernanke, successor to former chair Alan Greenspan. He served in this capacity from 2006 until 2014. (Courtesy of United States Federal Reserve via Wikimedia Commons)

were overseen by the Fed (Applebaum & Cho, 2009). Among them were Citigroup and Wachovia, both of which either invested heavily in subprime lending or purchased lenders that engaged largely in such practice.

Of course, what attracted these major institutions to subprime lending was the perceived profitability involved. As mentioned earlier, lenders were more concerned with booking large quantities rather than high-quality mortgages. Such numbers, regardless of the risks, served as indicators of the lender's success. When Lehman Brothers began engaging in subprime lending in 2006, one of its major competitors, Merrill Lynch, looked to acquire a similar subprime lender, New Century Mortgage. Meanwhile, mid-sized mortgage lenders such as Washington Mutual and Countrywide aggressively competed with one another over who could book what one analyst called "the flimsiest mortgages" (Dickey, 2010). One year later, Merrill Lynch and Countrywide were acquired by Bank of America, Lehman Brothers

Federal Reserve Chair Ben Bernanke meeting with United States President Barack Obama. (Courtesy of Pete Souza, official White House photographer, via Wikimedia Commons)

filed for bankruptcy, and Washington Mutual was acquired by Chase.

Nebulous Accounting: The Case of AIG. Seemingly adding insult to injury were the rewards the banks gave to their senior personnel for amassing such a large quantity of subprime mortgages. American International Group (AIG) was one of the businesses at the center of this firestorm. In 2009, AIG was starting to feel the effects of the subprime crisis after its financial products division had invested aggressively in the subprime market. The company lost $40 billion in 2008 alone because of its dealings in this arena. The federal government, however, was determined not to let a giant like AIG fail—the company was a major cog in the global economy, and many feared that its collapse would have devastating effects on other worldwide economies. To prevent collapse, the government intervened, infusing AIG with about $200 billion through the Troubled Assets Relief Program (TARP). This bailout was designed to enable AIG to recoup its losses and regain its footing as it phased out of subprime lending. The money was not exactly free, however; the government now owned most of AIG and required strict and transparent accounting (Saporito, 2009).

This accounting uncovered an issue that became one of the biggest political firestorms during the 2007–2010 recession. In many cases, subprime lenders were accused of "pumping up" sales figures on mortgages, as doing so entitled key executives to more significant bonuses (Davidson, Wiseman, & Waggoner,

2010). One of the most visible of these alleged activities was manifest once again in AIG. In March 2009, AIG reported that it had paid approximately $165 million in retention bonuses to executives. These individuals were at the helm of the subprime endeavor and were being rewarded for securing such volumes of mortgages ("Obama tries," 2009).

This infuriated President Barack Obama and congressional leaders on both sides of the aisle, with the public clamoring for some sort of retaliatory action. President Obama and Secretary of the Treasury Timothy Geithner demanded that AIG halt the bonuses, but their demands were largely ineffective. The executives were contractually obligated to receive the bonuses, according to the new AIG chief executive. In light of the potential lawsuits, forcing the executives to return the money was likely to cost more to the government than the bonuses themselves ("Obama tries," 2009).

To the further consternation of the government and the general public, routine reporting in 2010 revealed that AIG had classified about $2.3 billion in repurchase agreements (financial arrangements whereby a party offers securities such as stock as collateral for short-term cash) as sales transactions before these bonuses were paid out. In late 2008, AIG leadership had demanded higher levels of collateral to enter into such agreements, particularly in light of the fiscal climate. Because the collateral requirements were greater than in previous arrangements, such transactions would be seen as a sale. Although AIG flatly denied that the repurchase agreement inclusion was used for the bonus arrangement, critics quickly seized upon the information as more evidence of the apparent nefarious behavior of financial institutions that contributed to the fiscal crisis (Gallu, 2010).

Such accounting seemed reminiscent of other examples of perceived improper accounting measures leading up to and during the crisis. For example, in 2008, New Century was placed under the microscope for very similar circumstances when that company used allegedly inflated sales figures to pay out its bonuses (Reckard, 2008).

In 2014, former AIG executive Hank Greenberg filed a lawsuit with the U.S. Court of Federal Claims, arguing that the government's 2008 bailout of his former company was an unlawful seizure of the company's shareholders' private property. In 2015, a judge in the United States Court of Federal Claim found the government's bailout terms to be excessively harsh but awarded no damages to Greenberg, as the company would have been bankrupted without the government's bailout, leaving the company's shareholders with nothing.

ISSUES

The Road to Recovery. The U.S. financial crisis of 2007–2010 was one of the most impactful economic events since the Great Depression. The recession itself, which lasted 18 months, was one of the longest post-Depression recessions in history. During the crisis (which persisted after the recession came to an end), the economy simply staggered. The country's peak-to-trough decline in real GDP was more than 4 percent and monthly job losses were as high as 750,000. The unemployment rate peaked at 10 percent in October 2009. The government's intervention in the near collapse of the financial industry, coupled with steady, low interest rates and a continued commitment to stimulate jobs have helped the economy turn around in some ways. President Obama also signed the American Recovery and Reinvestment Act in 2009 to help create jobs and cut taxes to stabilize the middle class. The GDP was 2.2 percent annual growth rate in 2012, and the economy was adding about 125,000 jobs per month in 2010 and was up to 200,000 in late 2013. By August 2016, the unemployment rate had declined to 4.9 percent, although this figure remained above the prerecession unemployment rate, which was 4.4 percent in early 2007, and wages remained stagnant.

The recovery process after this crisis has been incremental and tentative. Most experts and political leaders have expressed cautious optimism that the recovery will be sustained. The July 2010 passage of a financial industry regulatory overhaul has been lauded as a major step toward prevention of the missteps and risk-taking that undid this sector.

Several conditions demand continued caution in declaring the apparent recovery successful. The tremendous damage caused by the mortgage crisis, for example, took a number of years to repair, and although the housing market rebounded, long-term effects are unknown. In 2012, the U.S. federal government settled with five major banks for $25 billion for their parts in the housing scandal, and it reached a large-scale agreement in 2013 with JP Morgan for

$14 billion for the sale of fraudulent mortgages. The government offered programs such as the Home Affordable Refinance Program (HARP) to allow for homeowners to renegotiate their mortgages, but few people initially took part. The government originally planned for three to four million homeowners to refinance under such programs, but only about one-quarter took advantage by June 2010. In 2011, the Federal Housing Finance Agency made adjustments to HARP in the hope that more homeowners would take advantage of the program. Meanwhile, more than 300,000 foreclosures took place monthly between 2009 and 2010. With banks holding enormous stocks of foreclosed mortgages—some studies suggested that it would take eight years to clear this backlog if the prerecession rate of sales resumed—housing prices remained static, compounding the issue of negative equity ("Double-dip," 2010).

Adding to the slow return to normalcy in the U.S. economy has been the credit environment. Lenders no longer offer flexible credit in the wake of the crisis, due both to the new cautionary mentality in financial institutions and the federal deficit, which was already high before the crisis and was exacerbated by financial institution bailouts, economic stimulus, and other programs. Small businesses, which account for about half of the jobs in the United States, stand to suffer the most because of this ongoing credit crunch ("How to measure," 2010). Lack of affordable credit continued to hamper businesses seeking to expand for many years after the recession. In 2014, more than five years after the recession officially ended, public spending as a portion of the country's GDP increased for the first time since the financial crisis, signaling that the economic recovery was beginning to take hold. However, the postrecession U.S. economy has seen significant increases in income and wealth inequality, with the top 1 percent of income earners capturing more than half of the income gains in the first three years of the recovery, and many low- and middle-income families remain less wealthy than they were prior to the recession.

CONCLUSION

Although the historical significance of the Great Depression led to the "retirement" of the use of the term *depression*, the semantics of its replacement, *recession*, do little to ease the concerns of an economically vibrant society. In truth, there are a great many parallels that have been drawn between the Depression and the Great Recession of 2007. Among the similarities are massive unemployment, long-term fiscal stagnancy, and even a Keynesian approach to reversing such conditions—massive government intervention in the traditionally private business country.

The severe conditions wrought by the combination of the housing bubble and the mortgage crisis created ripples that spread throughout the global economy. Although most economists agree that the three-year U.S. financial crisis was winding down by 2010, by 2016, unemployment and wages had not fully recovered to their prerecession levels.

TERMS AND CONCEPTS

American International Group (AIG): A major U.S. financial insurance institution that was the recipient of significant government bailout funds to prevent further, and possibly global, financial collapse.

American Recovery and Reinvestment Act: A 2009 law passed with the goal of creating new jobs, cutting taxes, investing in long-term economic growth, and providing funding for programs such as unemployment benefits.

Housing bubble: An uncorrelated increase in the price of residential real estate, which becomes unsustainable and can even result in negative equity for the homeowner.

Recession: An economic downturn in which growth declines over a sustained period (often two or more quarters).

Repurchase sgreement: A financial arrangement whereby a party offers securities such as stock as collateral for short-term cash.

Subprime lending: The practice of offering mortgages to individuals who are determined to be able to afford monthly payments despite poor credit histories or low incomes.

Troubled Assets Relief Program (TARP): A 2008 law that offered financial assistance to U.S. financial institutions on the brink of collapse.

BIBLIOGRAPHY

Applebaum, B., & Cho, D. (2009, December 21). Fed's approach to regulation left banks exposed to crisis. *The Washington Post*. A1. Retrieved from EBSCO Online Database Newspaper Source Plus.

Boyallian, P., & Ruiz-Verdu, P. (2017). Leverage, CEO risk-taking incentives, and bank failure during the 2009–2010 financial crisis. *Review of Finance*.

Burry, M. J. (2010, April 4). I saw the crisis coming — why didn't the Fed? *New York Times*. 10.

Davidson, P., Wiseman, P., & Waggoner, J. (2010, June 28). 7 things that helped break the economy … and how Congress aims to fix them. *USA Today*. 1B.

Dickey, R. (2010, May 12). Dissecting the global meltdown. *The Philadelphia Inquirer*.

Double-dip drama. (2010, June 26). *The Economist, 395*(8688), 34–35.

Federal housing finance agency. (2011, Oct 24). FHFA, Fannie Mae and Freddie Mac announce HARP changes. FHFA.

Freeman, M. (2005, June 21). Report: Housing market at risk. *San Diego Union-Tribune*.

Gallu, J. (2010, July 15). AIG says it counted as much as $2.3 billion of repos as sales. *Bloomberg Business Week*.

Harmon, J. (2010). Rising foreclosure activity in 75% of nation's top metros. *Mortgage Servicing News, 14*, 16.

How to measure the economic recovery. (2010, July). *Kiplinger's Personal Finance, 64*, 30–31.

Lozza, E., et al. (2016). Consumer sentiment after the global financial crisis. *International Journal of Market Research, 58*(5), 671–691.

Lynch, D. (2010, April 8). Greenspan says, "I was wrong 30% of the time." *USA Today*. 1B.

Moffat, M. (2010). Recession? Depression? What's the difference?

Obama tries to stop AIG bonuses: "How do they justify this outrage?" (2009, March 16). *Road to Rescue: The CNN Survival Guide*.

Paradise foreclosed. (2010, June 26). *Economist, 395*(8688), 5.

Peicuti, C. (2014). The Great Depression and the Great Recession: A comparative analysis of their analogies. *European Journal of Comparative Economics, 11*, 55–78.

Reckard, E. Scott. (2008, March 27). Lender inflated its profit, report says. *Los Angeles Times*.

Saporito, B. (2009, March 30). How AIG became too big to fail [Cover story]. *Time, 173*, 24–30.

Sharf, S. (2013, Nov 8). Jobs report: U.S. economy added 204k jobs in October, unemployment up to 7.3%. *Forbes*.

Tammy, J. (2015, October 11). About the Obama economy, supply siders go rather Keynesian. *Forbes*, 2.

World Bank. (2013). GDP growth (annual %).

Zandi, M. (2010, July 1). Perspectives on the US economy. *FDCH Congressional Testimony*.

SUGGESTED READING

Aliber, R. Z., & Kindleberge, C. P. (2015). *Manics, panics, and crashes: A history of financial crises* (7th ed.). New York: Palgrave.

Block, M., & Gonyea, D. (2010, June 30). Revisiting the creation of TARP. *All Things Considered (NPR)*.

Congdon, T. (2014). What were the causes of the Great Recession? *World Economics, 15*, 1–32.

Demyanyk, Y., & Hasan, I. (2009). Financial crises and bank failures: A review of prediction methods. *Omega, 35*, 315–324.

Johnston, C. W. (2013). Will the new banking regulations prevent the next U.S. financial crisis? *Journal of International Finance & Economics, 13*, 43–48.

Nguyen, T., & Pontell, H. (2010). Mortgage origination fraud and the global economic crisis. *Criminology & Public Policy, 9*, 591–612.

Schooley, D. K., & Worden, D. D. (2016). Perceived and realized risk tolerance: Changes during the 2008 financial crisis. *Journal of Financial Counseling and Planning, 27*(2), 265–276.

Weidenbaum, M. (2009). Reflections on the collapse of '07 and related matters. *Vital Speeches of the Day, 75*, 198–201.

Wessel, D. (2010, June 17). Rethinking home ownership. *Wall Street Journal — Eastern Edition, 255*. A2.

Essay by Michael P. Auerbach, MA

THEORY OF INTEREST

This paper addresses a critical component of Keynesian economics—his theory of interest. In addition to an overview of his works as well as modern, "neo-Keynesian" versions of his principles, the reader also gleans an understanding of the debate surrounding the applicability of Keynesian thought in a 21st-century economic environment.

OVERVIEW

Unbeknownst to many, John Maynard Keynes originally wanted to operate a railroad. Unfortunately, however, to do so, he had to pass a civil service examination, and the man who would become known as the "father of modern economics" received his lowest marks on the economics section. As Keynes would later recall, "I evidently knew more about economics than my examiners" ("Young John Maynard Keynes," 2007).

While Keynes's pursuit of a career on the rails did not come to fruition, his lack of discouragement at the civil service exam led him to become a central figure in the reinvigoration of the Western economy after the Great Depression and World War II. His theories on economic development reshaped the international community's perspective on how to address the ongoing fiscal crisis and left an impact on global economics that prevails today.

Of course, such accolades do not suggest that Keynes was free of controversy. In fact, Keynes's view that government must play a role in the revitalization of national economies and that the goal of economic redevelopment should be to bolster the demand side of a macroeconomy made him a target for those fearful of a leftist ideology in rebuilding the systems of the West. Even today, in the twenty-first century, Keynesian economics are consistently under fire by free market proponents and conservatives who view his theories as overly simplistic and even impractical in today's global economy.

This paper addresses a critical component of Keynesian economics—his theory of interest. In addition to an overview of his works as well as modern, "neo-Keynesian" versions of his principles, the reader gleans an understanding of the debate surrounding the applicability of Keynesian thought in a twenty-first-century economic environment.

Prof. Paul H. Douglas, right, of University of Chicago, & Prof. Alvin W. Hansen of Harvard University before Senate Unemployment & Relief Committee Hearings. (Courtesy of Library of Congress)

Keynes & the Future of Economics

In 1936, countries around the globe were mired in the Great Depression. Classical economic theories suggesting that the free market would correct itself (so-called *laissez-faire* economics; introduced by icons such as Adam Smith and John Stuart Mill) proved largely ineffectual in revitalizing the economies of the Western world. A new approach was clearly warranted, and the thinking of John Maynard Keynes seemed to offer just that alternative.

In his seminal work, *The General Theory of Employment, Interest, and Money*, Keynes advocated for a government that played a more significant role in economic affairs. By infusing monies into the demand side of the macroeconomy, Keynes suggested, economic systems under duress from recession and depression could become reinvigorated by increased consumer confidence, higher incomes, and a workforce well-suited to contribute to the economy.

Keynes's argument in that work was based on acknowledgement of three central, independent variables:

- The first of these was a combination of psychological factors: propensity to consume, the attitude concerning liquidity, and an expectation of future yield from capital assets.
- Second, Keynes posited, was the wage unit, which is determined by the bargains reached between employees and their employers.
- The last of these variables, Keynes argued, is the quantity of monies as determined by the central bank.

At the core of the interaction among these variables is what Keynes called the "liquidity preference schedule." Consumers, Keynes theorized, were in essence in control of the rate of interest (which is a price that a lender may charge a borrower in a loan situation). They could therefore choose to hoard their monies and assets or invest them in the markets, depending on how much in liquid assets they possessed. Keynes asserted that this choice would be a powerful determinant of the rate of interest. If national incomes and employment rates remained static, a state of equilibrium would exist. However, Keynes assumed that this equilibrium would not be consistent in light shifts in liquidity caused by changes in consumer behavior (Lutz, 2006).

As was the case for the predominance of Keynes's *General Theory*, the focus is on the demand side of a macroeconomy. Keynes asserted that governments seeking to reinvigorate their own economies through intervention (a shift in and of itself from the pure free-market economic model preferred by classical theorists) must focus on the consumer. In terms of his views on interest specifically, the consumer's attitudes concerning the economy would drive whether or not he or she will spend his or her liquid assets or retain it. Depending on the direction in which consumer behavior leads, rate of interest shifts.

As stated earlier, J. M. Keynes's notions introduced in *General Theory* were at best controversial. Part of the debate centered on the fact that his theory of interest was largely dependent upon ideas he proffered in a work published six years prior: *A Treatise on Money*. In *Treatise*, Keynes laid the groundwork for an argument that, in simplified terms, asserted that investment leads to inflation and savings to recession. The connection between the two works became frayed, due in part because debate with mainstream economists brought about modifications to Keynes's framework that disconnected *General Theory* from *Treatise* (Erturk, 2006).

Keynes's ideals created a firestorm of debate, but the controversy did not stem solely from those who maintained a conservative loyalty to the classical approach. There were many who at the time saw Keynes's work as needy of further exposition in order to ensure true validity. It is to this contemporary debate surrounding Keynes's theories that this paper turns next.

Peer Debate over the Keynesian School of Thought

Keynes's theories understandably set off controversy and invited pointed criticism. Some of it was politically motivated. After all, to free market conservatives (many of whom were actively concerned with the spread of communism) the idea that government should play an active role in a Western economy smacked of leftist ideology akin to Marxism. For others, Keynes was simply attempting to turn the establishment on its ear for revolution's sake.

Among the critiques was that of Friedrich August von Hayek, whose ideas would evolve into the school of thought known as Austrian economics. Hayek originally dismissed Keynes's theory of liquidity preference as far too rigid and only applicable in emergency situations in which the balance between supply and demand are in immediate peril. Hayek's views of Keynes, *General Theory*, and the liquidity preference were later revealed to be based on misinterpretation of Keynes's central message. In fact, Keynes made a point, in trying to help critics understand his ideas, of asserting that his main focal point, liquidity preference, was not the singular element in determining the interest rate (DeVecchi, 2006). Unfortunately, either due to the fact that Keynesian economics, by his own implication, was a work that still needed modification, or in order to answer to increasingly vocal critiques of his work in a conciliatory fashion, Keynes still needed to defend his views from a growing complement of peers.

One of Keynes's greatest critics prior to his death in 1946 was, in fact, a previous collaborator. Dennis Robertson worked closely with Keynes in the 1920s, long before *Treatise* or *General Theory*. Although those loyal to Keynes's ideas dismissed classical economic theory and anything prior to *General Theory* as irrelevant in the modern industrial economy, Robertson

Assistant Secretary, U.S. Treasury, Harry Dexter White (left) and John Maynard Keynes, honorary advisor to the U.K. Treasury at the inaugural meeting of the International Monetary Fund's Board of Governors in Savannah, Georgia, U.S., March 8, 1946. (Courtesy of International Monetary Fund via Wikimedia Commons)

took exception to accusations that he was the product of the antiquated world. In fact, Robertson retorted that it was Keynes who was not operating on solid ground—by seeking to discount the prewar theoretical environment, Keynes, he argued, was abandoning not only the precepts of classical economics but the time-honored, fundamental scientific practices of economic study that gave rise to economic thought.

Robertson, who in the 1920s was handpicked by Keynes to chair the Economics Department at Cambridge, attempted to move away from his personal feelings toward Keynes (a man by whom he felt betrayed for dismissing the very scientific precepts on which they had worked as colleagues) to provide a more academic repudiation of Keynes's theories. His assertion was that Keynes's view of the consumer as the central mitigating factor in the determination not only of price but of interest was far too rigid and, as a result, incomplete. Consumers do have a role,

Robertson admitted, but liquidity preference only worked within two regimes—an individual who was willing to spend his or her money and an individual who refused to spend.

Robertson argued that Keynes was operating from far too limited a position. By proffering that consumer income is the singular force behind fluctuations in interest rates, Robertson claimed, Keynes was discounting exogenous factors such as trade and a multitude of consumptive activities. These issues were complicated factors that demanded consideration in addition to income as determinants of interest rate changes (Higgins & Wright, 1998).

Keynesian economics obviously had its impacts on both the Depression-era and post–World War II international stages. With traditional economic development policy coming up short, leaders found themselves willing to think "outside of the box" in order to reestablish economic and fiscal order. It comes as no surprise, therefore, that Keynes's ideals of government intervention and state funding to bolster the consumer were received warmly by political leaders who sought to make life better for constituents. As the world moved out of wartime and the economy began improving, modern economic theorists began to wonder if Keynesian economics was becoming antiquated.

Interest Theory & the Future of Keynesian Economics
As the decades left Keynes to history in the Depression era, questions abound about the relevance of his theory of interest and liquidity preference and the quantity of money. Inflation, unemployment, international trade, and other issue areas that are commonplace in the twenty-first century seem to support the Robertson school of thought that suggests that there are a multitude of factors, both on the supply and demand sides of a macroeconomy, that impact price and interest rates. The rigidity of Keynes's view that consumer asset behavior dictates changes in interest rates seems too limited in a world in which many other factors seem to become manifest.

Still, Keynes's theories are widely under-analyzed and studied in a less-than-comprehensive manner. Most modern economists do not flatly refute the notion of liquidity preference as a major contributor to the determination of interest rates. The problem that skeptics see is in the perceived notion that Keynes believed that liquidity preference was the *sole* determinant in establishing interest rates.

Some modern economists see Keynes as an individual who provided a general set of guidelines, many of which are in fact compatible with classical and neoclassical economic theory. Their view is that gaps or rigidities in Keynes's theoretical structure, particularly with regard to liquidity preference and equilibrium as established by employment, may be general in nature and therefore open to interpretation, misinterpretation, and, in many ways, supplementation (Wright, 1945).

The offerings of Harvard professor Alvin Hansen create a similar situation concerning interpretations of Keynes's interest theory. The man some nicknamed "the American Keynes" criticized Keynes for calling classical interest theory indeterminate. Keynes, Hansen argued, was claiming that under a classical regime, the schedule relating savings to the rate of interest would shift as income changes, and incomes changed as interest rates changed as well. Income, according to Hansen's critique of Keynes's views, was an unpredictable factor that inevitably influences the direction in which the rate of interest shifts. Hansen pointed to what he saw as an irony in Keynes's "attack" on the classical motif—in Keynes's paradigm (in which interest rests at the intersection between the supply schedule of money and the liquidity preference schedule), income also exists as an X factor. Put simply, Keynes was, in Hansen's view, taking classical interest theory to task over the unpredictability of income, while Keynes's theory itself became indeterminate over the same unpredictability of income (Nevin, 1955).

Hansen's issue with Keynes proceeds with the assumption that Keynes's ideals, in failing to account for the very issue for which classical theory failed to account, were incomplete. This argument is difficult to confirm, for the aforementioned evolution of Keynes's interest theory (modified between *Treatise* and *General Theory*) was not a complete work in historical contexts. In fact, the theory of interest offered by Keynes was, by virtue of both the ongoing debate over his sea-change departure from classical theory and a change in the economy from its pre–World War II state to a modern, global industrial twenty-first-century economy.

The ambiguity of income's impact on interest, while the subject of debate among Keynes and those taking exception to Keynes's departure from classical theory, does appear to have piqued the interest of those who view Keynesian economics as a work on which exposition was not just possible but necessary.

Post-Keynesian economists have taken note of the holes in Keynesian and classical interest theories as they relate to income but have done so in such a way that they do not look at these flaws that are unworkable. Rather, they look to fill in those holes.

One post-Keynesian study, for example, supplements changes in wages with capacity utilization, a term that applies to the relationship between real and potential output. According to the study, an increase in real wages, by raising consumption demand, also increases productive capacity utilization. However, because the distribution of capacity utilization profits is evenly spread, the ambiguity of interest persists. Still, the application of productive capacity utilization (and the leveling effect it brings with it) in many ways fills in the gaps created by Keynesian and classical theorists and, at the very least, helps the observer understand the establishment of interest rates and supply-demand equilibrium (Meirelles & Lima, 2006).

The interest theory espoused by Keynes obviously established a legacy among modern economists, though this legacy is mixed at best, given the changing world and apparent shortcomings on the issue of income.

CONCLUSION

In one century, the world has undergone an incredible transformation. After World War I, it became clear that the world was moving toward an environment of interstate interconnectivity, with President Woodrow Wilson stressing the common global system with the introduction of the League of Nations. Two decades later, the Great Depression underscored this global environment, though not in the manner humanity had hoped—the U.S. market crash sent shockwaves around the world, and other nations succumbed to the Depression's malaise.

With an ever-evolving economic system that remained anemic, it became clear that a different policy was warranted. The urgency of economic development became more and more manifest. John Maynard Keynes, espousing a policy that favors the demand side of a macro-economy and government intervention that addresses the needs of consumers, became a central figure in that change in regimes.

Keynes's approach to economics entailed an emphasis on demand rather than the traditional view of business development as the central theme. Income,

according to Keynesian theory, is the central element that affects how the rate of interest increases or decreases. This point is, according to the theory, due to the fact that there are a variety of conditions under which a consumer will spend his or her money (or choose not to). Focusing on the consumer's liquidity preference schedule is therefore a pivotal part of economic recovery from such devastating conditions as the Depression.

The fact that Keynes's ideas were widely adopted by world governmental economic policy makers does not mean that his ideas were well-received by economists. That his concepts of demand-side government appropriations were new was not the issue—the controversy lay in the fact that Keynes arrived at his conclusions by apparently rejecting methods of economic study that had been the norm for nearly two centuries. Keynes had, in the eyes of his peers (many of whom had worked with him prior to his publication of *Treatise* and the tome in which his most controversial theories were introduced, *General Theory*), chosen to pursue his economic theories by rejecting not just the preferred focus of classical economics. He had arrived at his conclusions by rejecting the commonly accepted practices of economic research utilized by classical theory as well.

Keynes's theory of interest was of particular controversy in this regard, as the debate concerning his general theory of interest, as proffered in *General Theory*, can be placed in two categories. The first of these arenas is political—Keynes had distanced himself from the aforementioned well-established classical school of economic theory. He had even fomented the consternation of those peers and colleagues who had worked closely with Keynes himself within the classical regime. In an era of considerable mistrust toward the increasing promulgation of Marxism and communism, Keynes's apparent call for a reversal away from the free market system and one that relied on government intervention and/or interference was particularly abhorrent for some politically charged peers.

The second arena is that of a misunderstanding of Keynes's methodologies and data. Whether actual or perceived, this position asserted that Keynes's ideals were based largely on speculation and, more importantly, established parameters in the interest rate schedule that were far too rigid and dependent on one element (namely the liquidity preference schedule). There are many individuals, including the ones cited in this paper, who believe that the debate that immediately met Keynes's interest rate theory caused an exchange of ideas, reconsiderations, and modifications that left only the skeletal framework of what Keynes was expressing (and connecting to his largely under-analyzed earlier work, *Treatise*). For others, Keynes was simply laying a foundation on which others may build. His theories were not inflexible nor were they incomplete—they were dynamic and capable of evolving, should those who shared his perspective take the torch into the next era.

In the decades that followed Keynes's introduction of the theory of interest, as well as his other "revolutionary" theories of economic development, much has happened to change the world regime. Whereas pre-World War II nations could choose to limit their international commerce activities, the world of the latter twentieth and early twenty=first centuries relies on linkages between countries and systems. In fact, some may argue that, in business terms, national governments are becoming less relevant in comparison to multinational corporations and international business partnerships. Most nations (even those with Communist governments) have embraced some semblance of the free market model, and while government involvement is by no means nonexistent (most governments intervene when their economies experience downturns or when trade relations become imbalanced), there is some question as to the modern relevance of the theories of a man who at one time hoped to become a railroad operator. Perhaps a better understanding of the complete methodologies of J. M. Keynes will prove effective in determining whether there is a 21st-century application to be seen for one of the first relevant economic development theories of the early 20th century.

TERMS & CONCEPTS

Capacity utilization: Economic term identifying the relationship between real and potential production output.

Capital assets: Tangible property that cannot be easily liquidated into cash, such as land and real estate.

Interest: Price charged by a lender to a borrower as a condition of the transaction.

Liquidity preference: Keynesian economic indicator that identifies consumer behavior as it relates to investment or savings.

Macro-economy: Economic system comprised of aggregate demand and aggregate supply.

Wage unit: One of three central variables of consumer behavior in Keynes's theory of interest, referencing the salary agreement established between employer and employee.

BIBLIOGRAPHY

Chick, V., & Dow, S. (2013). Keynes, the long run, and the present crisis. *International Journal of Political Economy, 42*(1), 13–25.

DeVecchi, N. (2006). Hayek and the general theory. *European Journal of the History of Economic Thought, 13*(2), 233–258.

Erturk, K. A. (2006, January). Speculation, liquidity preference and monetary circulation. *The Levy Economics Institute's Working Paper Series.*

Higgins, A. L., & Wright, Jr., J. W. (1998). Keynes' antagonist. *American Economist, 42*(1), 82–89.

Lerner, A. P. (2013). Mr Keynes' 'general theory of employment, interest and money.' *International Labour Review,* 15236–46.

Lutz, F. (2006). *The theory of interest.* Aldine Transaction.

Meirelles, A. J. A., & Lima, G. T. (2006). Debt, financial fragility and economic growth. *Journal of Post-Keynesian Economics, 29*(1), 93–115.

Nevin, E. (1955). Professor Hansen and Keynesian interest theory. *Quarterly Journal of Economics, 69*(4), 637–643.

Wright, D. M. (1945). The future of Keynesian economics. *American Economic Review, 35*(3).

Young John Maynard Keynes. (2007). Anecdotage. com.

SUGGESTED READING

Cesaroni, G. (2001). The finance motive, the Keynesian theory of the rate of interest and the investment multiplier. *European Journal of the History of Economic Thought, 8*(1), 58–74.

Colander, D. (1999). Teaching Keynes in the 21st century. *Journal of Economic Education, 30*(4), 364–372.

Kregel, J. A. (1983). Post-Keynesian theory. *Journal of Economic Education, 14*(4), 32–43.

Wray, L. R. (2006). Keynes' approach to money. *Atlantic Economic Journal, 34*(2), 183–193.

Essay by Michael P. Auerbach, MA

Time Value of Money

This article focuses on the concept of time value of money. Although the concept has a major influence on individual, business, and government finances, this article highlights the concept's effects on individual and corporate finance. There is an introduction of corporate valuation and how corporations determine their worth. Understanding and calculating the worth of an organization allows the stakeholders to anticipate the present and future worth of the business. One can use this information in positioning the organization for growth, diversification, or merger. In addition, there is a discussion of how individuals can utilize modern portfolio theory to develop an investment strategy that makes money over time.

OVERVIEW

The time value of money has an impact on every sector of society, which includes individual, business, and government finance. Time value of money (TVM) is a basic principle in budgeting and investing. The time value of money tends to vary based on the situation. For example, the foundation of the concept relies on the premise that a dollar that one has today is worth more than the expectation that one will receive a dollar in the future. In essence, the money that one has today is worth more because the person can invest it and earn interest. Many would agree that the global economic system determines a basic time value of money according to the level of interest rates.

The foundation of the concept rests on the belief that one can determine the value that a single sum will grow to at some time in the future. This calculation is based on five elements. If one is given any four of the factors, the fifth factor can be calculated. According to Gallager and Andrew (1996), the five elements are interest rates, number of periods, payments, present value, and future value.

Interest: Charged for borrowing money; usually set as a percentage. There are two types of interest—simple and compound. Simple interest is computed on the original amount borrowed and is the return on the principal for one time period. Compound interest is calculated each period on the original amount borrowed and all unpaid interest accumulated to date.

Number of Periods: Evenly spaced intervals of time. Each interval corresponds to a compounding period for a single amount or a payment period for an annuity.

Payments: A series of equal, evenly spaced cash flows. In TVM calculations, payments must represent outflows (negative amounts) or inflows (positive amounts).

Present Value: An amount today that is equivalent to a future payment or series of payments that has been discounted by an appropriate interest rate. Since money has time value, the present value of a promised future amount is worth less the longer a person has to wait to receive it.

Future Value: The amount of money that an investment with a fixed, compounded interest rate will grow to by some future date. The investment can be a single sum deposited at the beginning of the first period, a series of equally spaced payments, or both.

TVM is considered to be an important aspect of financial management. The concept can be used to compare investment alternatives as well as solve a variety of financial calculations such as loans, mortgages, and

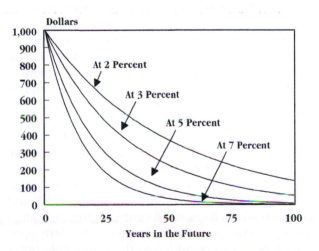

The time value of money describes the greater benefit of receiving money now rather than later. This graph shows the present value of $1,000, 100 years into the future. Curves represent constant discount rates of 2%, 3%, 5%, and 7%. (Courtesy of Congressional Budget Office (Congress of the United States) via Wikimedia Commons)

leases. One of the most popular ways to measure time value of money is through the rate of return that one can earn on an investment without losing any money.

TVM & Investments

It has been suggested that most Americans do not know how to save or prepare for their future. As a result, many financial investment companies have approached employers as well as individuals in an attempt to educate the masses on the benefits of investing. Some of the tips that have been provided by organizations, such as the American Association of Individual Investors, include the following:

- Build and maintain a cash reserve to meet short-term emergencies and other liquidity needs.
- Develop an overall investment strategy, even if it cannot be implemented immediately.
- Select mutual funds that fit into the overall investment strategy and then consider what the minimum initial investments are.
- Select a balanced fund for less aggressive investors or a broad base index fund for more aggressive investors. Build the portfolio after this initial investment has been completed.
- Review the percentage commitment to each stock market segment in order to determine when to add funds to the initial investment.
- Do not agonize over small deviations from the original allocation plan. Stay the course (pp. 1–2)!

Financial counselors may inquire about whether or not an organization has some type of retirement plan (i.e., 401 (k) plan) in place for their employees, or they may go directly to the employee for supplemental retirement opportunities. One popular approach that has emerged is the modern portfolio theory. Modern portfolio theory sounds like an academic and analytical concept; however, "it is the accepted approach to investment and portfolio management today" (American Association of Individual Investors, n.d.). The relationship between risk and return tends to form the foundation for investment theory. However, a third dimension, modern portfolio theory, can be added to the equation in order to create a framework that can assess investment opportunities that exist for the sole purpose of making money (Dunn, 2006).

APPLICATION

Modern Portfolio Theory

Modern portfolio theory (MPT) provides an opportunity for investors to utilize diversification in order to maximize the potential of their portfolio and assumes that the investor is adverse to risk. Therefore, the investor will take a risk only if he/she has determined that the risk will provide him/her with a higher expected return. In essence, the investor has to be willing to take on more risk in order to be compensated with higher returns.

The concept can be used by both individuals and corporations and can be used to determine how one can optimize his/her portfolio as well as what the price should be for a risky asset. According to the Association of Individual Investors, there are two parts of this approach:

- First, focus on the concept that the best combination of assets should be developed by focusing on how the various components perform relative to each other.
- Second, focus on the belief that the natural outcome of many people searching for underpriced securities in the markets should be an "efficient market" in which it is difficult to add value by finding underpriced securities, especially since it is expensive to do so (par. 4 and 5).

MPT was introduced by Harry Markowitz, an economist and college professor, when he wrote an article entitled "Portfolio Selection" in 1952. He eventually became a Nobel Prize recipient for his work in the field. Prior to his work, most investors focused only on the best way to assess risks and receive rewards on individual securities when determining what to include in the portfolio. Investors were advised to develop a portfolio based on the selection of those securities that would offer them the best opportunity to gain. Markowitz took this practice and formulized it by creating a mathematical formula of diversification. "The process for establishing an optimal (or efficient) portfolio generally uses historical measures for returns, risk (standard deviation) and correlation coefficients" ("Modern portfolio theory," n.d., para. 6). He suggested that investors focus on selecting portfolios that fit their risk-reward characteristics (Markowitz, 1959).

VIEWPOINT

Corporate Valuation

There are some specific measures that corporations must take in order to ensure that their entities have value over time. In order to effectively manage a company, it is important to know how much it is worth. If the organization does not know how much it is worth or what makes good business sense (i.e., acquisitions and mergers), there is potential to make fatal mistakes that may be detrimental to the organization's well-being. There are different ways one can determine the value of an organization, and some of those methods are discussed below.

Asset-Based Methods

Asset-based methods began with the "book value" of an organization's equity. An organization's equity is defined as the organization's assets minus its debt. Corporations are charged with two major responsibilities: acquire financial and productive resources and combine the resources in order to create new resources. Acquired resources are called assets, and the different types of assets are called equities. Therefore, the foundation for the basic accounting equation is "Assets = Equities." However, since equities can be divided into two groups, the basic accounting equation can be revised to read as "Assets = Liabilities + Owners' Equity."

Assets. Although assets consist of financial and productive resources, not all resources are considered to be assets. In order to determine whether a resource is considered to be an asset, it must satisfy all three of the following criteria:

- The resource must possess future value for the business. The future value must take the form of exchange ability (i.e., cash) or usability (i.e., equipment).
- The resource must be under the effective control of the business. However, legal ownership is not mandatory. As long as the resource can be freely used in business activities, the resource will met the asset criteria. An example would be a leased computer. Although the organization may use the computer, legal rights still belong to the leasing company.
- The resource must have a dollar value resulting from an identifiable event or events in the life of

the organization. The value assigned to the asset must be tracked to an exchange between the organization and others (Page & Hooper, 1985).
- If the resource does not meet all of the criteria, it cannot be reported as an asset.

Liabilities. When someone other than the owner provides an organization with an asset, the claims against the business take the form of a debt. Sources of assets from someone other than the owner are referred to as liabilities. Liabilities are the debts and legal obligations that a business incurs as the result of acquiring the assets from non-owners.

Owners' Equity. Some businesses may obtain assets via owner investment or sale of stock. When the owner supplies the organization with assets, the claim against those assets is called owners' equity (or stockholders' equity) in a financial report.

Another way to measure an organization's value is to determine its current working capital and its relationship to market capitalization. Working capital can be defined as the amount left once one has subtracted the organization's current liabilities from its current assets. Working capital is the amount of funds that an organization has ready access to for use in conducting its everyday business.

Shareholder equity helps one to determine the value of an organization when there is a need to calculate the book value. The book value of an organization is the value of an organization that can be found on the accounting ledger. To calculate book value per share, one has to take the organization's shareholders' equity and divide it by the current number of shares outstanding. The next step is to take the stock's current price and divide it by the current book value in order to get the price-to-book ratio.

Comparables

The most common way to value a company is to use its earnings. Earnings, also referred to as the net income or net profit, are the amount of cash that is available after the organization has paid its bills. In order to make a valid comparison, one has looked at earnings and measures them according to their earnings per share (EPS). An accountant may calculate the earnings per share by dividing the dollar amount of the earnings that is reported for an organization by the number of shares it currently has outstanding.

However, it should be noted that earnings per share alone does not mean anything. In order to evaluate an organization's earnings relative to its price, most financial professionals will use the price/earnings (P/E) ratio. The P/E ratio takes the stock price and divides it by the last four quarters' worth of earnings.

Free Cash Flow Methods

Cash flow is seen as the most common measurement for valuing public and private companies used by investment bankers. Cash flow is defined as the cash that flows through a company during the course of a quarter or the year after taking out all fixed expenses. Cash flow is normally defined as earnings before interest, taxes, depreciation, and amortization (EBITDA). Cash flow tends to be the only method that makes logical sense in most situations.

The argument for the discounted free cash flow method is that an organization's value can be estimated by forecasting future performance of the business and measuring the surplus cash flow generated by the organization. The surplus cash flows and cash flow shortfalls are discounted back to a present value and added together to arrive at a valuation. The discount factor used is adjusted for the financial risk of investing in the company. The mechanics of the method focuses investors on the internal operations of the company and its future.

The discounted cash flow method can be defined in six steps. Given the fact that this method is based on forecasts, it is crucial that the financial professionals of an organization have a good understanding of the business, its market, and its past operations. The steps in the discounted cash flow method are as follows:

- Develop debt free projections of the company's future operations. This is clearly the critical element in the valuation. The more closely the projections reflect a good understanding of the business and its realistic prospects, the more confident investors will be with the valuation it supports.
- Quantify positive and negative cash flow in each year of the projections. The cash flow being measured is the surplus cash generated by the business each year. In years when the company does not generate surplus cash, the cash shortfall is measured. So that borrowings will not distort the valuation, cash flow is calculated as if the company

had no debt. In other words, interest charges are backed out of the projections before cash flows are measured.

- Estimate a terminal value for the last year of the projections. Since it is impractical to project company operations out beyond three to five years in most cases, some assumptions must be made to estimate how much value will be contributed to the company by the cash flows generated after the last year in the projections. Without making such assumptions, the value generated by the discounted cash flow method would approximate the value of the company as if it ceased operations at the end of the projection period. One common and conservative assumption is the perpetuity assumption. This assumption assumes that the cash flow of the last projected year will continue forever and then discounts that cash flow back to the last year of the projections.
- Determine the discount factor to be applied to the cash flows. One of the key elements affecting the valuation generated by this method is the discount factor chosen. The larger the factor, the lower the valuation it will generate. This discount factor should reflect the business and investment risk involved. The less likely the company is to meet its projections, the higher the factor should be. Discount factors used most often are a compromise between the cost of borrowing and the cost of equity investment. If the cost of borrowed money is 10 percent and equity investors want 30 percent for their funds, the discount factor would be somewhere in between—in fact, the weighted-average cost of capital.
- Apply the discount factor to the cash flow surplus and shortfall of each year to the terminal value. The amount generated by each of these calculations will estimate the present value contribution of each year's future cash flow. Adding these values together estimates the company's present value assuming it is debt free.
- Subtract present long-term and short-term borrowings from the present value of future cash flows to estimate the company's present value (Giddy, n.d., p. 2).

Option-Based Valuation

Many financial professionals still have issues with the amount of risk and uncertainty in evaluating investments and acquisitions. Despite the use of net present value (NPV) and other valuation techniques, these individuals are often forced to rely on instinct when finalizing risky investment decisions. Given the shortcomings of NPV, real options analysis has been suggested as an alternative approach. This approach considers the risks associated with an investment while recognizing the ability of corporations to defer an investment until a later period or to make a partial investment instead. Basically, investment decisions are often made in a way that leaves some options open. The simple NPV rule does not provide accurate conclusions as to whether or not uncertainty can be managed. In acquisitions and other business decisions, flexibility is crucial, and the value of flexibility can be taken into account explicitly by using the real-options approach.

Financial options tend to be used for risk management in banks and firms. Real or embedded options are analogs of these financial options and can be used for evaluating investment decisions made under significant uncertainty. Real options can be identified in the form of opportunity to invest in a currently available innovative project with an additional consideration of the strategic value associated with the possibility of future and follow-up investments due to emergence of another related innovation in the future or the possibility of abandoning the project.

The option is worth something because the future value of the asset is uncertain. Uncertainty increases the value of the option. If the uncertainty is interpreted as the variance, there are possibilities for an organization to earn higher profits. The loss on the option is equal to the cost of acquiring it. If the project turns out to be nonprofitable, one may have the choice of not exercising the option. The real options approach is finding its place in corporate valuation.

CONCLUSION

The time value of money has an impact on every sector of society, which includes individual, business, and government finance. Time value of money (TVM) is a basic principle in budgeting and investing. The time value of money tends to vary based on the situation. For example, the foundation of the concept relies on the premise that a dollar that one has today is worth more than the expectation that one will receive a dollar in the future. In essence, the money that one has today is worth more because the

person can invest it and earn interest. Many would agree that the global economic system determines a basic time value of money according to the level of interest rates.

It has been suggested that most Americans do not know how to save or prepare for their future. Financial counselors may inquire about whether or not an organization has some type of retirement plan (i.e., 401 (k) plan) in place for their employees, or they may go directly to the employee for supplemental retirement opportunities.

In order to effectively manage a company, it is important to know how much it is worth. If the organization does not know how much it is worth or what makes good business sense (i.e., acquisitions and mergers), there is a potential to make fatal mistakes that may be detrimental to the organization's well-being.

TERMS & CONCEPTS

Assets: Any item of economic value owned by an individual or corporation, especially that which could be converted to cash.

Discounted cash flow analysis: A valuation method used to estimate the attractiveness of an investment opportunity.

Future value: Future value is the amount of money that an investment with a fixed, compounded interest rate will grow to by some future date. The investment can be a single sum deposited at the beginning of the first period, a series of equally spaced payments, or both.

Interest: A charge for borrowed money, usually set as a percentage. There are two types of interest—simple and compound. Simple interest is computed on the original amount borrowed and is the return on the principal for one period. Compound interest is calculated each period on the original amount borrowed and all unpaid interest accumulated to date.

Liabilities: Total assets minus total owners' equity.

Modern portfolio theory: A theory on how risk-averse investors can construct portfolios to optimize or maximize expected return based on a given level of market risk, emphasizing that risk is an inherent part of higher reward.

Number of periods: Evenly spaced intervals of time; each interval will correspond to a compounding period for a single amount or a payment period for an annuity.

Owners' equity: Total assets minus total liabilities.

Payments: A series of equal, evenly spaced cash flows. In TVM calculations, payments must represent outflows (negative amounts) or inflows (positive amounts).

Portfolio management: The art and science of making decisions about investment mix and policy, matching investments to objectives, asset allocation for individuals and institutions, and balancing risk vs. performance.

Present value: Present value is an amount today that is equivalent to a future payment or series of payments that has been discounted by an appropriate interest rate. Since money has time value, the present value of a promised future amount is worth less the longer a person has to wait to receive it.

BIBLIOGRAPHY

Abdullah, A. (2013). Examining the value of money in America over the long term (1792–2009). *International Journal of Economics & Finance, 5*(10), 58–84.

American Association of Individual Investors (n.d.). From theory to practice: How to apply MPT concepts to your 401(k) plan.

American Association of Individual Investors (n.d.). Investing basics: Investing questions that every successful investor should know how to answer.

American Association of Individual Investors (n.d.). The ten myths of retirement planning.

Dunn, B. (2006, August). Modern portfolio theory—with a twist: The new efficient frontier.

Ennis, H. M. (2012). Some theoretical considerations regarding net asset values for money market funds. *Economic Quarterly (10697225), 98*(4), 231–254.

Gallager, T., & Andrew, Jr., J. (1996). *Financial management: Principals and practices.* Upper Saddle River, NJ: Prentice Hall.

Giddy, I. (n.d.). Methods of corporate valuations.

Markowitz, H. (1959). *Portfolio selection: Efficient diversification of investments.* New York, NY: John Wiley.

Modern portfolio theory. (n.d.). *Money Online.*

Page, J., & Hooper, P. (1985). *Microcomputer accounting and business applications.* Reston: Reston Publishing Company, Inc.

Rosca, V. (2013). A model for measuring value for money in professional sports. *Theoretical & Applied Economics, 20*(7), 77–86.

SUGGESTED READING

Bland, L. (2005). A modern take on an old portfolio theory. *Money Management, 19*(16), 26.

Darwish, M. (2006, March). Imperfect production systems with imperfect preventive maintenance, inflation, and time value of money. *Asia-Pacific Journal of Operational Research, 23*(1), 89–105.

Gill, J. (2007). Your rates: Are they value for money? *Chartered Accountants Journal, 86*(10), 16–17.

Grundy, P. (2007). Value for money? *Circuits Assembly, 18*(11), 30–31.

Essay by Marie Gould

W

WILLS, TRUSTS, ESTATES, AND TAXATION

ABSTRACT

An estate is all that a person owns, both real and personal property, and is essentially a person's net worth. Within the context of estate planning, two other types of "estates" are also relevant. The taxable estate is that portion of the estate that will be subject to federal estate taxes and possibly state taxes. The probate estate is that portion of the estate that must be probated before it can be distributed. This article reviews wills and trusts, and other common components of most estate plans, in light of the two most relevant concerns: taxes and probate.

OVERVIEW

An estate is all that a person owns, both real and personal property, and is essentially a person's net worth. Within the context of estate planning, two other types of "estates" are also relevant. The taxable estate is that portion of the estate that will be subject to federal estate taxes and possibly state taxes. The probate estate is that portion of the estate that must be probated before it can be distributed. The interplay and content of these three values of estate will drive most estate planning. The general principle is to eliminate the probate and taxable estates to the greatest extent possible. This is done through estate planning arrangements that include wills, trusts, certain property ownership arrangements, and other devices.

The area of wills and estates is loaded with jargon. In this essay, three main ways that property can pass from one to another are discussed. This discussion requires the use of traditional technical language that should be addressed up front to avoid confusion and to attach modern simplified equivalent language where possible. A property can be passed along according to a will, under state law, and according to a trust.

Sometimes a will is called "last will and testament," but for all purposes, including legal uses, just the word *will* suffices. Traditionally, wills used the phrase "I give, devise, and bequeath." The modern approach is to use only the word *give*. A modern document titled "Will" that states "I give…" means exactly the same thing as a document titled "Last Will and Testament" that states "I give, devise, and bequeath." The will has

RLC **874** PAGE **2273**

300002   LAST WILL AND TESTAMENT

OF

TENNESSEE WILLIAMS

I, TENNESSEE WILLIAMS, of the City of Key West, Monroe County, Florida, being of sound mind and disposing memory, do hereby make, publish and declare this to be my Last Will and Testament, hereby revoking all Wills and Codicils by me heretofore made.

ARTICLE I.

I direct that all my just debts and funeral expenses be paid as soon as practicable after my decease.

ARTICLE II.

I do hereby give, to my good friend, LADY MARIA ST. JUST, of 9 Gerald Road, London, S.W.1, England, all of the royalties and other proceeds to which my Estate may be otherwise entitled from any and all uses in any and all media of my play presently entitled at this time "TWO CHARACTER PLAY".

ARTICLE III.

All the rest, residue and remainder of my estate, real, personal and mixed, of every kind and nature, and wherever situated, of which I may die seized or possessed, including without limitation, all property acquired by me or to which I may become

-1-

Last will and testament of Tennessee Williams. (Courtesy of Key West County Clerk's Office via Wikimedia Commons)

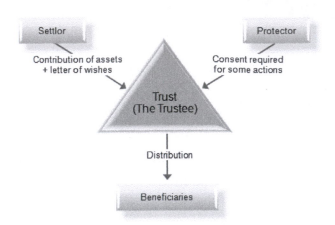

Chart of a basic trust. (Courtesy of Anja Bauer via Wikimedia Commons)

two basic parties: the person creating the will and the parties taking under the will. The person making the will is called the testator. As a technical matter, property distributed under a will is a legacy, devise, or bequest. A legacy is a gift of money, a devise is a gift of personal property, and a bequest is a gift of personal property other than money. The person taking then becomes a devisee or legatee. The delineations regarding the different types of gifts are sometimes used and not always used exactly as defined. For our purposes, and for most purposes, they need not be mentioned again, but if seen, they should be understood to relate to the passing of property under a will.

If a person did not make plans for his or her estate, or made plans that failed to address all property, state law dictates how the estate is to be distributed. A person who dies without making plans for his or her estate is termed an intestate or is said to have died intestate. The people who receive the property under state law are called distributes or heirs. The word *heir*, in this highly technical sense, refers only to people that receive property under state law; however, the word is more loosely used to refer to people that also receive property under a will.

Trusts are arrangements used to transfer property from one person to another. The person that establishes a trust can be called a settlor, trustor, or creator. The person who receives property under a trust arrangement is called a beneficiary. The word *beneficiary* is also generally used to mean any person who is designated to benefit from a legal arrangement, as in a will, a life insurance policy, etc.

In keeping with the modern approach, we will try to streamline our vocabulary. For our purposes,

any person making a will is a testator. Any person receiving under a will or under state law is an heir. Although in discussion it may seem otherwise, heirs are only heirs after the testator or intestate dies. Legally, no living person has heirs, only "heirs apparent." Anything that an heir receives is simply a gift or property. A person starting a trust will be called a settlor, and a person receiving property under the trust will called a beneficiary.

A will is a document that directs how a person's estate is to be distributed after his or her death. A will is a highly formal document that requires the testator to have capacity and must almost always be written, signed, and witnessed according to state law. A will can direct almost any distribution of property that a testator has an interest in at death to almost any heirs (except laws that prevent a spouse from being left out of a will). A will creates an interest in property only after the testator has died—until that time, the testator is free to change or revoke the will. Upon the testator's death, interested parties must present the will for probate in the appropriate court. Probate is a court-supervised process by which the validity of the will may be tested, and the debts and assets of the estate are collected. The executor is the person who actually collects the debts and assets of the estate to make the final distribution. Executors are usually appointed in the will and can be a relative, friend, lawyer, bank, or trust company. If the person named as executor declines the appointment or the will does not name an executor, the court will appoint the equivalent, called an administrator. The probate process is usually lengthy, taking an average of a year or more. The probate process is also expensive; it involves lawyers, accountants, appraisers, and filing fees for the court. For these reasons, it is wise to try to avoid probate.

Even though it is preferable to avoid probate to the greatest extent possible, everyone should have a will. First, if a person dies without a will, he or she is said to have died intestate. In that case, his or her property is distributed according the relevant state intestacy law. Intestacy laws represent a legislative judgment about how most people would want their property divided. Typically, the property would first go to a spouse and then be divided among children and grandchildren, then parents and siblings, and so on. In a case where virtually no family can be located, after a period of time, the property will ultimately go the state or escheat. To avoid the intestacy law and to distribute property exactly according to personal desires, a will or other estate plan is required. Wills also act as backups to other estate planning tools. Property may have been overlooked or newly acquired and not covered by some other arrangement. Wills are also important in that they allow a person to appoint personal and financial guardians for minor children.

There are several options to limit the property that passes under a will and through probate. Trusts, joint tenancies, certain bank account trusts, and life insurance are common options. A trust is a legal arrangement whereby a settlor splits ownership of his or her property into two parts, the legal title and the beneficial interest. The legal title to the property is conveyed to a fiduciary, called a trustee. The trustee holds and manages the property for the exclusive use of the beneficiary or beneficiaries, including pets in many states. A fiduciary is one who owes another the duties of good faith, trust, confidence, and candor and must exercise a high standard of care in managing another's money or property. In order to discharge those fiduciary duties, a trustee is generally required to apply, at least, the skill and prudence that a capable and careful person would exercise in conduct of his or her personal business. Trustees also have a duty of loyalty, which means that a trustee must administer the trust solely in the interests of the beneficiaries without regard to the interests of any third party. Among other obligations, the trustee also has the duty to preserve and protect the trust property, to keep the trust property separate from all other property, and to invest and make the trust property productive. The burden of trustee can be heavy, and many trustees are professionals. As a practical matter, a person should accept an appointment as trustee only with full knowledge of the scope of the commitment (Goldberg, 2007).

Once a settlor creates a trust, the settlor can still use trust property; in fact, the settlor can usually be the trustee and beneficiary under the trust so long as there is at least one other beneficiary. Trust arrangements, in this context, are sometimes referred to as inter vivos trusts, living trusts, or revocable trusts. All three terms refer to the same general arrangement where the settlor retains the right to use the property and can change the terms or revoke the trust at any time before death. This is opposed to an irrevocable trust, which does not allow the settlor to change it or revoke it after the trust has been established. At the grantor's death, the trust becomes irrevocable and

Last section of the third side handwritten 1616 will of William Shakspeare - only the signature written by Shakspeare. (Courtesy of William Shakespeare and unknown scribe via Wikimedia Commons)

can no longer be altered or revoked. At that point the trustee, usually named in the trust instrument, would take control of the trust and distribute the property to the beneficiaries as appropriate. Property held in trust avoids probate and can also be used to prevent a beneficiary from wasting an inheritance.

Trust property does not have to be distributed entirely at the grantor's death. The trust instrument can provide for any number of distributions to a beneficiary. A trust can provide for a periodic income distribution to the beneficiary until a certain age, at which the entire principal may be handed over. The trust can provide for discretion on the part of the trustee to distribute trust property according to a certain standard—for example, the education and health of a beneficiary or to keep the beneficiary comfortable according to a certain lifestyle. These types of trusts are generally called discretionary trusts or support trusts. A spendthrift trust is a type of trust that protects the beneficiary's interest in the trust from certain creditors.

A joint tenancy is a way for co-owners to hold property together, typically real property. The critical feature of the joint tenancy for estate planning purposes is called "the right of survivorship." With the right of survivorship, if one co-owner dies, that ownership automatically transfers to the other owner or owners. If two people own a house as joint tenants and one of them dies, the other owns the entire property. If three people own a property as joint tenants, when one dies, the other two each own half. The operation of the right of survivorship applies even if there were provisions in a will or trust to the contrary. The joint tenant ownership form should be compared to another co-ownership form called tenants in common. Tenants in common interests in property do not automatically vest in co-owners and are transferable by will or trust. A form of joint tenancy, available in some states exclusively for married couples, is called tenancy by the entireties (TBE). A TBE has the right of survivorship. While a co-ownership with a right of survivorship will avoid probate, it does not remove property from a person's taxable estate.

Joint tenancies can also be set-up in bank accounts. A joint tenancy in a bank account operates essentially the same way as joint tenants in real property. Unless otherwise arranged with dual consent, bank accounts with the right of survivorship (JTWROS) allow each tenant to withdraw all the funds in an account at any time. If a person intends to transfer his or her funds at death, a JTWROS account carries the risk that the other person may withdraw funds during the life of the primary depositor, or if dual consent is required, the primary depositor would need the consent of the other tenant to withdraw funds. To resolve this problem, bank accounts can be designated as a pay-on-death (POD) account. A POD account, sometimes called an informal trust, bank account trust, or Totten trust, allows a depositor to retain full control over the funds during his or her lifetime. Upon the depositor's death, the designated beneficiary can have immediate access to the funds by presenting proof of identity and a copy of the death certificate to the bank. Funds transferred by banks accounts are included in a decedent's taxable estate.

A related device that operates in the same manner as a POD bank account is called a transfer on death (TOD) designation. Transfer on death designations can be attached to stocks, mutual funds, bonds, and brokerage accounts. POD and TOD designations, like a joint tenant taking under a right of survivorship, will pass regardless of the terms of a will or trust. For example, if a person intended his or her children to share equally but left them accounts with unequal value, those children would have to agree to transfer money to equalize the shares (Goldwasser, 2006).

Life insurance is often a part of an estate plan. Life insurance proceeds go directly to the beneficiary named by the purchaser and do not go through probate. Insurance proceeds are a ready source of cash, a "liquid" asset that can be used for burial expenses, estates debts, and any estate taxes that may be due.

Other tools involved in the estate planning process are durable powers of attorney, health care proxies, and living wills. These documents do not transfer property in the event of death but help others to manage a person's affairs if they become incapacitated. A durable power of attorney is a document that allows another person to make transactions on behalf of the donor, or person giving the power. A donor can give a wide array of authority, exercisable during his or her life and without any further consent, to another, including the power to manage a business, use bank accounts, and buy and sell real property. A health care proxy nominates a person to make the health care decisions for another. Closely related to the health care proxy is the living will. A living will expresses a person's wishes with respect to life support in the event that he or she becomes terminally ill.

The digital age has ushered in a new form of property: digital assets, which can include e-mails, photographs, social media accounts, funds-transfer accounts (as through PayPal), and the like. However, the law has been slow to respond to this phenomenon in terms of who can access and control these assets after the owner dies and how. Meanwhile, unauthorized access of a person's digital accounts is considered an illegal violation of privacy and an act of hacking, posing a problem for executors and heirs (Bissett & Blair, 2014). The situation is further complicated by disparate terms of use for various service providers, such as e-mail clients (Bissett & Blair, 2014). As of mid-2015, about nineteen states had or were seeking to enact legislation that would grant permission to a fiduciary to access some or all of these digital assets. Some proposed laws would require the executor of an estate to obtain a court order first (McCarthy, 2015). Financial advisers have begun to recommend that individuals specify a fiduciary for that purpose and enumerate their various digital assets in their wills, just as they would for their tangible assets (Parthemer, Feffer, & Klein, 2014; Bissett & Blair, 2014).

APPLICATIONS

Through the use of trusts and other devices, probate can be largely eliminated, and property can pass relatively quickly and easily. However, the issue of taxes is a separate matter. While separate states may have taxes relevant to estates, this discussion focuses on federal estate tax considerations. Computing the precise amount of tax that may be owed by an estate and the precise legal measures that may be taken to avoid liability for taxes is difficult and often regarded as one of the most complicated fields of law. However, generally, a taxable estate is the gross estate minus the allowable deductions. The gross estate includes all property in which a person had an interest at death and life insurance proceeds, property transfers within three years of death, and trusts that a person established and retained certain powers in. Allowable deductions include funeral expenses, debts owed at death, and marital deduction (the amount passing to the surviving spouse) (Gallo, 2013). The size of a taxable estate can be reduced during life through the use of gifts. If, after gifts and allowable deductions, a taxable estate is still large enough to be potentially liable for tax, a unified credit can be used to erase part or all of the liability. The tax rates and the size of a taxable estate became a bone of contention, and federal legislation fluctuated for more than a decade. An estate of less than $2 million was exempt from estate tax for deaths occurring in 2007 and 2008. For deaths occurring in 2009, estates less than $3.5 million were exempt. The estate tax was repealed altogether for deaths occurring in 2010 (Clifford, 2006; IRS, 2006). In 2011 the estate tax was reinstated on estates over $5 million and indexed to inflation (Smith & Block, 2013). Consequently, the minimum estate value for which tax would be due to the Internal Revenue Service rose to $5.25 million in 2013, $5.34 million in 2014, and $5.43 million in 2015.

Estate tax and gifts are connected because gifts given during life lower the value of an estate and therefore the possibility of an estate tax. The gift tax applies to gifts that occur whenever property is transferred without the expectation of receiving something of equal value in return. Under that definition, selling something for less than what it is worth, or making a low-interest loan, may be a gift. While the general rule is that any gift is taxable, there are numerous nontaxable gifts including gifts for tuition and medical expenses paid directly to the institution, to a spouse, to political organizations, or to charities and any gifts less than the exclusion amount. The exclusion rule allows every person to give to any number of people nontaxable annual gifts so long as each recipient's total gift does not exceed $14,000 (beginning in 2013). However, tax is payable on an amount that exceeds $14,000. Married couples can enhance their gift giving to an individual with gift splitting, whereby half the gift comes from one spouse and half from the other. If a gift is still taxable after all those exceptions, unified credit can be used to eliminate it. The amount of the gift tax would be subtracted from the lifetime unified credit (IRS, 2006).

The unified credit eliminates or reduces both estate and gift tax. Each person has several hundred thousand to millions of dollars of credit as applied to gifts and estates. The amount of personal credit is a lifetime total, and each annual application of the credit during life reduces the total amount of credit. Thus the more credit applied to gifts, the less unified credit will be available to eliminate estate taxes at death.

According to a 2015 report by the congressional Joint Committee on Taxation, one-fifth of 1 percent, or 0.002 percent, of estates were subject to estate tax in 2013. For those larger estates, when both probate avoidance and tax reduction are at issue, more sophisticated estate planning vehicles are available. Those strategies can include life insurance trust, family limited liability partnerships or family limited liability companies, grantor retained annuity trusts, and other trusts to hold real estate for the benefit of children and certain charitable donations. Estate plans for these larger estates are exceedingly complex and are mentioned here to simply make the reader aware that estate planning does not end with wills, trusts, and other nonprobate transfers (Giarmarco, 2006).

The estate tax, or death tax, as it sometimes is called by opponents, is a political topic. Legislation that would have amounted to a near repeal of the estate tax after 2010 was stalled in the U.S. Senate in August of 2006. According the Joint Committee on Taxation, the legislation would have cost the government $268 billion between 2007–2016, or 80 percent of a full repeal. A repeal of the estate tax was then estimated to reduce federal revenue by $1 trillion over 20 years. In 2015, the Congressional Budget Office projected that estate taxes would bring the government $246 billion in revenue between 2016 and 2025. Opponents of the legislation also claimed that the repeal would remove a strong incentive for wealthy Americans to make charitable gifts through their estates, citing a possible 22 percent reduction in those gifts. Proponents of the legislation claimed that the estate tax law as it stood would devastate small businesses and farm owners (Schauer, 2006). On the state level, 15 states and the District of Columbia imposed a tax on estates as of 2015, with six also levying inheritance taxes (i.e., on the property transferred to heirs such as spouses, children, and other relatives), according to the Tax Foundation, a nonprofit think tank.

IRS Circular 230 Notice: To ensure compliance with requirements imposed by the IRS, we inform you that any U.S. tax advice contained in this communication (including any attachments) is not intended or written to be used, and cannot be used, for the purpose of (i) avoiding penalties under the Internal Revenue Code or (ii) promoting, marketing or recommending to another party any transaction or matter addressed herein.

Terms & Concepts

Beneficiary: A party designated to benefit from trust property. Generally, a party intended to benefit from any legal arrangement.

Convey: A legal transfer of ownership usually by writing.

Escheat: Process by which property left by a decedent and unclaimed by family or other takers is turned over to the state.

Fiduciary: A person who has a duty to act in the best interest of another, which involves certain duties in specific situations.

Intestate: Describes a person that dies without a will.

Intestacy law: State law that determines how an estate will be distributed in the absence of a will.

Inter vivos trusts: A trust that takes effect during the grantor's life; also called a living trust. Compare—testamentary trust: a trust created by a will that takes effect after the testator's death.

Liquid asset: Assets that can quickly be turned into cash, e.g., securities, marketable notes, or accounts receivable. Compare—illiquid asset: an asset not readily converted into cash because lack of demand, absence of an established market, or substantial cost or time required for liquidation (e.g., real property).

Probate estate: That portion of an estate that must be probated because the property passes under a will.

Probate: Court-supervised process that confirms the validity of a will and where assets and debts of an estate are collected and settled and then distributed.

Revocable trust: A condition inserted into a trust where the settlor retains the right to terminate the trust and recover the trust property.

Settlor, trustor, donor, or creator: Different names that refer to the person who places property in a trust.

Taxable estate: That portion of an estate subject to federal tax determined by the gross estate minus the allowable deductions.

Trust: A legally enforceable arrangement whereby a trustee holds legal title to property at the request of another (settlor) for the benefit of some third party (beneficiary).

Will: A document by which a person directs the distribution of his or her estate upon death.

Bibliography

Bissett, W., & Blair, A. W. (2014). Planning implications of new legislation for digital assets. *Journal of Financial Planning, 27*(12), 21–24.

Bogert, G. T. (1987). *Trusts* (6th ed.). Hornbook series student edition, St. Paul, MN: West Publishing.

Busch, J. (2013). Estate and inheritance tax updates and trends at the state level. *Journal of State Taxation, 31,* 35–48.

Clifford, D. (1992). *Plan your estate with a living trust* (2nd ed.). Berkeley, CA: Nolo Press.

Clifford, D. (2006) *Quick and legal will book* (4th ed.). Berkeley, CA: Nolo Press.

Gallo, J. J. (2013). Allocating assets between a bypass trust and a marital trust. *Journal of Financial Planning, 26,* 35–39.

Garner, B. (Ed.) (1999). *Black's Law Dictionary* (7th ed.). St. Paul, MN: West Publishing.

United States Internal Revenue Service, (2006) Publication 950, *Introduction to Estate and Gift Taxes.*

Giarmarco, J. (2006). Five levels of estate planning. *Advisor Today, 101,* 50–52.

McCarthy, E. (2015). Digital estate planning: Plugging the gap. *Retirement Advisor, 16*(8), 40–43.

Parthemer, M. R., Feffer, J. G., & Klein, S. A. (2014). Estate planning with digital assets—Where are we now? *Journal of Financial Service Professionals, 68*(2), 19–21.

Smith, A., & Block, S. (2013). Tax planning gets easier. *Kiplinger's Personal Finance, 67,* 11–12.

Suggested Reading

Basi, B., & Renwick, M. (2006). Where there's a will. *Industrial Distribution, 95,* 63–65.

Goldwasser, J. (2006). Estate planning LITE. *Kiplinger's Personal Finance, 60,* 93.

Ngai, V. (2015). Back to the basics of estate planning. *CPA Journal, 85*(1), 58–63.

Schauer, C. (2006). Estate tax repeal and the role of the CPA. *Sum News, 17,* 6–7.

Goldberg, S. (2007). In you they TRUST. *Kiplinger's Personal Finance, 61,* 90–92.

Essay by Seth M. Azria, JD

GLOSSARY

Accounting Information System: An organization's chronological list of debits and credits.

Accounting Methods: The rules for reporting income and expenses.

Accounting Profits: The difference between the total revenue and the cost of producing goods or services.

Accounts Payable: A financial account for paying debts owed to suppliers and others.

Accounts Receivable: The accounts for which payment is owed.

Actual Cost System: The recording of products costs based on the costs of materials, labor and overhead costs, allocated using the actual quantity of the allocation base experienced during the reporting period.

Adjusted Gross Income: An individual's total gross income minus specific deductions.

Aggregate Economy: In macroeconomics, aggregate demand (AD) or domestic final demand (DFD) is the total demand for final goods and services in an economy at a given time. It specifies the amounts of goods and services that will be purchased at all possible price levels. This is the demand for the gross domestic product of a country.

Angel Investors: Angel or Angel Investor defines an individual who offers capital to startup business in need of added value. Angel investors often boost the companies' financial worth due to their connections and expertise in the field.

Annual Percentage Rate: The simple interest rate or percentage which invested money earns over of period of one year.

Annual Report: A corporation's annual statement of financial operations. Annual reports include a balance sheet, income statement, auditor's report and a description of the company's operations.

Appreciation: The increased market value of an asset over time.

Arbitrage: Technology applied to business for processing data and transferring information.

Articles of Incorporation: A document that incorporators must file with the state to form a corporation and that sets out certain mandatory and optional information about the business and governance of the corporation.

Asset: A resource having economic value that an individual, corporation or country owns or controls with the expectation that it will provide future benefit.

Asset Allocation: How the assets in an investor's portfolio are allocated to difference investments based on how much risk the investor can tolerate.

Asset Management: In financial services, the management of a client's investments by a bank.

Asset Valuation: The determination of the net market value of a company's assets on a per share basis.

Audit: A formal assessment of an organizations' accounting records. Audits are traditionally performed by independent public accounting firms.

Balance Sheet: A document showing a firm's assets, liabilities and equity for a specified period of time.

Bank: Banks are commercial institutions licensed to receive deposits and whose primary business is making and receiving payments as well as supplying short-term loans to individuals.

Bankruptcy: A legal status of a person or other entity that cannot repay debts to creditors. In most jurisdictions, bankruptcy is imposed by a court order, often initiated by the debtor.

Bankruptcy Risk: Sometimes called insolvency risk. The risk for companies associated with having liabilities that exceed assets. Also called negative net worth.

Bear Market: A financial situation where the market sees falling prices.

Bid-Ask Spread (aka Spread): Refers to the difference between the current bid and the current ask (in over-the-counter trading) or offered (in exchange trading) of a given security. (Investor Words, 2007)

Bond: A certificate showing that an investor has loaned a company money to be paid back upon a specified maturity date.

Bond Fund: A collection of bonds, managed by financial experts, who used "pooled" money from numerous investors to establish a diversified portfolio.

Bond Issue: The act of offering a large set of bonds for sale to the public, the main source of bonds available for individual purchase.

Bond Laddering: A financial strategy involving the purchase of different bonds which have different maturity dates.

Broad-Based Index: An index that reflects the movement of the whole market.

Bull Market: A market where prices are increasing.

Business Environment: All of the internal and external factors that affect how the company functions including employees, customers, management, supply and demand and business regulations. An example of a part of a business environment is how well customers' expectations are met.

Business Model: Describes the rationale of how an organization creates, delivers, and captures value, in economic, social, cultural or other contexts. The process of business model construction is part of business strategy.

Business Process: A collection of related, structured activities or tasks that produce a specific service or product for a particular customer or customers.

Business Strategy: The context for specific business decisions and operating strategies.

Buyout: An investment transaction by which the ownership equity of a company, or a majority share of the stock of the company is acquired. The acquirer thereby "buys out" the present equity holders of the target company.

Capital: Capital is the combination of all durable investment goods, which are usually added and calculated with units of money.

Capital Asset: Includes property of any kind held by an assessee, whether connected with their business or profession or not connected with their business or profession. It includes all kinds of property, movable or immovable, tangible or intangible, fixed or circulating.

Capital Budgeting: Capital budgeting involves deciding which long-term projects are worthy of investing in and undertaking. Choosing such potential projects usually involved making comparisons of anticipated discounted cash flows and the internal rates of return.

Capital Expenditure: Money spent by a business or organization on acquiring or maintaining fixed assets, such as land, buildings, and equipment.

Capital Gain: The difference between the net cost of a security and the net sales price, if the cost is less than the price.

Capital Investment: Money a corporation uses to invest in a capital asset such as equipment or other long-term assets such as land or buildings.

Capital Loss: The difference between the net cost of a security and the net sales price, if the cost is more than the price.

Capital Structure: The total amount of a company's long-term debt, short-term debt, common equity and preferred equity. Companies use money from this fund to finance all general operations and expansion using different sources.

Cash: Legal tender or coins that can be used in the exchange of goods, debt or services. Sometimes also including the value of assets that can be converted into cash immediately, as reported by a company.

Cash Flow Statement: A document reporting the money going in and coming out of a firm.

Closely Held Corporation: Any company that has only a limited number of shareholders; its stock is publicly traded on occasion but not on a regular basis. These entities differ from privately owned firms that issue stock that is not publicly traded.

Commercial Bank: An institution that provides services such as accepting deposits, providing business loans, and offering basic investment products. Though commercial banks give their services to individual citizens, they usually invest more of their efforts to lending money to and taking deposits from companies.

Commodities: A term for projects of value, for which there is a demand. The resources are produced in large quantities by many different producers, the items from each are considered comparable – some examples include oil, soybeans and pork bellies.

Commodity Markets: A market where buyers and sellers of raw material (eg. wool, sugar, coffee, wheat, metals, etc.) trade.

Common Disaster: Situation in which two or more persons with joint property interests (such as an insured and the primary beneficiary of his or her life insurance policy) die at the same time, without a clear evidence to establish who died first and whose estate should receive the policy's benefits.

Common Law: The body of law derived from judicial decisions of courts and similar tribunals. The defining characteristic of "common law" is that it arises as precedent.

Compound Interest: Compound interest is the addition of interest to the principal sum of a loan or deposit, or in other words, interest on interest.

Contract: A voluntary arrangement between two or more parties that is enforceable by law as a binding legal agreement. Contract is a branch of the law of obligations in jurisdictions of the civil law tradition.

Corporation: A firm that is owned by stockholders and managed by professional administration.

Corporate Development: The activities that companies undertake to grow through inorganic means such as mergers and acquisitions, strategic alliances and joint ventures.

Cost-Benefit Analysis: Sometimes called benefit costs analysis (BCA), it is a systematic approach to estimating the strengths and weaknesses of alternatives (for example in transactions, activities, functional business requirements or projects investments); it is used to determine options that provide the best approach to achieve benefits while preserving savings.

Cost–Effectiveness Analysis: A form of economic analysis that compares the relative costs and outcomes (effects) of different courses of action. Cost-effectiveness analysis is distinct from cost–benefit analysis, which assigns a monetary value to the measure of effect.

Credit: The trust which allows one party to provide money or resources to another party where that second party does not reimburse the first party immediately, but instead promises either to repay or return those resources at a later date.

Credit Risk: A credit risk is the risk of default on a debt that may arise from a borrower failing to make required payments. In the first resort, the risk is that of the lender and includes lost principal and interest, disruption to cash flows, and increased collection costs.

Crowdfunding: The practice of funding a project or venture by raising many small amounts of money from a large number of people, typically via the Internet. Crowdfunding is a form of crowdsourcing and of alternative finance.

Cybercrime: Cybercrime, or computer oriented crime, is crime that involves a computer and a network. The computer may have been used in the commission of a crime, or it may be the target.

Day Trader: Investors who buy and sell stocks during the day with the goal being to make products as a stock's value changes throughout the day.

Debit: An entry recording an amount owed, listed on the left-hand side or column of an account.

Debt: A relationship where a borrower receives funds from a lender and is obligated to pay back the lending amount plus interest.

Debt Financing: Debt financing occurs when a firm advancing its capital through the means of selling bonds to individuals or institutions who are willing to invest. In exchange for the money lent, the investors become creditors and expect to be repaid with interest on the debt that was incurred.

Debt-to Equity Ratio: A calculation of a company's financial influence measured by dividing its total liabilities by stockholders' equity. It signifies what fraction of equity and debt the company is using to support its assets.

Demand: In economics, demand is the quantity of a commodity or a service that people are willing or able to buy at a certain price, per unit of time. The relationship between price and quantity demanded is also known as demand curve.

Demand and Supply Models: In microeconomics, supply and demand is an economic model of price determination in a market. It postulates that in a competitive market, the unit price for a particular good, or other traded item such as labor or liquid financial assets, will vary until it settles at a point where the quantity demanded (at the current price) will equal the quantity supplied (at the current price), resulting in an economic equilibrium for price and quantity transacted.

Digital Assets: Anything that exists in a binary format and comes with the right to use. Data that do not possess that right are not considered assets.

Double-Entry Bookkeeping: A system of bookkeeping so named because every entry to an account requires a corresponding and opposite entry to a different account.

Earnings Per Share: The portion of a company's profit allocated to each outstanding share of common stock. EPS serves as an indicator of a company's profitability.

EBITA: Earnings before interest, taxes, depreciation and amortization.

Elasticity: Refers to the degree to which individuals, consumers or producers change their demand or the amount supplied in response to price or income changes.

Enterprise: Describes the actions of someone who shows some initiative by taking a risk by setting up, investing in and running a business.

Enterprise Risk Management: A basic shift in the method that companies use in assessing and approaching risk involved in investments. Aon's ERM methodology uses companies' expertise in assessing and analyzing risk, recognizing causes for concern, and proactively creating methods to agree and conform to preexisting regulations.

Equity: In general, ownership in any asset after all debts connected to the asset are paid off.

Equity Capital: Money invested in a business by owners, stockholders or others who share in the profits.

Escheat: Escheat is a common law doctrine that transfers the property of a person who died without heirs to the crown or state. It serves to ensure that property is not left in "limbo" without recognized ownership.

Exchange Rate: In finance, an exchange rate is the rate at which one currency will be exchanged for another. It is also regarded as the value of one country's currency in relation to another currency.

External Audit: An external auditor performs an audit, in accordance with specific laws or rules, of the financial statements of a company, government entity, other legal entity, or organization, and is independent of the entity being audited. External auditors normally address their reports to the shareholders of a corporation.

Fair Market Value: A selling price for an item to which a buyer and seller can agree.

Fiat Money: Any money declared by a government to be legal tender.

Fiduciaries: Parties that hold something of value in trust for an individual or group.

Financial Accounting: Reporting of the financial position of an organization to external stakeholders.

Financial Management: The method of controlling economic resources such as accounting, economic reporting, budgeting and gathering accounts receivables, managing risks and insuring businesses.

Financial Markets: Markets where financial assets are traded.

Financial Statements: Documents that note the status of a company's assets, expenses, revenues and liabilities.

Firewalls: A network security system that monitors and controls incoming and outgoing network traffic based on predetermined security rules. A firewall typically establishes a barrier between a trusted internal network and an untrusted external network, such as the Internet.

First-In First-Out Costing: Means that the oldest inventory items are recorded as sold first but do not necessarily mean that the exact oldest physical object has been tracked and sold. In other words, the cost associated with the inventory that was purchased first is the cost expenses first.

Float: The amount of shares that are publicly owned and available to be traded. The float number is calculated by subtracting the number of restricted shares from the total number of outstanding shares. Also known as the "free float."

Floating Exchange Rate: An exchange rate system where the currency values is established by the foreign-exchange market based on the supply and demand for that individual currency compared to other currencies in the market.

Free Cash Flow: Refers to cash that is available for distribution among all security holders of a company. They include equity holders, debt holders, preferred stock holders, convertibles holders and so on.

Fund Accounting: Fund accounting is an accounting system for recording resources whose use has been limited by the donor, grant authority, governing agency, or other individuals or organizations or by law.

Futures: A term designating the standardized contracts covering the sale of commodities for future delivery on a futures exchange.

Futures Markets: Focus on margins as they relate to the initial deposit of "good faith" that is made to an account with the intent to then engage in a futures contract. The margin is also known as good faith due to its help in debiting daily losses that may be incurred.

General Partnerships: A general partnership, the basic form of partnership under common law, is in most countries an association of persons or an unincorporated company with the following major features: Must be created by agreement, proof of existence and estoppel.

Goodwill: Goodwill arises when a company acquires another entire business. The amount of goodwill is the cost to purchase the business minus the fair market value of the tangible assets, the intangible assets that can be identified, and the liabilities obtained in the purchase.

Gross Domestic Product: Gross domestic product is a monetary measure of the market value of all final goods and services produced in a period of time.

Growth: Economic expansion as measured by any of a number of indicators such as increased revenue, staffing and market share.

Growth Companies: Companies whose rate of growth considerably surpasses that of the typical in its category or the inclusive rate of financial gain.

Hacker: Any skilled computer expert that uses their technical knowledge to overcome a problem. While "hacker" can refer to any skilled computer programmer, the term has become associated in popular culture with a "security hacker", someone who, with their technical knowledge, uses bugs or exploits to break into computer systems.

Hedge: A transaction that offsets an exposure to fluctuations in financial prices of some other contract or business risk. It may consist of cash instruments or derivatives.

Hedge Fund: A fund generally used by wealthy entities outside of the purview of many rules and regulations that govern mutual funds. Since these funds are largely unregulated they allow for aggressive investment strategies that are unattainable but cannot be utilized in mutual funds. Examples include selling short, leverage, program trading, swaps, arbitrage and derivatives.

Historical Cost Accounting: A measure of value used in accounting in which the price of an asset on the balance sheet is based on its nominal or original cost when acquired by the company. The historical-cost method is used for assets in the United States under generally accepted accounting principles (GAAP).

Horizontal Merger: A merger or business consolidation that occurs between firms that operate in the same space, as competition tends to be higher and the synergies and potential gains in market share are much greater for merging firms in such an industry.

Hostile Mergers: The acquisition of one company (called the target company) by another (called the acquirer) that is accomplished by going directly to the company's shareholders or fighting to replace management to get the acquisition approved.

Identity Management: Identity management, also known as identity and access management is, in computer security, the security and business discipline that "enables the right individuals to access the right resources at the right times and for the right reasons".

Implied Contracts: An agreement created by actions of the parties involved, but it is not written or spoken. An implied contract is a legal substitute for a contract that is assumed to have been drawn. In this case, there is no written record nor any actual verbal agreement.

Income: Money received, especially on a regular basis, for work or through investments.

Income Statement: An income statement or profit and loss account is one of the financial statements of a company and shows the company's revenues and expenses during a particular period. It indicates how the revenues are transformed into the net income.

Indirect Costs: Indirect costs are costs that are not directly accountable to a cost object (such as a particular project, facility, function or product). Indirect costs may be either fixed or variable. Indirect costs include administration, personnel and security costs. These are those costs which are not directly related to production. Some indirect costs may be overhead. But some overhead costs can be directly attributed to a project and are direct costs. There are two types of indirect costs. One are the fixed indirect costs which contains activities or costs that are fixed for a particular project or company like transportation of labor to the working site, building temporary roads, etc. The other are recurring indirect costs which contains activities that repeat for a particular company like maintenance of records or payment of salaries.

Indirect Tax: An indirect tax is a tax collected by an intermediary from the person who bears the ultimate economic burden of the tax. The intermediary later files a tax return and forwards the tax proceeds to government with the return.

Inflation: The rate at which the general level of prices for goods and services rises.

Inherent Risk: An assessed level of raw or untreated risk; that is, the natural level of risk inherent in a process or activity without doing anything to reduce the likelihood or mitigate the severity of a mishap, or the amount of risk before the application of the risk reduction effects of controls. One of the main arguments against the use of inherent risk as a concept is the perceived difficulty in determining its level. Where the inherent risk can be assessed, it assists in identifying which controls are key.

Intangible Assets: An asset that lacks physical substance (unlike physical assets such as machinery and buildings) and usually is very hard to evaluate.

It includes patents, copyrights, franchises, goodwill, trademarks, trade names, the general interpretation also includes software and other intangible computer based assets. Contrary to other assets, they generally—though not necessarily—suffer from typical market failures of non-rivalry and non-excludability.

Interest: Cost of using money, conveyed as a rate per specific period of time, usually one year, which is known as an annual rate of interest.

Interest Rate: The price of borrowing money expressed in an annual percentage.

Internet: The world-wide system of computers that exchange information electronically.

Internet Security: A branch of computer security specifically related to the Internet, often involving browser security but also network security on a more general level, as it applies to other applications or operating systems as a whole.

Intestacy: The condition of the estate of a person who dies without having made a valid will or other binding declaration. Alternatively this may also apply where a will or declaration has been made, but only applies to part of the estate; the remaining estate forms the "intestate estate".

Intrapreneurship: A relatively recent concept that focuses on employees of a company that have many of the attributes of entrepreneurs. An intrapreneur is someone within a company that takes risks in an effort to solve a given problem.

Intrinsic Value: The present value of a firm's expected future net cash flows less the rate of return.

Investment: The use of money to create more money.

Investment Vehicle: Broad term defining any method by which money can be invested.

Job Order Costing: Job order costing or job costing is a system for assigning manufacturing costs to an individual product or batches of products. Generally, the job order costing system is used only when the products manufactured are sufficiently different from each other.

Joint Cost: A joint cost is a cost incurred in a joint process. Joint costs may include direct material, direct labor, and overhead costs incurred during a joint production process. A joint process is a production process in which one input yields multiple outputs.

Joint Tenancy: The holding of an estate or property jointly by two or more parties, the share of each passing to the other or others on death.

Joint Venture: A joint venture is a business entity created by two or more parties, generally characterized by shared ownership, shared returns and risks, and shared governance.

Just-In-Time Method: Just-in-time (JIT) is an inventory strategy companies employ to increase efficiency and decrease waste by receiving goods only as they are needed in the production process, thereby reducing inventory costs. This method requires producers to forecast demand accurately.

Key Performance Indicators: A performance indicator or key performance indicator is a type of performance measurement. KPIs evaluate the success of an organization or of a particular activity in which it engages.

Labor: Measure of work done by human beings.

Labor Markets: Labor economics seeks to understand the functioning and dynamics of the markets for wage labor. Labor markets or job markets function through the interaction of workers and employers.

Laissez-Faire Economics: An economic system in which transactions between private parties are free from government intervention such as regulation, privileges, tariffs, and subsidies.

Legal Liability: In law, liable means "responsible or answerable in law; legally obligated." Legal liability concerns both civil law and criminal law and can arise from various areas of law, such as contracts, torts, taxes, or fines given by government agencies.

Leverage: In general, the amount of debt used to finance a firm's assets.

Leveraged Buyout: When a company is taken over using borrowed money. The new company's assets are used as collateral for the borrowed finances.

Leveraged Capitalization: A technique employed to avoid involuntary acquisition. Using this strategy, a company takes on a significant amount of debt in order to repurchase stocks through a buyback offer or dispenses a significant dividend between current shareholders. The company share price then increases significantly, which makes the company less appealing as a takeover target.

Liability: A company's legal debts or obligations that arise during the course of business operations.

Limited Liability: The concept that neither the owners of a corporation, called shareholders, nor the directors or officers are personally liable for the obligations of the corporation. Generally, corporate owners risk only their original investment.

Liquidity: In business, economics or investment, market liquidity is a market's ability to purchase or sell an asset without causing drastic change in the asset's price.

Liquidity Risk: In the enterprise risk management model, the concept involves funding and market liquidity.

Loan: A transfer of an asset from a person or entity to another person or entity with the expectation that it will be repaid.

Macroeconomics: A branch of economics dealing with the performance, structure, behavior, and decision-making of an economy as a whole. This includes regional, national, and global economies.

Managerial Accounting: Financial reporting that is aimed at helping managers to make decisions.

Marginal Revenue: Marginal revenue (R') is the additional revenue that will be generated by increasing product sales by one unit. It can also be described as the unit revenue the last item sold has generated for the firm. As a result, it will have to lower the price of all units sold to increase sales by 1 unit.

Marginal Utility: In economics, utility is the satisfaction or benefit derived by consuming a product; thus the marginal utility of a good or service is the change in the utility from an increase in the consumption of that good or service.

Market: A market is one of the many varieties of systems, institutions, procedures, social relations and infrastructures whereby parties engage in exchange.

Mergers and Acquisitions: Mergers and acquisitions are transactions in which the ownership of companies, other business organizations or their operating units are transferred or combined.

Microeconomics: Microeconomics is a branch of economics that studies the behavior of individuals and firms in making decisions regarding the allocation of scarce resources and the interactions among these individuals and firms.

Mission Statement: A formal summary of the aims and values of a company, organization, or individual.

Money Markets: Money market securities are often considered a safe alternative to riskier ways of investing. They usually return a lower interest rate that aligns properly with the temporary cash storage and short-term future expectations.

Mortgage: A security instrument in which real property is pledged as collateral for the payment of a mortgage note.

Necessity Entrepreneurs: Those who start a business as they do not have another means of generating income.

Neoclassical Growth Theory: Neoclassical growth theory is an economic theory that outlines how a steady economic growth rate can be accomplished with the proper amounts of the three driving forces: labor, capital and technology.

Net Assets: Net assets are defined as total assets minus total liabilities. In a sole proprietorship the amount of net assets is reported as owner's equity. In a corporation the amount of net assets is reported as stockholders' equity.

Net Present Value: The difference between the present value of cash inflows and the present value of cash outflows. NPV is used in capital budgeting to analyze the profitability of an investment or project.

Network: Networking is a socioeconomic business activity by which businesspeople and entrepreneurs meet to form business relationships and to recognize, create, or act upon business opportunities, share information and seek potential partners for ventures.

New Growth Theory: An economic growth theory that posits humans' desires and unlimited wants foster ever-increasing productivity and economic growth. The new growth theory argues that real GDP per person will perpetually increase because of people's pursuit of profits.

Nonprofit: A non-profit organization, also known as a non-business entity, is dedicated to furthering a particular social cause or advocating for a shared point of view.

Non-Statistical Sampling: The selection of a test group that is based on the examiner's judgment, rather than a formal statistical method.

Normal Distribution: Normal (or Gaussian) distribution is a very common continuous probability distribution. Normal distributions are important in statistics and are often used in the natural and social sciences to represent real-valued random variables whose distributions are not known.

Note: A promissory note, sometimes referred to as a note payable, is a legal instrument (more particularly, a financial instrument and a debt instrument), in which one party (the maker or issuer) promises in writing to pay a determinate sum of money to the other (the payee), either at a fixed or determinable future time or on demand of the payee, under specific terms. If the promissory note is unconditional and readily saleable, it is called a negotiable instrument.

Nuisance Regulations: In a regulatory environment, the term "nuisance" embraces anything that results in an invasion of one's legal rights. A nuisance involves an unreasonable or unlawful use of property that results in material annoyance, inconvenience, discomfort, or injury to another person or to the public.

Objective Value: Prevailing value established by the market.

Operating Business Plan: It is a dynamic document that highlights the strengths and weakness of the company and guides the company toward learning and increased efficiency.

Operational Accountability: Operational accountability is demonstrated when governments issue accrual-based financial statements for the entire government. GASB Statement 34 requires reporting on operational accountability for all activities, including governmental activities, in consolidated government-wide statements.

Opportunity Costs: The cost of passing up the next best choice when making a decision. For example, if an asset such as capital is used for one purpose, the opportunity cost is the value of the next best purpose the asst could have been used for. (Investor Words, 2007)

Opportunity Entrepreneurs: Those who start a business because they spot an opportunity in the market which they want to pursue.

Oral Contracts: An oral contract is a contract, the terms of which have been agreed by spoken communication. There may be written or other physical evidence of an oral contract, for example where the parties write down what they have agreed, but the contract itself is not a written one.

Oversight: In business, oversight of a system or process is the responsibility for making sure that it works efficiently and correctly.

Over-the-Counter: Options are traded between private parties, an instrument is traded over-the-counter (OTC) if it trades under circumstances other than formal exchange.

Patient Capital: Patient capital is another name for long term capital. With patient capital, the investor is willing to make a financial investment in a business with no expectation of turning a quick profit. Instead, the investor is willing to forgo an immediate return in anticipation of more substantial returns down the road.

Performance: The overall results of general activities of an organization or investment over a certain period of time.

Personal Property: Personal property is generally considered property that is movable, as opposed to real property or real estate. In common law systems, personal property may also be called chattels or personalty.

Piggybacking: Piggybacking on Internet access is the practice of establishing a wireless Internet connection by using another subscriber's wireless Internet access service without the subscriber's explicit permission or knowledge. It is a legally and ethically controversial practice, with laws that vary by jurisdiction around the world.

Platform as a Service: This is a category of cloud computing services that provides a platform allowing customers to develop, run and manage applications without the complexity of building and maintaining the infrastructure typically associated with developing and launching an app.

Portfolio: A collection of investments held by an individual or group.

Portfolio Management: The process of creating and implementing decisions regarding investment mix and related policies. Other responsibilities include corresponding investments to their objectives, allocating assets for people and businesses and assessing the balance of risk versus performance.

Price: The quantity of payment or compensation given by one party to another in return for goods or services.

Primary Market: The part of the capital market that deals with issuing of new securities. Primary markets create long term instruments through which corporate entities raise funds from the capital market.

Private Equity: Equity capital available to companies or investors, but not quoted on a stock market. The finances obtained through private equity can be used for a variety of company activities such as developing new products and processes, expanding available capital, making acquisitions and strengthening a firm's balance sheet.

Private Equity Firms: Any type of non-public ownership equity security not listed on the public exchange. An investor who wants to sell private equity securities must find a buyer without the help of a public marketplace. There are three ways in which private equity firms usually obtain returns on their investments: An IPO, a sale or merger of the company they own, or a recapitalization.

Product Markets: Markets where finished goods and services are sold to consumers.

Profit Plan: This is a vital part of any business plan structure for a small or medium business. The goals of small business owners include ensuring that the business makes profits year-over-year, and that it is sustained over a period of time for growth.

Prospective Cost: Future costs that may be incurred or changed if an action is taken.

Proxy: An agent legally authorized to act on behalf of another party or a format that allows an investor to vote without being physically present at the meeting.

Proxy Server: In computer networks, a proxy server is a server that acts as an intermediary for requests from clients seeking resources from other servers.

Public Company: A public company, publicly traded company, publicly held company, publicly listed company, or public corporation is a corporation whose ownership is dispersed among the general public in many shares of stock which are freely traded on a stock exchange or in over-the-counter markets. In some jurisdictions, public companies over a certain size must be listed on an exchange.

Public Exchange: Trading venues open to all interested parties (many sellers and many buyers) that use a common technology platform and that are usually run by third parties or industry consortia.

Purchase Method: A method of accounting for a merger or combination in which one firm is considered to have purchased the assets of the other firm.

Real Property: In English common law, real property, real estate, realty, or immovable property is land which is the property of some person and all structures integrated with or affixed to the land, including crops, buildings, machinery, wells, dams, ponds, mines, canals, and roads, among other things.

Recession: In economics, a recession is a business cycle contraction which results in a general slowdown in economic activity.

Resource Markets: A resource market is a market where a business can go and purchase resources to produce goods and services.

Revocable Trust: A trust whereby provisions can be altered or canceled dependent on the grantor. During the life of the trust, income earned is distributed to the grantor, and only after death does property transfer to the beneficiaries.

Rider: An add-on provision to a basic insurance polity that provides additional benefits to the policyholder at an additional cost. Standard policies usually leave little room for modification or customization beyond choosing deductibles and coverage amounts.

Risk: Degree of uncertainty of return on an asset.

Risk Assessment: A technique used to measure two different quantities of risk: The size of the possible loss and the likelihood of the loss occurring.

Risk Averse Investor: An investor with a low tolerance for risk and who – with investment decisions – will choose to avoid risk more often than not. The risk averse investor can tolerate a lower return than high losses.

Risk Management: The ability to value assets over time in order to minimize the risk of loss of principle.

Risk-Return Tradeoff: Risk-averse investors require higher rates of return to induce them to invest in higher risk securities.

Sample Space: The range of values of a random variable.

Sampling Risk: Sampling risk is one of the many types of risks an auditor may face when performing the necessary procedure of audit sampling. Audit sampling exists because of the impractical and costly effects of examining all or 100% of a client's records or books. As a result, a "sample" of a client's accounts are examined.

Secondary Market: The secondary market, also called the aftermarket and follow on public offering is the financial market in which previously issued financial instruments such as stock, bonds, options, and futures are bought and sold.

Secured Creditors: Any creditor or lender that takes collateral for the extension of credit, loan or bond issuance. In the arena of personal finance, the most well-known secured creditors are mortgage lenders whose loans are secured either by a first or second lien on a property.

Security: A debt instrument when backed by collateral to assure compliance with a promise. Tradable instruments such as stocks and bonds that reflect an investor's ownership in, or debt obligations of, a company or government agency.

Share: A certificate that represents a single unit of possession in a business, mutual fund or limited partnership.

Shareholder Agreement: Also known as a stockholder agreement. It is a contract between the shareholders of a corporation.

Sole Proprietorship: An unincorporated business owned and run by one individual with no distinction between the business and you, the owner. You are entitled to all profits and are responsible for all your business's debts, losses and liabilities. You do not have to take any formal action to form one.

Start-Up: An entrepreneurial venture which is typically a newly emerged, fast-growing business that aims to meet a marketplace need by developing a viable business model around an innovative product, service, process or a platform.

Statistical Sampling: A technique of choosing a part of a population through calculating the mathematical probabilities involved. Such sampling helps to make more sound and scientific inferences having to do with the traits of the whole population.

Stock Certificate: Documentary proof of stock ownership. An item representing ownership rights in a corporation and signifying a claim to a relative share in the corporation's assets and profits.

Stock Market: The business transacted at a stock exchange.

Strategic Planning: A company's method of defining its personal strategy, plan or decision making process regarding the allocation of its resources intended to help in pursuing a strategy, such as its capital and people.

Strict Liability: The imposition of liability on a party without a finding of fault. The claimant need only prove that the tort occurred and that the defendant was responsible. The law imputes strict liability to situations it considers to be inherently dangerous.

Subprime Mortgage: A type of mortgage that is normally issued by a lending institution to borrowers with low credit ratings. As a result of the borrower's lower credit rating, a conventional mortgage is not offered because the lender views the borrower as having a larger-than-average risk of defaulting on the loan.

Subsidized Loans: Loans for undergraduate students with financial need, as determined by cost of attendance minus expected family contribution and other financial aid. They do not accrue interest while the student is in school at least half-time or during deferment periods.

Succession Planning: A process for identifying and developing new leaders who can replace old leaders when they leave, retire or die. It increases the availability of experienced and capable employees that are prepared to assume these roles as they become available.

Sunk Cost: A cost that already has been incurred and cannot be recovered.

Synergy: Synergy is a software application developed by Symless, for sharing a keyboard and mouse between multiple computers.

Target Market: A target market is the market a company wants to sell its products and services to, and it includes a targeted set of customers for whom it directs its marketing efforts. Identifying the target market is an essential step in the development of a marketing plan.

Time Value: Price put on the time an investor has to wait until and investment matures.

Time Value of Money: A dollar today is worth more than a dollar tomorrow or a dollar received later is worth less than one in hand today.

Tort: A wrongful act or an infringement of a right (other than under contract) leading to civil legal liability.

Trojan Horses: In computing, a Trojan horse, or Trojan, is any malicious computer program which misleads users of its true intent. The term is derived from the Ancient Greek story of the deceptive wooden horse that led to the fall of the city of Troy.

Trust: An arrangement in which someone's property or money is legally held or managed by someone else or by an organization (such as a bank) for usually a set period of time.

Universal Banks: Such banks participate in many kinds of banking activities. They are both an investment bank and a commercial bank as well as providing other financial services such as insurance.

Unsecured Creditors: An individual or institution that lends money without obtaining specified assets as collateral. This poses a higher risk to the creditor because it will have nothing to fall back on should the borrower default on the loan. A debenture holder is an unsecured creditor.

Valuation: The process of determining the current worth of an asset or company.

Venture: Venture is often used to refer to a start-up or enterprise business.

Venture Capitalists: A term that defines an investor that gives capital to start-up companies or offers support to small corporations hoping to expand. Capitalists, however, lack any form of access to public funding.

Vertical Merger: The business act in which one firm acquires either a customer or a supplier.

Virus: A piece of code that is capable of copying itself and typically has a detrimental effect, such as corrupting the system or destroying data.

Volatility: A statistical measure of the dispersion of returns for a given security or market index. Volatility can either be measured by using the standard deviation or variance between returns from that same security or market index. Commonly, the higher the volatility, the riskier the security.

Wage Unit: A unit of measurement for monetary quantities introduced by Keynes. A value expressed in wage units is equal to its price in money units divided by the wage (in money units) of a man-hour of labor.

Whistleblower: A whistleblower is a person who exposes any kind of information or activity that is deemed illegal, unethical, or not correct within an organization that is either private or public.

Written Contracts: An agreement made on a printed document that has been signed by both the lender and the borrower. Written contracts are legally binding and easier to enforce than oral contracts.

Zapping: To get rid of, destroy or kill, especially with sudden and concentrated application of force or energy.

INDEX

A

absolute assignment 400
absorption costing 175
access controls 299
Accord Implementation Group (AIG) 321
accountability 265
accounting complexity 6–7
accounting controls 31
Accounting Principles Board (APB) 3
accounting systems 23–31, 33–35, 37, 252
accounts receivables and inventories 38–42, 216
accretions 15–16
accumulated postretirement benefit obligation (APBO) 15
acquiring and creating resources 33
acquisition 109, 129
acquisition-related expenses 14
activist investors 163
activist shareholder 166
activity-based costing (ABC) 175–179, 181
activity-based management (ABM) 175, 181
actual cost system 176
Adelphia 219
adjusted grossed-up basis 16
adjusted gross income (AGI) 428, 431, 442
adjusting risk 45–46
administrative entrepreneur 207, 211
adverse opinion 72
aggregate economy 111
airline industry 110
alcohol taxes 387
algorithmic trading 276
Amazon.com 18
American Customer Service Index (ACSI) 428
American Enterprise Institute for Public Policy Research (AEI) 372
American Institute for Economic Research (AIER) 372
American Institute of Certified Public Accountants (AICPA) 31, 49, 55, 70, 226, 359, 365, 412
American International Group (AIG) 219, 456, 458
American Recovery and Reinvestment Act 458
Amkor Technology 152
Amphenol 152
Angel Capital Association (ACA) 126
angel investors 129, 236–237
antecedent debt 92

Apple Computer 152
application review 299
application software 148
application software development 299
apportionment 446
arbitrage 199
Arthur Andersen 57
artificial intelligence (AI) 328
Asia Economic Institute (AEI) 373
Asia Pacific Economic Cooperation (APEC) 46, 48, 84, 269
assets 37, 252, 469
Association to Advance Collegiate Schools of Business (AACSB) 221
assurance 31
assurance services 50–55
AT & T 152
attestation 72
attestation services 55
attest function 72
audit 54–55, 64–72, 228, 365
audit committee 62
audit program 72
audit risk 72
audit sampling 411, 412
audit services 56–62
avoidance powers 92

B

backflush costing 171, 176
balanced scorecard 181
Balance of payments (BOP) 80–86
balance sheets 176, 308–310
balancing debt and equity 163
bank account trust 474
bank failures 357
Bank of International Settlements 46, 48
bankruptcy 92–93
Bankruptcy Abuse Prevention and Consumer Protection Act (BAPCPA) 89–91, 93
Bankruptcy Act 1898 88
bankruptcy and organization 87–92
Bankruptcy Reform Act 1978 88
banks and banking 356–357
Banner Health 36, 181
barker 192

Basel Committee 318–322

Basel Committee on Banking Supervision 48

Basel Consultative Group (BCG) 322

batch-specific overhead costs 174

B2B hubs 76

bear market 418

Bear Stearns 92

before-tax target profit (BTP) 35

beneficiary 476

Bernie Madoff 219

Bezos, Jeff 19

bid-ask spread 279

Big Four accounting firms 54, 55

Big Six 411

binomial distribution 350–352

biodiesel hybrid bus 102

blocked funds 45

bonding programs 236

bond 228

bond markets 403

B-rated companies 164

B-ratings loans 91

breach 345

break-even analysis 168

Bretton Woods monetary system 44, 257, 259

Bricklin, Dave 36, 37

broker-dealer 279

Brookings Institution 372

budgeted balance sheet 36

budgeting 173

Bunnell, Ron 36, 181

Bureau of Economic Analysis (BEA) 83, 369

Bureau of National Affairs (BNA) 1, 7

business climate 105

business combination 4, 7

business conditions analysis 100–104

business continuity management (BCM) 54

Business Continuity Plans (BCPs) 422

business cycles 107–111, 259

business enterprise 211

business environment 154

business estate planning 112–117

business ethics 119–121, 213–216

business governance 52

business loan programs 235

business model 42, 78, 216

business owner's policies (BOPs) 394

business process 78

business strategy 154

business-to-business (B2B) e-business 74–78

business-to-consumer (B2C) e-business 78

business valuation templates 96, 98

Business Week 152

buyout of acquisitions 124–128

buyouts 124

buy-sell agreements 115, 117

by-product 176

C

cache memory 143

Cantillon entrepreneur 207, 211

capacity utilization 464

capital 237, 357

capital account 80, 86

capital asset(s) 464

capital asset pricing model (CAPM) 231–233

capital budgeting 48, 131–133, 305

capital expenditure(s) 109

capital expenditure analysis 168

capital structure 166

card protruding 144

carryback 16, 292

carryforward 16, 292

cash budget 36

cash flow(s) 38–39, 42, 133, 166

cash flow statements 309, 310

cash inflows 133

cash outflows 133

cash-out merger 9

Cassidy, Gerard 11

Catalog of Federal Domestic Assistance (CFDA) 363

central bank 358

certified public accountants (CPAs) 56, 62, 65, 218, 427, 441

channel partners 425

channel stuffing 40–42, 214

Chapter 7 89, 93

Chapter 11 89, 93

charter audits 298

Chartered Institute of Management Accountants (CIMA) 52

Chief audit executive (CAE) 30, 31

chose in action 400

Cisco model 77

Citibank 92

claimant 400

classical cycles 107, 111

classical interest theory 462

client 72
client computer 328
closely held businesses (CHB) 112, 117
cloud computing security 135–137
Coach 152
code of conduct 298
codification project 5, 7
codified 432, 437
Cognizant Tech Solutions 152
Colgate-Palmolive 152
Collins Industry Inc. 29
commercial banks 235, 237–238
commercial general liability (CGL) policy 345, 346, 394–395
Committee of Sponsoring Organizations of the Treadway Commission (COSO) 31
Committee on Corporate Reporting (CCR) 2
commodities 353, 354, 358
commodity markets 403
common disaster 400
common law 72
communications, networking and security 139–142
community land trusts (CLTs) 336
Community Reinvestment Act (CRA) 448, 451
co-movement 111
comparative cost analysis 168
compliance officer 42
compliance procedures 216
compounding 233
computer applications 144–148
concept filters 425
conglomerate mergers 9
consultants 154
consulting agreements 154
consumer equilibrium 382
consumption (sales) taxes 384
continuity plans 425
continuous data protection (CDP) 422
contra accounts 16
contract 345
contribution margin per unit (CMU) 35
control activities 25
control environment 24, 31
controller 42
Control Objectives for Information and Related Technology (COBIT) 293
control systems 205
convergence 252, 272
Convergence with U.S. GAAP 7

convey 476
Cooper, Cynthia 121
coordinated portfolio investment surveys (CPIS) 85
corporate accountability 155–160
Corporate bankruptcy 2005 88–89
corporate compliance 31
corporate culture 216
corporate development 124
corporate entrepreneurship 199, 201
corporate financial policy 162–166
corporate governance 52
corporate venturer 208
corporate venturing 201, 205
corporation 105, 154, 345
cost accounting 170–176, 181
cost accumulation 170
cost-benefit analysis (CBA) 185–188
cost-effectiveness analysis 184, 188
cost estimating 97
cost management systems (CMS) 172–179, 181
cost-minimization analysis 184
cost-utility analysis 184
cost/value/profit (CVP) analysis 33, 35
counterclaim 400
country risk 243
Cox, Chris 4
creator 476
credit 80
credit risk 160, 348, 351
crews 96
crippling debt 88
crowdfunding 189–192
current account 80, 86
curve shifts 377
cybercrime 147, 313, 316
cybercrime prevention 315
cyber entrepreneur 207–208

D
database 148
data encryption 425
data isolation 138
data leakage 140, 314
day trading 233
debentures 228
debit 80, 166
debt financing 234–236, 238
debt-to-equity (D/E) ratio 166
Decision driven 211

decision support system (DSS) 324, 328
deeds 333–334
Deets, Dan 36, 181
defaulted receivable 42
defendant 400
defense-in-depth system 314–315
deficit 86, 259
Defining Issues Test (DIT) 218
delinquent receivables 42
Dell business model 76–77
Deloitte and Touche 57
demand 286, 382
demand and supply models 377
demand and supply schedules 377–378
demand coefficients 379
demand schedule 286, 382
depression 259
derivatives markets 403
desktop publishing 148
developing countries 86, 272
development audits 294, 299
digital assets 474
dilution 15–16
direct costs 175, 179
direct foreign investment (DFI) 302, 305
direct labor costs 172, 176
direct materials 172, 176
disaster recovery planning (DRP) 54
disclaimer 401
disclaimer of opinion 72
disclaimer or qualified terminable interest property
        (QTIP) 116
disclosures 252
discounted cash flow (DCF) 131, 133, 305, 469
discounted value 134
discretionary trusts 474
distinctive capabilities 154
dividends 45
divestitures 109
document, content and knowledge management 54
Dodd-Frank Wall Street Reform 450
Dodd-Frank Wall Street Reform and Consumer
        Protection Act 223
dollar-unit sampling 411, 412
donor 476
dot.coms 18
double-entry bookkeeping 86, 148
Dow Jones Industrial Average 414
Dynergy 219

E
early-stage entrepreneurs 199
earned income tax credit (EITC) 440, 442
earnings per share (EPS) 16, 467
eavesdropping 141
eBay 18
EBITDA 16
e-commerce 18, 75–78, 140, 148, 316
economic analysis 188
Economic and monetary union (EMU) 403
Economic and Social Commission for Asia and the
        Pacific (ESCAP) 271
Economic Commission for Africa (ECA) 271
Economic Commission for Europe (ECE) 271
economic contraction 259
Economic Cycle Research Institute (ECRI) 373
economic development 105
economic expansion 259
Economic Growth and Tax Relief Reconciliation Act
        (EGTRRA) 114
economic indicator analysis 107
Economic Policy Institute (EPI) 371–372
economic rate of return (ERR) 134
economic stimulus package 105
effective tax rate (ETR) 432, 437
e-filing 440–442
egoism 223
e-hubs 77, 79
elasticity 378–379, 382
electronic archiving and data retention 54
electronic communication networks (ECNs) 277, 279
electronic document exchange 140
electronic exchanges 76, 79
electronic federal tax payment system (EFTPS) 445, 447
electronic funds transfer 140
electronic markets 76
email 140
emerging issues task force (EITF) 227
employee income tax 444–445
Employee Stock Ownership Plans (ESOPs) 10
encryption 138, 316
endogenous 111
Enron 56, 121, 122, 155, 160, 219, 278
enterprise 79, 148
enterprise resource planning (ERP) system 180, 181
enterprise risk 62
enterprise risk management (ERM) 61, 159–161
entrepreneur 205, 207
entrepreneurial behavior 205

entrepreneurial environment 209
entrepreneurship 194–195, 199–211
environmental scanning 205
equilibrium 286
equilibrium adjustments 283
equilibrium price 286, 377
equilibrium quantity 286
equitable income distribution 281
equity 166, 238, 252, 279
equity capital 238
equity investor 192
Ernst and Young survey 57, 60–61
error 73
escheat 476
established entrepreneurs 199
estates in land 330–332
estate tax 475
ethics in accounting 218–223
Euro 406
European Association of Securities Dealers Automated Quotation system (EASDAQ) 274
European Spreadsheet Risks Interest Group (EuSpRIG) 94, 97, 98
European Union (EU) 46, 48, 82, 449–450
exchange of commodities 356
exchange rate 86
exchange rate regimes 258–259
exchange traded funds (ETFs) 274
executive information systems 326, 328
exogenous 111
expected value 351
expenses 252
expert systems 326, 328
external audit 31
external auditor 62, 71, 73

F
factoring 39, 42
factory cost 176
factory overhead 172, 176
fair market value 117
fair value 252
fair value accounting (FVA) 248
fair value-based method 22
fair value method 20–21
fallen angels 166
False Claims Act (FCA) 118–120, 123, 155, 159, 161, 219
family owned businesses (FOB) 112, 117
Fannie Mae 95, 219, 448

FASB116 361, 366
FASB117 361–362, 366
FASB Codification Project 7
Federal Accounting Standards Advisory Board 226
Federal Deposit Insurance Corporation (FDIC) 357
federal government 188, 259
federal register 228
Federal Reserve Bank (Fed) 451
Federal Reserve Bank conference 242
Federal Reserve Bank of New York 80
federal tax code 437
fees, duties, and tariffs 384, 385
fiat currencies 254, 259
fiat money 353–356, 358
fiduciary 476
finance 246
financial accounting 33, 37, 80, 86, 181
Financial Accounting Foundation (FAF) 265
Financial Accounting Standards Board (FASB) 1, 7, 12, 16, 22, 224, 260, 266, 359
financial and accounting compliance 224–228
financial and stakeholder management 360
financial budgeting 35–36
financial buyers 125
financial consultants 152
financial controls 205
financial engineering 166
Financial Executives International (FEI) 2, 7, 411
financial institutions 238
financial markets 233, 402, 406
financial regulation 246
financial reporting 360–361
financial restatements 5–7, 62
financial risk 161
financial services agency 216
Financial Services Agency of Japan 213
firewalls 142, 143, 316
first-in first-out (FIFO) costing 170
first-time buyers 125
fiscal policy 259
floating exchange rate 258
footnote disclosure 13
Ford Explorer 105
Foreign Corrupt Practices Act (FCPA) 1977 26
foreign direct investment (FDI) 85
foreign exchange markets 403
foreseeable 345
Form 10-K 40
Form 10-Q 40

formula error 95
401(k) plans 15
Framework Convention on Tobacco Control (FCTC) 387
Frankston, Bob 36, 37
Freddie Mac 219, 448
free cash flow 133–134
friendly mergers 8
full sellers 125
functional hubs 77–78
fund accounting 361, 365
fundamental analysis 233
fundamental *vs.* technical financial analysis 230–232
funding new ventures 234–237
futures markets 403
futures trading 358
future value 465–466, 469

G

General Accounting Office (GAO) 64, 70, 293
General Agreement on Tariffs and Trade (GATT) 85
general and administrative costs 179
Generally Accepted Accounting Principles (GAAP) 1, 3–4, 7, 16, 33, 37, 38, 42, 50, 65, 224, 247, 263, 291, 292
General Motors Corp. 23–24
general partnerships 346
G-10 Group 318, 319, 322–323
gift/sale leaseback 114
Gilead Sciences 152
Gini coefficient 285, 286
Gini index 286
Glassman, C 6
Glass-Steagall Act 416
global 246
Global Crossing 219
global economy 269, 272
global entrepreneurship monitor (GEM) 196, 199
global finance 240–245
global financial crisis 2007-2010 449–450
global growth companies 151
globalization 2, 86, 246, 272, 418
globalization and international accounting 247–251
global markets 272
global money management 44–47
going-private transactions 166
gold currencies 254, 259
gold-exchange standard 44

Goldman Sachs group 92, 152
gold standard 43 254–259
goodwill 11, 17
Google 103, 104, 152
Government Accounting Standards Board (GASB) 6, 227, 261–266
Government Finance Officers Association (GFOA) 263, 266
government financial auditing 71
grace period 401
Gramm-Leach-Blilely Act 318, 323
great depression 389, 418
great recession 223
Great Society 359
greenbacks 358
"green" car market 102
Greene, Herbert H. 103
Green initiatives 434–435
gross domestic product (GDP) 107, 108, 369, 373, 453
growth 154
growth companies, consulting to, 149–154
growth cycles 107, 111
growth of nations, global economy 267–272
Gulf War 110

H

hacker 143, 316
Hand Formula 343, 346
harmonization 252
headline 437
hedge fund markets 403
hedge funds 406
high-growth companies 149, 154
Hilton Hotel Company 102
historical cost accounting (HCA) 248
home-based entrepreneur 207
home improvement supply industry 110–111
homeowner's insurance 393–394
horizontal merger 9
hostile mergers 9
household income 283
housing bubble 452, 458
human capital 271, 272
human resource management 109
Hummer 105
Hunterdone Healthcare, Inc. 36, 181
hybrid costing 171–172

I

identity access management 53

identity management 425

implied contracts 343

income 253

income distribution 281–286

income inequality 281, 286

income receipts 80

income statements 17, 308, 311

income tax 292, 384

income tax accounting 288–292

independent auditors 65

independent contractor 293

independent entrepreneur 207

independent exchange 76

independent software vendor 425

indirect costs 179

indirect taxes 437

industry-maker 207

inflation 259

informal trust 474

information and communication systems 25

information security management 53

information system 79

Information Systems Audit and Control Association (ISACA) 293–294, 297

information systems (IS) auditing 294–298

information technology (IT) 79, 143, 148, 328

infrastructure 266

infrastructure as a service (IaaS) 138

inherent risk 62

In-House/General Counsel 346

initial public offerings (IPOs) 18, 275, 279

installment sale 114, 117

insurance 346

insurance markets 403

insured 401

intangible assets 7

intentional damage 314

interest 464, 465, 469

interest theory 463

Internal Audit and Assurance Strategy (IAAS) 52–53, 55

internal auditor 71, 73

internal audits 26, 444

internal controls 24–31, 31

internal control structure 73

internal financial auditing 71

internal rate of return (IRR) 130–131, 134

Internal Revenue Code (IRC) 112, 432, 437

Internal Revenue Service (IRS) 19–20, 33, 443

international accounting 253

International accounting harmonization (IAH) system 248

International Accounting Standards (IAS) 250–251

International Accounting Standards Board (IASB) 226, 251, 253, 308

International Accounting Standards Committee (IASC) 248, 249, 308

International Association for Accounting Education and Research (IAAER) 220

International Auditing and Assurance Standards Board (IAASB) 297

international banking 406

International Banking Federation 406

international banking supervision 318–322

international business operations 305

international capital budgeting 44, 301–302, 305

international corporate finance 301–304

International Federation of Accountants (IFAC) 220

international finance 246

international financial accounting 306–310

international financial markets 402–405

International Financial Reporting Standards (IFRS) 1, 7, 247, 249–251, 308

international financial systems 46

International Monetary Fund (IMF) 46–48, 84–85, 244, 246, 256, 450

international monetary system 43, 44, 48

International Stock Market Exchanges 415

international strategy 305

internet access 140

Internet Age 387–388

internet security 312–314

Internet Tax Freedom Act (ITFA) 430, 431

interquartile range 351

inter vivos trusts 476

intestacy law 476

intestate 476

intrafirm debt 45

intrafirm sales 45

intrapreneurship 196, 201

intrinsic value-based method 22–23

intrinsic value method 21

inventory 42

inventory accounts 216

inventory costing methods 174

investment company/firm 418

investment programs 235–236

investments 129, 233, 238
investment vehicle 418
invoice backdating 40–41
invoices 38, 42
irrevocable proxies 115
IRS Revenue Ruling 59-60 114
IT governance 54
IT management applications 324–328

J
Jefferies Re-Org IndexSM 91
Jeffries index 91
JIT method. *see* just-in-time (JIT) method
job order costing 170, 176
Jobs, Steve 197
Johnson, Lyndon 426
joint cost 176
joint product and by-product costing 171
joint tenancy 473
joint ventures 207, 210
J. P. MorganChase 95
just-in-time (JIT) manufacturing 79
just-in-time (JIT) method 39, 42
just-in-time (JIT) production systems 171

K
key employee retention plans (KERPS) 90, 93
Keynesian economics 459–461
Keynes, John Maynard 438
key performance indicators (KPI) 6
knowledge seekers 303
Korea Economic Institute (KEI) 373
KPMG 57

L
labor income 283
labor market 286
labor productivity 176
laissez-faire economics 460–461
Lam Research 152
landlord-tenant relationships 338
land sale contracts 332
Langevoort, Donald C. 25
lapsed policy 401
law of demand 286, 382
law of property 332–339
law of supply 286, 382
Leading Economic Indicators (LEI) report 369
legal consultants 152

legal liability 70–71
legal risk 161
Lehman Brothers 92, 449, 455
letters of credit (LOCs) 406
leveraged buyouts (LBOs) 124, 125, 127–129, 166
leveraged recapitalizations 166–167
Levitt, Arthur 56–57
liabilities 34, 37, 253, 341–344, 469
liability risk management 341–344
life-cycle costing 181
life insurance 474
LIFO price index 408
limited liability company (LLC) 346
limited liability entity (LLE) 344
Lincoln, Abraham 353
liquid asset 476
liquidity 279
liquidity preference 460, 464
liquidity risk 161
Lloyd-La Follette Act 118, 120, 123, 155, 161
local area network (LAN) 143, 144, 148
locus of planning 205
logic bombs 141
logic errors 95
long-term capital management (LTCM) 279
long-term liabilities 11
Lorenz curve 284–286
loss distributions 347–351
Lotus 1-2-3 94
Lowe's Companies Inc. 110
low-growth companies 149
low-tech security mechanisms 316
Lufthansa German Airlines 110

M
Macroeconomics 368–373
macro-economy 464
managed exchange rate 258
management audits 295, 299
management buyers 125
management buyouts (MBOs) 124, 125, 127–129
management consultants 153
management information system (MIS) 328
manager 328
managerial accounting 34, 35, 37
manufacture 134
marginal revenue 286, 382
marginal utility 378, 382
market 286, 383

marketable title 332–333
market demand 105
market failure 287, 381–383
marketing and pricing 109
market risk 161, 323, 348, 352
markets 86, 272
market seekers 303
market structure 380–381
master budget 36
materials weakness 59, 62
mean 352
mechanical errors 95
median 352
merchandise trade 80
merger 129
mergers and acquisitions 9–16, 124
Merrill Lynch and Co. 92
metropolitan area network (MAN) 143
microeconomics 376–382
Microsoft Excel 94
MicroStrategy Inc. (MSTR) 57
mid-tier accounting firms 54
mission statement 214, 217
mobile and remote computing 54
mode 352
moderate-growth companies 149
modern portfolio theory (MPT) 466, 469
monetary policies 259, 373
money 353
money management 48
money markets 356, 358, 403
monitoring 25
Montreal Economic Institute (MEI) 373
Morgan, J. P. 92
moral conduct 217
moral hazard 19, 406
mortgages 334–335
multinational corporations (MNCs) 305, 403, 447
Mulvaney, Mick 183
myriad 124

N
NASDAQ technology index 18
National Association of Securities Dealers Automated Quotation system (NASDAQ) 274, 279, 414, 419
National Bureau of Economic Research (NBER) 107, 108
national deficits 373

National Federation of Independent Business (NFIB) 132
nations 86, 272
necessity entrepreneurs 196
negative income tax 389
negligence 346
neoclassical growth theory 268, 272
net identifiable assets 17
net operating loss (NOL) 17, 288–289, 293
net present value (NPV) 46, 131, 134, 188, 468–469
network 143, 148, 316
new common stock 90–91
new growth theory 268, 272
new international financial architecture (NIFA) 46–47
new venture 207
new venture formation 208–209
New York Mercantile Exchange (NYMEX) 354
New York Stock Exchange (NYSE) 166, 275, 414, 419
NII Holdings 152
No-FEAR Act 120–121, 123
nonprofit 366
nonprofit entrepreneur 208
nonprofit micro lenders 238
nonprofit organizations (NPOs) 359–364
nonprofit stakeholders 360
non-statistical sampling 411
nonvested stock. see restricted stock
normal distribution 350–352
North American Free Trade Agreement (NAFTA) 46, 48, 84, 269
North American Industry Classification System (NAICS) 134
note 228
Nucor 152
nuisance regulations 336–337
number of periods 465, 470

O
obsolete inventory disposal 40
occupy wall street 223
Office of Information and Regulatory Affairs (OIRA) 184–185
Office of Management and Budget (OMB) 359, 363, 366
old common stock 90
old target 17
Oliver Wyman Company 44, 48
OMB A-133 363

OMB Circular A-110 362, 366
OMB Circular A-122 362, 366
OMB Circular A-133 366
open invoices 410–411
operating business plan 154–155
operational accountability 266
operational auditing 71–73
operational costs 359
operational risk 161, 323, 352
operations audits 295, 299
operations management 328
operations research 328
opportunity costs 375
opportunity driven 207
opportunity entrepreneurs 196
Oracle 152
oral contracts 343
Organisation for Economic Co-operation and Development (OECD) 271–273
organizational justice 123
Original Institutional Economics (OIE) 368
origins and extensions of supply 379–380
other post-employment benefits (OPEB) 260, 263–266
output 287
oversight 364
Over-the-Counter (OTC) Bulletin Board 414–415
over-the-counter (OTC) security 93
owners' equity 34, 37, 470

P
Paccar 152
partial sellers 125
partnership relationship management (PRM) 425
patient capital 238
Paulson, Henry 4
payback period 131, 134
payments 465, 470
pay-on-death (POD) account 474
PayPal 474
payroll 445
payroll tax fund 447
pegged exchange rate 258
Pension Protection Act (PPA) 114
P/E ratio 468
performance 155
personal property 330
Peters, Don S. 29
piggybacking 140, 313
pink sheet 90, 93

pink sheet stocks 415
planning flexibility 205
planning horizon 205
plan of reorganization (POR) 93
platform as a service (PaaS) 138
policy 401
policy rationale 188
policy regimes 253, 272
political risk 45
pooling method 10
portal 79
portfolio management 470
portray risk 347
Pozen, Robert 5
pre-acquisition contingencies 13
predatory lending practices 217
premium 401
premium content 425
presentation software 148
present value (PV) 134, 465, 470
"pretty good privacy" (PGP) program 142
price 287
price controls 287, 383
price discovery 279
price elasticity 379
PricewaterhouseCoopers (PwC) 57, 58, 165
primary market 419
privacy management 54
private annuity 114, 117
private companies 2–3, 31
private equity 124
private equity firms 125
private equity (PE) funding 165, 166
private exchange 76
proactive financial advisors 417
probability density function 352
probability distribution 352
probate estate 476
process costing 170–171, 176
producers 287, 383
production and inventory control 109
production-efficiency seekers 303
product line-specific overhead costs 174
product-specific overhead costs 174
professional auditors 65
professional ethics 70
profit plan 36
program trading 276, 279
progress bar 192

property and liability insurance 394–400
property taxes 384
pro rata rights 238
proxy 228
proxy server 142
public companies 3–4
Public Companies Accounting Oversight Board (PCAOB) 3, 31, 226
public company 31
public exchange 76
public goods 382, 383
public policy 106
public-private partnerships 366
public problems 188
public problem-solving 188
public sector 183, 188
public trust 363–364
purchase method 11–14

Q

quantity demanded 287, 383
quantity supplied 287, 383
Quattro Pro 94
Questar 152

R

random variable 352
rating trends 164
raw-material seekers 303
real estate transactions 338
realize 17
real property 330
recession 111, 419, 453–454, 458
registrant 59, 62
regulatory agencies 217
relationship intelligence 425
repeat players 124–125
repurchase agreement 458
residual risk 63
resource markets 287, 381, 383
restricted stock 23
restructuring boutiques 91–93
return on equity (ROE) 275, 280
revenue 287, 383
revenues and custody of assets 364
revocable trust 476
rider 401
risk 316
risk assessment 24–25

risk-averse investors 417
risk-base audit 31, 53, 55
risk-based audit standards 32
risk management 109, 111, 425
Risk Management Association (RMA) 160
risk management strategy 109, 111
risk-return tradeoff 93
Rite Aid 219
Robertson 461–462
Roosevelt, Franklin D. 256, 453
royalties and license fees 45

S

sabotage 314
sale-leaseback transaction 336
salvage value 17
sample space 352
sampling risk 73
Sarbanes-Oxley (SOX) Act 4, 20, 23–24, 31, 37, 42, 98, 118, 120, 123, 155, 161, 214–215, 217, 220, 223, 227
Sarbanes-Oxley-section 404 32
SarbOx 404 compliance 59, 63
SBIC program. *see* Small Business Investment Companies (SBICs)
scavenging 141
SEC clarification statements 26–27
secondary market 280, 419
secured creditors 89
Securities and Exchange Commission (SEC) 1, 10, 32, 40, 42, 56–57, 90, 123, 165, 246, 419
security 143, 148, 316, 419
security and controlling information distribution 54
security interests 334
segregation of duties 299
serial entrepreneur 208
server 317, 328
service(s) 80
service activity management 327–328
service continuity controls 299
service efforts accomplishments (SEA) 263–264, 266
service resource management 327
service sector 328
settlor 476
share 238
share-based payment. *see* stock-based compensation
shareholder agreements 115, 117
shareholder value 167
short-term/current liabilities 11

short-term earning investment 164–166
simple random sampling 412
small business(es) 134
small business administration (SBA) 112, 234, 238
small business financial exchange 238
Small Business Investment Companies (SBICs) 126, 235–236
small business owner/operator 207
social media 192–193
social norms 223
social policy 389
social responsibility 217
social security 389
social welfare programs 366
Societe Generale 21–22
software as a service (SaaS) 138
sole proprietor 293
sole proprietorships 346
solvency 89, 93
Southwest Airlines Company 110
specialized taxes 384, 385
split-off point 171
sponsor 193
sport utility vehicles (SUVs) 105
spreadsheet 148
spreadsheet applications software 95–98
spreadsheet errors 98
spreadsheet modeling techniques 98
spreadsheet software 98
Spreadsheet Standards Review Board (SSRB) 94, 97, 98
spreadsheet templates 96, 98
Standard and Poor's 500 (S and P 500) company index 152
Standards Implementation Group (SIG) 321
Stanford Institute for Economic Policy Research (SIEPR) 372
start-up 238
statement on auditing standard 413
statistical applications 409–411
statistical correlation technique 412
statistical sampling technique 412
statutory tax rate 437
stealing/capturing data 314
stock-based compensation 18–22
stockbrokers 414
stock exchange 280
stockholder 89
stock markets 233, 274–278, 402, 413–416, 419

stock option 23
stock purchase plan 23
stock recapitalizations 115, 117
stock redemptions 115
strategic assets 155
strategic audit 55
strategic buyers 124
strategic controls 205
strategic plans 205
strategic tax review 437
strategy 317
Streamlined Sales and Use Tax Agreement (SSUTA) 388
strict liability 346
subcontractor information system (SIS) 96
subprime lending 454–455, 458
subprime mortgage 452
subsidized loans 45
succession planning 115, 117
sunk cost 176
Sunoco 152
supplier connectivity 425
supply 287, 383
supply and demand 282–283
supply schedule 287, 383
support trusts 474
surveys on the implementation of methodological standards for direct investment (SIMSDI) 85
SWOT analysis 205
synergy 148
system software controls 299
systems theory 328

T
tacit knowledge 205, 425
target 17
target costing 182
target market 79
taxable estate 471, 476
tax administration 389, 427–430
tax advantages 14
tax amnesty 431
taxation 384–387
tax code 293
tax collection 385–386
taxes and business strategy 444–446
taxes and social policy 386
tax evasion 428–429
tax impact on decisions 432–437

tax incentives 106
taxing entity 389
tax liability 442, 447
tax planning and preparation 439–443
tax reform 435, 437
tax risk assessment 433–434
tax risk management 432–433, 437
tax software 440
technical analysis 233
technologies 106
technology audits 295, 299
technology-media-telecom (TMT) 274–276, 280
technology stocks 417
tender offer 228
testator 472
third-party liability insurance 345
throughput costing 174
Tillman, Robert 110
time value of money (TVM) 465–469
tobacco taxes 386–387
tort 346
tort immunity 400
total fixed costs (TFC) 35
total service concept project (TSC) 326–327
Totten trust 474
trading 233
traditional entrepreneur 208
Traits 198
transfer on death (TOD) 474
transfer payment 188, 287
transfer pricing 45
transparency 280
trapdoors 313–314
Trojan horses 141
Troubled Assets Relief Program (TARP) 450, 452, 456, 458
Trump Organization 113
trust 476
trust arrangements 116
trustor 476
trust property 473
trust services 55
turnaround management services 92, 93
21st century IT applications 420–424
Tyco 56, 219

U
unconditional pledge 366
uniform sales tax 431

unilateral transfers 80
United Nations 271, 273
universal banks 92, 93
universalism 223
unsecured creditors 89
unwilling sellers 125
Urban Institute 372
U.S. Airline Deregulation Act 1978 110
U.S. economy 416–417
use tax 431
U.S. Financial Accounting Standards Board (FASB) 251
U.S. financial crisis (2007-2010) 453–456
U.S. Government Accountability Office (GAO) 295
U.S. Securities and Exchange Commission (SEC) 224, 275
U.S. Small Business Administration (SBA) 134
U.S. Stock Exchanges 414–415
utilitarianism 223

V
valuation 17
valuation allowances 293
value-added reseller (VAR) 425
value added tax (VAT) 430, 431
values 188
variable cost 176
VAT/GST rates 437
venture 238
venture capital 124, 129, 193
venture capitalists 236, 238
venture initiation 207
Verion Communications 152
vertical market application 425
vertical merger 9
vertical portals 77
vertical software applications 423
virtualization 138
virus 143, 317
VisiCalc 36, 37
voice mail 140
volatility 280
voting agreements 115
voting trusts 115, 117
vouching 73

W
wage unit 464
Wall Street Investment Firms 91–92

Walmart 114
warranty 401
Waste Management Inc. (WMI) 57
Watkins, Sherron 121, 123
WebMD 18
whistleblowers 118, 123, 161
wide area network (WAN) 143, 148
wills 472, 473, 476
wiretapping 141
wire transfers 406
word processing 148
workforce 106
working capital 38–39
World Bank 46, 48, 86, 246, 267, 273

WorldCom 56, 121, 219, 278
World Economic Forum (WEF) 151
World Health Organization (WHO) 387
World Trade Organization (WTO) 85
write-offs 444, 447
written contracts 341

Y
Yousafzai, Malala 196

Z
zapping 141, 314
zoning regulations 337